CRABBE: THE CRITICAL HERITAGE

THE CRITICAL HERITAGE SERIES

GENERAL EDITOR: B. C. SOUTHAM, M.A., B.LITT. (OXON.)
Formerly Department of English, Westfield College, University of London

For list of books in the series see back end paper

CRABBE

THE CRITICAL HERITAGE

Edited by
ARTHUR POLLARD
Professor of English, University of Hull

LONDON AND BOSTON: ROUTLEDGE & KEGAN PAUL

First published 1972
by Routledge & Kegan Paul Ltd
Broadway House, 68–74 Carter Lane
London EC4V 5EL and
9 Park Street
Boston, Mass. 02108, U.S.A.

ISBN 0 7100 7258 9

Printed in Great Britain
by W & J Mackay Limited, Chatham

To the memory of

URSULA

beloved companion
and helpmeet
from the first days of our marriage
to the last of her life

The Parish Register III, 581–6

General Editor's Preface

The reception given to a writer by his contemporaries and near contemporaries is evidence of considerable value to the student of literature. On one side we learn a great deal about the state of criticism at large and in particular about the development of critical attitudes towards a single writer; at the same time, through private comments in letters, journals or marginalia, we gain an insight upon the tastes and literary thought of individual readers of the period. Evidence of this kind helps us to understand the writer's historical situation, the nature of his immediate reading-public, and his response to these pressures.

The separate volumes in the *Critical Heritage Series* present a record of this early criticism. Clearly, for many of the highly productive and lengthily reviewed nineteenth- and twentieth-century writers, there exists an enormous body of material; and in these cases the volume editors have made a selection of the most important views, significant for their intrinsic critical worth or for their representative quality—perhaps even registering incomprehension!

For earlier writers, notably pre-eighteenth century, the materials are much scarcer and the historical period has been extended, sometimes far beyond the writer's lifetime, in order to show the inception and growth of critical views which were initially slow to appear.

In each volume the documents are headed by an Introduction, discussing the material assembled and relating the early stages of the author's reception to what we have come to identify as the critical tradition. The volumes will make available much material which would otherwise be difficult of access and it is hoped that the modern reader will be thereby helped towards an informed understanding of the ways in which literature has been read and judged.

B.C.S.

Contents

Acknowledgments

I should like to thank the Librarian and staff of the Brynmor Jones Library, University of Hull, for so kindly obtaining many of the periodicals which have been used in this collection. My thanks are also due to a number of colleagues, notably Dr J. A. Michie of the Department of English and Mr J. R. Jenkinson of the Department of Classics, and to Mr Roger Lonsdale of Balliol College, Oxford, and Dr Anthony Shipps of the University of Indiana, who helped to locate several quotations. Despite this help, the identity of a few quotations has continued to elude me. I owe a considerable debt to my secretary, Miss Ruth Green. The biggest obligation, as it always has been, is acknowledged in the dedication, now, alas too late for her to receive this recognition of it.

Introduction

'He is (or ought to be—for who reads him?) a living classic.'[1] In that one sentence Dr Leavis has stated the paradox of Crabbe's place in English literature. His status as a classic was indirectly urged by T. S. Eliot in an essay on Johnson's poetry[2] when he argued that

Those who demand of poetry a day dream, or a metamorphosis of their own feeble desires and lusts, or what they believe to be 'intensity' of passion, will not find much in Johnson. He is like Pope and Dryden, Crabbe and Landor, a poet for those who want poetry and not something else, some stay for their own vanity.

Discounting the Eliotian provocativeness (or arrogance, perhaps) one can see in this sentence, at the conclusion of his essay, the sort of poetry he is arguing for, albeit not so well as that he is arguing against. In saying that, we are immediately confronted with one of the familiarities, but also one of the difficulties, of Crabbe criticism. Eliot, not least, has reminded us that the most enlightening criticism is often that which is comparative, and right from Crabbe's own time (the inadequate 'Pope in worsted stockings' being only the most memorable) attempts have been made to define him by comparison. Often, however, they leave us at the end little better informed about what is 'poetry and not something else' in Crabbe than we were at the beginning.

Even this single sentence of Eliot's misses the mark for Crabbe, for in his later work there is much ' "intensity" of passion' within the action—whilst at the same time the narrative is told from a dry, detached point of view. It is not only Crabbe's place in English literature that is paradoxical. In literary history he stands between two distinct eras, the Augustan and the Romantic, belonging in part to both, yet owing total allegiance to neither. He writes in a form of the heroic couplet that can be variously considered as either freer or less controlled than that of the Augustans, and yet it fulfils Eliot's maxim that 'to have the virtues of good prose is the first and minimum requirement of good poetry.' I know that Crabbe's contemporary reviewers complained of the vagaries and inaccuracies of his grammar and vocabulary (see, for example, No. 28), and that he indisputably became increasingly prolix with the passage of the years, but we do well to remind ourselves, again in Eliot's words, that 'we ought to distinguish between poetry which is like *good* prose, and poetry which is like *bad* prose.' In this distinction Crabbe's belongs clearly to the first category. Of course, this is the place at which we are reminded of Hazlitt's question, 'Why not in prose?' The best answer I know is W. C. Roscoe's (No. 67), but there is another—have you ever read Crabbe's prose? Look at his letters, especially the later ones, look at the correct but lifeless expression of his dedications and prefaces—then look at his verse, and you will see how much he has exceeded 'the minimum requirement of good poetry'. But the fact that Hazlitt could ask his question is yet another of the paradoxes in Crabbe.

One more paradox lies in Crabbe's relationship with his birth-place. He could never escape from it, and yet he did not like it. E. M. Forster has remarked on this phenomenon[3], concluding that 'This attraction for the Aldeburgh district, combined with that strong repulsion from it, is characteristic of Crabbe's uncomfortable mind.' Within that uncomfortable mind he could be, as F. L. Lucas has so concisely summed it up, 'naïve, yet shrewd; straightforward, yet sardonic; blunt, yet tender; quiet, yet passionate; realistic, yet romantic'.[4] Yet this complicated, if not complex, poet was (and is) often dismissed as too narrow in his interests and in his response. At the same time as the critic is making such judgments, he is all too often aware that Crabbe, nonetheless, defies classification.

The quotation from Eliot which I have given in my first paragraph continues: 'I sometimes think that our own time, with its elaborate equipment of science and psychological analysis, is even less fitted than the Victorian age to appreciate poetry as poetry.' In this collection an attempt is made to see how Crabbe's own age responded to him volume by volume and then what the Victorians saw in him. The first point to make here is that Crabbe's first poem was published in 1780, his last in 1834. So often Crabbe seems to be thought of as the poet of *The Village* (indeed, there seems to be more than a hint of this in Eliot's remarks), but that poem was published in 1783 and belongs to the world of Johnson and Goldsmith and Cowper. Because they are also poems about people in small, close, tightly knit communities, there is often also a tendency to think of *The Parish Register* (1807) and *The Borough* (1810) as simply more extensive successors of *The Village*. They are, and they are not. Besides a somewhat mellower tone that no doubt came from maturity, experience and his own easier circumstances, these poems represent new departures, and in particular *The Borough* is, as Crabbe's son and biographer remarked, 'a great spring upwards'. In three ways at least—psychological analysis; evident, even at times obtrusive, moral concern; and the handling of verse and language in a manner far more characteristically his own than in the earlier poems—Crabbe struck out in new directions. What did the critics make of the poet newly emergent from over twenty years of silence? This is one of the questions to which these reviews should supply an answer. And what did they make of the incredibly prolific next few years? In other words, instead of seeing Crabbe as we too often tend to do (and were the Victorians here included doing just the same?) as one and the same throughout his career, we have the chance of seeing him through the eyes of his critics as they saw him at the several stages of that career. We also have the opportunity of seeing them at work, of tracing the movement of critical taste and the way in which this affected response to Crabbe himself. And how important this is for a writer who was praised by Johnson, the last Augustan, and who yet survived all the younger generation of the major Romantic poets! Yet another way in which this collection may help is in the search for an answer as to why he was so popular at a time when these latter poets were not. Why did the whirligig of taste swing so much in his favour and against them?

As we look beyond Crabbe's own time, we have the opportunity and the means of exploring the reaction against him. It is there, notably in Hazlitt, in Crabbe's own last years. Was Crabbe not 'Romantic' enough? Gilfillan (No. 65) was neither the first nor the last to be so much moved by 'The Hall of Justice' and 'Sir Eustace Grey', only perhaps the most fully explicit. Why did Crabbe's 'realism' and his discovery of what in effect was the short story in verse fail to appeal to the fiction-dominated Victorian age? Or is it, as the sentence from Eliot above might suggest, that somehow psychological analysis and poetry are uneasy bedfellows? But then why did Browning succeed and Crabbe descend to the doldrums or to the coteries of admiring enthusiasts? And why have we in this century failed to get much nearer to him? Was Leavis right in believing that Crabbe 'was hardly at the fine point of consciousness in his time',[5] and does this mean that each succeeding generation must struggle to find his characteristic and essential worth? FitzGerald was only one of many among those who would make 'cullings from' or 'readings in' Crabbe. The implications of such selection are clearly that, though much has vanished, much deserves to remain.

I

PUBLICATION AND PRINT RUNS

Crabbe's first work, *Inebriety* (1775), was printed and sold by C. Punchard in Ipswich. His next, *The Candidate*, was printed by John Nichols (*Literary Anecdotes*, VIII. 77), published by H. Payne and ran to 250 copies. Nichols also printed *The Library* in 200 copies for subscribers (ibid., VIII. 90). This latter poem ran to a second edition in 1783 and, like its successors, *The Village* and *The Newspaper*, was published by Dodsley. The print runs for these poems and for the second edition of *The Library* are not known, nor are those of the later works, namely, *Poems* (1807), *The Borough* (1810) and *Tales* (1812), all printed by John Brettell and published by Hatchard. There were nine editions of *Poems* and six of *The Borough* by 1817 and seven of *Tales* by 1815. Murray, who took over the remainder stock on becoming Crabbe's publisher, reissued the first two in their remaining 2,000 royal 8vo copies in 1820, together with an unknown number of foolscap 8vo copies of *Tales*, to the last of which he added a new edition of 750 copies as part of a seven-volume edition of the *Works*. The only new work of Crabbe's that Murray published was *Tales of the Hall* (1819), printed by Thomas Davison and issued first in 3,000 copies of a two-volume edition, followed in the same year by another of 1,500 copies and in 1820 by one in three volumes running to 3,000 copies. In 1823 Murray published a five-volume edition in foolscap 8vo (number of copies not known). Finally the *Poetical Works* of 1834 appeared in 7,000 copies of Volume I (which contained the *Life* by Crabbe's son) and 5,000 copies each of the other seven volumes. On 8 May 1846 Murray informed the younger Crabbe that this edition had 'come to a dead stand and there is no demand for it'. As a result, he published the *Works* in one volume in 1847, and this was followed by further editions in this form in 1854, 1867 and 1901.[6]

II

THE EARLY POEMS

The first of Crabbe's poems to be noticed by the reviewers was *The Candidate: a Poetical Epistle to the Authors of the Monthly Review* (1780). With that excessive modesty which marked the tone of his approach to the public throughout his life Crabbe sought the candid judgment of the

Monthly Reviewers upon his work. These last—or, rather, Edmund Cartwright, subsequently to become Crabbe's friend—duly responded. Behind a pretence of impartiality this review (No. 1) was suitably flattered at being thus singled out. The *Critical Review* was correspondingly annoyed by Crabbe's choice and proceeded to discover in the poem 'incurable METROMANIA', 'mad questions', 'ungrammatical transpositions' and 'unintelligible expressions' (No. 2), whilst with greater brevity the *Gentleman's Magazine* (No. 3) advised the Monthly Reviewers not to give the poet much encouragement.

Like its predecessor, Crabbe's next poem, *The Library* (1781), also appeared anonymously. It met a better fate. Cartwright in the *Monthly* considered it 'the production of no common pen' (No. 6), but the *Critical* was most outstanding in its praise (No. 4). With a precision missing from the *Monthly* and the *Gentleman's Magazine* it noted that the poem's 'rhymes are correct and the versification smooth and harmonious' and that there are lines which are 'manly, nervous, and poetical'. This is the critical vocabulary of the Augustan age, and whilst it fitted Crabbe's early works, it was less apt for the assessment of the later.

In his next poem, and the first incidentally to appear over his own name, *The Village* (1783), Crabbe's dissatisfaction with some of the poetical conventions of his day is evident. Dr. Johnson found the work 'original, vigorous, and elegant' (No. 7). In his reaction to the nostalgic pastoralism of Goldsmith and his like:

> I paint the Cot,
> As Truth will paint it, and as Bards will not.
> [I, 33–34]

Crabbe is both original and vigorous. Whether he is elegant is another matter. The *Critical Review* agreed with Crabbe's strictures, but it had also to point out that the subject was forsaken abruptly for the poem to conclude with a long encomium on members of the Rutland family (No. 8). The *Gentleman's Magazine*, though complimentary, noted Crabbe's insistence on 'the dark side of the landscape' (No. 10). Here was the first statement of a recurring criticism both in his own lifetime and ever since. Cartwright in the *Monthly Review* (No. 9) was even more explicit, complaining that the poet was asserting 'as a general proposition what can only be affirmed of individuals'. To this he added the charge of illogicality—'the second part contradicts the assertion of the first'. None the less, despite these criticisms, *The Village* received more serious attention than its predecessor.

In some respects, therefore, *The Newspaper* (1785) must have seemed an anticlimax. The *Gentleman's Magazine*, always the most perfunctory of the three reviews, did not notice it, and the other two (Nos 11 and 12) resorted to outline and quotation to conclude with fainter praise than they gave to *The Village* and unconcealed disappointment following the achievement of that poem. After this, being now established in the Church through the efforts mainly of Burke who had been impressed by *The Library*, Crabbe settled into twenty-two years of literary silence.

III

POEMS (1807)

He only re-emerged when the need for money to finance his son's university education compelled him to do so. The result was *Poems* (1807), a volume containing his early work, some of it revised, and a few new pieces, of which *The Parish Register* was the most important. In general, the new collection received a very favourable welcome. In this new generation the three periodicals which had reviewed Crabbe's earlier work were still in circulation, but their mode of reviewing—by maximum quotation and minimum comment—was now being superseded by the more extensive and detailed criticism characteristic of the new century. The *Critical Review* did not notice the 1807 poems, whilst the *Gentleman's Magazine* (No. 13), typically, dealt only in the most general comment. In the *Monthly Review* (No. 17) Denman, the future Lord Chief Justice, after a meandering start on the literary advice given to Crabbe by Johnson and Fox, and the usual long quotation and vague remarks, struck a more individual note in his last paragraph with its commendation of Crabbe's 'manly and powerful' language in contrast with the 'disgusting cant of idiot-simplicity'. This, however, only serves to remind us, first, that Jeffrey could do this kind of thing much better, and, secondly, to illustrate B. C. Nangle's point that under the younger Griffiths, who had succeeded his father as editor of the *Monthly Review*, 'an extremely able staff of men were placed in a strait jacket of restrictive prohibitions which hampered their free expression and which made their comments seem stodgy, dull and old-fashioned when set beside the new style of slashing, colourful and vivid writing in the *Edinburgh* and *Quarterly*'.[7]

The 1807 volume came, in fact, before the *Quarterly* began to appear (its first issue was February 1809), whilst the *Edinburgh*, though providing with the *Eclectic* the most extensive and, in the modern sense, critical estimation, was to produce both more penetrating and more balanced judgments in its consideration of later volumes. All Crabbe's subsequent works published in his lifetime would be reviewed by Jeffrey, and only the last of the *Edinburgh*'s reviews of Crabbe (on the *Life and Poetical Works* (1834)) would come from another pen, namely, that of Empson. In his *Contributions* (1844) Jeffrey gave more space to Crabbe than to any other poet on the grounds that Crabbe had had less justice done to him by comparison with the others. The review of the 1807 *Poems* (No. 16), whilst welcoming Crabbe back to the literary scene (as did a number of other periodicals), was not, by any means, the best of Jeffrey's considerations. It acknowledged Crabbe's force and truth in description and noted in 'The Hall of Justice' his ability to trace 'the tragic passions of pity and horror'. He also praised, with more than one use of the word, what he calls Crabbe's 'sarcasm'. Of his incidental criticisms we may remark his awareness that Crabbe's 'Chinese accuracy' may yet seem sometimes 'tedious and unnecessary'. This review is remarkable, however, for reasons other than the attention it gives to Crabbe. The criticism itself tends to decline into lengthy quotation and brief comment, but the real power and passion of the article—and this is a major reason why it is not among Jeffrey's finest assessments of Crabbe—lies in its extensive diversion on the shortcomings of the Lake Poets. Crabbe becomes a stick with which to beat Wordsworth. This collection is not the place to include such comments, but I have none the less excerpted a brief paragraph on Martha Ray to give something of the flavour of this criticism alongside and in contrast with what Jeffrey has to say about Crabbe.

The critics rightly saw *The Parish Register* as the major new contribution of the 1807 volume. Most of them welcomed it as a more extensive treatment of the area and topics Crabbe had considered in *The Village*. Though many noted the likenesses, there was little attempt at comparative judgment. The *Annual Review* (No. 19), however, made a succinct and just assessment in seeing the new work as 'on the whole less gloomy, less poetical, has no general plan, fewer general reflections, and more depth of thought'. Of the various character-sketches those of Phoebe Dawson and Richard Monday were most widely praised, whilst that of Isaac Ashford, the 'good peasant', also received some favour. The *Eclectic Review* (No. 21) praised it, but, alongside general criticisms conspicuous for their perspicacity (the reviewer was the underrated hymn-writer and critic, James Montgomery), there is a sermonising note upbraiding Crabbe's occasional lapses in moral seriousness—especially on death. By contrast, the *Anti-Jacobin Review* (No. 14) commended the proper balance of his sentiments on this subject as compared with 'the enthusiastic cant of those ignorant preachers whom the Methodists send forth in swarms'. This hint of sectarian animosity was at this time a cloud the size of a man's hand in the sky of Crabbe-criticism. It would not long remain so small.

IV

THE BOROUGH (1810)

Crabbe's fifties were a phenomenally productive period in his poetical life. Once he had returned with the 1807 *Poems*, he followed this volume first with *The Borough* (1810) and then with *Tales* (1812). 'This late spring of public favour' was to ripen, as Jeffrey hoped, into 'mature fame'. The poetry of community in *The Village* and then in the country parson's reflections on the 'simple annals of the VILLAGE POOR' in *The Parish Register* was developed and extended in Crabbe's recollections of his native Aldeburgh which form the staple of *The Borough*. Indeed, the *Monthly Review* (No. 22) was to characterize the new poem as Crabbe's '*Village*, extended beyond all reasonable limits', and the generous Jeffrey had to agree that a severe critic might find that 'its peculiarities are more obtrusive, its faults greater, and its beauties less' (No. 23). Grant in the *Quarterly* (No. 27) (though nineteenth-century writers thought it was Gifford[8]) discriminated more finely when he said: 'While the defects are more aggravated as well as more thickly sown, the beauties, though not less scantily doled out, are unquestionably touched with a more affecting grace and softness.' Crabbe's most ambitious poem to date was seen therefore as largely the mixture as before, except that there was more of it. In this excess some critics showed signs of surfeit. What was new was not striking enough, what was striking was not new enough.

The Borough was noticed by the old trio of the *Monthly*, the *Critical* (Nos 22 and 25) and the *Gentleman's* and by newer reviews which fall quite neatly into pairs—two religious periodicals, the *Eclectic Review* and the *Christian Observer* (Nos 24 and 29); two lesser publications of more recent origin, the *Monthly Mirror* and the *British Critic* (Nos 26 and 28); and finally what were to become the twin giants, the *Edinburgh* and the *Quarterly* (Nos 23 and 27). Of these, the last, together with the two religious reviews and the *Monthly Mirror* were largely hostile. By contrast, the *British Critic* was extremely laudatory. Jeffrey's essay in the

Edinburgh manifested that discriminating but sympathetic criticism which reveals the extent of his rapport with the poet and which made him the most reliable of Crabbe's contemporary critics.

The procedure of considering seriatim the several letters which constitute the poem was almost universally adopted, but the *Gentleman's Magazine* outdid the other journals in its characteristic mode of lengthy summary with little accompanying criticism. It discovered some 'truly Hogarthean traits—*ut Pictura Poesis*' in 'Elections' (Letter V), a comparison taken up at large by the *Monthly Review* (No. 22) which described Crabbe as 'the Hogarth of poetry', and for purposes of condemnation—with a quotation from Reynolds—by the *Christian Observer*. The *Monthly* preferred, however, to concentrate its censure upon the poet's 'want of arrangement' and his 'unfavourable opinion of mankind and his austere morality'. (Incidentally, it incorrectly ascribed the sin of Jachin (Letter XIX), pocketing the sacramental contribution, to Abel Keene (Letter XXI).) It also noted his increasing inclination to prolixity. To these the *Critical* (No. 25) added 'his occasionally prosaic familiarity almost to vulgarity [and] his carelessness of style'. The now familiar indictment was being built up, but the *Critical* also listed his qualities—'the faithfulness and spirit of his satire, his accurate delineation of almost every species of character, his easy and simple flow of poetical diction, his continual intermixture of pathetic and ludicrous observation, and the air of good nature, which tempers the rigour of his severest passages.'

To what would become the recurrent criticisms that are mentioned above two others were added. One of these was contained in the *Monthly Mirror* (No. 26) which began by lambasting what it called 'this frightful preface' with its 'attempts to anticipate every possible objection to every objectionable part of the poem, and to apologize for, and make exceptions to, the severity of its satire'. The *Eclectic* (No. 24) also rebuked Crabbe's 'solicitude' to mollify his satire as well as his servility to his patron. In addition, this review advanced the second objection—to Crabbe's attack on Dissenters in the fourth Letter of the poem.[9] In a lengthy five-page digression the reviewer condemned Crabbe as unfair to Dissenters as a body, as doubtfully accurate even in his portrayal of individuals and as questionably employing burlesque and buffoonery for the serious purpose of correcting religious eccentricity. The *Christian Observer* (No. 29) supported its contemporary in more ponderous tone and even extended its rebuke to 'the spirit of levity' with which Crabbe delineated the vicar (Letter III). By contrast, the Tory and High Church *British Critic* (No. 28) fervently and at length quoted the prose introduction to Letter IV with its 'very sensible and judicious remarks on the enthusiasts'.

The opposition of the *Edinburgh* and the new *Quarterly* under Gifford was both more subtle and more literary. Robert Grant, in the latter (No. 27), found Crabbe hostile to high imagination through his realism and went on to complain that, by distinction from the Dutch school of painters with whom he was often compared, Crabbe's realism was not even successful in itself because it lacked that 'happiness of execution' which the painters possessed. Crabbe's microscopic eye, whilst it made for 'minute accuracy', produced 'an air of littleness and technical precision'. Grant thought that Crabbe's great virtue was force, but it was accompanied by such defect of taste that the result was often coarseness. Whether one agrees with this or not, it has to be recognized as the most penetrating analysis of the poet's realism up to that date. It really attempts to examine what it was that laid so much of Crabbe's work open to the charge of being disgusting. It also seeks to explain why 'in his pity there seems to be more of contempt than of tenderness, and the objects of his compassion are at the same time the objects of his satire.' Grant, it will be seen, was basically anti-realist. Indeed, his review began with the claim that 'poetry . . . must flatter the imagination', 'drawing us away from the fatigues of reality'. Others made the same complaint, the *Christian Observer*, for example, noting the difference between Crabbe's subjects and those of Campbell and Scott.

Jeffrey (No. 23) presents us with the other side of the coin. He frankly accepted some of Crabbe's scenes and characters as disgusting, but he also examined at some length the nature of the disgusting in order to achieve a more precise definition and a more accurate separation of some of the poet's portraits than other reviews had achieved. He anticipated Grant by enlisting the roles of compassion and satire in determining what is disgusting: 'The only sufferers, then, upon whom we cannot bear to look, are those that excite pain by their wretchedness, while they are too depraved to be the objects of affection, and too weak and insignificant to be the causes of misery to others, or, consequently of indignation to the spectators.' This is a laudable attempt to deal with a difficult problem. It leads Jeffrey, however, to a condemnation of several characters in *The Borough*, among them Abel Keene, Blaney, Benbow—'and a good part of those of Grimes and Ellen Orford'! Something had gone wrong when these last two had to be included. With Grimes Jeffrey perhaps had failed to recognize the tragic depths of human suffering to be found even in the depraved. With all of them, however, he seems not to have allowed enough for the moral tenor of Crabbe's work. This is the more surprising when one realizes how most sensitively of all the critics he had recognized the poet's especial awareness of the universality of human experience to be found in common everyday life—'the truest and most pathetic pictures of natural feeling and common suffering. By the mere force of his art, and the novelty of his style, he forces us to attend to objects that are usually neglected, and to enter into feelings from which we are in general but too eager to escape.' To put it no higher than this, Jeffrey realized that, because we do not like a thing, it does not thereby become necessarily disgusting. He concluded the sentence quoted with the words—'and then trusts to nature for the effect of the representation'. In other words, he saw too, as so few of his fellow-critics did, that though Crabbe might sometimes oppress with redundant descriptive minutiae, his most powerful overall effects came not from what he said but from what he left unsaid, from poetry which works 'not so much in what it directly supplies to the imagination, as in what it enables it to supply to itself', from poetry of suggestion, that is, rather than from poetry of statement. Here is a fine perception of Crabbe the quintessential Romantic, not just the Gothicized Romantic of 'Sir Eustace Grey'. Why, oh why, then had Jeffrey been so harsh on Wordsworth? The next paragraph of this very review opens with a sentence that might have come from the Preface to the *Lyrical Ballads*: 'Now, the delineation of all that concerns the lower and most numerous classes of society is, in this respect, on a footing with the pictures of our primary affections,—that their originals are necessarily familiar to all men, and are inseparably associated with a multitude of their most interesting impressions.' Fundamental and universal, this, the romanticism of 'cottages, streets and villages', Jeffrey preferred to that of 'palaces, castles or camps'.

Jeffrey recognized also the task, 'in a great degree new and original in our language', which Crabbe had assumed as 'the satirist of low life'. One letter, in particular,—that on amusements—was widely commended for its light-hearted criticism. Generally speaking, Crabbe was praised for three qualities—his satire, together with his realism (when it was not disgusting) and his capacity for pathos. The tale of Thomas and Sally in Letter II received special mention in this last respect from the *Christian Observer* and the *British Critic*, whilst the *Quarterly* juxtaposed the very powerful but very similar descriptions of the ostracized parish-clerk (Letter XIX), Abel Keene (XXI) and Peter Grimes (XXII). The combination of low life and suffering, and especially merited suffering, presented the critics with a new problem of judgment (only Langhorne had ever, previously, approached this area of life in litera- ture). Their puzzlement is reflected in their judgments. The *Critical* (No. 25) praised the portrait of Jachin, for example, for its fine control of varying tone and the hostile *Monthly Mirror* (No. 26) thought this sketch commendable, whereas the *Eclectic* (No. 24), no doubt affected by religious bias, rejected it as morally objectionable. Nor was Jeffrey alone in his discomfort about Peter Grimes; the favourable *British Critic* (No. 28) was also repelled, whereas the *Gentleman's* thought this story 'depicted with a masterly hand' and the *Eclectic* (No. 24), in this case doubtless helped by its Evangelical view of human depravity, thought it 'the master-piece of the volume'.

Grant (No. 27), singling out 'Sir Eustace Grey' from the 1807 volume, praised Crabbe's psychological power; his 'delineations of the passions are so just—so touching of the gentle, and of the awful so tremendous'. Jeffrey (No. 23) at the end of his review also picked out this poem. At the same time he suggested that the poet's 'unrivalled gift in the delinea- tion of character which is now used only for the creation of detached portraits, might be turned to admirable account in maintaining the interest, and enhancing the probability of an extended train of adven- tures.' The poet was to heed this advice in his next work—in part.

V

TALES (1812)

Crabbe had set the critical world by the ears. 'The names of Voltaire and Crebillon never divided the critics of Paris into contrary parties more effectually than this world of ours is now set at variance by the disputed merits of Mr. Crabbe.' These were the words with which the *Critical Review* (No. 35) opened its examination of *Tales* (1812). It went on: 'The most remarkable feature in the present controversy is, that both parties are right. . . . Mr. Crabbe is absolutely and indubitably a poet in the sense which his admirers annex to the term . . . yet we must confess that his general style and disposition are such as in a great degree to bear out his objectors in their refusal.' To accentuate the struggle, Crabbe himself stepped into the arena with an answer to his critics.

The Preface to the 1812 collection (No. 30) is Crabbe's most explicit and most considered statement of the principles of his art. He noticed three objections, namely, lack of unity, excessive realism and deficient imaginative quality. Admitting the first, he yet claimed that 'something is gained by greater variety of incident and more minute display of character, by accuracy of description and diversity of scene.' On the second point he allowed that his work was not 'to be estimated with the more lofty and heroic kind of poems'; nevertheless, he claimed that faithful delineation of men and events as they are could yet be poetry, however much the critics might be reluctant to grant to a Crabbe what they would willingly concede to a Hogarth. This led him to a lengthy consideration of the last and most serious point, which had formed the core of the *Quarterly*'s strictures. Boldly ranging Chaucer, Dryden and Pope alongside himself, Crabbe argued for 'poetry without an atmosphere', claiming that faithful delineation of 'everyday concerns' might 'excite and interest [the reader's] feelings as the imaginary exploits, adventures and perils of romance'. As he told Mrs Leadbeater: 'I do not know that I could paint merely from my own fancy: and there is no cause why we should. Is there not diversity sufficient in society? and who can go, even but a little, into the assemblies of our fellow-wanderers from the way of perfect rectitude, and not find characters so varied and so pointed, that he need not call upon his imagination?'[10] And, just as he drew from experience rather than invention for his material, so also his appeal is to 'the plain sense and sober judgment of [his] readers rather than to the fancy and imagination'.[11] After this forthright apologia there were no reviewers' complaints about undue modesty in this Preface!

In some ways, indeed, the reviews of *Tales*, taken as a whole, are disappointing, particularly as Crabbe was now at the height of his fame (the collection ran into seven editions in three years). For one thing, many of the periodicals contented themselves largely with brief comment on each tale seriatim. For another, the most capable of the unsympathetic reviews, the *Quarterly*, chose not to notice either this volume or its only successor in the poet's lifetime, *Tales of the Hall*. The *Eclectic* (No. 36) remained cool: after despatching *The Borough* as 'on the whole . . . not a very pleasing poem', it thought that the new collection would hardly add to the poet's reputation. 'We seemed jogging on a broken-winded Pegasus through all the flats and bogs of Parnassus.' The *British Review* (No. 31), like the *Eclectic*, of Evangelical bias, also had faults to find, but yet had to conclude that the work was 'what no writer but one of original genius could have produced'. Here was the problem for the critics—so much power of original genius and yet so many glaring faults. Hence the opening of the *Critical*'s article (No. 35), the most perceptive that that journal ever devoted to Crabbe and, ironically, in one of the last numbers before its demise. But, as ever, Jeffrey in the *Edinburgh* (No. 33) was most judicious—generous without partiality, critical without carping.

What others had likened to 'short stories' (the *Monthly* (No. 34)) and 'episodes from longer poems' (the *British Critic* (No. 38)) Jeffrey chose to regard as 'mere supplementary chapters to *The Borough* or *The Parish Register*' and yet, so far as structure was concerned, he expressed himself 'satisfied with the length of the pieces he has given us'. These were sufficiently 'the extended train[s] of adventures' he had requested in his review of *The Borough*; he did not want the epic that Crabbe thought he was looking for. The main direction of Jeffrey's criticism of the new volume relates to repetition: 'The same tone—the same subjects—the same style, measure and versification; the same finished and minute delineation of things quite ordinary and common . . . the same strange mixture of [pathos] with starts of low humour . . .; the same kindly sympathy . . .;—and, finally, the same honours paid to the delicate affections and ennobling passions of humble life.' In three respects, however, there was improvement—first, 'a greater number of instances on which he has combined the natural language and manners of humble life with the energy of true passion'; second, the revelation of fine feelings in 'the middling orders'; and third, the new poems are 'more uniformly and directly moral and beneficial'. Some reviews—the *British Review* and the *British Critic* (Nos 31 and 38), for example—still complained of excessive gloom in certain tales, but Jeffrey was undoubtedly right in discovering a 'more amiable and consoling view of human nature', just as he was in noting Crabbe's new interest in higher social classes than hitherto, a fact that in the *Critical*'s view (No. 35) helped to make the *Tales* less 'obnoxious' than the previous volumes. The more insistent moral purpose was widely noted, by the *Gentleman's Magazine* and by the *British Review*, for instance, the latter even claiming that the new turn had gone so far as to produce 'an unity of piety with genius'.

In one respect, however, the reviews found no improvement whatever. One after another had found faults of execution in *The Borough*—the *Quarterly* (No. 27) considered the '*costume* of [Crabbe's] ideas . . . slovenly and ungraceful', mentioning particularly his abbreviated colloquial auxiliary verbs, the *Monthly Mirror* (No. 26) noticed clumsy triplet rhymes, the *Christian Observer* (No. 29) complained of 'ill advised fondness for antithesis' which the *Eclectic* (No. 24) preferred to describe as 'perpetual, snappish recurrence'. The last-named added monotonous versification, 'many very dull paragraphs, and numberless feeble lines' for good measure, whilst the *British Critic* (No. 28) singled out several inaccuracies of grammar and vocabulary. In the *Tales* the *British Review* (No. 31) thought Crabbe careless of all but rhyme and metre, but the *Eclectic* (No. 36) scornfully declared: 'It is nothing but prose measured, whether by ear or finger, into decasyllabic lines' and then showed the variety with which Crabbe altered the grammatical order, ignored quantity, was prodigal of triplets and alexandrines—and even then 'his verses are frequently as feeble as the following' with four lines as examples. Some of the more friendly reviews such as the *Edinburgh* (No. 33) noted Crabbe's faults of style—'not dignified—and neither very pure nor very easy', but, not possessing the animus of the *Eclectic* and no doubt by this time realizing that in this regard Crabbe was incorrigible, they contented themselves with brevity. The *Edinburgh* noticed that Crabbe's 'similes [were] almost all elaborate and ingenious, and rather seem to be furnished from the efforts of a fanciful mind, than to be exhaled by the spontaneous ferment of a heated imagination'. Crabbe's son quoted this in a note to the 1834 edition,[12] adding: 'Mr. Crabbe was much struck with the sagacity of this remark. On reading it, he said, "Jeffrey is quite right: my usual method has been to think of such illustrations, and insert them *after finishing a tale*." '

It was not faults of expression, however, that Jeffrey chose to emphasize. He rightly stressed Crabbe's stature as an observer of human nature: 'By far the most remarkable thing in his writings, is the prodigious mass of original observations and reflections they everywhere exhibit; and that extraordinary power of conceiving and representing an imaginary object, whether physical or intellectual, with such a rich and complete accompaniment of circumstances and details, as few ordinary observers either perceive or remember in realities.' That it was which made Jeffrey remark that Crabbe was 'the most original writer who has ever come before us', and that it was in the *Tales* that brought the poet to the high-water mark of his popularity.

VI

TALES OF THE HALL (1819)

On the strength of it John Murray paid Crabbe £3,000 for the copyright of his work and published his next volume, *Tales of the Hall* (1819).

The publisher lived to regret his bargain, for the poet's tide was on the ebb. Yet Murray was not alone in his miscalculation. The new work received much fuller notice than any of its predecessors, and though old complaints were reiterated, Crabbe's stature as a major poet was everywhere recognized, and at least three periodicals deliberately examined him in the broadest context—Wilson in *Blackwood's* (No. 43), opening with a comparison of him with Wordsworth and Burns as poets of the people, Jeffrey in the *Edinburgh* (No. 44) relating the poetic gift of observation to satire, sympathy and choice of character and incident, and finally the *Christian Observer* (No. 48) considering Crabbe against the traditional criteria of the poet's need both to please and to instruct. Journal after journal, recognizing how little Crabbe had changed, assumed that there could now be no further development and summarized his qualities; and yet they also looked back and saw some change. The *British Critic* (No. 45), whilst detecting some abatement in his severity, thought him more unequal than ever, and Jeffrey (No. 44) found both fewer faults and fewer beauties. With the *Christian Observer* (which, incidentally, like Jeffrey against Wordsworth years before, used Crabbe as a stick to beat Byron, who was then bringing out *Don Juan*), Jeffrey also discovered a new note—'Mr. C. seems to become more amorous as he grows older.' The confirmation of this surmise is to be found in the account of Crabbe's life between the publication of *Tales* and *Tales of the Hall*. His wife had died in 1813, he had moved to Trowbridge in 1814, and in the next years he formed friendships with a number of young women, one of whom he nearly married.[13] In my copy of *The Romance of an Elderly Poet*, which once belonged to Augustine Birrell, its erstwhile owner has written: 'Crabbe had *good taste* in women.'

It was Crabbe's view of life, and especially his choice of characters, which occupied the critics. There was the familiar complaint that his characters were too depraved. In this respect his views of life seemed contrary to experience (so the *British Critic* (No. 45)). The *Edinburgh Monthly Review* (No. 46) criticized his lack of selection, whilst at the same time recognizing him as 'the most moral of all living poets'; it even suggested that his arbitrariness was exaggerated by narrowness, by his concentration on class rather than individuals. It was the *Christian Observer* (No. 48) that, not surprisingly, pressed home the attack. Crabbe's fascination with the unpleasant was too much even for this Evangelical journal with its proper sense of man's inherent evil. His 'favoured objects . . . are a set of low, mean, pitiful and scoundrel passions, the sordid offspring of pure selfishness . . . His very virtues are of a creeping order; but his vices positively wallow in a kind of moral stench.' His pessimism was seen as sheer misanthropy, conveying 'an impression of the hatefulness of man, with the effect of scarcely wishing, because not hoping, to make him, by any efforts, better.' John Wilson (No. 43) in a sensitive first criticism of Crabbe, at once generous and just, answered this, using an image that comes again and again in considerations of the poet. He noted Crabbe's evident 'intense satisfaction in moral anatomy', and unpleasant though it might often be, Crabbe's poetry, he felt, opened up areas of human action and suffering new to many readers but none the less applicable to their experience: 'The power is almost miraculous with which he has stirred up human nature from its dregs, and shewn working in them the common spirit of humanity. Human nature becomes more various and wonderful in his hands . . . He lays before us scenes and characters from which in real life we would turn our eyes with intolerant disgust; and yet he forces us to own, that on such scenes and by such characters much the same kind of part is played that ourselves, and others like us, play on another stage.' Wilson also saw what others, fascinated by the evil in Crabbe even more than he was, failed to see—'the tenderness of the man's heart . . . we hear him, with a broken and melancholy voice, mourning over the woe and wickedness whose picture he has so faithfully drawn.'

Whether sympathetic or not, practically every review recognized at the end of Crabbe's career what had been evident from the beginning but what was now displayed in unsurpassed strength—the power of his observation ('he is peculiarly the poet of actual life', said the *Edinburgh Monthly Review* (No. 46)) and the depth of his pathos. It was the growth of this latter which prevented Crabbe from developing, as he might well have done, into a misanthropic satirist of the Swiftian brand. To the two qualities I have just noted Jeffrey rightly added 'the sure and profound sagacity' of many of Crabbe's remarks. Both Jeffrey in the *Edinburgh* (No. 44) and the critic of the *Eclectic* (No. 50) saw Crabbe as the greatest 'mannerist' of his time, but yet considered him inimitable because of 'his style of thought, and his materials for thinking'. The superficial manner might be parodied (as in *Rejected Addresses* (No. 39)); the essential style was beyond the reach of imitators. As Edward FitzGerald put it sixty years later in a letter to J. R. Lowell: 'Any Poetaster may improve three-fourths of the careless old Fellow's Verse: but it would puzzle a Poet to improve the better part' (No. 63g). Here, of course, lies the fundamental, and for many readers insuperable, problem with Crabbe.

His faults are all too evident; his virtues are much harder to come by, but how well they reward the effort they demand!

VII

POETICAL WORKS (1834)

Crabbe died in February 1832. Two years later an eight-volume edition of his works appeared. It contained a small collection of *Posthumous Tales* and was prefaced by a *Life* by his son, itself a minor biographical classic of the nineteenth century. Not surprisingly, the greater part of the work being already familiar, most reviewers concentrated their attention on the *Life*. They had, however, to devote some space to the new poems. These had not received their final touches, but there is no reason to think that they would have been much better if they had. Crabbe had already received too much criticism for his carelessness for us to believe that he would have taken pains at this late stage of his career. The periodicals damned with faint praise (as in the *Gentleman's Magazine* (No. 60)), or simply reported, as did the *Eclectic* (No. 59), that the new work would not affect the poet's reputation either way, or, as did both the *Edinburgh* and the *Quarterly* (Nos 61 and 55), found it decidedly inferior.

The *Edinburgh*'s reviewer was not Jeffrey but Empson, and perhaps for this reason the change of tone is remarkable. The old warmth has gone, and now we find the writer speculating on 'where Crabbe has not succeeded'. Empson, in fact, quoted the *Quarterly* of long years before (attributing its article wrongly to Gifford) and Crabbe's reply, but he came down on the side of the journal, concluding that Crabbe's 'imagination and his feelings stood him in marvellous little stead' and that to exchange the pain of fiction for that of reality is to gain but little indeed. Crabbe missed total truth, because he omitted the highest truth. Lockhart in the *Quarterly* had better things to say, emphasizing Crabbe's Christianity and the error of considering him a gloomy poet. The only other reviews which call for special mention are the American notices. That in the *North American Review* (No. 57) was very general and not very penetrating, but the *New York Review*'s (No. 62) is a systematic consideration, isolating the poet's originality, humanity, descriptive powers, pathos and religious attitude.

VIII

GENERAL STUDIES

One of the first general articles on Crabbe, as distinct from reviews of specific publications of his work, was that by T. N. Talfourd (then a mere twenty-year-old) in the *Pamphleteer* (1815) (No. 40). Apart from the youthfulness of the author, perhaps even because of it, it contains little that is remarkable. Talfourd saw Crabbe as the moral poet of humble life, inventive in his own way, but a faithful reproducer of things remembered rather than an imaginative creator.

The role of imagination, its nature or, as some claimed, its absence, is a central feature of the criticism of Crabbe, not least in the most notable unsympathetic assessments in his own lifetime, namely, those of Hazlitt and Wilson, the latter by 1827 much altered in his opinion as compared with the time when he reviewed *Tales of the Hall*. Hazlitt had characterized Crabbe as 'the most literal of our descriptive poets' in his *Lectures on the English Poets* (1818) (No. 41) which called forth a reply from R. H. Dana in an article on the lectures in the *North American Review* (1819) (No. 42). Hazlitt returned to the attack with redoubled force in an essay in the *London Magazine* (1821) (No. 52) which, with some alteration, later appeared in *The Spirit of the Age* (1825). 'Literal fidelity serves him in the place of invention . . . His Muse is not one of the daughters of Memory, but the old toothless mumbling dame herself.' Contrasting Pope's 'In the worst inn's worst room', a passage which Crabbe himself had cited in the Preface to the *Tales*, Hazlitt asserted: 'Pope describes what is striking, Crabbe would have described merely what was there'—or, changing the context a little, 'the non-essentials of every trifling incident'.[14] Varying the object of his attack, Hazlitt went on to find Crabbe 'sickly . . . querulous . . . fastidious . . . a sophist and a misanthrope in verse'. Not surprisingly—and how often the critics of the Romantic period did this—he praised 'Sir Eustace Grey'. He also praised 'Peter Grimes'; indeed, this poem and *The Village*, to which the sketch of Phoebe Dawson, incidentally, is erroneously allocated, receive a disproportionate amount of attention. The *Tales* are conceded to be 'more readable than his Poems', but the few lines that Hazlitt perfunctorily awards them at the end of the essay make one wonder whether he had read them, and there is no evidence that he even knew of the existence of *Tales of the Hall*.

Like Hazlitt, Wilson (No. 53) also felt that Crabbe was too contented simply to delineate. His failure to select suggested an absence of purpose, resulting in a sense of 'mere miscellaneousness'. Hazlitt had enlisted Pope; Wilson cited Wordsworth: 'If we should doubt for a moment the truth of Wordsworth's pictures, as pictures of reality, still we could not question his right to make them what they are.' Including Burns with Wordsworth, Wilson contended that 'Crabbe draws the face of things—they draw its spirit.' Wordsworth is an imaginative and a philosophic poet who elevates, Crabbe 'drives out of the region of poetry' with matter fit rather for 'the Committees of Mendicity or Police'. He writes as 'a sneering cynic'. He has no sense of the transcendental; there is nothing in the causes of his events.

Wilson's view of Wordsworth and Crabbe is supported by Wordsworth's own view of Crabbe. Indeed, the Romantic reaction to Crabbe might well be summed up as Hazlitt v. Jeffrey. For Wordsworth (No. 51a) 'nineteen out of 20 of Crabbe's Pictures are mere matters of fact'; for Coleridge (No. 51m) he has an 'absolute defect of the high imagination', whilst that faithful, even sycophantic, follower of the great Romantics, Crabb Robinson (No. 51n) thought that Crabbe's poems were a very 'unpoetical representation of human life'. On the other hand, Byron (No. 51c) declared that 'Crabbe's the man', as well as finding him, in the better known words, 'Nature's sternest painter, yet the best'. In a familiar image Carlyle (No. 51i) found Crabbe 'an anatomist in searching into the stormy passions of the human heart', whilst even more vividly Landor (No. 51o), through the mouth of Porson, noted Crabbe's psychological penetration when he said that the poet entered the human heart 'on all fours, and told the people what an ugly thing it is inside'. Croker (No. 51k) found poetical qualities to commend, but, in general, the praise derived from Crabbe's analysis of character and action.

With this in mind, one might think that Crabbe's reputation should have soared with the coming of the great age of the novel in the middle of the nineteenth century. It did not. Although *Tait's Magazine* in a fairly superficial review in 1834 thought that he had not at that time received his fair measure of praise, Gilfillan in the same journal in 1847 (No. 65) gave him a very cool appraisal. Twenty years later the *St. James's Magazine* (No. 69) granted that some doubted whether he deserved a place even in the second class of his contemporaries alongside Campbell, Scott and Moore, whilst at the end of the next decade, even though he goes on to say other things, the American critic G. E. Woodberry could write: 'We have done with Crabbe.' (No. 73). The dismissive criticisms were familiar enough—lack of imagination, a mind 'like a camera' (Frederick Sheldon, the *North American Review*, 1872 (No. 70)), narrow range, lack of selection, absence of overmastering purpose —and for Gilfillan, little humour. Many of these criticisms are not very profound and Gilfillan's is mannered to a degree, but, because they are representative of a fairly ordinary response, they are in some ways a better measure of the average reaction than the criticism of more sensitive judges.

Some of these latter are represented in the selection of Victorian views (No. 63). They include Clough and George Eliot who recall the pleasure of reading Crabbe in youth and Rossetti who declared a present enjoyment. Tennyson and Newman expressed their love of Crabbe and Hopkins placed him with characteristic precision and economy. Of this group only John Sterling, reviewing Tennyson, felt that Crabbe failed to make that leap from the sensitive observation, understanding and appreciation of the ordinary that transforms fact into poetry. Sterling saw poetry as 'a refuge from the hardness and narrowness of the actual world'.

The real enthusiast was FitzGerald, and with the work of W. C. Roscoe and Leslie Stephen his attempts to reinstate Crabbe deserve a special mention. Roscoe, writing in the *National Review* (1859) (No. 67), provides the most balanced and discriminating assessment of Crabbe to be made after his death in the whole of the nineteenth century. He accepted that 'it is low tide with Crabbe'; he accepted also that Crabbe is a poet 'without passion', that he has no wit, humour or profundity, no reasoning or systematic view of life; he conceded that 'once become sufficiently familiar with Crabbe to know what he has written, and there is nothing more to be gained from him.' He even went so far as to say that 'he handles life so as to take the bloom off it', but two views he firmly rejected. He could not agree that Crabbe was a mere descriptive realist—'He had imagination'; and he could not agree that Crabbe was either stern or gloomy—'The only passion which Crabbe really moves deeply is the one to which he was himself most accessible, that of pity.' That phrase 'to which he was himself most accessible' is important; it stresses the role of experience in Crabbe. Most critics saw the importance of experience in Crabbe's choice of material, but they also saw it so large that it obscured the form which Crabbe's imagination took. Roscoe, to his credit, observed in better perspective and emphasized the rare quality of 'receptive imagination' in Crabbe. The passage is worth quoting at length:

This adjective indicates the nature of the faculty in most minds; it is generally to a great extent passive, and partakes of the nature of a mirror in which the images of outer things are reflected. But in some men it is a more active and aggressive power; and this was particularly the case with Crabbe. His was a grasping tenacious imagination. Little Hartley Coleridge would have called it a 'catch-me-fast' faculty. He was a man of keen observation, but also something farther; he did more than see things; he laid fast hold of them, and held them up as it were to himself for contemplation; cast a vivid light on them; and when he gave them forth again, he gave not the crude fact, but the impression he had taken of it. If he did not transmute experience into poetry, he yet did something more than simply translate it into verse.

In Coleridgean terms, Crabbe had a very sensitive and comprehensive primary imagination which did not merely observe but also held fast as mental objects what had been received in sense-perception. His secondary imagination, whilst not profoundly re-creative, nevertheless vivified the mental objects which it received from the primary imagination. This is at once the most compact and most penetrating answer I know to Hazlitt's question: 'Why not insist on the unwelcome reality in plain prose?' Crabbe wrote in verse because, as Roscoe recognized, he 'dared to be true to himself'.

This sense of himself and this capacity for seeing others and being so affected by what he saw inevitably expressed itself through his insight into character. Roscoe noticed this, and so did Sheldon in his *North American Review* article (No. 70) which in an important measure is an attempt to interpret the poetry biographically. So also did Leslie Stephen (*Cornhill Magazine*, 1872) (No. 72), who not only noted the effects that Crabbe derived from trifling incidents, the sorrows of commonplace characters and especially the 'natural workings of evil passions' ('Nobody describes better the process of going to the dogs'), but also, incidentally, refined on Sheldon's biographical theory with his emphasis on the importance of Crabbe's early environment. His final word was for the power of Crabbe's pathos.

FitzGerald was a last and lonely admirer, an enthusiast rather than a critic, who sought to rescue his idol by judicious representation. If Crabbe would not select or prune, then FitzGerald would do it for him. He chose *Tales of the Hall*, in some ways the least likely poems, for the purpose (No. 74). His *Readings in Crabbe* was privately published in 1879. I have chosen three pieces from the next decade, in one of which T. E. Kebbel (No. 76) attempts to place Crabbe in a series of 'Great Writers'. His criticism is judicious, noting the poet's roles as psychologist, moralist, narrator and satirist and seeing that Crabbe has a grasp of the tragedy of humble life, but he has to concede the poet's lack of taste and slovenly style. Kebbel makes some illuminating comparisons, not least on the tragedy of humble life, between Crabbe and George Eliot, but more striking than the likenesses is the extended contrast that Patmore (No. 75) makes between Crabbe and Shelley. The last word is with Saintsbury (No. 77), who found Crabbe gloomy, insufficiently varied, lacking in music ('You could unrhyme him'—Could you?) and pictorial rather than poetic. This echoes Sterling (and others) of generations past, and it is a true verdict, but readers of two centuries, whilst recognizing its truth, have never been happy that it contains the whole truth.

Later generations have concurred with earlier critics in generally preferring the *Tales*, and of these the most popular have included 'The Parting Hour' (II), 'Procrastination' (IV), 'The Frank Courtship' (VI), 'The Lover's Journey' (X), 'Edward Shore' (XI), 'The Confidant' (XVI) and 'Resentment' (XVII). Of the *Tales of the Hall* only 'Sir Owen Dale' (XII) and 'Smugglers and Poachers' (XX) have attained anything like the same favour. These, with 'The Parish Clerk' (XIX), 'Ellen Orford' (XX), 'Peter Grimes' (XXII) and possibly one or two others from *The Borough*, represent the best of Crabbe.

IX

CRABBE'S REPUTATION ABROAD

Reference has been made above to American criticism of Crabbe, but some mention should also be included of those articles first published in Britain which were later reprinted in America. *Littell's Living Age*, for example, published Gilfillan's essay (No. 65) (Vol. XI, pp. 1–9), Roscoe's survey (No. 67) (LX, pp. 529–46) and Leslie Stephen's estimate (No. 72) (CXXIII, pp. 403–16).

Crabbe was included amongst *The British Poets of the Nineteenth Century* (pp. 1–193), published in English by Baudry in Paris (1827–8). This extensive selection included not only *The Library*, *The Newspaper* and a number of shorter poems but also *The Parish Register* and *Tales of the Hall*. The omissions—*The Village*, *The Borough* (except for the passage on prisons) and *Tales*—are, however, more remarkable than the inclusions. In 1829 Galignani published the *Poetical Works* in Paris. Translations include that of *The Parish Register* into Dutch by Sijbrandi in 1858 and of *The Newspaper* into German by Carl Abel in 1856. Long before this, however, in 1820, F. J. Jacobsen's *Briefe an eine deutsche Edelfrau über die neuesten englischen Dichter* included prose translations of a number of passages from Crabbe (e.g., parts of *Tales* I, IV, X, XI and XVII; the Phoebe Dawson episode in *The Parish Register*, Part II; and a number of shorter pieces from *The Borough*).

An important influence in extending foreign acquaintance with Crabbe seems to have been the section devoted to him in Allan Cunningham's *Biographical and Critical History of English Literature in the last fifty years*. Originally appearing as articles in the *Athenaeum* in 1833, this work was published in Baudry's Foreign Library in Paris in 1834. A French version came out in the *Revue des deux mondes* (New Series, IV), whilst A. Kaiser made a German translation (Leipzig, 1834). A copy of this latter was in the possession of Annette Droste, whose *Die Judenbuche* (1842) with its 'strong eighteenth-century atmosphere' of village life[15] may, though written in prose, have been influenced by Crabbe.

The French translation of Cunningham, we know, was used by the Russian S. P. Shevyrev, whilst Pushkin asked for Crabbe's works to be sent to him in a letter to Pletnev (26 March 1831). The Russian writer who acknowledges most fully his admiration of and debt to Crabbe, however, is Wilhelm Karlovich Kyukhel'beker (1797–1846). Imprisoned for his part in the Decembrist rising in 1825, Kyukhel'beker received a copy of Crabbe's poems in 1832. He was impressed by and sought to emulate Crabbe's faithful depiction of reality. The Ermil/Elisey episode of *Yury i Xenia* has likenesses to 'William Bailey' (*Tales of the Hall*, XIX), whilst *Sirota* ('The Orphan'), written in 1833–4, was avowedly based on Crabbe as a model (Diary, 16 October 1833) and recalls parts of 'Peter Grimes' (*The Borough*, XXII) and 'The Brothers' (*Tales*, XX).[16] The Russian critic, Druzhinin, published a study of *Crabbe and His Works* in 1857, and it has been suggested that through this Crabbe may also have influenced the work of Nekrassov with its emphasis on the sufferings of the peasants.[17] Whether this be so or not, Nekrassov's work resembles Crabbe's also in its facility, which reaches even to the extent of what some critics have called a lack of conscious craftsmanship. Maurice Baring, the most sensitive English interpreter of Russian literature, has made a detailed comparison, describing Nekrassov in the terms Byron applied to Crabbe, 'Russia's "sternest painter", and certainly one of her best'. He continues:[18]

He is a Russian Crabbe: nature and men are his subjects. . . . He is an uncompromising realist, like Crabbe, and idealizes nothing in his pictures of the peasant's life—like Crabbe, he has a deep note of pathos, and a keen but not so minute an eye for landscape. . . . Nekrassov's tales, taking into consideration the differences between the two countries, have a marked affinity, both in their subject matter, their variety, their stern realism, their pathos, their bitterness, and their observation of nature, with Crabbe's stories in verse.

Much the greatest interest in Crabbe in other countries, however, was that displayed in France. *La Revue britannique* (May 1827, pp. 61–70) included the remarks on Wordsworth, Crabbe and Campbell from Hazlitt's *The Spirit of the Age*, and in February 1835 there was an article 'La poésie domestique de la Grande-Bretagne' dealing with Burns, Crabbe, Cowper and Wordsworth, drawn from the *Retrospective Review*. The editor was Philarète Chasles, who with Amedée Pichot did more than anyone else to bring serious attention in France to English literature. He translated 'Peter Grimes' (*Revue de Paris*, 22 May 1831) and in *Revue des deux mondes* (15 October 1845) he contributed an article on 'La Poésie chartiste'. In *L'Angleterre au XIXe siècle* (1851) he was to declare: 'Quant à la poésie de la prison et de la pauvreté elle est, malgré le phénomène exceptionnel de Crabbe, inadmissible dans le monde de l'art' (p. 339). Étienne also ascribed the primacy to Crabbe among 'Les Poètes des pauvres en Angleterre' (*Revue des deux mondes*, 15 September 1856), noting that 'Son observation ingenieusement descriptive est un sorte de statistique.'

Perhaps this view of Crabbe may help to explain the limited appeal that his work seems to have had among the French poets of the nineteenth century. Only Sainte-Beuve appears to have been influenced to any degree. His early 'La Plaine' was modelled on Crabbe. He had, according to his review of Lamartine's *Jocelyn*, discovered the English poet through Pichot's *Voyage historique et littéraire en Angleterre et en Écosse* (1825). Professor George Lehmann has described Sainte-Beuve's moral epistle 'Monsieur Jean' (*Magasin pittoresque*, 25 November 1838) as 'a kind of hybrid derived from Crabbe and Boileau'.[19]

X

CRABBE IN THE TWENTIETH CENTURY

At the turn of the century Crabbe was included in the extensive English Men of Letters series. The volume was written by Alfred Ainger and published in 1903. In the manner of the series this work is mainly biographical but it also contains some useful critical observations seriatim. The substantial, and still standard, biography appeared a year or two later in 1906. It was René Huchon's *Un Poète réaliste anglais*, translated as *George Crabbe and His Times,1754–1832* (1907). This book is a veritable mine of detail, but its critical judgments tend to be rather pedestrian.

Crabbe's admirers have included the novelist E. M. Forster, poets as different as Edmund Blunden and Ezra Pound and critics as unlike as F. R. Leavis and Lilian Haddakin. To the introduction to the *Life*[20] Forster brought that sensitive but penetrating ability for character-analysis that we see in his novels, noting that Crabbe extended to most of his own creations 'a little pity, a little contempt, a little cynicism, but a much larger measure of reproof' so that 'an unusual atmosphere results; it is, so to speak, sub-Christian; there is an implication throughout of positive ideals, such as self-sacrifice and asceticism [*sic*], but they are rarely pressed.' Blunden, too, in the introduction to the Cresset Press *Life* (1947) emphasized Crabbe as the poet of psychological landscape. He also, as one might expect of him, emphasizes Crabbe's love of Suffolk and the sea. The relation of character and place is prominent in Forster's second essay, or rather lecture, on the poet, 'George Crabbe and Peter Grimes' delivered at the Aldeburgh Festival in 1948.

Forster reminds us that 'Peter Grimes' demonstrates Crabbe's 'sensitiveness to dreams' and other modern critics have dwelt on this aspect of the poet's work. Patrick Cruttwell, for example, although he entitles his article 'The Last Augustan',[21] emphasizes the 'phantasmagoria of the whole of Crabbe's essential life' and pays attention to 'The World of Dreams'. This poem and 'Sir Eustace Grey' are also the particular concern of M. H. Abrams[22] as opium-poems, portraying dreams with extremes of pleasure and pain. As the only two such (at any rate known at that time) they offer, he claims, 'an unexampled opportunity to observe the effect of opium on that mysterious phenomenon, poetic inspiration'. Alethea Hayter in a later study on the same subject[23] provides a fuller examination and had the advantage of the more considerable evidence offered by such poems as 'The Insanity of Ambitious Love' and 'Where am I now', first published in my *New Poems By George Crabbe* (1960).

For many critics, however, Crabbe is more simply the last Augustan. Varley Lang ('Crabbe and the Eighteenth Century'[24]) examines the poet's affinities with the earlier period in relation to pastoral, satire, humanism and neo-classic theory. In an article with the same title John Heath-Stubbs[25] urges that Crabbe is not a pre-Romantic and argues that his view of society is related to 'an organically conceived, functional ideal' and that his characters are directly in the tradition of Dryden and Pope. Crabbe features also as the last poet in Dr Leavis's survey of 'The Augustan Tradition and the Eighteenth Century',[26] where the very neglect into which he has fallen seems ascribable to the fact that he belonged so fully to a period earlier than his own: 'Crabbe . . . was hardly at the fine point of consciousness in his time. His sensibility belongs to an order that those who were most alive to the age—who had the most sensitive antennae—had ceased to find sympathetic.' Earlier, Ezra Pound in two short passages[27] appears to approve of the poet's Augustan affinities in first lamenting the nineteenth century's failure to follow Crabbe—'Only If'—and, secondly, in commending Crabbe's social vista.

Frank Whitehead[28] devotes a number of paragraphs to both the Augustan verse-texture and ideals of Crabbe's work, whilst stressing that 'if Augustan, he was an Augustan who lived and wrote throughout the period of the Romantic Revival'. It was Arthur Sale in his perceptive 'The Development of Crabbe's Narrative Art',[29] who decisively gave the placing of Crabbe a new direction. By emphasizing the later work he was able to isolate those qualities that have led to the poet's being considered, though not by Mr Sale, simply as a short-story writer in verse.

In an equally perceptive full-length study Lilian Haddakin among other things rejected this identification. She starts from Crabbe's insistence on 'the experiencing mind' and examines 'poetic aims and critical responses' before going on to consider what is meant by his phrase 'Poetry without an atmosphere'. She concludes with chapters on the pictorial element and the reasons why he was not 'a short-story writer who rearranged his prose in lines of a certain length'. Oliver Sigworth[31] has considered Crabbe's relationship with the eighteenth century and the Romantic movement, his achievement as nature poet and narrative poet and his critics, whilst R. L. Chamberlain[32] portrayed a richly developing Crabbe moving from a position 'hampered by Augustan modes and manners' to ever greater independence and success. Chamberlain is unusual in the high claims that he makes for the last work published in Crabbe's lifetime, *Tales of the Hall*. More recently, Howard Mills has edited *Tales, 1812 and Other Selected Poems* (1967), to which he has prefaced an introductory critical essay. The aim of the essay is stated to be an attempt 'to break open the simplifications about Crabbe, and so spread the reader's attention over a variety of critical approaches and the variety of his work'. In so doing, Mr Mills considers poetic development and personal experience, the social element, the moral element, language and the presentation of character and dramatic and 'romantic' poetry. This introduction has several interesting insights.

XI

CONCLUSION

We come then to the summary. Crabbe was accused of narrow photographic realism, of dwelling on coarseness and depravity, of missing the highest truth, of being excessively gloomy, of being deficient in genuine imagination. That is the debit side. For the other side of the account let him speak for himself:

> For this the poet looks the world around,
> Where form and life and reasoning man are found.
> He loves the mind in all its modes to trace,
> And all the manners of the changing race;
> Silent he walks the road of life along,
> And views the aims of its tumultuous throng;
> He finds what shapes the Proteus-passions take,
> And what strange waste of life and joy they make,
> And loves to show them in their varied ways,
> With honest blame or with unflattering praise.
> 'Tis good to know, 'tis pleasant to impart,
> These turns and movements of the human heart;
> The stronger features of the soul to paint,
> And make distinct the latent and the faint;
> Man as he is, to place in all men's view,
> Yet none with rancour, none with scorn pursue;
> Nor be it ever of my portraits told,—
> 'Here the strong lines of malice we behold.'—
>
> This let me hope, that when in public view
> I bring my pictures, men may feel them true;
> 'This is a likeness,' may they all declare,
> 'And I have seen him, but I know not where;'
> For I should mourn the mischief I had done,
> If as the likeness all would fix on one.
>   Man's vice and crime I combat as I can,
> But to his GOD and conscience leave the man;
> I search (a [Quixote!]) all the land about,

To find its giants and enchanters out,
(The giant-folly, the enchanter-vice,
Whom doubtless I shall vanquish in a trice;)
But is there man whom I would injure?—no!
I am to him a fellow, not a foe—
A fellow-sinner, who must rather dread
The bolt, than hurl it at another's head.
  No! let the guiltless, if there such be found,
Launch forth the spear, and deal the deadly wound;
How can I so the cause of virtue aid,
Who am myself attainted and afraid?
Yet, as I can, I point the powers of rhyme,
And, sparing criminals, attack the crime.

He is the realist who recognizes universality in ordinary everyday life—
'This is a likeness'; the explorer of the social scene—'all the manners of
the changing race'; the analyst of character—'what shapes the Proteus-
passions take'; the moralist, who differentiates 'With honest blame or
with unflattering praise'; the satirist—'Man's Vice and Crime I combat
as I can'; yet he is full of pity—'I am to him a fellow, not a foe'. It is
probably this last that appeals most; he had such a deep and sympathetic
understanding of poor, frail human nature. In our century which has
seen, more than most, man's inhumanity to man, the distorted passions
whence this arises and the suffering of soul and body it entails, Crabbe's
portrayal of the human condition and his broad, mature wisdom ought
to have stood him in better stead than they have done.

NOTES

1 F. R. Leavis, *Revaluation*, 1936, p. 125.
2 T. S. Eliot, Introduction to Johnson's *London* and *The Vanity of Human Wishes*, Hazlewood Books ed., 1930.
3 E. M. Forster, 'George Crabbe and Peter Grimes', *Two Cheers for Democracy*, 1951.
4 F. L. Lucas, *George Crabbe: An Anthology*, Cambridge, 1933, p. xix.
5 F. R. Leavis, *op. cit.*, p. 128.
6 Most of this section is based on investigations made by the late Mr K. Povey, formerly Librarian of the University of Liverpool Library.
7 *Monthly Review, 2nd Series, 1790–1815*, Oxford, 1955, p. vii.
8 See H. and H. C. Shine, *The Quarterly Review under Gifford*, Chapel Hill,

1949, p. 15, and R. B. Clark, *William Gifford, Tory Satirist, Critic and Editor*, New York, 1930, pp. 191–2.

9 For the background see the *Life of Crabbe* by his son, especially the beginning of Ch. VIII.

10 1 December 1816, *Life of Crabbe* by his son, Ch. IX.

11 Preface to *Tales*, 1812.

12 *Tales of the Hall*, II, 16.

13 See A. M. Broadley and W. Jerrold, *The Romance of an Elderly Poet*, 1913.

14 W. Hazlitt, *Lectures on the English Poets*, 1818.

15 See L. H. C. Thomas, ' "Die Judenbuche" and English Literature', *Modern Language Review*, lxiv, 1969, pp. 351–4. I am indebted to Professor Thomas for help with these references to the German reception of Crabbe's work.

16 These Russian references are based on Y. D. Levin, 'Kyukhel'beker and Crabbe', *Oxford Slavonic Papers*, 12, 1965, pp. 99–113.

17 See W. R. Morfill, *A History of Russia*, 1902, pp. 451–2.

18 M. Baring, *Russian Literature*, 1914, pp. 229–31.

19 G. Lehmann, *Sainte-Beuve*, 1961, p. 320.

20 E. M. Forster, Introduction to the *Life of Crabbe*, Oxford World Classics, 1932, p. xvii.

21 P. Cruttwell, 'The Last Augustan', *Hudson Review*, vii, 1954.

22 M. H. Abrams, *The Milk of Paradise*, 1934, pp. 13–20.

23 A. Hayter, *Opium and the Romantic Imagination*, 1968.

24 V. Lang, 'Crabbe and the Eighteenth Century', *English Literary History*, v, 1938.

25 J. Heath-Stubbs, 'Crabbe and the Eighteenth Century', *Penguin New Writing*, 25, 1945.

26 F. R. Leavis, *op. cit.*

27 E. Pound, *The Future*, 1917, and *An ABC of Reading*, 1934.

28 F. Whitehead, *George Crabbe: Selections*, 1955.

29 A. Sale, 'The Development of Crabbe's Narrative Art', *Cambridge Journal*, v, 1952.

30 L. Haddakin, *The Poetry of Crabbe*, 1953.

31 O. Sigworth, *Nature's Sternest Painter*, 1965.

32 R. L. Chamberlain, *George Crabbe*, 1965.

33 *The Borough*, XXIV, 426–65.

Note on the Text

Reference to Crabbe's text is usually shown by giving the first line together with the numbers of the lines in the text of A. W. Ward's Cambridge edition of Crabbe. The first line is omitted in quotations from the beginning of poems and in some instances where a group of quotations widely separated in the poem cited are given together. In the case of *The Library*, which underwent substantial revision, the first and last lines of quotations are given; readers will appreciate that contemporary quotation must necessarily have been from the first edition. In a few instances where the reviewer is quoting for stylistic purposes passages are given in full.

Reference is sometimes given to long passages quoted by reviewers upon which they had made little comment. The object of this is to provide some indication of reviewers' preferences.

THE CANDIDATE
A Poetical Epistle to the
Authors of the Monthly Review

(?) August 1780

---

1. Edmund Cartwright, unsigned notice, *Monthly Review*

September 1780, lxiii, 226–7

Cartwright (1743–1823) is better known as the reputed inventor of the power-loom. He and Crabbe became acquainted in the late 1780s when they were fellow-clergymen in Leicestershire. (See Introduction, p. 5.)

So usual is it for a disappointed Writer to vent his spleen upon the Reviewers, that we fully expected the poem before us, judging from its address, had been an effusion of that angry passion. It seems, however, we were mistaken. 'It is published,' says the Author, 'with a view of obtaining the opinion of the candid and judicious Reader, on the merits of the Writer as a Poet; very few, he apprehends, being in such cases sufficiently impartial to decide for themselves.' And, 'as to critics of acknowledged merit (we thank him for the acknowledgment), it is addressed to the Monthly Reviewers.'

The situation which we are drawn into by this address, is such as might bring upon us, on the one hand, the imputation of moroseness, should we not be softened by a compliment which few patrons can withstand; and on the other, should we treat this epistle with a lenity which the strictest impartiality would not justify, it might reasonably be suspected, that we had suffered our judgment to be duped by flattery. To avoid, therefore, every imputation or suspicion of either kind, let the Poem speak for itself.

> Say then, O ye who tell how authors speed . . .
> [166–211]

The Author of this Epistle, of whose merit our readers may probably by this time form no unfavourable opinion, will not, we are persuaded, think we mean

> —— to damn (as he expresses himself) with mutilated praise.

if we intimate that, beside some few other trifling inaccuracies, his rhymes are not always regulated by the purest standard of pronunciation: for instance, shone, moon, gods, abodes, &c. These are petty blemishes, which, should a future edition be called for, might easily be removed. And we would then also recommend to him to consider, whether his Poem, which bears evident marks of haste, might not admit of improvement in other respects; particularly one in which it is materially defective—the want of a subject to make a proper and forcible impression on the mind: where this is wanting, the best verses will lose their effect.

2. Unsigned notice, *Critical Review*

September 1780, 1, 233–4

The anonymous author of this Poetical Epistle is, it seems, an unfortunate gentleman, who having long laboured under a *cacoethes scribendi*, humbly requests the advice and assistance of Dr. G——, and his brethren of the faculty, concerned in the *Monthly Review*. The patient, it is observable, takes no notice of us Critical Reviewers, though we have been pretty famous for eradicating disorders of this kind. When the disease, however, increases, as it probably will, there is no doubt but we shall be called in. In the mean time, though we have received no fee, we shall (like the noble-minded physician to a certain news-paper) give our advice *gratis*. Temperance in this, as in almost every other case, is the grand specific, we shall confine our prescription, therefore, in a very few words; viz. *Abstinè à plumâ et atramento*; a safe, an easy, and we will venture to add, an infallible remedy. For the too visible symptoms of this poor man's malady, we refer our readers to the poem, where he says,

> We write enraptur'd, and we write in haste, . . .
>
> [57–8]

When he was young, he informs us,

> No envy entrance found, . . .
> Nor flattry's *silver'd* tale, nor sorrow's *sage*.
>
> [255, 257]

Sage, we suppose, is meant for another epithet for *Tale*, but surely this is a strange kind of *subintelligitur*, and our author, we believe, has no authority for it. Pretty early one morning, the Muse tells us,

> The vivid dew hung trembling on the thorn,
> And mists, like *creeping rocks*, arose to meet the morn.
>
> [271–2]

How *mists* can be like *rocks*, and what is meant by *creeping* ones, in particular, we cannot comprehend. Still less are we pleased with the unintelligible expressions of *shrouds well shrouded*, and *Hermes's own Cheapside*; nor are we fond of such compound epithets as, *woe-taught, fate-lop'd, song-invited, pine-prest, virtue-scorn'd, crowd-befitting,* &c. Whatever this writer may plead in his own behalf, we cannot entirely acquit him of pride, when he says,

> My song
> Shall please the sons of taste, and please them long.
>
> [330–1]

Though he is afterwards modest enough to add (speaking of himself)

> Faults he must own, tho' hard for him to find.
>
> [363]

Hard, however, as it is for *him*, faults may possibly be found by *others* in this poem. For our own parts, we cannot but be of opinion, that if this *Candidate* (which we suppose is his intention) sets up for the borough of Parnassus, he will most probably lose his election, as he does not seem to be possessed of a foot of land in that county.

3. Unsigned notice, *Gentleman's Magazine*

October 1780, 1, 475

If the authors addressed agree with us in their opinion of this candidate, they will not give him much encouragement to stand a poll at Parnassus; though we join issue with him in thinking, that, 'however little in this poem is worthy of applause, there is yet less that merits contempt.' But *mediocribus esse poetis,* &c.

THE LIBRARY

July 1781

When *The Library* was published, the opinion of Burke had its effect upon the conductors of the various periodical works of the time; the poet received commendatory *critiques* from the very gentlemen who had hitherto treated him with such contemptuous coldness; and though his name was not in the title-page, it was universally known.[1]

4. Unsigned notice, *Critical Review*

August 1781, lii, 148–50

A vein of good sense and philosophical reflection runs through this little performance, which distinguishes it from most modern poems, though the subject is not sufficiently interesting to recommend it to general attention. The rhymes are correct, and the versification smooth and harmonious. The author ranges his books scientifically, and carries us through natural philosophy, physic, romance, history, &c.—What he says of physical writers is not less true than severe; their aim, says he, is glorious.

> But man, who knows no good unmix'd and pure, . . .
> Their pen relentless kills through future times.
>
> [364–75]

These lines are manly, nervous, and poetical. We are still more pleased with the following description of romance, which is full of fancy and spirit.

> Hence, ye prophane! I feel a former dread . . .
> Fly Reason's power, and shun the light of Truth,
>
> [545–82]

[1]*Life of Crabbe* by his son, Ch. 4.

5. Unsigned notice, *Gentleman's Magazine*

October 1781, li, 474

We are led through 'a mighty maze, but not without a plan,' and introduced to books, not authors, of all sorts and sizes, 'mighty folios, well-ordered quartos, light octavos, and humbler duodecimos.' These form the phalanx, or line, of the leather-coated army that is here reviewed. After these, in the rear, by way of suttlers or trulls,

> undistinguished trifles swell the scene,
> The last new play, and *fritter'd magazine*.
> [133–4]

As the praise or censure of such a crew can be of no consequence to a general-officer, we shall dismiss him without either, and consign him to the patronage of

> Some generous friend, of ample power possess'd; . . .
> Some noble RUTLAND, Misery's friend and thine.
> [667–70]

The following lines, on the subject of 'Romance' are not destitute of poetical imagery:

> Hence, ye prophane! I feel a former dread . . .
> And Fear and Ignorance afford delight.
> [545–70]

6. Edmund Cartwright, unsigned notice,
Monthly Review

December 1781, lxv, 423–5

In the reflections with which this well-written poem commences, the Author observes the insufficiency of reason, or retirement, to alleviate the heavier afflictions of human life: and he proceeds:

> Not Hope herself, with all her flattering art, . . .
> Mild opiates here their sober influence shed.
>
> [28–62]

[Also quotes

> Now turn from these . . . (as in Ward, I, 529)
>
> Repent his anger, or withhold his rod.
>
> [234]

and

> But who are these? Methinks a noble mien . . .
> And Pain and Prudence make and mar the man.]
>
> [535–94]

After the specimens that have been given, to say what our sentiments are of this performance would be needless. The Reader will perceive it is the production of no common pen.

THE VILLAGE

May 1783

The Village was published in May, 1783; and its success exceeded the author's utmost expectations. It was praised in the leading journals; the sale was rapid and extensive; and my father's reputation was, by universal consent, greatly raised, and permanently established, by this poem. *The Library*, and *The Village*, are sufficient evidence of the care and zeal with which the young poet had studied Pope; and, without doubt, he had gradually, though in part perhaps unconciously, formed his own style mainly on that polished model. But even those early works, and especially *The Village*, fairly entitled Mr. Crabbe to a place far above the 'mechanick echoes' of the British Virgil. Both poems are framed on a regular classical plan,—perhaps, in that respect, they may be considered more complete and faultless than any of his later pieces; and though it is only here and there that they exhibit that rare union of force and minuteness for which the author was afterwards so highly distinguished, yet such traces of that marked and extraordinary peculiarity appeared in detached places—above all, in the description of the Parish Workhouse in *The Village*—that it is no wonder the new poet should at once have been hailed as a genius of no slender pretensions.[1]

---

[1] *Life,* Ch. 5.

7. Dr Johnson, letter to Sir Joshua Reynolds

4 March 1783

SIR,—I have sent you back Mr. Crabbe's poem, which I read with great delight. It is original, vigorous, and elegant. The alterations which I have made, I do not require him to adopt; for my lines are, perhaps, not often better than his own:[1] but he may take mine and his own together, and, perhaps, between them, produce something better than either. He is not to think his copy wantonly defaced: a wet sponge will wash all the red lines away, and leave the pages clean. His dedication will be least liked: it were better to contract it into a short sprightly address. I do not doubt of Mr. Crabbe's success. I am, sir, your most humble servant,

SAMUEL JOHNSON[2]

8. Unsigned notice, *Critical Review*

July 1783, lvi, 60–1

Though this gentleman seems to have taken the hint of his poem from Goldsmith's *Deserted Village*, he does not represent it, like that writer 'as the seat of indolence and ease,' but describes it with more justice, and almost an equal warmth of colouring, as too commonly the abode of toil, misery, and vice. He begins with ridiculing the idea of shepherds, who

[1] Boswell indicates that I. 15-20 were Johnson's. He also says: 'The sentiments of Mr. Crabbe's admirable poem, as to the false notions of rustic happiness and rustic virtue, were quite congenial with Dr. Johnson's own' (March 1783).

[2] In forwarding this letter to Crabbe, Reynolds wrote: 'If you knew how sparing Dr. Johnson deals out his praises, you would be very well content with that he says' (Huchon, *George Crabbe and His Times, 1754–1832*, 1907, pp. 145–6, n. 5).

in alternate verse, . . .

[I, 9–18]

The misery of the poor worn-out labourer and his family is thus described:

Ye gentle souls, who dream of rural ease, . . .

[I, 172–205]

The subsequent account of his sickness, death, &c. is, we fear, too true a picture. After enumerating the various vices prevalent in the country, which forcibly recalls Hamlet's observation, 'that the toe of the peasant comes so near the heel of our courtier, he galls his kibe,' we meet with the following striking reflection:

Yet why, you ask, these humble crimes relate, . . .

[II, 87–100]

This poem deserves much approbation, both for language and sentiment. The subject is broken off rather abruptly towards the conclusion, where we meet with a long encomium on the Duke of Rutland, and the hon. Captain Manners, who was killed in that memorable action in the West Indies, when the French fleet was defeated, and their admiral taken prisoner.

9. Edmund Cartwright, unsigned notice, *Monthly Review*

November 1783, lxix, 418–21

It has long been objected to the Pastoral Muse, that her principal employment is to delineate scenes that never existed, and to cheat the imagination by descriptions of pleasure that never can be enjoyed. Sensible of her deviation from Nature and propriety, the Author of the present poem has endeavoured to bring her back into the sober paths of truth and reality. It is not, however, improbable that he may have erred as much as those whom he condemns. For it may be questioned whether he, who represents a peasant's life as a life of unremitting labour and remediless anxiety; who describes his best years as embittered by insult and oppression, and his old age as squalid, comfortless, and destitute, gives a juster representation of rural enjoyments than they, who, running into a contrary extreme, paint the face of the country as wearing a perpetual smile, and its inhabitants as passing away their hours in uninterrupted pleasure, and unvaried tranquillity; such as are supposed to have prevailed in those fabled eras of existence,

> When youth was extacy, and age repose.

Mr. Crabbe divides his poem into two parts. In the first he principally confines himself to an enumeration of the miseries, which, he supposes, are peculiar to the poor villager. In this part there is a great deal of painting that is truly characteristic; and had not that indispensible rule, which both painters and poets should equally attend to, been reversed, namely, to form their individuals from ideas of general nature, it would have been unexceptionable.

> Say ye, opprest by some fantastic woes, . . .
> [I, 250–end]

In the second part the Author's good sense compels him to acknowledge, contrary to the tenor of what had gone before, that the poor have no reason to envy their superiors; that neither virtue nor vice, happiness nor misery, depend on either rank or station; that the peasant is frequently as vicious as the peer; and that the peer feels distress as poignantly as the peasant. He then points out to the latter a source of consolation, which, it is to be feared, would avail very little in the hour of affliction:

> Oh! if in life one noble chief appears, . . .
> [II, 107–16]

With a warm, though merited, panegyric on this gallant officer, and some consolatory compliments to his noble brother, the poem concludes. Considered as a whole, its most strenuous advocates must acknowledge it to be defective. The first part asserts as a general proportion what can only be affirmed of individuals; and the second part contradicts the assertion of the first. The chain of argument is illogical, and it is carried on, for the most part, without any apparently determinate object. It must not, however, be denied, that the poem contains many splendid lines, many descriptions that are picturesque and original, and such as will do credit to the ingenious Author of *The Library*.

10. Unsigned notice, *Gentleman's Magazine*

December 1783, liii, 1041–2

This poem, though on a hackneyed subject, treats it very differently from the ancient and modern writers of pastoral, representing only the dark side of the landscape, the poverty and misery attendant on the peasant—

> Theirs is your house that holds the parish poor . . .
> [I, 228–39 (1823 edn *Works*)]

As a specimen of the author's manner and versification, we will exhibit

> Anon a figure enters, quaintly neat . . .
> [I, 276–91]

> Fain would he ask the parish-priest to prove . . .
> [I, 298–317]

All no doubt well painted, and highly finished; but we hope not taken from the life . . .

THE NEWSPAPER

March 1785

11. Unsigned notice, *Critical Review*

April 1785, lix, 3–8

'The poem, says the author, which I now offer to the public, is, I believe, the only one written upon the subject; at least, it is the only one which I have knowledge of: and, fearing there may not be found in it many things to engage the reader's attention, I am willing to take the strongest hold I can upon him, by offering something which has the claim of novelty.'

This, we apprehend, is rather inaccurately expressed; for if, as he fears, many things are not found in it worthy notice, their nature cannot be altered by his subsequent claim to novelty. . . .

His talents are indeed more conspicuous in the pathetic and descriptive, than the satyric line. Humour he certainly possesses in no inconsiderable degree; but we do not perceive that force and spirit in the present poem, which is in general deemed essential to compositions of this kind. It is, however, a work of genius, and we shall therefore consider it with attention. . . .

> I sing of news, and all those vapid sheets, . . .
> [51–70]

These lines, though we think the eleventh exceptionable, are full of descriptive humour; and the simile which concludes them extremely apposite, though the expression, 'or thence ascend the sky,' seems of no use but to eke out the line. Possibly *and* should be substituted for *or*, which would make it much less objectionable. We fully allow the beauty and propriety of those that follow.

> Yet soon each reptile tribe is lost but these, . . .
> [71–6]

Though this performance does not appear so highly finished as *The Village*, it is certainly entitled to rank in the first class of modern productions.

12. Charles Burney, unsigned notice, *Monthly Review*

November 1785, lxxiii, 374–6

Burney (1757–1817) was the son of the musical historian and brother to Fanny, the novelist. He was a classical scholar of considerable renown.

This poem is a satire on the news-papers of the present day, which are lashed by the Author with much ingenuity. The versification is at once easy and forcible, and the rhimes are chaste, and carefully chosen; and though we do not think the poem equal to the Author's first production, the *Library*, we doubt not but that it will add another sprig of laurel to his wreath.

[Summary, quoting 251–84, 421–30 and 431–65.]

Mr. Crabbe seems to have chosen Pope as his model, and many passages of this poem are strongly marked imitations of the great Poet. Our Author will pardon us, if we say, too strongly marked. *Allusions* should rather be admitted, than *parodies*, in works of this nature. In some instances, perhaps, Mr. C. has not exhibited sufficient variety in his pauses; nor is his language *quite* poetical. He also has introduced the Alexandrine—we do not venture to say, *the needless Alexandrine*—too frequently into *The News-Paper*; a custom which, indeed, prevails much among modern poets:—but, in our opinion, it would be rather 'honoured in the *breach*, than the observance.'

But still the poem has uncommon merit, and sufficiently evinces, if it were possible to doubt it, after reading *The Library*, that the Author is possessed of genius, taste, and imagination, and a manly vein of poetry, such as is very uncommon in 'these degenerate days.'—He is, indeed, one of the very few,

> *Ingenium cui sit, cui mens divinior, atque os*
> *Magna sonaturum!*[1]

[1] If one has inborn genius, a diviner soul and tongue noble in utterance. Horace, *Satires*, I, iv, 43–4.

POEMS [1807]

October 1807

This preface is dated Muston, September, 1807; and in the same month the volume was published by Mr. Hatchard. It contained with the earlier series, *The Parish Register*, 'Sir Eustace Grey', 'The Birth of Flattery', and other minor pieces; and its success was not only decided, but nearly unprecedented. By *The Parish Register*, indeed, my father must be considered as having first assumed that station among British poets, which the world has now settled to be peculiarly his own. The same character was afterwards still more strikingly exemplified and illustrated—but it was henceforth the same; whereas there was but little in the earlier series that could have led to the expectation of such a performance as *The Register*. In the former works, a few minute descriptions had been introduced—but here there was nothing but a succession of such descriptions; in them there had been no tale—this was a chain of stories; they were didactic—here no moral inference is directly inculcated: finally, they were regularly constructed poems —this boldly defies any but the very slightest and most transparently artificial connections. Thus differing from his former self, his utter dissimilarity to any other author then enjoying public favour was still more striking; the manner of expression was as entirely his own as the singular minuteness of his delineation, and the strictness of his adherence to the literal truth of nature; and it was now universally admitted, that, with lesser peculiarities, he mingled the conscious strength, and, occasionally, the profound pathos, of a great original poet.

Nor was 'Sir Eustace Grey' less admired on other grounds, than *The Parish Register* was for the singular combination of excellences which I have been faintly alluding to, and which called forth the warmest eulogy of the most powerful critical authority of the time, which was moreover considered as the severest. The other periodical critics of the day agreed substantially with the Edinburgh Review; and I believe that within two days after the appearance of Mr. Jeffrey's admirable and generous article, Mr. Hatchard sold off the whole of the first edition of these poems.[1]

---

13. Unsigned reviews, *Gentleman's Magazine*

November 1807, lxxvii, 1033–40
and January 1808, lxxviii, 59

[The article begins with extensive reference to the preface]

If his fancy is somewhat chastened, his judgment is proportionally matured . . . 'The Register of Baptisms' affords some pleasing anecdotes. Let a pedantic Gardener serve as a specimen:

> Why Lonicera wilt thou name the child? . . .
> [611–42]

'The Marriage Register' gives the Author an opportunity of displaying his didactic powers;

> How fair these names, how much unlike they look. . . .
> [283–300 plus 6 lines replaced in later edn (Ward, I, 535)]

The Third and last Part, 'The Register of Burials' is pleasingly pathetic. . . .

. . . Much as we have admired the elegant diction of the former pieces with the chaste and natural description of rural life contained in them, we have no less reason to be satisfied with the interest excited by the concluding poems.

In 'The Birth of Flattery' there is much poetical playfulness.

The story of 'Sir Eustace Grey' is strongly impressive, and gives an affecting account of the progress of insanity on a proud and initiated mind.

---

[1] *Life*, Ch. 8.

The poor Sir Eustace!—Yet his hope . . .
[396–end]

In 'The Hall of Justice' our feelings are warmly excited for the poor wretched Vagrant, who, however great her errors, possesses a heart not insensible to compunction.

True, I was not to virtue train'd; . . .
[68–74]

Oh! by the GOD who loves to spare . . .
[119–26]

We have no hesitation in recommending a perusal of this interesting publication to the Amateurs of elegant Poetry.

14. Unsigned review, *Anti-Jacobin Review and Magazine*

December 1807, xxviii, 337–47

In our younger days we read Mr. Crabbe's admirable poems, *The Library* and *The Village*, with enthusiastic delight; and long endeavoured, but in vain, to procure *The Newspaper*. It was, therefore, with that kind of pleasure, which men experience on seeing an old friend after a long interval of absence, that we opened the volume before us; most happy, indeed, to renew our acquaintance with a companion at once so amusing, so interesting, and so instructive. After an attentive perusal of these Poems, we find our first opinion of the author's genius and merit strongly confirmed. We regard him, indeed, as fully entitled to rank with the first moral poets of the present age, nor would those of the past be injured by a comparison with him. . . .
. . . The author's own description of this poem will convey the best idea of it.

In the *Parish Register*, he (the reader) will find an endeavour once more to describe village manners, not by adopting the notion of pastoral simplicity, or assuming ideas of rustic barbarity, but by more natural views of the peasantry, considered as a mixed body of persons, sober or profligate, and from hence, in a great measure, contented or miserable. To this more general description are added the various characters which occur in the three parts of a register: baptisms, marriages, and burials.

In this endeavour Mr. Crabbe has most completely succeeded; his characters are ably drawn; his descriptions are highly poetical; and the moral reflections with which they are interspersed are excellent. Few poems are better calculated to interest the feelings, to meliorate the heart, and to inform the mind. They do great credit to the author's talents, while they reflect honour on his principles. . . .

Richard Monday—
To name an infant met our village sires . . .
[I, 688–766]

He may most truly be called the poet of nature who best delineates natural characters and natural scenes; and certainly no one displays more skill, in this kind of delineation, than Mr. Crabbe. All his scenes, and all his characters, are, indeed, taken from common life, and chiefly from rural life; they are such as every man *may* meet with, and such as most men, who live in the country, *do* meet with; but they are presented in a manner which heightens their natural effect, and are marked by many of those delicate touches which none but the hand of a master can give to a picture. . . .

Phoebe Dawson—
Two summers since, I saw at Lammas Fair . . .
[II, 131–246]

We now proceed to our extract from the last portion of the 'Register,' which contains a dismal catalogue of departed Christians, and affords an ample field for moral reflections, and for the impression of salutary admonitions. . . .

There was, 'tis said, and I believe a time . . .
[III, 1–74]

We much fear that more Christian pastors than Mr. Crabbe have to deplore the dearth of that true Christian knowledge, and the want of that true Christian spirit, which can alone entitle men to expect the advantages of the Christian covenant. The enthusiastic cant of those ignorant preachers whom the Methodists send forth in swarms, more destructive to the inhabitants than locusts would be to the fruits of the land, have materially tended to poison the source of true knowledge, and to substitute the fountain of presumption in its stead: and until our legislature shall adopt some effectual means for the preservation of Christianity against both the insidious and the open attacks of those mischievous assailants (who know little of Christianity but the name), the evil will continue to increase with additional rapidity, and will, at no remote period, spread over the whole kingdom.

There is much good satire well applied in *The Newspaper*, but we must not exceed our limits by farther quotations from the Poems, especially as we have some parts of the Preface still to notice. We could wish, however, that the author had enlarged this poem, as a considerable revolution has occurred in the management of newspapers since it was written, which would have afforded him ample food for satire, and which, indeed, call loudly for the satirical lash. Of the smaller poems we think *Sir Eustace Grey* and the *Hall of Justice* unquestionably the best, and the *Birth of Flattery* the least pleasing; but it is fair to add, that our dislike to allegorical poems in general may possibly influence our opinion. Of *The Library* and *The Village* too much cannot be said in their praise; it may, however, perhaps be objected to the latter, that if Goldsmith has fallen into one extreme in his delineation of village manners, Mr. Crabbe has here fallen into the other; and that Goldsmith's is the most pleasing delusion of the two. Still it must be acknowledged that there is much truth and nature even in the most disgusting scenes which Mr. C. exhibits. We are happy to see the apologetical note at the end of *The Village*, for it always appeared to us that the censure which the passage there alluded to conveyed on the clergy, was, in its *general* application, both severe and unjust. Mr. C. writes *nuptual* for *nuptial*, and *indure* for *endure*, for which there is, we believe, no authority, and which indeed no authority could justify. He also uses *projection* as synonymous with *project*, which though strictly *defensible*, is nevertheless extremely awkward and dissonant. The punctuation, too, throughout the volume, is extremely defective; whence we are led to suspect, that a point so essential was left entirely to the management of the printer.

(The review ends with a long quotation from the preface and a short comment on it.)

[Begins with a general survey of Crabbe's work.]

In *The Parish Register*, which is divided into three parts,—baptisms, marriages, and burials,—Mr. Crabbe continues to indulge his satirical propensity, not rudely indeed, nor wantonly, nor without much useful moral reflection, interesting narrative, and admirable description. . . .

> Here on a Sunday eve, when service ends . . .
> [I, 152–65]

The story of 'Sir Eustace Grey' is a fine proof of this writer's talent for the pathetic, which also appears in many other parts of the present volume. Hard must be the heart, depraved the mind, and profligate the manners of that reader, whose sympathy is not awakened by the recital of such sufferings, as those of 'the young Lord of Greyling Hall'. Of all the numerous representations which we have seen, whether on the stage or in the closet, of maniacal distress, this is one of the most natural, most sublime, and most affecting. Mr. Crabbe has, perhaps, been driven to the melancholy contemplation of insanity in all its wild variety of mood, and so, alas! to our misfortune, have we.

> Quis talia fando
> Temperet a lacrymis?[1]

The female gipsey's narrative, in the 'Hall of Justice', is not less interesting nor less poetical than the preceding. The plot is, indeed, like that of Horace Walpole's tragedy, 'the mysterious Mother', too horrible to dwell upon; but still it presents proper objects for abhorrence, and human beings must sometimes be taught what to abominate and to shun, as well as what to admire and to pursue.

A short but general encomium on 'Woman', suggested probably by a quotation from Mr. Ledyard, in Mr. Parke's Travels into Africa, concludes the book.

Our revisal of these poems has proved the most agreeable task that we have had to perform, since we commenced our critical labours; for

---

[1] Who, telling such things, could refrain from tears? Virgil, *Aeneid*, II, 6, 8.

their merit has secured us from all danger of misleading the public, and of either gratifying the vanity or wounding the pride of the author. His invention is ready, fertile, and multifarious: his description natural, striking, and rich: the structure of his verse has been formed according to the best models: his satire is keen and cuts home. We only regret that he has condescended now and then to introduce a line from other writers: this a poet, who is conscious of his own strength and native energies, should never do; unless when the follies and vices of obtrusive scribblers are to be exposed. Mr. Crabbe has enough of his own, and to spare: the peacock and the pheasant have no occasion for borrowed plumes.

We say nothing of another edition. These poems will go down to posterity, and be often found upon the same shelf with those of Dryden, Pope, Goldsmith, and Churchill.

16. Francis Jeffrey, unsigned review, *Edinburgh Review*

April 1808, xii, 131–51

Jeffrey (1773–1850) with Sydney Smith, Brougham and Horner founded the *Edinburgh Review* and was its first editor until 1829. He reviewed Crabbe extensively and sympathetically and gave him considerable space in his *Contributions to the Edinburgh Review*, 1844. His esteem for Crabbe was paralleled by his dislike of the Romantics, especially Wordsworth.

. . . Though the name of Crabbe has not hitherto been very common in the mouths of our poetical critics, we believe there are few real lovers of poetry to whom some of his sentiments and descriptions are not secretly familiar. There is a truth and a force in many of his delineations of rustic life, which is calculated to sink deep into the memory; and, being confirmed by daily observation, they are recalled upon innumerable occasions, when the ideal pictures of more fanciful authors have lost all their interest. For ourselves at least, we profess to be indebted to Mr. Crabbe for many of these strong impressions; and have known more than one of our unpoetical acquaintances who declared they could never pass by a parish workhouse, without thinking of the description of it they had read at school in the Poetical Extracts. The volume before us will renew, we trust, and extend many such impressions. It contains all the former productions of the author, with about double their bulk of new matter; most of it in the same taste and manner of composition with the former, and some of a kind of which we have had no previous example in this author. The whole, however, is of no ordinary merit, and will be found, we have little doubt, a sufficient warrant for Mr. Crabbe to take his place as one of the most original, nervous, and pathetic poets of the present century.

His characteristic, certainly, is force, and truth of description, joined for the most part to great selection and condensation of expression;—that kind of strength and originality which we meet with in Cowper, and that sort of diction and versification which we admire in Goldsmith. If he can be said to have imitated the manner of any author, it is Goldsmith, indeed, who has been the object of his imitation; and yet, his general train of thinking, and his views of society are so extremely opposite, that when *The Village* was first published, it was commonly considered as an antidote or answer to the more captivating representations of *The Deserted Village*. Compared with this celebrated author, he will be found, we think, to have more vigour and less delicacy; and, while he must be admitted to be inferior in the fine finish and uniform beauty of his composition, we cannot help considering him as superior, both in the variety and the truth of his pictures. Instead of that uniform tint of pensive tenderness which overspreads the whole poetry of Goldsmith, we find in Mr. Crabbe many gleams of gaiety and humour. Though his habitual views of life are more gloomy than those of his rival, his poetical temperament seems far more cheerful; and when the occasions of sorrow and rebuke are gone by, he can collect himself for sarcastic pleasantry, or unbend in innocent playfulness. His diction, though generally pure and powerful, is sometimes harsh, and sometimes quaint; and he has occasionally admitted a couplet or two in a state so unfinished, as to give a character of inelegance to the passages in which they occur. With a taste less disciplined and less fastidious than that of Goldsmith, he has, in our apprehension, a keener eye for observation, and a readier hand for the delineation of what he has observed. There is less poetical keeping in his whole performance; but the groups of which it consists, are conceived, we think, with equal genius, and drawn with greater spirit as well as greater fidelity.

It is not quite fair, perhaps, thus to draw a detailed parallel between a living poet, and one whose reputation has been sealed by death, and by the immutable sentence of a surviving generation. Yet there are so few of his contemporaries to whom Mr. Crabbe bears any resemblance, that we can scarcely explain our opinion of his merit, without comparing him to some of his predecessors. There is one set of writers, indeed, from whose works those of Mr. Crabbe might receive all that elucidation which results from contrast, and from an entire opposition in all points of taste and opinion. We allude now to the Wordsworths, and the Southeys, and Coleridges, and all that misguided fraternity, that, with good intentions and extraordinary talents, are labouring to bring back our poetry to the fantastical oddity and puling childishness of Withers, Quarles, or Marvel. These gentlemen write a great deal about rustic life, as well as Mr. Crabbe; and they even agree with him in dwelling much on its discomforts; but nothing can be more opposite than the views they take of the subject, or the manner in which they execute their representation of them.

Mr. Crabbe exhibits the common people of England pretty much as they are, and as they must appear to every one who will take the trouble of examining into their condition; at the same time that he renders his sketches in a very high degree interesting and beautiful,—by selecting what is most fit for description,—by grouping them into such forms as must catch the attention or awake the memory,—and by scattering over the whole, such traits of moral sensibility, of sarcasm, and of useful reflection, as every one must feel to be natural, and own to be powerful. The gentlemen of the new school, on the other hand, scarcely ever condescend to take their subjects from any description of persons that are at all known to the common inhabitants of the world; but invent for themselves certain whimsical and unheard of beings, to whom they impute some fantastical combination of feelings, and labour to excite our sympathy for them, either by placing them in incredible situations, or by some strained and exaggerated moralization of a vague and tragical description. Mr. Crabbe, in short, shows us something which we have all seen, or may see, in real life; and draws from it such feelings and such reflections as every human being must acknowledge that it is calculated to excite. He delights us by the truth, and vivid and picturesque beauty of his representations, and by the force and pathos of the sensations with which we feel that they ought to be connected. Mr. Wordsworth and his associates show us something that mere observation never yet suggested to any one. They introduce us to beings whose existence was not previously suspected by the acutest observers of nature, and excite an interest for them, more by an eloquent and refined analysis of their own capricious feelings, than by any obvious or very intelligible ground of sympathy in their situation. The common sympathies of our nature, and our general knowledge of human character, do not enable us either to understand, or to enter into the feelings of their characters. They are unique specimens and varieties of our kind, and must be studied under a separate classification.

[Comments on 'Matthew,' 'Martha Ray,' 'There was a boy,' 'Lucy,' etc. That on 'Martha Ray' reads: A frail damsel is a character common enough in all poems; and one upon which many fine and pathetic lines have been expended. Mr. Wordsworth has written more than three hundred lines on that subject: but, instead of new images of tenderness, or delicate representation of intelligible feelings, he has contrived to tell us nothing whatever of the unfortunate fair one, but that her name is Martha Ray; and that she goes up to the top of a hill, in a red cloak, and cries 'Oh misery!' All the rest of the poem is filled with a description of an old thorn and a pond, and of the silly stories which the neighbouring old women told about them.]

From these childish and absurd affections, we turn with pleasure to the manly sense and correct picturing of Mr. Crabbe; and, after being dazzled and made giddy with the elaborate raptures and obscure originalities of these new artists, it is refreshing to meet again with the nature and spirit of our old masters, in the nervous pages of the author now before us.

[Quotes from *The Village* at length.]

The next poem, and the longest in the volume, is now presented for the first time to the public. It is dedicated, like the former, to the delineation of rural life and characters, and is entitled, 'The Village [sic] Register'; and, upon a very simple but singular plan, is divided into three parts, viz. Baptisms, Marriages, and Burials. After an introductory and general view of village manners, the Reverend author proceeds to present his readers with an account of all the remarkable baptisms, marriages and funerals, that appear on his register for the preceding year, with a sketch of the character and behaviour of the respective parties, and such reflections and exhortations as are suggested by the subject. The poem consists, therefore, of a series of portraits taken from the middling and lower ranks of rustic life, and delineated on occasions at once more common and more interesting, than any other that could well be imagined. They are selected, we think, with great judgment, and drawn with inimitable accuracy and strength of colouring. They are finished with much more minuteness and detail, indeed, than the more general pictures in *The Village*, and, on this account, may appear occasionally deficient in comprehension, or in dignity. They are, no doubt, executed in some instances with a Chinese accuracy; and enter into details which many readers may pronounce tedious and unnecessary. Yet, there is a justness and force in the representation which is entitled to something more than indulgence; and though several of the groups are confessedly composed of low and disagreeable subjects, still, we think that some allowance is to be made for the author's plan of giving a full and exact view of village life, which could not possibly be accomplished without including those baser varieties. He aims at an important moral effect by this exhibition; and must not be defrauded either of that, or of the praise which is due to the coarser efforts of his pen, out of deference to the sickly delicacy of his more fastidious readers. We admit, however, that there is more carelessness, as well as more quaintness in this poem than in the other; and that he has now and then apparently heaped up circumstances rather to gratify his own taste for detail and accumulation, than to give any additional effect to his description. With this general observation, we beg the reader's attention to the following abstract and citations.

> Here, in cabal, a disputatious crew . . .
> [I, 170–81, 188–91, 194–7, 214–23, 230–68]

The miller's daughter—

> Then came the days [sic] of shame, the grievous night, . . .
> [I, 347–52, 371–80, 391–400]

Nathan—

> Fie, Nathan! fie! to let an artful jade . . .
> [II, 34–9 (as Ward, I, 534–5)]

Phoebe Dawson—

> Now, through the lane, up hill, and cross the green . . .
> [II, 165–86]

Lo! now with red rent cloak and bonnet black . . .
[II, 189–207, 211–26]

If present, railing, till he saw her pain'd; . . .
[II, 241–4]

The Lady of the Manor—

Forsaken stood the hall, . . .
[III, 235–47]

Isaac Ashford—

Next to these ladies, but in nought allied . . .
[III, 413–19, 425–6, 433–8]

I feel his absence in the hours of prayer . . .
[II, 491–502]

Mrs. Frankford—

Then died lamented, in the strength of life . . .
[III, 581–96]

Curious and sad, upon the fresh dug hill . . .
[III, 615–27]

We think this the most important of the new pieces in the volume; and have extended our account of it so much, that we can afford to say but little of the others. *The Library* and *The Newspaper* are republications. They are written with a good deal of terseness, sarcasm, and beauty; but the subjects are not very interesting, and they will rather be approved, we think, than admired or delighted in. We are not much taken either with 'The Birth of Flattery'. With many nervous lines and ingenious allusions, it has something of the languor which seems inseparable from an allegory which exceeds the length of an epigram.

'Sir Eustace Grey' is quite unlike any of the preceding compositions. It is written in a sort of lyric measure, and is intended to represent the perturbed fancies of the most terrible insanity settling by degrees into a sort of devotional enthusiasm. The opening stanza, spoken by a visitor in the madhouse, is very striking.

I'll know no more—the heart is torn . . .
[1–11]

There is great force, both of language and conception, in the wild narrative Sir Eustace gives of his frenzy; though we are not sure whether there is not something too elaborate, and too much worked up, in the picture. We give only one image, which we think is original. He supposed himself hurried along by two tormenting dæmons—

> Through lands we fled, o'er seas we flew . . .
> [192–211]

'The Hall of Justice', or the story of the Gypsy Convict, is another experiment of Mr. Crabbe's. It is very nervous—very shocking—and very powerfully represented. The woman is accused of stealing, and tells her story in impetuous and lofty language.

> My crime! this sick'ning child to feed, . . .
> [I, 9–12, 27–32, 37–42, 53–68]

> The night was dark, the lanes were deep, . . .
> [I, 89–96]

> I brought a lovely daughter forth, . . .
> [II, 49–56]

We have not room to give the sequel of this dreadful ballad. It certainly is not pleasing reading; but it is written with very unusual power of language, and shows Mr. Crabbe to have great mastery over the tragic passions of pity and horror. . . .

17. Thomas Denman, unsigned review, *Monthly Review*

June 1808, lvi, 170–9

Denman (1779–1854) became Lord Chief Justice. He reviewed for both the *Monthly* and the *Critical Reviews*.

[Begins with general remarks and quotations of Crabbe's reference to Fox in the preface.]

The Parish Register, which is the most considerable poem in this volume, and indeed occupies nearly a third part of it, may be characterized as a more expanded continuation of *The Village*. . . . He has presented us with a great variety of characters, which are discriminated with skill and spirit: while his incidents are in general judiciously selected, and told with peculiar felicity of narration, displaying occasionally much natural pathos, and uncommon powers of satire.

The miller's daughter—

> Then came the days of shame, the grievous night, . . .
> [I, 347–52, 357–60]

> Day after day was past in grief and pain, . . .
> [I, 371–402]

We insert the whole story of *Richard Monday*, which we consider as excellent in all its parts and of which the catastrophe in particular will be allowed to shew an intimate knowledge of human nature:

> To name an infant meet our village sires . . .
> [I, 688–766]

The village atheist—

> Last in my List, five untaught lads appear; . . .
> [I, 787–823]

The verses ['Reflections'] are intitled to very high praise. 'The motto, although it gave occasion to them, does not altogether express the sense of the writer; who meant to observe that some of our best acquisitions, and some of our nobler conquests, are rendered ineffectual by the passing away of opportunities, and the changes made by time; an argument that such acquirements and moral habits are reserved for a state of being, in which they may have uses here denied them.' (Pref. xxii.) We think that the same train of ideas likewise naturally suggests another moral respecting our conduct in society: but indeed it abounds with lessons the most awful and impressive, to every mind that is capable of serious reflection:

> When all the fiercer Passions cease . . .
> ['Reflections', 1–56]

'The Birth of Flattery' is nearly as good as most of the allegories which have been composed since the days of Spenser.—'Sir Eustace Grey', and 'The Hall of Justice', are very tragical stories, related with all the force and simplicity of the ballad style, while they are quite free from the insipid affection by which that style has been too frequently disgraced in the hands of its modern imitators.

> What though so pale his haggard Face, . . .
> ['Woman!', 13–28, 37–44]

. . . The style is not free from the faults of prolixity and obscurity in some passages, and *The Parish Register* will certainly admit of curtailment. On the whole, however, the volume deserves very superior commendation, as well for the flow of verse, and for the language, which is manly and powerful, equally remote from vicious ornament and the still more disgusting cant of idiot-simplicity, as for the sterling poetry and original powers of thought, of which it contains unquestionable proofs. One remark we add with pleasure, as prophetic of a still higher degree of excellence which the author may hereafter obtain:—his later productions are, in every respect, better and more perfect than those by which he first became known as a poet.

18. Unsigned review, *British Critic*

June 1808, xxxi, 590–5

In Mr. Crabbe we gratefully recognize one of the earlier friends of our youth, and whenever the recollection of his *Village*, and other poems, has glanced before us, the wonder has been excited, why the music which was cheered by Burke, encouraged by Johnson, and in some degree disciplined by Fox, should so long repose and conceal itself in inglorious solitude and silence. It does not appear that her slumbers, however profound, or however long, have contracted her powers or debilitated her energies. We discern and acknowledge the same excursive fancy, the same judicious selection, the same harmonious structure. . . .

The *Parish Register* is another successful effort to represent village manners, not with the chimerical over refined ideas of Arcadian simplicity, but as they actually exist among our peasantry; a mixture of good and evil propensities and habits, and their consequent effects, contentedness or wretchedness. . . .

> Dispos'd to wed, ev'n while you hasten, stay, . . .
> [II, 1–82 (and see Ward, I, 534–5)]

'The Birth of Flattery' is a beautiful effort of a sportive imagination, nevertheless this poem will perhaps be generally perused with less impression than any of the others. Allegory is out of fashion, and after having had some noble pictures before us to contemplate, the striking feature of which is truth, acknowledged and recognized by us all in the daily intercourse of life, we turn with languor to an ideal representation, to a fable, the moral of which, if any is intended, is not immediately obvious.

'Sir Eustace Grey' and the gypsey are of a very melancholy cast, and demonstrate uncommon powers of mind.

[Quotes 'Woman!']. . . .

19. Unsigned review, *Annual Review*

1808, vi, 513–21

The strongest writer whom it falls to our lot to mention in the poetical department of this year, is Mr. Crabbe. Feeling, energy, originality, minute observation, and vivid picture, are the characteristics of his style. . . .

This volume possesses in a high degree what is now certainly the rarest of poetical excellences—originality. Great indeed are its merits, its imperfections also are considerable; on both accounts it may be regarded as an excellent *study*, and therefore entitled to our particular attention. . . . An unrivalled vividness, and a certain painful truth of painting, characterize *The Village*. In plan, and still more in versification, this poem resembles that of Goldsmith—but here the likeness ends. Goldsmith saw his subject like a theorist as well as a poet—even the melancholy he excites is of a pleasing kind, and he lends a grace to his rustics themselves. Very different were the views and the situation of Mr. Crabbe. An actual and feeling spectator of the real sufferings of the poor in a dreary and inhospitable tract of the Suffolk coast, he snatches the pencil in a mingled emotion of pity and indignation,

> . . . to paint the cot,
> As truth will paint it, and as Bards will not.
> [I, 53–4]

His lines are not inferior in harmony, and certainly not in spirit nor in feeling, to any contained in *The Deserted Village*; but in fancy and elegance they cannot vie with that delightful poem. Mr. Crabbe is a kind of Dutch painter, who draws nothing that he does not, and any thing that he does see, which is capable of affording a picture, and a moral.

The Parish Register, which is the longest of the present volume, bears some relation by its subject to the poem we have just been noticing, but it is on the whole less gloomy, less poetical, has no general plan, fewer general reflections, and more depth of thought: in short it is the work of an older man. The experience of twenty years spent in a more agreeable part of the country, seems to have softened down the acuteness of those feelings that inspired *The Village*; and its author now appears the calm and impartial biographer of his parish.

Richard Monday—

> To name an infant meet our village sires . . .
> [I, 688–766]

Phoebe Dawson—

> Two summers since, I saw, at Lammas Fair . . .
> [II, 131–246]

Isaac Ashford—

> Next to these ladies, but in nought allied . . .
> [III, 413–52, 491–502]

. . . The student of life and manners can scarcely fail to be interested by the strong and faithful delineations here offered to his inspection, and the palled seeker after novelty will prefer their stimulant originality to the insipid elegance of many more ambitious votaries of the muses. To us it appears, that in the estimable branch of moral painting, the three specimens here selected are nearly perfect; and we are inclined to rank the master pieces in every branch above second-rate performances in any. *The Parish Register* contains several other portraits equal to these; with some of inferior merit, and a few which savour a little of that coarseness which the *rusticated* portion of our gentry and clergy find it so difficult to avoid contracting among clowns and cattle. The dramatic portions of this piece are not well managed; the speeches put into the mouths of peasants are not in *their* language, but this is a fault seldom shunned without incurring greater faults. A few slips of grammar, and some careless lines may also be remarked. Mr. C. is, we believe, the first poet who has snatched a simile from the wonderful experiments of Galvani—we wish he had not allowed himself so awkward a contraction of the name of that philosopher.[1]

> So two dead Limbs, when touch'd by *Galvin's* Wire,
> Move with new Life and feel awaken'd Fire;
> Quivering awhile, their flaccid Forms remain,
> Then turn to cold Torpidity, again.
> [II, 380–3]

If Mr. Crabbe has descended in the piece just criticized to a kind of

---

[1] Crabbe altered the second half of this line to 'touch'd by Galvani's wire'.

pedestrian style, it is not for want of the power to support a higher. His three earlier poems are always elegantly, and sometimes even richly versified, and several of his later ones unite dignity with spirit. The piece entitled 'Reflections', &c. which turns on the changes produced in the character and disposition by the approach of old age—the melancholy fact that experience comes too late, and the argument for a future state thence to be deduced, is truly admirable. . . .

> When all the fiercer passions cease . . .
> ['Reflections', 1–56]

> I'll know no more;—the heart is torn . . .
> ['Sir Eustace Grey', 1–27, 276–331]

. . . 'The Hall of Justice', is one which must not be overlooked. In structure it resembles Sir Eustace; being also in the form of a dialogue, in a lyric measure, between a magistrate and a poor gypsy woman, who relates her own story—a tale of vice and misery unfortunately too credible. The sentiments in some parts bear a resemblance to those of Mr. Wordsworth's 'Female Vagrant' but the incidents are totally different, and the expression is more concise and energetic, the conclusion too is satisfactory—the poor creature is one whom circumstances had made

> The slave, but not the friend of vice.
> [II, 60]

She had still that kind and degree of moral feeling which is denied we believe, to none of God's creatures who do not themselves take pains to smother it.

> True, I was not to Virtue train'd, . . .
> [II, 69–74]

In the benevolent magistrate she finds a humane protector, and the best of advisers. He gently reproves the vehemence of her despair, reminds her of the ransom paid for the sins of all; and points out the path of repentance and hope. On the whole this is one of the most interesting pieces in the volume, and is marked throughout with the strong stamp of a writer, little formed indeed to amuse or to captivate; but powerful to strike, to impress, to instruct, and sometimes to sadden and to humble the heart that can feel, and the mind that can reflect.

20. Unsigned reviews, *Universal Magazine*

November 1808–February 1809, 2nd Series, x, 434–8, 513–18, xi, 39–45, 127–32

It is not often that the labours of a reviewer are of that pleasing nature so as to make him contented with himself and his author. Called upon, as he most generally is, to expose the absurdities of false taste, the errors of ignorance, the unabashed boldness of impudence, and the pretensions of dullness, he is necessarily driven to harshness of language and severity of sentiment. It is a delightful repose to him when he happens to meet with a work whose merits are so numerous and conspicuous, and whose errors so few and unimportant, that he has little else to do than to resign his mind into his author's hands, and placidly to receive instruction and delight. Such has been the case in perusing the poems of Mr. Crabbe, and we hasten, with unfeigned pleasure, to communicate to our readers a portion of the pleasure we have felt. . . .

We hope, however, that if pastoral writers have drawn too placid and happy a picture of rural innocence and manners, Mr. Crabbe has, on the other hand, sketched too dark and gloomy a one. . . .

> Yes, thus the Muses sing of happy Swains, . . .
> [*The Village* I, 21–62]

Mr. Crabbe's manner frequently reminds us of Cowper, particularly when he is half ironical, half sarcastic. He has not indeed the vigour of Cowper, but he has his humour and his playfulness. . . .

[Quotes as 'felicitous simile'

> Why do I live, when I desire to be . . .
> [*ibid.*, 206–15]

and then

> Thus groan the Old, till, by disease opprest . . .
> [*ibid.*, 226–346]]

The second book of *The Village* falls far below the first; and the hyperbolical praise of Lord Robert Manners, of whom it can only be said that he died in the 24th year of his age, fighting for his country, carries its own censure with it, for who now remembers him? And yet, to read the following lines, who would not suppose that he had filled the world with his name like a Nelson or a Bonaparte?

So THOU, when every virtue, every grace, . . .
[II, 127–50]

Would all this exuberance of praise have been bestowed, had a young midshipman, the son of some obscure tradesman, died as bravely?—No. But for a *Lord* to perish so early it was quite another thing! Poetry is debased to prostitution when she gives to title what ought to be given to truth. The praise in the above lines is meanly hyperbolical; and we are surprised the author should retain it in 1808, when he finds that all those honours which he prophesied for his hero have been wisely withheld by his country. . . .

And hark! the riots of the Green begin, . . .
[II, 63–106]

The next poem in this volume is *The Parish Register*, divided into three parts. The idea is novel, and affords ample scope for the description of rural manners. The Village Register is considered as containing principally the annals of the poor; and under the distinct heads of *Baptisms*, *Marriages*, and *Burials*, such a view is taken of village customs, feelings, and prejudices, as interest the reader in the highest degree. Mr. Crabbe, indeed, is remarkably felicitous in his delineation of character as modified by the ordinary passions of human nature: and the moral maxims, which dignify his pages, embellished with the ornament of poetry, confer upon the labours of his muse a higher merit than can be claimed by verse, which is merely descriptive. . . .

The first part of *The Parish Register* is devoted to the consideration of village baptisms, and it is preceded by an introduction which delineates rural manners. Here, as in *The Village*, Mr. Crabbe colours darkly: he again strives to dispel the illusions which, probably, exist with regard to the supposed purity and innocence of rustic habits; and to shew that fields, and groves, and vallies, are no longer tenanted by those swains and virgins which pastoral poets represent. . . .

Fair scenes of peace! ye might detain us long, . . .
[I, 166–276]

Richard Monday—

To name an infant meet our village sires . . .
[I, 688–766]

Last in my List, five untaught lads appear; . . .
[I, 787–823]

Phoebe Dawson—

Two summers since, I saw, at Lammas Fair, . . .
[II, 131–246]

In the following, our readers will be pleased with the trio of similes with which it concludes:

Now to be wed, a well-match'd Couple came; . . .
[II, 358–83]

The third part of *The Parish Register* is devoted to the *Burials*; and here, where we expected most, we have been most disappointed. We looked for some of those tender delineations, those moral effusions, and that spirit of placid meditation with which the contemplation of mortality so naturally fills the heart. We hoped to find some affecting narrative, or some highly-wrought picture, which might please, even after the *Grave* of Blair. Why Mr. Crabbe has omitted all that we looked for, we have no right to ask; for, in works of imagination, an author must consult his genius, and not sign his own condemnation by an attempt beyond his powers. If motives like these operated upon Mr. Crabbe, his prudence deserves commendation.

Isaac Ashford—

Next to these ladies, but in nought allied . . .
[III, 413–502]

Natural and pathetic sentiments are but thinly scattered through this division of the poem; yet both nature and pathos are to be found in the following lines, which paint the melancholy emotions that throng to the mind when returned from the burial of those we love, and are beholding those objects that once occupied their minds, or delighted their view. He who has felt this distressing sensation; he whose eye has moistened at the sight of the most insignificant bauble that once belonged to departed friendship or love; he who has sighed with sorrow and anguish as he looked upon the vacant chair that once they sat in, or noticed the neglected avocation that was once theirs, will immediately recognize the melancholy accuracy of the following lines:

Arriv'd at Home, how then they gaz'd around . . .
[III, 619–34]

My Record ends:—But hark! ev'n now I hear . . .
[III, 801–970]

The next poem is *The Library*, which was published five and twenty years ago, and does not therefore demand from us that specific notice which it is our province to bestow only on new productions. The conception was happy, but it has not been employed with all that amplitude which would have afforded a wider scope for variety, for instructive observation, and for amusement. It might have been enlivened too by the introduction of character. It is not, however, without merit; and it has, in particular, the excellence of smooth versification, and a plain propriety of observation. . . .

Whilst thus engaged, high Views enlarge the Soul . . .
Most potent, grave and reverend Friends—Farewell!
[347–418]

Like some vast flood, unbounded, fierce, and strong, . . .
But freedom, that exalts the savage state, is gone.
[465–78]

What vent'rous race are ours! what mighty foes. . . .
And tell them, Such are all the toys they love.
[615–92]

The Newspaper, which is the next poem, is also, like *The Village* and *The Library*, a republication. It possesses a great portion of satirical humour, and some indignant reprobation. The character of a newspaper editor is drawn with a fidelity which truth herself may avouch.

Now be their Arts display'd, how first they choose . . .
[107–36]

Now sing, my Muse, what various Parts comprise . . .
[285–98]

'The Birth of Flattery', which follows next, possesses nothing very eminent. . . .

'Sir Eustace Grey', we think a very superior production, if we except a little childish inanity that sometimes prevails, and which we presume has been caught from the verbose and affected simplicity of Walter Scott, Wordsworth, *cum cæteris paribus*. The author says, that in this story 'an attempt is made to describe the wanderings of a mind first irritated by the consequences of error and misfortune, and afterwards soothed by a species of enthusiastic conversion still keeping him insane.'

A task, as he confesses, 'very difficult', yet Mr. Crabbe has succeeded to a certain degree. The language is adapted to the subject in a pleasing manner; and the abrupt transitions of Sir Eustace, not wholly incoherent, but preserving an almost evanescent chain of connexion, are proofs of Mr. Crabbe's skill. An ordinary poet would have made his hero talk in nothing but interjections.

> I'll know no more,—the Heart is torn . . .
> [1–147]

> Those Fiends, upon a shaking Fen . . .
> [268–331]

'The Hall of Justice' can have no moral effect; it brings detestable profligacy before the imagination, which cannot be compensated by any excellence of poetry. 'Woman!' with which the volume concludes, is a diffuse amplification of M. Ledyard's energetic praise of that ambiguous part of the creation.

Before we dismiss this volume from our consideration, we shall notice some errors, of various descriptions, which occurred to us in the perusal. Mr. Crabbe's poems are not likely to sink into speedy oblivion, and they are therefore entitled to more emendatory criticism than need be wasted on mere imbecility.

And first, we think the *Dedication* too much in the manner of those fawning hyperboles which disgrace the memory of Otway and Dryden. What is that infatuation which makes us look with admiration upon those qualities in a lord, that would be absolutely beneath notice in a private individual? Is it the miracle of nobility and common sense being united in the same person?

In *The Village* are some offences against harmony and against grammar:

> Where all that's wretched pave the way for death.
> [I, 261]

Here the verb should be in the singular, the nominative being evidently so, and the relative being put in the genitive singular.

> *For* him no hand the cordial cup applies.
> [I, 270]

> Without reply he rushes *on* the door.
> [I, 291]

In the above lines the prepositions *for* and *on* are used instead of *to*.

> Here too the Squire or squire-like farmer *talk*.
> [II, 55]

It is one of the simplest rules of grammar, that two or more substantives disjoined by the conjunction *or*, require the verb to be in the singular. It should, consequently, be *talks*.

The following reminds us of the Scotchman's phrase, 'I feel a stink':

> Or as Old Thames, borne down with decent pride,
> *Sees* his young streams run *warbling* at his side!
> [II, 200-1]

Mr. Crabbe would perform an acceptable service to the labouring part of the community, could he convince them that

> Toil, care, and patience *bless* th' abstemious few.
> *Parish Reg.* [I, 29]

> And cards, in curses torn, *lie* fragments on the floor.
> [I, 256]

There is, we believe, no precedent for making the verb, *to lie*, an active one.

> When to the wealthier farmers there *was* shown,
> Welcome unfeign'd, and plenty like their own.
> [I, 435-6]

It should be *were*, *plenty* and *welcome* being the nominatives.

> What if in both, *Life's bloomy flush* was lost.
> [II, 453]

This is copied from Goldsmith:

> And all the *bloomy flush of life* is gone.[1]

> Has then the hope that Heav'n its grief *approve*.
> [*The Parish Register*, III, 67]

It should be *approves*. Mr. Crabbe is culpably negligent in his frequency of this error.

> Death has his infant train; his bony arm
> *Strikes from the baby cheek the rosy charm*.
> [II, 191-2]

This last line is a strong metaphor, copied from a beautiful passage in the *Grave*.

[1] *The Deserted Village*, 128.

Dull Grave, thou spoil'st the dance of youthful blood,
Strik'st out the dimple from the cheek of mirth, &c.
[111–12]

Does not human flesh, in a putrescent state, generate worms like other corrupted animal substances? If so, Mr. Crabbe has more poetry than truth in the following lines:

Slow to the Vault they come with heavy tread, . . .
The Parish Register, [III, 284–93]

Mr. Crabbe again offends in what would call punishment down upon a schoolboy in the following line,

Some princes had it, or *was* said to have.
[III, 387]¹

So vile an antithesis as the following, in a serious poem, deserves to be reprobated,

I never colder, yet they *older* grew.
[III, 722]

And *villains* triumph when the worthless fall.
The Library [514]

Surely *villains* is here used for *virtue.*

For want like thine, a bog without a base,
Ingulph'st all gains, I gather for the place.
B. of Flattery [59–60]

The verb should be in the third person, not the second. *Want* is the nominative.

Which yet, *unview'd of* thee, a bog had been.
Ib. [300]

'Unview'd of' we suspect to be a provincial expression: we are certain it is a vulgar one.

If the minuteness of these strictures be objected to, our reply is that all error is prejudicial; and that what is good, clouded even with imperfections, will surely be better when those imperfections are removed.

---

1 'princes' is a misprint for 'princess'.

January 1809, v, 40–9

Montgomery (1771–1854), Radical politician, journalist and hymn-writer in succession is considered by the writer of the notice in the *Dictionary of National Biography* to be a critic of dull impartiality. His *Eclectic* comments on Crabbe do not support this criticism. See Introduction, p. 7.

Every man of moderate talents may step forth as an original writer, in any path of elegant literature to which his taste inclines him, if he will courageously exercise his powers on those subjects that are most frequently within his view, and of which he has the opportunity of acquiring the greatest knowledge. Of this noble and successful daring Mr. Crabbe is a signal example. His poetical qualifications are considerably limited: fancy, fervour, grace, and feeling, he has only in a low degree; his talents are chiefly of the middle order, but they are admirable in their kind, and he employs them to the utmost advantage. Strength, spirit, truth, and discrimination, are conspicuous in all his pieces; his peasant-characters are drawn with Dutch drollery, and his village-pictures finished with Flemish minuteness. His diction is copious and energetic, though frequently hard and prosaic; it remarkably abounds with antitheses, catchwords, and other products of artifice and labour. His verse is fluent, but exceedingly monotonous; the pause in his heroic measure falling sometimes through ten couplets in a page after the fourth and fifth syllables: but he often strikes out single lines of perfect excellence, sententious as proverbs, and pointed like epigrams. A vein of peculiar English humour runs through his details; a bitter pleasantry, a moody wit, a sarcastic sadness, that seems at once to frown and smile, to scorn and pity. He is a poet half way between Pope and Goldsmith; but he wants the taste of the one, and the tenderness of the other; we are often reminded of each, yet he never seems the servile imitator of either, while his style and his subjects, especially in facetious description, occasionally elevate him to an equality with both.

74

He sometimes borrows phrases, and even whole lines, from other authors; and as he does this from indolence, not from necessity, he deserves the discredit which such obligations throw upon his pages. One of his most masterly sketches in *The Parish Register*, that of the old blind Landlord, is ruined at the conclusion by the quotation of a line from the *Night Thoughts*, the substance of which the author had previously paraphrased in the context. No themes have been more hacknied in rhyme than the delights of villages, and the peace and innocence of country people; but as all the villages of former bards had been situated in Arcadia, Mr. Crabbe had nothing to do but to look at home, in his own parishes, (the one near a smuggling creek on the sea-coast, and the other among the flats of Leicestershire,) to become the most original poet that ever sang of village life and manners.

In the preface to this collection of his *new* and *republished* poems, Mr. Crabbe brings such critical recommendations in his hand, as ought perhaps to silence anonymous Reviewers. What can *we* say to '*His Grace the late Duke of Rutland, The Right Honourable the Lord Thurlow, Dr. Samuel Johnson, Mr. Burke, the Right Honourable Charles James Fox, Henry Richard Lord Holland, The Reverend Richard Turner*', &c. &c.? Truly we can do neither more nor less than make our bow, and retire in mute astonishment to find a poet in so much good company. However, we *will* whisper one surly hint in his ear, as he shews us to the door,—'Mr. C., you are much too obsequious to great folks not to provoke the spleen of little ones.' But if Mr. Crabbe is a willow in his Preface, he is an oak in *The Village*. This is his master-piece. It was published more than twenty years ago; the best parts of it are familiar to most readers of poetical miscellanies, having been frequently reprinted.

This piece ought to have concluded about the 106th line of the Second part: but Mr. C., not content with being the Censor of the Poor, most unseasonably becomes the Panegyrist of the Rich; at the *end* of *The Village* he has lighted a great bonfire of adulation to the Rutland family, and though he dances about it with abundant grace and gravity, we cannot help thinking that he ought to have chosen another time and place for demonstrations of gratitude to his munificent patrons.—. . .

The plan of [*The Parish Register*] has simplicity, and perhaps nothing else to recommend it; but the execution is intitled to very high praise; though there are some languid and heavy paragraphs, the humour and satire are well supported to the conclusion. . . .

Fair scene of peace! ye might detain us long . . .

[I, 166–211]

Here are no wheels for either wool or flax, . . .
[I, 230–68]

How fair these names, how much unlike they look . . .
[II, 283–300]

Here we cut short the description of these unmanageable fists, as the author ought to have done; but the thought was so good, that he could not resist the temptation of spoiling it in six more lines.—In this part, if we pardon the wedding scene, we must condemn the *three similes* of 'Old Hodge' and his 'Dame' [II, 372–83]: they are as sickening as the subject, on which the author seems to dwell with detestable delight.— The story of Phoebe Dawson deserves the applause which has been bestowed upon it by former critics: but the most affecting circumstance connected with it, we learn from the preface,—it was read to the late Mr. Fox on his death-bed, and was the last composition of the kind 'that engaged and amused the capacious, the candid, the benevolent mind of this great man.'

The third part, 'Burials' is, in our estimation, the most curious and valuable. The portraits are painted *from* life *in* death; when man appears what he *is*. And how *does* he generally appear in this Christian land? Let us hear a minister of the Church, who has had long and ample experience.

What I behold, are feverish fits of strife, . . .
[III, 29–58]

We are compelled reluctantly to pass over this striking description, without entering into a minute examination of its parts, all of which are most fearfully interesting. In the whole course of our reading, we never met with a phrase that chilled us with such horror, as one that occurs in the 16th line—'*Death's common-place!*' And is there indeed a common-place train of thought in death? and is this which our author has given, the faithful expression of it? There *is*, and *this* is the faithful expression of it! . . .

In the lines succeeding the above quotation,—in the character of his favourite Isaac Ashford,—in his Youth from Cambridge,—and in his Sir Eustace Grey, Mr. Crabbe takes special care to mark his abhorrence of sectaries and enthusiasts. We will only make one remark on this: were he better acquainted with those whom he despises and reprobates, he would find less of 'Death's common-place,' and more of 'the joy that springs from pardoning love' [III, 68] among them, in their last hours, than he finds in his *poetical* parish;—for we trust that in his *rectorial* parish, his precepts and example, his fervid zeal and holy faithfulness, induce many, if not all, of his flock, to choose 'the narrow way' that leads to eternal life.

That all our extracts from this singular poem may not be coarse and gloomy, we will copy the conclusion of Isaac Ashford's character, which is very natural, and mournfully pleasing.

At length, he found, when seventy years were run, . . .
[II, 465–502]

The poem of 'Sir Eustace Grey' presents a dreadful delineation of the woes and wanderings of a distracted mind. There are some very fine strokes of nature and truth in it, that display the author's profound knowledge of the human heart in its unconverted state. Of conversion he manifests his ignorance only; or else, if he knows what it is, he does not tell. The change wrought in the mind of the insane Sir Eustace, by 'a *methodistic* call,' when 'a sober and rational conversion could not have happened' to him, is either the greatest miracle or the greatest absurdity that we ever read of even in verse. We have not room to expose the contradiction involved in this monstrous story.

'The Hall of Justice' is a tale of excessive horror and abomination; there is a great deal of vigour, but very little poetry in it. We leave the few other pieces to their fortune.

THE BOROUGH

April 1810

The opinion of the leading reviews was again nearly unanimous; agreeing that *The Borough* had greater beauties and greater defects than its predecessor, *The Parish Register*. With such a decision an author may always be well pleased; for he is sure to take his rank with posterity by his beauties; defects, where there are great and real excellences, serve but to fill critical dissertations. In fact, though the character was still the same, and the blemishes sufficiently obvious, *The Borough* was a great spring upwards. The incidents and characters in *The Parish Register* are but excellent sketches:—there is hardly enough matter even in the most interesting description, not even in the story of Phoebe Dawson, to gain a firm hold of the reader's mind:—but, in the new publication, there was a sufficient evolution of event and character, not only to please the fancy, but grapple with the heart. I think the 'Highwayman's Tale', in the twenty-third letter (Prisons), is an instance in point. We see the virtuous young man, the happy lover, and the despairing felon in succession, and enough of each state to give full force to its contrasts. I know that my father was himself much affected when he drew that picture, as he had been, by his own confession, twice before; once at a very early period (see the 'Journal to Mira'), and again when he was describing the terrors of a poor distracted mind, in his 'Sir Eustace Grey'. The tale of the Condemned Felon arose from the following circumstances:—while he was struggling with poverty in London, he had some reason to fear that the brother of a very intimate friend, a wild and desperate character, was in Newgate under condemnation for a robbery. Having obtained permission to see the man who bore the same name, a glance at once relieved his mind from the dread of beholding his friend's brother; but still he never forgot the being he then saw before him. He was pacing the cell, or small yard, with a quick and hurried step; his eye was as glazed and abstracted as that of a corpse:

Since his dread sentence, nothing seem'd to be
As once it was; seeing he could not see,
Nor hearing hear aright . . .
Each sense was palsied!

[XXIII, 235–7, 233]

In the common-place book of the author the following observations were found relative to *The Borough*; and they apply
perhaps with still more propriety to his succeeding poems:—'I
have chiefly, if not exclusively, taken my subjects and characters
from that order of society where the least display of vanity is
generally to be found, which is placed between the humble and
the great. It is in this case of mankind that more originality of
character, more variety of fortune, will be met with; because, on
the one hand, they do not live in the eye of the world, and, therefore, are not kept in awe by the dread of observation and indecor-
um; neither, on the other, are they debarred by their want of
means from the cultivation of mind and the pursuits of wealth
and ambition, which are necessary to the development of character
displayed in the variety of situations to which this class is liable.'[1]

---

[1] *Life*, Ch. 8.

22. Thomas Denman, unsigned review, *Monthly Review*

April 1810, lxi, 396–409

Much amusement may be derived from drawing comparisons between the kindred arts, which address themselves to our taste and imagination; and it is an exercise that may sometimes afford no unprofitable employment to our general faculty of judging on subjects of this nature. The *belles lettres* and the fine arts bear a delightful analogy to each other; and though Dryden, in his epistle on painting, ought to have compared Michael Angelo, not Raffaelle, to Homer,—and Raffaelle, not Titian, to the Mantuan bard,—still we are indebted to him (though he was erroneous perhaps in the particular instance) for striking out such an idea. In conformity to it, we have heard Mr. Crabbe designated as the *Hogarth of Poetry*; and with reference to the force and truth of the descriptions of that deceased artist and this living poet, the moral effect of their combinations, their insight into human nature, and the particular mode and taste in which they love to study and represent it, we acknowledge much justice in the comparison. It might probably be this association which led us to expect, in *The Borough* of this author, something like a poetical counterpart to the series of the Election-pictures which were so admirably executed by the painting satirist: perhaps, indeed, the title itself naturally held forth some promise; and the actual state of our domestic politics appeared likely to have drawn attention towards this topic. We may at all events be permitted to retain our opinion that a more animated, interesting, and popular poem would have been produced by such a mode of treating the subject, than by that which has been in fact adopted.

As men, however, are only children of a larger growth, so Mr. Crabbe's *Borough* is neither more nor less than his *Village*, extended beyond all reasonable bounds. . . .

The settled, the *stagnant*, state of society, within the geographical limits of the writer's imaginary borough, is the subject of the poem: the reader is successively introduced to a set of characters in middling and low life; and though the pictures may be spiritedly drawn, and

faithfully accurate, they are only portraits,—detached, individual portraits,—illustrated sometimes indeed by a rather crowded allusive back-
ground, but without grouping, without historical painting, without
composition.

The want of arrangement and connection is more striking in this
poem than in any other of equal length that we remember. We
absolutely see no reason why any considerable passage in the whole
course of it should occupy its particular place; and if we began at the
last book, and read the books regularly backwards, or in any other
order whatever, it would be impossible to increase the confusion. In *The
Parish Register*, the several subjects were certainly united by a very
slender thread; yet we could listen with delighted sympathy to the
village-anecdote of a pastor who was paternally interested in the welfare
of all his flock, and connected with some of them by the ties of friendship and affection: but *here*, who writes the letters, who receives them,
and why or on what occasion they are composed, are questions to which
no answer is attempted. In fact, it seems rather whimsical that they
should be called *letters*, since they have nothing occasional, nothing
personal; and we must add that their style is, on the whole, deficient in
sprightliness and variety.

Mr. Crabbe's unfavourable opinion of mankind, and his austere
morality, remind us of the character of Persius given by Queen
Elizabeth, viz. a *crab-staff*. The author's own love of punning will forgive
this allusion; and we will transcribe the justification which he offers at
the conclusion of his work:

> No! 'tis not worldly gain, although by chance . . .
> [XXIV, 416-65]

We render full justice to these motives: but surely a more frequent
exhibition of the ability of virtue to triumph over our evil propensities
would be but a fair encouragement to frail human nature. To tell us that
there are certain temptations under which we cannot fail to yield, as
soon as they are adequately presented to us, is in fact to say that we are
puppets of an overpowering destiny; or the instruments of some such
cunning Devil, as he who tempted *Abel Keene*[1] to pocket the sacramental contributions for the relief of the poor. It may be also observed
that too much uniformity prevails in this poet's denunciation of vice;
and in particular that those who speak irreverently of the clergy are
visited somewhat too frequently with his just indignation.

[1] This is an error for Jachin (Letter XIX).

From what we have said, it may be collected that Mr. Crabbe has not, in our opinion, displayed any new talents in the work before us: but we have pleasure in stating, and in proving by our extracts, that the powers which he was known to possess are in some instances most vigorously developed.

> Yes, our election's past, and we've been free, . . .
> [V, 1–62, 115–26, 181–96]

. . . Our impression certainly is rather favourable to his preceding exertions; and we doubt whether any passage in this volume be quite so happily *hit off*, as the delineations of Isaac Ashford and Richard Monday, the Village Atheist, and the Parish Wedding, in *The Parish Register*: though persons are here described and their histories are related considerably more at length. The greatest portion of labour has been bestowed apparently on Blaney, an inhabitant of the Borough Alms-house, who has run through three fortunes with absurd extravagance, and becomes the most degraded of human beings in his old age. His early life is thus represented:

> Observe that tall pale veteran! what a look . . .
> [XIV, 1–28, 104–15, 142–51, 183–90]

> Again attend!—and see a man whose cares . . .
> [XVII, 214–55]

> The letter on itinerant players . . . to subsist upon except their credit.
> [Preface, Ward, I, p. 276]

It is impossible not to lament that a mind thus nervous and powerful should often waste itself in dilating on useless particulars, which are sometimes trifling, and not seldom revolting. In this point, a marked distinction prevails between the poet and the painter; for while the latter may introduce a thousand subordinate aids, which shall promote the general effect, the former would destroy the required prominency of the capital figures, by devoting much space and many words to a narration of minor circumstances. Yet even the highly-wrought tale of Peter Grimes is not entirely free from feeble minutiæ, though some parts of it are unquestionably very fine:

> Old Peter Grimes made fishing his employ . . .
> [XXII, 1–31, 40–58, 171–208, 278–375]

Whatever censures we may have deemed it right to bestow on such traits as appear to us to be the faults of this work, the length of our extracts will prove that in our judgment it contains much to admire; and if we were to quote all the verses that have pleased, affected, or shocked us, this article would not soon be brought to a conclusion. We abstain purposely from attempting to analyse so unmethodical a poem; and we have observed with surprise how little Mr. Crabbe seems to be sensible of the value of a plot, or a leading subject. It is remarkable that, in the immense number of his characters, no two are represented as bearing any relation to or influencing the feelings of each other.— Among the poor and their dwellings he is quite at home: but here the description is almost copied from his former poem, except that the dread of exact repetition has made the present less rich in particulars. At the same time, many good subjects for poetry are disregarded. Why is not this *Borough* bounded by some antient monastery, or bold Roman wall? Why is it not crowned by a towering castle, once the seat of baronial splendor and feudal contest, whose Keep secured the high-born captive, while its hall rang with shouts and minstrelsy? The history of this edifice might have carried us back in imagination to the factions of the two Roses; and, through the dismantling times of Cromwell, to the state in which its ruins might furnish hovels to the poor and vaults to the smuggler, while a few iron apartments still secured the fettered male-factor. A watch-fire might have gleamed over the waves from the sum-mit of some lofty rock, at whose base the fisherman could cultivate his garden and train his fruit-trees. A shipwreck is indeed described, but in such a manner as to make us rather share the alarm of those on shore, than feel the horrible calamity of the foundering crew.

No part of our critical duty is so irksome as that of stigmatizing the violation of propriety in language: but, in the works of an author of eminence, we cannot endure such barbarous contractions as *couldn't, they'd, there'll,* &c. &c.

In taking our leave of Mr. Crabbe, (but, we hope, for no long period,) we earnestly advise him, in his future efforts, to reject more boldly, to adopt more timidly, and to discriminate with greater caution. Unless they are controuled by a severe judgment, copiousness and facility are disadvantages, or at least snares, to the possessor. Gifted as Mr. C. is with uncommon poetical powers, he will be in danger of failing to produce a great poem, unless he can brook the labour of correcting, polishing, and re-writing, and submit to the sacrifice of resolutely expunging. In a beautiful passage in his preface, (p. vii.) in which he compares books to children, and says that all our pride is centred in those who are established in good company, but that all our fondness rests on those who are still at home, he admits his want of impartiality to draw a fair comparison between this and his former works. We have honestly endeavoured to assist his judgment; and we will not affront him by any apology for a freedom which is prompted only by respect for his talents, and anxiety for his reputation.

23. Francis Jeffrey, unsigned review, *Edinburgh Review*

April 1810, xvi, 30–55

We are very glad to meet with Mr. Crabbe so soon again; and particularly glad to find, that his early return has been occasioned, in part, by the encouragement he received on his last appearance. This late spring of public favour, we hope, he will yet live to see ripen into mature fame. We scarcely know any poet who deserves it better; and are quite certain there is none who is more secure of keeping with posterity whatever he may win from his contemporaries.

The present poem is precisely of the character of *The Village* and *The Parish Register*. It has the same peculiarities, and the same faults and beauties; though a severe critic might perhaps add, that its peculiarities are more obtrusive, its faults greater, and its beauties less. However that be, both faults and beauties are so plainly produced by the peculiarity, that it may be worth while, before giving any more particular account of it, to try if we can ascertain in what that consists.

And here we shall very speedily discover, that Mr. Crabbe is distinguished, from all other poets, both by the choice of his subjects, and by his manner of treating them. All his persons are taken from the lower ranks of life; and all his scenery from the most ordinary and familiar objects of nature or art. His characters and incidents, too, are as common as the elements out of which they are compounded are humble; and not only has he nothing prodigious or astonishing in any of his representations, but he has not even attempted to impart any of

the ordinary colours of poetry to those vulgar materials. He has no
moralizing swains or sentimental tradesmen; and scarcely ever seeks to
charm us by the artless manners or lowly virtues of his personages. On
the contrary, he has represented his villagers and humble burghers as
altogether as dissipated, and more dishonest and discontented, than the
profligates of higher life; and, instead of conducting us through blooming groves and pastoral meadows, has led us along filthy lanes and
crowded wharfs, to hospitals, alms-houses, and gin-shops. In some of
these delineations, he may be considered as the satirist of low life,—an
occupation sufficiently arduous, and in a great degree new and original
in our language. But by far the greater part of his poetry is of a different
and a higher character; and aims at moving or delighting us by lively,
touching, and finely contrasted representations of the dispositions,
sufferings, and occupations of those ordinary persons who form the far
greater part of our fellow-creatures. This, too, he has sought to effect,
merely by placing before us the clearest, most brief, and most striking
sketches of their external condition,—the most sagacious and unexpected strokes of character,—and the truest and most pathetic
pictures of natural feeling and common suffering. By the mere force
of his art, and the novelty of his style, he forces us to attend to objects
that are usually neglected, and to enter into feelings from which we are
in general but too eager to escape;—and then trusts to nature for the
effect of the representation.

It is obvious, at first sight, that this is not a task for an ordinary
hand; and that many ingenious writers, who make a very good figure
with battles, nymphs, and moonlight landscapes, would find themselves quite helpless if set down among streets, harbours, and taverns.
The difficulty of such subjects, in short, is sufficiently visible—and some
of the causes of that difficulty: but they have their advantages also;—
and of these, and their hazards, it seems natural to say a few words,
before entering more minutely into the merits of the work before us.

The first great advantage of such familiar subjects is, that every one
is necessarily perfectly well acquainted with the originals; and is therefore sure to feel all that pleasure, from a faithful representation of them,
which results from the perception of a perfect and successful imitation.
In the kindred art of painting, we find that this single consideration has
been sufficient to stamp a very high value upon accurate and lively
delineations of objects, in themselves the most uninteresting, and even
disagreeable; and no very inconsiderable part of the pleasure which
may be derived from Mr. Crabbe's poetry, may be referred to its mere

truth and fidelity, and to the brevity and clearness with which he sets before his readers, objects and characters with which they have been all their days familiar.

In his happier passages, however, he has a higher merit, and imparts a higher gratification. The chief delight of poetry consists, not so much in what it directly supplies to the imagination, as in what it enables it to supply itself;—not in warming the heart with its passing brightness, but in kindling its own lasting stores of light and heat;—not in hurrying the fancy along by a foreign and accidental impulse, but in setting it agoing, by touching its internal springs and principles of activity. Now, this highest and most delightful effect can only be produced by the poet's striking a note to which the heart and the affections naturally vibrate in unison;—by his rousing one of a large family of kindred impressions;—by his dropping the rich seed of his fancy upon the fertile and sheltered places of the imagination. But it is evident, that the emotions connected with common and familiar objects,—with objects which fill every man's memory, and are necessarily associated with all that he has felt or fancied, are of all others the most likely to answer this description, and to produce, where they can be raised to a sufficient height, this great effect in its utmost perfection. It is for this reason that the images and affections that belong to our *universal* nature, are always, if tolerably represented, infinitely more captivating, in spite of their apparent commonness and simplicity, than those that are peculiar situations, however they may come recommended by novelty or grandeur. The familiar feeling of maternal tenderness and anxiety, which is every day before our eyes, even in the brute creation,—and the enchantment of youthful love, which is nearly the same in all characters, ranks and situations,—still contribute more to the beauty and interest of poetry than all the misfortunes of princes, the jealousies of heroes, and the feats of giants, magicians, or ladies in armour. Every one can enter into the former set of feelings; and but a few into the latter. The one calls up a thousand familiar and long-remembered emotions,—and are answered and reflected on every side by the kindred impressions which experience or observation have traced upon every memory: while the other lights up but a transient and unfruitful blaze, and passes away without perpetuating itself in any corresponding sensation.

Now, the delineation of all that concerns the lower and most numerous classes of society, is, in this respect, on a footing with the pictures of our primary affections,—that their originals are necessarily familiar to all men, and are inseparably associated with a multitude of their most interesting impressions. Whatever may be our own condition, we all live surrounded with the poor, from infancy to age;—we hear daily of their sufferings and misfortunes;—and their toils, their crimes, or their pastimes, are our hourly spectacle. Many diligent readers of poetry know little, by their own experience, of palaces, castles or camps; and still less of princes, warriors and banditti;—but every one thoroughly understands every thing about cottages, streets and villages; and conceives, pretty correctly, the character and condition of sailors, ploughmen and artificers. If the poet can contrive, therefore, to create a sufficient interest in subjects like these, they will infallibly sink deeper into the mind, and be more prolific of kindred trains of emotion, than subjects of greater dignity. Nor is the difficulty of exciting such an interest by any means so great as is generally imagined. It is human nature, and human feelings, after all, that form the true source of interest in poetry of every description;—and the splendour and the marvels by which it is sometimes surrounded, serve no other purpose than to fix our attention on those workings of the heart, and those energies of the understanding, which alone command all the genuine sympathies of human beings,—and which may be found as abundantly in the breasts of cottagers as of kings. Wherever there are human beings, therefore, with feelings and characters to be represented, our attention may be fixed by the art of the poet,—by his judicious selection of circumstances,—by the force and vivacity of his style, and the clearness and brevity of his representations. In point of fact, we are all touched more deeply, as well as more frequently, in real life, with the sufferings of peasants than of princes; and sympathize much oftener, and more heartily, with the successes of the poor, than of the rich and distinguished. The occasions of such feelings are indeed so many, and so common, that they do not often leave any very permanent traces behind them, but pass away, and are effaced by the very rapidity of their succession. The business and the cares, and the pride of the world, obstruct the development of the emotions to which they would naturally give rise, and press so close and thick upon the mind, as to shut it, at most seasons, against the reflections that are perpetually seeking for admission. When we have leisure, however, to look quietly into our hearts, we shall find in them an infinite multitude of little fragments of sympathy with our brethren in humble life,—abortive movements of compassion, and embryos of kindness and concern, which had once fairly begun to live and germinate within them, though

87

withered and broken off by the selfish bustle and fever of our daily occupations. Now, all these may be revived and carried on to maturity by the art of the poet;—and, therefore, a powerful effort to interest us in the feelings of the humble and obscure, will usually call forth more deep, more numerous, and more permanent emotions, than can ever be excited by the fate of princesses and heroes. Independent of the circumstances to which we have already alluded, there are causes which make us at all times more ready to enter into the feelings of the humble, than of the exalted part of our species. Our sympathy with their enjoyments is enhanced by a certain mixture of pity for their general condition, which, by purifying it from that taint of envy which almost always adheres to our admiration of the great, renders it more welcome and satisfactory to our bosoms; while our concern for their sufferings is at once softened and endeared to us by the recollection of our own exemption from them, and by the feeling, that we frequently have it in our power to relieve them.

From these, and from other causes, it appears to us to be certain, that where subjects taken from humble life can be made sufficiently interesting to overcome the distaste and the prejudices with which the usages of polished society too generally lead us to regard them, the interest which they excite will commonly be more profound and more lasting than any that can be raised upon loftier themes; and the poet of *The Village* and *The Borough* be oftener, and longer read, than the poet of the Court or the Camp. The most popular passages of Shakespeare and Cowper, we think, are of this description: and there is much, both in the volume before us, and in Mr. Crabbe's former publications, to which we might now venture to refer, as proofs of the same doctrine. When such representations have once made an impression on the imagination, they are remembered daily, and for ever. We can neither look around, nor within us, without being reminded of their truth and their importance; and, while the more brilliant effusions of romantic fancy are recalled only at long intervals, and in rare situations, we feel that we cannot walk a step from our own doors, nor cast a glance back on our departed years, without being indebted to the poet of vulgar life for some striking image or touching reflection, of which the occasions were always before us, but,—till he taught us how to improve them,—were almost always allowed to escape.

Such, we conceive, are some of the advantages of the subjects which Mr. Crabbe has in a great measure introduced into modern poetry;— and such the grounds upon which we venture to predict the durability of the reputation which he has acquired. That they have their disadvantages also, is obvious; and it is no less obvious, that it is to these we must ascribe the greater part of the faults and deformities with which this author is fairly chargeable. The two great errors into which he has fallen, are—that he has described many things not worth describing;—and that he has frequently excited disgust, instead of pity or indignation, in the breasts of his readers. These faults are obvious,—and, we believe, are popularly laid to his charge: yet there is, in so far as we have observed, a degree of misconception as to the true grounds and limits of the charge, which we think it worth while to take this opportunity of correcting.

The poet of humble life *must* describe a great deal,—and must even describe, minutely, many things which possess in themselves no beauty or grandeur. The reader's fancy must be awaked,—and the power of his own pencil displayed:—a distinct locality and imaginary reality must be given to his characters and agents; and the ground colour of their common condition must be laid in, before his peculiar and selected groups can be presented with any effect or advantage. In the same way, he must study characters with a minute and anatomical precision; and must make both himself and his readers familiar with the ordinary traits and general family features of the beings among whom they are to move, before they can either understand, or take much interest in the individuals who are to engross their attention. Thus far, there is no excess or unnecessary minuteness. But this faculty of observation, and this power of description, hold out great temptations to go further. There is a pride and a delight in the exercise of all peculiar power; and the poet, who has learned to describe external objects exquisitely with a view to heighten the effect of his moral designs, and to draw characters with accuracy to help forward the interest of the pathos of the picture, will be in great danger of describing scenes, and drawing characters, for no other purpose, but to indulge his taste, and to display his talents. It cannot be denied, we think, that Mr. Crabbe has, on many occasions, proved unequal to this temptation. He is led away, every now and then, by his lively conception of external objects, and by his nice and sagacious observation of human character; and wantons and luxuriates in descriptions and moral portrait-painting, while his readers are left to wonder to what end so much industry has been exerted.

His chief fault, however, is his frequent lapse into disgusting representations; and this, we will confess, is an error for which we find it far more difficult either to account or to apologize. We are not, however, of the opinion which we have often heard stated, that he has represented human nature under too unfavourable an aspect, or that the distaste which his poetry sometimes produces, is owing merely to the painful nature of the scenes and subjects with which it abounds. On the contrary, we think he has given a juster, as well as a more striking picture, of the true character and situation of the lower orders of this country, than any other writer, whether in verse or in prose; and that he has made no more use of painful emotions than was necessary to the production of a pathetic effect.

All powerful and pathetic poetry, it is obvious, abounds in images of distress. The delight which it bestows partakes strongly of pain; and, by a sort of contradiction, which has long engaged the attention of the reflecting, the compositions that attract us most powerfully, and detain us the longest, are those that produce in us most of the effects of actual suffering and wretchedness. The solution of this paradox is to be found, we think, in the simple fact, that pain is a far stronger sensation than pleasure in human existence; and that the cardinal virtue of all things that are intended to delight the mind, is to produce a strong sensation. Life itself appears to consist in sensation; and the universal passion of all beings that have life, seems to be, that they should be made intensely conscious of it, by a succession of powerful and engrossing emotions. All the mere gratifications or natural pleasures that are in the power even of the most fortunate, are quite insufficient to fill this vast craving for sensation; and a more violent stimulus is sought for by those who have attained the vulgar heights of life, in the pains and dangers of war, —the agonies of gaming,—or the feverish toils of ambition. To those who have tasted of these potent cups, where the bitter however so obviously predominates, the security, the comforts, and what are called the enjoyments of common life, are intolerably insipid and disgusting. Nay, we think we have observed, that even those who, without any effort or exertion, have experienced unusual misery, frequently appear, in like manner, to acquire a taste for it, and come to look on the tranquillity of ordinary life with a kind of indifference not unmingled with contempt. It is certain, at least, that they dwell with most apparent satisfaction on the memory of those days, which have been marked by the deepest and most agonizing sorrows, and derive a certain delight from the recollections of those overwhelming sensations which once occasioned so fierce a throb in the languishing pulse of their existence.

If any thing of this kind, however, can be traced in real life,—if the passion for emotion be so strong, as to carry us, not in imagination, but in reality, over the rough edge of present pain,—it will not be difficult to explain, why it should be so attractive in the copies and fictions of poetry. There, as in real life, the great demand is for emotion; while the pain with which it may be attended, can scarcely, by any possibility, exceed the limits of endurance. The recollection, that it is but a copy and a fiction, is quite sufficient to keep it down to a moderate temperature, and to make it welcome as the sign or the harbinger of that agitation of which the soul is avaricious. It is not, then, from any peculiar quality in painful emotions that they become capable of affording the delight which attends them in tragic or pathetic poetry,—but merely from the circumstance of their being more intense and powerful than any other emotions of which the mind is susceptible. If it was the constitution of our nature to feel joy as keenly, or to sympathize with it as heartily as we do with sorrow, we have no doubt that no other sensation would ever be intentionally excited by the artists that minister to delight. But the fact is, that the pleasures of which we are capable, are slight and feeble, compared with the pains that we may endure; and that, feeble as they are, the sympathy which they excite falls much more short of the original emotion. When the object, therefore, is to obtain sensation, there can be no doubt to which of the fountains we shall repair; and if there be but few pains in real life which are not, in some measure, endeared to us by the emotions with which they are attended, we may be pretty sure, that the more distress we introduce into poetry, the more we shall rivet the attention and attract the admiration of the reader.

There is but one exception to this rule,—and it brings us back from the apology of Mr. Crabbe, to his condemnation. Every form of distress, whether it proceed from passion or from fortune, and whether it fall upon vice or virtue, adds to the interest and the charm of poetry —except only that which is connected with ideas of *disgust*,—the least taint of which disenchants the whole scene, and puts an end both to delight and sympathy. But what is it, it may be asked, that is the proper object of disgust? and what is the precise description of things which we think Mr. Crabbe so inexcusable for admitting? It is not easy to define a term at once so simple and so significant; but it may not be without its use, to indicate, in a general way, our conception of its force and comprehension.

It is needless, we suppose, to explain what are the objects of disgust in physical or external existences. These are sufficiently plain and unequivocal; and it is universally admitted, that all mention of them must be carefully excluded from every poetical description. With regard, again, to human character, action, and feeling, we should be inclined to term every thing disgusting, which represented misery, without making any appeal to our love or our admiration. If the suffering person be amiable, the delightful feeling of love and affection tempers the pain which the contemplation of suffering has a tendency to excite, and enhances it into the stronger, and therefore more attractive, sensation of pity. If there be great power or energy, however united to guilt or wretchedness, the mixture of administration exalts the emotion into something that is sublime and pleasing. Even in cases of mean and atrocious guilt, our sympathy with the victims upon whom it is practised, and our active indignation and desire of vengeance, reconcile us to the humiliating display, and make a compound that, upon the whole, is productive of pleasure.

The only sufferers, then, upon whom we cannot bear to look, are those that excite pain by their wretchedness, while they are too depraved to be the objects of affection, and too weak and insignificant to be the causes of misery to others, or, consequently, of indignation to the spectators. Such are the depraved, abject, diseased and neglected poor,—creatures in whom every thing amiable or respectable has been extinguished by sordid passions or brutal debauchery,—who have no means of doing the mischief of which they are capable,—whom every one despises, and no one can either love or fear. On the characters, the miseries, and the vices of such beings, we look with *disgust* merely: and, though it may perhaps serve some *moral* purpose, occasionally to set before us this humiliating spectacle of human nature sunk to utter worthlessness and insignificance, it is altogether in vain to think of exciting either pity or horror, by the truest and most forcible representations of their sufferings or of their enormities. They have no hold upon any of the feelings that lead us to take an interest in our fellow-creatures; —we turn away from them, therefore, with loathing and dispassionate aversion;—we feel our imaginations polluted by the intrusion of any images connected with them; and are offended and disgusted when we are forced to look closely upon those festering heaps of moral filth and corruption. It is with concern we add, that we know no writer who has sinned so deeply in this respect as Mr. Crabbe,—who has so often presented us with spectacles which it is purely painful and degrading to contemplate, and bestowed such powers of conception and expression in giving us distinct ideas of what we must abhor to remember. If Mr. Crabbe had been a person of ordinary talents, we might have accounted for his error, in some degree, by supposing, that his frequent success in treating of subjects which had been usually rejected by other poets, had at length led him to disregard, altogether, the common impressions of mankind as to what was allowable and what inadmissible in poetry, and to reckon the unalterable laws by which nature has regulated our sympathies, among the prejudices by which they were shackled and impaired. It is difficult, however, to conceive how a writer of his quick and exact observation should have failed to perceive, that there is not a single instance of a serious interest being excited by an object of disgust; and that Shakespeare himself, who has ventured every thing, has never ventured to shock our feelings with the crimes or the sufferings of beings absolutely without power or principle. Independent of universal practice, too, it is still more difficult to conceive how he should have overlooked the reason on which this practice is founded; for though it be generally true, that poetical representations of suffering and of guilt produce emotion, and consequently delight, yet it certainly did not require the penetration of Mr. Crabbe to discover, that there is a degree of depravity which counteracts our sympathy with suffering, and a degree of insignificance which extinguishes our interest in guilt. We abstain from giving any extracts in support of this accusation; but those who have perused the volume before us, will have already recollected the story of Frederic Thompson, of Abel Keene, of Blaney, of Benbow, and a good part of those of Grimes and Ellen Orford,—besides many shorter passages. It is now time, however, to give the reader a more particular account of the work which contains them. . . .

There is, of course, no unity or method in the poem,—which consists altogether of a succession of unconnected descriptions, and is still more miscellaneous in reality, than would be conjectured from the titles of its twenty-four separate compartments. As it does not admit of analysis, therefore, or even of a much more particular description, we can only give our readers a just idea of its execution, by extracting a few of the passages that appear to us most characteristic in each of the many styles it exhibits.

One of the first that strikes us, is the following very touching and beautiful picture of innocent love, misfortune, and resignation—all of them taking a tinge of additional sweetness and tenderness from the humble condition of the parties, and affording a striking illustration of the remarks we have ventured to make on the advantages of such subjects. The passage occurs in the second letter, where the author has been surveying, with a glance half pensive and half sarcastical, the monuments erected in the churchyard. He then proceeds—

Yes! there are real mourners—I have seen . . .
[II, 170–203, 206–63]

[As 'a passage in the same tone']—

. . . when first I came . . .
[XXIII, 237–44, 255–60, 271–84, 289–329]

If these extracts do not make the reader feel how deep and peculiar an interest may be excited by humble subjects, we should almost despair of bringing him over to our opinion, even by Mr. Crabbe's inimitable description and pathetic pleading for the parish poor. The subject is one of those, which to many will appear repulsive, and, to some fastidious natures perhaps, disgusting. Yet, if the most admirable painting of external objects,—the most minute and thorough knowledge of human character,—and that warm glow of active and rational benevolence which lends a guiding light to observation, and an enchanting colour to eloquence, can entitle a poet to praise—as they do entitle him to more substantial rewards—we are persuaded that the following passage will not be speedily forgotten.

Your plan I love not:—with a number you . . .
[XVIII, 109–18, 131–59, 170–94, 211–14]

These we take to be specimens of Mr. Crabbe's best style;—but he has great variety;—and some readers may be better pleased with his satirical vein,—which is both copious and original. The Vicar is an admirable sketch of what must be very difficult to draw;—a good, easy man, with no character at all;—his little, humble vanity;—his constant care to offend no one;—his mawkish and feeble gallantry—indolent good nature, and love of gossiping and trifling—are all very exactly, and very pleasingly delineated. We can only make room for the conclusion.

But let applause be dealt in all we may, . . .
[III, 81–90, 102–5, 154–65]

To the character of Blaney we have already objected, as offensive, from its extreme and impotent depravity. The first part of his history, however, is sketched with a masterly hand; and affords a good specimen

94

of that sententious and antithetical manner by which Mr. Crabbe sometimes reminds us of the style and versification of Pope.

> *Blaney*, a wealthy heir at twenty-one, . . .
> [XIV, 13–26, 29–32]

. . . There is nothing very interesting perhaps in [the] story [of
Clelia]; but the details of it show the wonderful accuracy of the author's
observation of character, and give it, and many of his other pieces, a
value of the same kind that some pictures are thought to derive from
the truth and minuteness of the *anatomy* which they display. There is
something original, too, and well conceived, in the tenacity with which
he represents this frivolous person, as adhering to her paltry characteristics under every change of circumstances. The concluding view is as
follows.

> Now friendless, sick and old, and wanting bread, . . .
> [XV, 174–193, 197–201]

The graphic powers of Mr. Crabbe, indeed, are too frequently
wasted on unworthy subjects. There is not, perhaps, in all English
poetry a more complete and highly finished piece of painting, than the
following description of a vast old boarded room or warehouse, which
was let out, it seems, in the Borough, as a kind of undivided lodging,
for beggars and vagabonds of every description. No Dutch painter ever
presented an interior more distinctly to the eye, or ever gave half such
a group to the imagination.

> That window view!—oil'd paper and old glass . . .
> [XVIII, 354–64, 369–97, 404–5]

[Also quotes IX, 112–16, 119–30 and XXII, 173–204 together with IX,
224–7, 244–62, 273–82, 285–96 and XXIV, 364–83, 388–407] . . .

We have now alluded, we believe, to what is best and most striking
in this poem; and, though we do not mean to quote any part of what
we consider as less successful, we must say, that there are large portions
of it which appear to us considerably inferior to most of the author's
former productions. The letter on the *Election*, we look on as a complete failure,—or at least as containing scarcely any thing of what it
ought to have contained. The letters on Law and Physic, too, are
tedious; and the general heads of Trades, Amusements, and Hospital
Government, by no means amusing. The Parish Clerk, too, we find
dull, and without effect; and have already given our opinion of Peter

Grimes, Abel Keene, and Benbow. We are struck, also, with several omissions in the picture of a maritime borough. Mr. Crabbe might have made a great deal of a press-gang; and, at all events, should have given us some wounded veteran sailors, and some voyagers with tales of wonder from foreign lands.

The style of this poem is distinguished, like all Mr. Crabbe's other performances, by great force and compression of diction,—a sort of sententious brevity, once thought essential to poetical composition but of which he is now the only living example. But though this is almost an unvarying characteristic of his style, it appears to us that there is great variety, and even some degree of unsteadiness and inconsistency in the tone of his expression and versification. His taste seems scarcely to be sufficiently fixed and settled as to these essential particulars: and, along with a certain quaint, broken, and harsh manner of his own, we think we can trace very frequent imitations of poets of the most opposite character. The following antithetical and half-punning lines of Pope, for instance,—

> Sleepless himself, to give his readers sleep;[1]

and—

> Whose trifling pleases, and whom trifles please;—[2]

have evidently been copied by Mr. Crabbe in the following and many others,—

> And, in the restless ocean, seek[3] for rest.
> [I, 230]
> Denying her who taught thee to deny.
> [XI, 304]
> Scraping they liv'd, but not a scrap they gave.
> [XIII, 14]
> Bound for a friend, whom honour could not bind.
> [XXIII, 97]
> Among the poor, for poor distinctions sigh'd.
> [XV, 177]

In the same way, the common, nicely balanced line of two members, which is so characteristic of the same author, has obviously been the

---

[1] *The Dunciad*, I, 93 (misquoted).
[2] The Second Epistle of the Second Book of Horace, 327 (misquoted).
[3] Crabbe wrote 'dip'.

model of our author in the following—

> That woe could wish, or vanity devise.
> [II, 114]
>
> Sick without pity, sorrowing without hope.
> [XII, 145]
>
> Gloom to the night, and pressure to the chain.
> [XXIII, 204]

—and a great multitude of others.

On the other hand, he appears to us to be frequently misled by Darwin into a sort of mock-heoric magnificence, upon ordinary occasions. The poet of *The Garden*, for instance, makes his nymphs

> Present the fragrant quintessence of tea.[1]

And the poet of the Dock-yards makes his carpenters

> Spread the warm pungence of o'erboiling tar.
> [I, 86]

Mr. Crabbe, indeed, does not scruple, on some occasions, to adopt the mock-heroic in good earnest. When the landlord of the Griffin becomes bankrupt, he says—

> Th' insolvent Griffin struck her wings sublime.
> [XV, 155]

—and introduces a very serious lamentation over the learned poverty of the curate, with this most misplaced piece of buffoonery—

> Oh! had he learn'd to make the wig he wears!
> [originally III, 202—Ward, I, p. 538]

One of his letters, too, begins with this wretched quibble—

> From Law to Physic stepping at our ease,
> We find a way to finish—by *degrees*.
> [originally VII, 1–2—Ward, I, p. 539]

There are many imitations of the peculiar rythm [sic] of Goldsmith and Campbell, too, as our readers must have observed in some of our longer specimens,—but these, though they do not always make a very harmonious combination, are better, at all events, than the tame heaviness and vulgarity of such verses as the following.

[1] E. Darwin, 'Loves of the Plants', II, 484.

As soon
Could he have thought gold issued from the moon.
[originally V, 167–8: Ward, I, 538]

A seaman's body—*there'll be more* taught.[1]
[I, 240]

Those who will not to any guide submit,
Nor find one creed to their conceptions fit—
True *Independents:* while they *Calvin* hate,
They heed as little what *Socinians* state.
[originally IV, 256–9: Ward, I, p. 538]

Here pits of crag, with spongy, plashy base,
To some enrich th' uncultivated space. &c. &c.
[I, 147–8]

Of the sudden, harsh turns, and broken conciseness which we think
peculiar to himself, the reader may take the following specimens—

Has your wife's brother, or your uncle's son,
Done ought amiss; or is he thought t' have done?
[V, 51–2]

Stepping from post to post he reach'd the chair;
And there he now reposes:—that's the Mayor.
[V, 179–80]

He has a sort of jingle, too, which we think is of his own invention;
—for instance,

For forms and feasts that sundry times have past,
And formal feasts that will for ever last.
[XXIV, 406–7]

We term it free and easy: and yet we
Find it no easy matter to be free.
[X, 191–2]

We had more remarks to make upon the taste and diction of this
author; and had noted several other little blemishes, which we meant
to have pointed out for his correction: but we have no longer room for
such minute criticism,—from which, indeed, neither the author nor
the reader would be likely to derive any great benefit. We take our
leave of Mr. Crabbe, therefore, by expressing our hopes that, since it is
proved that he *can* write fast, he will not allow his powers to languish
for want of exercise; and that we shall soon see him again repaying the

---

[1] Text reads 'to-night' for 'taught'.

public approbation, by entitling himself to a still larger share of it. An author generally knows his own forte so much better than any of his readers, that it is commonly a very foolish kind of presumption to offer any advice as to the direction of his efforts; but we own we have a very strong desire to see Mr. Crabbe apply his great powers to the construction of some interesting and connected story. He has great talents for narration; and that unrivalled gift in the delineation of character which is now used only for the creation of detached portraits, might be turned to admirable account in maintaining the interest, and enhancing the probability of an extended train of adventures. At present, it is impossible not to regret, that so much genius should be wasted in making us perfectly acquainted with individuals, of whom we are to know nothing but the characters. In such a poem, however, Mr. Crabbe must entirely lay aside the sarcastic and jocose style to which he has rather too great a propensity; but which we know, from what he has done in 'Sir Eustace Grey', that he can, when he pleases, entirely relinquish. That very powerful and original performance, indeed, the chief fault of which is, to be set too thick with images,—to be too strong and undiluted, in short, for the digestion of common readers,—makes us regret that its author should ever have stooped to be trifling and ingenious,—or condescended to tickle the imaginations of his readers, instead of touching the higher passions of their nature.

24. James Montgomery, unsigned review, *Eclectic Review*

June 1810, vi, 546–61

It is not without surprise and regret, that we see the name of the 'Rev. George Crabbe, LL.B.' appear once more upon a title page, unaccompanied by any tokens of noble patronage or insignia of ecclesiastical preferment. . . . Our principal reason, however, for wishing Mr. Crabbe a more effective patron and better preferment, is, that he would then have been under no temptation to *court* those advantages. It might be difficult to persuade some of our readers, that a benefice was an infallible cure for a servile or illiberal disposition. Yet it is evident there are stronger motives in the lower ranks of the sacred order than in the higher, to draw up flattering dedications, and lampoon the sectaries. With all our partiality for Mr. Crabbe we must own, that his present volume will unhappily confirm the disapprobation already excited against him, among men of an independent and catholic spirit. And if there be any room for supposing that his humble rank in the church has laid him under peculiar temptation to offend, we not only call upon our readers to share in our regret, but beseech them to moderate their resentment.

We, for our part, indeed, who are well known to possess a peculiar degree of candour in virtue of our office, superadded to the ordinary portion we enjoy in common with readers in general, are willing to excuse the soft tones and cringing attitudes which have offended us in Mr. Crabbe's addresses to his patron and the public, by attributing them to timidity rather than design. The effect, however, is extremely unfortunate. . . . The unmanly tone of the Dedication is also maintained with little intermission in the Preface. This preface is a tissue of explanations and apologies to the extent of nearly *thirty pages*; and is altogether most singularly tiresome, unnecessary, and injudicious. Such, we are to understand, are the blemishes of his performance, that no trouble can be too great to palliate them; and such the keenness of his wit and the asperity of his sarcasms, that fatal consequences, might ensue, were he not to provide a remedy in his prose, for the wounds that might be inflicted by his poetry. It will be scarcely believed to what extent Mr. Crabbe's solicitude is carried, without a specimen or two from this very singular preface.

In the first letter is nothing which particularly calls for remark, except possibly the last line—giving a promise to the reader that he should both smile and sigh in the perusal of the following letters. This may appear vain, and more than an author ought to promise; but let it be considered that the character assumed is that of a friend, who gives an account of objects, persons and events to his correspondent, and who was therefore at liberty, without any imputation of this kind, to suppose in what manner he would be affected by such descriptions. . . .

Then, again, his satire upon young physicians is so caustic, that he thinks it advisable to apply a digestive.

When I observe, under the article Physic, that the young and less experienced physician will write rather with a view of making himself known, than to investigate and publish some useful fact, I would not be thought to extend this remark to all the publications of such men.

In the same strain, Mr. C. hopes the solicitors will not be angry with his sarcasms on some of *their* fraternity: he trusts that his strictures on card-parties and strolling players will not be thought too severe; he is anxious to point out the difference between two of the characters he describes; he is solicitous to justify his remarks on Prisons, Poorhouses, and the advantages of Education; and he is greatly concerned lest the reader should tax him with plagiarism for certain apparent imitations, or with pedantry for his numerous mottos. After this, we scarcely need remark, that though the term *Borough* can hardly be pronounced by an independent Englishman without emotions of contempt and indignation, Mr. C. has carefully abstained from saying a syllable, even in the chapter upon *Elections*, which could displease a single individual, whether buyer or seller, among the crowds who traffic in political corruption. Indeed he expresses no little alarm, lest the very title of his poem should sound Jacobinical. It is far from being necessary, we admit, for a clergyman or a poet to embark in politics. But we had a right to expect, that the describer of a 'borough' should give some particular information as to the political constitution and condition which ascertain its *genus* and *differentia*,—which essentially distinguish it from other towns and other boroughs. And it would seem inevitable, too, for a man of integrity—a teacher of religion—who undertook the delineation of its moral aspect, to give due prominence to the most important and characteristic of its features. Nor could he be deterred from the discharge of this duty, by any deformity he might have had to represent. On the contrary, it could only have been some very powerful restraint, that prevented a poet, who delights in squalid subjects and gloomy colours, from exposing to public view the filthy haunts and slimy forms of corruption. We have yet to learn that the breach of moral and civil duties is then only unfit to be reprobated, when its occurrence is most frequent, and its consequences most fatal.

Having noticed a few of the symptoms of that timid and servile spirit with which by some means or other Mr. Crabbe is infected, we must proceed to mention his illiberality toward the 'enthusiasts'. . . .

> Canst thou, good sir, by thy superior skill, . . .
> [XXI, 267–89, 298–308]

The same kind of representation is given in another place, where the disciple is said to have become insane and committed suicide. Mr. Crabbe has made several attempts in this and his former writings, to confirm the popular prejudice that religion is apt to turn the brain. Perhaps he will tell us that it is not the tendency of religion, but of Calvinism, that he is so anxious to expose. We doubt if he can bring one instance, in which even Calvinism has had this effect, except upon a mind already in a morbid condition, or tainted with hereditary disease. It is not, however, Calvinism in particular, but Christianity in its simplest form, that is perverted by a disordered mind into the occasion of its lapses, and the aliment of its extravagant reveries. The only conceivable cause of error, is the apprehension of future punishment arising from despair of the divine clemency: but the dread of future punishment is inculcated in every part of Revelation; and a despair of the divine clemency, instead of springing from a belief in the system of Calvin, is neither more nor less than disbelief of the gospel he taught. . . .

Were it allowed, however, that Mr. C. has confirmed himself to the exact truth of the case in depicting the absurdities of individuals, we should nevertheless object to his sketches, because they will be understood to apply to whole societies. And whatever absurdities may prevail in these societies, we should still object to Mr. Crabbe's manner of exposing them, as in the first place unfair, and in the next pernicious. If a *fair* description were given of these 'enthusiasts' and 'fanatics,' (we speak generally, *not universally*) it would include so much of genuine devotion, strict sobriety, and zealous benevolence, so many of the dispositions and habits that conduce to domestic comfort, public peace, and national wealth, and among the lower orders at least so decided a superiority in intellect to those who are their equals in station, as would amply atone for a few harmless extravagancies and trivial mistakes. . . .

If burlesque and buffoonery were ever the proper method of correcting religious excentricities, and if ever it were a fit method for a clergyman to employ, it would be, when the greatest anxiety was evinced to counteract its pernicious tendency,—when a careful separation was made between piety itself and the errors with which it was associated, —and when the profoundest reverence was manifested for sound principles, enlightened zeal, and pure morality. The readers of the Reverend Mr. Crabbe's former publication will not be very forward to suppose, that his satire in the poem under review is thus checked and guarded. Among other passages that we fear have not the best tendency, is the story of Jachin,—a parish clerk, distinguished for his austerity of manners, but who was at length detected in pilfering from the communion-money, and sinking down, heart-broken with remorse and the public contempt, died miserably, at the moment when the vicar, who till then (it seems) had neglected him, came to inquire the state of his mind. A part of this story, which would be more creditable to Peter Pindar than to the Reverend George Crabbe, we shall transcribe.

This book-taught Man, with ready Mind receiv'd . . .
[XIX, 18-53]

As the author of these facetious lines is a clergyman, it is impossible he could intend to ridicule two received doctrines of Holy Writ, the agency of evil spirits on the mind, and the sinfulness of mental adultery. We should be happy to conceive of any good motive he could have, for representing the believer in these truths as a hypocrite and a thief, or for exhibiting them in terms of indecent and profane jocularity. It must be with a very ill grace that he will in future obey the injunction to Timothy, 'Young men likewise exhort to be sober minded.' Mr. Crabbe may think to defend himself, by saying the picture is taken from real life; a defence which will suit exactly as well for the venders of licentious pamphlets and obscene prints. . . .

Considering the moral tendency of this poem as unspeakably more important than its poetical merit, we make no apology for the length of these strictures. We must own the performance appears to us almost certain to do some harm, and almost incapable of doing any good; so that we feel some degree of reluctance to congratulate Mr. Crabbe, on the ability it discovers, and the reputation it will acquire. In our view, a most heavy responsibility attaches to the possession of leisure and talents; and it would have been a satisfaction to us to announce a poem from the pen of a clergyman, which might afford him consolation in his last moments, by a recollection of the hours he had employed in writing it, and an anticipation of its future utility. But though we are not constrained in this instance to revere his character or applaud his diligence, we willingly do honour to his genius. In spite of the prejudice which his preface is calculated to awaken, we have perused many parts of his poem with great satisfaction. In the impressive energy of his narrations, and the striking exactness of his descriptions, he probably excels all his contemporaries, and has little to fear from a comparison with any preceding poet. His subjects, we apprehend, are mostly taken from real life. They are, in general, far from pleasing; and appear selected to excite horror and disgust, rather than any gentler and finer sentiments. If they were the creatures of imagination, we should scarcely know in what order of poets to place him. But though he is not intitled to the praise of conceiving these subjects, his manner of representing them is truly admirable. . . .

The principal phænomena of the sea are described with much accuracy, and in a very easy style. We were pleased to observe that Mr. Crabbe's expertness is not confined to works of art, or the manners of human beings, but that he has an eye to seize and a hand to copy the wild and fleeting appearances of nature.

The lines which commence the second letter are so much to our taste, and go so far toward making some degree of atonement for the moral blemishes of the poem already noticed, that we willingly introduce them.

> 'What is a Church?'—let Truth and Reason speak, . . .
>   [II, 1–4]

This letter includes an indifferent descripiton of the church and monuments, with a well told and pathetic story.

In the third letter, which describes the Vicar and Curate, we should be at no loss to find room for censure. The terms in which the *frigidity* of the former is adverted to, and the address to 'male lilies,' produce an impression more conformable to the strain of sentiment Mr. C. has too often pursued, than to that sober and subdued state of the passions which it would be in character for him to recommend. The strength of the sensual appetites is surely an adequate competitor to the rational and spiritual powers of our nature, without being made the subject of poetical panegyric by a Christian moralist. This is another of the numerous instances, in which Mr. Crabbe has certainly not been prompted by an anxiety to employ his influence with the public in assisting the cause of virtue. . . .

[Quotation with brief comment on

> What said their Prophet?—Should'st thou disobey . . .
>   [IV, 228–45]

and

> Meantime Discretion bids the Tongue be still, . . .
>   [X, 145–88, 232–49]]

The character of Sir Denys Brand, governor of the almshouse, is a fine portrait of a very original and peculiar subject. It is needless to observe, how well Mr. Crabbe succeeds in this sort of delineation. He chooses his character well: his strokes are masterly, and his likenesses striking. We cannot particularize the distinguishing merits of those of Blaney the profligate, Clelia the vicious and worn-out coquette, Benbow the 'boon companion,' (the least interesting of all except for the memoir of a Squire Asgill which he is made to relate,) Jachin already alluded to, and Ellen Orford a signal example of patience under a complication of distress. In this last story, a horrible incident is introduced, like a ghastly corpse or frightful spectre in the back ground of a picture, not very obvious, but which the moment it is discerned chills the blood: it even surpasses the unnatural outrage related in his poem, intitled 'The Hall of Justice.' The art with which this discovery is intimated, would on any other occasion deserve praise. But we question the wisdom of familiarizing the mind with brutal profligacy and portentous crimes.

The story of Abel Keene is very singular. He is described as a quiet simple man, who grew old in the lowest rank of pedagogues, and at length became clerk in a countinghouse, where he was persuaded to turn infidel, beau, and debauchee. Our first extract contains part of his confessions, when worn out with age, and struggling, half-insane, between fear and presumption, remorse and infidelity.

The master-piece of the volume, however, for energy of conception and effect, is the story of Peter Grimes, a ruffian from his very infancy, a ferocious tyrant and suspected murderer, who finally became a madman, tormented with the most gloomy visions, and self-convicted of the most atrocious crimes. We have been exceedingly struck with the peculiar and unrivalled skill, with which Mr. Crabbe paints the horrors of a disordered imagination; a pre-eminence which we can only account for, by supposing it may have been his mournful privilege, for a considerable length of time, to watch the emotions and hear the ravings of the insane. . . .

On the whole, we must say [*The Borough*] is not a very pleasing poem, and we question whether its popularity will ever bear a due proportion to the talent which in many passages it displays. There is no unity in it, no subject on which the interest excited may be concentrated and fixed. Of the *borough*, we know and care as little as the last page as at the first; perhaps less, because the title raises a curiosity which the volume disappoints. The admirable descriptions of scenery and sketches of character have scarcely any connection and dependence, either mutual or common; and would lose no interest if detached. There is also a great sameness in the subjects; they are specifically different, but generically alike. As the poem is too long, this fault is peculiarly unfortunate. Moral reflections are interspersed, of which, generally, however, it were better to be silent; for what could we say in behalf of such lines as these?

> Vice, dreadful habit! when assum'd so long, . . .
> [originally between XII, 266–7; Ward I, p. 540]

There is often a point and an edge in the expression, when there is not much strength or temper in the thought. There is little to delight the fancy, and less to captivate the heart. The versification also is monotonous; the perpetual, snappish recurrence of antitheses is tiresome; there are many very dull paragraphs, and numberless feeble lines. Several couplets are patched up with expletive clauses; and as the rhymes are generally very good, the consequence is that they are sometimes better than the diction. On one occasion, Mr. C. mentions the singular phænomenon of a young woman's 'terrors doubling as her hopes withdrew,' and in the following couplet, the δεινη αναγκη of rhyme is but too tyrannical.

> These drew him back, till Juliet's hut appeared,
> Where love had drawn him when he should have—feared.
> [XI, 257–8]

It is quite needless to add any recommendation to our readers, to examine the poem for themselves.

25. Unsigned review, *Critical Review*

July 1810, xx, 291–305

We were much pleased at the announcement of the present publication, from a recollection of the great pleasure which Mr. Crabbe imparted to us on a former occasion. We, therefore, seized this new volume with avidity, and fairly read it through; and though we find it necessary to point out many considerable faults in it, yet upon the whole we are bound to confess that Mr. C's. powers of pleasing are not at all diminished. We suppose that most of our readers will know the works of this gentleman and remember his peculiarities, both good and bad; the faithfulness and spirit of his satire, his accurate delineation of almost every species of character, his easy and simple flow of poetical diction, his continual intermixture of pathetic and ludicrous observation, and the air of good nature, which tempers the rigour of his severest passages on the one hand; and on the other his frequently painful minuteness of description, his occasionally prosaic familiarity, approaching almost to vulgarity, his ignorance of 'the last and greatest art, the art to blot,' his carelessness of style, and above all, what is perfectly unwarrantable, his inaccuracies in language, and even in grammatical construction. The present work has all the above-mentioned characteristics, in as great a degree as Mr. C's. former publication; and on one score, we mean prolixity, is far more reprehensible. The narrative is frequently drawn out with a gossiping and tame tediousness, without either point or humour to rouse or keep alive the attention. The versification also is frequently very harsh, and there are numberless instances of such ungraceful contractions as 'he'd' for 'he would,' 'could'nt' for 'could not,' 'you'd' for 'you would,' &c. &c. there are even many pages of mere prose; and we cannot help mentioning the author's very unpoetical habit of giving two names to his heroes and heroines; such as Dolly Murray, Jacob Holmes, Abel Keene, Mister Smith, &c. &c. This frequently gives an air of drollery to the most pathetic passages, and is too familiar even for the most familiar narrative. Preceding the poem is a long rambling preface, which is a mere string of dull ill-written apologies, for what Mr. C. conceives to be exceptionable parts in his work: he here seems inclined to give a salve for many of the wounds, which his verses inflict, and evinces an evasiveness which in some degree detracts from that respect, which we are disposed to bear towards him. . . .

> All where the eye delights, yet dreads to roam, . . .
> [I, 200–5, 214–25, 229–32, 241–6, 261–70]

The Dutch minuteness, the particularity so observable in Mr. Crabbe's delineations, at the same time that it produces an air of truth and life, not unfrequently destroys the poetical effect which would arise from the contemplation of a whole, by confining the attention to the curiously laboured and sometimes servile development of the parts. Where the description is short, minuteness gives spirit; but if long, it degenerates into dryness and imbecility. . . .

The third Letter presents us with a pair of portraits, the Vicar and the Curate in the very best style of the author. The character of the mild but inanimate vicar, who is free from vice, because he is exempt from passion and feeling, who acts not wrong, because he has not energy to act at all, whose peace is never disturbed by the vices and schisms of his flock, but who feels deep chagrin because the good old christian custom of adorning churches with holly and misletoe is almost abolished; in short, whose virtue is without worth because it is without effort; whose benevolence evaporates in words; whose life is mere vegetation. This character is drawn with equal fidelity and animation.

> Fiddling and fishing were his arts: at times . . .
> [III, 102–5, 118–21, 126–9, 154–65]

Letter IV. After giving a concise account of Jews, Swedenburgians, Baptists, &c. our author dedicates the greater part of this letter to the description of the Calvinist and the Arminian. To render the impression more lively, he makes each of these fanatics give a specimen of his opinions in a sort of sermon versified: these copies of Methodist sermons have all the length and tediousness of their originals, without that *piquante* peculiarity of expression, which renders them so laughable in the mouths of the real preachers: the language is inanimate, prosaic, and, compared with Mr. Crabbe's usual power of satirical expression, exceedingly feeble.

We willingly pass from this subject to the next letter, which gives the history of a borough election. Here Mr. Crabbe is himself again. We believe there is nothing very original in the topics of his satire; but we never recollect to have seen them animadverted upon with such truth and spirit. . . .

The next three letters are dedicated to the professions of law and physic, and to trades. In the first, the author lashes with no unsparing hand the oppression and chicanery of certain law-practitioners, first generally and afterwards more particularly, in a striking picture of a man of the name of Swallow. This character bears a very observable resemblance to that of Sir Giles Overreach, in Massinger's play of *A New Way to pay Old Debts*. It is drawn, or rather dashed, with a bold and masterly hand; but we hope and think that the features are exaggerated into unnatural frightfulness. In our opinion, it would not be easy for a man at the present day to rest with such undisturbed triumph in his villainy. Some honest and equally skilful lawyer would detect his enormities, and drive the wretch from a fraternity, which he disgraced. The character is too long for transcription, and to select a part of it would be injurious to the whole. Mr. Crabbe has not succeeded so well in his history of the empyric: it contains no humour, and the language is tame; yet, at the same time, we have little doubt that some of the circumstances in it were copied from the life.

> Who would not lend a sympathising sigh, . . .
> [VII, 215–28]

[Brief comment on succeeding letters with quotation of IX, 131–52 and XII, 66–79.]

The XIIIth, XIVth, XVth, and XVIth Letters contain an account of the Alms-house, its trustees, and inhabitants. The character of Mr. Denys Brand, and his 'pride that affects humility', afford one proof, among many others, of Mr. Crabbe's power of keen observation. The character of Blaney, the old man with young vices, and the corrupt and frivolous Clelia, deserve to be repeatedly read for their great moral utility. The author has thought proper to apologize in his Preface for the portrait of Benbow: this was perfectly unnecessary, since it is perhaps the most useful character in the book. It is a lively picture of those worthless scoundrels, who are called *honest fellows*, because they get drunk with every body, and have the ignorant sort of good nature to be friends with every body over the bottle.

The best parts of the XVIIth Letter are a glowing description of a recovered patient, (which, however, is far beneath that most animated one in Gray's 'Ode on Vicissitude',) and the character of Eusebius, whom revilings and slander only stimulated to greater exertions of virtue.

Of the XVIIIth Letter we shall merely observe that its description of 'the large building, let out to several poor inhabitants,' is a specimen of his best and worst style. It has accuracy, truth, and vigour; but at the same time, is painfully and disgustingly minute.

Letters XIX, XX, XXI, and XXII. In these four Letters, we are presented with as many characters. The parish-clerk and the clerk in office, which the author in his Preface mentions, as perhaps too similar, needed not this apology. It is true they both fall from uprightness to vice; but in every feature which denotes character, they are totally dissimilar. The story of Jachin is told with most skill: after describing, with considerable humour, the rigid formalities of this cold-blooded pharisee, Mr. Crabbe very properly assumes a grave tone when treating of his crimes. Pope, in his character of Sir Balaam, to which, in some respects, this tale bears a resemblance, has not been equally cautious: he jokes throughout; and consigns his unhappy sinner to the gallows and the devil, with the same unconcerned levity as when he is talking of his additional pudding and gifts of farthings to the poor. Perhaps this gaiety suited Pope's Essay better than a more serious tone; but it would certainly have been indecorous and very ill placed in the Rev. Mr. Crabbe's narrative. It would be doing an injury to this exquisitely drawn character to give a partial quotation from it; and our limits will, by no means, admit us to give the whole.

We have little to remark on the very inferior story of the simple Abel Keene, who, in old age commences a *beau garçon* and a free-thinker, except that we wish that when he had hanged himself, he had not left behind such an immeasurably long account of his groanings and his crimes. To be serious, Mr. Crabbe seldom seems to know when he has said enough: his best thoughts are frequently amplified till what we began to read with pleasure is finished with a long and drawling yawn.

The story of Ellen Orford is indeed a pathetic tale, full of real woe, and is well introduced by a judicious and happy ridicule of the fantastic sorrows and absurd miseries, depicted in modern novels and romances.

Peter Grimes, the subject of the twenty-second Letter, is a male Brownrigg,[1] a ruffian who murders his three apprentices, after having

[1] Elizabeth Brownrigg was executed at Tyburn on 14 September 1767 for murdering one of her apprentices, Mary Clifford. She is commemorated in an inscription, parodying Southey and written by Canning and Frere in *The Anti-Jacobin*.

dealt the sacrilegious blow

> On the bare head, and laid his parent low.
> [XXII, 27]

The greater part of this hideous story is told in the Ordinary of Newgate style; but the conclusion, where the dying villain pours the wild
effusions of his guilt-distracted brain, is drawn with terrific strength.

> I saw my father on the water stand, . . .
> [XXII, 308–27]

Letter XXIII. Mr. Crabbe, alluding to this letter on prisons, apol-
ogizes in his Preface, for detaining his reader so long with the detail
of gloomy subjects; but remarks that the melancholy impression,
which they are so calculated to make on the mind, cannot be injurious,
because the real evils of life, which are continually before us, produce
no lasting or serious effects; and he adds, that it is a profitable exercise
of the mind to contemplate the evils and miseries of our nature. We
agree with him perfectly in this reasoning; but, at the same time, we
recollect that pleasure is a very material, and by most esteemed the
chief, end of poetry. Now this pleasure is weakened, and even changed
to disgust, by repeated stories of woe: surely, some method might have
been found to intermix the cheerful with the mournful, that both the
reader's pleasure and instruction might be unabated. We see no reason
why all the poor of the Borough, on whose history Mr. Crabbe enlarges, should be either atrociously criminal or heart-rendingly unfortunate: the scene might have admitted some poor, but cheerful, old
gossip, some veteran,

> Should'ring his crutch and shewing how fields were won,[1]

and many others, which we should have thought must have occurred
to the very extensive observation for which the author seems particularly eminent. . . .

Mr. Crabbe concludes by hoping, that malice may never be pre-
dicated of his portraits: quite the contrary; in the midst of all his severity, we see a very good-natured mind, and one that never, except in the
instance of the Methodists, at all exaggerates human folly, though it
must be confessed, that the author is rather fond of dwelling on the
weak side of human nature. But we fear that men, who have seen much,

---

[1] Goldsmith, The Deserted Village, 158.

if they tell what they see, must unfortunately communicate more evil, than good, respecting their species.

Upon the whole, we think, that the fame, which Mr. Crabbe has obtained, for simplicity, for pathos, for fidelity and spirit of descriptive satire, will be rather increased than shaken by the present publication; since his faults, though numerous, and even considerable, bear but a very small proportion to the great and various beauties which adorn his work.

In the present age of accurate orthography, punctuation, and typography, it is quite shameful to see the slovenly manner, in which either the reviser of the proof-sheets, or the printer of this volume has executed his task.

26. Unsigned reviews, *Monthly Mirror*

August and October 1810, viii,126–34, 280–4

Few poets seem to have laboured their productions more than Mr. Crabbe; and yet there are not many good poems which come out into the world in a more incorrect and raw material state, than the works of that gentleman. Mr. Crabbe, although he always looks at the dark side of things, (and this we conceive to have been the reason why Dr. Johnson applauded him so highly,) possesses an insight into character, and a vigour in the delineation of that character, which had he given his portraits a higher degree of finish, and a more concentrated air, would have constituted him the Chaucer of his day.

The poem before us describes the inhabitants of an English borough town on the sea-coast; and the several divisions of the poem are called with no great reason, '*letters*.' The work is introduced by a preface of forty pages, much of which ought to have been *postliminious*; for it is absolutely unintelligible to him, who has not perused the poem, of which, indeed, it looks more like a favourable *review*, than any thing else. We, as reviewers, must protest against this invasion of our province: we are put out of our bread, if every author is thus to become his own reviewer: the workman must not be his own overseer. This frightful preface attempts to anticipate every possible objection to every objectionable part of the poem, and to apologize for, and make exceptions to, the severity of its satire. The author's preface, indeed, is the smooth side of the neat's tongue, and his poem is the rough. . . .

Mr. Crabbe's great excellence is undoubtedly the delineation of character; and from the following passages of his preface, it will appear that he considers his poems as little better than the vehicles of his *dramatis personæ*, the frames of his portraits, the strings on which his pearls hang.

One of the governors of the Alms-House may be considered as too highly placed, for an author, who seldom ventures above middle life, to delineate; and indeed I had some idea of reserving him for another occasion, where he might have appeared with those of his own rank; but then it is most uncertain whether he would ever appear, and he has been so *many years prepared for the public, whenever opportunity might offer*, that I have at length given him place, and though with his inferiors, yet as a ruler over them.

The characters of the Hospital Directors *were written many years since*, and, so far as I was capable of judging, are drawn with *fidelity*. I mention this circumstance, that, if any reader should find a difference in the versification or expression, he will be thus enabled to account for it.

We would not have been without this character of Sir Denys Brand: it is one of Mr. Crabbe's most vigorous and original portraits.

His were no vulgar charities; none saw . . .
[XII, 142–226]

The character of the poor curate, the origin of which the author thus describes, is perhaps the most exquisite morsel in the volume; . . .

There cannot be a greater instance of Mr. Crabbe's profusion of verse and exhaustion of subject, than one which occurs in this character of the curate. We remember thinking the idea, almost as much exhausted as the patience of the diners, at the Literary Fund anniversary:[1] and yet we have, in the volume before us, the following paragraph thrown in as a make-weight:—

An angry dealer, vulgar, rich and proud, . . .
[III, 253–64]

Next to the character of the curate, we admire that of Jachin, the parish-clerk. His story distantly resembles that of Sir Balaam, and is

---

[1] The portrait of the curate in Letter III was read at the Literary Fund dinner in 1809.

told with some portion of Pope's spirit; but it is egregiously defective in the conciseness and condensation of that poet's verse. A parallel passage, which we shall mark, in the course of our extracts, from the character, will shew that Mr. Crabbe had Pope's Sir Balaam in his eye, when he drew his portrait of Jachin. . . .

Our worthy clerk had now arriv'd at fame . . .
[XIX, 122–41, 145–65, 174–98, 209–16, 221–49]

The remaining prominent characters are those of Ellen Orford, Abel Keene, and Peter Grimes. Their stories are all calculated to 'harrow up the soul;' and we are half inclined to wish that their 'blazon had not been to ears of flesh and blood.' There is, in Mr. Crabbe, a strange propensity to put things in their worst light; and if other poets have painted human nature better, he has certainly depicted her worse than she really is. The fact is, that Mr. Crabbe has lived a great deal in a smuggling neighbourhood, and has observed that the country there is a very different thing from what our Arcadian poets have represented it: he therefore very naturally falls into the other extreme, and sees nothing but vice in every village, and poverty in every cottage. The readers of books, who are mostly townspeople, are delighted to be told that there is quite as much vice and misery, and they know there is more poverty, in a house that looks upon fields, than in one that looks upon red bricks; and they eagerly believe in the truth of Mr. Crabbe's verse, especially since they perceive him able to discriminate and pourtray the characters of such men as themselves. They affect to pity the once happy cottager, and like no cottage but a *cottage ornée*. It is very true that 'the town has spoiled the country;' but there still is more simplicity, more virtue, and more happiness, in a village than in a town, in a town than in a city, and in a city than a metropolis; and a citizen's estimate of the country is not to be made from a borough-town near the coast. The story of Peter Grimes, who is a kind of male Brownrigg,[1] is either completely out of nature, or ought no more to be drawn for the determent of man, than a Portsmouth trull for a warning to the fair sex. There is no *cui bono* in such horrible delineations: they excite nothing but disgust. The misery of Ellen Orford, too, is worked up only to torture, without medicating our feelings. 'Terror,' says Rowe, 'is a proper subject for tragedy, but horror never;' and it is the same with all poetry. A poet may be allowed to excite our pity for the pain of others, with a view to purge our own passions; but he should never

1 See above, p. 110 n.

put us to real pain ourselves, with no view besides. There may be 'a pleasure in mourning;' but whatever the Edinburgh Review may say, there is none in mere pain, that we have ever discovered. . . .

Next to Mr. Crabbe's diffuseness, and seeming carelessness of verse, and the consequence of the latter fault, is his prosaicness. What possible rhythm is there in such lines as the following?

> All painful sense of obligation dies.
> [III, 313]

> It seems to us that our Reformers knew
> Th' important work they undertook to do.
> [IV, 84-5]

This last is prose, in which even the rhyme would not be discovered by the nicest ear, were it not printed as it is.

Mr. Crabbe's verse too is defaced by many clumsy triplets: what haste of composition does the following discover!

> All this experience tells the soul, and yet
> These moral men their pence and farthings set
> Against the terrors of the countless debt.
> [IV, 344-6]

Mr. Crabbe has many rhymes as rude and unpolished as this. In the following couplet, the words wear and tear may change places:

> Distress and hope—the mind's, the body's wear,
> The man's affliction, and the actor's tear.
> [XII, 76-7]

And, in the following, the word fact ought to be act too:

> For now, though willing with the worst to act,
> He wanted pow'rs for an important fact.
> [XII, 312-13]

But the most disgusting fault of Mr. Crabbe is his propensity to punning and bad pleasantry. Nothing can be meaner than the following.

> Lest some attorney (pardon me the name)
> Should wound a poor solicitor for fame.
> [VI, 51-2]

And those at p. 93, 140, 149, and 154, are not much better, and quite as much out of place. At p. 157, a young woman is christened *Juliet*, that her lover may be said to be her *Romeo* [XI, 236]; and at p. 288, it is said of Abel Keene that

> The righteous *Abel* turn'd the wretched *Cain*.
> [XXI, 93]

Lastly, at p. 300, we are presented with the following quibble:

> He *fish'd* by water, and he *filch'd* by land.
> [XXII, 43]

Of Mr. Crabbe's pleasantry, the first of the following passages will serve for a specimen of the ill-timed, and the rest for the downright bad:

> "Twas all a craft, they said, a cunning trade,
> Not she the priests, but priests religion made.
> So I *believ'd*.' No, Abel, to thy grief,
> So thou *relinquish'd* [st] all that was belief.
> [XXI, 236–9]

> 'Who deals?—you led—we've three by cards—had you
> *Honour* in hand?'—'Upon my *honour*, two!'
> [X, 73–4]

> 'Complain of me? and so you might, indeed,
> If I had ventured on that foolish lead,
> That fatal *heart*—but I forgot your play—
> Some folk have ever thrown their *hearts* away.'
> 'Yes, and their *diamonds;* I have heard of one,
> Who made a *beggar* of an only son.'
> [X, 155–60]

The poem abounds in minor faults: the following line affects to describe so much, that it describes nothing:

> And, *panting, sob* involuntary *sighs*.
> [X, 298]

Upon the whole, we are of opinion that Mr. Crabbe's poems, abounding as they do in masterly delineation of character, have yet been estimated too highly; and that posterity will be apt to look upon them, as we do upon the *Rasselas* of Mr. Crabbe's great admirer, as upon a gloomy and unedifying view of human life. We should be understood to compare the poet and the moralist, only in this one point: in others, *The Borough* and *Rasselas*, differ *toto cœlo*, the former being remarkable for the nicest discrimination of character, and the latter displaying nothing which can be entitled to the name of character.

Should Mr. Crabbe live to write another poem, which we heartily hope he may, let him seriously think of reversing the picture; let him give us some reason to be satisfied with life, some stimulus to exertion; at any rate let him correct his minor faults, of diffuseness of style, bad versification, and wretched pleasantry.

27. Robert Grant, unsigned review, *Quarterly Review*

November 1810, iv, 281–312

Grant (1779–1838), a lawyer who subsequently entered Parliament and became Governor of Bombay, is identified as the author of this review, often attributed to Gifford, by H. and H. C. Shine, *The Quarterly Review under Gifford*, Chapel Hill, 1949, p. 15. See also comment by R. B. Clark, *William Gifford, Tory Satirist, Critic and Editor*, New York, 1930, pp. 191–2.

. . . The peculiarity of this author is, that he wishes to discard every thing like illusion from poetry. He is the poet of reality, and of reality in low life. His opinions on this subject were announced in the opening of his first poem, *The Village*; and will be best explained by extracting from that work some lines which contain a general enunciation of his system.

> The village life, and ev'ry care that reigns . . .
> [I, 1–6, 15–22, 47–8, 53–4]

From these extracts, as well as from the constant tenor of his writings, it is clear, that Mr. Crabbe condemns the common representations of rural life and manners as fictitious; that he is determined in his own sketches of them to confine himself, with more than ordinary rigour, to truth and nature;—to draw only 'the real picture of the poor,' which, be it remembered, must necessarily, according to his opinion, be a

117

picture of sorrow and depravity. Now all this tends greatly to circumscribe, if not completely to destroy, the operation of illusion in poetry; and proceeds on what we conceive to be an entire misconception of the principles on which the pleasure of poetic reading depends. Notwithstanding the saving clause in favour of the privileges of Fancy, which is inserted in one of the preceding extracts, the doctrines of Mr. Crabbe appear to us essentially hostile to the highest exercise of the imagination, and we cannot therefore help regarding them with considerable doubt and jealousy.

To talk of binding down poetry to dry representations of the world as it is, seems idle; because it is precisely in order to escape from the world as it is, that we fly to poetry. We turn to it, not that we may see and feel what we see and feel in our daily experience, but that we may be refreshed by other emotions and fairer prospects—that we may take shelter from the realities of life in the paradise of fancy. To spread out a theatre on which this separate and intellectual kind of existence might be enjoyed, has in all ages been the great business of the speculative powers of the species. For this end new worlds have been framed, or the old embellished; imaginary joys and sorrows have been excited; the elements have been peopled with ideal beings. To this moral necessity, the divinities of ancient mythology owed their popularity, if not their birth; and when that visionary creation was dissolved, the same powerful instinct supplied the void with the fays and genii and enchantments of modern romance.

Poetry then, if it would answer the end of its being, must flatter the imagination. It must win the mind to the exercise of its contemplative faculties by striking out pictures on which it may dwell with complacency and delight. It does not follow that these pictures should be exclusively of a gay and smiling nature. The mind is notoriously so constituted as to enjoy, within certain limits, the fictitious representations of sad or terrible things.

But why, it is said, does poetry realize that which has no existence in nature? It is, at least, some answer to the question to observe, that, in this respect, poetry only does for us more perfectly what, without its assistance, we every day do for ourselves. It is to illusions, whether excited by the art of the poet, or by the secret magic of association, that life owes one of its first charms; and in both cases they give rise to feelings the same in their nature and in their practical effect. . . .

In tracing more particularly the modes by which poetry accomplishes its object of drawing us away from the fatigues of reality we shall find that, various as they are, they chiefly resolve themselves into two. That object may be effected by a diversion either to subjects that rouse and agitate the mind, as in the fictions of epic and chivalrous romance; or to such as soothe it, as in the representations of rural manners and scenery. Of these two methods, the latter, or that of the pastoral kind, has always, we are inclined to think, been somewhat the more popular. To the mind harassed and overburdened with care, there is something more comforting in the quietness of these subjects than in the tumult and pomp of more heroic distractions. They furnish, too, a more profound and sensible contrast to the bustling agitations of life. There are few of us, besides, to whom the idea of the country is not recommended by many tender and sacred associations;—by the recollection of early happiness and the pleasures of childhood, by the memory of our first hopes, and of companions who are now gone. Who has not sometimes figuratively adopted the language of the shepherd in Tasso?

> Ma poi ch' insieme con l' età fiorita
> Mancò la speme e la baldanza audace,
> Piansi i riposi di quest' umil vita,
> E sospirai la mia perduta pace.[1]

It may not be irrelevant to add, that the poetry which gratifies these breathings after the repose of humble life, may in every case be called pastoral; even if not in the vulgar acceptation of that name, yet according to its true and indeed its original intent. To affirm, that it is not of the essence of pastoral poetry to treat of sheep and shepherds, may seem a paradox; but the fact is, that these topics cannot be made essential to it, except by a sacrifice of its real to what we may term its verbal character. That which is its distinctive feature, and the efficient though not perhaps the ostensible cause of its popularity, is, that it diverts the mind from ordinary life by soothing and gentle means. It is one peculiar *mode* of answering the common end of all poetry. It takes us out of the cares of the world; and it does so, by transporting us to regions of innocent and quiet happiness. We are not snatched from the scene of combat by a whirlwind, but wafted away from it in the folds of some 'fair evening cloud.' A poem, therefore, may tell of nothing but flocks and swains; of loves carved on trees, and crooks wreathed with flowers;

---

[1] But when, as I grew older, hope and bold courage left me, I wept for the quiet of this humble life and sighed for the peace I had lost. *Gerusalemme Liberata*, VII, 13. Translation by Professor T. G. Griffith of the University of Manchester.

and yet if, while it gives us real pictures, it fail to keep alive that feeling of vernal refreshment and delight which such pictures are formed to inspire, it cannot be truly pastoral. To this main principle, of the *tone of mind* which such a composition ought to cherish, the most celebrated authors in this department have not sufficiently adverted. . . .

The visions of pastoral, like those of other poetry, can be said to convey false or incorrect impressions, only when they are regarded as exact likenesses of existing life and manners. So long as they are universally recognized to be visionary, they may be forgiven. If it be contended, that, in spite of the conviction of their falsehood, they yet insensibly affect the mind, and tend to unhinge us for the performance of our more homely and unromantic duties, by throwing an air of flatness over the incidents of common life;—this indeed is a serious charge, and demands some attention. It is analogous to the popular objection urged against all works of fiction, and especially against the higher kind of romance.

The mischievous influence, however, imputed to such writings, though it cannot entirely be denied to exist, is yet greatly overrated. In this, as in many other cases, Nature, even without the aid of a philosophical education, successfully struggles to accommodate herself to circumstances. The mind is soon taught, that swelling ideas and emotions of high-wrought delicacy, are unequal to the wear and tear of this *work-day* sphere. To reconcile the indulgence of its nobler sensations with the performance of practical duty, it insensibly learns to establish a distinction between the world of imagination and the world of sense; assigning to each its peculiar furniture of feelings and associations. To the one or the other of these departments whatever may be presented to it of virtue or of wisdom, is, without a conscious effort, referred.

We do not say that this division is, in every instance, systematically made; but, in every instance, a tendency towards it may be discovered. It is obvious to perceive, on what different grounds the same or nearly the same actions are judged, when they occur in ordinary life, and when they are found enshrined in the works of imagination. There are many virtues which are admired only in the records of fiction, and some which are admired only because they are fictitious.

The danger, to which we have adverted, seems then to be sufficiently removed by Nature itself; but it must be confessed, that the removal of it opens to us the view of another, into which a genius ardent but undisciplined, is not unlikely to fall. It is, that the line of distinction of which we have spoken, though drawn, will not be drawn in the right place. The masters of romance contrive to identify the good with the beautiful; and what they have thus identified, a mind trained in their school cannot easily be brought to separate. The captivating associations with which it has been taught to surround virtue, it acquires the habit of regarding not as her ornaments, but as her attributes; not as the fires which are kindled about her shrine, but as glimpses and emanations of her own essential beauty. . . .

But the question recurs, How are these dangers to be obviated? Are works of fiction, including, in that description, poetry ancient and modern, to be banished? If this principle be adopted, we must proceed a step farther, and banish also all the prose writers of antiquity. The pompous and enchanting eloquence of the ancient philosophers, orators, and historians, has done more than the *faërie* of all the novel writers from the creation till the present moment, to array virtue with that romantic brightness, which exercises so powerful a sorcery over the youthful imagination. . . .

But admitting (and it is surely an extravagant admission) that we have completely succeeded in the attempt to seclude the mind from these inflammatory compositions, what is the consequence? The power of fancy is neither destroyed, nor reduced to inaction. If it be repressed in one direction, it will break out in another; and will avenge itself on the bigotry that would have extirpated its energies, by devoting them to corruption and sensuality. This then is all that we have gained. We have extinguished the lights of heaven; but the darkness which we have left, is not solitude. The slumbers from which we have chased the better genii, will be haunted by the spectres of vice and folly.

It is not then by a vain effort to quench the imagination, that the dangers of which we have been speaking, are to be encountered. The only method by which a wise man would endeavour to meet them, is that of a skilful education, of which it is the object to train up all the intellectual powers in equal proportions and a mutual correspondence; to instil into the mind just and rational expectations of human life; and above all to encompass virtue with associations, if we may use the expression, more than mortal; associations, whose steady lustre may survive the waving and meteorous gleams of sentimental illusion.

The preceding observations relate generally to the principle of confining poetry to the realities of life; but they are peculiarly relevant, when that principle is applied to the realities of *low life*, because these, are of all others the most disgusting. If therefore the poet choose to illustrate the department of low life, it is peculiarly incumbent on him to select such of its features, as may at least be inoffensive. Should it be replied, that there is no room for such selection; then it follows, that he must altogether refrain from treating the subject, as utterly unworthy of his art. The truth however is, that there *is* room for selection. No department of life, however darkened by vice or sorrow, is without some brighter points on which the imagination may rest with complacency; and this is especially true, where rural scenes make part of the picture. We are not so absurd as to deny, that the country furnishes abundant examples of misery and depravity; but we deny that it furnishes none of a different kind. In common life every man instinctively acquires the habit of diverting his attention from unpleasing objects, and fixing it on those that are more agreeable; and all we ask is, that this practical rule should be adopted in poetry. The face of Nature under its daily and periodical varieties, the honest gaiety of rustic mirth, the flow of health and spirits which is inspired by the country, the delights which it brings to every sense—such are the pleasing topics which strike the most superficial observer. But a closer inspection will open to us more sacred gratifications. Wherever the relations of civilized society exist, particularly where a high standard of morals, however imperfectly acted upon, is yet publicly recognized, a groundwork is laid for the exercise of all the charities social and domestic. In the midst of profligacy and corruption, some trace of those charities still lingers; there is some spot which shelters domestic happiness; some undiscovered cleft, in which the seeds of the best affections have been cherished and are bearing fruit in silence. Poverty, however blighting in general, has graces which are peculiarly its own. The highest order of virtues can be developed only in a state of habitual suffering.

These are the realities which it is the duty of the poet to select for exhibition; and these, as they have nothing of illusion in themselves, it is not necessary to recommend by the magic of a richly-painted diction. Even presented to us in language the most precise and unadorned, they cannot fail to please; and please perhaps then most surely, when told in words of an almost abstract simplicity; words so limpid and colourless, that they seem only to discover to us the ideas, not to convey them, still less to lend them any additional sweetness or strength. Every reader will recollect some passages in our best authors which answer to this character; yet we cannot resist the temptation of exemplifying our position by an instance from Mr. Crabbe himself. What can be more *unfanciful*, and yet what more affecting, or more sublime, than his representation of a young woman watching over the gradual decay of her lover?

> Still long she nurs'd him; tender thoughts meantime . . .
> [*The Borough*, II, 222–9]

It must then be acknowledged that even the meanest station is not perfectly barren of interesting subjects; but the writer, who covets the praise of being a faithful transcriber rather than a generous interpreter of Nature, may be allowed to descend a step lower in the scale of exact delineation. There is a class of 'real pictures,' which is connected with no peculiar associations; and which may therefore, as far as the imagination is concerned, be called neutral. Of this nature are minute descriptions of agricultural pursuits, of ingenious mechanism, of the construction of buildings, of the implements of husbandry. Such descriptions are, in a long work, necessary, for the sake of variety; and are, at all times, if happily executed, grateful to the understanding, as specimens of intellectual skill and dexterity. But it is indispensable, that they should be strictly neutral. On this head much misconception has arisen from a confused apprehension of the analogy between poetry and painting. Because, in painting, low and even offensive subjects admitted, it is taken for granted that poetry also ought to have its Dutch school.

Without entering at length into this discussion, it may not be improperly suggested, that, even in painting, there is a limit, beyond which no prudent artist would venture to try the indulgence of the spectator. A variety of performances might be specified, in which the highest powers are in vain tasked to their utmost, to atone for the vulgarity and grossness of the subjects.

It may be suggested further, that the Dutch school is indebted for its celebrity, not in any part to the nature of its subjects, but exclusively to its happiness of execution. It professes to address only the eye; and its failings are lost and overlooked in the perfection of its mechanical excellence; in its grouping, and management of light and shade; in the harmony and radiance of its tones, and the luxuriance of its manner. The success of its productions is signally the triumph of colouring and composition. The subject, in a word, is the least part of these paintings. Poetry, on the other hand, is destitute of means to fascinate the external senses, and appeals to the mind alone. It is indeed popularly said, that words are the colours of poetry. But if this metaphor were just, it would, in the present case, be inapplicable. The new system which Mr. Crabbe patronizes, and to which therefore our remarks primarily refer, disclaims the attempt to disguise its *studies from Nature* under glowing and ornamental language.

We have hitherto considered the great principle on which our author proceeds. But this principle is not with him merely theoretical. Its impression visibly affects the character and impairs the merit of his writings.

The minute accuracy of relation which it inculcates, however favourable to the display of his uncommon powers of research, has a tendency to throw an air of littleness and technical precision over his performances. His description is frittered down, till instead of a spirited sketch, it becomes a tame detail. We will not say that he is incapable of large and comprehensive views; but he is surely somewhat slow to indulge in them. Thus his knowledge of man is never exhibited on a grand scale. It is clear and exact, but statistical rather than geographic; a knowledge of the individual rather than of the species. In his pictures there is little keeping; his figures, though singly admirable, are carelessly and clumsily grouped; and the whole drawing, while it abounds in free and masterly strokes, is yet deficient in depth and roundness.

The characteristic of Mr. Crabbe's writing is force; and this is the quality of which he most affects the praise. The finer parts of genius he neglects as useless or despises as weak. What he sees strongly, he makes a point of conscience to describe fearlessly. Occasionally perhaps this ambition of vigour drives him into unintentional vulgarity. Yet it cannot be disguised that he more commonly sins without this excuse: he admits coarseness on system. It is the original principle still operating. His sagacity in the discovery, and his ardour in the pursuit of offensive images are sometimes astonishing. His imagination never shrinks from the irksome task of threading the detail of vice and wretchedness.

The habit of anatomically tracing and recording the deformities of his fellow-creatures, has communicated to some of his descriptions an appearance of harshness and invective which, we are persuaded, has no counterpart in his feelings. He is evidently a man of great benevolence, but is apt to indulge in a caustic raillery which may be mistaken for ill-nature. In his pity there seems to be more of contempt than of tenderness, and the objects of his compassion are at the same time the objects of his satire. In the same manner he is jealous of giving his reader unmixed gratification; and even when his subject is inevitably pleasing, too often contrives, by the dexterous intervention of some less agreeable image, to dash the pleasure which he may have unwillingly inspired.

To the effect of his favourite doctrines also, we are disposed to ascribe it, that his perception of the beauties of nature has so little of inspiration about it. Living on the verge of fields, and groves, and streams, and breathing the very air which fans them, he is never tempted to forget himself in the contemplation of such scenes. A prospect of the country never thrills him as with the sudden consciousness of a new sense. We do not recollect that in any part of his writings he mentioned the singing of birds, except

> . . . the tuneless cry
> Of fishing Gull or clanging Golden-eye.
> [*The Borough*, XXII, 194–5]

It is consistent with this habit of mind that our author should evince little relish for the sentimental. From that whole class of intellectual pleasures he is not less averse in principle than in practice. He lives, if we may be allowed the expression, without an atmosphere. Every object is seen in its true situation and dimensions;—there is neither colour nor refraction. No poet was ever less of a visionary.

We are inclined to think that Mr. Crabbe's taste is not equal to his other powers; and this deficiency we attribute, partly indeed to the original constitution of his genius, but much more to the operation of local circumstances. A life of retirement is, perhaps, in no case, very favourable to the cultivation of taste. Unless the mind be sustained in its just position by the intercourse and encounter of living opinions, it is apt to be carried away by the current of some particular system, and contracts in science, as well as in morals, a spirit of favouritism and bigotry. The love of simplicity especially, which is natural to an intellect of strong and masculine proportions, is peculiarly liable to degenerate into a toleration of coarseness. Mr. Crabbe, however, seems to have been exposed to an influence doubly ungenial—that of solitude, in his hours of study; and in his hours of relaxation, that of the society with which his professional duties probably obliged him to become familiar. Even on a judgment the most happily tempered and vigilantly guarded, an intimate acquaintance with such a society, must have operated fatally; either by deadening its tact altogether, or by polishing it to an unnatural keenness; and its influence will be still greater on a mind naturally little fastidious, and predisposed perhaps to prefer strength to elegance.

The impression which results from a general view of our author's compositions, is such as we have stated. There are detached passages, however, in which he appears under a more engaging character. When he escapes from his favourite topics of vulgarity and misery,

> Cœtusque vulgares et udam
> Spernit humum,[1]

he throws off his defects, and purifies himself as he ascends into a purer region. Some of the most pleasing are also among the happiest of his efforts. The few sketches which he has condescended to give of rural life are distinguished not more for their truth, than for their sobriety and chasteness of manner. His love of circumstantial information is likely, in ordinary cases, to confound rather than inform, by inducing him to present us with a collection of unconnected and equally prominent facts, of which no arrangement is made, because there is no reason why one should have the precedence of another. But when the feelings are to be questioned, and the heart is to be laid bare, the same principle leads him closely to follow up nature; and thus we are conducted, step by step, to the highest point of interest. In the struggle of the passions, we delight to trace the workings of the soul; we love to mark the swell of every vein, and the throb of every pulse; every stroke that searches a new source of pity and terror we pursue with a busy and inquisitive sympathy. It is from this cause that Mr. Crabbe's delineations of the passions are so just—so touching of the gentle, and of the awful so tremendous. Remorse and madness have been rarely pourtrayed by a more powerful hand. For feeling, imagery, and agitation of thoughts, the lines in which Sir Eustace Grey tells the story of his insanity, are second to few modern productions. The contrast between the state of the madman, and the evening scene on which he was condemned to gaze, gives a tone of penetrating anguish to the following verses:—

> Upon that boundless plain below . . .
> [196–9, 204–11]

It may be remarked, that the emphatical expression, one dreadful *Now* is to be found in Cowley's Davideis.

There is great force in these two lines—

> I've dreaded all the guilty dread,
> And done what they would fear to do.
> [298–9]

---

[1] He spurns the vulgar crowds and the wet earth. Horace, *Odes*, III, 2, 23–4.

But that which gives the last finish to this vision of despair is contained in these words—

> And then, my dreams were such as nought
> Could yield, but my unhappy case.

[308–9]

Our author is no less successful, when he wishes to excite a milder interest, when he describes the calm of a virtuous old age, the cheerfulness of pious resignation, the sympathies of innocent love. His paintings of this nature are done in his best style; and though we perceive in them something of his usual dry and harsh manner, yet this peculiarity is now no longer a blemish, because it accords with the unpretending plainness of his subject.

It is, after all, on this portion of his works that he must build the fairest part of his reputation. The poetry, which speaks to the understanding alone, cannot permanently attract the mass of mankind; while that, which moves the passions and the heart, has already received the talisman of fame, and may securely commit itself to the affections of every coming age. It is very pleasing to perceive, that, in his best passages, Mr. Crabbe is, practically at least, a convert to the good old principle of paying some regard to fancy and taste in poetry. In these passages he works expressly for the imagination; not perhaps awakening its loftiest exertions, yet studiously courting its assistance, and conciliating its good will. He now accommodates himself to the more delicate sympathies of our nature, and flatters our prejudices by attaching to his pictures agreeable and interesting associations. Thus it is that, for his best success, he is indebted to something more than ungarnished reality. He is the Paladin, who, on the day of decisive combat, laid aside his mortal arms, and took only the magic lance. . . .

Our author is far from having abjured the system of delineating in verse subjects little grateful to poetry. No themes surely can be more untunable than those to which he has here attempered his lyre. It is observable too, that they are sought in a class of society yet lower than that which he has hitherto represented. The impurities of a rural hamlet were sufficiently repulsive;—what then must be those of a maritime borough? This gradual sinking in the scale of realities seems to us a direct consequence of that principle of Mr. Crabbe, on which we have in a former part of this article, hazarded some strictures. *The Borough* is purely the creature of that principle; the legitimate successor of *The Village* and *The Parish Register.*—Indeed, if the checks of fancy and taste

127

be removed from poetry, and admission be granted to images, of whatever description, provided they have the passport of reality, it is not easy to tell at what point the line of exclusion should be drawn, or why it should be drawn at all. No image of depravity, so long as it answers to some archetype in nature or art, can be refused the benefit of the general rule. The mind has acquired a relish for such strong painting, is not likely to be made fastidious by indulgence. When it has exhausted one department of life, it will look for fresh materials in that which is more highly rather than in that which is more faintly coloured. From the haunts of rustic debauchery, the transition is natural to the purlieus of Wapping.

By the choice of this subject, Mr. Crabbe has besides exposed himself to another inconvenience. It was the misfortune of his former poems that they were restricted to a narrow range. They treated of a particular class of men and manners, and therefore precluded those representations of general nature, which, it scarcely needs the authority of Johnson to convince us, are the only things that 'can please many and please long.'—But, with respect to the present poem, this circumstance prevails to a much greater degree. In the inhabitants of a sea-port there are obviously but few generic traces of nature to be detected. The mixed character of their pursuits, and their amphibious sort of life, throw their manners and customs into a striking cast of singularity, and make them almost a separate variety of the human race. Among the existing modifications of society, it may be questioned if there be one which is more distinctly specified, we might say individualized.

The volume before us exhibits all the characteristic qualities of its author; a genius of no common order, but impaired by system—a contempt for the *bienséances* of life, and a rage for its realities. The only 'imaginary personage (as Mr. Crabbe is pleased to style him) introduced into this poem, is a residing burgess in a large sea-port'; and this 'ideal friend' is brought in for the purpose of describing the 'Borough to the inhabitant of a village in the centre of the kingdom.' In other respects, the poem inherits the beauties and defects of its predecessors; but while the defects are more aggravated as well as more thickly sown, the beauties, though not less scantily doled out, are unquestionably touched with a more affecting grace and softness. Although, therefore, the effect of the whole may be far from lively, yet in the strength and pathos of single passages *The Borough* will not have many rivals. . . .

In the following description there is more fineness of execution. But, in spite of its singular accuracy and clearness, it is one of those unpleasing pictures, which are condemned alike by taste and by feeling.

> Say, wilt thou more of Scenes so sordid know? . . .
> [XVIII, 304–27, 344–53]

The lines that follow those which we have just quoted, are among the most successful of Mr. Crabbe's performances in the minute style; yet they develop a scene of such detailed guilt and wretchedness as no skill of execution can render palatable. This indeed, it must be confessed, is the case with no small part of the present volume. The characters of Thompson, Blaney, Clelia, and Benbow, excellently as they are in many particulars drawn, afford exhibitions of a depravity which can excite no emotions but those of disgust. Thus also the five letters on 'the Poor,' (Letters 18—22) contain a series of stories which successively rise above each other in horror.

In point of style our author is extremely negligent. Some of his better and more laboured parts are indeed distinguished by much vigour and compactness of expression; but he is too apt to write hastily, and of course writes diffusely. His best passages are sometimes injured by his namby-pamby feebleness; as in the case of the following ingenious, though not very intelligible, comparison, which is a counterpart to a celebrated simile on the *Essay on Man* [IV, 363–6].

> Though mild Benevolence our Priest possess'd,
> 'Twas but by wishes or by words express'd:
> Circles in water as they wider flow
> The less conspicuous in their progress grow;
> And when at last they touch upon the shore,
> Distinction ceases, and they're view'd no more:
> His Love, like that last Circle, all embrac'd,
> But with effect that never could be trac'd.
> [III, 142–9]

There is too a want of refinement, if we may so express it, about the *air* of his poetry; we do not here mean about its moral or intellectual parts, but about what may be termed its manners—its external deportment. The *costume* of his ideas is slovenly and ungraceful. He is indeed always at ease; but it is the ease of confident carelessness rather than of good-breeding. Thus the letter on Elections begins—

> Yes! our election's past: and we've been free,
> Somewhat as madmen without keepers be.
> [V, 1–2]

The substitution of *be* for *are* occurs more than once in our author; but, though it may be justified by the authority of Dryden, it can scarcely be reconciled to the rules of polished speech.

He thus describes a lady renouncing a cold and uncertain lover—

> The wondering Girl, no prude, but something nice,
> At length was chill'd by his unmelting ice;
> She found her tortoise held such sluggish pace,
> That she must turn and meet him in the chase:
> This not approving, she withdrew till one
> Came who appear'd with livelier hope to run.
>
> [III, 31–6]

Of a man whom the acquisition of wealth inspired with ambition for heraldic honours, we are told—

> he then conceiv'd the thought
> To *fish* for pedigree, but never *caught*.
>
> [XIII, 235–6]

We constantly meet with such phrases as '*he's pros'd*,' '*who're maids*,' '*he'd* now the power,' for *he had*; 'feeling *he's* none,' for *he has* none. In one place occur these rhymes:

> pray'rs and *alms*
> Will soon suppress these idly rais'd *alarms*.
>
> [XVII, 246–7]

In another—

> intent on *cards*,
> Oft he amus'd with riddles and *charardes*—for charades.
>
> [III, 104–5]

His humour, though at times peculiarly good, yet frequently trenches on buffoonery; and is sometimes, unintentionally, we are convinced, carried to the verge of profaneness. Of these qualities we shall not give any examples, but offer in their place a few puns—

> From Law to Physic stepping at our ease,
> We find a way to finish—by *degrees*.
>
> [originally VII, 1–2—Ward, I, p. 539]

> With the same Parts and Prospects, one a *Seat*
> Builds for himself; one finds it in the Fleet.
>
> [VIII, 37–8]

The character of a tradesman, who, having contributed by unkindness to the death of a brother, relieves his remorse by active charity, is thus concluded—

> And if he wrong'd one Brother,—Heav'n forgive
> The Man by whom so many *Brethren* live!
>
> [XVII, 168–9]

Some of his efforts are more happy. There is true epigrammatic point in the account of an old toper celebrating the former companions of his debaucheries.

> Each Hero's Worth with much delight he paints,
> Martyrs they were, and he would make them Saints.
>
> [XVI, 59–60]

But we have been too long detained by these specimens, and are impatient to gratify our readers with some of a different nature. And here we shall cordially agree with the most devoted of Mr. Crabbe's admirers.—Whatever may be our opinion on other points, we are ready to maintain, that few excellencies in poetry are beyond the reach of his nervous and versatile genius; a position which, if our limits allowed it, we should not despair to make good by a reference only to the work before us.

Our first extract shall be of the class which we have in a former place called neutral. It sets the object before us in the most vivid manner; but at the same time neither irritates nor pleases the imagination.

> Lo! yonder shed; observe its Garden-Ground, . . .
>
> [XVIII, 263–73]

For an easy vein of ridicule, terse expression, and just strokes of character, the description of the 'Card-Club' is admirable. It is one of those likenesses which, without knowing the original, we may pronounce to be perfect.

> Our eager Parties, when the lunar Light . . .
>
> [X, 113–88]

> A club there is of Smokers.—Dare you come . . .
>
> [X, 238–68]

> Oft have I travell'd in these tender tales . . .
>
> [XX, 33–42, 59–75]

The following sketch is truly in Mr. Crabbe's style. Without the romantic mellowness which envelopes the landscape of Goldsmith, or the freshness and hilarity of colouring which breathe in that of Graham,[1] it is perhaps superior to both in distinctness, animation, and firmness of touch; and to these is added a peculiar air of facility and freedom.

Thy Walks are ever pleasant; every Scene . . .
[I, 103–20]

As a contrast to this inland scene, we shall give an evening view on the sea-shore. The topics which it embraces have never, as far as we recollect, been so distinctly treated of in poetry; they are here recorded too in very appropriate numbers. The versification of the latter part of the passage particularly, is brilliant and *éveillée*, and has something of the pleasing restlessness of the ocean itself.

Now is it pleasant in the Summer-Eve, . . .
[IX, 77–90, 97–110]

A prospect of the ocean inspires Mr. Crabbe with congenial sublimity. The 'Winter Storm' is detailed with a masterly and interesting exactness. This is the opening of it—

All where the eye delights, yet dreads to roam, . . .
[I, 200–13]

We have already adverted to the talent which Mr. Crabbe possesses of delineating despair. That talent he has in this work exercised with a daring prodigality. There are no less than three very prominent representations of this kind; distinguished indeed from each other by varieties of circumstance and crime, but all bearing marks of the same dark and terrible pencil. . . .

In each lone place, dejected and dismay'd . . .
[XIX, 270–82]

And now we saw him on the Beach reclin'd, . . .
[XXI, 191–206]

When Tides were neap, and in the sultry day . . .
[XXII, 181–204, 223–31, 298–327]

In some of Mr. Crabbe's graver descriptions there is a tone of chastised and unambitious serenity, which has a powerful influence on the heart, and affects it like the quiet glow of a mild evening. Thus in the character of Eusebius—

---

[1] James Grahame (1765–1811), whose poems included *The Sabbath* (1804) and *British Georgics* (1809).

'Tis thine to wait on Woe! to soothe! to heal! . . .
[XVII, 78–87, 100–103]

Longinus somewhere mentions that it was a question among the
critics of his age whether the sublime could be produced by tenderness.[1]
If this question had not been already determined, the following history
would have gone far to bring it to a decision:

Yes! there are real Mourners—I have seen . . .
[II, 170–263]

We could prolong our extracts, and should be happy to adorn our
pages with the account of the 'water party,' the 'alms-house,' the
'highwayman's dream,' and some select sketches of character. But it is
time to draw to a close; and we shall content ourselves with throwing
together a few detached lines which struck us as eminently happy.

Of the inhabitants of the poor-house—

Nothing to bring them joy, to make them weep,
The day itself is like the night asleep.
[XVIII, 174–5]

A criminal under sentence of death is represented as absorbed in that
one prospect.

This makes his Features ghastly, gives the tone
Of his few words resemblance to a groan.
[XXIII, 253–4]

and, in his sleep, he

Dreams the very thirst that then will be.
[XXIII, 272]

These two lines are singularly expressive—

When half the pillow'd Man the Palsy chains,
And the blood falters in the bloated Veins.
[X, 364–5]

and the second of these that relate the finishing of the hospital—

Skill, Wealth, and Vanity, obtain the fame,
And Piety, the joy that makes no claim.
[XVII, 66–7]

The feeling of tenderness with which the dead are regarded is well
described—

1 *On the Sublime*, section 8.

133

Now to their Love and Worth of every kind,
A soft compunction turns th' afflicted Mind.
[II, 131–2]

From these specimens our readers will receive a very favourable
impression of the poetical talent of Mr. Crabbe; and of this impression
we are now content to leave them to the uninterrupted indulgence.
That it should be the tendency of the former part of our criticism, to
excite somewhat different feelings, would be to us a matter of much
self-reproach, if we were not convinced that, in commencing on a
writer at once of such powers and such celebrity, a frank exposition of
our sentiments was due both to him and to ourselves. Should these
imperfect strictures be fortunate enough to meet the eye of Mr. Crabbe,
we have so much reliance on his candour as to believe that he will
forgive their freedom. If however we are mistaken in this conjecture,
we can only express our hope that he may speedily revenge himself,
as he is well able, by the production of some work which shall compel
our unqualified praise.

28. Unsigned review, *British Critic*

March 1811, xxxvii, 236–47

We promised ourselves great satisfaction, and we may promise the
same to our readers, in the examination and reporting of this poem. It
cannot, in the nature of things, be an ordinary occurrence to meet with
a poem which stands much above the common class of compositions;
we must not expect to live on literary luxuries, and the daily bread of
the press certainly has no resemblance to Mr. Crabbe's *Borough*.

The talent of this author for accurate and lively delineation of
character, is already known and acknowledged; and we are inclined
to think that it is here displayed with more vigour and liveliness, than
even in his former works. He has the art, a truly poetic quality, of
rendering even the most trivial objects and events interesting; of
placing them exactly before the eyes of his reader; and of pointing out
those characteristics which every one must acknowledge to belong to
them, and yet no one perhaps before had marked with such precision.

As it is in the very conclusion of his poem that he speaks of his own general design in writing poetry, we shall, without scruple, go to that part for our first specimen. He has drawn in it, and evidently meant to draw his own character, which will therefore complete our description of him.

> For this the poet looks the world around . . .
> [XXIV, 426–45]

It does indeed appear to us, that he is as clear from the imputation of particular satire, as he is strong in his description of characters, which from their accuracy *might* be real. We only lament that in one or two instances he has drawn atrocious pictures of vice, which whoever believes to be natural, cannot but sigh for that nature which is capable of such depravity. That it is so must, we fear, be owned; but we cannot but a little wonder at the taste which dwells by preference on such representations. This observation, however, applies to a very small part of the poem: and chiefly to such characters as those of Blaney and Peter Grimes, which having once read, we never wish to see again. The more they have of truth and probability, the more curious but the more disgusting they must be felt. Mr. Crabbe's versification is well suited to his subjects; easy and flowing; sometimes apparently negligent; at others pointed and neat. The reader, as he proceeds, is neither fatigued by constant exertion, nor satiated by uniformity of style; he can read the letters with as much ease as if they were prose, with the frequently recurring stimulus of poetical effect, both in the thought and in the expressions. Comparing the present volume with the former poems of the author, we think it in general composed with more care; and if not always pointed with more felicity, yet certainly not often inferior.

The Borough, which the poet has undertaken to describe, is, like his human characters, not easily fixed to any one in particular. It is supposed to be situated on the sea coast, but that is all which can be ascertained; and as the author, by his own account, inhabits 'a village in the centre of the kingdom,' there are no means of guessing to which coast his footsteps would be turned, when he went to make poetical observations at a distance from home. It is likely indeed that his observations were made at various times, and in various excursions, through a long course of years. The subject, however, has enabled him to quit his usual scope of description, and to introduce new objects and new persons. Accustomed habits of thought have indeed led him to give a disproportionate share of his attention to the lowest classes of society; and it may be objected, not entirely without reason, that, out of twenty-four letters, nearly one half are given to the alms-house and other objects on a level with it. The only excuse for this fault, if it be a fault, will be found in the liveliness and originality of the descriptions and narratives which it produces. . . .

. . . There is nothing in his preface or in his book more calculated for general utility, than the following very sensible and judicious remarks on the enthusiasts, who are pictured in his fourth letter.

To those readers who have seen the journals of the first Methodists, or the extracts quoted from them by their opposers . . . to whose guidance they prostrate their spirit and understanding.

This picture is too correctly drawn, and too important in point of public instruction, to be passed over by us, whose anxious wish it is to guard the public, as far as in us lies, from all kinds of delusion; and to give as much circulation as we can to everything which may promise to be useful. But we now turn with increased pleasure to the poem itself, and to the objects which the art and genius of the writer bring before us.

With ceaseless motion comes and goes the tide . . .
[I, 37–60]

Hark! to those sounds, they're from distress at sea . . .
[I, 241–70]

[The reviewer praises 'the beautiful and affecting history' in Letter II.]

'Yes,' he replied, 'I'm happy, I confess, . . .
[III, 285–336]

In the last line, though Mr. C. has fallen upon a form of expression which has been ridiculed, we cannot but think that it has real pathos in his mode of application. So much do these letters abound with passages of strong and original effect, that we feel no danger but that of extending our specimens to an unreasonable length. . . .

The ample yards on either side contain . . .
[XI, 35–52]

Books cannot always please, however good; . . .
[XXIV, 402–25]

A few trifles have escaped his diligence, which a very little attention will rectify. A *bodger* (in [V, 193]) means, we suppose, a *botcher*, but we have never met with the word so corrupted. In [X, 384] *run* should be *runs*, rhyme and grammar are here at variance. In [XIII, 5–8], we have four successive lines with one rhyme. *Bows* for boughs, in [XVIII, 226], is a mere erratum. In [XIX, 192], should be 'did he tread.' In [XX, 126] we have *wed* for *wedded*, or did wed; this we presume is an error of system, as we find it in the author's former poems. We are almost ashamed to conclude our account of a poem of such high merit with observations so minute, they may serve, however, to prove that we have read the whole with strict attention, and this author is certainly not a man to contend that inaccuracies, either in grammar or in versification, ought to be continued.

29. Unsigned review, *Christian Observer*

August 1811, x, 502–11

His 'Letter on Sects' . . . occasioned a controversy between the writer and the editor of the *Christian Observer*, which appeared likely to become public. It ended, however, in mutual expressions of entire respect; and I am happy to think that the difference in their views was only such as different circumstances of education, &c., might cause between two sincere Christians.[1]

Mr. Crabbe has long been known the world as a writer of much originality and considerable merit; the successful cultivator of a field of poetry peculiar to himself. . . .

Mr. Crabbe must certainly be classed among the rural and domestic poets; but, from all others of this class he differs so widely, that his poetry must be considered as forming a distinct genus in the analysis of poetry. No topics, perhaps, have more frequently furnished materials to the poet than the manners, habits, and sentiments of the vulgar; but

---

[1] *Life*, Ch. 8.

it has been always hitherto thought necessary to exhibit them in some disguise, and to suffer them to borrow from fiction the delicacy and *amiableness* which nature had denied them. Turning from the corruption of towns and villages, the rural poets have generally repaired to the solitary cottage, or the hermit's cell, and the peace and innocence, which even there they failed to find, they have been accustomed to supply by their imagination. Far removed from this delicacy, Mr. Crabbe enters into a resolute detail of poverty, profligacy and disease; is more conversant with workhouses, than with grottos; and, instead of the sentimental distresses of Floras, Delias, and Strephons, enumerates the substantial grievances of Bridget Dawdle, Richard Monday, or Peter Grimes. He loves to exhibit his personages just as he finds them, in all their native coarseness and depravity, or in all their simple and unvarnished merit. They owe to his muse no favour, but that of drawing them from obscurity.

If such descriptions as those of Mr. Crabbe related to more polished scenes, and to persons of higher rank, they would properly be called *satires*. He has, therefore, been judiciously characterized as 'The *satirist of low life*.'[1] It is to the delineation of character and manners that he chiefly applies himself; and his delineation, if just, is at least severe. Though not unwilling to praise, and well able to give the charms of humble virtue their true energy and grace, it is by no means with an indulgent eye that he contemplates the scenes before him. He seems to be more on the watch for matter of censure than of panegyric, and paints the depravity which he finds in colours so vivid, that he has been thought to sacrifice resemblance to effect. Of this, however, we acquit him. Life supplies but too copious materials to the pen of the satirist, be his thirst for censure what it may. No doubt such characters as his Blaneys and his Grimeses may be found; but we believe the poet has gone somewhat out of his way to find them, and that they are of the very worst kinds which he could have selected.

If considered as a descriptive poet, Mr. Crabbe has also strong peculiarities. The pencil with which he delineates nature is obviously the same that he employs upon character. Little solicitous about the intrinsic beauty of his subject, his great aim seems to be to represent with fidelity and force; and he is anxious to leave nothing unrepresented which can add to the completeness of his picture, without considering whether it adds or not to its attraction.

The characteristics above pointed out are to be found in all the poems

[1] *Edinburgh Review* on Crabbe's *Borough*.

of this author; in none so strongly marked, perhaps, as in that which he last published.

The first of the twenty-four Letters of which this poem is composed, exhibits powers of description well calculated to raise the most advantageous prejudices in favour of the rest of the work. The busy and variegated prospect presented by a sea-town and its environs is sketched with great spirit and effect. The river, the quay, the limekilns, the walks, and the tea gardens, and, lastly, the ocean itself, in the terrors of its turbulence and in the majesty of its repose, are brought to the eye with a minuteness and accuracy which seems almost to blend the province of the painter with that of the poet. Those, to whom a sea prospect is at all familiar, cannot fail immediately to feel the *truth* of the following delineation.

> Be it the summer noon: a sandy space . . .
> [I, 173–93]

To the concluding simile, though it has a certain air of boldness and force, we must object, as too *recherché*, and little calculated, besides, to aid the imagination of the reader. To illustrate the agitation of the ocean by the wrath of a giant, is to explain what is familiar to every body by that which nobody knows any thing about.

In the next letter, we have the tale of Thomas and Sally— than which we will venture to pronounce there is no piece in the whole range of English poetry possessing superior power of genuine pathos—of that true pathetic, which flows from the purest and most elevated sources, undebased by any admixture of false sentiment or unchristian passion . . . .

> Still long she nursed him; tender thoughts, mean time . . .
> [II, 222–5]

After thus exhibiting his powers in the descriptive and the pathetic, Mr. Crabbe introduces us, in the succeeding Letter, to a very different style of composition; and gives a specimen of his talents for light and playful satire.

In the vicar of the parish, we are presented with a clerical trifler of a very entertaining cast; not of that ordinary class of foppish divines, who differ from other fops only in a slight distinction of dress—but a kind of Will Wimble, in orders.

> Fiddling and fishing were his arts—at times . . .
> [III, 102–5, 154–65]

Though our gravity is not quite proof against this recital of the vicar's qualities, and though we are very sorry to be obliged to find fault with an obliging, inoffensive, inconsequential being, whom every body else seems to have liked, it is nevertheless clear that this character cannot be allowed to pass without serious comment in the Christian Observer. As assigned to a clergyman, its triviality is too revolting to be comic; and we own that the spirit of levity in which the reverend author has pourtrayed it, and the smiling indulgence with which he treats it, led us to look forward with some anxiety to his letter on religious sects.

We hate illiberality, and are not so narrow as to maintain, that every thing in which religion is concerned must be discussed with a solemn air and a grave countenance; but when a Christian and a clergyman has occasion to describe a gross neglect of every Christian duty, an utter disregard of the clerical functions, an insensibility even to clerical decorum, and the death of an unregenerate sinner, we at least expect him to mingle with his satire some gravity of censure, and some fervour of compassion. . . .

In the Letter on Religious Sects, we shall first notice a passage [lines 190–209] in which the eternity of future punishment is considered as a doctrine but doubtfully inculcated in the Scriptures. We hope, and are inclined to believe, that the author did not mean to be so understood. His words are certainly to that purport; and it is at all events, unfortunate, that in an attack upon sectarians, he should himself appear to exhibit an instance of heterodoxy from which few sectarians would not recoil. We have a further charge, however, to make against this letter, and it is one that relates to its general spirit and tenor. It is no less than this: that the author has been witty at the expense of truth, and that, while professing to narrate facts, his muse has not scrupled to indulge herself in all the licence of fiction. We think it prudent, here, to insert this caveat, that by truth and fiction we do not mean veracity and falsehood. We do not say, that Mr. Crabbe has wilfully misrepresented; we simply say, that his representations are calculated to give impressions not warranted by fact. It is, in truth, the old error into which, somehow or other, those who attack religious sects are always falling; the error of investing fools, knaves, and madmen, with the name of Methodist, and then assailing Methodism itself with all the abuse which these fools, knaves, and madmen, so richly deserve. . . .

But though the injustice done by this author to the Methodists, and the other sectaries whom he has attacked, can be satisfactorily proved only by an appeal to fact, there is something in the nature of the attack itself, and in the manner in which it is conducted, which, independently of its injustice, calls for strong reprehension. He appears to us to have added to that class of writers, who, by putting the language and sentiments of religion into the mouth of meanness and imbecility, have been guilty of transferring to religion herself a portion of the dislike and contempt due to the qualities with which she is thus invidiously associated. Mr. Crabbe must have read the *Tartuffe* of Moliere, *The School for Scandal*, and the Spiritual *Quixote*; and it cannot, we think, have escaped him, that whatever might be the aim of these works, their tendency is not merely to expose hypocrisy or weakness, but that it is also to ridicule all persons professing morality or religion, with whatever discretion and sincerity that profession may be made. He must have observed, too, that this is accomplished by the obvious means of giving to fools and hypocrites much of the same language, many of the same sentiments, and some of the conduct by which every true Christian is distinguished; and then neglecting to trace the line between what is right in these persons and what is wrong, and taking care to present no contrasted characters, by whom the graces of real religion may be exemplified, and her honour redeemed.

It is not that these authors can be charged with violating truth. The subjects of their satire are not ideal. Though we believe them to be uncommon, they may, no doubt, occasionally be found. It is the unfair impression of which we complain—the invidious association which throws on the faith itself, the reproach of a few false professors.

Whether Mr. Crabbe, therefore, be correct or not, in attributing so much error and absurdity to his religious sectaries, we must still protest against the manner in which he has thought fit to expose these failings; and we make the protest not on behalf of the sects whom he satirizes, but of Religion, whose cause he supposes himself to defend. His Calvinistic and Arminian preachers, however reprehensible in taste and doctrine, have, by his own account, at least activity, energy, and apparent zeal. They refer to scripture. They speak strongly of the influence of the Spirit, and the agency of Satan. They profess a separation from the world, and holiness of heart and life. Now all these things are good and praiseworthy, and we are confident that Mr. Crabbe will allow them to be so. How is it, then, that he incorporates them, without any mark of distinction, in a mass of what is ridiculous and despicable? How is it that he, a minister of the established church, associates, with ludicrous and disgusting images, such qualities and such doctrines as those we have here mentioned, without warning his readers to what part alone he means to point their contempt? How is it that he has not made amends for this defect, by exhibiting the good principles of his sectaries in some other person or persons of character more consistent and respectable? The effect of his representation, as it now stands, will certainly be to persuade those who are already disposed to confound sincere piety with cant, that they are in reality the same thing; to convince them that zeal and spirituality are at least not essential to the religious character; and that they are chiefly, if not only, found among those whom neither taste nor reason can approve. . . .

It is impossible to read the description that follows, without the strongest emotions of terror and sympathy; and we think it must be allowed that in the conception of this passage, Mr. Crabbe has reached the high praise of sublimity.

> She gazed, she trembled, and tho' faint her call, . . .
> [IX, 238–54, 257–66]

> When tides are neap, and in the sultry day . . .
> [XXII, 181–95, 199–204, 223–31]

We have not attempted to present our readers with any analysis of this poem, for a very simple reason—that it is without a regular plan. It is totally destitute of what is called *unity of design*; and it is to this circumstance that we principally attribute that lassitude which, notwithstanding the numerous beauties it contains, we have frequently known its readers to experience. It has, indeed, what, in the almost antiquated language of criticism, is termed *unity of place*. The scene is uniformly laid in the 'Borough.' But, subject to this exception, it may be considered not as one poem, but as a miscellaneous collection of poems. The different parts are not essentially connected with each other, or with the whole. There is no continued action, or common catastrophe. We believe that in every poem of equal length with *The Borough*, a similar construction has been found to produce the same prejudicial effect. In Thompson's *Seasons* (to put a strong instance), we have a poem fertile in the most astonishing displays of genius, and much more regular than *The Borough* in its design: yet the want of connection between its parts has been always sensibly felt by the most ardent of its admirers.* The analogy of the different Seasons forms a chain too slight to confine the attention; and amidst all its varied beauties of imagery,

---

* See this defect noticed by Johnson, in his life of that poet.

sentiment, and versification, the interest of the poem languishes for want of method. It is not surprising, then, that in *The Borough* the same error should have been committed with impunity; but we think it is sur-prising that it should have been committed with this example, and a multitude of others, equally instructive, before the eyes of the author.

There are several other faults, not confined to the present poem, but exemplified in all the other works of Mr. Crabbe, as well as in that under review, which we reluctantly feel ourselves compelled, in our quality of critics, to point out. Among these, that which we consider as the principal, is the *choice of the subjects*. We have before noticed that Mr. Crabbe is fond of dealing in low life. But this is not all. Whatever in low life is most abhorrent and disgusting, vice, infamy, and disease, indigence, insanity, and despair, seem to be eagerly selected by this author as the images most animating and congenial to his muse, as the topics most favourable to inspiration. It is not enough that his hero should be vulgar; he must also be vile, and his fate must not only be tragical, but loathsome. No gleam of hope is allowed to pierce the dungeon which Mr. Crabbe exhibits: no tears of repentance to bedew the scaffold erected by *him*. We have not chosen to make any extracts which would put modesty to pain; but it is easy to perceive that, among the other objections to such kind of writing, it necessarily involves much indelicacy. In his pursuit of horrors, this author does not scruple to lay open the recesses of licentiousness, and to 'drag into day' the sickening deformities of low debauchery. We rejoice, however, to believe that it is to the temptation of being tragical alone that the fault is to be attributed, and that his *object* is never to be indelicate. But we entreat him to consider, whether the peculiarity of style, which gives birth to such passages, is not proved, by that circumstance alone, to be incon-sistent with good taste and with right principle.

Where his subjects are not revolting, they are often radically mean and uninteresting, such as no importance of moral can exalt, or splendour of fiction adorn. Quackery, elections, trades, inns, hospitals—what genius can hope to throw the least glimmering of poetic lustre upon materials so cold and coarse as these? It is with most impartial accuracy that he himself has characterized them, as

> Scenes yet unsung—which few would choose to sing.
> [XI, 8]

That he should have succeeded so well, in the management of such untractable materials, is certainly a decisive proof of his extraordinary powers as a poet.

We are aware that Mr. Crabbe's peculiarity, in the choice of his subjects, is the effect of deliberate intention, and part of the plan and character of composition which he has prescribed to himself. We know that he has said much, and has still much to say, in its defence. He will admit, that such topics are not, in themselves, the most eligible; and that, if he had had no predecessors in poetry, he would have applied himself exclusively to those of an opposite description; but he will observe, that he is born in a late age of poetry; that the most agreeable and advantageous topics are pre-occupied and worn threadbare; and that he seeks, therefore, in a change of subject, that originality which it is no longer possible, by any other means, to exhibit. If this is not the defence he would adopt, it is at least that which, in our opinion, may be the most plausibly urged in his favour. Yet it amounts to very little. It is, in effect, an admission, that the subjects are unfortunate, and it justifies their adoption merely on the ground of necessity. And even this justification, limited and disclaiming as it is, is unsupported by fact. We cannot admit that the era has yet arrived at which it is necessary to take up with the refuse materials of poetry; and, in proof of our opinion, it is only necessary, we conceive, to mention the names of Campbell and of Scott. It is obvious that Mr. Crabbe does not want the powers to raise him into that scale of public estimation which these distinguished poets now occupy. He is inferior to them only because his subjects keep him down; and while this is the case, he falls under the same sentence which a very competent judge has pronounced on those who, in the same taste, have cultivated the sister art.

'The painters who have applied themselves more particularly to low and vulgar characters, and who express with precision the various shades of passion as they are exhibited by vulgar minds (such as we see in the works of Hogarth), deserve great praise; but as their genius has been employed on low and confined subjects, the praise that we give must be limited as its object.'—Sir J. REYNOLDS' Discourse.

It only remains to notice two other blemishes in the poetry of Mr. Crabbe, of minor importance, indeed, to those which have been already specified, but too considerable to be overlooked. These are an ill-advised fondness for antithesis and point, and a slovenly system of versification.

Of the first, it would be easy to produce numerous examples. Let the following suffice.

Of sea-gulls, he says, that they

> clap the sleek white pinion to the breast,
> *And in the restless ocean dip for rest.*
> [I, 229–30]

The opposition here is merely verbal, and amounts to nothing more than a quibble.

In another place, he talks of

> The easy followers in the female train,
> *Led without love, and captives without chain.*
> [III, 67–8]

If this antithesis were as happy as it is otherwise, it would still be impossible to forgive the alliteration.

In the following page, the figure is very appropriately put into the mouth of the finical vicar, whose example, one might have thought, would have been a warning to Mr. Crabbe.

> Not without moral compliment—how they
> *Like flowers were sweet, and must like flowers decay.*
> [III, 89–90]

In his versification, we observe occasionally great harshness, and a want of the *limæ labor*; a fault the more remarkable, as, in its general features, it is, doubtless, formed upon that of Pope. The following disjointed paragraph may serve for example:

> The old foundation—but it is not clear
> When it was laid—you care not for the year;
> On this, as parts decay'd by time and storms
> Arose these varied disproportion'd forms;
> Yet, Gothic all: the learn'd who visit us,
> And our small wonders, have decided thus:
> 'Yon noble Gothic arch,' 'that Gothic door'—
> So have they said; of proof you'll need no more.
> [II, 25–32]

Another objection that we must make to Mr. Crabbe's versification is its general character of *monotony*. The cæsura is sometimes for nearly a page together in the middle of the line. Of this fault it is unnecessary to give a specimen. Every one who reads *The Borough* aloud will detect it at once in the heaviness of the recitation.

On the whole, we have seldom met with a poet who combines, with the very signal merit of Mr. Crabbe, a greater alloy of imperfection. If he were a young man, and a hasty composer, we should hope every thing from his maturer exertions; but when we read in his Preface, that he is 'anxious it should be generally known that sufficient time and application were bestowed upon this work' (*The Borough*), and that 'no material alteration would be effected by delay,' we confess that we dare no longer indulge the prospect of any material amendment in his style of composition, and fear that time may rather confirm his errors than extirpate them.

TALES

September 1812

In the early part of the year 1812, Mr. Crabbe published—(with a dedication to the Duchess Dowager of Rutland)—his *Tales in Verse*; a work as striking as, and far less objectionable than, its predecessor, *The Borough*; for here no flimsy connection is attempted between subjects naturally separate; nor consequently, was there such temptation to compel into verse matters essentially prosaic. The new tales had also the advantage of ampler scope and development than his preceding ones. The public voice was again highly favourable, and some of these relations were spoken of with the utmost warmth of commendation; as, 'The Parting Hour', 'The Patron', 'Edward Shore', and 'The Confidant'.[1]

30. Crabbe, Preface to *Tales*

This preface is Crabbe's most important statement of his own view of his art. It reflects on some of the criticisms made of his previous work and provides, incidentally, a typical example of his prose style.

That the appearance of the present Volume before the Public is occasioned by a favourable reception of the former two, I hesitate not to acknowledge; because, while the confession may be regarded as some proof of gratitude, or at least of attention from an Author to his Readers, it ought not to be considered as an indication of vanity. It is unquestionably very pleasant to be assured that our labours are well received; but,

[1] *Life*, Ch. 8.

nevertheless, this must not be taken for a just and full criterion of their merit: publications of great intrinsic value have been met with so much coolness, that a writer who succeeds in obtaining some degree of notice, should look upon himself rather as one favoured than meritorious, as gaining a prize from Fortune, and not a recompense for desert; and, on the contrary, as it is well known that books of very inferior kind have been at once pushed into the strong current of popularity, and are there kept buoyant by the force of the stream, the writer who acquires not this adventitious help, may be reckoned rather as unfortunate than undeserving; and from these opposite considerations it follows, that a man may speak of his success without incurring justly the odium of conceit, and may likewise acknowledge a disappointment without an adequate cause for humiliation or self-reproach.

But were it true that something of the complacency of self-approbation would insinuate itself into an author's mind with the idea of success, the sensation would not be that of unalloyed pleasure: it would perhaps assist him to bear, but it would not enable him to escape the mortification he must encounter from censures, which, though he may be unwilling to admit, yet he finds himself unable to confute; as well as from advice, which at the same time that he cannot but approve, he is compelled to reject.

Reproof and advice, it is probable, every author will receive, if we except those who meet so much of the former, that the latter is contemptuously denied them; now of these, reproof, though it may cause more temporary uneasiness, will in many cases create less difficulty, since errors may be corrected when opportunity occurs: but advice, I repeat, may be of such nature, that it will be painful to reject, and yet impossible to follow it; and in this predicament I conceive myself to be placed. There has been recommended to me, and from authority which neither inclination or prudence leads me to resist, in any new work I might undertake, an unity of subject, and that arrangement of my materials which connects the whole and gives additional interest to every part; in fact, if not an Epic Poem, strictly so denominated, yet such composition as would possess a regular succession of events, and a catastrophe to which every incident should be subservient, and which every character, in a greater or less degree, should conspire to accomplish.

In a Poem of this nature, the principal and inferior characters in some degrees resemble a General and his Army, where no one pursues his peculiar objects and adventures, or pursues them in unison with the movements and grand purposes of the whole body; where there is a community of interests and a subordination of actors: and it was upon this view of the subject, and of the necessity for such distribution of persons and events, that I found myself obliged to relinquish an undertaking, for which the characters I could command, and the adventures I could describe, were altogether unfitted.

But if these characters which seemed to be at my disposal were not such as would coalesce into one body, nor were of a nature to be commanded by one mind, so neither on examination did they appear as an unconnected multitude, accidentally collected, to be suddenly dispersed; but rather beings of whom might be formed groups and smaller societies, the relations of whose adventures and pursuits might bear that kind of similitude to an Heroic Poem, which these minor associations of men (as pilgrims on the way to their saint, or parties in search of amusement, travellers excited by curiosity, or adventurers in pursuit of gain) have in points of connection and importance with a regular and disciplined Army.

Allowing this comparison, it is manifest that while much is lost for want of unity of subject and grandeur of design, something is gained by greater variety of incident and more minute display of character, by accuracy of description, and diversity of scene: in these narratives we pass from gay to grave, from lively to severe, not only without impropriety, but with manifest advantage. In one continued and connected Poem, the Reader is, in general, highly gratified or severely disappointed; by many independent narratives, he has the renovation of hope, although he has been dissatisfied, and a prospect of reiterated pleasure should he find himself entertained.

I mean not, however, to compare these different modes of writing as if I were balancing their advantages and defects before I could give preference to either; with me the way I take is not a matter of choice, but of necessity: I present not my *Tales* to the Reader as if I had chosen the best method of ensuring his approbation, but as using the only means I possessed of engaging his attention.

It may be probably be remarked that Tales, however dissimilar, might have been connected by some associating circumstance to which the whole number might bear equal affinity, and that examples of such union are to be found in *Chaucer*, in *Boccace*, and other collectors and inventors of Tales, which considered in themselves are altogether independent; and to this idea I gave so much consideration as convinced me that I could not avail myself of the benefit of such artificial mode of affinity. To imitate the English Poet, characters must be found adapted to their several relations, and this is a point of great difficulty and hazard: much allowance seems to be required even for *Chaucer* himself, since it is difficult to conceive that on any occasion the devout and delicate *Prioress*, the courtly and valiant *Knight*, and '*the poure good Man the persone of a Towne*,' would be the voluntary companions of the drunken *Miller*, the licentious *Sompnour*, and 'the *Wanton Wife of Bath*,' and enter into that colloquial and travelling intimacy which, if a common pilgrimage to the shrine of *St. Thomas* may be said to excuse, I know nothing beside (and certainly nothing in these times) that would produce such effect. *Boccace*, it is true, avoids all difficulty of this kind, by not assigning to the ten relators of his hundred Tales any marked or peculiar characters; nor, though there are male and female in company, can the sex of the narrator be distinguished in the narration. To have followed the method of *Chaucer*, might have been of use, but could scarcely be adopted, from its difficulty; and to have taken that of the Italian writer, would have been perfectly easy, but could be of no service: the attempt at union therefore has been relinquished, and these relations are submitted to the Public, connected by no other circumstance than their being the productions of the same Author, and devoted to the same purpose, the entertainment of his Readers.

It has been already acknowledged, that these compositions have no pretensions to be estimated with the more lofty and heroic kind of Poems, but I feel great reluctance in admitting that they have not a fair and legitimate claim to the poetic character: in vulgar estimation, indeed, all that is not prose, passes for poetry; but I have not ambition of so humble a kind as to be satisfied with a concession which requires nothing in the Poet, except his ability for counting syllables; and I trust something more of the poetic character will be allowed to the succeeding pages, than what the heroes of the *Dunciad* might share with the Author: nor was I aware that by describing, as faithfully as I could, men, manners, and things, I was forfeiting a just title to a name which has been freely granted to many whom to equal and even to excel is but very stinted commendation.

In this case it appears that the usual comparison between Poetry and Painting entirely fails: the Artist who takes an accurate likeness of individuals, or a faithful representation of scenery, may not rank so high in the public estimation, as one who paints an historical event, or an heroic action; but he is nevertheless a painter, and his accuracy is so far from diminishing his reputation, that it procures for him in general

both fame and emolument: nor is it perhaps with strict justice determined that the credit and reputation of those verses which strongly and
faithfully delineate character and manners, should be lessened in the
opinion of the Public by the very accuracy, which gives value and
distinction to the productions of the pencil.

Nevertheless, it must be granted that the pretensions of any composition to be regarded as Poetry, will depend upon the definition of the
poetic character which he who undertakes to determine the question
has considered as decisive; and it is confessed also that one of great
authority may be adopted, by which the verses now before the Reader,
and many others which have probably amused and delighted him,
must be excluded: a definition like this will be found in the words
which the greatest of Poets, not divinely inspired, has given to the most
noble and valiant Duke of Athens—

> The Poet's eye, in a fine frenzy rolling,
> Doth glance from Heaven to Earth, from Earth to Heaven;
> And, as Imagination bodies forth
> The forms of things unknown, the Poet's pen
> Turns them to shapes, and gives to airy nothing
> A local habitation, and a name.*

Hence we observe the Poet is one who, in the excursions of his fancy
between heaven and earth, lights upon a kind of fairy-land in which
he places a creation of his own, where he embodies shapes, and gives
action and adventure to his ideal offspring; taking captive the imagination of his readers, he elevates them above the grossness of actual being,
into the soothing and pleasant atmosphere of supra-mundane existence:
there he obtains for his visionary inhabitants the interest that engages a
reader's attention without ruffling his feelings, and excites that moderate
kind of sympathy which the realities of nature oftentimes fail to produce, either because they are so familiar and insignificant that they
excite no determinate emotion, or are so harsh and powerful that the
feelings excited are grating and distasteful.

Be it then granted that (as *Duke Theseus* observes) '*such tricks hath
strong Imagination*,' and that such Poets '*are of imagination all compact*';
let it be further conceded, that theirs is a higher and more dignified
kind of composition, nay, the only kind that has pretensions to inspiration; still, that these Poets should so entirely engross the title as to

---

* *A Midsummer Night's Dream*, V, i.

exclude those who address their productions to the plain sense and sober judgment of their Readers, rather than to their fancy and imagination, I must repeat that I am unwilling to admit,—because I conceive that, by granting such right of exclusion, a vast deal of what has been hitherto received as genuine poetry would no longer be entitled to that appellation.

All that kind of satire wherein character is skilfully delineated, must (this criterion being allowed) no longer be esteemed as genuine Poetry; and for the same reason many affecting narratives which are founded on real events, and borrow no aid whatever from the imagination of the writer, must likewise be rejected: a considerable part of the Poems, as they have hitherto been denominated, of *Chaucer*, are of this naked and unveiled character; and there are in his Tales many pages of coarse, accurate, and minute, but very striking description. Many small Poems in a subsequent age of most impressive kind are adapted and addressed to the common sense of the Reader, and prevail by the strong language of truth and nature: they amused our ancestors, and they continue to engage our interest, and excite our feelings by the same powerful appeals to the heart and affections. In times less remote, *Dryden* has given us much of this Poetry, in which the force of expression and accuracy of description have neither needed nor obtained assistance from the fancy of the writer; the characters in his *Absalom and Achitophel* are instances of this, and more especially those of *Doeg* and *Ogg* in the second part: these, with all their grossness, and almost offensive accuracy, are found to possess that strength and spirit which has preserved from utter annihilation the dead bodies of *Tate* to whom they were inhumanly bound, happily with a fate the reverse of that caused by the cruelty of *Mezentius*; for there the living perished in the putrefaction of the dead, and here the dead are preserved by the vitality of the living. And, to bring forward one other example, it will be found that *Pope* himself has no small portion of this actuality of relation, this nudity of description, and poetry without an atmosphere;[1] the lines beginning '*In the worst inn's worst room*,' are an example, and many others may be seen in his Satires, Imitations, and above all in his *Dunciad*: the frequent absence of those '*Sports of Fancy*,' and '*Tricks of strong Imagination*,' have been so much observed, that some have ventured to question whether even this writer were a Poet; and though, as *Dr. Johnson* has remarked, it would be difficult to form a definition of one in which *Pope* should

---

[1] Crabbe seems to have taken up this phrase from the *Quarterly*'s review of *The Borough*. See p. 125 above.

not be admitted, yet they who doubted his claim, had, it is likely, provided for his exclusion by forming that kind of character for their Poet, in which this elegant versifier, for so he must be then named, should not be comprehended.

These things considered, an Author will find comfort in his expulsion from the rank and society of Poets, by reflecting that men much his superiors were likewise shut out, and more especially when he finds also that men not much his superiors are entitled to admission.

But in whatever degree I may venture to differ from any others in my notions of the qualifications and character of the true Poet, I most cordially assent to their opinion who assert that his principal exertions must be made to engage the attention of his Readers; and further, I must allow that the effect of Poetry should be to lift the mind from the painful realities of actual existence, from its every-day concerns, and its perpetually-occurring vexations, and to give it repose by substituting objects in their place which it may contemplate with some degree of interest and satisfaction: but what is there in all this, which may not be effected by a fair representation of existing character? nay, by a faithful delineation of those painful realities, those every-day concerns, and those perpetually-occurring vexations themselves, provided they be not (which is hardly to be supposed) the very concerns and distresses of the Reader? for when it is admitted that they have no particular relation to him, but are the troubles and anxieties of other men, they excite and interest his feelings as the imaginary exploits, adventures, and perils of romance;—they soothe his mind, and keep his curiosity pleasantly awake; they appear to have enough of reality to engage his sympathy, but possess not interest sufficient to create painful sensations. Fiction itself, we know, and every work of fancy, must for a time have the effect of realities; nay, the very enchanters, spirits, and monsters of *Ariosto* and *Spenser* must be present in the mind of the Reader while he is engaged by their operations, or they would be as the objects and incidents of a Nursery Tale to a rational understanding, altogether despised and neglected: in truth, I can but consider this pleasant effect upon the mind of a Reader, as depending neither upon the events related (whether they be actual or imaginary), nor upon the characters introduced (whether taken from life or fancy), but upon the manner in which the Poem itself is conducted; let that be judiciously managed, and the occurrences actually copied from life will have the same happy effect as the inventions of a creative fancy;— while, on the other hand, the imaginary persons and incidents to which the Poet has given '*a local habitation, and a name,*' will make upon the concurring feelings of the Reader, the same impressions with those taken from truth and nature, because they will appear to be derived from that source, and therefore of necessity will have a similar effect.

Having thus far presumed to claim for the ensuing pages the rank and title of Poetry, I attempt no more, nor venture to class or compare them with any other kinds of poetical composition; their place will doubtless be found for them.

A principal view and wish of the Poet must be to engage the mind of his Readers, as, failing in that point, he will scarcely succeed in any other: I therefore willingly confess that much of my time and assiduity has been devoted to this purpose; but, to the ambition of pleasing, no other sacrifices have, I trust, been made, than of my own labour and care. Nothing will be found that militates against the rules of propriety and good manners, nothing that offends against the more important precepts of morality and religion; and with this negative kind of merit, I commit my Book to the judgment and taste of the Reader,—not being willing to provoke his vigilance by professions of accuracy, nor to solicit his indulgence by apologies for mistakes.

31. Unsigned review, *British Review*

October 1812, iv, 51–64

To strike out a new path of interest or entertainment, either in poetry or prose, is become a task of some difficulty in this advanced age of literary competition. And it is no wonder if the struggle after novelty, where novelty is so hard to be found, should produce some anomalies in composition which rest their merit principally on their departure from long-existing practice. To this ambition of doing something not yet achieved, we are perhaps to attribute that rhythmetical prose which, but a short time ago, was a prevailing fashion, and from a similar cause we may perhaps deduce a late practice of writing poetry in the style and language of prose.

We are well aware that we are to look for the sublimest and most affecting passages of our greatest poets among those in which there is the least appearance of studied ornament, and the most unambitious use of language. The words in the passages to which we allude are usually taken warm and breathing from the intercourse of common life; but a reader of delicate ear and correct judgment soon becomes sensible that a certain secret in the arrangement and application of these homely words imparts to them, under the magical controul of these great masters, an effect not to be produced by the most shining assemblage of magnificent terms. For example in proof of the propriety of this observation, we may refer generally to Shakspeare and Milton.

But whatever may be the grace arising from a skilful combination of *single* words of low origin, the same poetical result is not to be produced by the adoption of the phraseology and idiom of vulgar life. Cowper descended lower than any bard had done before him, and it must be confessed that it required a general excellence like his to atone for the wilful negligences of his style in many parts. General excellence has a tendency to consecrate occasional faults; and Cowper's defects, like the scanty vest and rugged manners of Cato, have, insensibly perhaps, been an object of imitation to those who have had but little taste for his perfections. It is but justice, however, to this exquisite poet, and best of moral satirists, to remark, that he has, in numberless instances, produced, from the same sort of materials with which the plastic powers of Shakspeare and Milton wrought so successfully, the same surprizing fabrics.

But besides this beautiful application of ordinary terms, there is, it must be admitted, an ease, sporting on the very margin of negligence, which is very captivating in poetic composition, when its subject is the display of the manners or events of common life. But it fares with ease in composition, as it fares with what is usually called ease in behaviour: one is apt to suppose it consists merely in negation, and that to be graceful without the appearance of study, nothing is required but the absence of study. The supposition is natural, but very erroneous. Ease is, in truth, the consummation of art, and the last refinement of labour. It is not a blank, or meagre outline, but may be compared to a mellow assortment of colours, which gives repose to the eye, propagating its pleasing effects, and making all around it partake of its character. 'Componit furtim subsequiturque decor'.[1]

Among the various departments of writing, there are none either in prose or poetry to which true ease is more becoming than tales, such as

1 Grace follows her unseen to order all aright. Tibullus, III, 8, 8 (Loeb translation).

those in which Gower, Chaucer, and Boccaccio, have given us the picture of their own times. But in the ease which is so necessary to this species of writing, consists, if we mistake not, the difficulty of its execution, and the reason of the rarity of these productions since the age of the three contemporary geniuses to whom we have alluded. Such, indeed, is the merit of this *arduous ease* in the execution of the task of agreeable story-telling, that on this principally is founded the lofty reputation of Dryden, Swift, Prior, and Gay, Fontaine, Cervantes, and Marmontel; little else of their tales being their own except the manner of telling them. . . .

If these remarks are just (and we are afraid of their being considered as trite rather than paradoxical) in respect to the composition of tales in general, they are surely so in a peculiar degree when applied to tales composed in verse. It has been said of Chaucer by an eminent judge, that he was the first who taught his native language to express itself poetically, and that this was chiefly done by him in his tales. If for this we are to thank and commend the father of English poetry, we must, to be consistent, condemn those who, in this same walk of literature, force the muse to tread back her steps, and descend into that uncon-secrated region where poets seek only to come intelligibly to the point, express themselves like men of business, and relate their unvarnished tales, as honest men deliver matters of fact.

We have now brought our observations to a point, and we are sorry to say they center in the production which now lies before us. We are the more sorry to say it, because, from the specimens this gentleman has heretofore given us of his poetry, we are impressed with a very high respect for his genius and talents. In the present work his object seems to have been to secure himself on the side of rhyme and metre, and to leave everything else to chance. His poems remind us of the imitations of our English gardens, which we have formerly observed upon the continent, in which the ingenious owners, having no conception of any mode of controuling or regulating nature but by coercing her into quincunxes and parterres, contented themselves with paling in an area of ground, and then leaving its rambling vegetation to grow up at its leisure into a forest or wilderness. We are far from intending any reflection on Mr. Crabbe's general taste, or to compare him generally with the misjudging persons to whom we have alluded; but we mean by the similitude to mark in a strong manner our sense of the mistake into which we think he has been carried, by a love somewhat too un-distinguishing of nature and simplicity. In the area which Mr. Crabbe has inclosed, his most careless progress could not fail to leave the vestiges of genius, and many a magnificent feature would be sure to attest the creative hand of the proprietor.

We differ from some of his critics, who have blamed in very general terms the selection of his subjects. Fiction is not the only province of poetry. Some of its best energies have been displayed on the familiar incidents of domestic detail, the delineation of common character, and the vicissitudes of vulgar happiness and sorrow. It cannot, however, be denied, that there are some realities of existence so gross, or so trivial, as to be fairly out of the jurisdiction of the poet, and flatly incapable of any interest or embellishment. And we doubt whether it may not with justice be imputed to Mr. Crabbe, that, without sufficient consideration of these radical differences in the character of the subjects, which life in its ordinary walks suggests to the poet's search, he has regarded nothing as too low, too particular, too obscure, or too minute, to be swept into the inventory of his busy muse. The amiable maxim in the play 'Homo sum, humani nihil a me alienum puto',[1] he seems to apply to himself in his character of poet.

Independently of this objection, we really feel obliged to Mr. Crabbe for giving us a little of truth instead of fiction in his poetry. We have been so long assailed by the wonderful and terrific in the poems and romances of the present day; our tranquillity has been so long disturbed by knights and wizards, by Saracens and magicians, that it is some comfort to feel ourselves with Mr. Crabbe in a whole skin among beings like ourselves, and without a hippogryph or dragon at our elbow.

If Mr. Crabbe cannot claim an equal rank with Chaucer in the variety and compass of his powers, and is below him in bold delineation of character, he has in these tales proved himself happy in seizing the little peculiarities of mind, and those strong though small complexional tints and shades, which discriminate the heroes of the cottage and the counter. For descriptive imagery his subjects have afforded him but little opportunity, but those local characteristics and striking appearances of nature or art which are connected with the interest of his narrative, he knows well how to present in their most affecting forms.

There is one distinction between the performance of Mr. Crabbe and those of the writers (we except of course the other sex) who have trod the same path before him, which we should notice as reflecting

[1] I am a man and I do not regard anything concerning men as outside my concern. Terence, *Heautontimorumenos*, I, 25.

no small honour upon his muse, if we did not recollect the sacred function with which he is invested. His tales are free from every stain of indecency. In his closest copies of life he has not disgusted us with any gross exhibitions, or for the sake of gratifying a too numerous class of readers, has stooped to the indignity of titillating a loose imagination by allusions, jests, or descriptions of a vitiating or prurient tendency. We have so often spoken out upon this subject, that our readers will not be surprized at our now declaring, that with all our love of poetry and homage of genius, we would gladly consent to have all that now lives in verse of Chaucer and Prior blotted out of existence, if so we might be rid of the filthy tales which they have produced to the disgrace of their own memories, their own times, and of literature in general. . . .

Our author's stories are all of the most simple structure. Each turns upon a single event, and is designed to impress some useful lesson of prudence, some practical moral, coupled for the most part with a vivid display of contrast in character and manners. The reader is never embarrassed by the intricacy of the narrative; the actors are few; and the hero of the tale is conducted to the catastrophe, not by a series of surprising adventures, or an unexpected coincidence, or the disclosure of a long-buried mystery; but, a character being drawn and stated, and a situation supposed, (which situation is generally a very natural one, and such as is apt to determine a man's career of action), an ordinary train of consequences is made to follow in a succession agreeable to experience and the course of human affairs.

It must be confessed, however, that in most of the tales simplicity exceeds its proper measure. They want the necessary stamina of a story, and are incapable of exciting curiosity, or of fixing attention. In one or two of them the main incident is too ordinary, and the moral too trite to be worth the rhymes in which they are conveyed.

Another prevailing fault we are bound to notice, as it characterizes more or less every one of the tales, we mean an abruptness in passing from one fact, speaker, or scene, to another, leaving the chasm to be supplied by the reader as he can. By this practice, the poet has contrived, notwithstanding the simplicity of the story, to render it obscure, and to create frequent interruptions to the flow of the narrative. We do not say that sometimes this may not be done with good effect; but there is always danger that the facility with which a writer fills up in his own mind every break or omission, and smooths every transition, may lead him to suppose in the reader a similar promptitude;—a mistake too obvious to be enlarged upon.

The turn of Chaucer's mind was cheerful, and the gaiety of his disposition is reflected in his writings. They possess a festive humour, and a sportive variety of character, which is not found in the productions of Mr. Crabbe. The volume in our hands is not a mirror in which poor human nature, even in the social and educated man, sees a sprightly image of herself; and Mr. Crabbe must forgive us for hoping that the imperfection of the glass gives us back ourselves with some infidelity and distortion. His representation is the more painful, as it imports to be a faithful copy of living manners; and it is difficult to escape from the general sentence of degradation pronounced upon us, but by supposing the writer to speak a language dictated by a partial acquaintance with men, or provoked by particular disappointments. We are not apt to rate our fallen nature too high; but we cannot think the malignancy of conduct and temper which this volume describes so frequent in the present state of humanity, under the influence of religion and education, as to amount to more than exceptions to a rule, and if properly only exceptions, then it appears to us that they ought not to be exhibited as specimens of human character, unless under such circumstances as make them seem to be forced into existence by extraordinary incidents, encouragements, or provocations. The heart is rather hardened than corrected by these degrading views of its character. A tacit reservation in favour of oneself prevents its operation as a lesson of humility, while it shuts up the fountains of charity and benevolence towards our fellow creatures.

We have before remarked that this volume is free from the slightest tendency to what is immoral or indecent, but we have not remarked it as being extraordinary in a person of the author's holy vocation. It would be satire to remark as *extraordinary* the respect for religion which appears generally through the book. But as in the other works of Mr. Crabbe, we do not remember that he found an opportunity of making known his impressions on this subject, we were the more pleased at the indications dispersed over these tales, of an union of piety with genius. They meet together with propriety in a poem, which has discarded the *illusions* of poetry, and undertakes the task of improving us by examples which come home to our business and bosoms.

It is quite impossible to lay a fair specimen of this performance before our readers, without extracting a whole tale or two from the book. This, however, would be a method of doing him justice, which would not leave us room to do justice to the other publications which press upon our attention. By the perusal of the tale called 'The Mother', the reader will be able to judge of the author's sentiments on the power of religion. The circumstances of the story display no invention, and it is far from being the happiest as to style and manner. It contains, however, so pleasing and well wrought a picture of an interesting and virtuous maiden, that our female readers shall have an opportunity of being edified by it.

> A Village-maid unvex'd by want or love. . . .
> [VIII, 88–114]

The two most important poems in the volume are the 'Confidante' and 'Resentment.'

Summaries of the two, quoting

> Stafford, amus'd with books and fond of home, . . .
> [XVI, 462–590]

and

> Thus was the grieving man, with burthen'd ass. . . .
> [XVII, 341–422]

. . . That he has some faults as a writer we have ventured to suggest, but we are happy to add on the subject of those faults, that they seem all to be within the scope of his vigorous judgment to correct. His taste has been betrayed by too strong a bias to simplicity. But with all his faults he has supported his character as a powerful delineator of the passions, and a correct painter of moral scenes, as scientifically acquainted with the operations of feeling, and the springs of natural tenderness. If his style is mean, it is pure and grammatical, and there are sufficient specimens in this work of vigorous language, and elevated sentiment, to shew that, when he touches the bottom,—and he touches it too often,—he does so rather from choice than from necessity.

32. Unsigned review, *Scourge*

October 1812, iv, 386–94

It is seldom that the poetical or literary character of an individual remains unchanged through so long an interval as that which elapsed between the first productions of Mr. Crabbe, and the effusions of his age. The same views of life and human nature, the same predisposition to dwell with minuteness on the dark and unfavourable side of the poetical picture, and the same homeliness of diction, and affected ruggedness of verse, that impeded the success of the Village Curate [sic] among his early readers, are equally observable in his later volumes. His accuracy in the delineation of unpleasing objects, of the habitations of dependent and profligate indigence, of the smuggler's cottage, and the pauper's bed, of the noisome alley and the crowded ward, is not less apparent in the compositions of the reverend and respectable vicar, than in the effusions of the young and aspiring deacon, while his pictures of life are relieved by a greater variety of action, and his descriptions embellished by a more minute and diversified observation of the human character.

But unfortunately Mr. Crabbe, like all preceding votaries of literary fame, too easily intoxicated by public approbation, and unwilling to discriminate between those excellencies that have in themselves contributed to his success, and those deformities which have only been forgiven in consideration of the beauties by which they were accompanied, has thought it necessary, in his later works, to obtrude upon the public eye in all the prominence of display, every peculiarity of phraseology and versification, that the admirers of his early writings had most sincerely lamented, or the most earnestly corrected. He should have remembered that it was for the truth of his delineations, the force of his description, and the occasional pathos of his sentiment, that he had received the gratitude of the public and the praise of criticism. His quaintness of expression, his inaccuracy of rhyme, the ruggedness of his verse, his occasional attempts at wit, and the inanimate prosing that distinguished a considerable portion of his didactic efforts, were lamented as the unavoidable, or forgiven as the excusable, peculiarities of a poet, who atoned for their existence by great and various excellencies. The candid regarded them with indulgence, and the fastidious with an impatience proportioned to the gratification that they so frequently repressed or interrupted.

It is with pleasure that we have observed the Tales in Verse to be in a great measure purified from the asperities of diction, and those affectations of phraseology by which his last production was distinguished. But he still mistakes homeliness for simplicity, and in his fear of extravagance, is content to be prosaic. Though many occasions occur for the full display of all the enthusiasm of poetry, and all the splendor of rhetorical embellishment, he studiously avoids them. To tell his story in parallel lines of ten syllables seems to be his sole ambition; and even the reader who admires the intimate knowledge of life and human nature, the accurate discrimination of character, and the ingenuity of invention that his effusions display, must be disposed to regret that he has not occasionally assumed a more lofty and animated tone, nor given to his descriptions at once the accuracy of truth, and the pathos and energy of poetical eloquence.

As the faults of Mr. Crabbe's compositions will be sufficiently evident even in the extracts that we make to elucidate his characteristic excellencies, we shall proceed to the more pleasing task of pointing out a few of the latter to the admiration of our readers.

Considered merely as tales, the different essays contained in the present volumes have no pretentions to peculiar merit. They are usually indeed nothing more than the detail of a single incident, or the description of common-place occurrences, accompanied by appropriate reflections. A young man of genius relies on the professions of his patron, is disappointed, returns home and dies of a broken heart. A sailor leaves his sweetheart, and after a long absence, finds the object of his former love wealthy, and therefore unkind. A farmer's daughter returns from the boarding school, with ideas and manners too refined for rustic occupations, and with a disgust for the unpolished beings who surround her. She is reclaimed by the advice of a neighbouring widow, who relates her own history, and becomes the happy wife of a rustic neighbour. In describing the knavery of the lower classes, he is most luxuriant and successful: the volume abounds with descriptions of knavish stationers, and humble companions to country gentlewomen.

We recommend the following advice to the consideration of all juvenile satirists.

Hear me, my boy, thou hast a virtuous mind, . . .
[V, 247–72]
With spirit high John learn'd the world to brave . . .
[XIX, 29–56, 103–38]

The great merit of the tales, depends, indeed, on their gradual development of character; and our readers can obtain but a faint idea of their excellence from detached extracts. Yet we cannot deny ourselves the pleasure of quoting a single passage, of which the effect when taken in connection with the other parts of the tale, is almost electrical.

True, he was sure that Isaac would receive . . .
[XX, 160–1, 166–76; 254–9 and 334–55]

On the whole there is sufficient merit in these volumes, to charm the contemplative, and satisfy the fastidious. But the merit is all of one kind, and Mr. Crabbe had already convinced us, that he is not less able to delight the critic, by the splendor of his imagery, and the melody of his verse, than to instruct the philosopher, by his sombre delineations of life and character. When he again presents himself to the notice of the public, we hope that he will appear in a less homely garb, and with a more gay and animated countenance. At present he is only a fit companion for the guests of Duke Humphrey, or the gloomy frequenters of the tabernacle.

33. Francis Jeffrey, unsigned review, *Edinburgh Review*

November 1812, xx, 277–305

We are very thankful to Mr. Crabbe for these *Tales*; as we must always be for any thing that comes from his hands. But they are not exactly the tales which we wanted. We did not, however, wish him to write an Epic—as he seems from his preface to have imagined. We are perfectly satisfied with the length of the pieces he has given us; and delighted with their number and variety. In these respects the volume is exactly as we could have wished it. But we should have liked a little more of the deep and tragical passions—of those passions which exalt and overwhelm the soul—to whose stormy seat the modern muses can so rarely raise their flight—and which he has wielded with such terrific force in his 'Sir Eustace Grey,' and the 'Gipsey Woman.' What we wanted, in short, were tales something in the style of those two singular compositions—with less jocularity than prevails in the rest of his writings—rather more incidents—and rather fewer details.

The pieces before us are not of this description;—they are mere supplementary chapters to *The Borough*, or *The Parish Register*. The same tone—the same subjects—the same style, measure, and versification;—the same finished and minute delineation of things quite ordinary and common,—generally very engaging when employed upon external objects, but often fatiguing when directed merely to insignificant characters and habits;—the same strange mixture too of feelings that tear the heart and darken the imagination, with starts of low humour and patches of ludicrous imagery;—the same kindly sympathy with the humble and innocent pleasures of the poor and inelegant, and the same indulgence for their venial offences, contrasted with a strong sense of their frequent depravity, and too constant a recollection of the sufferings it produces;—and, finally, the same honours paid to the delicate affections and ennobling passions of humble life, with the same generous testimony to their frequent existence, mixed up as before with a reprobation sufficiently rigid, and a ridicule sufficiently severe, of their excesses and affections.

Holding this opinion then as to the substantial identity of *the fabric* of this volume, both as to materials and workmanship, with that of those which the author has lately given to the world, we cannot think of taking up the time of our readers, either by renewing the attempt which we formerly made to characterize the peculiar style of poetry which they all exemplify, or by resuming the observations which we then ventured to offer as to its merits or defects. If we were required to make a comparative estimate of the merits of the present publication, or to point out the shades of difference by which it is distinguished from those that have gone before it, we should say that it has fewer passages that excite that mixed feeling of pain and disgust which this author was formerly so much given to raise, and rather more perhaps of those in which his rare gifts of observation and description are lavished upon objects which no fidelity in the rendering, and no skill in the finishing can ever make interesting: But especially we should say that there are a greater number of instances on which he has combined the natural language and manners of humble life with the energy of true passion, and the beauty of generous affection,—in which he has traced out the course of those rich and lovely veins even in the rude and unpolished masses that lye at the bottom of society,—and unfolded, in the middling orders of the people, the workings of those finer feelings, and the stirrings of those loftier emotions which the partiality of other poets had hitherto attributed almost exclusively to actors on a higher scene.

We hope, too, that this more amiable and consoling view of human nature will have the effect of rendering Mr. Crabbe still more popular than we know that he already is, among that great body of the people from among whom almost all his subjects are taken, and for whose use his lessons are chiefly intended: and we say this the rather, because it appears to us that the volume now before us is more uniformly and directly moral and beneficial in its tendency than any of those which he has hitherto given to the public—consists less of mere curious description and gratuitous dissections of character, but inculcates for the most part some weighty and practical precept, and points right on to the cheerful path by which duty leads us forward to enjoyment. In this point of view, indeed, we think that many of the stories in the present volume may be ranked by the side of the inimitable tales of Miss Edgeworth; and are calculated to do nearly as much good among that part of the population with which they are principally occupied.

But it is not only on account of the moral benefit which we think they may derive from them, that we would peculiarly recommend the writings of Mr. Crabbe to that great proportion of our readers which must necessarily belong to the middling or humbler classes of the community. We are persuaded that they will derive more pleasure from them than readers of any other description. Those who do not belong to that rank of society with which this powerful writer is chiefly conversant in his poetry, or who have not at least gone much among them, and attended diligently to their characters and occupations, can neither be half aware of the exquisite fidelity of his delineations, nor feel in their full force the better part of the emotions which he has suggested. Vehement passion indeed is of all ranks and conditions; and its language and external indications nearly the same in all. Like highly rectified spirit, it blazes and enflames with equal force and brightness from whatever materials it is extracted. But all the softer and kindlier affections, all the social anxieties that mix with our daily hopes, and endear our home, and colour our existence, wear a different livery, and are written in a different character in almost every great *caste* or division of society; and the heart is warmed, and the spirit is touched by their delineation, exactly in the same proportion in which we are familiar with the types by which they are represented.—When Burns, in his better days, walked out in a fine summer morning with Dugald Stewart, and the latter observed to him what a beauty the scattered cottages, with their white walls and curling smoke shining in the silent sun, imparted to the landscape, the peasant poet answered, that *he* felt that beauty ten times more strongly than his companion; and that it was necessary to be a cottager to know what pure and tranquil pleasures nestled below those lowly roofs, or to read, in their external appearance, the signs of so many heartfelt and long-remembered enjoyments. In the same way, the humble and patient hopes—the depressing embarrassments—the little mortifications—the slender triumphs, and strange temptations which arise in middling life, and are the theme of Mr. Crabbe's finest and most touching representations,—can only be guessed at by those who glitter in the higher walks of existence; while they must raise many a tumultuous throb and many a fond recollection in the breasts of those to whom they reflect so truly the image of their own estates and reveal so clearly the secrets of their habitual sensations.

We cannot help thinking, therefore, that though such writings as are now before us must give great pleasure to all persons of taste and sensibility, they will give by far the greatest pleasure to those whose condition is least remote from that of the beings with whom they are occupied. But we think also, that it was wise and meritorious in Mr. Crabbe to occupy himself with such beings. In this country, there probably are not less than two hundred thousand persons who read for amusement or instruction among the middling classes* of society. In the higher classes, there are not as many as twenty thousand. It is easy to see therefore which a poet should choose to please for his own glory and emolument, and which he should wish to delight and amend out of mere philanthropy. The fact too we believe is, that a great part of the larger body are to the full as well educated and as high-minded as the smaller; and, though their taste may not be so correct and fastidious, we are persuaded that their sensibility is greater. The misfortune is, to

* By the middling classes, we mean almost all those who are below the sphere of what is called fashionable or public life, and who do not aim at distinction or notoriety beyond the circle of their equals in fortune and situation.

be sure, that they are extremely apt to affect the taste, and to counterfeit even that absurd disdain of their superiors, of which they are themselves the objects; and that poets have generally thought it safest to invest their interesting characters with all the trappings of splendid fortune and high station, chiefly because those who know least about such matters think it unworthy to sympathize in the adventures of those who are without them. For our own parts, however, we are quite positive, not only that persons in middling life would naturally be most touched with the emotions that belong to their own condition, but that those emotions are in themselves the most powerful, and consequently the best fitted for poetical or pathetical representation. Even with regard to the heroic and ambitious passions, as the vista is longer which leads from humble privacy to the natural objects of those passions; so, the career is likely to be longer and more impetuous, and its outset more marked by striking and contrasted emotions:—and as to all the more tender and less turbulent affections, upon which the beauty of the pathetic is altogether dependent, we apprehend it to be quite manifest, that their proper soil and *nidus* is the privacy and simplicity of humble life;—that their very elements are dissipated by the variety of objects that move for ever in the world of fashion; and their essence tainted by the cares and vanities that are diffused in the atmosphere of that lofty region. But we are wandering into a long dissertation, instead of making our readers acquainted with the book before us. The most satisfactory thing we can do, we believe, is to give them a plain account of its contents, with such quotations and remarks as may occur to us as we proceed.

The volume contains twenty-one tales;—the first of which is called 'The Dumb Orators.' This is not one of the most engaging; and is not judiciously placed at the portal to tempt hesitating readers to go forward. The fault, however, is entirely in the subject, which commands no strong or general interest; for it is perfectly well conceived and executed. . . .

Meetings, or public calls, he never miss'd—
[I, 45–73]

The second tale, entitled 'The Parting Hour,' is of a more tender character, and contains some passages of great beauty and pathos.

All things prepar'd, on the expected day . . .
[II, 109–28; 183–210, 213–36; 285–90, 295–300 and 325–34]

The close is extremely beautiful, and leaves upon the mind just that impression of sadness which is both salutary and delightful, because it is akin to pity, and mingled with admiration and esteem.

> Here his relation closes, but his mind . . .
> [II, 434-73]

The third tale is 'The Gentleman Farmer,' and is of a coarser texture than that we have just been considering,—though full of acute observation, and graphic delineation of ordinary characters. . . .

The next which is called 'Procrastination,' has something of the character of 'The Parting Hour'; but more painful and less refined. . . .

> Heav'n's spouse thou art not; nor can I believe . . .
> [IV, 267-318]

[Summarises 'The Patron' and quotes

> Cold grew the foggy morn; the day was brief . . .
> (V, 426-39, 444-57, 504-9, 626-31, 642-53)]

'The Frank Courtship,' which is the next in order, is rather in the merry vein; and contains even less than Mr. Crabbe's usual moderate allowance of incident.

> The couple gaz'd, were silent, and the Maid . . .
> [VI, 337-52]

'The Widow's Tale' is also rather of the facetious order.

. . . The account of her horrors, on first coming down, is in Mr. Crabbe's best style of Dutch painting—a little coarse, and needlessly minute—but perfectly true, and marvellously coloured.

> Us'd to *spare* meals, dispos'd in manner pure . . .
> [VII, 7-30]

'The Mother' is not one of the most felicitous of Mr. Crabbe's imaginations. . . .

'Arabella', again, is somewhat jocular. . . .

> Let us proceed:—Twelve brilliant years were past . . .
> [IX, 226-49]

'The Lover's Journey' is a pretty fancy; and very well executed,—at least as to the descriptions it contains. . . .

The following picture of a *fen* is what few other artists would have thought of attempting, and no other could possibly have executed.

When next appear'd a *dam*,—so call the place,— . . .
[X, 102–28]

The features of the fine country are less perfectly drawn: But what, indeed, could be made of the vulgar fine country of *England*? If Mr. Crabbe had had the good fortune to live among *our* Highland hills, and lakes, and upland woods—our living floods sweeping the forests of pine—our lonely vales and rough copse-covered cliffs; what a delicious picture would his unrivalled powers have enabled him to give to the world!—But we have no right to complain, while we have such pictures as this of a group of Gypsies. It is evidently finished *con amore*, and does appear to us to be absolutely perfect, both in its moral and its physical expression.

Again, the country was enclos'd, a wide . . .
[X, 141–95]

The next story, which is entitled 'Edward Shore,' also contains many passages of exquisite beauty. . . .
The ultimate downfall of this lofty mind, with its agonizing gleams of transitory recollection, form a picture, than which we do not know if the whole range of our poetry, rich as it is in representations of disordered intellect, furnishes anything more touching, or delineated with more truth and delicacy.

Harmless at length th' unhappy man was found . . .
[XI, 432–67]

'Squire Thomas' is not nearly so interesting . . .
'Jesse and Colin' pleases us better . . .
There is a great deal of goodheartedness in this tale, and a kind of moral beauty, which has lent more than usual elegance to the simple pictures it presents. We are tempted to extract a good part of the *denouement*.

Then when she dares not, would not, cannot go . . .
[XIII, 409–42, 461–76, 486–506, 509–14]

'The Struggles of Conscience,' though visibly laboured, and, we should suspect, a favourite with the author, pleases us less than any tale in the volume. . . .
'The Squire and the Priest' we do not like much better. . . .
'The Confidant' is more interesting; though not altogether pleasing . . .

'Resentment' is one of the pieces in which Mr. Crabbe has exercised his extraordinary powers of giving pain—though not gratuitously in this instance,—nor without inculcating a strong lesson of forgiveness and compassion.

. . . Of all the pictures of mendicant poverty that have ever been brought forward in prose or verse—in charity sermons or seditious harangues—we know of none half so moving or complete—so powerful and so true—as is contained in the following passages.

A dreadful winter came, each day severe . . .
[XVII, 351–9, 366–73, 389–96, 401–12]

'The Wager' is not of this tragical complexion . . .

'The Convert' is rather dull—though it teaches a lesson that may be useful in these fanatic times. . . .

'The Brothers' restores us again to human sympathies.

. . . The great art of the story consists in the plausible excuses with which the ungrateful brother always contrives to cover his wickedness. This cannot be exemplified in an extract; but we shall give a few lines as a specimen.

Cold as he grew, still *Isaac* strove to show, . . .
[XX, 207–30, 280–91, 300–11]

The last tale in the volume, entitled 'The Learned Boy,' is not the most interesting in the collection . . .

We have thus gone through this volume with a degree of minuteness for which we are not sure that even our poetical readers will all be disposed to thank us. But considering Mr. Crabbe as, upon the whole, the most original writer who has ever come before us; and being at the same time of opinion, that his writings are destined to a still more extensive popularity than they have yet obtained, we could not resist the temptation of contributing our little aid to the fulfilment of that destiny. It is chiefly for the same reason that we have directed our remarks rather to the moral than the literary qualities of his works; —to his genius at least, rather than his taste—and to his thoughts rather than his figures of speech. By far the most remarkable thing in his writings, is the prodigious mass of original observations and reflections they everywhere exhibit; and that extraordinary power of conceiving and representing an imaginary object, whether physical or intellectual, with such a rich and complete accompaniment of circumstances and details, as few ordinary observers either perceive or remember in realities;—a power which, though often greatly misapplied, must for ever entitle him to the very first rank among descriptive poets; and, when directed to worthy objects, to a rank inferior to none in the highest departments of poetry.

In such an author, the attributes of style and versification may fairly be considered as secondary;—and yet, if we were to go minutely into them, they would afford room for a still longer chapter than that which we are now concluding. He cannot be said to be uniformly, or even generally, an elegant writer. His style is not dignified—and neither very pure nor very easy. Its characters are force, precision, and familiarity;— now and then obscure—sometimes vulgar, and sometimes quaint. With a great deal of tenderness, and occasional fits of the sublime of despair and agony, there is a want of habitual fire, and of a tone of enthusiasm in the general tenor of his writings. He seems to recollect rather than invent; and frequently brings forward his statements more in the temper of a cautious and conscientious witness, than of a fervent orator or impassioned spectator. His similes are almost all elaborate and ingenious, and rather seem to be furnished from the efforts of a fanciful mind, than to be exhaled by the spontaneous ferment of a heated imagination. His versification again is frequently harsh and heavy, and his diction flat and prosaic;—both seeming to be altogether neglected in his zeal for the accuracy and complete rendering of his conceptions. These defects too are infinitely greater in his recent than in his early compositions. *The Village* is written, upon the whole, in a flowing and sonorous strain of versification; and 'Sir Eustace Grey,' though a late publication, is in general remarkably rich and melodious. It is chiefly in his narratives and curious descriptions that these faults of diction and measure are conspicuous. Where he is warmed by his subject, and becomes fairly indignant or pathetic, his language is often very sweet and beautiful. He has no fixed system or manner of versification; but mixes several very opposite styles, as it were by accident, and not in general very judiciously;—what is peculiar to himself is not good, and strikes us as being both abrupt and affected.

He may profit, if he pleases, by these hints—and, if he pleases, he may laugh at them. It is no great matter. If he will only write a few more Tales of the kind we have suggested at the beginning of this article, we shall engage for it that he shall have our praises—and those of more fastidious critics,—whatever be the qualities of his style or versification.

34. Thomas Denman, unsigned review, *Monthly Review*

December 1812, lxix, 352–64

Very few of our poets have run a more singular career than the author of this volume. After having exhibited, at an early age, such specimens of talent as insured him general popularity and critical approbation, and might have stimulated the most languid and the least ambitious to farther exertions, he remained contented with the garlands of his youth for five-and-twenty years: but when, after the lapse of that long period, he resumed his labors, he produced in a short time three considerable works, each exceeding the aggregate of all that he had accomplished before. We trust that he will annually proceed, for many years to come, to excite our wonder in the same manner; and that each successive volume will continue to deserve the praise, which we think is justly due to the present, of improving in all the qualities of a youthful muse,— in grace and spirit, in copiousness, vigor, and sensibility.

Perhaps those of our readers, who have already judged for themselves on the merit of these poems, will arrest us here at the outset; and, while they admit the title of Mr. Crabbe to all the other parts of our panegyric, they will vehemently exclaim against the notion of his deserving any compliments on the score of grace or elegance. We flatter ourselves, however, that our position will be established in all its parts to the satisfaction of this class of censors; to whom, on the other hand, we will frankly own that great concessions are also to be made. That a large proportion of these compositions is wholly without grace, and opposed to elegance,—that they are in several places loaded with unnecessary rubbish, and degraded by useless vulgarity,—it is, we fear, impossible to deny. We lament this the more because it seems to be the result of a system, and might have been easily avoided by the writer of such passages as we shall presently lay before our readers; and we acknowledge that, in our estimation, indiscriminating minuteness and coarse particularity are not to be justified by the additional air of probability, with which they are supposed to invest a fictitious narrative. Not that we complain, after the manner of some contemporary critics, to whom this most patient and reasonable of authors has not refused to offer a reply, that the illusion of his fiction is *too* perfect; that the legitimate object of poetry is to deceive the reader; and that, therefore, (for such is the argument) the deception becomes faulty when it most nearly resembles reality: but we are disposed to question whether verisimilitude be in truth increased by an enumeration of such particulars, as we are sure would be omitted and overlooked by a person who was relating a series of real facts. Richardson, indeed, who wished to create between his reader and his *dramatis personæ* such a degree of intimacy as should outlast nine close volumes, might be excused for describing even the china cups and the chintz furniture. Teniers and Wilkie, on the other hand, may minutely delineate pots, pans, and cabbages, the alembic of the alchemist, the various machines employed by the conjuror, and the ragged hat and starved face of the blind fidler, because all these things may be kept in due subordination to the principal purpose and leading effect of the respective pictures. In short stories, however, the main interest of which depends commonly on a single crisis, the minor ingredients of character are wasted, and the leading features are alone required; while a full detail of little circumstances occupies the same space in a poem (or probably much more), as the grand and decisive events which are calculated to excite the strongest feelings. Confusion is likewise apt to be produced between different tales; and we must add that, in this age of parody, the temptation to caricature such obvious defects becomes almost irresistible. In truth, on some occasions this author might, himself, be suspected of the wish to burlesque his own prevailing style, by pushing it to a ridiculous excess.

This extensive admission of the prominent vice in the writing of Mr. Crabbe will secure us from the suspicion of being actuated by blind partiality to that gentleman, in the opinion which we have formed of his merits: but, as his mildness under critical reproof is exemplary, and as he has frequently done us the honor of noticing our remarks and sometimes of adopting our advice, we will just observe that his reason for declining to attempt a more considerable work appears to us to savor of modesty or indolence, rather than to proceed on a just appreciation of his own powers; and that our objection to the want of unity in his poem of *The Borough*, the subject of which admitted a general bond of connection, does not apply to a professed collection of tales, every one of which is in itself a perfect narrative.

The Tales before us are twenty-one in number, and very dissimilar in quality. The first in order contains one very well drawn character, but has little else to recommend it; and the last of the series, borrowed from the 108th number of the *Tatler*, relates how a foolish boy was horse-whipped by his father out of the errors of Atheism into the faith of a good Christian. We prefer every other tale in the volume to these two. . . .

[There follows a lengthy summary with quotation of Tales II and V.]

'The Lover's Journey' is a delightful poem; and 'Edward Shore' is a deeply affecting story. . . .

'Resentment' is a dreadful but (we fear) not an unnatural story: its catastrophe has too great an affinity to that of 'The Brothers.' In these two stories, and 'The Confidant,' Mr. Crabbe has displayed his uncommon keenness of searching into the mind of man, united with a remarkable power of affecting the feelings: in most of the remaining tales, he has been satisfied with the former. 'Arabella' and 'The Mother' are admirable in this class. 'Jesse and Colin' combines some excellent traits of ordinary life with all the interest of a genuine pastoral.

. . . One or two observations still remain to be offered. First, the author's style is improved by the paring away of awkward and uncouth phrases, which were objectionable in some of his former works: but, secondly, the narrative is too often disfigured by a very unpleasant habit of attempting to pun. '*High-applauding* voice, that gained him *high applause*;' [I, 474], '*Choice* of rare songs, and garlands of *choice* flowers; And all the hungry mind *without a choice*,' [V, 22–3] &c. &c. Examples of this kind seem to take for granted not only that all puns must be witty, but that all jingles of words must be puns. One instance occurs of a real pun, though not very happy in itself, inhumanly obtruded on the reader in the most affecting moment of one of the best stories. We allude to that in the second and third lines of the hundredth page [V, 616–17], and earnestly hope to see it expunged from the next edition.[1]

On Mr. Crabbe's general character as a poet, we deem it scarcely necessary now to offer a single word. The public has pronounced, and this volume is not likely to alter their verdict. If, indeed, we were compelled to institute a comparison between it and its precursors, we should be inclined to say decidedly that it sometimes attains a higher degree of poetical merit, but should doubt whether it did not also exhibit a larger portion of what might have been advantageously

[1] It was, in the fourth edition (1813).

spared:—'Lesser than Macbeth, yet much greater; not so happy, yet far happier.'

After having perused the quotations which we have made, the reader will learn with a smile that the writer of them has received an intimation from some of his critical supervisors that, whatever credit he may deserve as a faithful delineator of men, manners, and things, he must not aspire to the name of a POET; at which he seems not a little distressed. In the preface, he labors the point at some length, with infinite humility and diffidence, and endeavours to shew that he ought in fairness to be comprised within any legitimate definition of the word. We will not, however, venture to prophecy what turns of language the enlightened metaphysics of modern times may produce: but this we will offer by way of consolation to Mr. Crabbe, that, when his name is struck off the roll of poets, not only Romeo's Apothecary, and Chamont's Witch, Pope's Sir Balaam, and his Death of Buckingham, but the better half of Shakespeare's plays, must no longer bear the name of poetry.

35. Unsigned review, *Critical Review*

December 1812, ii, 561–79

The names of Voltaire and Crebillon never divided the critics of Paris into contrary parties more effectually than this world of ours is now set at variance by the disputed merits of Mr. Crabbe. It is not unusual at the present day to find one's self in a society of which one half is loud in extolling him as *a poet* in the truest sense of the word—as the *inventor* or *creator* (ὁ ποιητης) of a new field for the exercise of the imagination—and on that account worthy of a comparison with the greatest original geniuses of antiquity—while the other is roused to indignation by the bare idea of what appears to them so exaggerated and almost blasphemous an elevation, and, running headlong to the contrary extreme, refuses him even the name of a poet, and all pretensions to the alleged qualifications of poetry, to the high honours of invention and imagination, whatever. The most remarkable feature in the present controversy is, that both parties are right, at least in their premises, whatever may be the consequence as to the conclusions they respectively draw from them. Mr. Crabbe is absolutely and indubitably a poet in the sense which his admirers annex to the term; and, although in the other and more popular acceptation of the phrase, we cannot admit in the full extent which is sometimes contended for, his want of all pretension to the dignity demanded by him, yet we must confess that his general style and disposition are such as in a great degree to bear out his objectors in their refusal. On examining the subject more in detail, we find ourselves also compelled to admit the justice of almost every censure and of almost every praise that he has received; and, to reconcile these apparent contradictions, and try both praise and censure by the test afforded us in his most recent publication, will be the principal object of our present article.

On the appearance of his last work, *The Borough*, he received from some of his warmest panegyrists a piece of advice which we thought at the time rather misplaced, and which we are not at all sorry to find was lost upon its object. Mr. Crabbe was recommended, as we recollect, to turn his thoughts thenceforward to the construction of some interesting and connected story. Now we never imagined that Pope would have made any thing of his intended epic on the conquest of this island by Brute the Trojan; and it is surely no ill compliment to Mr. Crabbe to suppose that he also would have failed where Pope was not qualified to succeed. A resemblance has before been remarked in the genius of these two poets; and we think that a strong resemblance certainly does exist, and that it consists in a happy perception of strong individual traits of character, and a peculiar power of delineating them, which go far towards constituting the whole excellence of satirical and didactic poetry, but a very small way in exciting dramatic or epic interest. In many of the qualities which are necessary to these far different purposes, we conceive Mr. Crabbe to be altogether deficient; and of this a stronger proof can scarcely be afforded than by his present publication, which, though he has chosen to give to it the title of *Tales*, consists rather of insulated descriptions of character and manners than of that species of narrative to which the denomination of fable properly applies. Out of the twenty-one separate pieces with which we are here presented, by far the greater number, at least, such as 'The Dumb Orators,' 'The Gentleman Farmer,' 'The Frank Courtship,' 'The Widow's Tale,'

'Arabella,' 'The Lover's Journey,' 'Edward Shore,' 'The precipitate Choice,' 'The Struggles of Conscience,' 'The Convert,' 'The Learned Boy,' and others, wear much more the appearance of characters to be inserted in some description or satirical essay than of separate historical narrations, which demand the interest of incident as well as of character to support them; and (although we are little disposed on our own parts to quarrel with mere names, which are in themselves indifferent), we think that many of the objections which will be made to the present publication, might probably have been avoided, if some such title as that of 'Characteristic Sketches of Life,' had been given to it, instead of that which the author has assumed.

In order to complete the catalogue of pieces which the volume contains, and at the same time to divide them into the three classes, which we think may be fairly instituted to receive them, we will now enumerate the titles in the following order. Those which appear to us to contain the largest portion of Mr. Crabbe's peculiar and acknowledged beauties, and to have afforded the widest scope to the exercise of his powers, are 'The parting Hour,' 'The Patron,' 'The Lover's Journey,' 'Edward Shore,' to which we would perhaps add 'The Confidant,' and 'Resentment.' In those which follow, 'The Dumb Orators,' 'The Gentleman Farmer,' 'Procrastination,' 'The Frank Courtship,' 'The Widow's Tale,' 'The Mother,' 'Arabella,' 'Jesse and Colin,' 'The Wager,' 'The Convert,' and 'The Brothers,' either his faults and his beauties have been so equally dealt, or his powers have been so much cramped by the defect of the subject, that they may be fairly set down in a middling or neutral class—but 'The Struggles of Conscience,' 'Squire Thomas, or the precipitate Choice,' 'Advice, or the Squire and the Priest,' and 'The Learned Boy,' are performances which deserve a much smaller share of indulgence, and must therefore be set down among the decidedly bad. Not but in the very best there are unfortunate blemishes, by the aid of which Mr. Crabbe's detractors may turn the whole into ridicule; while in the very worst there are traces of genius and talent, which in the opinion of his admirers may, perhaps, redeem all their defects; and as for those which we have classed as neutrals, they may, (we think) very fairly be admitted into the higher, or degraded to the lower rank, according to the general inclination of the reader in favour of the author or otherwise.

The excellencies of Mr. Crabbe have thus been summed up by some of his most devoted lovers—force and truth of description—selection and condensation of expression. He is said to possess the strength and originality of Cowper. His versification is compared to that of Gold-smith. His language is commended for its strength and purity. His taste for the talents of selecting and grouping his objects. His descriptions for their minute resemblance and 'Chinese' accuracy. His reflections for their moral sensibility, and their alternate tone of sarcasm and pathos. With regard to the subjects he has chosen, the interest excited by humble life is said to be general, profound, and lasting. The most popular passages even of Shakespeare himself are of this nature; and if there is often no intrinsic beauty in the objects which he describes, the truth of nature nevertheless demands the description of them. Nay, the poet, as the painter, of low life *must* descend to particulars which in other subjects would be impertinent and obtrusive. A 'distinct locality and imaginary reality' must be given to his pictures. His objects must be distinguished with 'a minute and anatomical precision.' Thus, in the judgment of these writers, much of what at first sight and unconnected with the general design of his works, would necessarily be condemned as vulgar, bald, or prosaic, is in fact necessary to the completion of that design, and therefore to be ranked in the class of beauties rather than of defects.

In our opinion, Mr. Crabbe amply deserves every commendation which has thus been bestowed upon him; and, before we proceed to contemplate the other side of the picture, we shall present to our readers a few out of the many specimens which we might select from the volume now before us, in justification of our opinion. Our first extracts shall be from 'The Lover's Journey,' which, considered not as a tale, but (as we before denominated it) a sketch of character, merits every praise which it is possible for the warmest friends of the author to bestow upon it.

[Extensive quotation includes X, 1–17; 103–19, 124–8 and 141–97.]

The merits of this beautiful poem are too obvious to require any further illustration than that of our copious analysis; and we shall only advert to one of its minor excellencies, which might otherwise escape the reader's attention, that which we may venture to call its geographical precision and accuracy. Various as are the descriptions of natural scenery which it embraces, it is easy to believe that the whole may fall within the compass of a twenty miles' ride on the eastern coast of the island; and there is a truth, and (to adopt the expression of some former critics) a 'distinct locality' about it, which almost persuades us that Mr. Crabbe has himself (we will not say on a similar occasion) taken the very ride which he here describes, and that his pictures are neither drawn from imagination, nor strung together by the fancy, but taken from reality in the very succession in which he has placed them. . . .

In the tale of 'Edward Shore,' we are presented with a most powerful, though terrible, picture, of genius, confident in itself and in its imagined virtues, falling a victim to its own overweening strength, and becoming a prey to passions which terminate in madness. The opening verses are equally striking, from the boldness of sentiment and of versification.

> Genius! thou gift of Heav'n! thou light divine! . . .
> [XI, 1–30]

> Despis'd, asham'd; his noble views before . . .
> [XI, 309–31]

The unhappy man, deserted by human pride, and untaught to seek divine consolation and forgiveness, flies for relief to every species of vicious excess, and at last becomes a raving maniac. The gradual change of this horrible state of nature into the less fearful but yet more degraded condition of childish idiotism, is touched with a pencil which this most powerful painter alone possesses.

> Harmless at length th' unhappy man was found, . . .
> [XI, 432–5]

In this last stage of the afflicting history, and as a relief to the gloomy horror which it tends to inspire, one of those exquisitely touching traits of nature is introduced, which Mr. Crabbe knows how to command at pleasure, and which would alone be sufficient to stamp him with the rare character of a true and original poet.

> And as she trembling speaks, his lively eyes
> [XI, 450–7]

[Also quotes VI, 1–32, 153–67 and II, 436–73.]

Without disputing any more than is necessary about words, for which, (as words merely), we again repeat, we have no value, it does appear to us an extremely childish perversion of language to deny the praise of poetry to such passages as those we have now had the pleasure of laying before our readers. But we are told that Mr. Crabbe is only the poet of reality, whose wish and aim it is to discard every thing like illusion; that, on the contrary, men fly to poetry for the express purpose of getting rid of reality; that the office of poetry is to flatter the imagination merely; that the pleasures of poetry depend entirely on illusion, &c. &c.[1] all which, with great submission, appears to us the most absurd and inconsiderate jargon; the meaning of which, (if any meaning whatever can be collected from it) is, not simply that Mr. Crabbe is no poet, but that all didactic and all descriptive writers of all ages are equally to be excluded from that denomination; that Pope is a mere stringer of verses—nay, more, that (with the exception of a few flights of imagination which we find scattered in their works), Homer and Shakespeare are equally undeserving of the title; and, moreover, that there is no writer past or present among all those, whom the common consent of the world has classed among the poets, who is not improperly so classed, with the saving (perhaps) of Mr. Southey alone. But Mr. Crabbe does not stand in need of the poor defence of hyperbole against a charge so very hyperbolic. He answers it himself much more satisfactorily than we can pretend to do it for him.

But in whatever degree . . .—

[Quotes from Preface to *Tales*—pp. 153–4 above.]

But although the defence of Mr. Crabbe is easy, and has been in his own hands (as we consider) most complete, against a censure so indiscriminate and extravagant, there is no writer who enjoys a similar degree of reputation with himself, equally obnoxious to fair and honest criticism on points with regard to which his own rules of poetry will afford him no justification. It is true that we feel no *actual* pain in what does not concern ourselves; but Mr. Crabbe will not pretend to say that the imagination may not be painfully affected by the mere relation of what does not immediately concern the individual; and if the manner in which the imagination is affected be *merely* painful, we presume he will not attempt to deny that the means by which that effect is produced are contrary to the true end and purpose of poetry. It is most truly remarked that distress, in order to be interesting, must be unattended with disgust; that there is 'a degree of depravity which counteracts our sympathy with suffering, and of insignificance which extinguishes our interest in guilt.' It has also been observed, and that by no unfriendly critic, that no poet has ever sinned so deeply in violation of this rule as the author now before us. The present volume contains

[1] Cf. *Quarterly Review*, Nov. 1810 (No. 27 above).

much less of what is strictly obnoxious to this censure than either of his former works. The subjects of which it treats are raised one step higher in the scale of humanity. The 'depraved, abject, diseased, and neglected poor,' are no longer the objects which he employs his pencil to pourtray; and, in a less abject view of society, that of our yeomanry, our mechanics, little tradesmen, and inferior gentry, there rarely presents itself to our view any picture of unmixed disgust and uninteresting depravity. Yet such characters as those which are designed in 'The Mother,' 'Squire Thomas,' 'The Learned Boy,' and perhaps some few more of these pieces, can hardly be considered as entirely free from the objection to which we now refer. We have one further remark to make as to the class of subjects which he has now chosen for the exercise of his talents; and that is, that while it tends, in a great degree, to exempt him from the force of the objection which has been so frequently made to his former writings, it has an equal tendency to diminish one of the principal sources of the gratification which his readers have hitherto derived from him. The characters and habits, the vices and sufferings of the poor, possessed much of that interest which is attached to novelty —to the description of scenes which, though familiar as to the sort of sympathy which they are intended to excite, are nevertheless, not *personally* familiar, or of constant and every-day occurrence to the generality of readers. Every step which the poet advances in the rank of his subjects, approaches them nearer to that of his readers; the charm of novelty is altogether wanting to the description of scenes which resemble those of our own fire-sides; and it is in treating of the characters and habits of the middle ranks of society, that the relief of fable and incident to diversify the narrative becomes more than ever indispensable.

Another topic of censure to which this poet has exposed himself, the force of which, the present volume is rather calculated to augment than to obviate, is his indiscriminate love of minute detail, of unnecessary, uninteresting, *prosing* circumstance. We do not agree with those who deny the closeness of the analogy which has been generally conceived to exist between the arts of poetry and painting, and, without going to China for our illustration, shall be content to acquiesce in the strong resemblance which has been pointed out between the style of Crabbe's descriptive poetry and that of what is called the Dutch school of painting. But the best masters of that school are at least as remarkable for the force, brilliancy, and (to employ a metaphor which the subject seems to justify,) the *terseness* of their execution, as for the minuteness of detail which is their most prominent quality; and the poet, who forgetting this important ingredient, squanders himself away in tedious and flat circumstantiality, may indeed resemble *the school* to which he is assimilated in the eyes of the superficial and tasteless observer, but will never be ranked by the connoisseur or the critic on the same level with Teniers, Ostade, or Vandevelde. It is not his love of minuteness and detail which ought to be objected to Mr. Crabbe, but his want of taste and discrimination in rendering those qualities subservient to the general effect of his picture. The *'distant locality and imaginary reality'* which this faculty of particularizing is said to confer, may be obtained at too great an expence of the time and patience of the reader. At all events, what possible advantage is gained to the interest of, for instance, 'The Lover's Journey,' by his telling us in measured prose that the gentleman whom he calls Orlando, was really christened John, and that his mistress's appellation in the parish register was not Laura, but Susan; and that the more poetical names of Orlando and Laura were conferred on them not by their god-fathers and god-mothers, but by those ideal worthies, love and fancy? Of what possible importance is it that the contested election which gave rise to the connection, the consequences of which are so feelingly and exquisitely pourtrayed in the tale of 'The Patron,' was carried on between Sir Godfrey Ball and Lord Frederick Damer, the son of the Earl of Fitzdonnel? And a thousand other the like insignificant and impertinent pieces of newspaper information?

There is an easy familiarity which, when kept within decent bounds, is a peculiarly fit vehicle for the introduction of a long narration; and Dryden may, in this particular, have served Mr. Crabbe for a model worthy of imitation. But vulgarity is far removed from that frank good-humoured air which tends to ingratiate the reader at the outset, and to give him precisely that complacent impression with which it is the poet's interest that he should proceed. The impression which Mr. Crabbe's blunt ploughman-like familiarity is calculated to produce is very different, and if he had displayed the same disgusting and repulsive coarseness in the introductions to his earlier works, that he has since suffered to grow upon him, bold indeed must have been the man who could have ventured to explore the hidden treasures of so unpromising a superficies. The commencement of almost every tale in this collection is in this perverted taste:

> Gwynn was a farmer, whom the farmers all,
> Who dwelt around, the *gentleman* would call.
> [III]

A borough bailiff, who to law was train'd,
A wife and sons in decent state maintain'd.
[V]

Grave Jonas Kindred, Sybil Kindred's sire,
Was six feet high, and look'd six inches higher.
[VI]

To farmer Moss, in Langar Vale, came down
His only daughter, from her school in town—.
[VII]

Of a fair town, where Dr. Rack was guide, &c.
[IX]

'Squire Thomas flatter'd long a wealthy aunt, &c.
[XII]

A serious toyman in the city dwelt,
Who much concern for his religion felt.
[XIV]

Than old George Fletcher, on the British coast
Dwelt not a seaman who had more to boast.
Kind, simple, and sincere,—he seldom spoke,
But sometimes sang and chorus'd 'Hearts of Oak!'
[XX]

An honest man was farmer Jones, and true,
He did by all, as all by him should do.
[XXI]

What reader, unacquainted with Mr. Crabbe's previous reputation, would think of reading a single line more of an author who forces himself into his notice with such vulgar effrontery, and who thinks to gain by repelling him, like the beggar at the corner of the street who thrusts his stump of an arm into the passenger's face, in order to compel his attention and extort his alms? Who does not turn from the obtrusive mendicant in disgust, and escape his importunities if the swiftness of his feet will only enable him to elude them?

We forbear to instance any of the passages in which the same offensive vulgarity arrests or startles us in almost every page of some, and occasionally even in his best and most interesting pieces. Another observation to which he is fairly liable, is that his very virtues are often pushed to such an excess as to become glaring and capital defects. For instance, he has been commended for his force and compression, his

183

sententious brevity and manly strength of language. It is singular enough that in the same author such admirable qualities as those which we have just cited, and their very opposites, of tame languid diffuseness, and 'namby-pamby feebleness,' should be found co-existent. Yet so it certainly is with Mr. Crabbe. We have now, however, only to do with the former, and to say that he sometimes pushes those very excellencies for which he has been justly admired, to their vicious extremes of abrupt conciseness, quaint mannerism, and antithetical jingle. They even carry him so low as to the mean pedestrian vice of punning; and that species of *wit* which is habitually condemned, even in the freedom of conversation, is thus, (we believe,) for the first time, introduced into the regions of serious, descriptive or didactic, poetry.

It has been remarked that he is always at ease, but that his ease is rather that of confident carelessness than of good breeding. This reflection is too general, and by no means universally applicable. We are quite sure that many passages of all his works have been deeply studied, and (if we mistake not) some have been many times written and re-written before they were committed to the press. Nevertheless, he is very often, we may perhaps say most generally, careless both of his thoughts and language to an extent that we have seldom seen paralleled in any writer who has so much value for his reputation as Mr. Crabbe undoubtedly possesses.

All these defects, however, when collected together, cannot counter-balance the many claims which Mr. Crabbe possesses upon our admiration and gratitude. The worst perhaps is that they are so glaringly obvious to the whole world, while his beauties are of a nature which few, comparatively speaking, know how properly to estimate. His style is more apt to provoke the dangerous ridicule of parody than that of any poet of the present day.[1] The very best of poets, may be and have been parodied, but not till long after their merits have been sufficiently understood and established, to bear the severest test of ridicule. Mr. Crabbe only irresistably incites the reader to the exercise of this species of wit, even while he is fresh from the first perusal of him. The disadvantage attending the excitement of such a propensity is obvious. Thousands are endowed with a sense of ridicule, while a hundred only possess a refined and intelligent taste; and out of that more select number, perhaps there are very few who are able to resist the influence of ridicule when once excited. Ridicule is not, nor ever ought to be made, the test either of moral or of political truth—nevertheless no man

[1] See No. 39 below.

should be so confident in his virtue or his talents as to venture wantonly to incur its hostility.

36. Unsigned review, *Eclectic Review*

December 1812, viii, 1240–53

We have heard Mr. Crabbe called of the school of Pope and Dryden. Mr. Crabbe, to be sure, writes in rhymed heroic couplets, and so did they; Dryden was careless, and so is he; Pope had humour, and so has he. But has he that pregnancy of imagination, and that unselecting copiousness of resources, which always crowded the mind of Dryden with more matter than was wanting, more than could be reduced to proper sequency and order? Has he that boundless command of diction, and that facility of versifying, which enabled Dryden to clothe and adorn his ideas, however unfitted for poetry by their remoteness, in 'words that burn,' and numbers so musically full? Has he Dryden's metaphysical and argumentative turn of mind—his love for subtle and scholastic disputation? Surely not. Has he, then, the trimness and terseness and classical elegance of Pope—his diligence and selection—his compression and condensation and energy—his light and playful fancies—or the naiveté and delicacy and cutting fineness of his satire? In all these qualities we think Mr. Crabbe assuredly wanting.

Mr. Crabbe, in our opinion, is of his own school. And if originality, merely as originality, be merit, this merit, we are inclined to think, his volumes possess. The *Tales* are so much in the manner of his former poems, that we shall not be wandering far out of our way, if we give a page or two to the consideration of the characteristics of his poetry in general.

Mr. C.'s grand fault lies in the choice of his subjects. It has all along been avowedly his aim to paint life, or rather the most loathsome and painful forms of life, in their true colours; to speak the truth, and nothing but the truth:

I paint the cot
As truth will paint it, and as bards will not.
Village. B. 1.

And truly there is something specious in the idea of rejecting all that imagination had added to nature, and substituting sober truth and sound good sense in the place of fictitious ornament, and 'pleasant lies.' But if the end of poetry be to relax and recreate the mind, it must be attained by drawing away the attention from the low pursuits and sordid cares, from the pains and sorrows of real life, at least whatever is vulgar and disgusting in them, to an imaginary state of greater beauty, purity, and blessedness. Undoubtedly, the poet must retain enough of this world, to cheat the mind into a belief of what he adds thereunto: the figures in the pictures of the Muse must appear to be real flesh and blood: we must be acquainted with their dress; their features must express passions that we have known; or we are not interested about them. But then the poet will select what is most amiable in this world around him: what is displeasing and disgusting, he will keep back, or soften down, or disguise; and withal he will add fancies of his own, that are in unison with realities; and thus the imagination of the reader will be for a while beguiled into Elysium, and receive unreproved pleasure in the contemplation of 'airy nothings.' To determine the relative quantities of truth and fiction to be employed, would require a poetical calculus of much greater delicacy than we are possest of: but we suspect that the general propension is in favour of fiction. How else can the Corydons and σἀτυρισχοι of the Greek pastoral—the palaces and caverns and enchantments of eastern story—the knights and palfreys and distresses of the chivalrous romances—the pomp and delicacy and declamation of French tragedy—or even the sensibility and kindliness of Mr. Wordsworth's leach-gatherers and ragamuffins,—how else can these get or keep possession of the mind? The heroes of Homer and the epic muse, indeed, approximate somewhat more to *workday* men and women; they have the passions and feelings, and something of the manners of mortality. Yet even in the simple narrations of Homer how much is witheld that in reality offends? how much of strength and beauty and magnanimity is given to the admiration of the reader?

But Mr. C. is all for naked and unornamented reality. Accordingly in his volumes is to be found whatever is uninteresting and unattractive —all the petty cares and trifling inconveniences that disquiet life—dirt, and drunkenness, and squabbling wives and ruined tradesmen. Ecce signum.

[Give a brief account of *Tales* I and IV.]

We do not know that we have picked out the two most uninteresting of the tales. Lest the reader should think that the manner of telling makes up for the deficiency of matter, we must subjoin a quotation or two. We have but to open the book.

> When the sage Widow *Dinah's* grief descried, . . .
> [IV, 72–99]

> With pain I've seen, these wrangling wits among . . .
> [V,329–63]

> The Uncle died, and when the Nephew read . . .
> [XIV, 60–81]

We assure our readers, it is very seldom that Mr. C.'s style in these volumes rises above these specimens. It is nothing but prose measured, whether by ear or finger into decasyllabic lines. Nor are there any little ebullitions of fancy, bubbling and playing through the desert waste; very little of simile, or metaphor, or allusion; and what there is, of this kind.

> For all that Honour brings against the force
> Of headlong passion, aids its rapid course;
> Its slight resistance but provokes the fire,
> As wood-work stops the flame, and then conveys it higher.
> [XI, 289–92]

> Each new idea more inflam'd his ire,
> As fuel thrown upon a rising fire:
> [XV, 316–17]

> As heaviest weights the deepest rivers pass,
> While icy chains fast bind the solid mass;
> So, born of feelings, faith remains secure,
> Long as their firmness and their strength endure:
> But when the waters in their channel glide,
> A bridge must bear us o'er the threat'ning tide;
> Such bridge is Reason, and there Faith relies,
> Whether the varying spirits fall or rise.
> [XIX, 95–102]

> 'Nor good nor evil can you beings name,
> Who are but Rooks *and* Castles in the game;
> Superior natures with their puppets play,
> Till, bagg'd or buried, all are swept away.'
> [XI, 362–5]

Our next objection to Mr. C.'s poetry, is the wearisome minuteness of his details.* Every description is encumbered with an endless enumeration of particulars. He will copy a dress, a chamber, or an alley, with more than Chinese accuracy. And every circumstance is touched with equal strength,—the slightest as diligently laboured as the most important. We have heard of sculptors, who have laid out as much pains upon a shoe-tye, as a forehead. But does not Mr. C. know, that the reader of poetry must owe half his pleasure to his own fancies and associations? Some metaphysicians have asserted, that the secondary qualities of bodies exist only in the percipient mind; that the heat of fire, and the colours of the rainbow, and the sweetness of honey are not in exterior things, but in the mind that receives the ideas of them. This is very poor doctrine in metaphysics, but there is something very much like it in poetry. Half of the beauty of the most beautiful poem exists in the mind of the reader. He hears of Eve, that 'grace was in all her steps, &c.': of Dido, that she was 'pulcherrima Dido,' and he conjures up the form of 'her he loves the best.' But had Milton told us that his heroine was little and languishing, had light hair and blue eyes, &c. &c. what would have become of him whose mistress should be a commanding beauty, of jet-black eyes and raven locks? Thus, therefore, to particularize description is most grievously to fetter the imagination. Where out of the infinity of ways from one point to another, the poet has chosen one, the reader cannot take another. The reader must have the *setting* of the poet's air; he must lay the colours on the poet's outline. Our remarks are necessarily very general; *we*, though not writing poetry, follow our own rule, in leaving something to the limitation of the judicious reader. Now for an instance or two.

Fix'd were their habits; they arose betimes . . .
[VI, 41–52]

The Lover rode as hasty lovers ride . . .
[X, 62–73, 98–128]

Lastly, a word or two with Mr. Crabbe on his carelessness. If one order of words will not do, Mr. C. will try another and another, till he makes his verse; and truly ten syllables can seldom be found so unbending, as not to form metre some way or other.

* We shall not quarrel about names; but Mr. C's choice is somewhat odd; Dinah, Jonas, Josiah, Judith, Isaac, Allen Booth, John Dighton, Stephen Jones, Sybil Kindred, &c.

To learn how frail is man, how humble then should be.
[XI, 319]

. . . he would not then upbraid.
And by that proof she every instant gives.
[XIII, 257]

And George exclaim, Ah, what to this is wealth.
[XX, 147—misquoted]

Thus the auxiliary and the verb are continually most ungracefully separated.

And was with saving care and prudence blest.
[I, 22]

He sometimes could among a number trace.
[II, 256]

The pronoun and the verb.

That all your wealth you to deception owe.
[XII, 304]

He is sometimes ungrammatical.

Pain mixt with pity in our bosoms rise.
[II, 13]

Blaze not with fairy-light the phosphor-fly.
[II, 461]

His quantity is incorrect.

While others, daring, yet imbécile, fly.
[XXI, 175]

The mind sunk slowly to infántine ease.
[XI, 425]

With all these helps, however, and that of triplets and alexandrines to boot, of which he is very liberal, he cannot always get his verse.

That, if they improve not, still enlarge the mind.
[XIX, 331]

It shock'd his spirit to be esteem'd unfit.
[XX, 264]

His rhymes are not always of the best.

> With tyrant-craft he then was still and calm,
> But raised in private terror and alarm.
>
> [XIV, 349–50]

His verses are frequently as feeble as the following.

> All things prepar'd, *on the* expected day.
>
> [II, 109]

> And what became *of the* forsaken maid.
>
> [II, 244]

> Blamed *by the* mild, approved *by the* severe.
>
> [I, 72]

> *To the* base toil *of a* dependent mind.
>
> [VII, 23]

Mr. C. is fond of antithetic lines, yet they are sometimes very carelessly managed.

> Where joy was laughter, and profaneness wit.
>
> [XV, 14]

> With heart half broken, and with scraps ill fed.
>
> [XX, 275]

All these things individually are nothing, but much in the aggregate. A face may lose as much by being pitted with the small-pox, as by having the nose awry.

We turn with pleasure to the excellencies of Mr. Crabbe. And among the first of these, we place his power in the pathetic. Every body remembers the Dying Seaman, and the Malefactor's Dream. Such passages, indeed, will be looked for in vain in the work before us; but still there is pathos. There is something touching in the tale called 'The Parting Hour':—the opening lines are striking.

[II, 1–14, followed by 175–212, 432–3 and 450–73.]

Mr. Crabbe, again, though his descriptions are mostly affected with that tedious minuteness we have already spoken of, can certainly describe with the hand of a master. Here is a beautiful description of the closing autumn.

> Cold grew the foggy morn, the day was brief . . .
>
> [V, 426–33]

> Again the country was enclos'd, a wide . . .
>
> [X, 141–95]

In portrait-painting. Mr. C. is often successful.

Counter meantime selected, doubted, weigh'd . . .
[XVIII, 62–79]

But in this instant *Sybil's* eye had seen . . .
[VI, 341–52]

Friends now appear'd, but in the Man was seen . . .
[XI, 416–67]

These passages certainly possess excellence. On the whole, however, we are very far from thinking that these tales will add to the reputation of the author of *The Village* and *The Borough*. Lovers as we are of poetry, it was with no little difficulty that we toiled through this heavy mass of verse. We seemed jogging on a broken-winded Pegasus through all the flats and bogs of Parnassus. We do hope that, when Mr. Crabbe has it in contemplation to appear again before the public, he will employ a little more judgment in the selection of his subjects, a little more fancy in their decoration, and withal a little more time in preparing ten thousand verses for the press.

One word at parting. Mr. C. says a great deal about religion and grace in these volumes. Not having been able perfectly to comprehend his opinions on these subjects, we shall only venture to assure him that virtue is the certain companion of grace, and feeling in no wise incompatible with reason.

37. Unsigned reviews, *Universal Magazine*

February and March 1813, xix, 128–33 and 219–24

From being among the most scrupulous or indolent of modern poets, Mr. Crabbe appears to have been awakened to a just confidence in his own powers, and, at length, to follow, in the pursuit of fame, with a vigour unshackled by his wonted timidity, and animated by the experience of success. Were we to state in a few words our opinion of the distinguishing excellencies of this gentleman's poetry, we should say, they consisted in a singular adherence to nature, both in her external forms and invisible operations; in description, equally true and powerful of animate and inanimate objects; in the clearness, force, and unlaboured elegance of his diction; in his rejection of petty graces, and his contempt of fantastic decoration. Of all species of poetical writing, it is that on which the mind will endure to remain the longest: it never palls upon the appetite, but nourishes and invigorates at the same time that it refreshes and delights. What Cicero says of letters in general may, with no impropriety, be predicted of Mr. Crabbe's productions, they are grateful at all seasons, by the fire side and in the field, *nobiscum peregrinantur rusticantur*.[1] They resemble that fruit of simple, but peculiar flavour, neither lusciously sweet nor harshly acid, which excites while it assuages thirst; and though it exercises and stimulates the taste, leaves it unexposed to the chances of intoxication.

Undoubtedly, the grand and prominent virtue of this writer is the closeness and accuracy with which he has pursued the footsteps of nature, and traced her through all her windings. His pictures are of things and feelings that actually or sensibly exist, that are recognized by every eye, or appropriated in every breast, not as they appear magnificently attired and strangely grand in the dreams of poesy or the fairy landscapes of a creative imagination. A great question might be raised as to what order of poetry, the highest dignity and merit may belong, but few, we believe, will be disposed to deny Mr. Crabbe's pretensions to be included in the catalogue of genuine bards. In a modest preface to his new publication, he has mildly asserted his claim to a character to which he had been long raised by the according approbation of his readers. If he does not boast of having assumed the *cecropius cothurnus*, or sung his lay in the lofty strain of epic composition, he has demonstrated powers and endowments which have extorted a consentaneous acquiescence in his title to an exalted rank among modern poets. Without meaning any hyperbolical encomium, we think we can attest a kindred resemblance between his mind and that of our greatest dramatic genius, as the excellencies by which he is distinguished seem to us to be closely allied to those which are most essential to the power and triumph of the drama. Accurate exhibitions of nature in her simplest but most interesting forms, incidents skilfully invented to absorb the attention, and managed so as to stir every latent affection, and to make us acquainted with the secrets of our own hearts, are the instruments with which the tragic muse achieves her noblest ends. The art of other poets

[1] They accompany us in our wanderings and are with us in our country retreats. *Pro Archia*, 7. 16.

consists in giving to their original drawings an adventitious and imposing richness, in embellishing them with new colouring and tints of brilliancy taken from the stores of their own swelling and exuberant fancy. Mr. Crabbe, on the other hand, never departs from the truth of his subject, never seeks to adorn the simplicity of his prototype with the trappings of his own conceit, or to display it otherwise than it exists, either in its native deformity or its own untransformed and unborrowed beauty. Nothing can seduce him from the observance of this stern and self-imposed necessity; he worships nature with a spirit of intolerant idolatry, and seems to entertain a silent scorn of those who pay their incense at any other shrine.

Good sense, indeed, and liberality of opinion, are prominent features in the character of all his writings; his views of life are rational and sober, clouded sometimes by the shadows of constitutional gloom, but always evincing the force and freshness of a vigorous and penetrating judgment.

The sorrows which he paints and deplores are never fantastic; his incidents do not often displease us by their improbability or their insignificance, and his sentiment uniformly appears to grow out of, rather than to be engrafted upon his subject. In his pages, nature is not distorted or encumbered with unnecessary appendages; nor passion, however deep and genuine, swelled beyond its true and legitimate dimensions.

The present work, which bears the simple appellation of *Tales* though it seems to differ from the principle of his previous productions, affords no important deviation from the general design and style of the execution. The author had before presented us with a gallery of portraits, and interesting sketches of familiar groups; he has now produced a series of historical delineations, and exercised his powers in narrative composition, and in the structure of connected trains of character and incident. There are twenty-one distinct stories, or epic poems in miniature, each of which has its separate title and peculiar design. It is manifest, that the latitude of such a plan gave him the command of more varied materials than he could apply, consistently with the character of pure and limited description, that appertained to the 'village-register' and *The Borough*. His persons and adventures were before drawn from sources bounded by local or artificial distinctions, such as were afforded by the narrow scenes of country towns and hamlets, and the humble occupations of peasants and fishermen. He has, in his *Tales*, taken a wider survey of mankind; he has drawn his supplies from the ample magazines of human life under all its modifications, and ranged at his own discretion through all the forms and diversities of the moral world. In the enjoyment of this unbounded licence it is not to exact too much, to require some excellency which we missed before, and the exclusion, at least, of those faults which were, perhaps, inseparable from the nature of his previous themes. We are of opinion, that the just and natural demand has been answered, and that if there are fewer splendid and highly wrought passages, there are likewise fewer defects and deformities than may be discovered in his other productions.

This sort of poetical novel writing, of which the history of literature furnishes so few examples, is, we apprehend, governed by the same principles as its kindred composition in prose, but susceptible of greater dignity. Verse always adds to the importance and impressiveness of every subject on which it is employed. It necessarily excludes mean extremities, and, in some degree, paltry incidents and contemptible characters. This is the broad line of demarcation between tragedy and comedy, which modern dramatic writers have so assiduously laboured to obliterate. As the antients were utterly ignorant of romance, they have left us, with the exception of their comedies, (their satires necessarily afford very imperfect glimpses) no minute representations of familiar life, or lively views of domestic manners and prejudices. Now there are causes, we think, which render dramatic writing a comparatively inadequate exponent of these useful and delightful pictures. The laws which preside over the drama are of the severest kind, and a play so constructed, as entirely to satisfy a critical judgment, is therefore one of the rarest and most curious productions of human genius. But however indulgent the tests applied, still the restrictions imposed by the very nature of the work itself are such as to exclude almost all the advantages of narrative and epistolary composition. . . .

The first of the Tales before us is entitled 'The Dumb Orators,' and although not without its merits, and exhibiting, frequently, traces of the powerful hand that produced it, is not such as to extort from us any very warm eulogium. It is, perhaps, the least interesting and instructive of the collection; and as it contains no incident to withdraw us from a consideration of the author's design, so the design itself seems scarcely of importance sufficient to deserve the labour and dignity of invention to support or illustrate it. That ostentatious ignorance and presumptive loquacity may be overawed by the presence of superior talent and virtue, is a truth which fiction can hardly serve to elucidate, and which those only can have to learn whom experience alone will teach.

In the second or 'The Parting Hour'; Mr. Crabbe has made ample amends for the vacuity and listlessness of its predecessor, and exerted the full vigour of his unrivalled powers for pathetic and picturesque description. In none other of his published compositions has he succeeded in exciting an interest more profound, or sympathies of a higher order, than this beautiful and melancholy picture of a life doomed to the experience of the most heart-striking emotions, and chequered by every variety of affliction and disappointment. . . .

> At length a prospect came that seem'd to smile . . .
> [II, 93–130, 181–212, 305–40]

In 'The Patron,' the author has left us nothing to censure or desire; for it is, in all respects, a finished and glowing picture. The errors of a youth of genius condemned to poverty, but yielding to the seductions of an ardent temperament, and fascinated by the visions of a glowing imagination, leading finally to disappointment, despair, and death, are depicted with the hand of a master. That Mr. Crabbe found the original in the life and fate of the unfortunate Chatterton we think highly probable; and not even in the history of that surprising boy is there to be found a more interesting exemplification of the wanderings of an enthusiastic mind, fired by passion and bounding with fancy; or of the perils that attend the course of such a spirit when spurning at the sober control of experience, and freed from the discipline of the severer studies. . . .

> Now was the Sister of his Patron seen,— . . .
> [V, 172–205, 351–91, 577–606, 654–87, 716–27]

We are decidedly of opinion, that next to the two stories from which we have made our quotations, the best tales are 'Procrastination,' 'The Gentleman Farmer,' 'The Mother,' 'Edward Shore,' 'The Confidant,' and 'The Brothers.' There is much good description, much of accurate drawing and homely doctrine in 'The Lover's Journey,' 'The Convert,' 'Resentment,' and 'The Wager.' We cannot, however, avoid saying, that there is little either of entertainment or instruction to be gleaned from 'The Frank Courtship,' 'Squire Thomas,' 'The Squire and Priest,' or 'The Learned Boy.'

It ought not to be omitted, that the conclusion of the story of Edward Shore contains one of the best descriptions in the English language of the rise and progress of an incurable insanity.

We have already stated an opinion of the fitness and capabilities of this species of composition as a true representative of the features and varying colours of life and manners. Perhaps it might be urged, that modern times present materials for such productions with far greater fecundity and profusion than could be expected from the character of earlier ages. The relations of men towards each other have been greatly multiplied and changed by the progress of intelligence and the diffusion of property, and the taste and refinement of the cultivated orders have reached a much higher point than, perhaps, it was possible to attain under the more simple forms of ancient society. The sentiments and understandings of the whole community have been so much raised and enlarged, that it often requires no small share of sagacity and discernment to find the genuine and real causes of action under the veil of those decorums and punctilios by which the social intercourse of modern life is polished and defended. It is curious to consider the connection which subsists between the various causes that influence public happiness and prosperity. The silent revolution in the face and character of European society, to which we have just adverted, has affected its political frame no less than its civil condition. It has tempered the insolence of despotism, harmonized the conflicting interests of mixed governments, and assuaged the pride and austerity of republics. It has exalted human nature by instructing it in the grand lesson of commanding itself, while it has fortified it by controuling the ambition of individuals and confining it within streams, which are all, in some degree, tributary to the grand reservoir of national welfare and honour.

Such then are the advantages of which Mr. Crabbe might have availed himself in the construction of some epic but familiar story. In his present work he has declined this task, as above his strength or acquirements, and remained satisfied with giving a dress and scenery to characters and incidents already treasured in his mind, and which he was unwilling to conceal till he had moulded and fashioned them into due subserviency to some comprehensive plan. We do not know that we have any right to complain, although we may regret that, with more eagerness, our author should still manifest as little ambition as before. The present work, like his former, continues rather to prove his great powers than their real extent, or the uses to which they might be applied. There are marks of haste too in this last performance, which if not of the glaring kind, are sufficiently obvious to those who have admired the elaborate finish and completion of his first production.

We have, perhaps, already said enough of the general merits and peculiar character of Mr. Crabbe's poetry; yet, as he himself has expressed some doubts as to the place which he is entitled to occupy, we cannot resist the temptation of offering a few reflections on that question. With respect to the more mechanical part of the composition, in what relates to style merely, and the structure of the versification, we have been, in contemplating it, forcibly reminded of the vigour and facility, the natural flow, combined with the masculine energy that distinguish the poetry of Dryden. Nor have we observed any eminent deviation from that regularity of cadence and habitual melody which Pope and Goldsmith have communicated to poetical diction. If he be inferior to Dryden in variety, and in the rapidity with which the latter pours forth a succession of original ideas, he has some points of superiority both over him and his disciple Pope. The latter supplied, in delicacy of taste and nice discrimination, what he fell short of in the force and majesty of his master. Mr. Crabbe has not only the merit of describing natural emotions and external objects with as much spirit as either, and with more correctness, but he has succeeded in one of the higher provinces of poetry, which Dryden knew himself too well to attempt, and which Pope has attempted almost in vain. Nothing—no, not even the magical scenes of Otway, can surpass the intense and irresistible pathos of some of our author's delineations, heightened as that pathos is by that stern truth and that devoted fidelity of expression which form the basis of all his designs. Like a wise general, he always directs his attack against the citadel of the heart, and victorious there, has reason to be satisfied with his achievement. It is no subtraction from this glory to admit that he has not the command of playful imagery, which belonged to Pope, or his polish and vivacity; that the fastidious taste and romantic tenderness of Goldsmith and Campbell are not discoverable in his productions. These, perhaps, are the poets to whom he may, with the least impropriety, be compared, and, in striking the balance of their respective merits, it is necessary that we should consider how far their combination in the same writer is possible, and in what degree the attainment of the one kind of excellence operates to the exclusion of the other. Our own opinion is, that if Mr. Crabbe has failed in the distinguishing characteristics of his predecessors and rivals, his failure proceeds, in a great measure, from his not aiming at them, and from his having followed the inclination of his genius in the pursuit of different and incompatible objects. Fascinating as the paintings and imagination of Pope frequently are, and gratified as we are, at all times, by his delicacy of perception and scrupulosity of taste, yet his writings seem ever to appeal to the head rather than to the feelings. He never causes us to forget our critical functions, but challenges the full severity of judgment; and, while he comes forth from his probation with the secured applause of the understanding, remain but little cherished in the warm affection of our common nature. The success of Goldsmith and Campbell is derived partly from a peculiar felicity of diction, and, in no small degree, from their habit of substituting the aids of a luxuriant fancy, animated and guided by the most exquisite sensibility, for those rigid copies of nature, and those simple but powerful appeals to the heart, which are the prominent features in Mr. Crabbe's poetical character, as they were in that of the father of poetry.

We have thus spoken of Mr. Crabbe's merits as we think they deserve, and are but little disposed to fatigue the reader's attention further by any laborious detection of subaltern defects, or occasional remissions of vigour and correctness. There are, it is not to be disguised, such examples to be found in the publication before us, as in, perhaps, every long and arduous exercise of intellectual power. If Homer sleeps, Mr. Crabbe may be allowed, at intervals, to nod and repose his collected might till the due period of its exertion. We have been struck, upon the general perusal, with an air of monotony, arising from the too great uniformity observed in the mode of balancing his lines. The cæsural pause falls with too little variation at the same point, and hence the ear is oppressed too frequently with a sense of languor. It is not easy, in the conduct of pure narrative, to avoid degenerating sometimes into prose; and Mr. Crabbe is certainly sometimes prosaic. He appears, at once, to be inflamed with a passion for the antithetical, and to labour after its concealment in his systematic preference of simplicity. This struggle is the 'worm in the bud' that mars the damask purity of his poetical fame. In the collision of these opposite pursuits he is now splendid and powerful—now mean, harsh, and repulsive. The work is indisputably deformed by many asperities of language; and whilst it exhibits, on the other hand, a still greater number of glittering points and pleasing eminences, brings to our minds the image of that unequal scenery, where vallies buried in shade are intermingled with hills, whose summits refract rays of every hue.

We had selected several instances in exemplification of these latter remarks, but, upon the whole, deem it superfluous to illustrate blemishes, or enforce such moderate censure. We cannot, however, take our leave of Mr. Crabbe without noticing one merit of the highest kind, if considered in relation to its consequences. He is not less the poet of morality than the poet of nature, and, like Miss Edgeworth, (an artist to whose genius his own bears some affinity) he has learned to bend the pride of his ambition, and the prowess of his genius into subserviency to objects associated with the moral improvement and happiness of his species. Never was fiction rendered a more powerful ally to truth, never poetry a clearer guide to practice, or fancy a more faithful and honest minister to the understanding. We shall conclude with observing, that notwithstanding all the faults to which we have just adverted, it is easy to perceive that our author has been animated by a severe and self-denying spirit that amply evinces the patient and candid temper with which he has received the criticisms and appreciated the award of public opinion upon his former labours. It cannot, however, be matter of surprise, that a mind like Mr. Crabbe's which could prolong its early diffidence through so many years of laborious seclusion, should even, after gaining the tribute due to its success, continue to exercise over its subsequent effusions the same humble caution and generous austerity which secured to it its original and indefeasible title to poetical renown.

38. Unsigned review, *British Critic*

April 1813, xli, 380–6

In Mr. Crabbe's Poems, already known to the public, every discriminating reader must have remarked very original delineation of character, marked by strong and sometimes even coarse features; a fertile invention of incident, with a propensity to display rather the bad than the favourable side of human nature; an easy flow of narrative versification, sometimes negligent and harsh, more frequently pointed and appropriate. A style, in short, perfectly his own, and happily imitated, though with more of caricature than in most of the other specimens, in the *Rejected Addresses*.[1]

Exactly the same is the character of the present volume; so exactly,

[1] Quoted below, No. 39.

that it has more the appearance of a collection of episodes, cut out of longer poems, like his former compositions, than of a set of tales, originally written and intended as such. We can hardly, indeed, persuade ourselves that the personages here exhibited were not primarily intended to figure in *The Village, The Parish Register,* or *The Borough,* though for some reason laid aside, and thus reserved for another form of publication. This remark is by no means intended as a reproach. Mr. Crabbe's former poems had too much excellence, for any one to be offended at the family likeness observed in the present, however strong.

The collection contains twenty-one tales, much varied in their subjects, except perhaps that the most striking circumstance in the 17th and 20th is rather too nearly the same. The first is perhaps inferior to most of the rest. In interest it certainly is; recording only the separate triumphs of two orators, as each spoke upon, what is vulgarly called, his own dunghill. The second, entitled 'The Parting Hour,' has something peculiarly touching in the picture it displays.

> They parted, thus by hope and fortune led, . . .
> [II, 181–252, 283–312]

The tale is well continued to the end, and is extremely pleasing. 'The Gentleman Farmer,' (tale 3,) gives the well touched history of a man, who determining to be completely independent, but not drawing his independence from religious sources, becomes, by very natural steps, a complete dupe and slave. Tale 4, entitled 'Procrastination;' the 9th, called 'The Mother;' the 11th, 'Edward Shore;' the 12th, 'Squire Thomas;' the 14th, 'The Struggles of Conscience;' the 17th, 'Resentment;' and the 20th, 'The Brothers,' all give, more or less, those gloomy views of life and character, which, however excellent in narration and invention, afford probably but little gratification to the majority of readers. The more they have to boast of truth and probability, the more the heart sinks at the reflection that such things may, and possibly have been true. Of 'The Squire and Priest,' (tale 15,) it is not easy to see the drift. The best we can make of it is, that the zeal of a young man, not governed by discretion, at once impedes his fortunes, and fails to produce the most desirable effects, even where it succeeds. But his zeal is certainly honest and upright, and though it seems to be hinted that it is methodistical, there is nothing fanatical either in his expressions or conduct. 'The Convert,' (tale 19,) seems to contain merely the versified history of a bookselling adventurer in London, well known as his own biographer, and as having been alternately a convert, an apostate, and a re-convert to the fanatics.[1] The 21st, 'The Learned Boy,' is a disgusting history of a stupid lad, and except that it collaterally throws some contempt upon atheistical presumption, is little worthy of notice.

But 'The Frank Courtship,' (tale 6,) 'The Widow,' (7,) 'The Lover's Journey,' (10,) 'Jesse and Colin,' (13,) 'The Confidant,' (16,) are pleasing in all respects, and admirably told, particularly 'Jesse.' 'The Patron,' (5,) is a melancholy tale, but pleasing, of the disappointments of a youthful poet. 'Arabella,' (9,) and 'The Wager,' (18,) are rather humourous, particularly the latter. Some of those, however, which are not on the whole satisfactory, have passages of high beauty. Of this nature is the following, from the unpleasant tale of 'The Mother.' It describes the declining days of a very ill-used daughter.

> While quickly thus the mortal part declin'd . . .
> [VIII, 302–40]

> 'Hear me, my Boy, thou hast a virtuous mind— . . .
> [V, 247–72]

> Such was his fall; and *Edward*, from that time, . . .
> [XI, 307–31]

. . . The language of Mr. Crabbe is in general pure, but blemishes are to be found. In the passage last quoted '*flown*' is used for 'flowed,' by a solecism similar to the vulgar mistake of 'overflown' for 'overflowed.' These come from *fly*, not *flow*. He uses *wed* for *wedded*; 'was wed,' which is perhaps provincial. It occurs several times. Of passages faultily obscure several might be pointed out. The press has been, in general, well corrected; but pages 274 and 5 present some remarkable errors, as 'now' for *own*, in the former 'these' for *there* in the latter, and perhaps 'danger' for *dagger*. [XV, 208, 248, 247].

If we are to sum up, in conclusion, our general opinion of the book, it is briefly this: it is strongly marked with the characteristic peculiarities of the author; but it is what no writer but one of original genius could have produced, and what no reader, who delights in accurate pictures of human character, can peruse without delight.

---

[1] James Lackington (1746–1815).

39. James Smith, 'The Theatre',
Rejected Addresses

1812

James Smith (1775–1839) was the author of this early and excellent parody of Crabbe in the collection in which he collaborated with his brother Horace. It is proof of Charles Mathews' view of him as 'the only man who can write clever nonsense'.

THE THEATRE

Interior of a Theatre described.—Pit gradually fills.—The check-taker.—Pit full.—The orchestra tuned.—One fiddle rather dilatory.—Is reproved—and repents.—Evolutions of a play-bill.—Its final settlement on the spikes.—The gods taken to task—and why.—Motley group of playgoers.—Holywell Street, St. Pancras.—Emanuel Jennings binds his son apprentice.—Not in London—and why.—Episode of the hat.

'Tis sweet to view, from half-past five to six,
Our long wax-candles, with short cotton wicks,
Touch'd by the lamplighter's Promethean art,
Start into light and make the lighter start;
To see red Phœbus through the gallery pane
Tinge with his beam the beams of Drury-Lane
While gradual parties fill our widen'd pit,
And gape, and gaze, and wonder, ere they sit.
    At first, while vacant seats give choice and ease;
Distant or near, they settle where they please;
But when the multitude contracts the span,
And seats are rare, they settle where they can.

Now the full benches, to late comers, doom
No room for standing, miscall'd *standing room*.

Hark! the check-taker moody silence breaks,
And bawling 'Pit full,' gives the check he takes;
Yet onward still the gathering numbers cram,
Contending crowders should the frequent damn,
And all is bustle, squeeze, row, jabbering, and jam.

See to their desks Apollo's sons repair;
Swift rides the rosin o'er the horse's hair;
In unison their various tones to tune
Murmurs the hautboy, growls the hoarse bassoon;
In soft vibration sighs the whispering lute,
Tang goes the harpsichord, too-too the flute,
Brays the loud trumpet, squeaks the fiddle sharp,
Winds the French-horn, and twangs the tingling harp;
Till, like great Jove, the leader, figuring in,
Attunes to order the chaotic din.
Now all seems hush'd—but no, one fiddle will
Give, half-ashamed, a tiny flourish still;
Foil'd in his crash, the leader of the clan
Reproves with frowns the dilatory man;
Then on his candlestick three taps his bow,
Nods a new signal, and away they go.

Perchance, while pit and gallery cry, 'Hats off,'
And awed Consumption checks his chided cough,
Some giggling daughter of the Queen of Love
Drops, reft of pin, her play-bill from above;
Like Icarus, while laughing galleries clap,
Soars, ducks, and dives in air the printed scrap;
But, wiser far than he, combustion fears,
And, as it flies, eludes the chandeliers;
Till sinking gradual, with repeated twirl,
It settles, curling, on a fiddler's curl;
Who from his powder'd pate the intruder strikes,
And, for mere malice, sticks it on the spikes.

Say, why these Babel strains from Babel tongues?

Who's that calls 'Silence' with such leathern lungs?
He, who, in quest of quiet, 'silence' hoots,
Is apt to make the hubbub he imputes.

What various swains our motley walls contain!
Fashion from Moorfields, honour from Chick Lane;
Bankers from Paper Buildings here resort,
Bankrupts from Golden Square and Riches Court;
From the Haymarket canting rogues in grain,
Gulls from the Poultry, sots from Water Lane;
The lottery cormorant, the auction shark,
The full-price master, and the half-price clerk;
Boys who long linger at the gallery door,
With pence twice five, they want but two-pence more,
Till some Samaritan the two-pence spares,
And sends them jumping up the gallery stairs.

Critics we boast who ne'er their malice balk,
But talk their minds, we wish they'd mind their talk;
Big-worded bullies, who by quarrels live,
Who give the lie, and tell the lie they give;
Jews from St. Mary Axe, for jobs so wary,
That for old clothes they'd even axe St. Mary;
And bucks with pockets empty as their pate,
Lax in their gaiters, laxer in their gait,
Who oft, when we our house lock up, carouse
With tippling tipstaves in a lock-up house.

Yet here, as elsewhere, chance can joy bestow,
Where scowling Fortune seem'd to threaten woe.

John Richard William Alexander Dwyer
Was footman to Justinian Stubbs, Esquire;
But when John Dwyer listed in the Blues,
Emanuel Jennings polish'd Stubbs's shoes.
Emanuel Jennings brought his youngest boy
Up as a corn-cutter, a safe employ;
In Holywell Street, St. Pancras, he was bred
(At number twenty-seven, it is said),
Facing the pump, and near the Granby's Head:

He would have bound him to some shop in town,
But with a premium he could not come down;
Pat was the urchin's name, a red hair'd youth,
Fonder of purl and skittle-grounds than truth.

Silence, ye gods! to keep your tongues in awe,
The muse shall tell an accident she saw.

Pat Jennings in the upper gallery sat,
But, leaning forward, Jennings lost his hat;
Down from the gallery the beaver flew,
And spurn'd the one to settle in the two.
How shall he act? Pay at the gallery door
Two shillings for what cost, when new, but four?
Or till half-price, to save his shilling, wait,
And gain his hat again at half-past eight?
Now, while his fears anticipate a thief,
John Mullins whispers, Take my handkerchief.
Thank you, cries Pat, but one won't make a line;
Take mine, cried Wilson, and cried Stokes, take mine.
A motley cable soon Pat Jennings ties,
Where Spital-fields with real India vies.
Like Iris' bow, down darts the painted hue,
Starr'd, striped, and spotted, yellow, red, and blue,
Old calico, torn silk, and muslin new.
George Green below, with palpitating hand,
Loops the last 'kerchief to the beaver's band.
Upsoars the prize; the youth, with joy unfeign'd,
Regain'd the felt, and felt what he regain'd,
While to the applauding galleries grateful Pat
Made a low bow, and touch'd the ransom'd hat.

40. T. N. Talfourd on Crabbe as historian of the poor

1815

Sir Thomas Noon Talfourd (1795–1854) contributed to early issues of the *Pamphleteer*. This review appeared in v, 437–43, in an article 'A Sketch of the History of Poetry'. It contains some instructive comparisons.

It will be universally admitted even by those who do not regard him as a *poet* that MR. CRABBE is a moral writer of great excellence. He does not indeed aspire to enforce the more obvious and striking duties—to present us with admirable examples of heroic virtue, or to display the sad effects of the daring and odious vices—but he sets forth the humbler charities, and traces out the miserable and often fatal consequences, which flow from habits and affectations which we are disposed to consider as venial. The evils that by the very mention appal us are perhaps seldom to be prevented by any serious exhortation;—the turbulence of the passion which hurries on its victims to destruction is in general too fierce to be opposed by reasoning; for no one is so entangled with sophistry as to need to be convinced of its tendency. The lesser vices, on the other hand, are often veiled by the name of imprudence, they approach us in inviting forms; and even border closely on the virtues which it is most the fashion to admire. He, therefore, who will detect these in their artful disguises, and trace out the folly and the sorrows which arise from their pursuit, is a better moralist than the pompous declaimer on the cardinal virtues, or the eloquent reasoner who demonstrates with irresistible force that bloody ambition is pernicious—that war destroys mankind—or that robbery and murder are sinful. The youth who has learned the consequences of procrastination, or the anguish that results from stepping out of our sphere in life, from such simple yet weighty productions, will have received far more practical benefit, than if he had been sympathizing with George Barnwell, and learning from that inimitable extract of the Newgate Calendar, that to kill an uncle is the probable course to the scaffold. In this respect, Mr. Crabbe bears a striking resemblance to Miss Edgeworth in her admirable delineations of humble life; though in his tales of sorrow he has infinitely more compassion for his victims and pity for the frailties of our species. Yet there are many who cannot deny the practical utility of his writings, who refuse to admit them to be poetry—because their persons are confined to the inferior classes of society—because they do not elevate us with delight—and rather present us with portraits of actual existence than transport us into worlds created by original genius.

The first objection will, however, have very little weight with those who are not dazzled by the glare of French criticism. The human heart —the native seat of English poets—is ever the same in its more important varieties and may be rendered equally interesting by the magic touches of the writer. Thus, although Shakespeare has most frequently drawn the characters of kings and princes, it is one of his peculiar excellencies that he has drawn them as *men*. There is very little of nobility or royalty in any of his heroes: his Romans have not much of the Roman in them—or of any artificial distinctions as removed from the great leading traits which are impressed on the deep chords of the species. If they are majestic, it is the intellectual greatness of the man and not the stateliness of the prince by which we are awed into reverence. It is not in the higher ranks of life where feeling has been frittered away by excessive refinements, where the heart has been deadened by unmeaning courtesy and variable fashion, that we should expect to find imagination running into luxuriance, or passion bursting out in terrible energy. The joys which are to be found in the affections of nature, in homely virtues which nestle among the middle class of men; in domestic tenderness and youthful love—are not felt so deeply, even when they are felt at all, in that lofty region where life is like a calm and polished stream upon which men move in a round of amusements and gaieties. It is in the midst of struggles with fortune, ardent aspirings which look through long and stormy vistas to the objects of their desire; fluctuations which perpetually call for sympathy and awaken the lovelier charities—that they expand and florish. As these are the ranks which have produced the finest minds, which have raised us in the scale of being, it cannot be unnatural for genius occasionally to glance at the walks of its infancy and to celebrate the persons with whom it was then familiar. They are not only interesting to those who are acquainted with their peculiar emotions, and who enter into all their full-swoln joys and heart rending distresses, but to them who have always occupied more exalted stations. We look on the poor without envy, their sorrows affect us more naturally than the grief of those who are surrounded with luxury even in the midst of their distresses; and whom we feel a secret gratification in beholding reduced to participate in the common lot of humanity. A celebration of their 'short and simple annals' revives within us a thousand sensations of pity which their woes have excited—and a thousand pictures of real anguish softened by the recollection that we are often able to console and relieve it. To a good mind, these representations will be full of mysterious delight, they will convey to it a thrill of unearthly rapture by reviving the emotions produced by numberless acts of charity and kindness; while the acts themselves have faded from the memory, though duly observed and registered in heaven.

Excepting, indeed, in the excitement of these associations, Mr. Crabbe does not often affect us through the medium of delight. The sensations he produces are painful and often oppressive, from the fidelity with which his pictures are drawn and the universal dominion of the feelings which his narrative produces. But it should be remembered that men seek not only after what is commonly denominated pleasure, but after powerful sensation, or to speak more accurately, they search for pleasure not only in the sources of peace and tranquillity, but in the stormy vehemence of passion. Life itself, the first of blessings, is carried to a higher degree of vividness, in proportion as all the faculties of the spirit are called into fervid exercise. The same principle which makes us desire to live impels us to wish to feel with intenseness. Even suspense, the greatest perhaps of torments, is frequently sought with avidity, and we cling even to sorrow, we nurse and feed melancholy, as a relief from the dull insipidity of inaction. The dangers of enterprize, the agonies of gaming, the terrors of superstition, owe their continuance to a strange satisfaction in the whirl and depth of the desires. So the belief even of eternal torments, with its dark and terrible sublimity, is defended by its advocates, less as a solemn truth of scripture, than as an idea producing stupendous and inconceivable terrors—which has become a favorite contemplation with men who imagine themselves personally secure. All mankind too look back on past afflictions with a sacred and inconceivable pleasure, and cherish the memory of their distresses with a joy far beyond the measure of ordinary gladness. Man is not only born to trouble but fitted to endure it. By a kindly disposition of his nature he snatches his finest enjoyments from sufferings without which even bliss would become tasteless. Those who wonder why heaven should have permitted sorrow and evil to enter a world which it might have preserved in the purities of an immortal Eden, forget that as without the one very little virtue could have been produced, so without the other happiness, however perfect, would scarcely have been perceived by the recipient. The common breathings and actions of healthy existence are full of pleasure, but we do not perceive it because they form the usual state of our being; but we enjoy them at every pore after they have been suspended. So heaven, with its unbroken repose, would have been comparatively joyless, had we not here become familiar with affliction, over which we shall delight to brood when we arrive at the universal haven. It is upon this principle that we are charmed with the deepest melancholy tragedies than by the liveliest specimens of gaiety. And it is upon this principle too that Mr. Crabbe has outstepped the generality of writers in their natural delineations of sorrow, has stripped off the glittering tapestry and the ceremonial pomp by which the heroes of ancient story are excluded from the full weight of human sympathies. He has dared to tear away all the obstructions to our grief—all the ornaments by which its course was diverted, and mingled with milder and less overpowering sensations. Hence it is no wonder that he should be regarded with aversion by the giddy and the worldling, all who are exclusively in love with the garishness of joy—and who cannot endure the shock of those homely and awful sensations which are the favorite food of prouder and more lofty spirits.

Nor will the last objection, that Mr. Crabbe is not an *inventive* poet, avail the opposers of his fame. It is true that he has not 'exhausted worlds and then imagined new'—and that, in general, he has presented us with pictures which are so real and so unadorned, that we acknowledge them as the exact representations of reality rather than as the offspring of fancy. But the truth is that we err by ascribing a wrong sense to the word *invention*, which we use as if it imported some actual production of the mind composed of materials which are wholly new. Whereas in reality we are capable of no ideas but those which we receive through the medium of our senses, we can imagine no new words that we do not build from the fragments of the old—we can paint no emotion whose scattered elements do not subsist within us, we can describe no Paradise without the forms and the colors by which we are surrounded. The whole of imaginative imagery from the dome of Olympus down to the palaces of Mr. Southey, composed of rainbow and wreathed fire, is but a various association of images with which the meanest are familiar. It is no doubt perfectly true that no beings exactly similar to Milton's devils ever existed, and that no living mortal has ever beheld a scene of such perfect loveliness as his Eden. But it is no less certain than those which subsisted in the mind of man and in the beauties of external creation. Shakespeare, although generally acknowledged to be a greater *inventive* genius, did not even go near so far as this—for his persons are such as have often lived and his descriptions are exacter copies of nature. Indeed if imagining new things was the standard of the poet's highest property, the Arabian nights entertainments and the curse of Kehama are infinitely superior to Homer, Milton, or Shakespeare. We are, therefore, to regard the faculty of *invention* as a power, not of *creating* new substances, but of *discovering* what already exists. It is this which developes the workings of the heart, and opens rich stores of wisdom and thought of which we were before unconscious. The accusation against Mr. Crabbe then is no more than this, that instead of blending together a variety of images collected from different parts of nature, and throwing their glory over the range of his poetry, he has ventured to confine himself to the class which he has chosen—to pour over it no external sanctity, to adorn it with no extrinsic graces, but to unfold its stores of richness and beauty as they appear to the undazzled eye of a gifted and accurate observer.

It is true that this experiment was hazardous, nor are we prepared to maintain that it has in every respect succeeded. The effort has at all events given abundant proof of a potent and original genius. His power of accurate description is quite unrivalled; and if he has not sought to array nature in fresh charms, to pour a brighter green over her tufted groves and luxuriant recesses, he has exhibited the rare faculty of displaying one moment the most revolting of her external forms and, at another, of shadowing out her wildest and most striking productions. He is peculiarly conversant with that amiable satire which at once laughs at and loves, the easy good-humoured ridicule which so gently relieves the pathos of *The Vicar of Wakefield* and *The Deserted Village*, though he is destitute of the uniform sweetness and flowing versification of Goldsmith. In his softer and more delicate touches he resembles Cowper—that pure spirit whose saddest melancholy was full of kind-heartedness and relieved by the sweetest pictures of devotion; who loved the most humble retirements of nature, and listened, as to heavenly consolation, to her softest voices. Like him, Mr. Crabbe abounds in touching representations of every-day incidents and feelings, although he unfortunately substitutes a cumbrous pomp for his graceful ease, and wants the pervading enthusiasm which gives vitality to his finest conceptions. He has entered the lowly walks of life, not for the purpose of grouping, among their seclusions, elegances which belong to a different region, or even of filling them with perfect and undashed pictures of refined and gentle affections; but he has done more than any living writer, except Miss Edgeworth, to render them what others have been contented to feign. It is true that in his minute representations of hardhearted villainy, he has often bordered on the shocking and disgustful; but there will generally be found, as in the works of Hogarth, some kind and gentle touch which sobers the whole scene—some amiable object, which from his consummate skill, operates not in the way of contrast, but mellows and throws a softness over the most revolting figures, and leaves the heart, after all its lacerations, to a sweet and consoling repose.

Although it is true that Mr. Crabbe is often wearisome in his minute pictures of common circumstances and mean occupations, there is perhaps something in this minuteness that more than overpays our attention. It gives to the whole a strong appearance of truth, a vivid distinctness, which heightens, in an inconceivable degree, the more touching and lofty part of his narrations. Every one knows the peculiar interest he has always felt for the heroes of the *Iliad*—how completely he has identified himself with their sensations, and been rapt into the very costume and manner of the period to which the action is referred. Perhaps there are few human emotions so glowing—few of the loves and desires of our youth so free from decay—as the breathless anxiety, the engrossing interest, with which we first perused the works of Homer, and fought among battles decided by the interference of deities whose existence we can scarcely imagine. As we are contented to enjoy the charm, without analysing the materials from which it is produced, we are, in general, little aware how much of this effect is to be ascribed to the seeming accuracy with which the every-day employments and common habits of the shepherd-heroes are delineated, while those pictures form an admirable relief to the bustling and terrible scenes on which they border. In this respect, Richardson, of all writers, most nearly resembles Homer. We see all his characters in their undress, and engaged in the usual pleasures and occupations of life, in which it requires no effort to believe them actually to exist. Thus we slip into their privacy, and become their friends and confidents, before we are aware

—till the interest we feel for them is raised to an inconceivable height—and when we come to the deeper and more surprising parts of the story, we feel for them, not only as real persons, but as old acquaintances, and are overwhelmed and melted by our own emotions before we can relieve ourselves by forcing on our remembrance, that the woes we are deploring are fictitious. This is one of those master keys by which this wonderful writer subdues our hearts to this pleasure. The reader who should peruse only his terrible and pathetic scenes, with a previous knowledge of the history, would have a very slight conception of their wonder-working magic. We must go through with patience and attention, the whole of his dull routs, and journies, and dialogues, in order to feel the force of his dreadful pictures—as we must gaze on the champions of Troy, devouring their short repasts, and buckling on their armor, if we would go with them into the thickest terrors of the combat. It is the same, though of course in an inferior degree, with the tediousness of Mr. Crabbe; he paints the scene in which his humble heroes act and suffer with such seeming fidelity and truth, that it is almost impossible to believe the transactions and woes to be ideal. They seem remembered rather than invented,—and in all their parts have a reality so painful, that we are glad to escape from them into lighter fancies—without paying due homage to the genius of an author, who in his power over the heart belongs to the good old school of our English poets.

41. Hazlitt on 'still life of tragedy' in Crabbe

1818

The forthrightness of William Hazlitt (1778–1830), almost to the point of idiosyncrasy, is well illustrated in his criticism of Crabbe. This passage comes from 'On Thomson and Cowper' in *Lectures on the English Poets* (1818).

Crabbe is, if not the most natural, the most literal of our descriptive poets. He exhibits the smallest circumstances of the smallest things. He gives the very costume of meanness; the non-essentials of every trifling incident. He is his own landscape painter, and engraver too. His pastoral scenes seem pricked on paper in little dotted lines. He describes the interior of a cottage like a person sent there to distrain for rent. He has an eye to the number of arms in an old worm-eaten chair, and takes care to inform himself and the reader whether a joint-stool stands upon three legs or upon four. If a settle by the fire-side stands awry, it gives him as much disturbance as a tottering world; and he records the rent in a ragged counterpane as an event in history. He is equally curious in his backgrounds and in his figures. You know the christian and sur-names of every one of his heroes,—the dates of their achievements, whether on a Sunday or a Monday,—their place of birth and burial, the colour of their clothes, and of their hair, and whether they squinted or not. He takes an inventory of the human heart exactly in the same man-ner as of the furniture of a sick-room: his sentiments have very much the air of fixtures; he gives you the petrification of a sigh, and carves a tear, to the life, in stone. Almost all his characters are tired of their lives, and you heartily wish them dead. They remind one of anatomical preservations; or may be said to bear the same relation to actual life that a stuffed cat in a glass-case does to the real one purring on the hearth: the skin is the same, but the life and the sense of heat is gone. Crabbe's poetry is like a museum, or curiosity-shop: every thing has the same posthumous appearance, the same inanimateness and identity of char-acter. If Bloomfield is too much of the Farmer's Boy, Crabbe is too much of the parish beadle, an overseer of the country poor. He has no delight beyond the walls of a workhouse, and his officious zeal would convert the world into a vast infirmary. He is a kind of Ordinary, not of Newgate, but of nature. His poetical morality is taken from Burn's *Justice*, or the Statutes against Vagrants. He sets his own imagination in the stocks, and his Muse, like Malvolio, 'wears cruel garters'. He collects all the petty vices of the human heart, and superintends, as in a panopticon, a select circle of rural malefactors. He makes out the poor to be as bad as the rich—a sort of vermin for the others to hunt down and trample upon, and this he thinks a good piece of work. With him there are but two moral categories, riches and poverty, authority and dependence. His parish apprentice, Richard Monday, and his wealthy baronet, Sir Richard Monday, of Monday-place, are the same individual—the extremes of the same character, and of his whole system. 'The latter end of his Commonwealth does not forget the beginning.'[1] But his parish ethics are the very worst model for a state: anything more degrading and helpless cannot well be imagined. He exhibits just the contrary view of human life to that which Gay has done in his *Beggar's Opera*. In a word, Crabbe is the only poet who has attempted and succeeded in the *still life* of tragedy: who gives the stagnation of hope and fear—the deformity of vice without the temptation—the pain of sympathy without the interest—and who seems to rely, for the delight he is to convey to his reader, on the truth and accuracy with which he describes only what is disagreeable. . . .

[1] *The Tempest* II, i, 152 (misquoted).

42. R. H. Dana replies to Hazlitt

1819

Richard Henry Dana (1787–1879) reviewed extensively for the *North American Review*. This article on 'Hazlitt's English Poets' appeared in viii (1819), 315–18. He also wrote poetry; his 'Buccaneer' shows the influence of Crabbe and Wordsworth.

If variety of powers in a single mind be accounted genius, who among modern poets shall be placed before Crabbe? We do not mean by this, that certain quickness and aptitude for any thing, no matter what, by which some men perform pretty well whatever they choose to undertake, or like Bunyan's 'Talkative,' can discourse you what you will; 'will talk of things heavenly or things earthly, things moral or things evangelical, things sacred or things profane, things past or things to come, things foreign or things at home, things more essential or things circumstantial.'—This is what we call smartness, or sometimes dignify with the title of talent. But it is rather a misfortune than a blessing to the man who possesses it, and to his neighbours; for he will have an active part in whatever is done or said, yet all that comes from him is, at most, but second best. Yet his versatility astonishes the bystanders. What would he be, could he condescend to devote his powers to a single pursuit! He would be only a second rate man in that. His change is his weakness, a want of a particular bent of mind, arising not from an intense universal love, but a knowing all things superficially, and a caring little for any thing. We mean not that variety of powers which makes a man turn poet, politician, divine, artist, mathematician, metaphysician, chemist, and botanist, with the alterations of fashion or whim, but that by which one feels and sees in all its changes and relations the particular object for which nature seems solely to have made him. And this variety has Crabbe beyond any man since the days of Shakspeare. Reading Shakspeare is studying the world; and though we would not apply this in any thing like its full extent to Crabbe, yet we do not hesitate to say, that such a variety of characters, with the growth and

215

gradual change in each individual, the most secret thoughts, and the course of the passions from a perfect calm to their most violent tossings, and all the humours of men, cannot be found so fully brought together, and distinctly made out, in any other author since Shakspeare and our old dramatists. Nor is this done by a cold anatomical process or anxious repetition. Though every variation is distinctly marked, and made visible to us, there is no appearance of labour, nor are we left standing as mere lookers-on. It is not a dissection of character as has been sometimes said. The men and women are living and moving beings, suffering and acting; we take a deep interest in all their concerns, and are moved to terrour or deep grief, to gaiety or laughter, with them. Nothing but the dramatic form could imbody us more completely in them. Notwithstanding there is such a multitude of characters, and none of them, except Sir Eustace Grey, lying higher than the middle class of society, or engaged in any but the ordinary pursuits of life, yet no repetition is produced.—As in life, some have a general resemblance, but particular differences prevent a flat sameness.

No one is a stronger master of the passions. Peter Grimes, the Patron, Edward Shore, the Parish Clerk,—it is endless to go on naming them,— take hold of us with a power that we have not felt since the time of our old poets, except now and then in Lord Byron. He is quite as good too in playful sarcasm and humour. The bland Vicar,[1] whom 'sectaries liked—he never troubled them,' moved to complaining by nothing but innovations in forms and ceremonies, who extracted 'moral compliment' from flowers, for the ladies, the fire of whose love burnt like a very glow-worm, and who declared his passion with all the uncontrolled ardour of Slender,—who protested to Mistress Ann Page 'that he loved her as well as he loved any woman in Gloucestershire,'—the whole story of this once 'ruddy and fair' youth, whose arts were 'fiddling and fishing,' is sustained throughout, and is one of the most delightfully sarcastic and humorous tales ever read. There are the same particularity, clearness, and nice observation in his descriptions, but with no marks of the tool. His scenes are just the very places in which his men and women should be set down, or rather such as they appear to have grown up in from children; so that the occupations of his people, their characters and the scenes amidst which they live, are in perfect keeping with each other, and brought together just as they should be. And this gives a feeling, sentiment, and reality to his description. Where else could Peter Grimes have been placed than where he is?

[1] *The Borough*, III.

> . . . when tides were neap,—
> There anchoring, Peter chose from man to hide,
> There hang his head, and view the lazy tide
> In its hot slimy channel slowly glide.[1]
> [*The Borough*, XXII, 181, 185–7]

But we forget that Peter Grimes, for power and development of character unequalled before or since, even by Crabbe himself, and placed in the midst of scenery painted with an originality and poetry which we have scarce seen before, is shut out by Crabbe's earliest and warmest admirers, the Edinburgh Reviewers, because it was thought necessary to write a dissertation under the title of the word 'disgusting,' and found convenient to sacrifice him as an example. For an exemplification of their principle, they might as well have taken Macbeth or Iago, for Peter could equally with them cause a poetical dread.—Crabbe's versification has been compared to Pope's. There is very seldom a resemblance. It is easy and familiar, when his subject is so, and rises with it. It is infinitely more varied than Pope's, though not so much broken as Cowper's rhyming verse. His language, strongly idiomatic, has no bad words in it, and is very eloquent and poetic when he chooses.

We do assure Mr. Hazlitt, that if he and master Leigh Hunt[1] undertake to turn such gentlemen as Crabbe into the kitchen, they will soon have the parlour all to themselves. They may amuse each other as much as they like, and admire their own forms and the tie of their cravats, in the full length mirror,—there will be but four of them, Hunt and Hazlitt in the glass, and Hunt and Hazlitt out of it, all equally agreeable. . . .

[1] See below, No. 51(h).

TALES OF THE HALL

July 1819

In June, 1819, the *Tales of the Hall* were published by Mr. Murray; who, for them and the remaining copyright of all my father's previous poems, gave the munificent sum of 3000 l. The new work had, at least, as general approbation as any that had gone before it; and was not the less liked for its opening views of a higher class of society than he had hitherto dealt much in.[1]

43. John Wilson ('Christopher North'), unsigned review, *Blackwood's Edinburgh Magazine*

July 1819, v, 469–83

John Wilson (1785–1854) was associated with *Blackwood's* from its beginning in 1817. The definite, sometimes exaggerated and occasionally contradictory nature of his criticism is illustrated in his writing on Crabbe (see also No. 53).

Burns, Wordsworth, and Crabbe, are the three poets who, in our days, have most successfully sought the subjects and scenes of their inspiration in the character and life of the People. While most of our other great poets have in imagination travelled into foreign countries, and endeavoured to add to those profounder emotions which all representations of human passion necessarily excite, that more lively impression of novelty and surprise produced by the difference of national manners, and all the varieties of external nature—or have restricted themselves,

[1] *Life*, Ch. 9.

as, for example, in the splendid instance of Scott, to one romantic era of history—those Three have, in almost all their noblest compositions, grappled closely with the feelings which at all times constitute the hearts and souls of our own Islanders, so that the haunt of their song may be said to have lain in the wide and magnificent regions of the British character. Accordingly, their poetry has been more deeply felt, where it has been felt at all, than that of any of their contemporaries. No poet ever so lived in the love of the people of his native country as Burns now lives; and his poetry has intermingled itself so vitally with the best feelings of their nature, that it will exist in Scotland while Scotland retains her character for knowledge, morality, and religion. Crabbe is, confessedly, the most original and vivid painter of the vast varieties of common life, that England has ever produced; and while several living poets possess a more splendid and imposing reputation, we are greatly mistaken if he has not taken a firmer hold than any other, on the melancholy convictions of men's hearts ruminating on the good and evil of this mysterious world. Wordsworth, again, has produced poetry reflecting the shadows of our existence, which has met with a very singular kind of reception among the people of Britain. For, while he is considered by some as a totally misguided man of genius, and by some as a versifier of no merit at all, he is looked on by others, and among them minds of the first order, as the poet who has seen deeper into the constitution of the human soul than any other since the days of Shakspeare. Though, therefore, not yet a popular poet, (in the noblest sense of the word popular,) like Burns and Crabbe, Wordsworth has exerted a power over the mind of his age, perhaps, of deeper and more permanent operation than that of all the rest of the poetry by which it has been elevated and adorned. There is not a man of poetical genius in Britain who is not under manifold obligations to his pure and angelic muse; and though the responses of her inspiration have been neglected or scorned by the vulgar and the low, they have been listened to with the deepest delight by all kindred spirits, and have breathed a character of simplicity and grandeur over the whole poetry of the age.

But though we have thus classed these three great poets together, as the poets of human nature, who, in modern times, have thought nothing that belongs to human nature in our country unworthy of their regard, nothing surely can be more different than the views they take of its forms and shews, as well as the moods and emotions which the contemplation of all these awakens in their hearts. Each is in strength a king—but the boundaries of their kingdoms are marked by clear lines of light—and they achieved their greatest conquests without the invasion of each other's territory.

Burns is by far the greatest poet that ever sprung from the bosom of the People, and lived and died in a lowly condition of life. Indeed no country in the world, but Scotland, could have produced such a man—and Burns will, through all posterity, be an object of intense and delighted interest, as the glorious representative of the national and intellectual character of his country. He was born a poet, if ever man was, and to his native genius alone is owing the perpetuity of his fame. For he manifestly never studied poetry as an art, nor reasoned on its principles—nor looked abroad, with the wide ken of intellect, for objects and subjects on which to pour out his inspiration. The condition of the peasantry of Scotland—the happiest, perhaps, that Providence ever allowed to the children of labour—was not surveyed and speculated on by Burns as the field of poetry, but as the field of his own existence; and he chronicled the events that passed there, not as food for his imagination as a poet, but as food for his heart as a man. Hence, when genius impelled him to write poetry, poetry came gushing freshly up from the well of his human affections. . . .

He wrote not to please or surprise others, but in his own delight; and even after he discovered the power of his talent to kindle the sparks of nature wherever they slumbered, the effect to be produced seems never to have been considered by him,—informed, as he was, by the spirit within him, that his poetry was sure to produce that passion in the hearts of other men from which it boiled over in his own. Whatever, therefore, be the faults, or defects, or deficiencies, of the poetry of Burns—and no doubt it has many—it has, beyond all the poetry that ever was written, this greatest of all merits—intense, passionate, life-pervading, and life-breathing truth.

Wordsworth, on the other hand, is a man of high intellect and profound sensibility, meditating in solitude on the phenomena of human nature. He sometimes seems to our imagination like a man contemplating from the shore the terrors of the sea, not surely with apathy, but with a solemn and almost unimpassioned sense of the awful mysteries of Providence. This seeming self-abstraction from the turmoil of life gives to his highest poetry a still and religious character that is truly sublime—though, at the same time, it often leads to a sort of mysticism, and carries the poet out of those sympathies which are engendered in human hearts by a sense of our common imperfections. Perhaps it would not be wrong to say, that his creed is sometimes too austere, and that it deals, almost unmercifully, with misguided sensibilities and perverted passions. Such, at least, is a feeling that occasionally steals upon us from the loftiest passages of *The Excursion*, in which the poet, desirous of soaring to heaven, forgets that he is a frail child of earth, and would in vain free his human nature from those essential passions, which, in the pride of intellect, he seems unduly to despise!

But the sentiment which we have now very imperfectly expressed, refers almost entirely to the higher morals of *The Excursion*, and has little or no respect to that poetry of Wordsworth in which he has painted the character and life of certain classes of the English People. True, that he stands to a certain degree aloof from the subjects of his description, but he ever looks on them all with tenderness and benignity. Their cares and anxieties are indeed not his own, and therefore, in painting them, he does not, like Burns, identify himself with the creatures of his poetry. But, at the same time, he graciously and humanely descends into the lowliest walks of life—and knowing that humanity is sacred, he views its spirit with reverence. Though far above the beings whose nature he delineates, he yet comes down in his wisdom to their humble level, and strives to cherish that spirit

> Which gives to all the same intent,
> When life is pure and innocent.

The natural disposition of his mind inclines him to dwell rather on the mild, gentle, and benignant affections, than on the more agitating passions. Indeed, in almost all cases, the passions of his agents subside into affections—and a feeling of tranquillity and repose is breathed from his saddest pictures of human sorrow. It seems to be part of his creed, that neither vice nor misery should be allowed in the representations of the poet, to stand prominently and permanently forward, and that poetry should give a true but a beautiful reflection of life. Certain it is, that of all the poets of this age, or perhaps any age, Wordsworth holds the most cheering and consolatory faith—and that we at all times rise from his poetry, not only with an abatement of those fears and perplexities which the dark aspect of the world often flings over our hearts, but almost with a scorn of the impotence of grief, and certainly with a confiding trust in the perfect goodness of the Deity. We would appeal, for the truth of these remarks, to all who have studied the Two Books of *The Excursion*, entitled, 'The Church-Yard among the Mountains'. There, in narrating the history of the humble dead, Wordsworth does not fear to speak of their frailties, their errors, and their woes. It is indeed beautifully characteristic of the benignant wisdom of the man, that when he undertakes the task of laying open the hearts of his fellow mortals, he prefers the dead to the living, because he is willing that erring humanity should enjoy the privilege of the grave, and that his own soul should be filled with that charity which is breathed from the silence of the house of God. It is needless to say with what profound pathos the poet speaks of life thus surrounded with the images of death—how more beautiful beauty rises from the grave—how more quietly innocence seems there to slumber—and how awful is the rest of guilt.

General and indeed vague as is this account of the genius of Wordsworth, perhaps it may serve, by the power of contrast, to bring into more prominent view the peculiar genius of Crabbe. He delights to look over society with a keen, scrutinizing, and somewhat stern eye, as if resolved that the human heart should not be suffered to conceal one single secret from his inquisitorial authority. He has evidently an intense satisfaction in moral anatomy; and in the course of his dissections, he lays bare, with an unshrinking hand, the very arteries of the heart. It will, we believe, be found, that he has always a humane purpose,— though conscious of our own frailties, as we all are, we cannot help sometimes accusing him of unrelenting severity. When he finds a wound, he never fails to probe it to the bottom.

Of all men of this age, he is the best portrait-painter. He is never contented with a single flowing sketch of a character—they must all be drawn full-length—to the very life—and with all their most minute and characteristic features even of dress and manners. He seems to have known them all personally; and when he describes them, he does so as if he thought that he would be guilty of a kind of falsehood, in omitting the description of a single peculiarity. Accordingly, to make the picture in all things a perfect likeness, he very often enters into details that weary, nay, even disgust—and not unfrequently a character is forced, obtruded as it were, on our acquaintance, of whose disagreeable existence we were before happily ignorant. His observation of men and manners has been so extensive and so minute, that his power of raising up living characters is wholly without limitation; and Mr. Crabbe has thrown open a gallery, in which single portraits and groupes of figures follow each other in endless procession, habited in all the varieties of dress that distinguish the professions, orders, and occupations of the whole of human society.

Perhaps the very highest poetical enthusiasm is not compatible with such exquisite acuteness of discernment, or if it be, the continual exercise of that faculty must at least serve to abate it. Accordingly, the views which Mr. Crabbe does in general take of human life, are not of a very lofty kind; and he rarely, if ever, either in principle or feeling, exhibits the idealism of nature. Accustomed thus to look on men as they exist and act, he not only does not fear, but he absolutely loves to view their vices and their miseries; and hence has his poetry been accused, and perhaps with some reason, of giving too dark a picture of life. But, at the same time, we must remember, what those haunts of life are into which his spirit has wandered. Throughout a great part of his poetry, he has chosen to describe certain kinds of society and people, of which no other poet we know could have made any thing at all. The power is almost miraculous with which he has stirred up human nature from its very dregs, and shewn working in them the common spirit of humanity. Human life becomes more various and wonderful in his hands, pregnant with passion as it seems to be, throughout the lowest debasement of profligacy and ignorance. He lays before us scenes and characters from which in real life we would turn our eyes with intolerant disgust; and yet he forces us to own, that on such scenes and by such characters much the same kind of part is played that ourselves, and others like us, play on another stage. He leaves it to other poets to carry us into the company of shepherds and dalesmen, in the heart of pastoral peace; and sets us down in crowds of fierce and sullen men, contending against each other, in lawful or in lawless life, with all the energies of exasperated passion. Mr. Hazlitt, in his *Lectures on English Poets*,[1] has said, that in Crabbe we find the still life of tragedy. To us it appears, on the other hand, that till Crabbe wrote, we knew not what direful tragedies are for ever steeping in tears or in blood the footsteps of the humblest of our race; and that he has opened, as it were, a theatre on which the homely actors that pass before us assume no disguise—on which every catastrophe borrows its terror from truth, and every scene seems shifted by the very hands of nature.

In all the poetry of this extraordinary man, we see a constant display of the passions as they are excited and exacerbated by the customs, and laws, and institutions of society. Love, anger, hatred, melancholy, despair, and remorse, in all their infinite modifications, as exhibited by different natures and under different circumstances, are rife throughout all his works; and a perpetual conflict is seen carried on among all the feelings and principles of our nature, that can render that nature happy or miserable. We see love breaking through in desperation, but never

[1] See above, No. 41.

223

with impunity, the barriers of human laws; or in hopelessness dying beneath them, with or without its victim. The stream of life flows over a rugged and precipitous channel in the poetry of Crabbe, and we are rarely indeed allowed to sail down it in a reverie or a dream. The pleasure he excites is almost always a troubled pleasure, and accompanied with tears and sighs, or with the profounder agitation of a sorrow that springs out of the conviction forced upon us of the most imperfect nature, and therefore the most imperfect happiness of man.

Now, if all this were done in the mere pride of genius and power, we should look on Mr. Crabbe in any other light than as the benefactor of his species. But in the midst of all his skill—all his art—we see often—indeed always—the tenderness of the man's heart; and we hear him, with a broken and melancholy voice, mourning over the woe and wickedness whose picture he has so faithfully drawn. Never in any one instance (and he claims this most boldly in his preface) has he sought to veil or to varnish vice—to confuse our notions of right and wrong—to depreciate moral worth, or exaggerate the value of worldly accomplishments—to cheat us out of our highest sympathies due to defeated or victorious virtue, or to induce us, in blindfolded folly, to bestow them on splendid guilt and dazzling crime. It is his to read aloud to us the records of our own hearts—the book of fate—and he does not close the leaves because too often stained with rueful tears. This world is a world of sin and sorrow, and he thinks, and thinks rightly, that it becomes him who has a gifted sight into its inmost heart, to speak of the triumphs of that sin, and the wretchedness of that sorrow, to beings who are all born to pass under that two-fold yoke. We do not believe that a bad or even an imperfect moral can be legitimately drawn from the spirit of any of Mr. Crabbe's poetry.

We have said this now, because we know that he has been called a gloomy, which must mean, if any accusation is implied in the term, a false moralist. No doubt, to persons who read his poetry superficially and by snatches and glances, it may seem to give too dark a picture of life,—but this, we are convinced, is not the feeling which the study of the whole awakens. Here and there, he presents us with images of almost perfect beauty, innocence, and happiness—but as such things are seldom seen, and soon disappear in real life, it seems to be Mr. Crabbe's opinion, that so likewise, ought they to start out with sudden and transitory smiles among the darker, the more solemn, or the gloomy pictures of his poetry. It is certain that there are, in this writer, passages of as pure and profound pathos as in any English poet—that he dwells with as holy a delight as any other on the settled countenance of peace, and that, in his wanderings through the mazes of human destiny, his heart burns within him, when his eyes are, at times, charmed away from the troubles and the wickedness of life to its repose and its virtue.

There is, however, one point on which we cannot agree with Mr. Crabbe, and on which we feel that we may, without arrogance, affirm that he is wrong. He has not made that use of religion in poetry which a poet, a philosopher, and a Christian such as he is, might—and ought to have made. On this subject, however, we intend to speak fully soon, and to shew that no poetry which aspires to the character of a picture of man and nature can be otherwise than imperfect from which are excluded, or but partially introduced, the consideration and illustration of the influence of religion on the whole structure of society and life. . . .

The *Tales of the Hall* consist of many poems, in which the lives of so vast a number of individuals are unfolded, that it may almost be said that a general view is given in them of the moral character of the people of England. There is something very happy in the plan of that one poem to which all the different stories belong; and the interest that we are made to take in the destinies of the persons who recite the narrative imparts so great a charm to the whole, that our feelings never flag, but with increasing sympathy and delight watch the fortunes of every successive actor that is brought to figure before us. . . . There is great tenderness and beauty in all that relates to the affection of the brothers, and the contrast of their characters is throughout most admirably sustained. . . .

Strong as this painting is, its strength can be fully felt by those alone who have read the whole story of 'Ruth,' and of all her wild and confounding afflictions. Never was hopeless distress, day by day persecuted unto the death, delineated with such fearful truth—but the whole description so hangs together in its darkness, that no fragments could present an adequate idea of the desolation.

'Thus my poor Ruth was wretched and undone, . . .
[V, 233–52, 416–67]

I knew not then their worth; and, had I known, . . .
[VIII, 681–746]

Years past away, and where he lived, and how, . . .
[III, 237–95, 302–24]

Dark and despairing though this picture be, our next quotation shall be one yet more terrible. In the hands of ordinary writers, tales of seduction are such maudlin things, that one almost loses his horror for the wretched criminals in pity of the still more wretched writers. But Crabbe bears us down with him into the depths of agony, and terrifies us with a holy fear of the punishment, which even on earth eats into the adulterer's heart. The story of Farmer Ellis, might, we think, have stood by itself, instead of being introduced merely as part of another story—but Mr. Crabbe very frequently brings forward his very finest things, as illustrations of others of inferior interest, or as accessories to less momentous matter. . . .

'Hear me, Sir Owen:—I had sought them long, . . .
[XII, 696–890]

This is somewhat superior to Kotzebue's Stranger and Mrs. Haller. Farmer Ellis is but a homely person, it is true—but he is an Englishman, and he behaves like one, with the dagger of grief festering in his heart. Nothing can be more affecting than his conduct in granting an asylum in a lonely spot on his own grounds to the repentant wretch who had once been so dear to him—a sanctuary, as it were, where she may live within the protection of her husband's humanity, though for ever divorced from his love—and where the melancholy man knows that she is making her peace with God, in a calm haven provided for her against the waves of the world by him whose earthly happiness she had for ever destroyed. Never did a more sublime moral belong to a tale of guilt.

But we shall now lay before our readers a picture of gentler sorrows— . . .

Nor pass the pebbled cottage as you rise . . .
[XVIII, 61–6, 84–99; 286–99; 300–45, 348–51]

For the present we close our extracts from these admirable volumes with some passages from the last of the *Tales*, which is entitled 'Smugglers and Poachers,' and which is perhaps the most characteristic of them all, of Mr. Crabbe's genius. It opens in this beautiful and natural way.

[XXI, 1–27; 28–35; 349–402; 465–86; 541–93; 621–32.]

We had much more to say of Mr. Crabbe and his genius, but we must wait till another opportunity. We cannot, however, bid farewell to him, for the present, without observing, with real delight, that while old age has not at all impaired the vigour of his intellect, or blunted the acuteness of his observation, it seems to have mellowed and softened his feelings just to the degree that his best friends may have once thought desirable—and that while he still looks on human life with the same philosophic eye, and spares none of its follies or its vices, he thinks of it with somewhat of a gentler and more pitying spirit, as of one who has well understood it all, and who looks back upon its agitations and its guilt as on a troubled and unintelligible scene, from which, in the course of nature, he may soon be removed in the strength of that trust which can only be inspired by that religion of which he has so long been a conscientious minister.

44. Francis Jeffrey, unsigned review, *Edinburgh Review*

July 1819, xxxii, 118–48

Mr. Crabbe is the greatest *mannerist*, perhaps, of all our living poets, and it is rather unfortunate that the most prominent features of his mannerism are not the most pleasing. The homely, quaint, and prosaic style— the flat, and often broken and jingling versification—the eternal full-lengths of low and worthless characters,—with their accustomed garnishings of sly jokes and familiar moralizing—are all on the surface of his writings; and are almost unavoidably the things by which we are first reminded of him, when we take up any of his new productions. Yet they are not the things that truly constitute his peculiar manner, or give that character by which he will, and ought to be, remembered with future generations. It is plain, indeed, that they are things that will make nobody remembered—and can never, therefore, be really characteristic of some of the most original and powerful poetry that the world ever saw.

Mr. C., accordingly, has other gifts; and those not less peculiar or less strongly marked than the blemishes with which they are contrasted —an unrivalled and almost magical power of observation, resulting in descriptions so true to nature as to strike us rather as transcripts than imitations—an anatomy of character and feeling not less exquisite and searching—an occasional touch of matchless tenderness—and a deep and dreadful pathetic, interspersed by fits, and strangely interwoven with the most minute and humble of his details. Add to all this the sure and profound sagacity of the remarks with which he every now and then startles us in the midst of very unambitious discussions;—and the weight and terseness of the maxims which he drops, like oracular responses, on occasions that give no promise of such a revelation;—and last, though not least, that sweet and seldom sounded chord of lyrical inspiration, the lightest touch of which instantly charms away all harshness from his numbers, and all lowness from his themes—and at once exalts him to a level with the most energetic and inventive poets of his age.

These, we think, are the true characteristics of the genius of this great writer; and it is in their mixture with the oddities and defects to which we have already alluded, that the peculiarity of his manner seems to us substantially to consist. The ingredients may all of them be found, we suppose, in other writers; but their combination—in such proportions at least as occur in this instance—may safely be pronounced to be original.

Extraordinary, however, as this combination must appear, it does not seem very difficult to conceive in what way it may have arisen; and, so far from regarding it as a proof of singular humorousness, caprice or affection in the individual, we are rather inclined to hold that something approaching to it must be the natural result of a long habit of observation in a man of genius, possessed of that temper and disposition which is the usual accompaniment of such a habit; and that the same strangely compounded and apparently incongruous assemblage of themes and sentiments would be frequently produced under such circumstances—if authors had oftener the courage to write from their own impressions, and had less fear of the laugh or wonder of the more shallow and barren part of their readers.

A great talent for observation, and a delight in the exercise of it—the power and the practice of dissecting and disentangling that subtle and complicated tissue of habit, and self-love, and affection, which constitute human character—seems to us, in all cases, to imply a contemplative, rather than an active disposition. It can only exist, indeed, where there is a good deal of social sympathy; for, without this, the occupation could excite no interest, and afford no satisfaction—but only such a measure and sort of sympathy as is gratified by being a spectator, and not an actor on the great theatre of life—and leads its possessor rather to look on with eagerness on the feats and the fortunes of others, than to take a share for himself in the game that is played before him. Some stirring and vigorous spirits there are, no doubt, in which this taste and talent is combined with a more thorough and effective sympathy; and leads to the study of men's characters by an actual and hearty participation in their various passions and pursuits;—though it is to be remarked, that when such persons embody their observations in writing, they will generally be found to show their characters in action, rather than to describe them in the abstract; and to let their various personages disclose themselves and their peculiarities, as it were spontaneously, and without help or preparation, in their ordinary conduct and speech—of all which we have a very splendid and striking example in the 'Tales of My Landlord,' and the other pieces of that extraordinary writer. In the common case, however, a great observer, we believe, will be found, pretty certainly, to be a person of a shy and retiring temper,—who does not mingle enough with the people he surveys, to be heated with their passions, or infected with their delusions—and who has usually been led, indeed, to take up the office of a looker on, from some little infirmity of nerves, or weakness of spirits, which has unfitted him from playing a more active part on the busy scene of existence.

Now, it is very obvious, we think, that this contemplative turn, and this alienation from the vulgar pursuits of mankind, must, in the first place, produce a great contempt for most of those pursuits, and the objects they seek to obtain—a levelling of the factitious distinctions which human pride and vanity have established in the world, and a mingled scorn and compassion for the lofty pretensions under which men so often disguise the nothingness of their chosen occupations. When the many-coloured scene of life, with all its petty agitations, its shifting pomps, and perishable passions, is surveyed by one who does not mix in its business, it is impossible that it should not appear a very pitiable and almost ridiculous affair; or that the heart should not echo back the brief and emphatic exclamation of the mighty dramatist,

> Life's a poor player,
> Who frets and struts his hour upon the stage,
> And then is heard no more.[1]

Or the more sarcastic amplification of it, in the words of our great moral poet—

[1] *Macbeth*, V, v.

Behold the Child, by Nature's kindly law,
Pleased with a rattle, tickled with a straw;
Some livelier plaything gives our Youth delight,
A little louder, but as empty quite:
Scarfs, garters, gold our riper years engage,
And beads and prayerbooks are the *toys* of Age:
Pleased with this bauble still as that before,
Till tired we sleep—and *Life's poor play is o'er*![1]

This is the more solemn view of the subject:—but the first fruits of observation are most commonly found to issue in Satire—the unmasking the vain pretenders to wisdom and worth and happiness with whom society is infested, and holding up to the derision of mankind those meannesses of the great, those miseries of the fortunate, and those

Fears of the brave, and follies of the wise,[2]

which the eye of a dispassionate observer so quickly detects under the glittering exterior by which they would fain be disguised—and which bring pretty much to a level the intellect and morals and enjoyments of the great mass of mankind.

This misanthropic end has unquestionably been by far the most common result of a habit of observation, and that in which its effects have most generally terminated:—Yet we cannot bring ourselves to think that it is their just or natural termination. Something, no doubt, will depend on the temper of the individual, and the proportions in which the gall and the milk of human kindness have been originally mingled in his composition.—Yet satirists, we think, have not in general been ill-natured persons—and we are inclined rather to ascribe this limited and uncharitable application of their powers of observation to their love of fame and popularity,—which are well known to be best secured by successful ridicule or invective—or quite as probably, indeed, to the narrowness and insufficiency of their observations themselves, and the imperfection of their talents for their due conduct and extension.—It is certain, at least, we think, that the satirist makes use but of half the discoveries of the observer; and teaches but half—and the worser half— of the lessons which may be deduced from his occupation.—He puts down, indeed, the proud pretensions of the great and arrogant, and levels the vain distinctions which human ambition has established among the brethren of mankind—he

[1] Pope, *Essay on Man*, II, 275–82.
[2] Johnson, *Vanity of Human Wishes*, 316.

Bare[s] the mean heart that lurks beneath a Star,[1]

—and destroys the illusions which would limit our sympathy to the forward and figuring persons of this world—the favourites of fame and fortune.—But the true result of observation should be not so much to cast down the proud, as to raise up the lowly—not so much to extinguish our sympathy with the powerful and renowned, as to extend it to all those who, in humbler conditions, have the same claims on our esteem or affection.—It is not surely the natural consequence of learning to judge truly of the characters of men, that we should despise or be indifferent about them all;—and though we have learned to see through the false glare which plays round the envied summits of existence, and to know how little dignity, or happiness, or worth, or wisdom, may sometimes belong to the possessors of power and fortune and learning and renown,—it does not follow, by any means, that we should look upon the whole of human life as a mere deceit and imposture, or think the concerns of our species fit subjects only for scorn and derision. Our promptitude to admire and to envy will indeed be corrected, our enthusiasm abated, and our distrust of appearances increased;—but the sympathies and affections of our nature will continue, and be better directed—our love of our kind will not be diminished—and our indulgence for their faults and follies, if we read our lesson aright, will be signally strengthened and confirmed. The true and proper effect, therefore, of a habit of observation, and a thorough and penetrating knowledge of human character, will be, not to extinguish our sympathy but to extend it—to turn, no doubt, many a throb of admiration, and many a sigh of love into a smile of derision or of pity, but at the same time to reveal much that commands our homage and excites our affection in those humble and unexplored regions of the heart and understanding which never engage the attention of the incurious,—and to bring the whole family of mankind nearer to a level, by finding out latent merits as well as latent defects in all its members, and compensating the flaws that are detected in the boasted ornaments of life, by bringing to light the richness and the lustre that sleep in the mines beneath its surface.

We are afraid some of our readers may not at once perceive the application of these profound remarks to the subject immediately before us. But there are others, we doubt not, who do not need to be told, that they are intended to explain how Mr. Crabbe, and other persons with the same gift of observation, should so often busy themselves with what

---

1 Pope, *Imitations of Horace, Satires* II, i, 103.

may be considered as low and vulgar characters; and, declining all deal-
ings with heroes and heroic topics, should not only venture to seek for
an interest in the concerns of ordinary mortals, but actually intersperse
small pieces of ridicule with their undignified pathos, and endeavour to
make their readers look on their books with the same mingled feelings
of compassion and amusement, with which—unnatural as it may appear
to the readers of poetry—they, and all judicious observers, actually look
upon human life and human nature. This, we are persuaded, is the true
key to the greater part of the peculiarities of the author before us; and
though we have disserted upon it a little longer than was necessary,
we really think it may enable our readers to comprehend him, and
our remarks on him, something better than they could have done
without it.

There is, as everybody must have felt, a strange mixture of satire and
sympathy in all his productions—a great kindliness and compassion for
the errors and sufferings of our poor human nature—but a strong distrust of its heroic virtues and high pretensions. His heart is always open
to pity, and all the milder emotions—but there is little aspiration after
the grand and sublime of character, nor very much encouragement for
raptures and ecstacies of any description. These, he seems to think, are
things rather too fine for the said poor human nature—and that, in our
low and erring condition, it is a little ridiculous to pretend, either to
very exalted and immaculate virtue, or very pure and exquisite happiness. He not only never meddles, therefore, with the delicate distresses
and noble fires of the heroes and heroines of tragic and epic fable, but
may generally be detected indulging in a lurking sneer at the pomp and
vanity of all such superfine imaginations—and turning to draw men in
their true postures and dimensions, and with all the imperfections that
actually belong to their condition:—the prosperous and happy over-
shadowed with passing clouds of *ennui,* and disturbed with little flaws
of bad humour and discontent—the great and wise beset at times with
strange weaknesses and meannesses and paltry vexations—and even the
most virtuous and enlightened falling far below the standard of poetical
perfection—and stooping every now and then to paltry jealousies and
prejudices—or sinking into shabby sensualities,—or meditating on their
own excellence and importance, with a ludicrous and lamentable
anxiety.

This is one side of the picture; and characterizes sufficiently the
satirical vein of our author: But the other is the most extensive and
important. In rejecting the vulgar sources of interest in poetical nar-

ratives, and reducing his ideal persons to the standard of reality, Mr. C. does by no means seek to extinguish the sparks of human sympathy within us, or to throw any damp on the curiosity with which we naturally explore the characters of each other. On the contrary, he has afforded new and more wholesome food for all those propensities—and, by placing before us those details which our pride or fastidiousness is so apt to overlook, has disclosed, in all their truth and simplicity, the native and unadulterated workings of those affections which are at the bottom of all social interest, and are really rendered less touching by the exaggerations of more ambitious artists—while he exhibits, with admirable force and endless variety, all those combinations of passions and opinions, and all that cross-play of selfishness and vanity, and indolence and ambition, and habit and reason, which make up the intellectual character of individuals, and present to every one an instructive picture of his neighbour or himself. Seeing, by the perfection of his art, the master passions in their springs, and the high capacities in their rudiments —and having acquired the gift of tracing all the propensities and marking tendencies of our plastic nature, in their first slight indications, or from the very disguises they so often love to assume, he does not need, in order to draw out his characters in all their life and distinctness, the vulgar demonstration of those striking and decided actions by which their maturity is proclaimed even to the careless and inattentive;—but delights to point out to his readers, the seeds or tender filaments of those talents and feelings and singularities which wait only for occasion and opportunity to burst out and astonish the world—and to accustom them to trace, in characters and actions apparently of the most ordinary description, the self-same attributes that, under other circumstances, would attract universal attention, and furnish themes for the most popular and impassioned descriptions.

That he should not be guided in the choice of his subject by any regard to the rank or condition which his persons hold in society, may easily be imagined; and, with a view to the ends he aims at, might readily be forgiven. But we fear that his passion for observation, and the delight he takes in tracing out and analyzing all the little traits that indicate character, and all the little circumstances that influence it, have sometimes led him to be careless about his selection of the instances in which it was to be exhibited, or at least to select them upon principles very different from those which give them an interest in the eyes of ordinary readers. For the purposes of mere anatomy, the physiologist, who examines plants only to study their internal structure, and to make himself master of all the contrivances by which their various functions are performed, pays no regard to the brilliancy of their hues, the sweetness of their odours, or the graces of their form. Those who come to him for the sole purpose of acquiring knowledge, may participate perhaps in this indifference; but the world at large will wonder at them—and he will engage fewer pupils to listen to his instructions, than if he had condescended in some degree to consult their predilections in the beginning. It is the same case, we think, in many respects, with Mr. Crabbe. Relying for the interest he is to produce, on the curious expositions he is to make of the elements of human character; or at least finding his own chief gratification in those subtle investigations, he seems to care very little upon what particular individuals he pitches for the purpose of these demonstrations. Almost every human mind, he seems to think, may serve to display that fine and mysterious mechanism which it is his delight to explore and explain;—and almost every condition, and every history of life, afford occasions to show how it may be put into action, and pass through its various combinations. It seems, therefore, almost as if he had caught up the first dozen or two of persons that came across him in the ordinary walks of life,—and then opening up his little window in their breasts,—and applying his tests and instruments of observation, had set himself about such a minute and curious scrutiny of their whole habits, history, adventures and dispositions, as he thought must ultimately create not only a familiarity, but an interest, which the first aspect of the subject was far enough from leading any one to expect. That he succeeds more frequently than could have been anticipated, we are very willing to allow. But we cannot help feeling also, that a little more pains bestowed in the selection of his characters, would have made his power of observation and description tell with tenfold effect; and that, in spite of the exquisite truth of his delineations, and the fineness of the perceptions by which he was enabled to make them, it is impossible to take any considerable interest in many of his personages, or to avoid feeling some degree of fatigue at the minute and patient exposition that is made of all that belongs to them.

These remarks are a little too general, we believe—and are not introduced with strict propriety at the head of our *fourth* article on Mr. Crabbe's productions. They have drawn out, however, to such a length, that we can afford to say but little of the work immediately before us. It is marked with all the characteristics that we have noticed, either now or formerly, as distinctive of his poetry. On the whole, however, it has certainly fewer of the grosser faults—and fewer too, perhaps, of the more exquisite passages which occur in his former publications. There is nothing at least that has struck us, in going over these volumes, as equal in elegance to Phoebe Dawson in 'The Register', or in pathetic affect to the Convict's Dream, or Edward Shore, or the Parting Hour, or the Sailor dying beside his sweetheart. On the other hand, there is far less that is horrible, and nothing that can be said to be absolutely disgusting; and the picture which is afforded of society and human nature is, on the whole, much less painful and degrading. There is both less misery and less guilt; and, while the same searching and unsparing glance is sent into all the dark caverns of the breast, and the truth brought forth with the same stern impartiality, the result is more comfortable and cheering. The greater part of the characters are rather more elevated in station, and milder and more amiable in disposition; while the accidents of life are more mercifully managed, and fortunate circumstances more liberally allowed. It is rather remarkable, too, that Mr. C. seems to become more amorous as he grows older,—the interest of almost all the stories in this collection turning on the tender passion—and many of them on its most romantic varieties.

The plan of the work,—for it has rather more of plan and unity than any of the former,—is abundantly simple. Two brothers, both past middle age, meet together for the first time since their infancy, in the Hall of their native parish, which the elder and richer had purchased as a place of retirement for his declining age—and there tell each other their own history, and then that of their guests, neighbours, and acquaintances. . . .

Though their own stories and descriptions are not, in our opinion, the best in the work, it is but fair to introduce these narrative brothers and their Hall a little more particularly to our readers. The history of the elder and more austere, is not particularly probable—nor very interesting; but it affords many passages extremely characteristic of the author. . . .

The following passage, we think, might be quoted as a fair epitome of his poetry—its strength and its weakness—its faults, its oddities, and its beauties.

Something one day occurr'd about a bill . . .
[VII, 470–512, 517–24, 543–63]

She views his distress with some confusion, and more contempt; and at last endeavours to sooth him, by saying and singing, as follows.

'Come, my dear friend, discard that look of care . . .
[VII, 593–98, 609–14, 626–41]

We were lately rash enough, we think, to say, that we had no poets
so unlike as Mr. Crabbe and Mr. Moore: But poets of their mettle can
put out critics when they please. This little song [626–41] is more like
Mr. Moore than any thing we ever saw under the hand of a professed
imitator; and if Mr. Crabbe's amatory propensities continue to increase
with the years, as they have done, the bard of Lalla Rookh may still have
a formidable rival. . . .

Soften'd, I said—'Be mine the hand and heart, . . .
[VII, 694–705]

He chose his native village, and the hill . . .
[I, 23–35, 55–8, 65–74]

[Summary of the story of the younger brother, Richard.]
I sought the town, and to the ocean gave . . .
[IV, 295–304, 309–33, 339–42; 365–8, 371–4, 377–82, 387–94]

[Some account of 'Ruth', *Tales of the Hall* V, with following quotations.]
'Ruth—I may tell, too oft had she been told— . . .
[V, 119–28, 184–98, 416–63]

[Some account of 'The Sisters', *Tales of the Hall* VIII, with following
quotations.]
Thus lived the sisters, far from power removed.
[VIII, 255–64, 631–52, 681–710, 837–96]

The Preceptor Husband is exceedingly well managed—but it is rather
too facetious for our present mood . . .

'The Maid's Story' is rather long—though it has many passages that
must be favourites with Mr. Crabbe's admirers. 'Sir Owen Dale' is too
long also; but it is one of the best in the collection. . . .

Twice the year came round— . . .
[XII, 698–722, 736–44, 755–82, 833–49, 884–96]

We always quote too much of Mr. Crabbe:—perhaps because the
pattern of his Arabesque is so large, that there is no getting a fair specimen of it without taking in a good space. But we must take warning
this time, and forbear—or at least pick out but a few little morsels as we
pass hastily along. One of the best managed of all the tales, is that entitled 'Delay has danger.' . . .

The introduction to this story is in Mr. Crabbe's best style of concise and minute description.

[XIII, 1–16.]

We cannot give any part of the long and finely converging details by which the catastrophe is brought about: But we are tempted to venture on the catastrophe itself, for the sake chiefly of the right English melancholy autumnal landscape with which it concludes.

> In that weak moment, when disdain and pride, . . .
> [XIII, 688–724]

The moral autumn is quite as gloomy, and far more hopeless.

> Five years had past, and what was Henry then? . . .
> [XIII, 733–64]

'The Natural Death of Love' is perhaps the best written of all the pieces before us. . . .
'Gretna Green' is a strong picture of the happiness that may be expected from a premature marriage between a silly mercenary girl, and a brutal selfwilled boy. . . .

> The boy repented, and grew savage soon; . . .
> [XV, 375–80, 395–400, 414–29]

'Lady Barbara, or the Ghost' is a long-story, and not very pleasing. . . .

> I resisted—O! my God, what shame. . . .
> [XVI, 925–46]

'The Widow,' with her three husbands, is not quite so lively as the wife of Bath with her five:—but it is a very amusing, as well as a very instructive legend, and exhibits a rich variety of those striking intellectual portraits which mark the hand of our poetical Rembrandt. The serene close of her eventful life, is highly exemplary.

> The widow'd lady to her cot retired, . . .
> [XVII, 521–9]

'Ellen' is a painful story—and not quite intelligible.
. . . Not the least explanation is given of the extraordinary message which produced all [the] misery; and though there are some striking touches of passion, and some fine description in this poem, it is by far the least satisfactory of any in the collection.

'William Bailey' is the best of the tales of humble life that we find in these volumes; and is curiously and characteristically compounded of pathos and pleasantry,—affecting incidents, and keen and sarcastic remarks: But it would take too much room to give any intelligible account of it. 'The Cathedral Walk' has something of the same character; though what it has of story is of far inferior interest, and in truth poor enough. . . .

The last regular Tale is 'The Poachers', and it is sad and tragical. . . .

[XXI, 1–27 and 623–32.]

We shall be abused by our political and fastidious readers for the length of this article. But we cannot repent of it. It will give as much pleasure, we believe, and do as much good, as many of the articles that are meant for their gratification; and, if it appear absurd to quote so largely from a popular and accessible work, it should be remembered, that no work of this magnitude passes into circulation with half the rapidity of our Journal—and that Mr. Crabbe is so unequal a writer, and at times so unattractive, as to require, more than any other of his degree, some explanation of his system, and some specimens of his powers, from those experienced and intrepid readers whose business it is to pioneer for the lazier sort, and to give some account of what they are to meet with on their journey. To be sure, all this is less necessary now than it was on Mr. Crabbe's first reappearance nine or ten years ago; and though it may not be altogether without its use even at present, it may be as well to confess, that we have rather consulted our own gratification than our readers' improvement, in what we have now said of him; and hope they will forgive us.

45. Unsigned review, *British Critic*

September 1819, n.s. xii, 285–301

We love a Poem which will bear to be outrageously abused: not one, we mean, in which it is impossible to find any thing worth praising; but one which deserves so much praise, and will *have* so much, in spite of all we can say against it, that we may, without compassion, venture to fall foul of every thing that displeases or dissatisfies us. Mr. Crabbe, of all our contemporary Poets, certainly takes most pains to gratify this propensity in us; and we shall by no means scruple to indulge in it to the full. He sometimes writes so well, that our task, if we mean to give him his due, must be that of citation only; and sometimes so much otherwise, that, if he is the shrewd man we take him to be, he will be much obliged to us for omitting the testimonies upon which our opinions have been founded. Our admiration, when we give it, ought, we think, to possess no little value in his eyes; for we very honestly promise that we like neither his general matter nor manner. Our tastes have been formed in direct opposition to, what is foolishly called, his school; and if we cannot but acknowledge that the power of his genius not unfrequently dashes aside all our prejudices, it is a confession, be it remembered, won from professed adversaries of his style, and therefore the more honourable to him.

If such have been our feelings in respect of Mr. Crabbe's former publications, they must recur, with increased vigour, on a perusal of that which is now before us. We think that he has never yet written so unequally; and we fear we may add never with so great a preponderance of his peculiar faults. It is almost too late in this gentleman's career to venture upon any analysis of his poetical character. The opinions of our readers upon his excellencies and defects, are probably, by this time, as decidedly formed as our own are; for Mr. Crabbe is now an acquaintance of long standing. Nevertheless, as we have taken the liberty of avowing our opposition to his practice of poetry, we are, perhaps, bound, in justice to ourselves, to say a few words in palliation of this temerity.

The pleasure arising from Poetry is drawn, as we imagine, very much from the same sources as that which is derived from Painting; and the analogy which subsists between these sister arts is so strong, that they may always, with safe reasoning, be permitted to illustrate one another. Every body knows, at a glance, the difference between a picture of the Italian, or of the Flemish school; and everybody, we doubt not, receives a very distinct pleasure from either of the two. In the landscapes of the one we are carried to an enchanted land, to the gardens of Alcinous, or Armida, with prolonged vistas, and melting distances, and a prodigality of woods and waters, which nature has been too chary to lavish on any single existing spot. In the other we are presented with dreary flats, and slimy fens, and an eternal perspective of those dams, dykes, and wind-mills, which man has so profusely forced on nature wherever he seeks to cultivate her face against her will. The artist, in either case, is an equally faithful copyist. The one selects, blends, and adjusts, the choicest objects which he has treasured in his memory, into an imaginary whole. The other, neither adding nor extenuating, sketches the scene before him very much in the same manner as his camera obscura would present it. This difference pervades every branch of the art from the ad vivum half-caricature likenesses of our English Deighton, to Titian's demi-heroic portraits: from the last scene in the Harlot's Progress, to the Death of Cleopatra; from the Fiddling Boors of Teniers, to the Apollo and the Muses of Raphael. The ground-work in all these is essentially the same, Nature; but it is nature sublimated or depressed, in propor-tion as the artist's predominating quality is observation, or imagination.

We do not know whether we shall have been anticipated in the application which we wish to make of these remarks to Mr. Crabbe's poetry; but we are certain, that our objections to it rest on some such principles as these; Man, as he finds him in individual reality, not as imagination may frame him, by combining the analogous qualities of separate characters; Man, in his worky-day, not his Sunday clothes; Man, as we meet him in the streets, and sit with him by our fire-sides, is the model from which Mr. Crabbe professes to draw. Now, though it may be a question how far this subject, under the strict limitations pro-posed, is susceptible of the very highest poetry, there can be no question at all that it may admit very pleasing poetry; for to turn back to our former illustration, there is no reason why an admirer of Claude should not be an admirer of Cuyp also, though in different degrees. If, there-fore, we only thought that Mr. Crabbe contented himself with the choice of an inferior style, we would, without another word, award him the praise of having compassed the full excellence of which that style is capable; unfortunately, however, from a fear of not being sufficiently natural, we apprehend that this poet very often is not sufficiently just. We will not deny, that such characters as he has exhibited sometimes exist; nay, on the contrary, we rather feel confident that, in most instances, he has, perhaps unconsciously, sketched his first outline from the life. But we cannot bring ourselves to believe, that the *average* character of our species is to be found in his pages; if it be so, our standard of it has been as much elevated above temperate, as we conceive his to be depressed below zero. Nor again do his views of human life at all accord with those which experience has induced us to form; and in our search after truth we would just as soon accept the gaudy and glittering periods of some Minerva-press novelist, as the morose and melancholy strains of this uncomfortable bard. Life is neither a garden, nor a wilderness; it bears, like the earth which we inhabit, spots enough both of culture and of desolation; and he who is not perversely desirous to pitch his tent either at the Equator or the Poles, may, for the most part, meet with a zone which is at least tolerably habitable.

We are no friends to the cheerless doctrine of the utter depravation of our nature, in discussions of far higher moment; but in poetry it is altogether misplaced and insufferable. The chief aim of this art can be nothing but to give pleasure;

Delectando pariterque monendo,[1]

if we chuse, but always remembering, that the monition must be subservient to the delight. Now what pleasure is there in contemplating the evil side only? in turning from all that is bright, and golden, and sunny, to the chill, the misty, and the dark? If human nature really is Mr. Crabbe's theme, it is the human nature of Hobbes, in which, for the bond of universal love, is substituted a barrier of universal hatred, and every man is asserted to be an adversary to his brother. It is the social plan of Mandeville, in which, what little good we possess is declared to be the produce of conflicting evils. No one will suspect us of implying that Mr. Crabbe is a disciple of these selfish and detestable sophists any farther than his poetical morals are concerned. The well-known Christian uprightness and benevolence of his private life, are sufficient testimonies that his practical ethics are drawn from a source which pours forth none but living waters.

Again, even if Mr. Crabbe's delineations were more correct than we admit them to be, we contend, that in good taste there is much in them

---

[1] By delighting and advising equally. Horace, *Ars Poetica*, 344.

that ought to be kept out of sight. We do not know that we love demigods and heroes much more than Mr. Crabbe appears to do; and we certainly have been more powerfully moved by Lillo than by Racine; still, if the descent into poetical lower life of necessity is to introduce us to all those details which we so carefully shrink from in real lower life, we had much rather continue in good company above stairs. It is his fear of generalization, we think, which has led Mr. Crabbe into this mistake. He never omits; and yet there is quite as much good taste in omission as in selection. In the line which he has chosen this is a fault of the first magnitude; and one which evidently increases in proportion to the keenness with which he observes, and the force with which he describes; so that it is scarcely too much to say, that he would give more pleasure if he wrote with less genius. We shall, perhaps, make these remarks clearer, by one more reference to painting. It is not that we wish everything to be elevated, but that we wish nothing to be mean; we require only that the artist should not think himself bound to paint that which is offensive, simply because it is natural. When Teniers, with his irresistible comic perversity, cannot help giving one of his figures a dirty job to do, he generally has the decency to put him in the distance, or to turn his back upon the spectators. We know that the arena of the Coliseum was once wattled round with pigsties; and that the Parthenon is still profaned with heaps of many mingled filth! but Piranesi and Stuart, in their respective drawings, have judiciously sunk these inopportune accompaniments. The portrait-painter learns this lesson practically. Agesilaus, with his club-foot, Alexander, with his wry-neck, Charles XII, with his dirty-face, and 'unkempt locks,' lose half their heroism if their defects are preserved on canvas; and that easel will stand long untenanted whose master will not condescend to humour little peculiarities of countenance.

Now with Mr. Crabbe, not a wart, a wrinkle, or a freckle, escapes faithful notice; nay, sometimes, we are convinced, that he reddens the rubicundity of a nose, and distorts the obliquity of an eye. It would be no impeachment to his genius if he forebore this unpleasing practice; for the *laid essentiel* requires far lower powers for its representation than the *beau ideal*. Any bungler can daub vulgar monsters on a sign-post, and the Chinese paint red dragons in abundance. The conception of beauty is much less easy than that of deformity; and we know not in what points the genius of our greatest master of song has displayed itself more transcendantly than in his delicious pictures of the primæval garden. If we were asked in what other part of his immortal poem he had exemplified the delicacy of his tact by forbearance, we should point to his Lazar-house. In this, if he had not generalized, if with the minute poet he had *walked the hospital*, he would have excited not terror but disgust; instead of shuddering at the fearfully-sublime catalogue of bodily ills to which our nature is exposed, we should have sickened at the Pharmacopoeia of drugs, cataplasms, and electuaries, by which they are mitigated.

One word more, in this invidious part of our task, on Mr. Crabbe's versification, it is the most untunable in our language, the merest scrannel scraping that ever grated on mortal ear. Quarles is an Apollo to this Pan. In the XXII Books of the two octavo volumes now before us, we can scarcely recollect a single couplet that tripped easily from the tongue; and yet whenever the poet turns from the heroic to any other metre, his verse becomes rich music. We cannot pretend to search after principles which may account for this extraordinary deficiency of skill in the rhythm to which he has been most accustomed.

We have dwelt long upon Mr. Crabbe's faults, and we shall touch so very briefly on his acknowledged merits, that we may perhaps be deemed not to admit them as sincerely and cordially as we profess to do; but we are convinced, that the best mode of displaying the many excellencies of this singularly unequal writer, is by silently permitting the passages in which they break forth to speak for themselves. We consider him unrivalled in microscopic observation of certain peculiarities of the human heart—in unveiling one class of feelings which do not most openly present themselves to the common view. He is a skilful anatomist of a diseased patient; and, if we may continue the metaphor, the preparations which he makes from the dissected parts retain a freshness and shew of life, which no other hand has been able to give. Herein indeed is the surest proof of his genius; and it is in this that its originality displays itself not less than its power. We know not how to describe the manner by which he *compels* such vivid interest into his pictures—there is no high finishing, no delicacy of touch about them; the strokes are broad and coarse, but the brush is incessantly at work, and colour is plaistered upon colour, till the figures stand out of the canvas almost as it were in bas relief. Life is not kindled in them by a Promethean or an electric spark; but their animator has discovered the που στω of Archimedes, and throws them into what attitudes he pleases by mere force of the lever. His machine is one of infinite pressure, and weight is heaped on weight in it, till like the Recusant, under the *peine forte et dure*, his characters must speak or die. Add to this, a subdued tone of humour, more caustic than playful—a melancholy for the most part bitter, but sometimes highly pathetic—a facility of presenting reflections not the most obvious in very familiar forms—a love of virtue, without any great willingness to believe in its prevalence—and it will readily be seen, that Mr. Crabbe, though not a very pleasing, may yet be, and assuredly is, a very powerful writer. . . .

The stories, which, we will not say are interwoven with, but are scattered over this extraordinary main plot, are related either by the brothers in their private conversations, or by various neighbours, whom they visit; and few of them have more interest in themselves than the great Epic round which they cluster as a nucleus—nothing indeed could present less promise than the cursory glances which we caught when we first ran through the uncut pages of these volumes with our paper-knife; but, as we mean to show presently, this is not the way to travel in Mr. Crabbe's country. His poetry puts us in mind of our last journey over Salisbury Plain, when after paying the post-boy double to gallop over many a dreary mile of flat and unvaried barrenness, we pulled him up in a hurry at Stone Henge, or the Vale of Pewsey, and could scarcely stop long enough for our contentment.

The story of Ruth, the daughter of a man and his wife, with whom Richard becomes acquainted in a seaport town, strikingly exemplifies Mr. Crabbe's peculiarity of style. In character, incident, and language, every thing is most obvious and familiar; it might be a newspaper paragraph, or the minutes of evidence on a coroner's jury; it is told as the merest village-gossip would tell it, bestowing 'all her tediousness' upon her hearers, and is worked up with most distressing power; for the catastrophe unnecessarily harrows the feelings, without producing a correspondent moral effect. We rise from it with an oppressive and painful conviction, that such things may occur, probably have occurred, in real life; and that their solution must for ever be denied to our present faculties.

'There was a teacher, where my husband went— . . .
[V, 253–89; 302–17; 416–63]

Richard tells his own wooing in a different strain—the first acquaintance—the insensible transition from friendship to love—his hope—his causeless jealousy—his suspense—his apprehension—his happiness—are portrayed, somewhat at length it must be confessed, and with a certain mannerism which marks them as Mr. Crabbe's own; but they form altogether one of his most happy specimens. The elder brother recounts

his unsuccessful amour in return, and neither so agreeably nor intelligibly as Richard. We pardon him, however, on account of his unexpected introduction of the two pleasing and harmonious stanzas
below.

> My Damon was the first to wake . . .
> [VII, 626–41]

The still more exquisite lines which we shall next cite, will be read
with astonishment by those who are only acquainted with Mr. Crabbe's
muse in her slipshod heroic shamble. We recollect no composition of
the same kind in our language which has more genuine pathos or nicer-
attuned melody.

> Let me not have this gloomy view, . . .
> [VIII, 837–96]

'The Preceptor Husband' is of a lighter kind, though from four lines
in it our fair readers might imagine otherwise.

> Calix, and coral, pericarp, and fruit——
> Lunate, and lyrate, runcinate, retuse——
> Latent, and patent, patulous, and plane——
> Panduriform, pinnatifid, premorse.——
> [IX, 280, 285, 288, 287]

Nor should we be much surprised if, like Mr. Crabbe's heroine, they
thought a husband who dealt in terms of such obscurity somewhat
tiresome.

'Sir Owen Dale' is another of those tales, which are exclusively
Mr. Crabbe's property. . . .

> O! that I saw her with her soul on fire, . . .
> [XII, 303–14 and 752–97]

'Delay has Danger,' and 'Gretna Green,' are well told and we doubt
not are founded on real incidents. 'Ellen' we do not understand. 'The
Cathedral Walk' and 'Lady Barbara' are both somewhat (we wish we
could find a milder word) silly; but of the two, we like the sham ghost
better than the real one.

'The Natural Death of Love' belongs to that class of stories, in which
Mr. Crabbe most successfully displays his extraordinary power of being
disagreeable; it is elaborately conceived, abounds in nice observation, is
more carefully finished perhaps than any tale in the volumes, and yet is
one which we heartily wish he had never written. It does not force tears

from us like 'Ruth', but it frets and worries and irritates us. To the poet, least of all writers, even in sport, belongs the vulgar task of chilling our best feelings, and stripping life of its choicest graces; and imagination from the noblest of our faculties becomes the most odious, when it is employed in representing all that is amiable in our nature, as hollow and illusive. In the present instance, this is done for the benefit of heartless rakes and disappointed bachelors, not less at the expense of truth than of good taste.

One story more, and we must conclude; it is the crowning stone and *chef d'œuvre* of the volumes, and contains in its own compass every fault and merit by which Mr. Crabbe is distinguished from his contemporaries. Two foundling brothers, James (or *Jemes*, as Mr. Crabbe makes him rhyme to 'schemes') and Robert, evince from childhood the most opposite dispositions. James is sedate, temperate, and slow; Robert quick, prompt, and generous.

> In fact, this *youth* was generous—that was just, . . .
> [XXI, 53–6 and 535–95]

It is impossible not to admit that, with all their carelessness and coarseness of execution in some parts, there is infinite power of conception in most of the passages which we have extracted. We imagine that Mr. Crabbe writes with great rapidity, and never blots; two qualities in an author as little preparative for immortality as any we could mention. We are convinced, however, that no small portion of his poetry will live in spite of all the oppressive pains he takes to kill it, and when in some future anthology he

> Shakes off the dust and rears his reverend head,[1]

although he may be somewhat extenuated in size he will have increased materially in vigour. If he would permit us to make a *corps d'elite* of his lines, we would promise to burn all our obnoxious criticism, and in so doing we should perform a duty not a little grateful to ourselves, and which, indeed, Mr. Crabbe might justly demand at our hands.

---

[1] Pope, *Essay on Criticism*, 700.

46. Unsigned review, *Edinburgh Monthly Review*

September 1819, ii, 287–302

These volumes make us proud of our calling. The unmerited neglect into which Mr. Crabbe's earliest publication fell, had disinclined him from again appearing as an author. His active mind had too many resources to be dependant on the stimulus of popularity; and was probably too conscious of its own powers to court what seemed to be capriciously refused him. The notice of his poems in a celebrated Journal, twenty years after their original publication, brought him forward again from his retirement. We envy the feelings of the man, who, when he takes up the volumes which Mr. Crabbe has published since, can say to himself 'It is to me that my countrymen owe this rich addition to their stores of improvement and pleasure.'

Once possessed of the public ear, Mr. Crabbe is sure of retaining it. From every successive publication he may safely anticipate an increase of his well-earned fame. His is not the poetry that cloys; nor are his the powers which exhaust themselves in youth. He was never distinguished by the strength of his fancy; if we employ that somewhat ambiguous term to denote the faculty which delights in creations of its own, and can breathe only amidst more majestic grandeur, and brighter beauty and tenderer grace than the realities of life supply. He was never distinguished for that blaze of imagery with which a sportive and versatile muse fatigues at last the eye of the beholder. He was never distinguished for that high-wrought elegance of diction, which refines itself either into weakness or obscurity; for that melody of numbers, which steals the mind of the listener from meaning to sound. All these are charms which either decline with the flowers of our spring, or which exert only a secondary and transient power over the mind most alive to their value. The attributes of Mr. Crabbe's poetry are keen discrimination, manly sense, high moral feeling, graphic description, and vigorous language. Though he has a poet's eye and a poet's tongue, his mind is a calm, sober, well-regulated mind; which, even when the passions are its theme, describes them not as existing in itself, but as traced in others

247

by its intuitive glance, through all the graces of their tenderness, and all the terrors of their grandeur.

Hence it appears to us, that, as Mr. Crabbe advances in life, his poetry improves. We are disposed, upon the whole, to think the volumes now before us the best of his works. The range of observation which they include is widened; it stretches more into the middling rank of life, instead of limiting its descriptions to the poor. We think, too, that although nothing of his shrewdness is lost, he has abated somewhat in his severity. When he first began the anatomy of the human heart, he tasked his ingenuity rather too much for new discoveries, and fettered himself a little too much with system. Where an anomalous fact presented itself, he could not rest till he had traced its origin to the quarter where he expected it to spring, till he had brought it into harmony with the appearances around it. He seems now more content to take the facts as he finds them. When something good occurs along with much that is villanous, he no longer insists upon tracing it to a worthless motive. The characters which he employs his glowing pencil to depict, he no longer forces to be more uniformly consistent than he finds them to be in actual nature.

Crabbe is peculiarly the poet of actual life. Among all those, who, in our day, have made human nature the theme of their song, we think his descriptions the most impressive, because they are by far the *truest*. Cowper (whom he resembles often in purpose, though in manner they are utterly unlike) looked at the world 'through the loop-holes of retreat.' The shyness which held him back from his fellow-men during almost the whole maturity of his intellect, necessarily narrowed his opportunities for observing individual character. His views of life are less coloured from nature, than worked up from meditation and theory; his sketches of character, though often drawn with great liveliness, and oftener with great sweetness and grace, are the pictures of a *class*, rather than such portraits of *individuals*, as by certain nameless traits convince you at once of their living identity. Rogers quits his retreat and walks abroad a little—but it is chiefly in the neighbourhood of his own tranquil home, and on the gravel walks of his own *ferme orné*; where, though there may be poverty near, it is not squalid, though there may be sorrow, it is not inelegant. Byron looks down upon human life from his hill of storms; and its objects alternately appear to him too remote and trifling for distant vision, or are seen of supernatural dimensions through the mists which he gathers around him. Wordsworth exhibits it in a phantasmagoria. He presents to you, not living creatures, but the vivid images of forms which he himself has fashioned, which he moves by his own agency, and tints with his own colours. From all these faults Crabbe is free. He mingles easily with the world. He has none of the shyness which kept poor Cowper aloof from his fellows; none of the shrinking fastidiousness with which Rogers hides unpicturesque evil. He does not, like Byron, claim a superiority to his fellow men, which unfits him for being their historian; nor does he, like Wordsworth, lay them on the bed of *Procrustes*, and screw them into forms and attitudes of his own devising. He describes in the most appropriate and vigorous language what he himself has seen, and what his reader seldom fails to recognize. This is the great charm of his writing; a charm which would have been felt in prose as well as in poetry. We are far indeed from joining with those against whom he asserts (in the preface to a former work) his own right to the name of poet; nor do we wish him other than what he is. But we are satisfied, that his particular turn of mind would qualify him for the composition of prose essays not less instructive than amusing; and that it depends only on himself to be the Theophrastes or La Bruyere of English literature.

This particular turn of mind has been strengthened, we have no doubt, by his professional habits; and, while it qualifies him admirably for the performance of his duties, must afford to himself both pleasure and profit from the intercourse which a clergyman holds with his parishioners in the most interesting hours of life. He sees them under the strongest emotions of their nature—amidst those uncontrollable workings of sorrow, or shame,—amidst the joy with which they enter on the new relations of life—amidst the elevation with which they are enabled to die. All this Mr. Crabbe has seen; and he has described it *all*. His principle of selection is not very strict. Either his taste is not refined enough to guard him at all times from the description of what is unseemly and disgusting; or rather the habits of his mind prevent such parts of human conduct from appearing disgusting and unseemly to him. He looks upon them as the surgeon does on the wound which ordinary beholders would abhor to touch. He estimates it as affording both an exercise for his skill, and the means of benefiting a fellow creature. Of the benefit of his fellow creatures Mr. Crabbe is never for a moment unmindful. He is the most moral of all living poets. Cowper himself was not more so. He has the cause of religion and virtue on his lips and in his heart. We may doubt sometimes whether the means be judiciously chosen through which he endeavours to advance their interests. We may doubt, for example, whether the detection of hypocrisy, and the unsparing severity with which he exhibits sectarianism, be the fittest means in the present day for benefiting religion. We may doubt whether a display of the pleasures associated with the performance of duty, be not a better method of pleading the cause of virtue, than a detail of the agony, and shame, and ruin of vice. But the choice of means is one thing, and the purpose for which they are chosen is another. The cause for which he pleads, has in Mr. Crabbe an advocate thoroughly sincere and zealous, and as eminently successful, we trust, as the means which he has chosen will permit. We know indeed no writer more thoroughly practical. No man, who feels the stirrings of evil within him, can rise from the perusal of such volumes as these, without saying to himself, 'Here is my own individual case. This is the very march of my own feelings and wishes. Here is my own precise danger. Here I must seek to plant a guard, or this very guilt and misery will be mine.'

This is a work which obviously does not admit of analysis. . . .

In the third book, the rector relates the history of one of their early companions, a second Dick Tinto.[1] There is great power in the last sad scenes of this melancholy tale. The passage is very much in Mr. Crabbe's peculiar manner. The description of the furniture of the work-house, though a refined taste would not have ventured on it, adds to the truth and impression of the picture; and the mixed feeling with which the artist consigns his last favourite sketch to the flames is finely imagined.

I saw him next where he had lately come, . . .
[III, 253–324] . . .

In the seventh book, George repays his brother's confidence. His tale, we think, is by no means so happy [as Richard's]. George, we suspect, is one of the few among the characters described in these volumes to whose personal acquaintance Mr. Crabbe could not introduce us, were we so fortunate as to visit him at his rectory. There are two different eras in the character; each is natural enough in itself, but they do not appear to us to harmonize into one living whole; nor is the mock heroic style in which George relates the dreams of his youth, (though calculated, no doubt, to mark the mixture of shame and attachment with which he looks back to them,) well suited to the confidential air of his communication with a brother.

Years now had flown, nor was the passion cured . . .
[VII, 428–61, 810–28]

[1] In Scott's *The Bride of Lammermoor* and *St. Ronan's Well*.

The story of Sir Owen Dale, which the rector relates in the twelfth book, contains by far the most splendid passages in these volumes. Its plot is revolting, and not very probable. . . .

> She show'd a cool, respectful air; . . .
> [XII, 219–32, 236–44, 821–38, 844–9, 859–916]

The 'dangers of delay' are illustrated in the thirteenth book, by the case of a young man, who in a short absence from his betrothed bride, yields, half unconsciously, to the power of another mistress. The fourteenth, 'the natural death of love,' combines, with much pretty poetry, and much shrewd sarcasm, a great deal of sensible counsel to young wedded people. The fifteenth, 'Gretna Green', is a strongly woven tissue of the sordid and the sensual. The sixteenth is a ghost story. We should have been much better pleased had the subject been omitted. This seems intended as an instance of a case in which it was not *a priori* improbable that a ghost might be allowed to appear, on account of the importance of the warning to be conveyed. But really it required no ghost to tell a lady already arrived at the years of discretion, that, if she married a boy, no happiness was likely to follow from so absurd a connection. The seventeenth is an amusing history of a widow, who in two of her three marriages had been indulged, and in one restrained.

> What gives our tale its moral? Here we find . . .
> [XVII, 530–44]

The eighteenth is a pretty, though not a very profitable tale. The subject of it, as we understand from the preface, was suggested by Mr. Rogers; and it is more within his walk than Mr. Crabbe's.

> As past the day, the week, the month, the year . . .
> [XVIII, 320–45]

'William Bailey' is exceptionable in point of morality. It is a shred of the German School. A frail fair one, after years of penitence, is rewarded with the hand of the man who had loved her in purer and happier days. Hints are given of palliating circumstances in her case; but, had they been more explicit, and more satisfactory than they are, this was none of the departments where it was all necessary for Mr. Crabbe to relax his high standard of purity. We wish that this tale were modified or cancelled, though there is much pretty writing in it.

To the twentieth tale also we object. It not only reverts to the injudicious theme of apparitions, but is unpleasantly managed in itself.

After we have been prepared, with sufficient, and far more than sufficient solemnity, for an interview in the aisles of a cathedral between a
lovelorn maiden, and the spirit of her departed bridegroom, the spirit
proves to be a brutal ruffian who has been employed in rifling the dead.

The twenty-first is one of those tales of crime and misery in which
Mr. Crabbe has terrible power. . . .

> She saw him fetter'd, full of grief, alone . . .
> [XXI, 349–96, 623–32]

This outline bears such a sort of resemblance to the work before us,
as the blank profile does to the human face divine. It is in the volumes
themselves that our readers must seek the living transcript of Mr.
Crabbe's genius, with all the shrewdness of its observation, and all the
liveliness of its sarcasm, and all the loftiness of its moral feeling, and all
the vigour of its eloquence.

47. Unsigned review, *New Monthly Magazine*

September 1819, xii, 198–205

[Begins with a partial summary, quoting II, 120–31; 138–45; 184–207;
III, 287–324; 428–38; V, 199–240; 416–63; VI, 120–43; 323–87; VII,
58–85, 118–44; 191–209; 535–63; 714–26; 727–76.]

The above extracts are sufficient specimens of the author's style of thinking, his powers of description and versification. The first volume, to
which we confine our present remarks, consists of eleven books. The
poet does not aspire to the praise of heroic invention; he does not seek
to astonish by the wonderful, or dazzle by the continued splendor of
fancy. He has avoided the faults of extravagance and chosen a walk
which is exposed to the opposite defect. The subjects are selected from
the incidents of *daily life* and compounded of the affections, the hopes
and fears, the frailties, vicissitudes and misfortunes to which we are all

liable, and are in constant action around us. His thorough knowledge of the human heart has not impaired his sympathies for, nor lessened his love of his fellow-creatures. Although their classes have been, almost, all described before, his characters, in general, derive an interest from their admirable truth. Old bachelors and old maids have been frequently delineated; but George, the elder brother, in the first book and the old bachelor, in book x, the sisters Jane and Lucy, in book viii, and the two spinster friends, in book xi, possess the freshness of original portraits, painted by the hand of a master, and placed before us in new lights and under different combinations. In some, the single figure may be said to fill the canvas, in others, each figure in the group, gives and receives a relative value. It is no easy task to produce novelty. No doubt, by having repeated the same characters in his present work, he has increased his difficulties; lost an opportunity of variety, and incurred, in some degree, the charge of sameness in these instances. Richard, his married man, poor, proud, tenderly loving and beloved, is drawn with great vigour and warmth: as a husband and father, he lays hold of our interests, with all the glow and animation of life itself. The tyrant of the village school is only a slight outline, with little to distinguish him from the Thwackums of preceding writers. Barlow, the sordid lover, and Bloomer, the perfidious, are every day to be found in nature. His sectarian *teacher* is of the modern race; and we have not met with any more forcible picture of hardened religious pride and hypocritical selfishness. In the affecting story of poor Ruth, the danger of preventing marriage, where two hearts are united, and the cruelty of pressing that ceremony against the inclinations, are strikingly exemplified. His preceptor husband is a literary novelty, and his fraudulent banker, a clever copy of an original, which is now rather too often to be met with in this country. . . .

[There follows a lengthy passage on Crabbe's 'commendable effort to do away with national prejudice' in his portrayal of the Irish captain and the Scottish doctor in this tale, in which the reviewer praises Crabbe's 'fine sense of patriotism and Christian duty'!]

This poet's wit is just; but neither so far-sought, nor so abundant, as to sparkle at the expense of more important essentials. There is a delicate pleasantry in his humour, which is more agreeable because it is wholly unforced, and not a leading feature in his composition. His descriptions are varied, and he leads us with an easy transition from the groves and stately apartments of Binning Hall, to the bleak, half-roofless garret of Cecil, the seducer, or the workhouse of the unfortunate painter. He paints the one with force, like the calm glow of a fine sunset; and delineates the homely furniture and suffering tenants in the other with minute fidelity, without exciting disgust by offensive images and objects. His landscapes have all the beauty of local prospects: they delight us by bringing to our recollection scenes in which we have passed days of pleasure, or wandered in hours of musing melancholy. His versification is that which has been long in use, and of which we have given sufficient specimens for our readers to judge for themselves in the preceding extracts. He is fond of triplets; and in the close of an heroic climax, the effect is heightened by that form and by

The deep mouthed verse and long resounding line:[1]

but this poet walks on earth amidst his listening fellow-mortals, and his triplets occur as frequently in the middle as in the close of a descriptive period.

Mr. Crabbe is not one of those who delight in drawing scenes of horror, and characters, whose turpitude renders our species loathsome in the contemplation! The good and the amiable, the contented and happy, are so judiciously intermingled in his pages with the unfortunate, the erring, and the wicked, as to soften the effect of the latter, and give the former a salutary influence on the mind. In each of his tales, he furnishes salutary lessons of life, and evinces the power of rendering guilt hateful without hardening the heart against the guilty: we detest the offence, but are filled with a compassionate interest for the offender, and would, if possible, save him from the consequences of his crimes. His instances of depravity are not brought forward to favour a doubt of Divine Providence, or querulous spirit of misanthropy, but to encourage all that is praiseworthy in our nature, and to render vice itself an excitement to virtue. His sentiments are purified by a religious sense, warm and constant, but so mild, unobtrusive, and blended with kind affections and soothing charities, that it may be termed a social piety, which makes the bands of duty light and pleasant, and operates as a perpetual inducement to benevolence. His morality is not the blind rigor of a bigot, who includes all virtue in a profession of belief; separates good works, the fruit, from the tree of faith, on which they ought to flourish in perpetual season, and pleads a love of God as a justification for hating and persecuting his fellow-creatures. We have been amused, soothed, delighted, instructed and bettered, by the perusal of these volumes; and we are inclined to think, that, when the works of some of his *brilliant* contem-

[1] ? Misquotation of Pope, *Epistle to Augustus*, 268.

poraries are consigned to forgetfulness, *The Tales of the Hall* will be read with applause, and the name of Crabbe be pronounced with increasing esteem and regard by posterity.

48. Unsigned review, *Christian Observer*

October 1819, xviii, 650–68

In the cursory survey, to which we are annually invited, of the laudable and sometimes splendid display of British genius in the exhibition of pictures at Somerset House, we strongly participate in the pleasure very generally felt at being directed to some new production, from the inimitable pencil of our modern genius, Mr. Wilkie. We have noticed, in succession, his admirable and close delineation of the Blind Fidler, the Rent Day, the Card-players, &c.; and no fresh effort of this truly spirited and exact, though characteristically low-life, painter, has induced those feelings of satiety in our gaping mood, which we consider it the first privilege of the true artist *never* to produce.

It is with feelings not very dissimilar, that we hear, amidst the often splendid trash which exhibits itself for daily or monthly inspection in the scribbling world, of another set of tales and delineations, from the pen of our able and faithful copyist of nature in her lowly forms, the Rev. George Crabbe. As readers of poetry, we still own to the magic power held over our minds by nearly the same manner, and quite the same original force, in the present delineations of life and manners, with those which rivetted us on former occasions: and the judgment that has thrown an interval of seven years between the present and the last effusions of this satiric muse, has secured to us quite a sufficiency of novelty, at least in matter if not in style, to renew all the interest which we felt in its first productions. The question, indeed, whether this highly successful pourtrayer of almost the *only* subjects he professes to choose for the exercise of his art, be in truth a poet or not, seems to us to be just as moot a point as whether the aforesaid artist, Mr. Wilkie, be a painter or not. We have very much mistaken the meaning of the latter term, if it is to be confined to the Raffaelles, the Rubenses, the Wests, the Davids, and other *epic composers*, whether of ancient or modern times: and if the term poet belong only to a Homer, or a Tasso, a Milton, or a Southey, we shall require another edition of Johnson's poets, and must lash the memory of that great critic, for having inscribed amongst his worthies the names of a Butler, a Churchill, or even a Dryden, and a Pope. If by the force of vivid conceptions, aided by the magic of an artificial and harmonious diction, to raise strong emotions, whether of pity, fear, desire, or hate towards persons, or at events with which we are conscious of no immediate and direct concern, be the very essence and genuine effect of all true poetry, however otherwise technically defined; then must the above last mentioned names, and Mr. Crabbe's with them, be admitted to the full freedom of the Pierian band: and though it may not have been the fortune or genius of this or that man to raise exactly this or that class of sensations, in the imaginative faculties of their readers, yet the power of raising any strong sensations of whatever kind, pleasing or displeasing, by such methods, must be considered as equally entitling the exercise of that power to the dignified name of poetic genius.

One class of sensations, it is most true, our popular modern poet Mr. Crabbe does not raise, nor even profess an attempt to raise, in the breast of his readers. It is one of which, considering his very strong mind and great superiority in another department of poetry, we should almost hesitate in averring, what is, notwithstanding, our belief, that he is completely destitute in his own soul; at least destitute to a degree surprisingly beyond the ordinary run of the 'irritable tribe' whom he so much surpasses in his peculiar way. To the feelings of the genuine and lofty *epic*, we must pronounce our decided opinion that Mr. Crabbe is, as a writer, wholly insensible. To explain, in two words, what we mean by the term 'epic' or 'heroic,' we should state, that whatever is above life, above ordinary life, as experienced in our quotidian intercourse with our fellow-beings, may be ranked under that title. Great powers, great virtues, even great vices, and great sufferings may all be considered as the proper objects of the epic feeling. The greatness of the object seems to communicate itself to, or rather to derive itself from, a corresponding sentiment in the mind of the poet. It appears as much in the character he draws, as in the numbers of his song: and there is in the whole matter and method of his discourse, such a lofty aspiring, such a stately march, such a splendid, and sometimes scarcely measured, ambition of thought and expression, that, except for a felicity which the pagans might well call inspiration, the heroic inventor is in hourly danger of out-reaching his aim, and toppling over into the sublimely ridiculous.

> But not to one in this benighted age
> Is that diviner inspiration giv'n,
> Which shone in Shakespear's and in Milton's page—
> The pomp and prodigality of Heav'n.[1]

To this inspiration, if Mr. Crabbe possesses not the slightest claim, he has at least the merit of not advancing any. Like his fellow-satirist, he has chosen, by profession, 'to expatiate over' the humbler, but, perhaps, more appropriate, 'field of man:' he has chosen by his writings to awaken chiefly those sensations which arise in reading Pope's Satirical Letters, his *Dunciad*, and other essays of a like nature; and if that great poet is only to be called such in his 'Messiah,' *Windsor Forest*, Epistles, or 'Rape of the Lock,' then, indeed, Mr. Crabbe must renounce any participation with him in that name: and the only question that will further remain is this, Would Mr. Pope himself have chosen to rest his title to poetic fame on any one species of his own compositions, to the exclusion of the rest?

That Mr. Crabbe does claim, at least, so much as the name of poet, will be seen in his own preface to his former work, the *Tales*;[2] and to that very rational and spirited preface we shall content ourselves with referring such of our readers as may, after accompanying us through the present work, the *Tales of the Hall*, still retain an opinion, that they furnish inadequate evidence of his title to that high and distinguished name.

So far, indeed, has Mr. Crabbe chosen to rest his honourable claims, on grounds totally distinct from *epic* composition, that he has gone beyond all his predecessors of name and note to whom we might have referred, in rejecting the very front or colour of that ambitious style. With much ability for the regular heroic march of song, and no lack, we should presume, of resources from whence to draw his 'sesquipedalia verba,' we find him, we might almost say, forcing himself to reject those which come ready to his hand, and descending, even by unnatural efforts, from his loftiest measures to that 'sermo pedestris' which he seems determined to make the grand characteristic of all his writings. Hence not only are his openings most ordinarily in that low and *chatty*

[1] Gray, 'Stanzas to Mr. Bentley', 17–20.
[2] See above, No. 30.

257

sort of language, which goes quite beyond the prudent modesty recommended by the great Roman critic[1] in the first steppings of his heroic muse; but even in the mid-height of his career, when the native force of his mind seems instinctively to have lashed him into something of the nobler darings of thought and style, he takes care to let us know, before he finishes his sentence, how much he despises the praise at which we fancied he was aspiring, and ends not uncommonly the finest passage with an effect not unlike that of a race-horse who flings a shoe at the last heat, or an alderman who finishes a luxurious feast by breaking with his last morsel an unsound tooth. Instances will, we are persuaded, frequently occur, in the course of the many quotations we shall have to give from the volumes before us, of this quaint and unaccountable taste: unaccountable perhaps on any ground, but that of supposing our poet afraid of the slightest imputation, of what might be termed in any sense of the word enthusiastic; desirous of keeping his head perfectly cool, and shewing it to be so amidst scenes the most qualified to arouse the liveliest sensations of the soul; and perhaps acting upon the questionable principle of a forcible contrast, in which the careless and familiar attitude of the poet himself should set off the growing and the deepening effects, lights and shadows, of the picture before him.

We think it necessary to say thus much on the style of our author, because we may be considered in some measure as patrons of it, whilst we quote, with more or less approbation, passages of the deepest interest and greatest merit on other grounds; and that we may be saved, likewise, the trouble of referring to such comparatively minor defects, when we may feel ourselves called upon to detract from our critical and poetic praise, by some more serious considerations of a moral and religious nature. These considerations will naturally arise in the progress of our review; but at present we are unwilling to detain our readers further from the Tales themselves, or to suspend the varied interest which they are calculated to excite, in every breast not wholly dead to those peculiar feelings of sympathy with the vices, weaknesses, and sufferings of mankind, which Mr. Crabbe knows so well how to touch.

The *Tales of the Hall* so far depart from the author's previous plans, as to stand in a sort of connexion with one another throughout the whole, by means of a preliminary tale not deficient in interest, which runs its thread along the entire texture of the piece. Whether he thinks such a plan may give a little more the appearance of original invention than the former disjointed method he had pursued, or whether a little

[1] Horace, *Ars Poetica*.

more pains, or a little more aptitude in his materials, or a little more experience, persuaded and directed him to that regularity of composition which he had acknowledged on a former occasion beyond his reach, certain it is that he has conformed himself in this instance, more to the generally recognized mode of all superior tale-bearers, from Boccace downwards, through the illustrious undertaker of a Thousand and One Stories to form the amusement of as many nights for the Arabian tyrant, to the final splendors of our new and modish, rather than moral, poet of *Lallah Rook*. The device has its merit, though not worth much cost of time or pains. We forget who tells the tale, if the tale itself is worth our hearing. The persons relating, if remarkably amiable or remarkably romantic, or any otherwise remarkably interesting, perhaps a little take off from our close and undivided attention to the wonders they are telling. The improbability, moreover, continually strikes us of so many marvellous occurrences having come under the cognizance of any one or two persons, however conversant with 'the varied scenes of crowded life.' A poem which is, after all, nothing but a congeries of episodes, can scarcely be called, by any Aristotelian disciple, a regular composition. And if the tales be considered as a series of interesting dramas, and the relaters of them the actors, it cannot add much interest or effect to the several pieces, to know the character of the players: this has a large family, that has a country box, this is a decent man, that a profligate, &c.

> It was an ancient, venerable hall . . .
> [I, 43–74]

(Italicising as follows:

> Its worth was poor, *and so the whole was sold*
> [52]

and

> Work of past ages; *and the brick-built place*
> *Where he resided was in much disgrace.*
> [59–60].)

The words in Italics are, if not a strong, yet some illustration of our meaning, in commenting on that free-will insertion of low *colloquialism* with which our author chooses perpetually to dash his most interesting passages; a mixture which, for our own part, we think by no means necessary to keep up that perfectly easy and natural flow that Mr. Crabbe, when he pleases, can so well combine with much grace and harmony of language.

The Hall thus graphically described has a visitor, in the person of

Richard, younger and half-brother to George its possessor. The portraiture of the guest is worked with no common care; and his free and engaging manners, with much of a liberal cast of mind, and certain early free-thinking habits, now sobered down by the well tried, and well beloved services of a wise and affectionate wife, are admirably drawn.

[The summary then notes the 'interesting story' of Ruth (Book V) and the 'highly wrought tale' of Sir Owen Dale (Book XII), and concludes as follows:]

Three other personages, in the neighbourhood, form the subjects respectively of the three next books; of which 'the Widow,' still pretty, after the disruption of her three-fold knot, is the most amusing; 'Ellen,' the most provokingly sad and disappointing;* and 'William Bailey,' affording the liveliest series of incident, carried through the heights of love in a cottage, and the depths of vice in a great house below-stairs. A sufficiently dull story succeeds, in book twenty, of 'a Cathedral Walk,' with sundry remarks on ghosts, and at the end an appropriate and laughable mistake, by a romantic maid, of a resurrection-man for a pure and sainted apparition. A more touching and truly tragical scene, or rather drama, succeeds, in the twenty-first book, in connexion with the portentous subject of 'Smugglers and Poachers.' And, finally, the closing book brings us back to our 'two Brothers,' and after a very decently managed state of sentimental suspense, in which Richard's characteristic nicety of feeling and delicacy of honour betray him into some natural mistakes, respecting his brother's intentions and the worthy Rector Jacques's sentiments of friendship, and even his Matilda's tenderness towards him, the whole matter is closed in the following happy *denouement* from the lips of the homely but honest and fraternal George, on the very morning of Richard's looked-for departure.

'No! I would have thee, Brother, all my own, . . .
[XXII, 380–417; 477–92, 496–510]

Without attempting any thing further in the way of an account of the contents of these, we must call them, volumes of true poetic merit, as most *readers* have probably ascertained, from personal acquaintance, before now; we shall proceed to such few, but free, observations on

* It is a curious fact, and might lead to some curious speculations on the difference between fiction and truth, that the story of Ellen, decidedly the most inexplicable, and that of Lady Barbara's Ghost, nearly the most dull and unmeaning in the volumes before us, are acknowledged in the preface as not original inventions, and actually communicated by friends, as true stories, we presume, or 'founded on truth'.

particular parts, and on the whole performance, as have occurred to us in the perusal. To these observations a passage in Mr. Crabbe's own sprightly preface may, perhaps, afford us a convenient *text*. It is as follows:—

The first intention of the poet must be to please; for, if he means to instruct, he must render the instruction which he hopes to convey palatable and pleasant. I will not assume the tone of a moralist, nor promise that my relations shall be beneficial to mankind; but I have endeavoured, not unsuccessfully I trust, that, in whatsoever I have related or described, there should be nothing introduced which has a tendency to excuse the vices of man, by associating with them sentiments that demand our respect, and talents that compel our admiration. There is nothing in these pages which has the mischievous effect of confounding truth and error, or confusing our ideas of right and wrong. [p. xviii.]

Now the questions which arise to our minds from this passage, and on which we found our observations, are these three:—Does Mr. Crabbe please us? Does he instruct us? Does he rightly define the first duty of the poet as being to please, or properly disclaim the assumption that his relations shall be beneficial to mankind?

To the first of these questions we say, that the word 'please' must be taken in a large sense, in order to answer it, on the present occasion, in the affirmative. If the test of pleasure conferred be the general desire to purchase and to read, then Mr. Crabbe wants nothing further to prove that he is a *pleasing* poet; since we know no poet more generally read, or made more frequently the topic of interesting and animated conversation. But when we listen to the remarks no less frequently recurring in the course of such conversations; and when we look into the pages of our brother critics, whether of greater or humbler note, and find so many persons literally writhing under the horrors of the song, and gasping after terms to express their shocked and severely pained feelings, at many of the ideas lastingly impressed on their brain; it certainly conveys to us the notion of something the very contrary to pleasure, and we begin to think our worthy divine has failed in 'the first intention of the poet.' We hear, indeed, of the eagerness with which auditors will rush into the stuffed theatre, to have their sensibilities harrowed by the adventures of a Lear, or a Macbeth; and this, we are still told, is being 'pleased.' But even here there are limits; and the Athenians of old, those most determined playgoers, were for hanging the poet who cruelly and unjustly murdered his hero. We know, too, that people will crowd to an execution; nay, we doubt not we should have multitudes of 'pleased' spectators, were they admissible into the surgery or dissecting room; and yet we apprehend neither the hangman nor the chirurgeon would be ranked amongst the tribe of those whose 'first intention is to please.' Mr. Crabbe is a fine dissector: his moral knife lays open to universal gaze, with a firm and unshaken touch, and in horrible truth and fidelity, the breathing vitals, the *spirantia exta* of his victims. The mental sufferings he seems to take a delight in pourtraying are often worked up with a poignancy that would leave the very cruellest spectator, a Domitian himself, or a French mob, nothing more to desire; and when pursued, as it is occasionally, to the death of the unhappy sufferer, can any thing more nearly approach the *merit* of the before-mentioned unfortunate Athenian Poet?

He then was sitting on a workhouse-bed, . . .
[III, 261–324]

. . . From ten to twelve of Mr. Crabbe's two and twenty books would afford materials for the deepest tragedies. The comparative languor of some other of the books which exhibit endeavours of an opposite description, leave us little doubt as to the style of thought most congenial to the author's own peculiar mind. We desire, however, here to speak with very large exceptions in Mr. Crabbe's favour; as we hesitate not to affirm, that some of the most pleasing descriptions of domestic happiness, and the bosom's joy, to be found any where in the language, may be traced in this author's pages. His playful efforts, likewise, or rather his playfully satirical efforts, are occasionally very happy and truly amusing. Of this the comely 'Widow,' in the seventeenth book, whose 'thrice-slain peace' had scarcely left a wrinkle on her brow, may be adduced as an excellent specimen, with all her pretty wayward infantile fancies; save and except that these also were the death, and a cruel one, of her first ruined husband!

Water was near them, and her mind afloat; . . .
[XVII, 136–40]

Many of his windings up at last, have the merit of allaying a small portion of the irritated feelings produced by the substance of the story, and seem intended to act as a sort of entertainment after the horrors of the piece; but we must add, they generally come in too late to our assistance, are too short, and fail by scarcely forming any constituent part of the drama. On the whole, we sum up our sentence on this head, by declaring our opinion, that Mr. Crabbe is not, as he stands at present *in the piece*, a pleasing poet; that his great power and constant inclination lie in pourtraying all the varied feelings and shadows, deeper and deeper still of woe and vice; but that he gives a sufficient indication of his power in an opposite manner to make us covet, and even demand as our right, some more pleasing and animating pictures from his pen—some pictures which may, without deviating from truth, exhibit her in her fairer forms and more inviting colours. We assign, it is true, a more arduous task to our poet than any he has yet attempted, as beauty is more difficult of delineation than deformity, and the simple magnificence of wisdom and virtue and truth and peace, in their purest earthly forms, more unattainable to the ordinary pencil, than the harsh, and wrinkled, and ever-shifting features of falsehood and folly, and vice and wretchedness: but why should not the attempt be made, with powers of genius like those of Mr. Crabbe?

The next question which demands our attention, and a very grave one, is this—Does Mr. Crabbe instruct us? To this we most readily reply, in spite of his own modest disclaimer, which we reserve as a dry question for our last topic, that it is his laudable intention to do so. We as firmly believe, that Mr. Crabbe intends to benefit mankind by his labours as to please them; and *if* he fails, or as *far* as he fails in either, we have no hesitation in ascribing both alike, rather to error in judgment than to any perversity of will. The points of instruction in which we perceive no failure in our poet's able productions, are, 1. That nice delineation of character in general, as far as *his* characters go, which must ever be considered as highly conducive to the cultivation of that discriminative faculty which is so useful in our intercourse with mankind; and, 2. and near akin to this, The perpetual recurrence of inimitable home strokes in the course even of his commonest details, which go very far in assisting us to form a correct judgment of our own minds and our own motives. As an instance of the former, what can be more in point, or more admirably discriminating, than the following portion of the respective characters of 'The Two Sisters,' Jane and Lucy?

> Lucy loved all that grew upon the ground, . . .
> [VIII, 120–71]

Instances of the latter point of instruction occur so frequently in Mr. Crabbe's pages, that it seems an injustice to select only one or two as specimens of the rest. Perhaps, however, the following fearful outline of a state of mind, as common as it is lamentable, may not be without its use to whom it may concern.

'Tis said th' offending man will sometimes sigh, . . .
[III, 428–38]

O! that unknown to him the pair had flown
[XV, 227–32]

3. We consider Mr. Crabbe's writings beneficial, as a direct satire
on some of the most common, and therefore, perhaps, most fatal errors
which meet us in our ordinary plans of life, or general intercourse with
mankind. In the early history of George, he gives us a hearty laugh at
adult bachelor romance, that is, till he conducts to a scene of ghastly
interest in the presence chamber of his actual intended, where a more
distressing moral forces itself upon us, in descriptions scarcely *producible*
of the

> something he had seen
> So pale and slim, and tawdry and unclean,
> With haggard looks of vice and woe the prey;
> Laughing in languor, miserably gay, &c. &c. &c.
> [VII, 549–52]

The arts of the seducer, the speculator, and such other vermin and
pests of society, are exposed with a force which may be of much practical use; the 'righte pleasante storie' of two brothers falling murder-
ously by each other's hands makes us equally hate the game laws and
their breach; whilst the consequences of unguarded marriages, and the
proper method of guarding any from disappointment, and guiding them
to their truest and most lasting bliss, form perhaps one of the most
frequent, varied, and most edifying admonitory results of the entire
volumes before us. Of this latter head of instruction, 'The Natural
Death of Love,' would afford us, had we time for more quotation, some
very interesting specimens; particularly the exquisite description of the
married duties at the close. But we forbear; and only add, that the tale,
which occurs before, of Sir Owen Dale, one of the highest wrought, and
most striking in the volume, gives us a very fine tragical lecture on the
moral death of *Revenge*; and whilst it inflicts a most heart-rending, but
true poetical justice on an unhappy run-away wife and her paramour,
presents one of the most touching examples of forgiveness in the
husband, so touching, as to overcome even the Shylock-heart of Sir
Owen himself, and induce him to transfer his own lost bliss to his happier
rival, or rather successor in love. In a word, we consider Mr. Crabbe as
in the main poetically just: if his crimes are disgusting, it must be allowed
that so likewise are his punishments, and we fully concede to him the

merit of never 'excusing the vices of man, by associating with them sentiments that demand our respect, and talents that compel our admiration.'

Something, however, and indeed much remains to be said on the opposite side of the question, and we cannot help offering rather a strong opinion, that Mr. Crabbe fails in the point of instruction in his poems in two or three very important ways. First of all, we think he errs in making so many of his examples purely negative, and presenting to us the large mass of mankind and womankind, as only to be scorned for their vices, and scarcely ever to be pitied for their manifold and deserved misfortunes. Aristotle, it is true, makes it the office of tragedy to purify the mind by pity and terror: and if Mr. Crabbe's heroes and heroines rose to a certain pitch of gigantic action, or sunk to any thing like a state of honourable misfortune, we fully allow such an advantage might follow. But these are not the favoured objects of Mr. Crabbe's portraiture, which rather are a set of low, mean, pitiful, and scoundrel passions, the sordid offspring of pure selfishness, and proper and fit cause of a debasing and squalid wretchedness, such as we look for in the dungeon, or shudder at in the hospital. His very virtues are of a creeping order; but his vices positively wallow in a kind of moral stench: and both indicate a something in our poor mortal frame even lower than our avowed and too lamentable frailty; a lowness that nothing can raise; a total incapacity for any thing great, generous, and godlike. We approve, because the Scriptures approve, every description of fallen human nature that shall make it, in its own proper worth and merit, 'abominable,' and 'none righteous; no, not one.' But we do not wish to see its capacities traduced; its high and noble destinies trampled in the dust: nor do we willingly behold even man in his worst estate as 'less than the archangel ruined; and the excess of glory obscured.'[1] We think ill both of the impression and the effect with which we rise from descriptions of human nature like many of Mr. Crabbe's; an impression of the hatefulness of man, with the effect of scarcely wishing, because not hoping, to make him by any efforts, better. How shockingly, indeed, must the fall of man not only have debased but annihilated his capacities, if this be really the case! how much changed from that primeval innocence and towering dignity of character!

> For contemplation He and valour form'd—
> For softness She and sweet attractive grace.[2]

---

[1] Milton, *Paradise Lost*, I, 593–4.
[2] *Ibid.*, IV, 297–8.

How much below the hopes and feelings once entertained towards him even in his fallen state! 'For God so loved the world that he gave his only begotten Son, that every one that believeth in him should not perish, but have everlasting life.'

And this, again, leads us to say, that in the pages of Mr. Crabbe, Christianity itself—we say it with pain—seems to us degraded from its high and privileged authority; and the pure and undefiled religion of Jesus Christ, more than once unfeelingly confounded with the most horrid and polluted mixtures, is almost at all times exposed as a totally insufficient antidote either to the ills or the vices of mankind. By a most sad and disheartening process, Mr. Crabbe seems to make his characters, for the most part, good at first, such as their goodness is, and bad afterwards; and it seems to us as if his works might not be inaptly titled, The Triumphs of Vice. Virtue, resolution, honour, conscience, which with him seem to have existed previously in the mind, are all chased away before the breath of temptation, like chaff before the wind: and, instead of tracing the gradual and glorious transitions from bad to good, from the first corruptions of nature to the happy improvements of Divine grace, through the medium of the first and purest of religions, we have to view in Mr. Crabbe's pages the puny efforts of a spurious or lowborn innocence of nature, gradually or hastily subsiding into the depths of a miserable and overwhelming depravity.

> Still there was virtue, but a rolling stone . . .
>
> [XII, 579–92]

Who would have thought this dire foreboding of a future fall, to belong to the amiable and delightful vicar's niece in 'Sir Owen Dale,' all 'softness, gentleness, and ease,' surrounded by her three darling girls, and a loving and attentive though rather coarse husband, and

> . . . health with competence, and peace with love.
>
> [520]

See here ere long—must we behold it, or, having beheld it, repeat it?—

> In that vile garret which I cannot paint,
> The sight was loathsome, and the smell was faint.
> . . . reclined unmoved, her bosom bare
> To her *companion's* unimpassioned stare. . . .
> Sure it was all a grievous odious scene,
> Where all was dismal, melancholy, mean,
> Foul with compelled neglect, unwholsome and unclean.
>
> [755–6, 769–70, 839–41]

It is true, the repentance of one or *both* is hinted at—

> I believe *her* mind
> Is now enlightened—I am *sure* resigned:
> . . . *he* was past
> All human aid, and shortly breathed his last,
> But his heart open'd and he lived to see
> Guilt in himself, and find a friend in me.
>   [860-1, 867-9]

We should add, that we think these very traits of repentance, and, as it may happen, palliations or aggravations of guilt, are of so slight and equivocal a nature, as very much to perplex the true boundaries of vice and virtue. We do not understand in the sad self-inflicted end of the unfortunate Ruth, what moral exactly is meant to be conveyed in the following lines.

> She had—pray, Heav'n!—she had that world in sight
> Where frailty mercy finds, and wrong has right;
> But sure, in this, her portion such has been,
> Well had it still remain'd a world unseen.
>   [V, 460-3]

But we cannot leave the above-mentioned story of Ruth, without expressing our heartiest disapprobation of that other inveterate practice of Mr. Crabbe's, namely, the associating the name, profession, and *notions* of a something like religious faith, with the very worst features in heart and practice. The 'reptile' described in that story,

> who beneath a show
> Of peevish zeal, let carnal wishes grow;
> Proud and yet mean, forbidding and yet full
> Of eager appetites, devout and dull;
>   [380-3]

is but a match for other like characters drawn by the satirical pen of Mr. Crabbe, and which again meet us in 'the Maid's Story' and 'William Bailey;' and to one and all we must say, though we are wholly unwilling to be thought the patrons of Dissent, Methodism or cant; nay, though we have met ourselves accidentally with such horrid combinations as that which our poet describes; yet that we protest most solemnly in the name of our common faith against any equivocal associations on serious subjects, where it, above all, behoves us to speak out plainly, and so as not to be misunderstood; and that we from our heart condemn the too common practice of joining scriptural terms and ideas, such as zeal, devotion, experience, faith, &c. &c. with those detestable abuses to which the best things are most easily liable. Does Mr. Crabbe really mean to insinuate, that the more zeal, and warmth, and devotedness to the cause of Christ and his Gospel, persons may shew, the more they are to be suspected of nefarious designs and disgraceful lusts? Or are the clergy or our venerable establishment so much his debtors as to stand exempted in his view from all those vices, open or nameless, with which he would exclusively charge dissenting teachers? Or, finally, does he mean that all alike, whether preachers or professors, regular or irregular, of our holy religion, shall each in their way be suspected, be forcibly and of right accused of some mal-designs and malpractices at bottom; only with this difference, that to the regular shall be attributed the decent, and to the irregular the indecent, vices of humanity?

. . . It is preposterous to say that any sect or set of men, professing Bible principles, in whatever varieties, admit immorality and vice as a part of their creed. No man commits adultery, lies, or steals, but against his principles; and, if he is a professor of a pretended reformed creed, against very strong principles. . . .

We had intended to make some observations on the remarkable preponderance, in these volumes, of love stories; and the various feelings, bad and good (not always the latter), detailed in connexion with the passion of love. We are not surprised that one who can paint this subject so well, should be ambitious of painting it often: nor can we wonder that one desirous, like Mr. Crabbe, of raising some of the strongest *home-emotions* in the hearts of his readers, should fix upon that passion which is well known to bear an undisputed sovereignty over the entire animal economy of nature. But this very last-named circumstance makes us doubt the propriety of assisting nature, where in point of fact she needs so little assistance. The business of *instruction* is to allay what is naturally predominant in the human soul, and to arouse its slumbering and oppressed faculties.

. . . These representations, we are persuaded, are much calculated to awaken ideas far beyond the exact words of the narration, and to familiarize the tender and susceptible mind with vice in its most mischievous, because most insidious, forms: and the subsequent operation of those past, but *never forgotten*, feelings upon minds afterwards imbued with better principles, we often think leads far more to those inconsistencies in practice, those sad and humiliating conflicts between 'the flesh and the Spirit,' satirized by Mr. Crabbe himself, than all the lectures of Methodism, or the cant of Antinomianism.

. . . We still should have coveted from such a pen, even in its 'moments of leisure and amusement,' something more definitely instructive, though not less interesting, than the present work. . . .

The question which we had reserved for our final consideration, and which we must now, for obvious reasons, spare ourselves and our readers the trouble of discussing at any length—viz. whether the poet's first intention ought to be to please, and his attempt to instruct quite a contingency—does, we think, in the case now before us, admit but of one solution. Indeed, talents in general, of so interesting, so distinguished, so rare, and so highly privileged an order, as those of the true poet, by whomsoever possessed, do to us seem in their first exercise most imperatively to demand a leading tribute of glory to their Great Giver, as well as of benefit to His creatures, whom it is always HIS first intention to instruct. Nor do we imagine the cause of poetry would at all suffer by such an intention. We might, indeed, hear a little less of certain obvious and questionable feelings of our nature, on which poets, intending first to please, are too apt to dwell with a fondness 'akin to sickliness.' But instead of these, we should have the effusions of a vigorous and masculine understanding, leading us to all that is great and noble and generous in our common nature, and bearing us on lofty measures and daring thoughts, as on eagle-wings, towards heaven. We should learn from the Muse so regulated, perhaps less of the love of the sex, but more of the love of human kind, the love of virtue, the love of country, the love of God. In tracing the angel-flight of such a bard, we should feel not the less interest in his subject from our admiration of the man; something, on the other hand, of the greatness of the writer would insensibly communicate itself to the breast of the reader.[1] Praise so obtained, would, we should think, be dear to any poet, if worthy of the name; and the laurels so obtained most honourable indeed. Such laurels, let us hope, we may yet have, in his declining years, to place with unreserved applause on the brows of our now respected Mr. Crabbe: such laurels we unre-

[1] Crabbe felt that an aim of such a height was purposeless. In a letter of 11 November 1819 (*Spectator*, 25 February 1932, p. 245) he wrote:

I take as an Act of Kindness your sending to me that number of the *Christian Observer* in which my late Book has been reviewed . . . Little I am afraid can be effected by the Muse of most moral and even seraphic Endowments: the Urania of Milton and the—I know not what to call her—of Young included: Creating in the Reader a general Sobriety and some Elevation of Mind is all I think that can be expected or that will be found to arise from the perusal of the more serious and sublime poetry, but even if I thought more might be done, a Writer must consider whether he be capable of doing it. I endeavour to take up the Burden that fits my Shoulders, and I fear that under one of more weighty and precious kind, I should stumble and fall.

servedly concede as the just meed of the virtuous triumphs of Mr. Southey's maturer muse: and justly may England boast of more than a proportionate share of names, living and dead, from whom it were injustice to withhold the wreath. But if there be ONE, of either world, from whom that wreath shall be withheld; ONE from whom at least posterity shall snatch it with indignation, and who has himself, in the phrensy of an ignoble malevolence, torn it to atoms and trampled it in the dust; it is that man whose writings display the resources of the finest genius in dark and unnatural connexion with the worst qualities of a perverted heart. Shall we say *their* first and *sole* intention is to please? If so, it is to please that they may corrupt; to smile, that they may slay. Their author speaks indeed of love, but he so speaks as to warn his stripling imitators of the dangerous illusions of the song. With a cold and satiate mind he seems to paint and revel in all the scenes of imagined debauchery; and in the 'garnished nuisance' of a late work, scarce conceals, beneath the thinly scattered flowers on the surface, the semblance of a conscience, which, if authors are like their works, we should fear is dead to every just and legitimate feeling— 'Lust hard by hate.'—How long, indeed, an abused British public, and our fair countrywomen in particular, will suffer themselves to be held in the silken chains of a poetical enchantment; and how long admire a writer, who has to offer to their admiration a brighter gem, it is true, than any which sparkles in his coronet, the jewel of a rich and brilliant fancy; is more than we can tell. We have done our duty in seizing this opportunity, of which we are not ambitious of the repetition, to offer our friendly warning. For our own parts, we as little envy the reputation of an intimacy with such works, as we do the merit of their first production. If, according to the disgusting sarcasm of their author, the knowledge of their mischief will only further inflame, amongst those from whom we should hope better things, the curiosity to peruse them, we shall still have performed a duty: we must be satisfied with our good intentions, and with the thanks of those who *will* thank us. The wretched author might himself, perhaps, one day thank us, if, by any feeble representations of our own, or the stronger protests of other critics, his works should be *less sold* (the only calamity we apprehend, such authors *feel*), and consequently his mind brought to a new position of self-recollection and inquiry. At present, feelings of the strongest pity for the man mingle with our severer reflections on his detestable though fascinating poetry: and not only whilst enjoying our own fire-side comforts and domestic bliss, in all the plenitude and all the dulness of a contented mediocrity, but even whilst contemplating the penniless obscurity and anguished despair of Mr. Crabbe's imaginary 'Patronized Boy' on his death-bed, if we are compelled to look abroad for a more pitiable object, we see it in one foolishly patronized to his own undoing by an ill-thinking multitude, who neither half relish nor half understand his poetry; we see it in the victim at once of passion and popularity, the self-exiled, the self-tormenting author of *Don Juan*.

With such a fearful *negative* example before our eyes, in Mr. Crabbe's own compendious manner, 'one moral let us draw,'—viz. the error of those who use the finest talents in poetry 'to please, and not to instruct.' And whilst we are very far from considering such a case as applicable, in any of its darker and more appropriate shades, to the writings of Mr. Crabbe, we are still prompt to offer a salutary warning to the writers as well as the readers of poetry; and to lay it down as always a questionable, and often a hazardous, principle in such works, to rest their credit rather on their pleasing than their instructive qualities. In Mr. Crabbe we cannot but see a genius of a very bright order, with a substance of good sense and sound feeling, to our minds a thousand times superior to the factitious and rhodomontading sentiment of the other writer, whose lyrical measures would even find some match from the pen of our present poet, if we are to judge from one or two exquisite specimens scattered up and down his works, and one particularly at the conclusion of the Maid's story,[1] beginning

> Let me not have this gloomy view . . .
> [VIII, 837-40]

We now take our leave of Mr. Crabbe; and should this slight notice of his late work ever chance to meet his eye, we should wish it to bear to his mind the assurance of our unfeigned respect for his very distinguished talents, our sincere thanks for the entertainment afforded us by his interesting work, and our unfeigned hope of meeting him again, on ground (we ask no more) at once worthy the power of his song, and capable of embalming all its worth in the records of an admiring posterity.

---

[1] This is an error: the reference is to 'The Sisters'.

49. Unsigned review, *Monthly Review*

November 1819, xc, 225–38

A strange revolution certainly has occurred in the poetical taste of
England: the pleasure which was derived from the perusal of poetry,
a few years ago, was very different from that of its present readers; and
many qualifications were then necessary to render a poet popular, from
which he now enjoys a complete dispensation. Among these, we may
enumerate some sort of dignity or elegance in the subject,—a selection
of picturesque circumstances,—and an adaptation of proper or adorned
phraseology to the characters and incidents of the piece. All this, however, has passed away; and provided that the one indispensable quality
of *energy* be infused into the leading action, or, perhaps, of extravagant
wickedness in the *leading actor*, with *occasional* felicity in the expression,
neither slovenliness of style nor ruggedness of versification in the
general frame-work of the poem will prove any obstacle to its eminent
success.

The prevailing effect of the works of our elder poetical artists often
reminded us of the chastised and elegant pleasure, that is derived from
the productions in the sister-art of painting which either belong to the
school of Italy, or are formed on that professed model. Our contemporary poets, on the contrary, have in their few laboured passages a
Dutch minuteness of detail; and, generally careless of the grandeur or
refinement of their subject-matter, they are satisfied with dressing their
boors in appropriate trowsers, and painting the signposts of their ale-
houses with broadly contrasted colours. In a word, poetry has been
called down from that exalted region in which it was the delight of a
few cultivated minds, and is now lowered to the pitch of the meanest
intellect, and made the food of the vulgar. Its '*decent drapery*' is torn
away, and its *ideal beauty* is prostrate in the dust. As we really feel
ashamed, however, to reiterate these obvious truths in the ears of our
countrymen, we shall be satisfied with the numerous protests which we
have already entered, in the pages of our Review, against this degradation of the heavenly art of poetry, with the consequent debasement of
our literary taste and tone altogether; and we shall turn from a general

question, which cannot be very acceptable to those who seem to have made up their minds respecting it, to a more particular discussion of the merits and defects of the work immediately before us.

It will not be expected that we should again draw a studied character of an author, who has for so many years (although with a long interval of silence, and, in our judgment, with a very altered manner on his re-appearance) submitted his efforts to the public tribunal. The class of subjects, with which Mr. Crabbe successfully began his poetical career, still indeed continues to employ him: but, to our conception, he has been encouraged by the prevailing relaxation of taste in poetry, till he has been carried, in the train of familiar and prosaic versification, to such an extreme liberty both of thought and language, that his present lucubrations bear only that resemblance to the compositions of our classical school of rhyme, which the caricatures of Rowlandson bear to the cartoons of Raphael. Yet, with all this verbose garrulity of metrical conversation, this every-day talking in rhyme, he frequently displays a vigour and correctness of description, a deep observation on the human heart, or a striking trait of manners, which place him at the head of the moral painters of the age. Low as that age has fallen in literary taste, Mr. Crabbe feels it to be no longer necessary to study the conciseness and the classical precision which marked his earlier couplets. He has in his view no Johnson, no Burke, now to satisfy; and, accordingly, he is contented with a rare couplet or two of finished excellence, while in the great majority of rhymes he cares little for cadence and less for expression, and, above all his other faults, offends by a tautology that is equally feeble and unpoetical.

Our readers shall now have an opportunity of judging whether we have overcharged the picture of imperfection. At the same time, we beg them to bear in mind the portion of praise which we are eager to bestow on this old favourite of the public; and, if *they* also are of the number of the indulgent *spoilers* of the muse, and can forgive *all* her other defects if she be but *energetic* on certain marked occasions, then, we have no doubt, they will deem our objections quite hypercritical and obsolete: while they dwell with undiminished delight on the nervous and the natural portraits of this Hogarth of English poetry, as his warmer admirers will be ready to denominate him.

Two brothers, who have been educated in a wholly different manner, and have not met during the greater portion of their lives, are brought together at last, and amuse themselves by mutual narratives. The events of their own youth, and the fruits of their experience in ample converse with mankind, form the subject of their happy after-dinner colloquies: but the connecting matter, by which their stories are united, is generally of so prosaic a description, that we have been tempted to wish even for a recurrence to the Gothic mixture of prose and verse in Moore's *Lalla Rookh*, rather than be required frequently to peruse such *stuff* as we are about to quote. We use this degrading expression, not only because we think it is amply deserved, but because we are yet anxious (in spite of the faint hope of prevailing on a corrupted taste to attend to such suggestions) to do all that *we* can to mark with reprobation that audacity, which would palm on the public such *admeasurements of prose* for *real poetry*. The lines in italics are among those which we condemn:

Book the Seventh.[1]
The morning shone in cloudless beauty bright;
Richard his letters read with much delight—
George from his pillow rose in happy tone,
'His bosom's lord sate lightly on his throne.'
They read the morning news—they saw the sky
Inviting call'd them, and the earth was dry.

[1–6]

Book the Tenth.
Save their kind friend the rector, Richard yet
Had not a favourite of his brother met.

[1–2]

Book the Eleventh.
Three days remain'd their friend, and then again
The brothers left, themselves to entertain.

[1–2]

'*Themselves to entertain!*'—and this is the manner in which a popular poet is to abuse his advantages, and to laugh in the easy, good-humoured, faces of his unsuspicious readers!

Well—be it so—the time is gone,
When Dryden pour'd a matchless lay;
When Pope's unclouded morning shone,
Or gentle Goldsmith's evening ray.

Book the Twelfth.—Sir Owen Dale.
Again the brothers saw their friend the PRIEST.
Who shared the comforts he so much INCREASED;

---

1 This should read 'Eighth'.

Absent of late—and thus Squire ADDRESS'D
With welcome smile, his ancient friend and GUEST.
[1-4]

Priest and *increas'd*, *address'd* and *guest*, would perhaps, twenty or thirty years ago, have been considered as terminations of too similar a kind to furnish four successive rhymes: but to object to such matters *now* would be to speak unintelligibly to many readers, and hypercritically to many more.

Book the Thirteenth.
Three weeks had past, and Richard rambles now
Far as the dinners of the day allow;
He rode to Farley Grange and Finley Mere,
That house so ancient, and that lake so clear;
He rode to Ripley through that river gay,
Where in the shallow stream the loaches play, &c. &c.
[1-6]

We would ask any dispassionate person, whether it would be more '*difficile* than to *whistle*,' to go on scribbling ten feet after ten feet of verse (by courtesy so called) in perfect unison with the foregoing?

We have not selected these introductory fragments because they are worse, in any degree, than hundreds of their brethren throughout these volumes, but because they *are introductions*; and because they shew, plainly, to any unprejudiced reader, the little pains which Mr. Crabbe has taken (although he seems to deceive himself on this point in his preface) in *composing* the present work: that is, in all but certain favourite, and no doubt very powerful, passages. The inartificial thread on which all the stories are strung, the absolute *prose* of these connecting portions of the *Tales of the Hall*, to any *old* reader of *old* poetry, must be great drawbacks from his own pleasure, and from the merit of the whole performance. As to us, we confess that such patches of familiar conversation, interspersed occasionally with high and heart-rending subjects of feeling, have the effect of a pail of dirty water flung into a face which has just begun to be agitated with some heroic emotion!

Let us now, for a while, turn to a far more pleasant occupation, than this of vituperative criticism on the writings of a man of acknowledged *genius*. We only wish that some *good* dæmon would whisper in his ear, —'Crabbe, have a *taste*,' and then these anomalies would never have occurred, to debase his vigorous and often pathetic efforts.

The beginning of the second book is very good:

275

[II, 1-34.]

It is obvious that some *verbiage* and some unnecessary minuteness disfigure this eloquent delineation; and these are Mr. Crabbe's predominant offences, even in his best moments: but we perceive a manly tone and poetical illustration in this extract, which we will not offend our readers by more distinctly pointing out. We must, however, once more call their attention to that beautiful simile, (blemished by bad grammar,)

> Till the heart rested, and could calmly feel,
> *Till the shook compass felt the settling steel.*
>
> [5-6]

The fate of an unsuccessful painter is forcibly described in the third book; and much in this passage carries us back to Mr. Crabbe's earliest, and, as we shall always maintain, his happiest manner. If it may be thought that a Dutch particularity of description occurs in some of the lines, which borders rather on the ludicrous than the pathetic, and a familiarity in others with which it is difficult to sympathize in due decasyllabic majesty of sorrow, still the most fastidious judges must, we think, be struck with the whole effect; and looser critics will, no doubt, lavish all their random panegyric on it.

> Now Charles his bread by daily labours sought, . . .
>
> [III, 218-68]

> Hither, it seem'd, the fainting man was brought,
> *Found* without food,—it was no longer *sought.*
>
> [269-70]

The sort of antithesis, or rather of pun, in this last line is very frequent in the present author, sometimes happy enough, and rising to the epigrammatic terseness of Young: but almost always wanting the elegance of that writer in his more pointed couplets, and often descending to the poorest degrees of paronomasia.

When Mr. Crabbe deals in *general* description, he occasionally hits the true tone of poetry. Thus, in the preceding extract, such a couplet as

> Where, in her narrow courts and garrets, hide
> The grieving sons of genius, want, and pride,
>
> [241-2]

affords *us*, at least, incomparably more pleasure than his 'yellow tea-

276

pot,' and 'cold black tea;' although these last may furnish a good hint or two for the school of Wilkie. It is, however, to the conclusion of the picture that we give the highest praise; and we may add that the capricious patronage of the great is morally satirized in this story:

> Poor Charles! unnoticed by thy titled friend, . . .
> [III, 296–324]

As a relief to his scenes of moral sadness, Mr. Crabbe often refreshes us in these volumes with some lively natural description, and with the cheering effect which the varied appearances of nature produce on a young and susceptible mind. Thus, in Richard's account of his own early adventures, we have the subjoined animating and touching picture:

> I loved to walk where none had walk'd before, . . .
> [IV, 447–85]

We should now advert to one of the most finished parts of the work, and present our readers with an ample extract from the principal adventure in the life of George: but mere want of room obliges us to refer them to the seventh book, where they will find a description of the fate of an 'unfortunate' female, which has perhaps seldom if ever been exceeded in moral or in pathetic effect. With regard to the hero of the story, (George,) we are indeed disposed to address him in those impressive words of Horace:

> —— ah miser!
> Quantâ laboras in Charybdi;
> Digne, puer, meliore flammâ!¹

Mr. Crabbe certainly excels in the humorous, as well as in the tender; and we are inclined to think, indeed, that his success would be still more perfect (more *uniform* we are certain it would be,) in the first than in the latter style of poetry. A selection of circumstances, a delicacy of touch and taste both in their colouring and their grouping, are surely requisite for the full effect of a *pathetic* description: but *humour* will be felt where broader strokes, and wilder composition altogether, are adopted; and the mixture of sham prose with real verse,—the Hudibrastic mixture in a word,—will here rather heighten than diminish the whole result. Let Mr. Crabbe forgive us for suggesting this to him; and still farther

¹ Wretched boy, worthy of a nobler flame, in what a whirlpool are you toiling! *Odes* I, 27, 18–20. Horace has 'laborabas' in line 19.

for taking up the epithet *Hudibrastic* again, and asking him whether he does not consider the present age to be particularly in want of *another Hudibras*? In that case, who is so calculated as himself to do justice to this great theme; to dissipate, by the powerful *flail of ridicule*, the chaff of religious doctrine that floats among us, and to separate it from the wheat? We call on him to throw his great talents into this useful, this worthy, channel.

That he thinks with ourselves on the subject of the overflowing methodism of the day, his works furnish abundant proofs; and that he has the peculiar tact to render his exposure of this melancholy absurdity very effectual, we could also prove by ample quotation. Let our readers turn to the 'Maid's Story,' and there they will see strong indications of the admirable power in question; the power of sneering even super-stitious folly out of countenance! . . .

> But 'twas a mother's spleen; and she indeed . . .
> [XI, 498–563]

The story of Sir Owen Dale, who, in revenge for the coquetry of a lady whom he has wooed, induces a young friend to court her, with the generous aim of breaking her heart, is extravagant and idle enough: but the tale intitled 'Delay has Danger' is in many parts excellent. The be-ginning, as usual, is rather *prosy*: but both the humour and the pathos heighten and deepen as we proceed. . . .

In the major part of this tale, ycleped 'The Natural Death of Love,' we do not perceive much merit, except of the comic kind; and why the two characters should hold a dialogue under the names of 'Henry and Emma,' unless to excite a somewhat odious comparison,[1] we are at a loss to imagine. The conclusion of the story is beautiful, and does equal honour to the talents and the feelings of the author; who, indeed, on many occasions, has shewn a power of painting the true deep tender-ness of conjugal affection, with a force and a variety altogether his own.

We are compelled, though with great reluctance, to pass rapidly over the remainder of this volume. 'Gretna Green' is a disgusting picture of human folly and wickedness: but, no doubt, such medicines have their effect where strong disorders prevail. 'Lady Barbara, or the Ghost,' is a very extraordinary tale, powerfully interesting, and painfully dis-tressing too, in its catastrophe. How great is the author's success in des-cribing that most melancholy of human feelings, the decline and change of the affections! but, surely, this subject at least is too sacred to have any

---

[1] Presumably with Prior's poem of this name.

ludicrous images and low familiarities mixed with it. We must again call on our *'whispering dæmon'* to do his work.—'The Widow' is one of those happy pictures of common life, which are calculated to throw strong ridicule on the affection of delicate feelings in vulgar minds.

'Ellen' is in parts very affecting, but in parts revoltingly ridiculous. The manner in which the long-absent lover is described as *calling* on his mistress, (and *sending up his name by the servant!*) might be selected as a specimen of the triumphant burlesque on this modern style of '*Conversation Poetry.*' We cannot but be very angry with a writer, who so woefully debases his own superiority as to mix the most incongruous feelings together, and to excite in us the most genuine tears and the broadest grin at the same instant. If this be not to destroy all distinctions, '*confundere sacra profanis,*' in the imagination, we know not what excess deserves the character of that confusion.

The story of 'William Bailey' is not, we think, so good in its moral effect as the great majority of Mr. Crabbe's productions. . . .

'The Cathedral Walk' is a good exposure of ghost-stories;—after which, however, we suspect the author to have more than a Johnsonian hankering.

The tale of 'Smugglers and Poachers' is in this poet's happiest and most original manner. Here is, almost, the tremendous vigour of 'The Hall of Justice;' and all that we have to regret (a regret, we fear, that the growing *democracy of poetical taste* will nearly confine to ourselves) is the inveterate fondness for the *vulgar violent* and the *vulgar pathetic*, which bids fair to place all our heroes and heroines among the menial ranks of society, and to introduce a sort *of High Life below Stairs* into the best efforts of the imagination.

We must find room for the following nervous description:

> Now met the lawless clan—in secret met, . . .
> [XXI, 465–86]

> *Cedite Germani* Prædones, *cedite Galli;*[1]

or, more properly, *Gaëli.*

> Yield, German *Robbers*; Scotch *Marauders*, yield;
> And thou, great *Corsair*, quit the plunder'd field.

[1] My colleague, Mr J. R. Jenkinson of the Department of Classics in the University of Hull, suggests that this may be an adaptation of

> Cedite Romani scriptores, cedite Grai!
> Propertius II, 34, 65.

We will match Mr. Crabbe's 'Smugglers and Poachers' against them all: nay, we will throw 'Peter Bell,' the pedlar of Mr. Wordsworth, even in his best and most sniveling moment, into the opposite scale, and yet maintain our opinion.

For one instant, however, we would ask, where is the moral use, or where is the poetic probability, (if the former be too serious a question,) of investing such rapscallions with all the dignity of the loftiest passions or setting them forth with all the eloquence of the most thrilling descriptions?

The most touching book of the whole is, according to our opinion, the last; and here we part, in pain indeed, with Mr. Crabbe. May we meet again; and under still happier auspices!—the mixed feelings in Richard's mind, on the day of his intended departure from his friendly brother; the natural touches of disappointment in not meeting with every thing about him as warm as his own heart; and then the sudden discovery that George's fraternal affection is still superior to his own; are altogether really charming;—and the gentle retired wife, in the distant back-ground of the picture, completes the magic of the whole scene. We must leave it to our readers; and, summoning all our courage, and gulping down all our immediate feelings, we will once more beg this author to tell us why *he* (of all men) publishes such lines as

To seek the firm of Clutterbuck and Co.?
[VII, 473]

50. Unsigned review, *Eclectic Review*

February 1820, n.s.xiii, 114–33

Mr. Crabbe has written a long preface to these Tales, for the singular purpose of shewing that no preface was necessary; that the reasons which induce an author to bespeak the attention of his readers to a prefatory address, do not at all apply to his own case; that he is not uninformed of the place assigned him as a writer, and that with the degree of public favour which he enjoys, he has no reason to be dissatisfied.

His motive for writing it, was, he tells us, the fear 'that it would appear to his readers like arrogancy, to send two volumes of considerable magnitude from the press without preface or apology.' This fear was assuredly groundless; but for our own part, we are always glad to meet with a preface: it is often the most characteristic part of a volume, and how uninteresting and superfluous soever in every other point of view, it seldom fails to discover to us some trait of the writer's mind, which renders us better acquainted with the man. We were, however, unfeignedly surprised to find Mr. Crabbe disclaiming 'the tone of a moralist,' and, diffident of any beneficial effect from these 'relations,' contenting himself with the hope, that nothing in his pages would be found of a mischievous tendency. Though not sanguine ourselves as to the moral benefit likely to result from his labours, we had candidly given our reverend Author credit for worthier intentions. This did not arise from our thinking, as he is aware some will think, 'that a minister of religion in the decline of life, should have no leisure for such amusements as these,'—for whom, he says, 'I have no reply,'—but from our imagining that an individual sustaining the responsibility of the sacred office, superadded to that which attaches to every possessor of distinguishing genius, would naturally propose to himself some moral purpose as the end even of his amusements, were it only that to himself he might seem something better, in the decline of life, than a trifler. Why Mr. Crabbe should have deemed it advisable to undeceive us on this point, we find it difficult to conjecture; but we subjoin what purports to be an explanation.

For them I have no reply;—but to those who are more indulgent to the propensities, the studies, and the habits of mankind, I offer some apology when I produce these volumes, not as the occupations of my life, but the fruits of my leisure, the employment of that time which, if not given to them, had passed in the vacuity of unrecorded idleness, or had been lost in the indulgence of unregistered thoughts and fancies, that melt away in the instant they are conceived, and '*leave not a wreck behind.*' [p. xx.]

It is obvious, that in reference to the productions of a writer of acknowledged talent and established fame, who has, to a certain extent, the command of the public attention, the moral tendency of what proceeds from his pen, forms the most interesting consideration, more especially as it can scarcely be of a negative character. And Mr. Crabbe has laid himself so very open to severe censure by the injurious and even irreligious tendency of some of his former Tales, that we should have been glad to find him disposed, on appearing again before the public after the lapse of six years, to repair, or offer some atonement for, the wrong. And he does affirm that 'there is nothing in these pages which has the mischievous effect of confounding truth and error, or confusing our ideas of right and wrong.'

> I know not, [he adds] which is most injurious to the yielding minds of the young, to render virtue less respectable by making its possessors ridiculous, or by describing vice with so many fascinating qualities, that it is either lost in the assemblage, or pardoned by the association. Man's heart is sufficiently prone to make excuse for man's infirmity; and needs not the aid of poetry, or eloquence, to take from vice its native deformity. A character may be respectable with all its faults, but it must not be made respectable by them. It is grievous when genius will condescend to place strong and evil spirits in a commanding view, or excite our pity and admiration for men of talents, degraded by crime, when struggling with misfortune. It is but too true, that great and wicked men may be so presented to us, as to demand our applause, when they should excite our abhorrence; but it is surely for the interest of mankind, and our own self direction, that we should ever keep at unapproachable distance, our respect and our reproach.

These remarks are exceedingly just, and do the Writer credit. His poetry is, to an exemplary degree, clear of the offence he reprobates, that of rendering vice fascinating. We wish we could wholly acquit him of the opposite offence. But although he is not chargeable with rendering virtue less respectable by the direct method of ridiculing its possessors, yet, under the pretence of lashing hypocrisy and fanaticism, he has not scrupled to countenance the most unjust and pernicious prejudices against those whose religious profession singularizes them from their neighbours. . . .

There is less of this in the present volumes, than in the *Tales*, or *The Borough*; a circumstance which we should readily have set down to the account of the Author's better informed judgement, or improved taste, were it not for the gross profaneness which still characterizes his ridicule whenever an opportunity of the kind appears to present itself. In 'The Maid's Story,' Frederick, a young collegian, is successively exhibited as a Methodist teacher, a soldier, an infidel, and a strolling player. Mr. Crabbe would probably say, that he drew the character from real life; and the character has all the verisimilitude of life. We think it the more probable that the Author has, at some time or other, become acquainted with an apostate of this description, because his notions of the 'Sect' to which Frederick is attached, are precisely such as Mr. Crabbe would be likely to obtain through such a channel. It is at least from witnesses just as competent and as credible, that he has obtained the materials for his portraiture of Methodism.

[XI, 690 and 508–14, 535–6, 527–8.]

A man who boldly ridicules that cardinal doctrine of the Reformation, Justification by Faith, and who can bring in for the purpose of burlesque, so beautiful a Scriptural allusion as the one introduced in the first of these specimens, may with great consistency, himself being a clergyman, sneer at conversion as a substitute for episcopal ordination. After this, it is perfectly unnecessary to comment on any want of liberality discovered in his estimate of the Dissenters from that Church whose priest he is; such, for instance, as is implied in the sentiments of the Squire, who

——viewed the Church as *liberal* minds will view, . . .
[I, 138–45]

Our Author prides himself on his knowledge of the world, and his insight into human character. . . .

And he does possess in a very extraordinary degree, the power of describing with anatomical accuracy, as well as picturesque force, every morbid variety of the moral subject. He has been a diligent observer, and he is a no less skilful dissector. But his knowledge is purely that which is derived from close observation; and the field of his observation has exclusively been what we must designate by that equivocal phrase—the world. It is, in other words, the worldly,—the polite and gay, or the base and mean, the careless or the hopeless worldling,—that supply the materials of his parish registers. It is the world in all its naked barrenness and dreariness, it is the human character in its native weakness and obliquity, it is life as a tissue of vanity and vexation, that he unfolds to us. His tales are all half elegy, half satire. He tells us what he has seen, and he *must* have seen what he paints so well. But the heart of a reflecting man would often faint at what he sees, were it not for the relief afforded by recurring to what he can imagine and what he loves to believe. Mr. Crabbe, however, sternly sets himself to combat the illusions which imagination would throw over the scene. He is for banishing fiction even from poetry. He would have us walk through the world with the sobriety and self possession with which we should walk the hospital, treasuring up all the dirty facts and painful occurrences we meet with, as so much knowledge that may turn to our private use in practice. What is displeasing, what is disgusting, is not the less acceptable to him if it presents some fresh variety of human nature. Dugald Stewart has remarked on the traces of early habits of association, which may be detected in writers upon abstract subjects, in their frequent recurrence to some one favourite method of analogical illustration: as for instance, the writer who shall be perpetually speaking of coils and springs and regulating principles in reference to the phenomena of mind, shall prove to be the son of a watchmaker; and in another, who is for ever borrowing his metaphors from the art of healing, we shall recognize the medical student. In like manner, in our clerical Poet there still survives the Surgeon and Apothecary of Aldborough. Not that his phraseology smells of the 'Pharmacopeia,' but his poetical system, though he disavows any specific theory on the subject, bears the marks of a professional view of men and things, strikingly analogous to that with which the medical practitioner is doomed to be familiar. This is a view the very reverse of that which would seem to favour the purpose of the poet; but it suits Mr. Crabbe, and, if we admit it as an axiom of *Common Sense*, that

> None but a bard his own true line can tell,
> He chooses right who executes it well.[1]

we must congratulate him upon a choice of subject so peculiarly adapted to that modification of taste and that passion for bare reality, which his early habits may be supposed to have induced.

But if the ideal was of necessity to be excluded from his Tales, a relief might still have been obtained from another source, which should have been in perfect harmony with the soberest hues of life. If we are forbidden the boyish indulgence of fancy, we might at least be allowed the manly consolations of faith. But this same professional habit of viewing things, is apt to render a man insensible of the want of any such expedient. Besides, Mr. Crabbe tells us that he does not assume the tone of a moralist, and we must, therefore, take him as he is.

What he is, as a poet, our readers cannot require to be informed. As a didactic writer, he is pointed, axiomatic, and often energetic, yet not unfrequently trite and feeble. His descriptions have generally the merit of a Dutch accuracy: sometimes they are strikingly picturesque and even beautiful. But in the delineation of character, lies his distinguishing excellence; and in some of his narrations, which vary from the humblest degree and kind of interest, (sometimes, indeed, bordering upon

[1] C. H. Terrot, *Common Sense*, 199–200. See below, No. 51 (j).

the tiresome,) to a style of the deepest pathos, he has perhaps never been surpassed. The present volumes will not detract from his reputation, as a powerful, though far from being always a pleasing writer.

The plan, or story, which serves to connect these Tales into a series, is, as in the case of Mr. Crabbe's former publications, slight and inartificial. . . .

'Tis to thy own possession that we go . . .
[XXII, 478–92]

Years past away, and where he lived, and how, . . .
[III, 237–68, 302–24]

I loved to walk where none had walk'd before, . . .
[IV, 447–76]

The story of Ruth is one of those deeply tragical and, at the same time, revolting tales which it is an insult to the reader's feelings for the narrator to offer as mere amusement. Nothing short of a valuable moral lesson, as the evident purpose of the recital, can compensate for having the imagination disturbed with such images of disgusting horror. . . .

We must again remind our readers that the Reverend Mr. Crabbe does not assume 'the tone of a moralist,' and, therefore, if this tale should seem intended to palliate the crime of suicide, and to sanction the pernicious delusion that misfortune will claim a retributive compensation in the world 'where frailty mercy finds, and wrong has right;' they must recollect that he does not 'promise that his relations shall be beneficial to mankind.' And further, if it should appear to them, that 'a minister of religion, in the decline of life,' might find some worthier amusement than holding up the teachers of any religious sect to suspicion and reproach, not as the promulgators of false doctrine, but specifically as hypocrites, as gross, and vulgar, and sensual, thus siding with the vilest of mankind in their blind and malignant hostility against the ministers of religion, and becoming a pander to their bigotry and hatred,—for them, be it remembered, Mr. Crabbe has 'no reply.'

Other readers, when they find an author is making a profligate use of his talents, may, at the first impulse of disgust or indignation, throw away the volume; but the critic must proceed. We felt ourselves continually to stand in need of this inducement in persevering through Mr. Crabbe's volumes; so often was the pleasure he is always capable of affording, suspended by the positively disagreeable qualities of the narration, or the worse than ill-chosen nature of his subject. We will not deny that we found ourselves repaid for our perseverance. The reflections suggested by such passages as the one above cited, were so much the more painful, as they were accompanied with the conviction that these Tales, with all their faults, are likely to become a permanent accession to our poetical literature, which will thus receive a fresh portion of that deleterious matter by which its moral tendency is already rendered too adverse to the spirit of the religion of Christ.

The next Tale, which concludes Richard's adventures, and details the progress and successful termination of his courtship, is of a more pleasing cast. There is a great deal of natural feeling in the relation. A lover's recital is apt, however, to border so closely upon the ridiculous, from the causeless fears, the unreasonable jealousies, and what seems to others the amusing eagerness and abstraction of mind, incident to the period of his probation, that it is scarcely susceptible of deep interest. We scarcely know whether the Poet means that we should listen in sober gravity, or with the smile of a grey-haired senior on looking back upon the pleasing frenzy of his youth. Mr. Crabbe cannot be *amatory* with grace; nor can he be sportive. In the succeeding Tale, the 'Elder Brother's' narrative of his strange romantic passion for a beauty whom he one day rescued from danger, and is unable to meet with or hear of again, till he accidentally discovers her in London, ruined and depraved, —the reference *en badinage*, to the 'lunacy sublime' which so long enthralled his reason, is quite in character, and the character suits Mr. Crabbe. But the love song which has been adduced as an instance of his success in a style hitherto unattempted by him, we regard as affording a decided proof of his inadequacy to the attempt: it has little point, little propriety or elegance, and no feeling, and the 'Damon' is almost burlesque. No sooner, however, does Mr. Crabbe arrive at that period in the story which affords scope for pathos, than he is all himself again. The idea in the last three lines of the following extract, is extremely beautiful.

—there came, at length, request . . .
[VII, 714–26, 750–1, 767–76]

'The Sisters' is an interesting and not uninstructive story: the characters are very natural and well discriminated, and the incidents are of a kind with which real life has of late but too much abounded. Like most of the Tales, it leaves a melancholy impression upon the mind, such as the Writer seems to delight in producing. Melancholy is the very element of his fancy, and in this instance it has seemed to supply an inspiration which has called forth the unusual effort of some lyrical stanzas. They are in the moodiest strain, and breathe all that is morbid in feeling; but some of the verses have a redeeming beauty, and the last in particular is very striking. As Mr. Crabbe so rarely indulges in this style of composition, we must do him the justice of extracting some of the stanzas.

> Let me not have this gloomy view, . . .
> [VIII, 837–56, 861–4, 869–72, 877–56]

In our opinion, the poem would not have lost any of its beauty if it had appeared in the form in which we have given it, with the omission of the intermediate twelve lines. . . .

'The Maid's Story,' which concludes the first volume, is replete with that interest which arises from the minute delineation of human character and the manners of the world. It is for the most part a satire, abounding with the marks of shrewd observation, and not destitute of a kind of cynical humour. We have by anticipation animadverted on the chief deformity in the tale in a moral point of view, the character of Frederick. That of Grandmamma, and the humble one of Biddy, claim a more honourable distinction.

> Poor grandmamma among the gentry dwelt . . .
> [XI, 235–61, 391–408, 429–34]

We shall have less temptation to multiply our extracts in proceeding to give an account of the second Volume. With the exception of the first story, the tales are all of inferior interest, the subjects being, for the most part, instances of uninstructive distress, or of uninteresting and disgusting folly and meanness. For example, 'Delay has Danger' is the title of a narrative which shews how a silly young fellow was half-entrapped, half induced by pique, to break his engagement to a woman he loved, by marrying one, in far inferior circumstances, whom he despised, and how he thereby had to endure for the rest of his days, a burden of self-contempt, in addition to the contempt of all his friends, in which the reader sincerely participates. 'The Natural Death of Love' is a conversation rather than a tale, which contains some wholesome but rather common-place doctrine and advice on the subject of conjugal happiness. 'Gretna Green' is a revolting picture of an extreme case of duplicity and folly, terminating in a more than usual measure of domestic unhappiness. 'Lady Barbara, or the Ghost' is a warning against indiscreet second marriages, where the disparity of years adds impropriety to the venture. It is rather obscurely and feebly written, and has little merit of any kind to compensate for the unpleasing nature of the story. Mr. Crabbe tells us, that he was indebted to a friend for the outline of the tale, which may partly account for the inferiority of its execution, as he had to work upon the ideas of another, instead of following the bent of his own fancy. He acknowledges a similar obligation with respect to the story of Ellen in Book xviii. The obligation does not, in this instance, any more than in the former, appear to be very considerable. The story, even if it be true, we should still pronounce improbable; and the inexplicable perverseness of the lady is irreconcileable either with the common forms of social courtesy, or the natural operations of feeling. We cannot concede our pity to folly so wilful, and to suffering so entirely self-inflicted. Cecil's is a more natural character, and a more likely fate.

The thrice-married Widow is another of those unpleasing Tales which this Writer is fond of telling; not deficient in shrewd remark, and lively description, and knowledge of the world, but wholly destitute of those qualities which are adapted either to captivate the fancy or to interest the feelings. The prominent character is vulgar, heartless, and insipid; the incidents are the common business of common life; and the tone of the Narrator is as frigid, and cynical, and dry, as divinity grafted upon physic may be expected to make a man. If this, and the Tales just adverted to, can answer any beneficial purpose, it is well; and their unpleasing character becomes in that case a consideration wholly subordinate; but as poetry, a person must have a strangely modified taste, not to say, a sensibility a little the worse for wear, who can experience in the perusal, any of that pleasure which works of taste are adapted and designed to awaken. The same remarks will apply, with some qualification, to the remaining stories of William Bailey, the Cathedral Walk, and Smugglers and Poachers. In the last, however, there is more of the poet displayed in the vivid description of the workings of the imagination, and the strong beatings of the 'naked human heart.' The subject is the very reverse of pleasing, but the terror and gloom which hang over it, have charms for the imagination, which supply the deficiency of other sources of interest.

We have reserved for our concluding extracts, the story of Sir Owen Dale, to which we referred as an exception to the inferior character of the second volume. It is one of the best in the work, and its moral tendency is excellent. . . .

With steady and delicate hand, Mr. Crabbe traces the steps by which the domestic happiness of Ellis is for ever blasted, not forgetting his own just remark, that there are crimes which 'they almost share who paint them well.' Vice is never fascinating in his pages, nor does the description supply an impulse at variance with the moral of the Tale.

> A lovely being, who could please too well; . . .
> [XII, 550–6, 587–92; 621–4; 752–814, 844–9,
> 859–70, 878–90]

Compared with Mr. Crabbe's former volumes, the *Tales of the Hall*, exhibit, we think, no marks of decay or exhaustion of faculty, and they are, upon the whole, less obnoxious to criticism than some of his productions. A few inadvertencies, and an occasional negligence of style, may have been noticed in our extracts; but upon these, we have deemed it perfectly unnecessary to remark. The Author is himself too old a practitioner to stand in need of hints from any of our profession, relative to the *minutiæ* of composition; and, of all the writers of the day, he is the one the least likely to tempt into a reproduction of his faults, a tribe of imitators. Although a mannerist, his manner is not of a kind to seduce a copyist: it is in general, too cool, too dry to take even with his admirers as a model, nor would it be endurable at second hand. But what places Mr. Crabbe peculiarly beyond the reach of imitation, is not so much his manner, as his style of thought, and his material for thinking. Few poetical writers are more entirely free from egotism, or seem to have their own feelings and concerns so little implicated in their productions; and yet, there are few whose works bear more decided marks of individuality of character. To be the author of these *Tales*, a man must have passed through a noviciate of no ordinary kind, must have been subjected to the modifying process of circumstances which serve to account for whatever is morbid in his feelings, and for much that is excellent in his faculties; and he must have lived long, and seen much of life, in order to have acquired that treasure of good and evil knowledge from which Mr. Crabbe draws his seemingly inexhaustible materials. On all these accounts, we deem him safe from the impertinence of imitation; and an originality of this substantial nature affords, perhaps—the best security for the permanence of a Writer's literary existence.

51. Comments by Crabbe's contemporaries

(a) WILLIAM WORDSWORTH. To Samuel Rogers, 29 September 1805: . . . Crabbe's *verses*; for *poetry* in no sense can they be called. . . . I remember that I mentioned in my last that there was nothing in the last publication so good as the description of the Parish workhouse, Apothecary, etc. This is true—and it is no less true that the passage which I commended is of no great merit, because the description, at the best of no high order, is in the instance of the apothecary, inconsistent, that is, false. It, no doubt, sometimes happens, but, as far as my experience goes, very rarely, that Country Practitioners neglect, and brutally treat, their Patients; but what kind of men are they who do so?—not Apothecaries like Crabbe's Professional, pragmatical Coxcombs, 'generally neat, all pride, and business, bustle, and conceit,' no, but drunken reprobates, frequenters of boxing-matches, cock-fightings, and horse-races—these are the men who are hard-hearted with their Patients, but any man who attaches so much importance to his profession as to have strongly caught, in his dress and manner, the outward formalities of it, may easily indeed be much occupied with himself, but he will not behave towards his 'Victims,' as Mr. Crabbe calls them, in the manner he has chosen to describe. After all, if the Picture were true to nature, what claim would it have to be called Poetry? At the best, it is the meanest kind of satire, except the purely personal. The sum of all is, that nineteen out of twenty of Crabbe's Pictures are mere matters of fact; with which the Muses have just about as much to do as they have with a Collection of medical reports, or of Law Cases. (P. W. Clayden, *Rogers and His Contemporaries*, 1889, I, 49.)

28 May 1815: He also blamed Crabbe for his unpoetical mode of considering human nature and society. (*Henry Crabb Robinson on Books and Their Writers*, ed. E. J. Morley, 1938, I, 168.)

1819: Of Crabbe, he spoke in terms of almost unmingled praise, conceiving that his works would be turned to, with curiosity and pleasure, when the rapid march of improvement, in another century, had altered the manners, and situation, of the peasantry of England. . . . (*The Brothers Wiffen*, ed. S. R. Pattison, 1880, 38.)

Lockhart to his wife, 25 August 1825: Wordsworth says Crabbe is always an addition to our classical literature, whether he be or be not a poet. He attributes his want of popularity to a want of *flow* of *feeling*,— a general dryness and knottiness of style and matter *which it does not soothe the mind to dwell upon.* . . . (*Familiar Letters of Sir Walter Scott*, ed. D. Douglas, Boston, 1894, II, 343.)

c. 1831: . . . [W.] told Anne a story, the object of which, as she understood it, was to show that Crabbe had no imagination. Crabbe, Sir George Beaumont, and Wordsworth were sitting together in Murray's room in Albemarle Street. Sir George, after sealing a letter, blew out the candle which had enabled him to do so, and exchanging a look with Wordsworth, began to admire in silence the undulating thread of smoke which slowly arose from the expiring wick, when Crabbe put on the extinguisher. (Diary of Sir Walter Scott in *Prose Works of William Wordsworth*, ed. A. B. Grosart, 1870, III, 503.)

To George Crabbe the son, February 1834: . . . the extracts made such an impression upon me, that *I* can also repeat them. The two lines

> Far the happiest they
> The moping idiot and the madman gay
> [*The Village*, I, 238–9]

struck my youthful feelings particularly—tho' facts, as far as they had then come under my knowledge, did not support the description; inasmuch as idiots and lunatics among the humbler Classes of society were not to be found in Workhouses—in the parts of the North where I was brought up,—but were mostly at large, and too often the butt of thoughtless Children. Any testimony from me to the merit of your revered Father's Works would I feel be superfluous, if not impertinent. They will last, from their combined merits as Poetry and Truth full as long as any thing that has been expressed in Verse since they first made their appearance. . . . (*The Letters of William and Dorothy Wordsworth, The Later Years*, ed. E. de Selincourt, Oxford, 1939, 1376–7.)

1840: Wordsworth considers him a dull man in conversation. He said he did not either give information, nor did he enliven any subject by discussion. He spoke highly of his writings as admirable specimens of the kind, but he does not like the misanthropic vein which runs through them. He was surprised to hear from my mother that Crabbe's prose style was stiff and artificial in his letters. He said that generally good writers of verse wrote good prose, especially good letters. (*Autobiography of Mrs. Fletcher*, Edinburgh, 1874, 216.)

1843: The way in which the incident [in 'Lucy Gray'] was treated, and the spiritualising of the character, might furnish hints for contrasting the imaginative influences, which I have endeavoured to throw over common life, with Crabbe's matter-of-fact style of handling subjects of the same kind. This is not spoken to his disparagement, far from it; but to direct the attention of thoughtful readers into whose hands these notes may fall, to a comparison that may enlarge the circle of their sensibilities, and tend to produce in them a catholic judgment. (Note by Isabella Fenwick in *Prose Works of William Wordsworth*, ed, A. B. Grosart, 1876, III, 16.)

1843: Crabbe obviously for the most part preferred the company of women to that of men; for this among other reasons, that he did not like to be put upon the stretch in general conversation. Accordingly, in miscellaneous society his talk was so much below what might have been expected from a man so deservedly celebrated, that to me it seemed trifling. It must upon other occasions have been of a different character, as I found in our rambles together on Hampstead Heath; and not so much so from a readiness to communicate his knowledge of life and manners as of natural history in all its branches. His mind was inquisitive, and he seems to have taken refuge from a remembrance of the distresses he had gone through in these studies and the employments to which they led. Moreover such contemplations might tend profitably to counterbalance the painful truths which he had collected from his intercourse with mankind. Had I been more intimate with him I should have ventured to touch upon his office as a Minister of the Gospel, and how far his heart and soul were in it, so as to make him a zealous and diligent labourer. In poetry, tho' he wrote much, as we all know, he assuredly was not so. I happened once to speak of pains as necessary to produce merit of a certain kind which I highly valued. His observation was, 'It is not worth while.' You are right, thought I, if the labour encroaches upon the time due to teach truth as a steward of the mysteries of God; but if poetry is to be produced at all, make what you do produce as good as you can. Mr. Rogers once told me that he expressed his regret to Crabbe that he wrote in his later works so much less correctly than in his earlier. 'Yes,' replied he, 'but then I had a reputation to make; now I can afford to relax.' Whether it was from a modest estimate of his own qualifications or from causes less creditable, his motives for writing verse and his hopes and aims were not so high as is to be desired. After being silent for more than twenty years he again applied himself to poetry, upon the spur of applause he received from the periodical publications of the day, as he himself tells us in one of his Prefaces. Is it not to be lamented a man who was so conversant with permanent truth, and whose writings are so valuable an acquisition to our country's literature, should have *required* an impulse from such a quarter? (*op. cit.*, III, 191–2.)

(b) ROBERT SOUTHEY. To J. N. White, 30 September 1808: With Crabbe's poems I have been acquainted for about twenty years, having read them when a schoolboy on their first publication, and, by the help of the Elegant Extracts, remembered from that time what was best worth remembering. You rightly compare him to Goldsmith. He is an imitator, or rather an *antithesizer*, of Goldsmith, if such a word may be coined for the occasion. His merit is precisely the same as Goldsmith's,—that of describing actual things clearly and strikingly; but there is a wide difference between the colouring of the two poets. Goldsmith threw a sunshine over all his pictures, like that of one of our water-colour artists when he paints for ladies,—a light and a beauty not to be found in Nature, though not more brilliant or beautiful than what Nature really affords. Crabbe's have a gloom, which is also not in Nature,—not the shade of a heavy day, of mist, or of clouds, but the dark and overcharged shadows of one who paints by lamp-light,— whose very lights have a gloominess. In part this is explained by his history. He had formed an attachment in early life to a young woman who, like himself, was absolutely without fortune; he wrote his poems to obtain patronage and preferment. In those days there was not much good poetry, and hardly any negligent [? intelligent] criticism. He *pushed* (as the world says) for patronage with these poems, and suc- ceeded; got preferment sufficient, and married. It was not long before his wife became deranged, and when all this was told me by one who knew him well, five years ago, he was still almost confined in his own house, anxiously waiting upon this wife in her long and hopeless malady. A sad history! It is no wonder that he gives so melancholy a picture of human life. (*Letters*, ed. J. W. Warter, 1856, II, 90–1.)

To C. W. W. Wynn, 22 July 1819: I was not disappointed with Crabbe's Tales. He is a decided mannerist, but so are all original writers in all ages; nor is it possible for a poet to avoid it if he writes much in the same key and upon the same class of subjects. Crabbe's poems will have a great and lasting value as pictures of domestic life, elucidating the moral history of these times,—times which must hold a most conspicuous place in history. He knows his own powers, and never aims above his reach. In this age, when the public are greedy for novelties, and abundantly supplied with them, an author may easily commit the error of giving them too much of the same kind of thing. But this will not be thought a fault hereafter, when the kind is good, or the thing good of its kind. (*Life and Correspondence*, ed. C. C. Southey, 1850, IV, 355–6.)

(c) BYRON. 1809:

> There be who say, in these enlightened days,
> That splendid lies are all the poet's praise;
> That strained Invention, ever on the wing,
> Alone impels the modern Bard to sing:
> 'Tis true, that all who rhyme—nay, all who write,
> Shrink from that fatal word to Genius—Trite;
> Yet Truth sometimes will lend her noblest fires,
> And decorate the verse herself inspires:
> This fact in Virtue's name let CRABBE attest:
> Though Nature's sternest Painter, yet the best.

(English Bards and Scotch Reviewers, 849–58.)

To John Murray, 15 September 1817: With regard to poetry in general, I am convinced, the more I think of it, that he and *all* of us—Scott, Southey, Wordsworth, Moore, Campbell, I,—are all in the wrong, one as much as another; that we are upon a wrong revolutionary poetical system, or systems, not worth a damn in itself, and from which none but Rogers and Crabbe are free; and that the present and next generations will finally be of this opinion. I am the more confirmed in this by having lately gone over some of our classics, particularly *Pope*, whom I tried in this way,—I took Moore's poems and my own and some others, and went over them side by side with Pope's, and I was really astonished (I ought not to have been so) and mortified at the ineffable distance in point of sense, harmony, effect, and even *Imagination*, passion, and *Invention*, between the little Queen Anne's man, and us of the Lower Empire. Depend upon it, it is all Horace then, and Claudian now, among us; and if I had to begin again, I would model myself accordingly. Crabbe's the man, but he has got a coarse and impracticable subject. (*Works: Letters and Journals*, ed. R. E. Prothero, 1922, IV, 169–70.)

(d) FRANCIS HORNER. To Jeffrey, 16 July 1810: I must not conclude without thanking you very gratefully for the pleasure I received in reading your extracts from Crabbe's *Borough*; some of which, particularly the 'Convict's Dream,' leave far behind all that any other living poet has written. (*Memoirs and Correspondence*, 1843, II, 53.)

(e) SIR SAMUEL ROMILLY. 1810: I do not at all agree to the judgment which has been passed upon Crabbe's poem. So far from being the worst of his poems, I think great part of it infinitely superior to every thing that he had before written. Much, it is true, of *The Borough* is very tiresome and languid; but the horrible story of Ellen Orford, the description of the condemned convict, and of the sailor who dies in the arms of his mistress, [XX, XXIII, II] and many other passages, show more genius than anything that has lately appeared. It is true that in general his subjects are extremely disgusting. I cannot, however, but think that it is useful to compel that class of persons, among whom alone he will find readers, to enter with him into poorhouses and prisons, and inspect and closely examine the various objects of wretchedness which they contain. (*Memoirs*, 1840, II, 163.)

(f) SIR JAMES MACKINTOSH. 1 March 1812: I have finished C (*The Borough*). I acknowledge his almost unparalleled power of painting, sometimes humourous, sometimes tender, and often aiming only at likeness, without selection of objects, or intention to excite any particular class of feelings; but the constant recurrence of this one talent, during a long poem is tiresome. Sometimes he reminds me of Hogarth. (*Life*, (1835 edn), II, 218.)

(g) JANE AUSTEN. To Cassandra Austen, 21 October [1813]: No; I have never seen the death of Mrs. Crabbe. I have only just been making out from one of his prefaces that he probably was married. It is almost ridiculous. Poor woman! I will comfort *him* as well as I can, but I do not undertake to be good to her children. She had better not leave any. (*Letters*, ed. R. W. Chapman, Oxford, 1932, 358.)

To Cassandra Austen, 6 November [1813]: Miss Lee I found very conversible: she admires Crabbe as she ought. (*op. cit.*, 370.)

(h) LEIGH HUNT. 1814:

> 'Your Majesty then,' said the Gaius, 'don't know
> That a person nam'd Crabbe has been waiting below?
> He has taken his chair in the kitchen, they say.'
> 'Indeed!' said Apollo, 'Oh pray let him stay:
> He'll be much better pleased to be with 'em down stairs,
> And will find ye all out with your cookings and cares:—
> But mind that you treat him as well as you're able,
> And let him have part of what goes from the table.'

Mr. Crabbe is unquestionably a man of genius, possessing imagination, observation, originality: he has even powers of the pathetic and the terrible, but with all these fine elements of poetry, is singularly deficient in taste, his familiarity continually bordering on the vulgar, and his seriousness on the morbid and the shocking. His versification, where the force of his thoughts does not compel you to forget it, is a strange kind of bustle between the lameness of Cowper and the slipshod vigour of Churchill, though I am afraid it has more of the former than the latter. When he would strike out a line particularly grand or melodious, he has evidently no other notion of one than what Pope or Darwin has given him. Yet even in his versification, he has contrived, by the colloquial turn of his language and his primitive mention of persons by their christian as well as surname, to have an air of his own; and indeed there is not a greater mannerist in the whole circle of poetry, either in a good or bad sense. His main talent, both in character and description, lies in strong and homely pieces of detail, which he brings before you as clearly and to the life as in a camera obscura, and in which he has been improperly compared to the Dutch painters, for in addition to their finish and identification, he fills the very commonest of his scenes with sentiment and an interest. (*The Feast of the Poets*, 1814, 103–10 and note.)

(i) THOMAS CARLYLE. To Robert Mitchell, 15 July 1816: In addition to great powers of correct description, he possesses all the sagacity of an anatomist in searching into the stormy passions of the human heart —and all the apathy of an antomist in describing them. (*Early Letters*, ed. C. E. Norton, 1886, I, 73.)

(j) C. H. TERROT. 1819:

> We still have bards, who with aspiring head,
> Rise o'er the crazed, the dying and the dead.

For instance, there's old Crabbe—though some may deem
He shows small taste in choosing of a theme;
None but a bard his own true lines can tell—
He chooses right who executes it well.
And Crabbe has done it well: although his verse
Be somewhat rude, 'tis pregnant, strong and terse:
And he has feeling—I who never weep,
And o'er a Werther's woes am apt to sleep,
Even I, though somewhat rude, can feel for wo
Such as I've known, or such as I may know;
Even I can feel at tales of love or strife,
Stamped, as are his, with traits of real life,
He knows the human heart (which, by the way,
Is more than some Psychologists can say.)
He knows it well; and draws with faithful pen,
Nor Corsairs, Pedlars, Waggoners,—but Men.
And then his back-ground—how the figures glow
With all the mimic art of Gerald Dow,
Each in itself a picture—while the soul
Of one great moral breathes throughout the whole.

(*Common Sense: A Poem*, 1819, 195–216, in *British Review*, xxix, March 1820.)

(k) J. W. CROKER. To John Murray, 18 July 1819: I had Crabbe's tales with me on shipboard, and they were a treasure. I never was so much taken with anything. The tales are in general so well conducted that, in prose, they would be interesting as mere stories; but to this are added such an admirable *case* and *force* of diction, such good pleasantry, such high principles, such a strain of poetry, such a profundity of observation, and such a gaiety of illustration as I never before, I think, saw collected. He imagines his stories with the humour and truth of Chaucer, and tells them with the copious terseness of Dryden, and the tender and thoughtful simplicity of Cowper. This high commendation does not apply to the whole of the tales, nor, perhaps, to the whole of any one. There are sad exceptions here and there, which might easily be removed, but on the whole it is a delightful book. (*Croker Papers*, 1884, I, 146.)

(l) JOHN CLARE. To John Taylor, 1820: I have written about the Woodman as you find the Sketch in these papers as one character for it but I must avoid satire as much as possible I like the 'all ten' measure best of any now and shall keep on wi't doubtless they will next say in so doing I imitate Crabb as they guessed by the same means I imitated Burns (last winter). *Tales* I lik'd here & there a touch but there is a d-d many affectations among them which seems to be the favourite of the parson poet. (*Letters*, ed. J. W. and Anne Tibble, 1950, 75.)

(m) SAMUEL TAYLOR COLERIDGE. 5 March 1834: I think Crabbe and Southey are something alike; but Crabbe's poems are founded on observation and real life—Southey's on fancy and books. In facility they are equal, though Crabbe's English is of course not upon a level with Southey's, which is next door to faultless. But in Crabbe there is an absolute defect of the high imagination; he gives me little or no pleasure: yet, no doubt, he has much power of a certain kind, and it is good to cultivate, even at some pains, a catholic taste in literature. I read all sorts of books with some pleasure except modern sermons and treatises on political economy. (*Table Talk, Coleridge's Miscellaneous Criticism*, ed. T. M. Raysor, 1930, 432–3.)

(n) HENRY CRABB ROBINSON. Extract from Diary for 29 December 1835: I awoke early and read in bed what I finished soon after breakfast. This *Life* has not much to interest me, because there is not much that interests me in Crabbe's poetry; I take no pleasure in his unpoetical representations of human life, and though no one can dispute that he had a powerful pen and could faithfully portray what he saw, yet he had an eye only for the sad realities of life. As Mrs. Barbauld said to me many years ago: 'I shall never be tired of Goldsmith's *Deserted Village*—I shall never look again into Crabbe's *Village*.' Indeed this impression is so strong that I have never read his later works—I know little about them. I feel infinite respect for Crabbe and may read some two or three of his poems that I may have something like an idea of him. (*Diary . . . An Abridgement*, ed. D. Hudson, 1967, 147.)

(o) WALTER SAVAGE LANDOR. Extract from *Imaginary Conversations*: English—Southey and Porson, 1842: PORSON. Crabbe wrote with a twopenny nail, and scratched rough truths and rogues' facts on mud walls. There is, however, much in his poetry, and more in his moral character to admire. Comparing the smartnesses of Crabbe with Young's, I can not help thinking that the reverend doctor must have wandered in his Night Thoughts rather too near the future vicar's future mother, so striking is the resemblance. But the vicar, if he was fonder of low company, has greatly more nature and sympathy, greatly more vigour and compression. Young moralised at a distance on some external appearances of the human heart; Crabbe entered it *on all fours*, and told the people what an ugly thing it is inside. (*Complete Works*, ed. T. E. Welby, 1931 (reprinted 1969), V, 168–9.)

52. Hazlitt attacks Crabbe

1821

From 'Living Authors—No. V, Crabbe', *London Magazine*, May 1821, iii, 484–90. It was reprinted in a revised form in *The Spirit of the Age*, 1825.

The object of Mr. Crabbe's writings seems to be, to show what an unpoetical world we live in: or rather, perhaps, the very reverse of this conclusion might be drawn from them; for it might be said, that if this is poetry, there is nothing but poetry in the world. Our author's style might be cited as an answer to Audrey's inquiry, 'Is poetry a true thing?' If the most feigning poetry is the truest, Mr. Crabbe is of all poets the least poetical. There are here no ornaments, no flights of fancy, no illusions of sentiment, no tinsel of words. His song is one sad reality, one unraised, unvaried note of unavailing woe. Literal fidelity serves him in the place of invention; he assumes importance by a number of petty details; he rivets attention by being prolix. He not only deals in incessant matters of fact, but in matters of fact of the most familiar, the least animating, and most unpleasant kind; but he relies for the effect of novelty on the microscopic minuteness with which he dissects the most trivial objects—and, for the interest he excites on the unshrinking determination with which he handles the most painful. His poetry has an official and professional air. He is called out to cases of difficult births, of fractured limbs, or breaches of the peace; and makes out a parish register of accidents and offences. He takes the most trite, the most gross and obvious, and revolting part of nature, for the subject of his elaborate descriptions; but it is nature still, and Nature is a great and mighty goddess. 'Great is Diana of the Ephesians.' It is well for the reverend author that it is so. Individuality is, in his theory, the only definition of poetry. Whatever is, he hitches into rhyme. Whoever makes an exact image of any thing on the earth below, according to him, must succeed—and he has succeeded. Mr. Crabbe is one of the most popular and admired of our living writers. That he is so, can be accounted for on no other principle than the strong ties that bind us to the world about us, and our involuntary yearnings after whatever in any manner powerfully and directly reminds us of it. His Muse is not one of the daughters of Memory, but the old toothless mumbling dame herself, doling out the gossip and scandal of the neighbourhood, recounting, *totidem verbis et literis*, what happens in every place in the kingdom every hour in the year, and fastening always on the worst as the most palatable morsels. But she is a circumstantial old lady, communicative, scrupulous, leaving nothing to the imagination, harping on the smallest grievances, a village oracle and critic, most veritable, most identical, bringing us acquainted with persons and things just as they happened, and giving us a local interest in all she knows and tells. The springs of Helicon are, in general, supposed to be a living stream, bubbling and sparkling, and making sweet music as it flows; but Mr. Crabbe's fountain of the Muses is a stagnant pool, dull, motionless, choked up with weeds and corruption; it reflects no light from heaven, it emits no cheerful sound:—his Pegasus has not floating wings, but feet, cloven feet that scorn the low ground they tread upon;—no flowers of love, of hope, or joy spring here, or they bloom only to wither in a moment;—our poet's verse does not put a spirit of youth in every thing, but a spirit of fear, despondency, and decay; it is not an electric spark to kindle and expand, but acts like the torpedo-touch to deaden and contract: it lends no rainbow tints to fancy, it aids no soothing feelings in the heart, it gladdens no prospect, it stirs no wish; in its view the current of life runs slow, dull, cold, dispirited, half-underground, muddy and clogged with all creeping things. The world is one vast infirmary; the hill of Parnassus is a penitentiary; to read him is a penance; yet we read on! Mr. Crabbe is a *fascinating* writer. He contrives to 'turn diseases to commodities,' and makes a virtue of necessity. He puts us out of conceit with this world, which perhaps a severe divine should do; yet does not, as a charitable divine ought, point to another. His morbid feelings droop and cling to the earth; grovel, where they should soar; and throw a dead weight on every aspiration of the soul after the good or beautiful. By degrees, we submit and are reconciled to our fate, like patients to a physician, or prisoners in the condemned cell. We can only explain this by saying, as we said before, that Mr. Crabbe gives us one part of nature, the mean, the little, the disgusting, the distressing; that he does this thoroughly, with the hand of a master; and we forgive all the rest!—

Mr. Crabbe's first poems were published so long ago as the year 1782, and received the approbation of Dr. Johnson only a little before he died. This was a testimony from an enemy, for Dr. Johnson was not an admirer of the simple in style, or minute in description. Still he was an acute, strong-minded man, and could see truth, when it was presented to him, even through the mist of his prejudices and his theories. There was something in Mr. Crabbe's intricate points that did not, after all, so ill accord with the Doctor's purblind vision; and he knew quite enough of the petty ills of life to judge of the merit of our poet's descriptions, though he himself chose to slur them over in high-sounding dogmas or general invectives. Mr. Crabbe's earliest poem of *The Village* was recommended to the notice of Dr. Johnson by Sir Joshua Reynolds; and we cannot help thinking that a taste for that sort of poetry, which leans for support on the truth and fidelity of its imitations of nature, began to display itself much about the time, and, in a good measure, in consequence of the direction of the public taste to the subject of painting. Book-learning, the accumulation of wordy commonplaces, the gaudy pretensions of poetical diction, had enfeebled and perverted our eye for nature: the study of the fine arts, which came into fashion about forty years ago, and was then first considered as a polite accomplishment, would tend imperceptibly to restore it. Painting is essentially an imitative art; it cannot subsist for a moment on empty generalities: the critic, therefore, who has been used to this sort of substantial entertainment, would be disposed to read poetry with the eye of a connoisseur, would be little captivated with smooth, polished, unmeaning periods, and would turn with double eagerness and relish to the force and precision of individual details, transferred as it were to the page from the canvas. Thus an admirer of Teniers or Hobbima might think little of the pastoral sketches of Pope or Goldsmith: even Thompson describes not so much the naked object as what he sees in his mind's eye, surrounded and glowing with the mild, bland, genial vapours of his brain:—but the adept in Dutch interiors, hovels, and pig-styes must find in such a writer as Crabbe a man after his own heart. He is the very thing itself; he paints in words, instead of colours: that's all the difference. As Mr. Crabbe is not a painter, only because he does not use a brush and colours, so he is for the most part a poet, only because he writes in lines of ten syllables. All the rest might be found in a news-paper, an old magazine, or a county-register. Our author is himself a little jealous of the prudish fidelity of his homely Muse, and tries to justify himself by precedents. He brings, as a parallel instance of merely literal description, Pope's lines on the gay Duke of Buckingham, be-ginning, 'In the worst inn's worst room see Villiers lies!'[1] But surely nothing can be more dissimilar. Pope describes what is striking, Crabbe would have described merely what was there. The objects in Pope stand out to the fancy from the mixture of the mean with the gaudy, from the contrast of the scene and the character. There is an appeal to the imagination; you see what is passing from a poetical point of view. In Crabbe there is no foil, no contrast, no impulse given to the mind. It is all on a level and of a piece. In fact, there is so little connection between the subject-matter of Mr. Crabbe's lines, and the ornament of rhyme which is tacked to them, that many of his verses read like serious bur-lesque, and the parodies which have been made upon them are hardly so quaint as the originals.

Mr. Crabbe's great fault is certainly that he is a sickly, a querulous, a fastidious poet. He sings the country, and he sings it in a pitiful tone. He chooses this subject only to take the charm out of it, and to dispel the illusion, the glory, and the dream; which had hovered over it in golden verse from Theocritus to Cowper. He sets out with professing to overturn the theory which had hallowed a shepherd's life, and made the names of grove and valley music in our ears, to give us truth in its stead; but why not lay aside the fool's cap and bells at once, why not insist on the unwelcome reality in plain prose? If our author is a poet, why trouble himself with statistics? If he is a statistic writer, why set his ill news to harsh and grating verse? The philosopher in painting the dark side of human nature may have reason on his side, and a moral lesson or a remedy in view. The tragic poet, who shows the sad vi-cissitudes of things, and the disappointments of the passions, at least strengthens our yearnings after imaginary good, and lends wings to our desires, by which we, 'at one bound, high overleap all bound' of actual suffering. But Mr. Crabbe does neither. He gives us discoloured paint-ings of things—helpless, repining, unprofitable, unedifying distress. He is not a philosopher, but a sophist, and misanthrope in verse: a namby-pamby Mandeville, a Malthus turned metrical romancer. He professes

[1] See Preface to *Tales* (No. 30 above).

historical fidelity; but his vein is not dramatic: he does not give us the *pros* and *cons* of that versatile gipsey, Nature. He does not indulge his fancy or sympathise with us, or tell us how the poor feel; but how he should feel in their situation, which we do not want to know. He does not weave the web of their lives of a mingled yarn, good and ill together, but clothes them all in the same overseer's dingy linsey-woolsey, or tinges them with a green and yellow melancholy. He blocks out all possibility of good, cancels the hope, or even the wish for it, as a weakness; check-mates Tityrus and Virgil at the game of pastoral cross-purposes, disables all his adversary's white pieces, and leaves none but black ones on the board. The situation of a country clergyman is not necessarily favourable to the cultivation of the Muse. He is set down, perhaps, as he thinks, in a small curacy for life, and he takes his revenge by imprisoning the reader's imagination in luckless verse. Shut out from social converse, from learned colleges and halls, where he passed his youth, he has no cordial fellow-feeling with the unlettered manners of the *Village* or the *Borough*, and he describes his neighbours as more uncomfortable and discontented than himself. All this while he dedicates successive volumes to rising generations of noble patrons; and while he desolates a line of coast with sterile, blighting lines, the only leaf of his books where honour, beauty, worth, or pleasure bloom, is that inscribed to the Rutland family! But enough of this; and to our task of quotation. The poem of *The Village* sets off nearly as follows:

> No: cast by Fortune on a frowning coast, . . .
> [I, 49–62]

This plea, we would remark by the way, is more plausible than satisfactory. By associating pleasing ideas with the poor, we incline the rich to extend their good offices to them. The cottage twined round with real myrtles, or with the poet's wreath, will invite the hand of kindly assistance sooner than Mr. Crabbe's naked 'ruin'd shed;' for though unusual, unexpected distress excites compassion, that which is uniform and remediless produces nothing but disgust and indifference. Repulsive objects (or those which are painted so) do not conciliate affection, or soften the heart.

> Lo! where the heath, with withering brake grown o'er, . . .
> [*ibid.*, 63–84]*

---

* [At line 70] This is a pleasing line; because the unconsciousness to the mischief in the child is a playful relief to the mind, and the picturesqueness of the imagery gives it double point and *naiveté*.

This is a specimen of Mr. Crabbe's taste in landscape-painting, of the power, the accuracy, and the hardness of his pencil. If this were merely a spot upon the canvas, which might act as a foil to more luxuriant and happier scenes, it would be well. But our valetudinarian 'travels from Dan to Beersheba, and cries it is all barren.' Or if he lights 'in a favouring hour' on some more favoured spot, where plenty smiles around, then his hand to his human figures, and the balance of the account is still very much against Providence, and the blessings of the English Constitution. Let us see.—

> But these are scenes where Nature's niggard hand . . .
> [*ibid.*, 131–53]*

Grant all this to be true; nay, let it be told, but not told in 'mincing poetry.' Next comes the WORKHOUSE, and this, it must be owned, is a master-piece of description, and the climax of the author's inverted system of rural optimism.

> Thus groan the Old, till by disease opprest, . . .
> [*ibid.*, 226–49, 262–73, 318–46]

To put our taste in poetry, and the fairness of our opinion of Mr. Crabbe's in particular, to the test at once, we will confess, that we think the two lines we have marked in italics,

> Him now they follow to his grave, and stand
> Silent and sad, and gazing, hand in hand—

worth nearly all the rest of his verses put together, and an unanswerable condemnation of their general tendency and spirit. It is images,

---

* [At line 144] This seems almost a parody on the lines in Shakspeare.
> Not all these, laid in bed majestical,
> Can sleep so soundly as the wretched slave,
> Who with a body fill'd and vacant mind,
> Gets him to rest, cramm'd with distressful bread;
> Never sees horrid night, the child of hell;
> But like a lackey, from the rise to set,
> Sweats in the eye of Phœbus, and all night
> Sleeps in Elysium; next day, after dawn,
> Doth rise and help Hyperion to his horse;
> And follows so the ever-running year
> With profitable labour to his grave:
> And, but for ceremony, such a wretch,
> Winding up days with toil and nights with sleep,
> Hath the forehand and vantage of a king.
> *Henry V.*

Who shall decide where two such authorities disagree!

such as these, that the polished mirror of the poet's mind ought chiefly
to convey; that cast their soothing, startling reflection over the length
of human life, and grace with their amiable innocence its closing scenes;
while its less alluring and more sombre tints sink in, and are lost in an
absorbent ground of unrelieved prose. Poetry should be the handmaid
of the imagination, and the foster-nurse of pleasure and beauty: Mr.
Crabbe's Muse is a determined enemy to the imagination, and a spy on
nature.

Before we proceed, we shall just mark a few of those quaintnesses
of expression, by which our descriptive poet has endeavoured to vary
his style from common prose, and so far has succeeded. Speaking of
Quarle he says,—

> Of Hermit Quarle we read, in island rare,
> Far from mankind and seeming far from care;
> Safe from all want, and sound in every limb;
> Yes! there was he, and there was care with him.
>
> [*The Parish Register*, I, 107–10]

> Here are no wheels for either wool or flax,
> But packs of cards—made up of sundry packs.
>
> [*ibid.*, I, 230–1]

> Fresh were his features, his attire was new;
> Clean was his linen, and his jacket blue:
> Of finest *jean*, his trowsers, tight and trim,
> Brush'd the large buckle at the silver rim.
>
> [*ibid.*, I, 301–4]

To compare small things with great, this last touch of minute description is not unlike that in Theseus's description of his hounds,—

> With ears that sweep away the morning dew.
>
> [*Midsummer Night's Dream*, IV, i, 118]

> Alas! your reverence, wanton thoughts, I grant,
> Were once my motive, now the thoughts of want.
> Women like me, as ducks in a decoy,
> Swim down a stream, and seem to swim in joy.
>
> [*The Parish Register*, I, 453–6]

> But from the day, that fatal day she spied
> The pride of Daniel, Daniel was her pride.
>
> [*ibid.*, II, 319–20]

As an instance of the *curiosa felicitas* in descriptive allusion (among many others) take the following. Our author, referring to the names of the genteeler couples, written in the parish-register, thus 'morals' on the circumstance:—

> How fair these names, how much unlike they look . . .
> [*ibid.*, II, 283–300]

The Library and *The Newspaper*, in the same volume, are heavy and common-place. Mr. Crabbe merely sermonizes in his didactic poetry. He must pierce below the surface to get at his genuine vein. He is properly himself only in the petty and the painful. The Birth of Flattery is a homely, incondite lay. The writer is no more like Spenser than he is like Pope. The ballad of Sir Eustace Grey is a production of great power and genius. The poet, in treating of the wanderings of a maniac, has given a loose to his conception of imaginary and preternatural evils. But they are of a sort that chill, rather than melt the mind; they repel instead of haunting it. They might be said to be square, portable horrors, physical, external,—not shadowy, not malleable; they do not arise out of any passion in the mind of the sufferer, nor touch the reader with involuntary sympathy. Beds of ice, seas of fire, shaking bogs, and fields of snow, are disagreeable matters of fact; and though their contact has a powerful effect on the senses, we soon shake them off in fancy. Let any one compare this fictitious legend with the unadorned, unvarnished tale of Peter Grimes, and he will see in what Mr. Crabbe's characteristic strength lies. He is a most potent copyist of actual nature, though not otherwise a great poet. In the case of Sir Eustace, he cannot conjure up airy phantoms from a disordered imagination; but he makes honest Peter, the fisherman of the Borough, see visions in the mud where he had drowned his 'prentice-boys, that are as ghastly and bewitching as any mermaid. We cannot resist giving the scene of this striking story, which is in our author's exclusive manner. 'Within that circle none durst walk but he.'

> Thus by himself compell'd to live each day, . . .
> [XXII, 171–204]

This is an exact facsimile of some of the most unlovely parts of the creation. Indeed the whole of Mr. Crabbe's *Borough*, from which the above passage is taken, is done so to the life, that it seems almost like some sea-monster, crawled out of the neighbouring slime, and harbouring a breed of strange vermin, with a strong local scent of tar and bulge-water.—Mr. Crabbe's *Tales* are more readable than his *Poems*. But in proportion as their interest increases, they become more oppressive. They turn, one and all, upon the same sort of teazing, helpless, mechanical, unimaginative distress;—and though it is not easy to lay them down, you never wish to take them up again. Still in this way they are highly finished, striking, and original portraits,—worked out with an eye to nature, and an intimate knowledge of the small and intricate folds of the human heart. Some of the best are the Confidant, the story of Silly Shore, the Young Poet, the Painter;—the episode of Phœbe Dawson in *The Village*[1] is one of the most tender and pensive; and the character of the methodist parson, who persecutes the sailor's widow with his godly, selfish love, is one of the most profound. In a word, if Mr. Crabbe's writings do not add greatly to the store of entertaining and delightful fiction, yet they will remain 'as a thorn in the side of poetry,' perhaps for a century to come.

53. John Wilson reinforces the attack

1827

In an unsigned article 'Preface to A Review of the Chronicles of the Canongate', *Blackwood's Magazine*, November 1827, xxii, 537–40.

Now, we are thus led pleasantly to a point, from which we had intended to begin, on the very first dip of our pen into the dolphin—namely, to the consideration of what are called the Lower Orders, as the subjects of fictitious composition with a moral aim, scope, and tendency. Not to go deeply or widely into such inquiry, suffice it to say, that there must be, and long have been, much of true grandeur and nobility of nature in those orders of the people, that, omitting

[1] Phoebe Dawson appears in *The Parish Register*.

many other names, have furnished materials for the very highest powers to mould and work upon—of Crabbe, Burns, Wordsworth, and Scott.

The Whigs say they are distinguished by their enlightened love of the people. If so, we are a Whig. But an enlightened love of the people may be shown in many other ways than by advocating Annual or Triennial Parliaments, wishing to extend Suffrage till it be almost universal, founding Mechanical Institutions, pulling down Hospitals, and abolishing the Poor Laws. It may be shown by studying their character, and holding it up to affection and admiration, in works of which a delight in the virtues that adorn their condition is the life and the soul. Now, most men of genius who have been Whigs,—and bigoted as we fear we are in politics, we do not deny that men of genius there have been, who have at least been but indifferent Tories—have been too highly aristocratical, to stoop to employ their genius on such vulgar subject-matter as the Poor. It seemed as if the smoke of their cribs and cabins came offensively 'between the wind and their nobility.' We may be wrong—and if so, we hope, and do not fear, that some Whig magazine or newspaper will have the kindness to set us right—but we cannot help thinking that your Tory man of genius has generally had the warmest side towards the lower orders—has shewn himself, in his representation of human life, most familiar at the Farmer's Ingle, and in the Shepherd's Shieling, and even in the Workshop or Dwelling house of the Artificer. Mr. Crabbe, we think, is a Whig—Wordsworth and Scott are Tories. Now, much as we admire Mr. Crabbe's extraordinary talents for observation and description, we cannot for our souls love and venerate him as a poet, as we love and venerate Scott and Wordsworth. Burns was Whiggish—but that is nothing to the purpose, for he was himself a poor man and proud—and pride and poverty will make a Whig of the only and dutiful son of a father believing in the divine right of kings. Besides, he had not become a Whig, when at the plough tail he wrote the Saturday Night, and the Address to the Daisy—and during the composition of his love lyrics, he was a manifest Tory. Let us say a few words, then, about Crabbe, and Burns, and Wordsworth, and Scott—not with the view of illustrating this whim of ours about Whig and Tory poets, but simply by way of whiling away a fireside hour or two with some general discussion of their competitive merits.

Crabbe is a writer of masculine genius, who, on whatever he touches, leaves marks of a vigorous hand. It may be said, that he seldom fully treats a subject. He tells a story; he carries through his narrative right forward, from beginning to end. This the reader can depend upon. But that he will draw out the resources of his subject, that he will bring out into fulness of effect its mournfulness, its beauty, its gloomy grandeur, or even its bitterness and indignation, this is not to be counted on. What parts will be given with detail, a tedious dialogue, or a scene of anguish—what will be wrought with poetical colouring, a passage of mere indifference, or of great importance, to the whole—of this the reader can anticipate nothing. He is on no certainty with his author, till a thing is done. A defect, surely; since great part of the whole effect of poetry lies in continually raising and fulfilling expectation.

Two features of Mr. Crabbe's poetry seem chiefly to characterize it in popular opinion. He is regarded as a poet having great acquaintance with the realities of ordinary life; and as a writer, making his representations of human nature just within the verge of calumny—whose statements are not false, but the impressions they leave are.

Mr. Crabbe would too often seem to have no other purpose than to take from the life of the people subjects for *delineation*, as if he felt that his talent were to delineate, and had no higher end than to exercise it. They are studies of an artist—a great one, undoubtedly—who amuses himself with drawing from nature, without any very particular choice, as it might seem, of the subject. The temper of his spirit, the cast of his genius, it may be said, determine a choice of the subject, as well as of the manner of handling it, as is evinced by the common impression of the gloom and bitterness of his poetry. It may be so. Yet we doubt if this will imply anything more than that he exercises the talent in which he excels, in the manner in which he excels in it. He can paint reality, often in its own vividness, sometimes in its own hardness. He does not refuse himself to greatness, to beauty, to pathos, when he finds it; but he is just as ready—it would be unjust to say readier—to paint coarseness, meanness, and that callousness of depraved hearts, of which the sight almost shuts up the consciousness of feeling in our own. Now, there can be little doubt that a man who will walk through lower life in this country, with an eye eager to catch only striking subjects for his pencil, will paint much below the just tone of poetry, and will leave by his works an unfavourable, perhaps a revolting, impression of his genius and his subject. What is worst in such life is most conspicuous—what is good is unobtrusive.

Notwithstanding any truth there may be in these observations, it will be difficult to every one to escape from the common impression, that when Mr. Crabbe begins to rail, he is at home; and that when he gets among scenes of dark passions, among revenges and hates, or begins to tread the haunts of outlaws, he walks with more command, and his verse takes more the strain of a genial inspiration. If so, he might have been a greater poet; and the absence of all purpose, the mere miscellaneousness of his poetry in general, would show that he has not sufficiently known himself.

Mr. Crabbe's stories are seldom poetically hung together. His causes are not poetical causes. They are downright reality. Something that happened o' Wednesday—hard matter of fact. Not that there is any deficiency of improbable causes upon occasion, either, but there is no principle or consistency—an incongruous mixture of romance and the news of the next Parish.

Perhaps the very best parts of Mr. Crabbe are unconnected passages, descriptions, anecdotes, or character which is drawn under one purpose and dispatched—like the landlady who died holding her keys,[1] where one conception carries the writer through, before he has got time to grow cold upon it. There certainly is a want of depth of mind in the mind of this poet—of thought. What can be thrown off at once is done well, but what goes further is incomplete. There is neither the fulness of nature, nor the fulness of an artist's composition, but a baldness and a fortuitous concatenation. For our own part, we often and often feel, in reading Crabbe, that had he known more about the matter, he would have drawn his pen through many of his very ablest compositions, from beginning to end, saying, 'This seemed to me to be all true, but I now see that it is all false.' For the whole imagery, and much of the sentiment of a poem, may be true to nature; and yet, either the absence or presence of *something* may utterly vitiate it, and render it libellous. The poet who composes coolly from cool observation—and Mr. Crabbe seems to us to be such a poet—will be much more apt to overlook and to fall into blunders, omissions, mistakes, and errors, than the poet, whose quiet eye, (such as Wordsworth for instance), not unwatchful of his brethren, sees where the noblest harvests are to be reaped, while 'it broods and sleeps on its own heart.'

It is one bold and generous enterprise of genius to draw poetry from the ordinary lives of ordinary men. It is trusting in the depth and power of nature to believe, that even in such life her spirit is not extinct nor suppressed, that it can be found there, and drawn forth into expression, and that there is a sympathy alive to receive its just representations.

[1] Widow Goe, *The Parish Register*, III, 184.

This Burns did by the impulse of native genius. This Wordsworth has done under the guidance of philosophic thought. This Crabbe too has done—almost unwillingly as it might seem—when the strong conceptions of his working mind have carried him away for a little while from his bare delineations of reality. For the ordinary view that has reigned in Mr. Crabbe's composition of poetry, might seem to be that words and numbers might make anything into verse; and not that higher view which seems to prevail in Burns and Wordsworth, that the spirit of delineation may make anything into poetry. What does indeed lie in common life—what it can yield to poetry—what it may bear within itself far above poetry—no one can tell; neither a town critic of one score, with a brown curled wig, nor a country minister of fourscore years, with smooth, silvery, natural hair. That it will yield materials to poetry such as would not have been expected till genius produced them, we now know as a fact of our late literature, and a fact that will be to the immortal glory of the age.

Now, observe, that in what is drawn from the life of the people, it is not to be said that life is to be exalted. In Wordsworth, indeed, it is exalted—almost universally. In Burns it is sometimes—but generally not. This much, however, seems certain,—it ought never to be degraded. In Crabbe it often is degraded. Crabbe draws the face of things —they draw its spirit. Wordsworth draws the life of the people, as a part of that universal nature which he contemplates and loves. Burns, as the life which himself has lived; in which he has found his joy and his sorrow; which he loves as his own, as having been that of his forefathers, and which he hopes and trusts, will be the life of his children. Crabbe writes of it as an observer, fond of criticizing, and somewhat inclined to disparage. If we should doubt for a moment the truth of Wordsworth's pictures, as pictures of reality, still we could not question his right to make them what they are; and such imaginary representations of men in his scenes of nature, seem fit inhabitants of those scenes. If the character be ideal, the elements of the character are in nature. But there is far more than this in that poetry of Wordsworth devoted to the delineation of humble life. For it is not enough to say, that he has drawn with love and reverence that natural life of man which he has so earnestly contemplated—but in the midst of his pictures his own presence is felt. And his reader does not go on, without feeling himself bound continually in dearer love to him who has opened up for him the secrets of his own spirit, without recognizing in himself the enlarging capacity, the growing power, the unfolding sensibilities, into which a strong sympathy has infused new energies of life.

With respect to Burns, we have simple belief—and are satisfied. He writes with a genial fervour of love—with a beating heart. The tide of life which rolled in his veins flowed through his song. Yet his genius, too, has cast its own lights upon that picture. There are touches there which were not borrowed from nature, and peoplings of fancy in the midst of acknowledged realities. Every one who reads, feels that he is not moved merely, softened, amused by the representatives of living nature, but that he is borne along in an unison of feeling and thought with the poet himself. He feels himself elate in new strength, while he accompanies the steps of the fine, free, bold, rustic genius, ranging its own heights, or searching the secret paths that lead to its own beloved haunts of peculiar and appropriate inspiration. Or our patriotic heart leaps within us when we look

> On him, who walked in glory and in joy,
> Following his plough upon the mountain side.
> [Wordsworth, 'Resolution and Independence']

As to Crabbe, if we believe, it is often just what we try not to do. He gives us a picture of reality, which repels our belief while it commands it. He drives us out of the region of poetry; and if we are compelled to believe, we ask why we must meet that in a volume of poems, which ought to have been evidence before the Committees of Mendicity or Police?

Unlike to that of Burns or Wordsworth, may it not be said that the genius of this author alienates the spirit of his reader? For not only is there a continual painful sense that he is describing a life, which, though he has considered shrewdly, he has never justly known; but there is felt a yet more demanding consciousness of the repression within ourselves of feelings, of the contraction within ourselves of thought. We often make positive loss from accompanying his steps, and no acquisition. We leave off, saddened, disheartened, dispirited, and weak. We have found no friend in the poet, to whom we were willing to surrender our hearts, but too often a sneering cynic, who shows us insultingly that he knows and understands the beauty we prize, and then plucks it to pieces before our very face.

How heavily in general does the narrative of Crabbe drag on! Not because there is not life in the manner of relation, but because there is no life in the story itself he relates—because there is seldom or never genius breathing in the linking together of the incidents he has selected from the ongoings of human beings before his eyes. Instead of the deep-thrilling and often occult and mysterious Causation which indeed reigns over life, and of which great poets and writers of romance have in their representations caught shadowy and fearful reflections, he binds his events together by threads lying on life's surface. His events are not the living brood of a dark and mighty Power, which spring up on the earth to affright and trouble it. They walk over it in orderly and regular pro-cession, in mechanical obedience to the marshalling hand of their Choregus. The highest poetical conception of incident or story may be illustrated out of the old Greek Fable, by the terrific passions cast into human breasts from the hands of avenging deities—by the overhanging fate which pursues the steps of Œdipus, guiding him in its darkness to unwilling crime—by the decrees which enjoin Orestes to the act of worldly retribution, and then punish him in its fulfilment. These dark dim visions of the world of man, which show him living in part in intelligible sufferings, and in part under unintelligible agencies, if they exaggerate his condition, show it at least in the colours in which it appears to the troubled and awful imagination. They shew the strong-limbed mariner tossing on the billows which he buffets, whirling in their eddies, living yet by the struggles of his human strength, but un-knowing at what moment he may be dashed in pieces, or swallowed up, and discovering, by the lightnings that blaze over him, nothing but the sea on which he is tempest-driven. The Fables of Shakespeare, as they appear in his works, are created in imagination, and hold a middle place between this fearful Causation, and the ordinary realities of life. They are realities half-shadowed. The stories of Crabbe are on the other extreme point of the line. His causes of events are sedulously chosen out of the most intelligible, and incontestable realities; and he makes the current of human life run yet shallower than it appears even to the undiscerning eyes of ordinary experience.

POETICAL WORKS (WITH LIFE)

January–September 1834

This collected edition included *Posthumous Tales* in addition to the works published in the poet's lifetime. The reviewers concentrated their attention on the *Life* by Crabbe's son, George. The extracts below do not include criticism of the biography at any length.

54. 'Farewell, dear Crabbe!'

1834

The following verses form the conclusion of the *Life*. They are by John Shute Duncan (1769–1844), Fellow of New College, Oxford (1791–1829) and a barrister. They represent a fair summary of Crabbe's poetic qualities.

Farewell, dear CRABBE! thou meekest of mankind,
With heart all fervour, and all strength of mind.
With tenderest sympathy for others' woes,
Fearless, all guile and malice to expose:
Steadfast of purpose in pursuit of right,
To drag forth dark hypocrisy to light,
To brand th' oppressor, and to shame the proud,
To shield the righteous from the slanderous crowd;
To error lenient and to frailty mild,
Repentance ever was thy welcome child:
In every state, as husband, parent, friend,
Scholar, or bard, thou couldst the Christian blend.
Thy verse from Nature's face each feature drew,
Each lovely charm, each mole and wrinkle too.

314

No dreamy incidents of wild romance,
With whirling shadows, wilder'd minds entrance;
But plain realities the mind engage,
With pictured warnings through each polished page.
Hogarth of Song! be this they perfect praise:—
Truth prompted, and Truth purified thy lays;
The God of Truth has given thy verse and thee
Truth's holy palm—His Immortality.

55. J. G. Lockhart, unsigned reviews, *Quarterly Review*

January 1834, l, 468–508 and October 1834, lii, 184–203

Lockhart, Scott's biographer and son-in-law, edited the *Quarterly* from 1825. This review was published by John Murray, who was also Crabbe's publisher, and no doubt through Murray Lockhart helped with the revision of *Posthumous Tales*.

This is the first of a series of eight volumes, in which we are about to have before us the life, journals, and annotated poems of Mr. Crabbe, in the same portable shape, and at the same rate of cost, as the *Life and Works of Lord Byron*, and the poetry of Sir Walter Scott; illustrated, moreover, in the same exquisite manner, by designs from our best artists. We hardly doubt that this attempt to extend the circulation of Crabbe's poetry, especially among the less affluent classes of the community, will be attended with as much success as either of the previous adventures to which we have alluded. Placed by Byron, Scott, Fox, and Canning, and, we believe, by every one of his eminent contemporaries, in the very highest rank of excellence, Crabbe has never yet become familiar to hundreds of thousands of English readers well qualified to appreciate and enjoy his merits. 'The poet of the poor,' as his son justly styles him, has hitherto found little favour except with the rich; and yet, of all English authors, he is the one who has sympathized the most profoundly and tenderly with the virtues and the sorrows of humble life—who has best understood the fervours of lowly love and affection—and painted the anxieties and vicissitudes of toil and penury with the closest fidelity and the most touching pathos. In his works the peasant and the mechanic will find everything to elevate their aspirations, and yet nothing to quicken envy and uncharitableness. He is a Christian poet—his satire is strong, but never rancorous—his lessons of virtue are earnest but modest—his reprehensions of vice severe but brotherly. He only needs an introduction into the cottage, to supplant there for ever the affected sentimentality and gross sensualism of authors immeasurably below him in vigour and capacity of mind, as well as in dignity of heart and character, who have, from accidental circumstances, outrun him for a season in the race of popularity.

When about seven-and-twenty years ago, Crabbe, after half a lifetime spent in retirement and silence, broke upon the world for the second time in his *Parish Register* and 'Sir Eustace Grey,' a great deal of very pretty writing was bestowed on the illustration of three deep propositions:—namely, (this was not a very novel one,) that poetry is read for the sake of the excitement it gives to our minds and feelings; that painful emotions are more energetic and exciting than pleasurable ones; and that, as Mr. Crabbe dealt more exclusively than any other modern poet in sad and dismal subjects, he must eventually, of course, outstrip all his rivals in popular favour. The world has outlived all reverence for such juvenile pedantry as made the staple and glory of the school of criticism we have been alluding to: in other words, it has come to be the fashion to test metaphysical generalizations (as they were called) by fact; and the slightest application of that criterion must be sufficient for the utter demolition of the ingenuities in question. Every man that lays his hand on his own breast, knows perfectly well that painful emotions are not necessarily more powerful than pleasurable ones. Is there anything of *pain* in the enthusiasm of the chase; or

> In the stern joy which warriors feel
> In foemen worthy of their steel;
> [Scott, *The Lady of the Lake*, V, st. 10]

or in the rapture of successful love, or the generous glow of active benevolence? And then, as to the probable ultra-popularity of a poet whose claim should be founded on his exclusive devotion to themes of woe and calamity, is it not wonderful that it should not have occurred even to a metaphysician to ask who, *de facto*, are the most universally popular of the great poets of past ages? Is Homer less popular than Euripides? Who is, and ever has been, the most popular of all Roman writers?—who but the one that has hardly one touch of melancholy in his composition—the most thoroughly worldly, shrewd, good-humoured painter of life and manners that ever handled a pen—Horace? Is Dante more popular than Ariosto? Racine than Rabelais? Calderon than Cervantes? or Klopstock than Goethe? Here, at home, who are and ever will be the most popular of our own poets? Speaking of works of any considerable bulk, which can be named beside those of Shakespeare and Pope? And will any man pretend that Shakespeare's tragedy has at any time enjoyed more favour than his comedy, or that Pope has counted one worshipper of his pathos for a hundred admirers of his wit? We need not go into the works of Mr. Crabbe's own contemporaries. If he himself were never to gain general favour except by reason of the painful emotions he excites, we should still despair of his fate; but the truth is, Crabbe can hardly be said to deal more largely in such emotions than either Byron, or Wordsworth, or Moore; and indeed, no poet ever was, or ever will be, popular in this country that deals exclusively in such materials. The national taste is, on the whole, a manly one; it is felt that life is made up of light and shadow in pretty equal proportions—and the only art that can permanently fix and please us, is that which has scope enough to reflect life in its own contrasts. Crabbe's deep, and sometimes dreadful pathos, tells on us a thousand times more than it would otherwise have done, by reason of the wit, the humour, the playful humanity with which he relieves it. A short piece of thorough anguish is very well; but we venture to say that the habitual readers of Crabbe (and most of those who read him at all have him constantly in their hands) do not turn the most frequently to 'Sir Eustace Grey,' or 'Peter Grimes.' We should as soon expect to be told that Allan's 'Pressgang' has been more liked than his 'Shepherds' House-heating,' or that Wilkie's 'Distraining for Rent' has been a more lucrative print than 'Blindman's Buff' or 'The Chelsea Pensioners.'

The vulgar impression that Crabbe is throughout a gloomy author, we ascribe to the choice of certain specimens of his earliest poetry in the 'Elegant Extracts'[1]—the only specimens of him that had been at all

[1] Collected by Vicesimus Knox, 1789.

generally known at the time when most of those who have criticized his later works were young. That exquisitely-finished, but heart-sickening description, in particular, of the poor-house in *The Village*, fixed itself on every imagination; and when *The Register* and *Borough* came out, the reviewers, unconscious perhaps of the early prejudice that was influencing them, selected quotations mainly of the same class. Generalizing critics are apt to think more of their own theory than of their author's practice; and we assert, without hesitation, that it would be easy to select from Crabbe a volume at least of most powerful, most exciting, and most characteristic poetry, which should hardly, in a single line, touch on any but the pleasurable emotions of our nature; of cunning but altogether unvenomed ridicule; of solemn but unsadden-ing morality; and of that gentle pathos which is a far more delicious luxury than ever sprung from gaiety of spirit. . . .

★ ★ ★ ★

. . . We mean, at present, to confine ourselves to the easy and humble task of reviewing, in a very cursory manner, the last volume of the younger Crabbe's edition of his father's poetical works—that which consists entirely of new matter. In the other volumes of the series, various little pieces have for the first time been published—and some of these appear to us highly meritorious: indeed, the dialogue called 'Flirtation' (in vol. v.) is a fair specimen of his lightest humour; and 'The World of Dreams' (vol. iv.), though obviously unfinished in some parts, is on the whole a lyrical composition of extraordinary power, interest, and beauty. But the editor reserved unbroken for his con-cluding volume those *Tales* which the poet himself had destined and prepared for posthumous publication; and to these we must give the space that we have now at our disposal. . . .

The posthumous volume offers, indeed, no tale entitled to be talked of in the same breath with the highest efforts of Crabbe's genius—no 'Peter Grimes'—no 'Ellen Orford'—no 'Sir Owen Dale'—no 'Patron' —no 'Lady Barbara;' but it contains, nevertheless a series of stories, scarcely one of which any lover of the man and the poet would wish to have been suppressed: every one of them presenting us with pithy couplets, which will be treasured up and remembered while the English language lasts; and some of them, notwithstanding what the editor candidly says as to the general want of the *limæ labor*, displaying not only his skill as an analyst of character, but in a strong light also his peculiar mastery of versification. The example of Lord Byron's 'Corsair' and 'Lara' had not, we suspect, been lost upon him. In some of these pieces he has a freedom and breadth of execution which we doubt if he ever before equalled in the metre to which he commonly adhered —insomuch, that in place of a 'Pope in worsted stockings' (as James Smith has called him), we seem now and then to be more reminded of a Dryden in a one-horse chaise.

One of the most amusing of these stories is the first of them, entitled 'Silford Hall, or the Happy Day.' . . .

> Small as it was, the place could boast a School, . . .

[I, 7–17; 78–93, 121–45, 164–9; 220–3, 238–47; 302–5, 315–38, 347–64; 384–415; 426–31; 463–76, 477–94.]

Crabbe is never greater than in dreams. We have already alluded to that lyric recently published, which no one could have written but the author of 'Sir Eustace Grey.' In a lighter vein, what can be better than the dreams of Peter Perkin, when, having explored all the galleries and libraries, and saloons of Silford Hall, he is told the housekeeper's dinner will not be for an hour yet—walks abroad into the gardens, and falls asleep under some huge oaks, as old, he doubts not, as Julius Cæsar?—

> I am so happy, and have such delight, . . .
> [I, 661–99; parts of *Poetical Works*, 1834, VIII, 32–4]
> Dream on, dear boy! . . .
> [Ward III, 534–6.]

The 'Family of Love' is perhaps the best tale in this volume. . . .

> He had a sturdy multitude to guide, . . .

[II, 120–45; 164–83; 214–53, 264–80; 342–9; 354–95; 400–22, 427–30; 435–6; 447–54, 459–62; 471–6.]

The story of 'The Equal Marriage' is a much shorter one than this truly excellent 'Family of Love;' and the subject is neither an interesting nor a new one—the sudden break-up of all affection and all comfort, consequent on the termination of the honeymoon allotted to a rake and a coquette, who have mutually deceived each other, and in so far themselves. . . .

[III, 1–19, 26–34, 43–60; 240–66.]

From 'Rachel,' the only thoroughly sad story in this volume, we extract the following picture of a deserted and heart-broken woman:—

> One calm, cold evening, when the moon was high, . . .
> [IV, 121–6, 149–51]

'Villars' is the history of a creature of imagination, tormented by the levity and, indeed, vice of a beautiful woman whom his infatuated admiration compels him on every occasion to forgive: there is, we have no doubt, truth in the conception—but the conclusion has not been adequately developed. The following sketch is in the best style of Crabbe's coast scenery:—

Villars long since, as he indulged his spleen . . .
[V, 399–416]

. . . This plan[1] is essentially much the same with that of the *Tales of the Hall*; but the characters of the 'Poet' and the 'Friend,' in whose dialogue these histories are brought out, have been left almost blanks, which is a sad falling off. The scene, however, seems to be undoubtedly laid at Aldborough; and, indeed, the following lines in the introductory section are little more than the versification of a passage in Mr. Crabbe's diary, describing his sensations on visiting his native place in very advanced life, which was inserted by his son in the Biographical Memoir—

Yes!—twenty years have pass'd, and I am come, . . .
[VI, 63–74, 77–86, 89–92]

My grave informer doubted, then replied, . . .
[VII, 58–76, 82–4; VIII, 1–8, 83–100]

'The Ancient Mansion' is one of the best pieces in this collection. . . .

Her servants all, if so we may describe . . .
[X, 32–7, 42–7; 58–60, 70–101; 114–65]

How bows the market, when from stall to stall . . .
[XI, 55–70, 101–8, 121–30, 137–8, 141–2]

Miranda sees her morning levee fill'd . . .
[XIII, 24–41, 74–81, 86–93; 110–15, 132–50]

. . . 'Belinda Waters', a most Crabbish portraiture of a fine dainty miss:—

She sees her father oft engross'd by cares, . . .
[XV, 22–31, 34–43; 99–117]

'The Will' and 'The Cousins' are among the most powerful of these tales; and 'The Boat Race,' 'Master William, or Lad's Love,' 'Danvers and Rayner,' 'Preaching and Practice'—in short, almost every piece in

---

[1] Of 'The Farewell and Return' (Tales VI–XXII).

the volume—might furnish us with some extract, grave or gay, which would much adorn our pages. But we believe we have already quoted quite enough to convey a fair notion of what this legacy amounts to. It is on the whole decidedly inferior, in most respects, to any other volume of the author's poetry; but still it is perhaps more *amusing* than any of the rest of them: it is full of playfulness and good-humour, and the stories are, with hardly an exception, such as we can fancy the good old man to have taken delight in telling to his grandchildren, when the curtains were drawn down and the fire burnt bright on a winter's evening, in the rectory parlour of Trowbridge. 'Why, sir,' said Johnson at Dunvegan—(anno ætat. 64)—'a man grows better-humoured as he grows older. He improves by experience.' It is pleasing to trace the gradually-increasing prevalence of the softer feelings in the heart of Crabbe, when removed from the stern influences of his early distress. . . .

56. Unsigned review, *Tait's Edinburgh Magazine*

April 1834, n.s. i, 161–8

Although Crabbe has enjoyed no sparing meed of applause from many whose praise was of itself a passport to distinction, his admirers have hitherto been select rather than numerous. We think that he has not yet been honoured according to his deserts. At no period of his career, perhaps, can he have been justly called a popular writer: of late, he has certainly been undeservedly neglected. As regards the present genera-tion of readers, this is easily accounted for. In aspect and manner, our poet belongs, in some degree, to a former age. The author, whose earlier efforts were fostered by Burke, whose tales had been criticized by Johnson, and had beguiled the sufferings of Fox during his last illness, was lost amidst the crowd of brilliant writers that rose to celebrity after the commencement of the present century. And although he reappeared, after a long interval, with powers mellowed and confirmed by time; still he might, in some measure, be regarded as one of an obsolete school, by those who were engrossed by the dazzling productions of Scott, and Southey, and Byron. The captivations of a new vein of poetic imagery, rich, fanciful, and picturesque beyond precedent, would naturally divert the multitude of readers from an author who still adhered to the older fashion, and who made no attempt to recommend the strict and often homely truth of his pictures, by splendour of colouring or variety of tone, by the romance of his fables, or the dignity of his personages. But the temporary excitement, whether of novelty or of fashion, has now subsided; and our author and his illustrious rivals are alike denizens of the past. The time is perhaps arrived, when we may better perceive and appreciate the relative truth of their labours.

The opinion generally prevalent as to the character of Crabbe's writings, would of itself prove how little they have been consulted by the mass of readers. We believe that by the majority of these he would be represented as the painter *par excellence* of vice, indigence, and misery; the harsh anatomist of all unlovely diseases of the moral and physical world, apt and diligent in his ungrateful occupation, but destitute of the capacity to conceive or enjoy those fairer creations, which are Poetry's chosen offspring. And yet how false and unjust will such a description appear to those who are conversant with our author;—how much of unaffected beauty and generous feeling—what a store of genial, quiet humour and original reflection were here overlooked! He was, indeed, too clear-sighted and honest to substitute mere pleasant inventions for the real lineaments of life and nature, which he had closely inspected ere he ventured to portray. His pursuit of truth, it must be confessed, often led him amidst scenes which rarely attract the idler or the visionary: he came forth as the chronicler of common life; and how frequently is the web of daily existence chequered with sombre colours! Yet his eye could recognize beauty in the lowliest places: he was no wilful maligner of human nature; but resolutely gazed upon it in its rudest aspect, and with a master's hand transferred its lights and shadows to his canvass. Herein his merit resides;—the secret of his genius lay in a perspicacity which allowed no detail of his subject to escape him, and a conscientiousness that refused to decorate it with foreign ornaments. In the scenes with which he was most conversant, the shade predominated over the sunshine: in his characters we see evil blended with, and at times quenching the good: it was thus with the men by whom he was surrounded. It cannot be objected to him, that one circumstance of care or suffering is overcharged in the description; his delineation may be stern, but it is no caricature. Although he feared not to record what he knew, he wrote no 'scandalous chronicle' of human nature. He strictly fulfilled the purpose so well announced in his own words:—

> Come then fair Truth, and let me clearly see
> The minds I paint, as they are seen in thee!
> To me their merits and their faults impart.
> Give me to say, 'Frail Being, such thou art';
> And clearly let me view the naked human heart.
> [*Tales of the Hall*, I, 121–5]

Such being the author's object, it were unfair to condemn the sobriety of his pictures, unless it appear that he has omitted the beauties, or exaggerated the defects of their original. . . .

Crabbe was not deficient in imagination. The poem of Sir Eustace Grey would suffice to prove this, were other proof wanting. But the power with which realities attracted his mind repressed the exercise of this faculty, and determined his preference for a class of composition, in which his unrivalled accuracy of perception, and his graphic vigour found entire occupation. It is as a descriptive poet that he sought to excel; by his success in this capacity he must be judged. It would be unreasonable to reproach him for the absence of qualities foreign to the object he pursued. And if we examine his writings with the due advertence to their aim, which is a chief duty of honest criticism, how admirable will his success appear! What vivid truth in his landscapes! Every feature is brought out with precision—every touch tells; yet the effect, as a whole, is perfect. His epithets are pregnant with feeling, and bespeak a familiar acquaintance with the object represented. Nothing is vague or inconsistent; his accessaries are in the finest keeping, and aid the conception of the reader. Our poet does not love to generalize, but executes his task with a careful and firm hand, producing his effect by a series of well-chosen details, each confirming the impression he seeks to convey. His choice of subjects may be objected to by the fastidious. True, he depicts no Tempè or Arcadia; his scenes are drawn from our workday world, nor has he always selected even here the fairest portions. His acquaintance with the richer beauties of nature was not extensive. Yet he could discern a charm in the wild and barren places of the earth; and the boldness with which he has preserved their express features is in our eyes a merit of the highest order. With all our love for ideal beauty, we should have regretted his departure from a province peculiarly his own, in pursuit of embellishments belonging to another region. Each has its own place and season; and we deem it the highest excellence of Crabbe's descriptive passages, as works of art, that they are so perfectly sincere, so free from any intermixture of a character at variance with the appropriate features of the scene.

It is impossible, in an article like the present, to display his excellence in this department by adequate specimens. Those which we select, almost at random, are not offered as such: they can but be viewed as fragments, which lose much of their force by being separated from the context. Here is an autumn scene, the calm repose of which must, we think, be felt by every lover of nature. The turn at the close of the passage is a happy instance of our author's skill in combining his observation of external objects with the moral progress of his story.

It was a fair and mild autumnal sky . . .
[*Tales of the Hall*, IV, 46–64]

The freshness and truth of Crabbe's sea views could only have been produced by one who, from early youth, had known the aspect of the deep in all its changes. He loved it as a familiar friend, and was ever happiest when within reach of its sound. Had his poems no other merit, they would be dear to us for the sake of this ocean-love of his. How fondly he dwells on the picture that memory was continually bringing before him!

Pleasant it was to view the sea-gulls strive . . .
[*ibid.*, IV, 463–76]

This, however graphic and instinct with the true marine flavour, is far from being the best of his sea pictures. They abound in all his poems, and form a series which it would be difficult to parallel in the works of any other author. . . .

Lo! where the heath, with withering brake grown o'er, . . .
[*The Village*, I, 63–84]

A similar vigour of touch distinguishes Crabbe's sketches of human character. They are drawn *ad vivum*: the great book of nature alone could have supplied him with such a multitude of figures, so life-like, distinct, and full of genuine character. At every page we start on recognizing some known individual,—some vivid trait which arouses a tribe of forgotten associations,—some personification, embodying a truth which had laid in our minds indistinct and naked until now. His power in depicting the features and essential forms of common life bespeaks the practised observer; and he traces the workings of the passions on every variety of character, with a precision the result of a profound knowledge of humanity. At every step we are met by a new incitement to reflection and inquiry. But this is not all. To Crabbe we are in a great measure indebted for the discovery of the thrilling interest claimed by the sorrows and accidents of obscure life—a province upon which the eye of genius had seldom before ventured to look with earnestness and patience. He has displayed the fallacy of many idle impressions, touching the humble and the poor, which indifference alone could have allowed to exist so long undisturbed. From the haunts of toil and indigence he brings the personages of a drama, grave and mournful, indeed, but fraught with instruction to the student of human nature. With the eloquence of the poet, and the sympathetic earnestness of a fellow-sufferer, he displays the true circumstances of life struggling with want and care,—its stern passions,—its patient virtues,—its scenes of squalid distress, or of decent poverty,—the endurance, the ambition, the despair of this neglected sphere of existence. In this he has done good service. We had need of a faithful chronicler to tell us what our poorer fellow mortals feel, and suffer, and enjoy; and if the record be rather sad than cheerful, it is well that we should be awakened to the knowledge that it is so. On purely aesthetic grounds, his advertence to this topic is commendable. The subject was new and striking: its development, in the hands of a master like Crabbe, affords abundant food for all the soft and strong emotions, and is susceptible of genuine poetic elevation, nay, sublimity. For it cannot be too often repeated—that the soul of poetry is truth; and none but a sickly judgment will be offended by its accents, merely because it is too faithful to be evermore prophesying smooth things. . . .

> Theirs is yon house that holds the parish poor, . . .
> [*The Village*, I, 228–39, 260–73]

> Curious and sad, upon the fresh-dug hill, . . .
> [*The Parish Register*, III, 615–28]

Now, let us see how exquisitely the poet could feel and depict the grace which love can impart to the hours of sickness and death. In the following passage, all is sweetness and repose. It is the close of a tale of constancy and love; the sailor has returned to die in the arms of his betrothed:—

> One day he lighter seemed, and they forgot . . .
> [*The Borough*, II, 232–51]

Assuredly, he who could thus describe the tender ministry of woman's love,

> And paint its presence beautifying death,

had no lack of the gentler sympathies of the poet's nature, no feeble perception of the spirit which makes suffering forget to sorrow, and life, with all its trials, wear a smile of hope.

It has, indeed, been said, and we believe it, that it is the lively sense of happiness alone which can teach the poet thoroughly to conceive the severity of its privation. The genius which inspired the passage above quoted is equally present in this strongly contrasted description of the last hours in a conscience-striken existence:

> In each lone place, dejected and dismay'd, . . .
> [*ibid.*, XIX, 270–88]

. . . He was himself somewhat of a humourist, and is never more successful than in the portraiture of such characters, or where he pleasantly reveals the minor absurdities of habit or caprice. In the following cordial passage, we fancy we can recognize some traits of dear old Gilbert White of Selborne, that most amiable of all naturalists:—

> He had no system, and forebore to read . . .
> He show'd the flowers, the stamina, the style, . . .
> [*Tales of the Hall*, IX, 279–305]

We do not think that Crabbe has ever been surpassed in the delineation of those minor peculiarities of habit, action, and propensity, which are in ordinary life the chief indications of character, yet which it requires a fine perception to distinguish and define, so slightly are they raised above the general surface. The subjoined passage has been justly celebrated; although well known, it cannot be too often praised.

> Six years had past, and forty ere the six . . .
> [*ibid.*, X, 458–86]

> 'Sir Denys Brand! and on so poor a steed!' . . .
> [*The Borough*, XIII, 199–216]

In what may be termed the historical analysis of character, Crabbe has few rivals. His patience, minuteness, and care are inimitable. He traces the operation of passions, of original tendencies, of external accidents, as they combine to influence action and feeling in different ages and natures, with a fidelity almost approaching intuition. He employs no glaring contrasts, no abrupt transitions. Every step is noticed and prepared; we observe the progress of habit and will as they advance towards virtue or vice, until we are placed in sight of the inevitable consequence. Nor is this power of our author employed on graver subjects alone. He takes an equal delight in pursuing throughout a long career, the eccentricities of a whimsical or humorous character, and dwells upon their changes with a most captivating *gusto*. Of his severer tone of remark, it should be observed, that it is never heard, but in the censure of arrogance, folly, or baseness, when the force of his sarcasm commands our entire approbation.

But we must now touch upon our author's chief defect, as the Poet of Human Life. Of that higher philosophy which not only perceives, but can reconcile the contending elements of suffering and action, we find no appearance in his writings. He is purely descriptive and historical. He lays the materials of existence before us in all their fulness; but there is no attempt on his part to arrange or explain them. He is, like ourselves, a mere spectator; more clear-sighted, and wise, and compassionate than the rest, yet still a spectator alone. He sees life but in fragments, nor does he appear to have any conception of a harmony, of a whole. He does not even aid us in unravelling the tangled web that has just passed through his hands: gently or firmly, as the texture of the various threads may require, he seizes upon them; and as he found them, so does he lay them down. He is no expounder of mysteries. The charge of kindling, amidst the darkest perplexities of life, the beacons of Hope and Belief, and universal love, is the highest function of poetry. We have no reason to believe that Crabbe was conscious of this attribute of his art; he wrote as though it had no existence. Let us not be misunderstood. Crabbe was a wise, and pious, and benevolent man. It is not of the rigour of his darkest pictures that we complain; but that we find in them no glimmering of that light which is ever present to the thoroughly gifted teacher, amidst the deepest gloom of life's afflictions. He never learned, perhaps was not endowed with the perception of the highest function of his art. In his pictures of affection, and endurance, and self-sacrifice, we see poetry unconsciously vindicating her office; but the effect is casual and interrupted. And in estimating

Crabbe's poetical merits, we are bound to award him praise as a faithful recorder of all that he knew, and an observer, diligent, but partial. Of that greater praise which attends the full comprehension of our history, we can afford him no share.

It would be unjust to conclude this sketch of our author without some notice, however brief, of his lyrical powers. The few specimens which he has produced in this province, are sufficient to shew how distinguished a place he might have attained in it, had not another claimed the preference. In rapidity, force, and flow of language, and power of conception, and in a certain tenderness, which pervades the whole, his poem of Sir Eustace Grey has few equals,—it may be placed amidst the best of our lyrical compositions. We regret that we cannot extract the whole.

> Yes! I had youth and rosy health, . . .
> [52–83, 116–31, 180–203, 232–59]

Of softer beauty is the following exquisite song of a heart-broken maiden, crazed by the perfidy of her lover, and sighing gently to be at rest. The melody of the numbers is faultless, and beautifully harmonizes with the graceful pathos of the subject.

> Let me not have this gloomy view . . .
> [*Tales of the Hall*, VIII, 837–76]

In general, Crabbe's style is vigorous and correct, plain, and free from redundant epithets;—at times it sinks to the level of the commonest prose, and perhaps never quite reaches the sustained elevation which his subject occasionally requires. The structure of his verse is not in general remarkable for melody; though passages might be found in his writings of easy and flowing versification, worthy of Pope himself. A fondness for verbal points and appositions, approaching at times the nature of quibbles, is observable in his earlier efforts; in his last published work, the *Tales of the Hall*, such instances rarely occur. Their effect, however, is not, on the whole, unpleasing; their occasional introduction gives pungency to his descriptive passages, and affords considerable gratification to the ear.

57. O. W. B. Peabody, unsigned review, *North American Review*

July 1834, xxxix, 135–66

Peabody (1799–1848), lawyer and man of letters, was a frequent contributor to the *North American Review* (edited by his brother-in-law, Alexander H. Everett) after 1830.

[Mainly devoted to a summary of the *Life*.]

Gay's Pastorals, intentionally coarse and ludicrous as they are, are more true to nature than those of Pope; because these were never designed to be faithful to nature, but only to present a pleasing copy of a work of ancient art. Goldsmith's descriptions have more of truth about them, but the sunlight rests on these as on our landscape in the Indian summer; there is a soft haze which veils the ruder features of the prospect, and the dreary sky and gathering storm are kept entirely from the view. Crabbe's error was just the opposite one; he was himself familiar with all the dark shades of village life, and in his own depressed and sad circumstances, they occupied and filled his imagination; he had himself experienced what others only sung, and had found it cheerless as the valley of the shadow of death. We all know how much our impressions of scenery and modes of life are governed by our feelings; the brightest sun is cold and melancholy to the mourner, and the dreariest landscape pleasing to the eye, when we ourselves are happy. Crabbe saw the country with pleasure, and left it without regret; to him it presented no recollections but those of disappointed hope: and he accordingly describes it with a stern and powerful hand, without compunction or mercy, and with colors too severely true.

. . . Mr. Crabbe inverted the maxims of the Greek painter, in the execution of his portrait of the Queen of Love; instead of selecting and combining beauties, he left no blemish or deformity untouched, and produced a whole, every part of which might be true to nature, while its general impression was as false as it was frightful. But moral defects are the first to be forgiven: men were weary of the small poets who had undertaken to amuse them in the absence of the chief performers, and were glad to welcome one, who revived the ancient inspiration; they saw in Crabbe a poet of real abilities, who, if he resorted to old themes, treated them in a manner rarely witnessed before; they saw a model of versification, as finished and far more vigorous than that of Goldsmith, and inferior in his own language only to Pope. No wonder, under these circumstances, that the impression which he made was strong and lasting. . . .

Mr. Crabbe is certainly entitled to the praise of a reformer. Before his day, no poet would have dreamed of resorting to humble life for any thing beyond a theme of ludicrous caricature, or the personages of a Beggar's Opera. Even at the present time, critics are apt to shake their heads with looks of peculiar wisdom, when they come in contact with such innovations: they are willing to admit that *The Borough* is well enough in its way, but deem the effort to invest such objects with poetical attraction as hopeless as to draw the living waters from the rock. The poets themselves have yielded to this prejudice, and instead of copying from nature, when they wish to introduce a peasant, have made him as unlike reality, as is the waxen image to the animated frame; the man of their creation has no affinity with merely mortal flesh and blood. We might as well expect in real life to meet a phoenix, as one of their sentimental swains, musing in rapture as he goes forth to his daily task, or following the plough with unutterable joy and glory. We know that there is enough in humble life which has no claim to the title of poetical, and so there is in every other condition; but we are not sure, that the materials of poetry are not more abundant in a lowly, than in an elevated sphere; for feeling is there unfettered by those conventional restraints, which operate like law on natural freedom: . . .

When all the exhalations of prejudice and of fashion shall have passed away, the moral interest will be more equally distributed among the different conditions of life. The simple energy and truth of Crabbe will be more valued by the many, than they have been heretofore; if his intellectual vision does not, like that of the most glorious of the sons of light, comprehend all space, it will be acknowledged to be keen, wide, and faithful. Shakspeare, from his watchtower, caught every change of many-colored life; the great volume of our nature was wide open before him; and whether he unveils the humble bosom, or describes the fierce struggles of jealousy, ambition or remorse, or the sorrow quickened into madness of the credulous old king, no one ever thought of doubting that the portraiture was real. Crabbe generally aspired to no such wide extent of observation, though when he has attempted it, his success is complete; he saw and studied all the beings around him with no less interest and care, than he pursued his researches into the secrets of inanimate nature; and what he undertakes to describe, neither Scott nor Shakspeare could have painted better. His purpose is a moral one; he never aims to dazzle or to please; he conceals no defect, softens no deformity, and aims not to exaggerate a single beauty; he makes few sacrifices on the altar of fastidious taste: whoever admires him, admires him for his plain truth and manly power. In these remarks, we refer of course to his later writings; for the prevalent defect of the earlier ones has been already pointed out. As he went onward in the way of life, he became a cool, thoughtful, philosophical and somewhat sarcastic observer, with tolerable charity for human vice and folly, but with principle enough to describe them as they are. . . .

58. Unsigned review, *Monthly Review*

September 1834, n.s.iii, 101–15

Mr. Crabbe is said to have remarked, that he derived less pleasure from the contemplation of a beautiful prospect, than from standing in the highway, to watch the faces of the passers by; and the remark, we think, serves to afford an explanation of the character of his later writings. Natural beauty excites but a small share of his enthusiasm; it is rare for him to dwell on any lovely scene, though he occasionally describes those of an opposite character with great vividness: with the exception of the ocean, with which many of the associations of his childhood were connected, and whose changing aspects he portrays with remarkable force of colouring, the grand and beautiful in nature have few charms for him. Motives,—feelings,—passions,—all that relates to human character and action,—these are the points which he seizes on with a master's hand, and unfolds with a stern energy and truth, which con-vince us that he is engaged with no creations of fancy, but is describing what he has actually seen and studied. No English poet since the time of Shakspeare has painted those diversities of character, which one meets in the ordinary intercourse of life, with equal fidelity or with equal effect. He sees them not through a distorted medium, nor within the shade of intervening objects: he has obtained that point of philosophical elevation, neither so lofty as to confuse the sight, nor so low as to confine it, where every object appears in a true light and in its just proportions; the result of his observation are neither things of speculation nor of fancy, but the strong, distinct, vivid portraitures of classes of our race.

Mr. Crabbe is certainly entitled to the praise of a reformer. Before his day, no poet would have dreamed of resorting to humble life for any thing beyond a theme of ludicrous caricature, or the personages of a Beggar's Opera. Even at the present time, critics are apt to shake their heads with looks of peculiar wisdom, when they come in contact with such innovations: they are willing to admit that *The Borough* is well enough in its way, but deem the effort to invest such subjects with poetical attraction as hopeless as to draw the living waters from the rock. The poets themselves have yielded to this prejudice, and, instead of copying nature, when they wish to introduce a peasant, have made him as unlike reality, as is the waxen image to the animated frame; the man of their creation has no affinity with merely mortal flesh and blood. We might as well expect in real life to meet a phœnix, as one of their sentimental swains, musing in rapture as he goes forth to his daily task, or following the plough with unutterable joy and glory. We know that there is enough in humble life which has no claim to the title of poetical and so there is in every other condition; but we are not sure, that the materials of poetry are not more abundant in a lowly, than in an elevated sphere; for feeling is there unfettered by those conventional restraints, which operate like law on natural freedom: the stern rebuke of opinion, which has as much power over those who move in the elevated social walks, as the eye of the keeper over the madman, loses its authority; passion walks abroad without control, and the reluctant step of the slave is exchanged for the free and elastic movements of the mountaineer. So it is with the utterance of deep emotions; the natural expression of feeling is never vulgar, and those who deem it so, show only that they do not know what they condemn. . . .

The simple energy and truth of Crabbe will be more valued by the many, than they have been heretofore; if his intellectual vision does not, like that of the most glorious of the sons of light, comprehend all space it will be acknowledged to be keen, wide, and faithful. Shakspeare, from his watch-tower, caught every change of many-coloured life; the great volume of our nature was wide open before him; and whether he unveils the humble bosom, or describes the fierce struggles of jealousy, ambition or remorse, or the sorrow quickened into madness of the credulous old king, no one ever thought of doubting that the portraiture was real. Crabbe generally aspired to no such wide extent of observation, though, when he has attempted it, his success is complete; he saw and studied all the beings around him with no less interest and care than he perused his researches into the secrets of inanimate nature; and what he undertakes to describe, neither Scott nor Shakspeare could have painted better. His purpose is a moral one; he never aims to dazzle or to please; he conceals no defect, softens no deformity, and aims not to exaggerate a single beauty; he makes few sacrifices on the altar of fastidious taste: whoever admires him, admires him for his plain truth and manly power. . . .

59. Unsigned review, *Eclectic Review*

October 1834, xii (3rd series), 305–14

Apart from the merits of the poetry, the [*Posthumous*] *Tales* possess intrinsic interest, as the lessons of a grey and reverend Moralist, who, if wont to take a sombre view of life, was far removed from misanthropy, and moved with cheerful benevolence in the sphere of unpoetical realities, which he has compelled Poetry to recognize and record. His very benevolence served to arm his mind, and sheathe his feelings, against the painful impressions which the scenes and facts he describes are in themselves adapted to produce, and thus rendered him, perhaps, in some degree insensible of their unpleasing character. There is no reason to think that he delighted in satirizing human nature. He took the subjects as they turned up to his observation, and preferred those which presented the stronger lines and deeper shades. Like a true botanist, who bestows equal attention on the weed and the flower, and is less at home in the garden, where the very beauty is artificial, than in the lane or meadow, our Poetical Anthropologist found equal luxury in analysing and copying the most unsightly and worthless and the most lovely specimens of human nature. There is a pleasure in observation, as an exercise of the faculties, apart from that which may be derived from its results. Such pleasure Crabbe seems to have found in observing what he has so accurately delineated with the fidelity of a Teniers or a Cuyp; the love of nature, in his mind, standing in stead of the love of beauty, and the homeliest background being as pleasing to his eye as the loveliest landscape. Such was the mind, and such, accordingly, is the poetry of Crabbe.

By far the most interesting tale in the present volume is the first, which almost partakes of an autobiographical character. . . .

> Through rooms immense, and galleries wide and tall . . .
>   [I, 300–16, 510–37; and parts of Dream
>   on, dear Boy! . . . (Ward III, 534–6).]

[X, *in toto*.]

In the former volumes, there are inserted a few smaller pieces hitherto unpublished. The most interesting is a lyrical composition, entitled, 'The World of Dreams,' (in vol. iv.,) which is not unworthy of the Author of Eustace Grey, although not equal in power and beauty to that remarkable production. It has been remarked, that the present volume, if inferior in vigour to any other volume of the Author's poetry, is perhaps more amusing than any other, and displays more mild good-humour. 'A man,' said Johnson, 'grows better-humoured as he grows older.'* This depends, however, upon the qualities of the man. Age mellows some tempers, and sours others.

* See *Quarterly Review*, No. 55 above.

60. Unsigned review, *Gentleman's Magazine*

December 1834, n.s. ii, 563-75

A poet is generally followed at no very considerable distance by his servant the critic; and, as his rank and fame increases, in the same proportion is the number of his followers enlarged. Such persons as Scott and Byron had a whole clan at their heels for many years; most of them a sort of gentlemen ushers, and persons of very polite behaviour, attached to their chiefs, and anxious to point out their excellencies; while Mr. Keats, or Mr. * * * were per force contented with the small services of a single attendant. The author of the volumes before us has had his full share of critical accompaniment; and his successive volumes of Poetry have for twice ten years served as whetstones to the wit and acuteness of many clever and ambitious commentators, not only differing much from each other in their various decisions, but even from themselves;* and shifting round the vane of praise or censure, as caprice suggested, or the breath of public favour blew. Yet as Mr. Crabbe never suffered severely from the fiery darts of the wicked, which were occasionally launched at his poetical fame, so we think, on the other hand, that he was never indebted to any modern scholiast, any Aristarchus, or Servius, for the rapid and lofty elevation of his fame. He was personally unknown to the world of Literature; he had no modern patrons to supply the place of Johnson or of Burke; he had no Mæcenas in Albemarle-street, no friendly Sosius in Burlington-street. The style and subjects of his earlier Muse were not calculated to delight the fastidious saloons of the rich, to satisfy the severe taste of the learned, or to win the timid applauses of the fair; no particular favour was shown to his early attempts to mount Parnassus: he did not follow in the class of his brother bards, or, by belonging to their school, propitiate their favour.

Multa Poetarum veniet manus, auxilio quæ

* Sir Egerton Brydges has said with justice, that 'though the critical disquisitions on poetry in the leading Reviews, separately taken, are in many cases written with great talent and taste, yet it is impossible to unite them into any uniform or consistent theory. One writer forgets, and one demolishes, what the first had advanced; not to speak of the same writer changing his critical code, as his taste improves and his views enlarge.'

Sit mihi, nam multo plures sumus, ac veluti te
Judice [sic—sc. Judaei] cogemus in hanc concedere turbam.[1]

Mr. Crabbe derived no enlargement of mind, no extended reach of observation, from the diversified views of society and manners which travel affords; nor was he conversant with that deep, rich, and refined literature,—those *literæ exquisitæ et reconditæ,*—which belong to the scholar exclusively, and open to him the peculiar mysteries of antiquity, and the profound and unerring principles of art; and yet by the vigour of his talents, and his poetical genius, supported by great industry, activity, and observation, working on his materials with the patience and zeal of an artist, he won his way progressively to the possession of a reputation which few of his contemporaries have surpassed, and which no change or caprice of public taste can lower or impair. We cannot presume to say how much of the poetry of the present day will descend to posterity, and what proportion of each writer will be preserved from oblivion by the Andersons and Chalmers's of a future age.* But we may confidently assert, that if a selection is to be made by a more severe and critical generation, removed alike from *our* prejudices and partialities, from the works of our contemporaries, Mr. Crabbe's book will be seen sailing down the sacred river of Immortality, with as large and full-spread sail, and weighty cargo, as any of his rivals.† When he first put in his claim to the 'honest fame' of a poet, there were some qualities in his poetry, which were conducive to his success, while there were others that seemed for awhile to retard the progress of its growth in public favour, and repelled the enthusiastic applause which has since

* 'Posterity will hang with rapture on the *half* of Campbell,—the *fourth* part of Byron, the *sixth* of Scott, the *scattered tithes of Crabbe*, and the *three per cent.* of Southey,' &c. So said the *Edinburgh Review* in 1819; what would they say in 1834?

† Of Mr. Crabbe's early poetry, *The Village* is far superior in poetic vigour and effect to the *Library* or *Newspaper*. The cause, we conceive, is to be found in the poet's early habits of observation, his knowledge of the humble walks of life, and his interest in the occupations and scenes of the society around him; while his deficiency in book-learning in the one case, and his recluse and private life, and consequent want of familiar acquaintance with the world, in the other, rendered his two later poems comparatively flat and feeble. The 'Parish Register' was a surprising improvement on the former poems; in variety of incident, liveliness of detail, and dramatic power representing the passions, as well as in a better style of versification. *The Borough* is on the whole inferior. There is more description and reflection, and less of well-drawn character and well-arranged story. The description of the religious sects is too long; but it improves much in the latter part; and there are some well-conceived portraits, among which 'Blaney,' and the 'Parish Clerk', are conspicuous. With the latter person we are well acquainted. Old Jasper's [sic—sc. Jachin's] picture is drawn alike with fidelity and force.

1 A large group of poets will come to my aid—for we are in a great majority—and we, like the Jews, will force you to join our number. Horace, *Satires*, I, 4, 141–3.

decidedly rewarded his labours. Of the first kind must be mentioned what he derived from the subject and style of his fictitious narratives. . . . Mr. Crabbe stept in with an attempt to excite interest in themes far more humble, familiar, and domestic. The other poets were weaving their rich and florid tapestry, and embroidering their costly arras with purple colours and threads of gold; Mr. Crabbe took a plain ground-work for his subject, and spoke in 'the language of the heart.' He trusted to the fidelity of his narrative, and to the dramatic development of his passions and characters: in fact, to his sympathy with nature. He did not go to the palace of the Caliph, or the harem of the Sultan, to the land of the citron or the palm, to the den of the Greek pirate, or the seraglio of the Turkish Pasha, for subjects which were to excite interest, and kindle passion: but he sought them in the common life around him, in the cottages and hamlets of his own county and neighbourhood, in the occupations and details, the joys and distresses, the virtues and the crimes, the smiles and the tears of the humblest ranks, and the most depressed and despised society, 'men cruel, sensual, selfish, cold.' . . .

It is perhaps true, that two poets had preceded Mr. Crabbe at no great distance of time, who had as it were gradually prepared the public mind to sympathize with the familiar scenes, the humble occupations, the ordinary feelings, and the petty joys and distresses of village life;* and so far they possessed a claim to the merit of having enlarged the boundaries of the empire of poetic fiction, and restored her lost but lawful possessions; but *Cowper*, who was one to whom we allude, had a feminine tenderness of disposition, a refined and nervous temperament, and a highly excited moral and religious feeling, which would have shrunk with aversion and disgust from scenes which Crabbe dared and delighted to pourtray; and *Goldsmith* never would have possessed patience or skill to collect the rich materials, which, duly arranged and worked up, form the fine and masterly groups of Mr. Crabbe's painting. Beautiful as is the poetry of Goldsmith, and delicate and delightful the breath of that soft and pensive melancholy that harmonizes the whole, yet even in his tenderest reflections we feel that we are rather sympathizing with the poet himself, than with the subjects of his poetry; that we do not weep over distresses which we believe existed only in the poet's conception, or are at least much exaggerated in his

* In dramatic poetry, George Lillo has the claim of transferring sympathy from heroes and kings to subjects of common and familiar life, to merchants and 'prentice-boys, distressed gentlemen, and unfortunate ladies.

descriptions; that we do not join in his lamentation over the decay of a system and state of society, which could no more exist, than the golden pictures of pastoral simplicity and happiness; and through the enchanted veil of his poetry, we catch constant glimpses of the unfinished and imperfect argument behind.*

But we have said that there were also qualities connected with Mr. Crabbe's poetical system, which were at first unfavourable to its reception, and which may in some measure affect it even at the present day. We allude to his materials being so largely collected from the coarse and repulsive realities of common life, seen in its most degrading and unfavourable form; and from the fabric of his tales being formed of the unmodified passions, the wild delusions, the paltry jealousies and mean repinings, the loathsome crimes, the brutal sensuality, and the hardened selfishness of the ignorant and poor. Some readers might be repelled from scenes like these, so powerfully pourtrayed, by delicacy of taste; and some by sensitiveness of feeling. The poetic pleasure would to them be lost in the real and positive pain. How much the selection of such subjects acted against him; how mistaken his theory was called, and how misguided his judgment, some leading publications of the day, if looked back to, will clearly show. Time, however, has much softened the severity of this early judgment; and in his later volumes Mr. Crabbe has risen in his descriptions more to the middle walks of life, and has escaped from the whirlwinds of passion and crime to regions of suffering more modified and mild, to more mixed and general views of life, to more familiar subjects of interest, and a more social spirit of observation; he has found ample scope for his powers of pathos and reflection in pictures which awake universal sympathy and pity; of the blossoms of youth and beauty dropping untasted and unknown; of the sickness of the heart from hopes too long deferred; of misplaced affections, and unrequited tenderness, and unfortunate love. Though it must be allowed that there is much which to the most favourable mind will give disgust and pain, in Mr. Crabbe's *anatomical* plates of the human heart; though with a stern and unrelenting hand he has sometimes swept away all the bright creations of Fancy's loom, dispelled the magic allusions and charms which Poetry had long delighted to cast over the naked and

---

* Goldsmith lamented that in his time 'it was not as of old, when every rood of ground maintained its man'; he also enlarges on the evil and cruelty of emigration. We should like to know, under his own argument, how many men this same rood of ground would have to maintain at the present day; and as he would prohibit commerce, in what state of comfort, or with what advantages, those 'rude forefathers of the hamlet' would now be living.

repulsive realities of life, and shown in their hideous and true forms, the cruel, the cowardly, and the false;—yet there is in the vigour of his genius, in the fidelity of his representations, in the force, the fullness, the spirit of his details, in the grouping of his characters, in the weight and wisdom of his sentiments, enough to compensate for many defects; while what Mr. Wordsworth calls the great and simple affections, the elementary feelings, and the essential passions, are all at his command. One thing is certain, that the force and truth of Mr. Crabbe's delineations must be owing to the unusual keenness of his observation, and the unwearied industry of his research. Thus he collected all the minute particulars of the subjects he described, grouped every circumstance with philosophical skill, and then surrounded them with that richness of accompaniment and representation, that gave to truth and reality their fullness of effect. He is an artist perfect in his line, a painter of nature. In no instance can he be detected slurring over a part of a subject from inability to fill up the details; he is never ignorant, fantastic, or superficial. One perceives at once, that his touch is that of a person who feels himself master of his subject. One can distinguish what he draws from books, and what from nature and life; and that when he called, like Hamlet, for his tablets to inscribe his thoughts, it was not in his *study alone* that he found it meet to put down his thoughts. Look at the Pastorals of Philips or of Pope, or of any other of the wits of the day. The first thing you find is, that every thing is *false*,—false descriptions, false imagery, false thoughts, false situations; that the poet had no truth to delineate, no facts to work from, no nature to copy, no experience to direct; that there never were such people, such situations, or such scenes. Therefore all is fantastic, and inconsistent, and incongruous, all paint and varnish and tinsel. 'The shepherds are all embroidered, and acquit themselves in a ball better than our English dancing-masters. I have seen a couple of Rivers appear in red stockings, and Alpheus, instead of having his head covered with sedges and bullrushes, making love in a fair full-bottomed periwig, and a plume of feathers.' But our Suffolk poet is a very different workman. The boors of Teniers and Ostade are not more true to nature than Crabbe's fishermen and smugglers. They are the identical persons whom the poet's eye and mind saw, and whose images he reflected in his poetic mirror to his readers; while both in the painter and the poet, the particular individual described, is in fact a finely embodied abstraction of his whole class, with all his distinguishing peculiarities brought fully into view. To these poetical excellencies, Mr. Crabbe adds a dry caustic kind of humour, appearing Proteus-like in the different forms of a gibe or a pun, (sometimes badly out of place! '*Punica* se quantis attollit gloria *rebus*!'[1]) or sly and pointed raillery and ridicule: and when he pleases—alas! far too seldom—he can rise to strains exquisitely touching and refined; he can sweep the strings of the lyre with a master's hand, and pour forth verses as tender and as graceful as the lost Simonides. Of his versification, it is seldom 'of a higher mood.' It is not formed on any refined principles of art, nor modelled after any eminent authority, but it is germane to the matter; it is pitched in a key that harmonizes with the subject, and sufficiently good to satisfy the taste. Many verses filled with sense and observation, are condensed into close expression, vigorous and sinewy in their structure, yet natural and harmonious. Sometimes he approaches the easy and negligent graces of Goldsmith, sometimes affects the smart conciseness and pregnant brevity of Pope, and sometimes the intentional ruggedness of Cowper. Occasionally, his lines are slovenly, inharmonious, and tame, with unpardonable elisions, quaint expressions, and defective rhymes; while very seldom does Mr. Crabbe delight us with specimens of that fine musical rhythm, those enchanting cadences, that flowing melody, those graceful idioms, and those exquisite touches of finished elegance, which we meet with in our best poets, from Dryden to Rogers. Still, in his least successful parts, there is nothing false, tawdry, or affected; no Della Crusca ornaments or gilding, or frippery; no second-hand thoughts, no indistinct images, and vague dreaming words. We may blame his negligence, and sometimes dislike his vulgarity; but we confess his truth and power. When he speaks, we feel it is Nature herself, who

————effert animi motus, interprete linguâ.[2]

But in this very truth and absolute fidelity of imitation, so distinguishable in Mr. Crabbe's poetry, may be found perhaps the cause why its merit has not gained universal consent. The world which he describes, is a world to the higher ranks of society, we grieve to say, almost unknown. The squalid habits of the poor, the abodes of want, profligacy, and disease; the petty arts of the mean, and the shuffling stratagems of the cunning; the severe denials, and unrelenting parsimony of the needy; the boisterous joys and disgusting carousals of the 'rude waissailers;' the hopes and fears, the plans and employments and occupations of com-

1 With what great things shall Punic glory be upheld! *Aeneid*, IV, 49.
2 With the tongue as interpreter she utters the emotions of the soul. Horace, *Ars Poetica*, III.

mon life are things which seldom fall within the scope of their observation, or become familiar subjects of meditation. To those whose eyes have been used to glide along the fine and delicate threads of polished life, all below is coarse, repulsive, and disagreeable; their sympathies have seldom been turned into that channel. Now we are quite sure that, without descending into the sordid details of the poor-house, or roadside tavern, or the hospital, or absolutely mixing with the 'fæces Romuli,' the more we partake of Mr. Crabbe's intimate knowledge of the people whom he described, the more strongly we shall appreciate the force and truth of his delineations, and feel the spirit of his tragic pencil; and as a philosophical critic says, that to understand Sophocles, we must study him beside the statues of Laocoon and Niobe; so we say, to do justice to Mr. Crabbe, and to receive due delight ourselves, we must not refuse to possess some acquaintance with the neglected and forlorn community which he describes. . . .

The first poem we meet with is called 'Silford Hall, or The Happy Day.' It is supposed to be suggested by the Poet's recollection of his own boyish visits, when the apprentice of an apothecary, to Cheveley. There is no attempt in it to move the passions, and no extraordinary incidents to arouse the curiosity. The merit of the piece is in the truth and reality of the description, in the happy combination of incidents, in the elegance of the reflections, and in the harmonious effect produced by the succession of various gentle feelings and pleasing impressions; in short, in the elegance of the execution. A poem consisting of such materials, affords delight by the very tranquillity and repose of the subject. . . .

> The matron kindly to the boy replied, . . .
> [I, 345–66]

The next story, 'The Family of Love,' is in Mr. Crabbe's best style . . .

> Dear Captain Elliot, how your friends you read! . . .
> [II, 762–804]

'The Equal Marriage' is clear and spirited, and the mutual reproaches of the disenchanted pair, as soon as the veil of the imagination has been torn away, and the false fires of a foolish love extinguished, are truly imagined and described.

> Still they can speak—and 'tis some comfort still, . . .
> [III, 235–74, 294–301]

The tale of Rachael possesses no novelty of incident. 'It's an old tale, and often told,' of an absent lover and a faithful mistress; but the description of the effect of the sudden appearance and as sudden departure of the lover, after a long absence, on a mind broken, wearied, and misled, is finely painted, and the following lines are unsurpassed for their melancholy truth and beauty:

> He tried to sooth her, but retired afraid . . .
> [IV, 147–51]

Parts of the story of 'Villars' are good in the execution, but it is not an agreeable picture; and we think that neither the morality, the delicacy, nor the feeling of the author, would approve or applaud a husband who takes to his bosom a wife who had been living in adulterous estrangement, and who at last is forcibly and unwillingly separated from her guilty paramour. This is not the only tale in Mr. Crabbe's works, where a false humanity triumphs over all honour, and a sense of justice connected with every pure and tender emotion, and virtuous principle, and honourable feeling. It may do very well in a German play, but we did not expect to find it in Mr. Crabbe's poems. The guilt is unfortunately such, as nothing on earth can expiate without lowering the moral purity of the feeling that pardons. Forgiveness must be sought elsewhere, and may be obtained; but here, to use the words of Young,

> If I forgive, the world will call me kind:
> If I receive her in my arms again,
> The world will call me very—very kind.
> [*The Revenge*, Act IV (misquoted)]

The 'Ancient Mansion' is well described, the accompaniments judiciously chosen, and the description conveyed in some of Mr. Crabbe's best versification. We can only afford room for the latter part.

> Here I behold no puny works of art
> [X, 67–99]

In the 'Wife and the Widow,' the concluding verses are neatly and forcibly expressed, as is also the character of the frivolous and foolish Belinda Waters, who after coquetting long, at last marries a poor surgeon's mate, and suffers accordingly.

> She *wonders* much—as why they live so ill, . . .
> [XV, 99–111]

'Danvers and Rayner' is a good story of a purse-proud parvenu; and the disenchantment of the lover at the end, is told with humour, though it is too long for us to give. 'Master William, or Lad's Love,' is of the same kind, where a quixotic and romantic youth falls in love with the gardener's niece; and his fancy invests her with such perfections as to make him even hesitate in venturing to declare his love. The dream is sadly broken in pieces by a sudden disclosure, abruptly made, that she is going to be married to the *Footman*.

> Who takes her arm? and oh! what villain dares . . .
>
> [XIX, 194–215]

'The Will' is excellent, natural in its design, and well finished in its detail, but perhaps falling off a little towards the end; and the story of 'The Cousins' admirably delineates the unsuspecting and disinterested feelings of a young woman, and her all-confiding lover; and the cold . calculating selfishness, duplicity, and hardheartedness of a treacherous worldy-minded man.

And thus at length we are arrived at the end of this pleasing and clever volume, which the editors judged rightly in giving to the public. Of Mr. Crabbe's former fame it has in no manner impaired the lustre; while to the public it has afforded a few more hours of innocent gratification. If compared to his former productions, a critical and curious eye may perhaps detect in some cases a feebleness of execution, and an incompleteness of design:—may find the colouring of a fainter hue, and some few of the tales deficient in power and spirit—but we cannot see that the best of them are at all below the level of Mr. Crabbe's general power of writing. We have not, it is true, those tempestuous descriptions of his earlier scenes; the terrific and heart-rending descriptions that are to be found in Ellen Orford, or in that half-dæmon and half-brute Peter Grimes, or in the Prisons; but in these perhaps the tragic distress has not been sufficiently softened and subdued by the ideal and poetical, which ought always to maintain their elevated dominion over the violence of passion, while the reason and the taste are to be satisfied even among the most engrossing and painful impressions. We have alluded to those earlier paintings by our great artist, of debased humanity, where the whole soul has become diseased by crime; the moral nature disappeared in dark perspective behind the savage and sensual; and where the gloom and blackness that brooded over it, were only occasionally broken through by the electric fires of the unhallowed and ungovernable will. There are, too, the not less affecting scenes of a heart withering away in an uncongenial atmosphere, and in defenceless misery; where a long and fatal sorrow, grown up from early emotions, and youthful feelings, and modest and delicate desires, is first seen by a few sunny tears and tender alarms, and timid hopes; afterwards in patient resignation, and silent suffering, and virgin pride; then, as blow followed blow, and a fresh tide of calamity rushed in e'er the former had ebbed away, the progress of misery is beheld gradually increasing in power, and growing sterner in feature, unfortunately mastering all other passions and feelings, till it gains entire possession of every faculty, banishing even hope itself, and making its habitation the receptacle of thoughts and images more forlorn and fearful than the grave. There is a life, alas!—thrice happy they who know not of it—that is said to resemble one single—one endless sigh!

Such were the masterly productions of Mr. Crabbe's muse, in the fulness of his strength, and when his genius was in its meridian power and heat. The present Tales belong rather to the subdued and chastened fancy which shed a mild gleam on the evening of his poetical life. They hold, as it were, a middle place between the deeply tragic and the ludicrous; serious some, some pathetic, and some almost conversational and familiar. Yet they exhibit the same knowledge of the human heart; the same profound view—'of the life of nature and her mysterious springs,' —the inconsistencies of disappointed passion, and the wanderings of a misguided and distressed mind; the same picturesque situations; the same power of collecting all the impressions in one focus to bear with the greatest effect; the same fine harmonies and contrasts, colours delicate or strong, allusions playful or pathetic, grave or gay; the same discrimination and selection of facts, images and illustrations; with the same occasional superfluity of detail, weakness of expression, and tameness of versification.

61. William Empson, unsigned review, *Edinburgh Review*

January 1835, lx, 255–96

Empson (1791–1852) was a regular contributor to the *Edinburgh Review* from 1823, becoming editor in 1847.

Next to the life, the substantial novelty of the present edition is the posthumous poems. They will, of course, be more or less attractive, according as the poetry of Crabbe is more or less popular in itself; and according to the relative degree of merit subsisting between the new productions and the old. In our opinion, there can be no manner of doubt (nor have we heard a doubt any where expressed) but that the new poems are decidedly inferior. The other question—the nature and degree of Crabbe's popularity as a poet—is a simple question of fact. It is one, at the same time, on which a great body of conflicting evidence is much in the way of all who like only positive opinions. Thus much, however, is plain. In case it should turn out that Crabbe is not the favourite poet of his age, this certainly will not have happened from any want of a clear stage and some favour.

. . . The two gentlemen who negotiated with Mr. Murray on the part of Crabbe, both (we are told) what is called 'exquisite judges of literary merit,' have been found at issue with the purchasers of poetry; and the discovery of the real 'state of public taste at that moment,' has unfortunately been made at Mr. Murray's expense. A wide discrepance of taste and evidence, on a question of this kind, is a fact no less curious than desirable to have explained. We believe Mr. Moore to be correct in his view of the public taste. Our only doubt is, on the propriety of his limiting the reproach of a want of taste in this respect to the public of any particular moment. If the copyright, which was bought for £3000, was bought at two-thirds above its market value, there have been few purchasers, only because as yet there have been but few readers. Why have there been few readers? and what are the signs that

345

the number is increasing? In these matters, we feel a reasonable jealousy of appeals to posterity from the present age; and are desirous first of knowing what is the principle upon which a literary reaction, on the part of a penitent or enlightened future, is expected to proceed. Mr. Elliott says that Crabbe is thought unnatural in America. According to his hypothesis, the Americans are not sufficiently acquainted with the miseries of English society to duly appreciate the fidelity of the descriptions. As to that, let him look at the great towns and the banks of the Mississippi, and let him ask Mr. Owen, Dr. Tuckerman, or any of the Howards of the United States. But the battle for subsistence is not man's worst or only trial; and a small part of the drop of vitriol which Crabbe delights to let fall into his Castalian fountain, arises from want of bread. A difference in the physical or political condition of their respective populations, cannot account for a different estimate of Crabbe's poetry in the two countries. But, in fact, we doubt exceedingly whether the supposed difference of estimate exists. On the contrary, Mr. Croker concurs with Mr. Moore in the opinion, that his works have not obtained at home so extensive, or at least so brilliant a reputation as those of some of his contemporaries. For this Mr. Croker proceeds to assign certain reasons; and in the precise degree that they may chance to be the true ones, the less probability is there that posterity will reverse the present verdict. It was anticipated, on a former occasion, in this Journal, that the growth of the middle classes would increase the proportion of Crabbe's admirers. For, in those classes, it was supposed, that his warmest admirers would be found, in consequence of the associations which naturally existed between his subjects and themselves. But if it be true that his poetry has never acquired the degree of popularity to which it was otherwise entitled, because he has 'taken a view of life too minute, too humiliating, too painful, and too just,' what is the final result for which we ought in reality to be prepared? These are the words of Mr. Croker. The objection, thus re-stated, is identically the same which was anticipated long ago by Scott of Amwell. In direct contradiction to the supposition of Mr. Elliott, that where Crabbe has not succeeded, it is from an incapacity on the part of the reader to appreciate his truth—the present objection assumes that his comparative failure even at home has arisen from his being too painful and too true. When Mr. Croker expects that he will nevertheless stand higher with posterity, the grounds of that expectation ought to have been explained. Future antiquarians may put an additional value on him for their own purposes. The objection appears otherwise as permanent as human nature. Representations of pain, both physical and moral, require to be ennobled before they can become the materials of enjoyment. Even then they are a source of pleasure sufficiently mysterious. Pictures of martyrdom and mortifications do not bear a price in proportion to their merit as pictures. The crowd in a gallery look another way. Children, it is true, may be pleased in Crabbe with the perfect imitation of all that they understand. Quakers may be captivated by the downright plainness and perspicuity of the moral. Artists and connoisseurs may go further. They will admire in these poems the clear and microscopic observation of ordinary existence, delineated, as it is, with the marvellous exactness of Miss Austin's [sic] novels, and carried into a variety of regions where she durst never venture. There are certain minds also of such a powerful texture, as to relish the realities of life in their most pungent forms;— whom the cellar and the garret, the dissecting-room and the guillotine, feed with the excitement that they love. For them, the nearer a hard and coarse reality is approached by a vivid fiction, so much the better. Crabbe may command these several classes; and with them of course the happy few who love the Muses under every form. Yet, nevertheless, it may be true, that Crabbe shall not have communicated to the greater portion of the readers of poetry, that specific gratification which they expect to find there, and without which no author can be universally and permanently read.

Mr. Gifford was originally one of Crabbe's severest judges; observing that he sinned on principle, 'removing the checks of fancy and taste from poetry.' The poet replied, that he had no theory of poetical composition; that he professed to paint *man as he is*; that, whatever effect poetry could produce might be produced, as he conceived, by the poetry which transcribed real events and characters, as well as where invention stood aloof, at the distance of two or three removes from fact; that any difference in the happiness of their effects between these two methods, would depend upon the manner in which the poem itself was conducted; and that nothing could be more ridiculous than a definition of poetry, which would end by excluding Pope. To all this, thus generalized, we quite agree. But when it is added, that the magic of this species of literature consists in its transporting us from the objects which surround us—it is evident that this is only part of the case, the negative part; no more than what it possesses in common with the sciences, and with every thing strong enough to lay hold of the attention. The positive part remains to be disposed of. This introduces the important consideration—what are the other objects which, when you remove the present from out of our immediate sight, you proceed to substitute in their room? A person will gain but little, if the new objects to which the poet carries him are quite as painful as the cares which he has left at home, and from which he was seeking to escape. A mistake on this point is something more than a difference in the manner of conducting the poem. Crabbe lays it down, that all that is necessary in these substituted objects is, that they be capable of being contemplated 'with some degree of interest and satisfaction.' Whatever 'pleasant effect' is produced upon a reader by transporting him out of himself, may be obtained (he says) 'by a fair representation of existing character, nay, by a faithful delineation of the painful realities, the everyday concerns, and vexations of actual existence, provided they be not the very concerns and distresses of the reader.'[1] This sounds to us, notwithstanding his disclaimer, something very like a theory. It introduces us to subjects and to a spirit so new in poetry, that, independent of all the quaint and vigorous peculiarities of his style, its author necessarily became the most original writer of his age. Other writers had taken far darker views of human nature and human life, but at the same time kept comparatively clear of the objections against Crabbe; for nobody can complain that he is not indulgent to our weaknesses; jocular in and out of season; or that he does not love the jingle of a conceit, as well as any rhyming predecessor, who 'for a tricksy word defied the matter.' He has none of the gloom of Young, the pensiveness of Goldsmith, the Calvinism of Cowper, or the misanthropy of Byron. The difference is, that, by adopting a higher tone, they became, whenever they succeeded, touching or sublime; whereas his principle of versifying for the most part the concerns and vexations of his neighbour's house, made it a thousand to one but that so much of what was homely and disagreeable got into his descriptions, as seriously to damage their popular effect. The experiment, how far poetry may be made to speak the truth, the whole truth, and nothing but the truth, was never so extensively made before. His readers at once admit that he has spoken the truth, and nothing but the truth. Relying on observation, and not on inspiration, he was so far faithful to nature, as to step neither beyond it nor above it. But the whole truth is what, in comparison, he very seldom tries to speak. He seldom speaks the higher truths belonging to the more aspiring part of our nature. And this he acknowledges, when he admits that, being 'to satire prone,' he chiefly confined himself to those cases which were most capable of being satirically exposed:

[1] See above No. 30, p. 153.

My muse, which calmly looks around, nor more,
Muse of the mad, the foolish, and the poor.
[*Tales of the Hall*, VI, 23–4 (original reading)—see Ward, II, 489.]

His imagination and his feelings stood him in marvellous little stead. As an Englishman, living in perilous times, he tried heroic subjects. In compliment to his profession, (for, in one of his prefaces, he volunteers a superfluous and scarcely sincere apology,) he tried religious ones. Out of obedience to his critics, he tried plots of greater variety and connexion. All equally in vain. Considering the efforts he made to extend his sphere of power, he is a most eminent instance either of the strength of first associations, or of a singular correspondence between native capacity and early opportunities. It is impossible to say which. He lived to know the mountains and the world; but he preferred his Fen-Flora and village life; and to the last, Suffolk scenery and Aldborough manners maintained almost exclusive possession of the genius of Crabbe.

If the posthumous poems of Crabbe were as good as what were published in his lifetime, they could have merely sustained his popularity at the point which it had attained. But they are not as good. The new poems consist of three classes, of unequal interest and merit. The first are sundry juvenile attempts, saved either by accidents or design from the conflagrations of condemned manuscripts, which the editor has recorded. The insignificance of these early prolusions excuses the neglect with which they were originally received, whether by the public generally, or by the individuals to whom they were privately addressed. . . .

The second class in the posthumous poems consists of a collection of occasional verses from all quarters. The poet seems (looking at their quality) to have paid in the greater part of these contributions, much in the same humour that a conscript joins his regiment. We cannot suppose that he ever dreamed of their publication. Among the minor poems not before published, those every way the least worthy of his talents are his compliments to fine ladies. Crabbe never spoke a truer word than when he said, that the language of panegyric did not sit well on him. The Duchess of Rutland and Lady Jersey do not owe him much for common place adulation below the average of Album poetry. Among his spontaneous productions, 'The World of Dreams' recalls 'Sir Eustace Grey' by a higher affinity than that of its measure. But none of these smaller pieces are more striking than two little amatory elegiacs,[1]

[1] 'The Friend in Love', and 'Wilt thou never smile again'.

349

evidently written under one of those mortifications to which the sexagenarian admirer of beauty is exposed. Personal excitement restored to the old man on these occasions the lyrical spirit which descended on him so sparingly, yet so powerfully, in his better days. . . .

The last and most important addition to his poetry—the posthumous tales—is comprised in the last volume. These, reckoning in a stray one, called 'Flirtation,' and which, though clever, is coarse enough for poetical justice to have given its heroine a harder name, are twenty-three in number. Crabbe had prepared them, put them by, and bequeathed them for publication. On this point, therefore, the editors had little discretion left. They are fully aware that their father greatly erred in supposing that they are much like his former tales in execution. The execution is almost every thing in a Flemish picture; and the difference between the two cases in the present instance, is the difference between the finish of Teniers and of Ostade. Something must be allowed for declining years—something for the confidence of success, and for his indifference to the sentence of reviewers, when he should be himself quietly at rest in the chancel of Trowbridge Church. The presence, however, of some of his literary advisers is what he has wanted most. The Aldborough gossip, that Burke and Johnson had so cobbled the early manuscripts that their author did not know them again, is an amusing example of the spiteful exaggeration that follows poets, as well as prophets, in their own country. Crabbe, however, who professed to recognize the ascendency of his friends, was, in truth, wonderfully docile for an author; and we may be certain, that neither his earlier nor his later domestic critics would have permitted these stories to have gone to sleep in their recess, on the faith of their having received the author's last corrections. Crabbe suggests, that the new series will be found sufficiently different from the former ones in events and characters, to have the attraction of novelty. In this also, we think, he is mistaken. He saw himself a successive gradation in his other writings, beyond what his readers have been generally aware of. One uniform tone of narrative and reflection contributed to conceal from the public the fact, that the characters in the 'Parish Register' belonged to the lower orders; those in *The Borough* (which is, in truth, Aldborough, only Aldborough magnified) to the middle ranks of society; and those in the *Tales of the Hall* to a still superior class of cultivated minds and habits. A passage or two in the latter 'London Journal' had led us to anticipate the introduction of a new caste of *dramatis personæ* on his scene. But they are all from the same familiar chronicle as before. The same spirit also has presided over their fate. Of the stories contained in the new series, seventeen form the history of a town, as set forth in the 'Farewell and Return.' The plot is simple enough. A young man takes leave of his native place, and comes back, to look up his old acquaintance, after an absence of twenty years. The interest of each story turns upon the sudden juxtaposition of the two periods. It is the contrast between the rising and setting sun. 'Now look upon this picture, and on that!' Alas for human life, if Crabbe is to tell its fortune! He can afford but two pleasant changes out of all the alternations which he has prepared for 'the Return.' A wretched, or (what is worse for the purposes of poetry) an uncomfortable catastrophe hangs over the rest. Crabbe claims for himself that he paints '*man as he is.*' In this case, he surely has not been lucky in the scene of his observations. The fair proportion of good luck is surely considerably more than what is here allowed us. A false representation in literature of the average virtue or happiness of life, is not necessarily, as we have seen it called by writers who praise Crabbe for his truth, false morality. Provided that the distinction between vice and virtue, and between the natural consequences of both, is not mystified or denied, the cause of morality will not suffer from any such exaggerations, whether on the favourable or unfavourable side of the account, as a reasonable person is likely to commit. Violent extremes either way—*optimism or pessimism*—besides being absurd, must be pernicious. But, to a certain extent, a habit of looking at the bright side of every thing is far from being a fault or weakness. On the contrary, a little optical delusion of this kind is a habit of sufficient moral importance to make it worth the while, both of individuals and of society, to countenance and confirm it. The general question, however, which we have above examined, and to which the contents of his last volume force us for a moment to recur, is not whether 'Nature's sternest painter is the best,'—by best, meaning either the truest or the most moral. It is an easier point which criticism and experiment have to settle—simply, whether the sternest painter is likely to be the most popular. If our view of them is correct, the posthumous tales are exposed to the same steady and silent opposition as their predecessors have sustained. They are likely, too, to make a less vigorous resistance, as they have less merit of other kinds to compensate for their defects. The strong enchantment of immortal harmony is wanting, which might carry away the reader, as the music and excitement of a battle keep the soldier insensible to his wounds. Poetry and painting, before they can affect mankind at large, in the manner that many of Crabbe's admirers have expected and still insist that mankind ought to be affected by him, must appeal to a higher nature than the average condition of ordinary life. The sense of this necessity has been, of olden time, the secret of the sublime and beautiful. Thence the name, the *belle arti*. There are general admirers, to whom no sort of poetry comes amiss—whose universal power of association and of sympathy makes them delighted and at home with Coleridge as well as Crabbe, and every intermediate son of song. But the poetical associations of most minds are much more limited. The poetry, which depends for its principal effect upon accurate descriptions of familiar life, risks being generally regarded pretty much as Crabbe himself regards the unheroic friendships of modern days.

> Yes! there are sober friendships, made for use, . . .
> [XVII, 41-6]

In case the descriptive artist takes a pleasure in giving pain, by recalling subjects which disgust and annoy, mortify and depress, his descent in his art is something worse than a degeneracy from festival apparel down to good and useful clothing. Ordinary people will as soon think of walking out in a hair-shirt, as of seeking for his company.

We have not space for any analysis of the several stories comprised in the new series. That of 'Villiers' [i.e. 'Villars'] is perhaps the most striking. Some of them are amusing as stories, and almost all of them contain examples of his epigrammatic surveillance of ordinary life, and of his humorous or caustic verses.

Wilkie, Leslie, and Allen are said to be designing from Crabbe. They should leave the following sketch (it occurs in the fearful story of the Dealer and Clerk) for Landseer:—

> There watch'd a cur before the miser's gate, . . .
> [XVI, 171-91]

Gentlemen, who are wanting a wife, and are in danger of falling captive in the doll line, will do well to look at the case of 'Belinda Waters;' one of the pretty misses of idle civilization,—lovely, useless, and at her very best, only negatively good:

> Of food she knows but this, that we are fed:— . . .
> [XV, 26-9, 99-105, 118-25]

Crabbe has, however, no great confidence in male discretion. In the common alternative of wives—the ornamental or the useful—the

Helen of Homer or the Helen of Miss Edgeworth; or say (that model of work-a-day virtue) Jeannie Deans—a lover is certain, he thinks, to prefer the worst. Left to repent at leisure, he will never have long to wait. For, according to Crabbe's theory of life, the ordeal of afflictions always is at hand. 'The Wife and Widow' is the account of a most excellent and exemplary woman—closing with an interrogatory, whether men are duly sensible of so much strong but simple merit.

> No! ask of man the fair one whom he loves, . . .
> [XVI, 130–69]

The story of 'Rayner,' a *nouveau riche*, who moves off to a place left him by a relation, contains a pithy and comic notice of the embarrassment attending the ambiguous nomenclature of our ornamental times:

> Now, lo! the Rayners all at Hulver Place— . . .
> [XVII, 199–202]

The following sketch in 'The Cousins,' of the quietness of a sick chamber is perfect; you can hear a pin drop, and see the parties. It looks to be sure, more like a view taken by the attorney than by the divine:—

> The uncle now to his last bed confined, . . .
> [XXI, 193–200]

Crabbe has, in these *Tales*, repeated himself a little in some of his events and characters. 'The Equal Marriage' too nearly resembles 'Henry and Emma,' and is far inferior. 'The Alms-house Merchant' is part and parcel of our old acquaintance in *The Borough*. . . .

62. Unsigned review, *New York Review*

March 1837, i, 96–109

Amidst the diversity and ceaseless change of opinion with respect to most modern poets, it is pleasing to turn to one whose merits have constantly been admitted. While others have risen and fallen with the varying scale of popular taste, Crabbe preserved one consistent character for excellence, neither elevated, nor depressed by any transient burst of excitement. The reader who approaches his works has no false veil of prejudice to remove before he can enter upon their enjoyment. . . .

There is a popular idea that our author deals only in the severer traits of nature; that he is ever groping in poor houses and dungeons, among the vicious and unfortunate; that his pages abound with harshness and gloom; that he pictures only the *penseroso* of life in its most repulsive aspect.—This is not the character of the great poet of actual life. He has been more just to nature. In his moral anatomy of society, he has laid bare many errors and misfortunes of the species. He has painted life as it came before him, and never violated truth for sickly sentiment. He has drawn a portion of society—the village poor—as they truly exist. But he has found too 'the soul of goodness in things evil.'—The tares and wheat of this world spring up together, and in whatever rank of men there must be much good. No one observes this truth more than our poet; and in his darkest pictures we have gleams of the kindliest virtues. The severity of Crabbe's muse consists in the faithful portraiture of nature. If man is not always happy, it is not the poet's fault. There is too much of sober reality in life to make the picture other than it is. This Crabbe knows, for he writes of scenes under his own observation. He lived amidst the people he describes, felt their little occasional joys, and saddened over their many misfortunes. But in the gloomiest character he never 'oversteps the modesty of nature.' He does not accumulate horrors for effect. He has no extravagant and unnatural heroes pouring forth their morbid sentiment in his pages. There is no sickly affectation, but a pure and healthy portrait of life—of life it may be in its unhappiest, but in its least artificial development, where society has done little to alter its rough uneducated tones, where the actual feelings and passions of man may be traced at every footstep.

In our analysis of the poetry of Crabbe, we would first notice his *originality*. He struck out for himself a new walk in literature. Other poets had dwelt in fiction, and spoken the language of imagination. They had reviewed the relations of society, and mastered life in its general aspect. From their retirement they had watched the characters of men and moralized over their foibles. Their round of observation had at length grown familiar, and in fact seemed destined for ever to copy the same features, and repeat the same sentiments. If they at times extended their view from the court and town, to the scenes of the country, it was to clothe the inhabitants in the imaginary simplicity of shepherds and shepherdesses as innocent and simple, and quite as characterless as their flocks. The conventional qualities of Damons, Strephons, and Chloes had been stereotyped in verse, till the reader was wearied with the repetition. Crabbe was the first to break this chain of studied refinements. He turned the waters of poetry from the worn-out ground of letters to the fresh and uncultivated soil. Long before the Lake school appeared, he had taught the world poetry might descend to the philosophy of common life, might enter into the sympathies and hopes of man, might be familiar with his most ordinary emotions without losing the least of its lofty energy. He was the first poet of the poor. He first carried the light of poetry into the rude cabin of the villager, and re corded the humble history of poverty. No other author, ancient or modern, can supply the peculiar place of Crabbe. He stands distinct from every other class of writers.

A chief element of the interest of our author lies in the *spirit of humanity* breathed through his verse.—In the fine phrase of Shakspeare 'all his senses have but human conditions.'[1] He loves man purely as man. He suffers no prejudice to divert his philanthropy. He has the true feeling of sympathy for life. We constantly meet with traits of unmingled charity in his writings. He recognizes the humblest joys and sorrows of existence. With such passages as the following, we wonder that he could ever be thought only stern and forbidding. It is highly characteristic of his kindly feeling for all that conduces to virtuous happiness, however lowly. He is describing a village scene in *The Parish Register*.

> Here on a Sunday eve, when service ends . . .
> [I, 152–65]

Let no one complain of Crabbe's severity and gloom. With the first power as a moral poet, his nature is never satiric. We may believe him

[1] *Henry V*, IV, i.

when in one of his occasional pieces he says:

> I love not the satiric Muse:
> No man on earth would I abuse;
> Nor with empoison'd verses grieve
> The most offending son of Eve.—

Crabbe's forte is *description*. He excels in drawing the *minutiæ* of the picture. He does not depend for success on a few great outlines, but on repeated touches. He particularizes every feature till we have the whole scene vividly before us. He brings the subject fully out upon the canvas. Every circumstance tells.—As in the paintings of Wilkie, nothing is neglected. The sketch of the parish poor-house in *The Village*, is a well known example. As a more incidental instance of this power of picturesque illustration, there is a brief narrative of a baptism which occurs in *The Parish Register*.

> Her boy was born—no lads nor lasses came . . .
> [I, 373–82]

The latter portion of this passage is in the spirit of Gray, and we are closely reminded of a line in the *Elegy*, where is described so vividly,

> The swallow twittering on the straw-built shed;
> [line 18]

but Crabbe has connected the inanimate picture with living nature by the contrast in his verse.

It is time that we should approach one of the higher qualities of our poet. He is a powerful master of *pathos*. Gifford, alluding to a portion of *The Borough*, remarks, 'Longinus somewhere mentions, that it was a question among the critics of his age, whether the sublime could be produced by tenderness. If this question had not been already determined, this history would have gone far to bring it to a decision.' The praise is just. It is a simple tale of real life. A village maiden is betrothed to her lover. Prudence deters them from marriage, till he had gained a competence from the sea. He makes one voyage more for the last, but before he returned, disease had seized upon his constitution, and he reaches home—to die.

> Still long she nursed him: tender thoughts meantime . . .
> [*The Borough*, II, 222–63]

With all true poets, Crabbe is not merely a moral, but a *religious* author. For poets at the present day to omit this grand feature of man and his relations, in that view of his character and principles which poetry must embody, is to struggle against the whole sense of truth, and, apart from the want of piety, must betray the awkwardness of an imperfect work. All great poems have been based upon the national faith; from Homer and the Athenian tragedies, to Milton, and latest of all, Wordsworth, religion has formed the groundwork of genuine poetry. There may be light and frivolous verse, but *unhallowed poetry* is a contradiction in terms. There is something cold and heartless in that portrait of life, which omits its most important feature—its relation to eternity. The very happiness of such a pictures is unsatisfying; but its sorrow, unalleviated by hope, is cheerless indeed. There is a cruel mockery in exposing the woes and sufferings of life, without the antidote to the baneful misery; in conducting weary existence to its close, without a joy in this world or a hope for the next. No such barren moralist is Crabbe. Virtue may be unrewarded here, but it will be recompensed hereafter; and we are directed to the consolation. Religion is never obtruded on the attention, but its hallowed influence is constantly experienced. The history of Isaac Ashford may illustrate our remarks. It is in Crabbe's best manner.

> Next to these ladies, but in naught allied . . .
> [*The Parish Register*, III, 413–68; 487–502]

It has been objected against Crabbe that he has modelled himself after Pope; and he has been considered by some—ignorant of the true character of his writings—but a mere imitator. Horace Smith has favored this injustice by a note to the *Rejected Addresses*,[1] where, merely for the sake of the point, Crabbe is characterized as 'Pope in worsted stockings.' It is not the first instance in which truth has been sacrificed to a witticism. No intelligent reader of their poetry can confound the different merits of Pope and Crabbe. They belong to independent schools. The excellence of one consists in the perfection of the Artificial, the merit of the other lies in the purer love of the Natural. Pope reflects the nice shades of a court life, and adapts himself to the polished society around him. He lives among lords and ladies. He penetrates beneath the surface of character, but it is within the circle of a court, and after a classical model. Out of Queen Anne's reign he would have been nothing. We can form no idea of him removed from the wits and gentlemen of his day. He is a master of elegance, and has power as a satirist; can dilate upon the virtues of Atticus, or heighten the crimes of

[1] See No. 39 above.

Atossa. He can follow where one has gone before. He can revive the felicity of Horace, or the vehemence of Juvenal. Out of the track of the artificial, the conventional, he is nothing; within it he reigns supreme. Crabbe is of another order. He has no model to copy after. He throws himself upon a subject that derives no aid from romance or classic association. He paints the least popular part of society. He has to overcome a powerful prejudice against his characters. He suggests where art can avail him little; where his whole success must depend upon nature. His personages have nothing in them to please the taste, or enlist the fancy of the polished. They come before us at every disadvantage. They are out of the pale of good society. They have no relish of high life to add interest to their virtues, or throw a softening shadow over their crimes. They do not belong to the court standard. According to Touchstone's scale they would infallibly be condemned 'If thou never wast at court, thou art in a parlous state, shepherd!' But they have something in their composition prior to and independent of this artificial excitement. They are vigorous specimens of human nature in its elementary traits, and have their whole charm in being simply men. They interest us as they feel and suffer, as they truly exist in themselves, not as they act in an outward pageant. They have the feelings and passions of the species, and their example comes home to our own breasts. It is in this respect that 'one touch of Nature makes the whole world kin.' The Artificial must be content with admiration; the Natural claims our sympathy. This is the distinction. Pope tickles the sense with fine periods, or gains the fancy by a sparkling picture, while Crabbe leaves an impression on the heart. There may not be a single line to be quoted for its brilliancy, like a finished couplet of Pope, but the passage from our author shall convey a force and reality, the bard of Twickenham—were he twice the master of art he is—could never attain.

A word of *apology* for the poetry of Crabbe is hardly needed. Time was when this might be necessary, but a returning sense of justice is rapidly coming over the age, and the world is fast acknowledging that the relations of life, however simple, afford a true ground of poetry. It is pleasing to remark this change in favor of sound taste. Wordsworth, but lately neglected, begins to receive his due honors. He is no longer laughed at for his childishness. This is a triumph of humanity; for it permits the poor and humble as well as the great to feel they too have emotions and sympathies worthy of poesy; that their simple hopes may also be 'married to immortal verse.' If we have taught a man self-respect, we have led him to the path of virtue. When he feels that his existence, however unobtruded upon the world, is an object of sacred regard to the poet, he must think more nobly of himself and live more wisely. The age is made better by such works as *The Lyrical Ballads*, and *The Borough*. Question not their claim to poetry. The denial is not founded on a proper understanding of the art. Poetry is born not only of the lofty and the imaginative, but of the simple and pathetic. The attendant of human feelings and human passions, it exists alike for the means and the extremes of life. Wherever man is separated from the gross earth beneath him, and connected by any link with the vast and beautiful above him; wherever there exists an image of a greater good than the conditions of sense offer; wherever the limited, intellectual and moral part of our nature sighs after the great and the perfect; wherever any of the mysterious links of the chain binding together the present with the untried future, are visible,—there, in their just degree live the nature and spirit of poetry. 'Soaring in the high region of its fancies,' it may approach 'the azure throne, the sapphire blaze.' It may be 'choir-ing to the young-eyed cherubim,' and it may sing of 'the humblest flower that decks the mead,' or speak of the smallest hope that breaks the darkness of the least educated. It is not to be limited in its applica-tion. It is not built on learning, or founded on the canons of the critic. It is itself the foundation of all just critical laws. Its fresh source is in the human heart; its province is in the wide map of human relations; it is bounded only by the horizon of human emotion; its heritage is the race of man,—and its task-work is to connect and blend the sentiment of the true, the good, the beautiful, the infinite and eternal, with all the passions and emotions that beat in the heart of universal humanity.

63. Victorian views of Crabbe

(a) JOHN STERLING. Extract from review of Tennyson's *Poems* (1842), in the *Quarterly Review*, lxx, September 1842:

Of all our recent writers the one who might seem at first sight to have most nearly succeeded in this quest after the poetic *Sangreal* is Crabbe. No one has ranged so widely through all classes, employed so many diverse elements of circumstance and character. But nowhere, or very, very rarely, do we find in him that eager sweetness, a fiery spirituous essence, yet bland as honey, wanting which all poetry is but an attempt more or less laudable, and after all, a failure. Shooting arrows at the moon, one man's bow shoots higher than another's; but the shafts of all alike fall back to earth, and bring us no light upon their points. It needs a strange supernatural power to achieve the impossible, and fix the silver shaft within the orb that shoots in turn its rays of silver back into our human bosoms.

Crabbe is always an instructive and forceful, almost always even an interesting writer. His works have an imperishable value as records of his time; and it even may be said that few parts of them but would have found an appropriate place in some of the reports of our various commissions for inquiring into the state of the country. Observation, prudence, acuteness, uprightness, self-balancing vigour of mind are everywhere seen, and are exerted on the whole wide field of common life. All that is wanting is the enthusiastic sympathy, the jubilant love, whose utterance is melody, and without which all art is little better than a laborious ploughing of the sand, and then sowing the sand itself for seed along the fruitless furrow.

In poetry we seek, and find, a refuge from the hardness and narrowness of the actual world. But using the very substance of this Actual for poetry, its positiveness, shrewdness, detailedness, incongruity, and adding no new peculiar power from within, we do no otherwise than if we should take shelter from rain under the end of a roof-spout.

(b) JOHN RUSKIN. Extract from letter to Miss J. Wedderburn, 24 April 1849. (*Letters of Ruskin*, I, 93: *Works*, ed. E. J. Cook and A. Wedderburn, 1909, Vol. XXXVI):

Cultivate your taste for the horrible and chasten it: I am not sure whether you have taste for the beautiful—I strongly doubt it—but you can always avoid what is paltry; your strong love of truth may make you (as a painter) a kind of Crabbe, something disagreeable perhaps at times, but always majestic and powerful, so only that you keep serious. . .

(c) J. H. NEWMAN. (*The Idea of a University*, 1873 edn, I, 150):
[i] This poem [*Tales of the Hall*], let me say, I read on its first publication, above thirty years ago, with extreme delight and have never lost my love of it; and on taking it up lately, found I was even more touched by it than heretofore. A work which can please in youth and age, seems to fulfil (in logical language) the *accidental definition* of a Classic. [A further course of twenty years has past, and I bear the same witness in favour of this Poem.]

[ii] Crabbe 'turned back to a versification having more of Dryden [than of Pope in it].
(*Ibid.*, I, 326)

(d) D. G. ROSSETTI. Extract from letter to William Allingham, 23 January 1855. (*Letters of D. G. Rossetti*, ed. O. Doughty and J. R. Wahl, 1965, I, 241):
. . . I am awfully sleepy and stupid, or should try to say something about the book I have read for a long while back—Crabbe, whose poems were known to me long ago, but not at all familiarly till now. I fancy one might read him oftener and much later than Wordsworth —than almost anyone.

(e) A. H. CLOUGH. Extract from letter to F. J. Child, 14 November 1856. (*Correspondence*, ed. F. L. Mulhauser, 1957, 522):
. . . I have been reading pretty nearly through Crabbe lately. Have you republished Crabbe? If not, you ought to do so. There is no one more purely English (in the Dutch manner), no one who better represents the general result through the country of the last century.—His descriptions remind even me of things I used to see, hear, and hear of in my boyhood. And sometimes, though rarely, he has really the highest merit—e.g. Ruth in the *Tales of the Hall* [V]. The *Life* prefaced to Murray's Edition is very amusing, chiefly because of the naive way in which the son talks about his father.

(f) GEORGE ELIOT. Extract from letter to William Allingham, 26 March 1874. (*The George Eliot Letters*, ed. G. S. Haight, 1956, VI, 33):
. . . In the far-off days of my early teens I used to enjoy Crabbe, but if my imperfect memory does him justice your narrative of homely life is touched with a higher poetry than his.

(g) FITZGERALD.[1] [i] Extract from letter to C. E. Norton, 22 December 1876. (*Letters and Literary Remains*, ed. W. A. Wright, 1889, I, 394–5):
I have been reading with real satisfaction, and delight, Mr. L. Stephen's *Hours in a Library*: only, as I have told his Sister in law, I should have liked to put in a word or two for Crabbe. I think I could furnish L. S. with many Epigrams, of a very subtle sort, from Crabbe: and several paragraphs, if not pages, of comic humour as light as Molière. Both which L. S. seems to doubt in what he calls 'our excellent Crabbe,' who was not so 'excellent' (in the goody sense) as L. S. seems to intimate. But then Crabbe is my Great Gun. He will outlive ——, —— and Co. in spite of his Carelessness. So think I again.

His Son, Vicar of a Parish near here [Bredfield, Suffolk], and very like the Father in face, was a great Friend of mine. He detested Poetry (sc. verse), and I believe had never read his Father through till some twenty years ago when I lent him the Book. Yet I used to tell him he threw out sparks now and then. As one day when we were talking of some Squires who cut down Trees (which all magnanimous Men respect and love), my old Vicar cried out 'How *scandalously they misuse the Globe!'* He was a very noble, courageous, generous Man, and worshipped his Father in his way. I always thought I could hear this Son in that fine passage which closes the *Tales of The Hall*, when the Elder Brother surprises the Younger by the gift of that House and Domain which are to keep them close Neighbours for ever.

> Here on that lawn your Boys and Girls shall run,
> And gambol, when the daily task is done;
> From yonder Window shall their Mother view
> The happy tribe, and smile at all they do:
> While you, more gravely hiding your Delight,
> *Shall cry—'O, childish!'—and enjoy the Sight.*
> [XXII, 487–92]

By way of pendant to this, pray read the concluding lines of the long, ill-told, Story of 'Smugglers and Poachers.' Or shall I fill up my

---

[1] See also No. 74 below.

Letter with them? This is a sad Picture to match that sunny one.

> As men may children at their sports behold,
> And smile to see them, tho' unmoved and cold,
> Smile at the recollected Games, and then
> Depart, and mix in the Affairs of men;
> So Rachel looks upon the World, and sees
> It can no longer pain, no longer please:
> But just detain the passing Thought; just cause
> A little smile of Pity, or Applause—
> And then the recollected Soul repairs
> Her slumbering Hope, and heeds her own Affairs.

I wish some American Publisher would publish my Edition of *Tales of the Hall*, edited by means of Scissors and Paste, with a few words of plain Prose to bridge over whole tracts of bad Verse; not meaning to improve the original, but to seduce hasty Readers to study it.

[ii] Extract from letter to C. E. Norton, 1 February 1877. (*Ibid.*, I, 398–9):

I thought, after I had written my last, that I ought not to have said anything of an American Publisher of Crabbe as it might (as it has done) set you on thinking how to provide one for me. I spoke of America, knowing that no one in England would do such a thing, and not knowing if Crabbe were more read in your Country than in his own. Some years ago I got some one to ask Murray if he would publish a Selection from all Crabbe's Poems: as has been done to Wordsworth and others. But Murray (to whom Crabbe's collected *Works* have always been a loss) would not meddle. . . . You shall one day see my *Tales of the Hall*, when I can get it decently arranged, and written out (what is to be written), and then you shall judge of what chance it has of success. I want neither any profit, whether of money, or reputation: I only want to have Crabbe read more than he is. Women and young People never will like him, I think: but I believe every thinking man will like him more as he grows older; see if this be not so with yourself and your friends. Your Mother's Recollection of him is, I am sure, the just one: Crabbe never showed himself in Company, unless to a very close and experienced observer: his Company manner was exactly the reverse of his Books: almost, as Moore says, '*doucereux*;' the apologetic politeness of the old School over-done, as by one who was not born to it. But Campbell observed his 'shrewd Vigilance' awake under all his 'politesse,' and John Murray said that Crabbe said uncommon things in so common a way that they escaped recognition. It appears, I think, that he not only said, but wrote, such things: even to such Readers as Mr. Stephen; who can see very little Humour, and no Epigram, in him. I will engage to find plenty of both. I think Mr. Stephen could hardly have read the later Books: viz. *Tales of the Hall*, and the *Posthumous Poems*: which, though careless and incomplete, contain Crabbe's most mature Self, I think. Enough of him for the present: and altogether enough, unless I wish to become a 'seccatore' by my repeated, long letters. . . '

[iii] Extract from letter to J. R. Lowell, 13 June 1879. (*Ibid.,* I, 440, 442): I was curious to know what an American, and of your Quality, would say of Crabbe. The manner and topics (Whig, Tory &c.) are almost obsolete in this country, though I remember them well: how then must they appear to you and yours? The 'Ceremoniousness' you speak of is overdone for Crabbe's time: he overdid it in his familiar intercourse, so as to disappoint everybody who expected 'Nature's sternest Poet' &c.; but he was all the while observing. I know not why he persists in his Thee and Thou, which certainly Country Squires did not talk of, except for an occasional Joke, at the time his Poem dates from, 1819: and I warned my Readers in that still-born Preface to change that form into simple 'You.' If this Book leaves a melancholy impression on you, what then would all his others? Leslie Stephen says his Humour is heavy (Q^y is not his Tragedy?), and wonders how Miss Austen could admire him as it appears she did; and you discern a relation between her and him. I find plenty of grave humour in this Book: in the Spinster, the Bachelor, the Widow &c. All which I pointed out (in the still-born) to L. S. . . . He says too that Crabbe is 'incapable of Epigram,' which also you do not agree in; Epigrams more of Humour than Wit; sometimes only hinted, as in those two last lines of that disagreeable, and rather incomprehensible 'Sir Owen Dale.'[1] I think he will do in the land of Cervantes still. . . .

This Letter shall sleep a night too before Travelling. Next Morning. Revenons à notre Crabbe. 'Principles and Pew' very bad.[2] 'The Flowers &c. cut by busy hands &c.' are, or were, common on the leaden roofs of old Houses, Churches &c.[3] I made him stop at 'Till the Does ventured on our Solitude,' without adding '*We were so still!*,' which is quite 'de trop.' You will see by the enclosed prefatory Notice what I have

[1] XII, 915–16.
[2] *Tales of the Hall*, I, 139.
[3] *Ibid.*, I, 73–4.

done in the matter, as little as I could in doing what was to be done. My own Copy is full of improvements. Yes, for any Poetaster may improve three-fourths of the careless old Fellow's Verse: but it would puzzle a Poet to improve the better part. I think that Crabbe differs from Pope in this thing for one: that he aims at Truth, not at Wit, in his Epigram. How almost graceful he can sometimes be too!

> What we beheld in Love's perspective Glass
> Has pass'd away—one Sigh! and let it pass.
>   [*Tales of the Hall*, XIV 407–8]

[iv] Extract from letter to W. Aldis Wright, 1 August 1879. (*More Letters*, 1901, 220):
Crabbe's Humour. I think Stephen speaks rather of Stories than of single Lines: of both of which he might have found good samples in the *Tales* and the *Posthumous*; I doubt if he ever got so far in the *Works*: if he did, he, or I, must be very obtuse on that score. Please to read about the two Kinds of Friendship at the Beginning of 'Danvers and Rayner'[1]; and of the Suitors that a Woman likes to have in store, if ever wanted, in 'Barnaby the Shopman':

> Lovers like these, as Dresses thrown aside, etc.
>   [*Posthumous Tales*, VIII, 59]

I do believe that *you* give my old Boy his due credit. His verbal Jokes are as bad as—Shakespeare's.'

[v] Letter to C. E. Norton, 1 May 1888. (*Letters and Literary Remains*, 1889, I, 449–52):
I must thank you for the Crabbe Review[2] you sent me, though, had it been your own writing, I should probably not tell you how very good I think it. I am somewhat disappointed that Mr. Woodberry dismisses Crabbe's 'Trials at Humour' as summarily as Mr. Leslie Stephen does; it was mainly for the Humour's sake that I made my little work: Humour so evident to me in so many of the Tales (and Conversations), and which I meant to try and get a hearing for in the short Preface I had written in case the Book had been published. I thought these Tales showed the 'stern Painter' softened by his Grand Climacteric, removed from the gloom and sadness of his early associations, and looking to the Follies rather than to the Vices of Men, and treating them often in some-

---

[1] *Posthumous Tales*, XVII.
[2] See below, No. 73.

thing of a Molière way, only with some pathetic humour mixt, so as these Tales were almost the only one of his Works which left an agreeable impression behind them. But if so good a Judge as Mr. Woodberry does not see all this, I certainly could not have persuaded John Bull to see it: and perhaps am wrong myself in seeing what is not there.

I doubt not that Mr. Woodberry is quite right in what he says of Crabbe not having Imagination to draw that Soul from Nature of which he enumerates the phenomena: but he at any rate does so enumerate and select them as to suggest something more to his Reader, something more than mere catalogue could suggest. He may go yet further in such a description, as that other Autumnal one in 'Delay has Danger,' beginning—

> Early he rose, and look'd with many a sigh, . . .
> [*Tales of the Hall*, XIII, 701 ff]

Where, as he says, the Decay and gloom of Nature seem reflected in—nay, as it were, to take a reflection from—the Hero's troubled Soul. In the Autumn Scene which Mr. Woodberry quotes,[1] and contrasts with those of other more imaginative Poets, would not a more imaginative representation of the scene have been out of character with the English Country Squire who sees and reflects on it? As would have been more evident if Mr. W. had quoted a line or two further—

> While the dead foliage dropt from loftier trees
> The Squire beheld not with his wonted ease,
> But to his own reflections made reply,
> And said aloud—'Yes, doubtless we must die.'
> [*ibid.*, 61-4]

οἴη περ φύλλων γενεή—[2]

This Dramatic Picture touches me more than Mr. Arnold.

One thing more I will say, that I do not know where old Wordsworth condemned Crabbe as unpoetical (except in the truly 'priggish' candle case) though I doubt not that Mr. Woodberry does know. We all know that of Crabbe's *Village* one passage was one of the first that struck young Wordsworth: and when Crabbe's son was editing his Father's Poems in 1834, old Wordsworth wrote to him that, because of their combined Truth and Poetry, those Poems would last as long at least as any that had been written since, including Wordsworth's own.

1 *Tales of the Hall*, IV, 46 ff.
2 As is the generation of leaves. *Iliad*, VI, 146.

And Wordsworth was too honest, as well as too exclusive, to write so
much even to a Son of the dead Poet, without meaning all he said.

I should not have written all this were it not that I think so much of
Mr. Woodberry's Paper; but I doubt I could not persuade him to think
more of my old Man than he sees good to think for himself. I rejoice
that he thinks even so well of the Poet: even if his modified Praise does
not induce others to try and think likewise. The verses he quotes—

> Where is that virtue which the generous boy &c.

made my heart glow—yes, even out at my Eyes—though so familiar to
me. Only in my private Copy, instead of

> When Vice had triumph—*who his tear bestow'd*
> On injured merit—

in place of that '*bestowed Tear*,' I cannot help reading

> When Vice and Insolence in triumph rode &c.

which is, of course, only for myself, and you, it seems: for I never mentioned that, and some scores of such impudencies.

[vi] Letter to R. C. Trench, 9 May 1880. (*Ibid.*, I, 452–3):
You are old enough, like myself, to remember People reading and talking of Crabbe. I know not if you did so yourself; but you know that no
one, unless as old as ourselves, does so now. As he has always been one
of my Apollos, in spite of so many a cracked string, I wanted to get a
few others to listen a little as I did; and so printed the Volume which I
send you: printed it, not by way of improving, or superseding, the
original, but to entice some to read the original in all its length, and (one
must say) uncouth and wearisome '*longueurs*' and want of what is now
called 'Art.' These *Tales* are perhaps as open to that charge as any of his;
and, moreover, not principally made up of that 'sternest' stuff which
Byron celebrated as being most characteristic of him. When writing
these *Tales*, the Poet had reached his Grand Climacteric, and liked to
look on somewhat of the sunnier side of things: more on the Comedy
than the Tragedy of Human Life: and hence these *Tales* are, with all
their faults, the one work of his which leaves me (ten years past my
grand Climacteric also) with a pleasant Impression. So I tried to make
others think; but I was told by Friends whose Judgment I could trust
that no Public would listen to me. . . . And so I paid for my printing,
and kept my Book to be given away to some few as old as myself, and

brought up in somewhat of another Fashion than what now reigns. And so I now take heart to send it to you whose Poems and Writings prove that you belong to another, and, as I think, far better School, whether you care for Crabbe or not. I dare say you will feel bound to acknowledge the Book; but pray do so, if at all, by a simple acknowledgment of its receipt; I mean, so far as I am concerned in it: any word about Crabbe I shall be glad to have if you care to write it; but I always maintain it best to say nothing, unless to find fault, with what is sent to one in this Book Line. And so to be done by.

(h) G. M. HOPKINS. Extract from letter to R. W. Dixon, 16 December 1881. (*Correspondence of G. M. Hopkins and R. W. Dixon*, ed. C. C. Abbott, 1935, 99):
I suppose Crabbe to have been in form a descendant of the school of Pope, with a strong and modern realistic eye.

(i) TENNYSON 1883. (Hallam Tennyson, *Tennyson: A Memoir*, 1924, II, 287):
He liked Crabbe much, and thought that there was great force in his homely tragic stories. 'He has a world of his own. There is a tramp, tramp, tramp, a merciless sledge-hammer thud about his lines which suits his subjects.'

64. An early American assessment

1846

Henry Theodore Tuckerman (1813–71), *Thoughts on the Poets*, 1846, pp. 122–36.

[There is a brief biographical introduction.]

Crabbe was no stoic. He could not conceal his feelings, and was a novel reader all his life. He had suffered enough to teach him to feel for others. There was a rare and winning simplicity in his manners. He was remarkably unambitious for a son of the muses; and sought mental delight according to his instincts rather than from prescribed rules. Manly and independent, with an active and exuberant mind, his character won him as many suffrages as his verse. His attachments, we are told, knew no decline and his heart seemed to mellow rather than grow frigid, with the lapse of time. We discover, in his life and writings, a kind of Indian summer benignly invading the winter of age. Such was Crabbe as a man. His fame, as a poet, is owing in some degree to the time of his appearance. It was his fortune to come forward during one of those lapses in the visits of the muse which invariably insure her a warmer welcome. Perhaps on this very account his merits have been somewhat exaggerated and vaguely defined,—at least by those whose early taste was permanently influenced by his genius. . . .

The bards of the visible world, who love to designate its every feature, evince their observation by a happy term or most apt allusion, as when Bryant calls the hills 'rock-ribbed,' and the ocean a 'gray and melancholy waste.' Crabbe owes his popularity both to the sphere and quality of his observation. In these, almost exclusively, consists his originality. The form of his verse, the tone of his sentiment, and the play of his fancy, are, by no means, remarkable. He interests us from the comparatively unhackneyed field he selected, and the peculiar manner in which he unfolds its treasures. He seized upon characters and events before thought unworthy of the minstrel. He turned, in a great measure, from the grand and elegant materials of poetry, and sought his themes amid the common-place and the vulgar. Nor was he aided in this course by any elevated theory of his own, like that of Wordsworth. He carried no magic torch into the dark labyrinths he explored, but was satisfied to open them to the light of day. Indeed, Crabbe seems to have reversed all the ordinary principles of the art. His effects arise rather from sterility than luxuriance. His success seems the result rather of a matter-of-fact than an illusive process. The oft-quoted question of the mathematician to the bard—'what does it all prove?' Crabbe often literally answers; and to this trait we cannot but refer the admiration in which this writer was held by Johnson, Gifford, and Jeffrey. These critics often failed to appreciate the more exalted and delicate displays of modern poetry; but in Crabbe there was a pointed sense and tangible meaning that harmonized with their perceptions. Of poets in general we are accustomed to say, that they weave imaginary charms around reality; and, like the wave that sparkles above a wreck, or the flowery turf that conceals a sepulchre, interpose a rosy veil to beguile us from pain. But Crabbe often labours to strip life of its bright dreams, and portrays, with as keen a relish, the anatomical frame as the round and blooming flesh. He bears us not away from the limits of the present by the comprehensive views he presents; but, on the contrary, is continually fixing our attention upon the minute details of existence, and the minor shades of experience. He seeks not to keep out of sight the meaner aspects of life, or relieve, with the glow of imagination, the dark traits of the actual. With a bold and industrious scrutiny he plunges into the gloomy particulars of human wretchedness; and, like some of the Dutch limners, engages our attention, not by the unearthly graces, but the appalling truthfulness of his pictures. Unlike Goldsmith, instead of casting a halo of romance around rustic life, he elaborately exposes its discomforts. He sometimes, indeed, paints the enchantments of love, but often only to contrast them with the worst trials of matrimony; and woman's beauty is frequently described with zest in his pages, only to afford occasion to dwell upon its decay.

It is evident, that to such a writer of verse many of the loftier and finer elements of the poet were wanting. The noble point, in a mind of this order, is integrity. The redeeming sentiment in Crabbe's nature was honesty, in its broadest and most efficient sense. What he saw he faithfully told. The pictures, clearly displayed to his mind, he copied to the life. He carried into verse a kind of dauntless simplicity, an almost Puritan loyalty to his convictions. He appears like one thoroughly determined to tell the homely truth in rhyme. Poetry has been called the 'flower of experience.' If we adopt this definition literally, Crabbe has small claims to the name of poet. He searched not so much for the meek violet and the blushing rose, as the weeds and briars that skirt the path of human destiny. Where, then, it may be asked, is his attraction? The picturesque and the affecting do not, as he has demonstrated, exist only in alliance with beauty. The tangled brake may win the eye, in certain moods, as strongly as the garden; and a desolate moor is often more impressive than a verdant hill-side. So rich and mysterious a thing is the human heart, so fearfully interesting is life, that there is a profound meaning in its mere elements. When these are laid bare, there is room for conjecture and discovery. We approach the revelations as we would the fathomless caves of the sea, if they were opened to our gaze. Some of Salvator's landscapes, consisting mainly of a ship's hulk and a lonely strand, are more interesting than a combination of meadow, forest, and temples, by an inferior hand; and, on the same principle, one of Crabbe's free and true sketches is better than the timid composition of a more refined writer. Byron calls him 'Nature's sternest painter, yet the best;'[1] and he has been well styled by another, the Hogarth of verse. There is something that excites our veneration in reality, whether in character or literature. 'To the poet,' says Carlyle, 'we say first of all, *see*.' And just so far as Crabbe *saw*, (where the object admits,) he is poetical. There is a vast range which he not only failed to explore, but did not even approach. There is a world of delicate feeling, and exalted idealism of which he seems to have been almost unconscious. Of the deeper sympathies it may be questioned if he had any real experience. And yet we are to recognize in him no ordinary element of poetry—that insight which enabled him to perceive and to depict in so graphic a style, particular phases of life. We trace, too, in his writings a rare appreciation of many characteristics of our nature. He found these among the ignorant, where passion is poorly disguised. He acted as an interpreter between those whom refinement and social cultivation widely separated. He did much to diminish the force of the proverb, that 'one half the world know not how the other half live;' and to direct attention to the actual world and the passing hour, as fraught with an import and an interest, which habit alone prevents us from discovering.

Crabbe was rather a man of science than an enthusiast. He looked upon nature with minute curiosity oftener than with vague delight. This is indicated by many of his descriptions, which are almost as special as the reports of a natural historian. He calls sea-nettles 'living jellies,'

[1] See above, No. 51(c).

and speaks of kelp as floating on 'bladdery beads.' Like Friar Lawrence, too, he thought that 'muckle is the power and grace that lies in herbs, plants, stones, and their true qualities.' Through life he was an assiduous collector of botanical and geological specimens. His partiality for detail is exhibited in many of his allusions to the sea-side; and they afford a remarkable contrast to the enlarged and undefined associations, which the same scene awakened in the mind of Byron. Crabbe loved nature, but it was in a very intelligent and unimpassioned way. When Lockhart took him to Salisbury Crags, he was interested by their strata far more than the prospect they afforded. How light a sway music held over him, may be realized from the fact that he once wrote the greater part of a poem in a London concert-room, to keep himself awake. The tone of his mind is revealed by the manner in which he wooed the muse. From his own artless letters we cannot but discover that much of his verse was produced by a mechanical process. His best metaphors, he tells us, were inserted after the tale itself was completed. He confesses his surprise that, in two or three instances, he was much affected by what he wrote, which is proof enough of the uninspired spirit in which many of his compositions were conceived. 'I rhyme at Hampstead with a great deal of facility,' says one of his letters. Accordingly his writings fall much below the works 'produced too slowly ever to decay.' In fact, with all his peculiar merits, Crabbe was often a mere rhymer, and the cultivated lover of poetry, who feels a delicate reverence for its more perfect models, will find many of his voluminous heroics unimpressive and tedious. But interwoven with these, is many a picture of human misery, many a display of coarse passion and unmitigated grief, of delusive joy and haggard want, of vulgar selfishness and moral truth, that awaken sympathy even to pain, and win admiration for the masterly execution of the artist. Much of the poetry of Crabbe, however, is of such a character that we can conceive of its being written in almost any quantity. He began to write not so much from impulse alone, as motives of self-improvement and interest. When his situation was comfortable, he ceased versifying for a long interval, and resumed the occupation because he was encouraged to do so by the support of the public. Only occasionally, and in particular respects, does he excite wonder. The form and spirit of his works are seldom exalted above ordinary associations. Hence they are more easily imitated, and in the *Rejected Addresses*, one of the closest parodies is that of Crabbe.[1] The department he originally chose was almost uninvaded, and he was singularly fitted to

[1] See above, No. 39.

occupy it with success. In addition to his graphic ability, and the studied fidelity of his portraiture, which were his great intellectual advantages, there were others arising from the warmth and excellence of his heart. He sympathized enough with human nature to understand its weaknesses and wants. His pathos is sometimes inimitable; and superadded to these rare qualifications, we must allow him a felicity of diction, a fluency and propriety in the use of language, which, if it made him sometimes diffuse, at others gave a remarkable freedom and point to his verses.

Illustrations of these qualities abound in Crabbe's writings. His similes convey a good idea of his prevailing tendency to avail himself of prosaic associations, which in ordinary hands, would utterly fail of their intended effect:

> For all that honour brings against the force
> Of headlong passion, aids its rapid course;
> Its slight resistance but provokes the fire,
> As wood-work stops the flame and then conveys it higher.
> [*Tales*, XI, 289–92]

> As various colours in a painted ball
> While it has rest, are seen distinctly all;
> Till whirled around by some exterior force,
> They all are blended in the rapid course;
> So in repose and not by passion swayed,
> We saw the difference by their habits made;
> But tried by strong emotions, they became
> Filled with one love, and were in heart the same.
> [*Tales of the Hall*, II, 25–32]

The following are specimens of his homely minuteness.

[*The Borough*, I, 54–5; IX, 18–23; IX, 137–44; X, 242–3 and *The Parish Register*, I, 257–68, 301–4, 469–72, 554–7.]

His fondness for antitheses is often exemplified;

> The easy followers in the female train,
> Led without love, and captives without chain.
> [*The Borough*, III, 67–8]

> Opposed to these we have a prouder kind,
> Rash without heat and without raptures blind.
> [*ibid.*, IV, 28–9]

Hour after hour, men thus contending sit,
Grave without sense, and pointed without wit.
[*ibid.*, X, 75–6]

Gained[1] without skill, without inquiry bought,
Lost without love, and borrowed without thought.
[*ibid.*, XIV, 17–18]

It is amusing, with the old complaints of the indefiniteness of poetry fresh in the mind, to encounter such literal rhyming as the following,— a sailor is addressing his recreant mistress:

Nay, speak at once, and Dinah, let me know,
Means't thou to take me, now I'm wreck'd, in tow?
Be fair, nor longer keep me in the dark,
Am I forsaken for a trimmer spark?
[*Tales*, IV, 263–6]

Grave Jonas Kindred, Sybil Kindred's sire,
Was six feet high, and look'd six inches higher.
[*ibid.*, VI, 1–2]

A tender, timid maid, who knew not how
To pass a pig-sty, or to face a cow.
[*ibid.*, VII, 3–4]

Where one huge, wooden bowl before them stood.
Filled with huge balls of farinaceous food,
With bacon most[2] saline, where never lean
Beneath the brown and bristly rind was seen.
[*ibid.*, 19–22]

As a male turkey straggling on the green . . .
[*ibid.*, I, 368–83]

No image appears too humble for Crabbe:

For these occasions forth his knowledge sprung,
As mustard quickens on a bed of dung.
[*ibid.*, III, 214–5]

When his graphic power is applied to a different order of subjects and accompanied with more sentiment, we behold the legitimate evidences of his title to the name of poet:

[*The Borough*, I, 113–20; *The Village*, I, 228–39, 63–92, 172–9].

---

[1] Should read 'Gamed'.
[2] Should read 'mass'.

No small portion of the interest Crabbe's writings have excited, is to be ascribed to his ingenious stories. Some of them are entertaining from the incidents they narrate, and others on account of the sagacious remarks with which they are interwoven. These attractions often co-exist with but a slight degree of poetic merit, beyond correct versification and an occasional metaphor. Most of the tales are founded in real circumstances, and the characters were drawn, with some modification, from existent originals. Scarcely a feature of romance or even improbability belong to these singular narratives. They are usually domestic in their nature, and excite curiosity because so near to common experience. As proofs of inventive genius they are often striking, and if couched in elegant prose or a dramatic form, would, in some cases, be far more effective. Lamb tried the latter experiment in one instance, with marked success.* These rhymed histories of events and personages within the range of ordinary life, seem admirably calculated to win the less imaginative to a love of poetry. Crabbe has proved a most serviceable pioneer to the timid haunters of Parnassus, and decked with alluring trophies, the outskirts of the land of song. We can easily understand how a certain order of minds relish his poems better than any other writings in the same department of literature. There is a singular tone of every-day truth and practical sense about them. They deal with the tangible realities around us. They unfold 'the artful workings of a vulgar mind,' and depict with amusing exactitude, the hourly trials of existence. A gipsy group, a dissipated burgess, the victims of profligacy, the mean resentments of ignorant minds, a coarse tyrant, a vindictive woman, a fen or a fishing boat—those beings and objects which meet us by the way-side of the world, the common, the real, the more rude elements of life, are set before us in the pages of Crabbe, in the most bold relief and affecting contrast. There is often a gloom, an unrelieved wretchedness, an absolute degradation about these delineations, which weighs upon the spirits—the sadness of a tragedy without its ideal grandeur or its poetic consolation. But the redeeming influence of such creations lies in the melancholy but wholesome truths they convey. The mists that shroud the dwellings of the wretched are rolled away, the wounds of the social system are laid bare, and the sternest facts of experience are proclaimed. This process was greatly required in Great Britain when Crabbe appeared as the bard of the poor. He arrayed the dark history of their needs and oppression in a guise which would attract the eye of taste. He led many a luxurious peer to the haunts of

* *The Wife's Trial.*

poverty. He carried home to the souls of the pampered and proud, a startling revelation of the distress and crime that hung unnoticed around their steps. He fulfilled, in his day, the same benevolent office which, in a different style, has since been so ably continued by Dickens. These two writers have published to the world, the condition of the English poor, in characters of light; and thrown the whole force of their genius into an appeal from the injustice of society and the abuses of civilization.

65. Gilfillan's 'spasmodic' criticism

From *Tait's Edinburgh Magazine*, March 1847, xiv, 141–7; reprinted in *A Second Gallery of Literary Portraits*, 1850. His work is marked by a colourful style and strong likes and dislikes.

To be the Poet of the waste places of Creation—to adopt the orphans of the Mighty Mother—to wed her dowerless daughters—to find out the beauty which has been spilt in tiny drops in her more unlovely regions —to echo the low music which arises from even her stillest and most sterile spots—was the mission of Crabbe, as a descriptive poet. He preferred the Leahs to the Rachels of Nature: and this he did not merely that his lot had cast him amid such scenes, and that early associations had taught him a profound interest in them, but apparently from native taste. He actually loved that beauty which stands shivering on the brink of barrenness—loved it for its timidity and its loneliness. Nay, he seemed to love barrenness itself; brooding over its dull page till there arose from it a strange lustre, which his eye distinctly sees, and which in part he makes visible to his readers. It was even as the darkness of cells has been sometimes peopled to the view of the solitary prisoner, and spiders seemed angels, in the depths of his dungeon. We can fancy, too, in Crabbe's mind, a feeling of pity for those unloved spots, and those neglected glories. We can fancy him saying, 'Let the gay and the aspiring mate with Nature in her towering altitudes, and flatter her more favoured scenes; I will go after her into her secret retirements, bring out her bashful beauties, praise what none are willing to praise, and love what there are very few to love.' From his early circumstances besides, there had stolen over his soul a shade of settled though subdued gloom. And for sympathy with this, he betook himself to the sterner and sadder aspects of Nature, where he saw, or seemed to see, his own feelings reflected, as in a sea of melancholy faces, in dull skies, waste moorlands, the low beach, and the moaning of the waves upon it, as if weary of their eternal wanderings. Such, too, at moments, was the feeling of Burns, when he strode on the scaur of the Nith, and saw the waters red and turbid below; or walked in a windy day by the side of a plantation, and heard the 'sound of a going' upon the tops of the trees: or when he exclaimed, with a calm simplicity of bitterness which is most affecting—

> The leafless trees my fancy please,
> Their fate resembles mine.
> ['Winter, A Dirge', 15-16]

Crabbe, as a descriptive poet, differs from other modern masters of the art, alike in his selection of subjects, and in his mode of treating the subjects he does select. Byron moves over nature with a fastidious and aristocratic step—touching only upon objects already interesting or ennobled, upon battle fields, castellated ruins, Italian palaces, or Alpine peaks. This, at least, is true of his *Childe Harold*, and his earlier pieces. In the later productions of his pen, he goes to the opposite extreme, and alights, with a daring yet dainty foot, upon all shunned and forbidden things—reminds us of the raven in the Deluge, which found rest for the sole of her foot upon carcasses, where the dove durst not stand—rushes in where modesty and reserve alike have forbidden entrance—and ventures, though still not like a lost archangel, to tread the burning marle of Hell, the dim gulph of Hades, the shadowy ruins of the Pre-Adamitic world, and the crystal pavement of Heaven.—Moore practises a principle of more delicate selection, resembling some nice fly which should alight only upon flowers, whether natural or artificial, if so that flowers they seemed to be; thus, from sunny bowers, and moonlit roses, and gardens, and blushing skies, and ladies' dresses, does the Bard of Erin extract his finest poetry.—Shelley and Coleridge attach themselves almost exclusively to the great—understanding this term in a wide sense, as including much that is grotesque and much that is homely, which the magic of their genius sublimates to a proper pitch of keeping with the rest. Their usual walk is swelling and buskined: their common talk is of great rivers, great forests, great seas, great continents; or else of comets, suns, constellations, and firmaments—as that of all half-mad, wholly miserable, and opium-fed genius is apt to be.—Sir Walter Scott, who seldom grappled with the gloomier and grander features of his country's scenery, (did he ever describe Glenco or Foyers, or the wildernesses around Ben mac Dhui?) had—need we say? the most exquisite eye for all picturesque and romantic aspects, in sea, shore, or sky; and in the quick perception of this element of the picturesque lay his principal, if not only descriptive power.—Wordsworth, again, seems always to be standing above, though not stooping over, the objects he describes. He seldom looks up in rapt admiration of what is above; the bending furze-bush and the lowly broom—the nest lying in the level clover-field—the tarn sinking away seemingly before his eye into darker depths —the prospect from the mountain summit cast far beneath him; at highest, the star burning low upon the mountain's ridge, like an 'untended watchfire:'—these are the objects which he loves to describe, and these may stand as emblems of his lowly yet aspiring genius.— Crabbe, on the other hand, 'stoops to conquer'—nay, goes down on his knees, that he may more accurately describe such objects as the marsh given over to desolation from immemorial time—the slush left by the sea, and revealing the dead body of the suicide—the bare crag and the stunted tree, diversifying the scenery of the saline wilderness—the house on the heath, creaking in the storm, and telling strange stories of misery and crime—the pine in some wintry wood, which had acted as the gallows of some miserable man—the gorse surrounding with yellow light the encampment of the gypsies—the few timid flowers, or 'weeds of glorious feature,' which adorn the brink of ocean—the snow putting out the fire of the pauper, or lying unmelted on his pillow of death—the web of the spider blinding the cottager's window—the wheel turned by the meagre hand of contented or cursing penury—the cards trembling in the grasp of the desperate debauchee—the day stocking forming the cap by night, and the *garter at midnight*—the dunghill becoming the accidental grave of the drunkard—the poor-house of forty years ago, with its patched windows, its dirty environs, its moist and miserable walls, its inmates all snuff, and selfishness, and sin—the receptacle of the outlawed members of English society (how different from 'Poosie Nancy's!'), with its gin-gendered quarrels, its appalling blasphemies, its deep debauches, its ferocity without fun, its huddled murders, and its shrieks of disease dumb in the uproar around—the Bedlam of forty years ago, with its straw on end under the restlessness of the insane; its music of groans, and shrieks and mutterings of still more melancholy meaning; its keepers cold and stern, as the snow-covered cliffs above the wintry cataract; its songs dying away in despairing gurgles down the miserable throat; its cells how devoid of monastic silence; its confusion worse confounded, of gibbering idiocy, monomania absorbed and absent from itself as well as from the world, and howling frenzy; its daylight saddened as it shines into the dim, vacant, or glaring eyes of those wretched men; and its moonbeams shedding a more congenial ray upon the solitude, or the sick-bed, or the death-bed of derangement:—such familiar faces of want, guilt, and woe —of nakedness, sterility, and shame, does Crabbe delight in showing us; and is, in very truth—

Nature's sternest painter, yet the best.

In his mode of managing his descriptions, Crabbe is equally peculiar. Objects, in themselves counted commonplace or disgusting, frequently became impressive, and even sublime, when surrounded by interesting circumstances—when shown in the moonlight of memory—when linked to strong passion—or when touched by the ray of imagination. Then, in Emerson's words, even the corpse is found to have added a solemn ornament to the house where it lay. But it is the peculiarity and the daring of this poet, that he often, not always, tries us with truth and nothing but truth, as if to bring the question to an issue—whether, in Nature, absolute truth be not essential though severe poetry. On this question, certainly, issue was never so fully joined before. In even Wordsworth's eye there is a misty glimmer of imagination, through which all objects, low as well as high, are seen. Even his 'five blue eggs' *gleam* upon him through a light which comes not from themselves—which comes, it may be, from the Great Bear, or Arcturus and his sons. And, when he does—as in some of his feebler verses—strive to see out of this medium, he drops his mantle, loses his vision, and describes little better than would his own 'Old Cumberland Beggar.'—Shakspeare in his witches' caldron, and Burns in his 'haly table,' are shockingly circumstantial;—but the element of imagination creeps in amid all the disgusting details, and the light that never was on sea or shore disdains not to rest on 'eye of newt,' 'toe of frog,' 'baboon's blood,' the garter that strangled the babe, the grey hairs sticking to the haft of the parricidal knife, and all the rest of the fell ingredients.—Crabbe, on the other hand, would have described the five blue eggs, and besides the materials of the nest, and the kind of hedge where it was built—like a bird-nesting schoolboy; but he would never have given the 'gleam.' He would, as accurately as Hecate, Canidia, or Cuttysark, have given an inventory of the ingredients of the hell-broth, or of the curiosities on the haly table, had they been presented to his eye; but could not have conceived them, nor would have slipped in, that one flashing word, that single cross ray of imagination, which it required to elevate and startle them into high ideal life. And yet in reading his pictures of poor-houses, &c. we are compelled to say, 'Well, that is poetry after all, for it is truth; but it is poetry of comparatively a low order—it is the last gasp of the poetic spirit: and, moreover, perfect and matchless as it is in its kind, it is not worthy of the powers of its author, who can, and has, at other times risen into much loftier ground.'

We may illustrate still farther what we mean by comparing the different ways in which Crabbe and Foster[1] (certainly a *prose* poet) deal with a library. Crabbe describes minutely and successfully the outer features of the volumes, their colours, clasps, the stubborn ridges of their bindings, the illustrations which adorn them, &c. so well that you feel yourself among them, and they become sensible to touch almost as to sight. But there he stops, and sadly fails, we think, in bringing out the living and moral interest which gathers around a multitude of books, or even around a single volume. This Foster has amply done. The speaking silence of a number of books, where, though it were the wide Bodleian or Vatican, not one whisper could be heard, and yet, where, as in an antichamber, so many great spirits are waiting to deliver their messages—their churchyard stillness continuing even when their readers are moving to the pages, in joy or agony, as to the sound of martial instruments—their awakening, as from deep slumber, to speak with miraculous organ, like the shell which has only to be lifted, and 'pleased it remembers its august abodes, and murmurs as the ocean murmurs there'—their power, so silent and sublime, of drawing tears, kindling blushes, awakening laughter, calming or quickening the motions of the life's blood, lulling to repose, or rousing to restlessness, often giving life to the soul, and sometimes giving death to the body—the meaning which radiates from their quiet countenances—the tale of shame or glory which their title pages tell—the memories suggested by the character of their authors, and of the readers who have throughout successive centuries perused them—the thrilling thoughts excited by the sight of names and notes inscribed on their margins or blank pages by hands long since mouldered in the dust, or by those dear to us as our

[1] John Foster (1770–1843), *Essay Introductory to Doddridge's Rise and Progress of Religion*, 1825.

life's blood, who had been snatched from our sides—the aspects of gaiety or of gloom connected with the bindings and the age of volumes —the effects of sunshine playing as if on a congregation of happy faces, making the duskiest shine, and the gloomiest be glad—or of shadow suffusing a sombre air over all—the joy of the proprietor of a large library who feels that Nebuchadnezzar watching great Babylon, or Napoleon reviewing his legions, will not stand comparison with himself seated amid the broad maps, and rich prints, and numerous volumes which his wealth has enabled him to collect, and his wisdom entitled him to enjoy—all such hieroglyphics of interest and meaning has Foster included and interpreted in one gloomy but noble meditation, and his introduction to Doddridge is the true 'Poem on the Library.'

In Crabbe's descriptions the great want is of selection. He writes inventories. He describes all that his eye sees with cold, stern, lingering accuracy—he marks down all the items of wretchedness, poverty, and vulgar sin—counts the rags of the mendicant—and, as Hazlitt has it, describes a cottage like one who has entered it to distrain for rent.[1] His copies, consequently, would be as displeasing as their originals, were it not that imagination is so much less vivid than eyesight, that we can endure in picture what we cannot in reality, and that our own minds, while reading, can cast that softening and ideal veil over disgusting objects which the poet himself has not sought, or has failed to do. Just as in viewing even the actual scene, we might have seen it through the medium of imaginative illusion, so the same medium will more probably invest, and beautify its transcript in the pages of the poet.

As a moral poet and sketcher of men, Crabbe is characterized by a similar choice of subject, and the same stern fidelity. The mingled yarn of man's every-day life—the plain homely virtues, or the robust and burly vices of Englishmen—the quiet tears which fall on humble beds —the passions which flame up in lowly bosoms—the *amari aliquid*—the deep and permanent bitterness which lies at the heart of the down-trodden English poor—the comedies and tragedies of the fireside—the lovers' quarrels—the unhappy marriages—the vicissitudes of common fortunes—the early deaths—the odd characters—the lingering superstitions—all the elements, in short, which make up the simple annals of lowly or middling society, are the materials of this poet's song. Had he been a Scottish clergyman we should have said that he had versified his Session-book; and certainly many curious chapters of human life might be derived from such a document, and much light cast upon the devious

[1] See above No. 41, p. 213.

windings and desperate wickedness of the heart, as well as upon that in-extinguishable instinct of good which resides in it. Crabbe, perhaps, has confined himself too exclusively to this circle of common things which he found lying around him. He has seldom burst its confines, and touched the loftier themes, and snatched the higher laurels which were also within his reach. He has contented himself with being a Lillo (with occasional touches of Shakspeare) instead of something far greater. He has, however, in spite of this self-injustice, effected much. He has proved that a poet, who looks resolutely around him—who stays at home—who draws the realities which are near him, instead of the phantoms that are afar—who feels and records the passion and poetry of his daily life—may found a firm and enduring reputation. With the dubious exception of Cowper, no one has made out this point so effectually as Crabbe.

And in his mode of treating such themes, what strikes us first is his perfect coolness. Few poets have reached that calm of his which reminds us of Nature's own great quiet eye, looking down upon her monstrous births, her strange anomalies, and her more ungainly forms. Thus Crabbe sees the loathsome, and does not loathe—handles the horrible, and shudders not—feels with firm finger the palpitating pulse of the infanticide or the murderer—and snuffs a certain sweet odour in the evil savours of putrefying misery and crime. This delight, however, is not an inhuman, but entirely an artistic delight—perhaps, indeed, springing from the very strength and width of his sympathies. We admire as well as wonder at that almost *asbestos* quality of his mind, through which he retains his composure and critical circumspection so cool amid the con-flagrations of passionate subjects, which might have burned others to ashes. Few, indeed, can walk through such fiery furnaces unscathed. But Crabbe—what an admirable physician had he made to a Lunatic Asy-lum! How severely would he have sifted out every grain of poetry from those tumultuous exposures of the human mind! What clean breasts had he forced the patients to make! What tales had he wrung out from them, to which Lewis' tales of terror were feeble and trite! How he would have commanded them, by his mild, steady, and piercing eye! And yet how calm would his brain have remained, when others, even of a more prosaic mould, were reeling in sympathy with the surrounding delirium! It were, indeed, worth while inquiring how much of this coolness resulted from Crabbe's early practice as a surgeon. That com-bination of warm inward sympathy and outward phlegm—of impulsive benevolence and mechanical activity—of heart all fire and manner all ice—which distinguishes his poetry, is very characteristic to the medical profession.

In correspondence with this, Crabbe generally leans to the darker side of things. This, perhaps, accounts for his favour in the sight of Byron, who saw his own eagle-eyed fury at man corroborated by Crabbe's stern and near-sighted vision. And it was accounted for partly by Crabbe's early profession, partly by his early circumstances, and partly by the clerical office he assumed. Nothing so tends to sour us with mankind as a general refusal on their part to give us bread. How can a man love a race which seems combined to starve him? This misanthropical influence Crabbe did not entirely escape. As a medical man, too, he had come in contact with little else than man's human miseries and diseases; and as a clergyman, he had occasion to see much sin and sorrow: and these, combining with the melancholy incidental to the poetic temperament, materially discoloured his view of life. He became a searcher of dark—of the darkest bosoms; and we see him sitting in the gloom of the hearts of thieves, murderers, and maniacs, and watching the remorse, rancour, fury, dull disgust, ungratified appetite, and ferocious or stupified despair, which are their inmates. And even when he pictures livelier scenes and happier characters, there steals over them a shade of sadness, reflected from his favourite subjects, as a dark, sinister countenance in a room will throw a gloom over many happy and beautiful faces beside it.

In his pictures of life, we find an unfrequent but true pathos. This is not often, however, of the profoundest or most heart-rending kind. The grief he paints is not that which refuses to be comforted—whose expressions, like Agamemnon's face, must be veiled—which dilates almost to despair, and complains almost to blasphemy—and which, when it looks to Heaven, it is

> With that frantic air
> Which seems to ask if a God be there.

Crabbe's, as exhibited in 'Phœbe Dawson,'[1] and other of his tales, is gentle, submissive; and its pathetic effects are produced by the simple recital of circumstances which might, and often have occurred. It reminds us of the pathos of 'Rosamond Gray,' that beautiful story of Lamb's, of which we once, we regret to say, presumptuously pronounced an unfavourable opinion, but which has since commended itself to our heart of hearts, and compelled that tribute in tears which we

[1] *The Parish Register*, II, 105 ff.

had denied it in words. Hazlitt is totally wrong when he says that Crabbe carves a tear to the life in marble, as if his pathos were hard and cold. Be it the statuary of woe—has it, consequently, no truth or power? Have the chiselled tears of the Niobe never awakened other tears, fresh and burning, from their fountain? Horace's *vis me flere*, &c.[1] is not always a true principle. As the wit, who laughs not himself, often excites most laughter in others, so the calm recital of an affecting narrative acts as the meek rod of Moses applied to the rock, and is answered in gushing torrents. You close Crabbe's tale of grief, almost ashamed that you have left so quiet a thing pointed and starred with tears. His pages, while sometimes wet with pathos, are never moist with humour. His satire is often pointed with wit, and sometimes irritates into invective; but of that glad, genial, and bright-eyed thing we call humour (how well *named*, in its oily softness and gentle glitter!) he has little or none. Compare, in order to see this, his *Borough* with the *Annals of the Parish*. How dry, though powerful, the one; how sappy the other! How profound the one; how pawky the other! Crabbe goes through his Borough, like a scavenger with a rough, stark, and stiff besom, sweeping up all the filth: Galt, like a knowing watchman of the old school—a *canny Charlie* —keeping a sharp look-out, but not averse to a sly joke, and having an eye to the humours as well as misdemeanours of the streets. Even his wit is not of the finest grain. It deals too much in verbal quibbles, puns, and antitheses with their points broken off. His puns are neither good nor bad—the most fatal and anti-ideal description of a pun that can be given. His quibbles are good enough to have excited the laugh of his curate, or gardener; but he forgets that the public is not so indulgent. And though often treading in Pope's track, he wants entirely those touches of satire, at once the lightest and the most withering, as if dropped from the fingers of a malignant fairy—those faint whispers of poetic perdition— those drops of concentrated bitterness—those fatal bodkin-stabs—and those invectives, glittering all over with the polish of profound malignity—which are Pope's glory as a writer, and his shame as a man.

We have repeatedly expressed our opinion, that in Crabbe there lay a higher power than he ever exerted. We find evidence of this in his 'Hall of Justice' and his 'Eustace Grey.' In these he is fairly in earnest. No longer dozing by his parlour fire over *The Newspaper*, or napping in a corner of his *Library*, or peeping in through the windows of the 'Workhouse,' or recording the select scandal of *The Borough*—he is away out into the wide and open fields of highest passion and imagination. What

[1] You wish me to weep. *Ars Poetica*, 102.

a tale that 'Hall of Justice' hears—to be paralleled only in the 'Thousand and One Nights of the Halls of Eblis!'—a tale of misery, rape, murder, and furious despair; told, too, in language of such lurid fire as has been seen to shine o'er the graves of the dead! But, in 'Eustace Grey,' our author's genius reaches its climax. Never was madness—in its misery—its remorse—the dark companions, 'the ill-favoured ones,' who cling to it in its wild way and will not let it go, although it curse them with the eloquence of Hell—the visions it sees—the scenery it creates and carries about with it in dreadful keeping—and the language it uses, high aspiring but broken, as the wing of a struck eagle—so strongly and melt-ingly revealed. And, yet, around the dismal tale there hangs the breath of beauty, and, like poor Lear, Sir Eustace goes about crowned with flowers—the flowers of earthly poetry—and of a hope which is not of the earth. And, at the close, we feel to the author all that strange grati-tude which our souls are constituted to entertain to those who have most powerfully wrung and tortured them.

Would that Crabbe had given us a century of such things. We would have preferred to the *Tales of the Hall*, 'Tales of Greyling Hall,' or more tidings from 'The Hall of Justice.' It had been a darker Decameron and brought out more effectually—what the 'Village Poorhouse,' and the sketches of Elliott have since done—the passions, miseries, crushed aspirations, and latent poetry, which dwell in the hearts of the plun-dered poor; as well as the wretchedness which, more punctually than their veriest menial, waits often behind the chairs, and hands the golden dishes of the great.

We have not space nor time to dilate on his other works individually. We prefer, in glancing back upon them as a whole, trying to answer the following questions: 1st, What was Crabbe's object as a moral poet? 2dly, How far is he original as an artist? 3dly, What is his relative posi-tion to his great contemporaries? And, 4thly, what is likely to be his fate with posterity? 1st, His object.—The great distinction between man and man, and author and author, is purpose. It is the edge and point of character; it is the stamp and the superscription of genius; it is the direction on the letter of talent. Character without it is blunt and torpid. Talent without it is a letter, which, undirected, goes no whither. Genius without it is bullion, sluggish, splendid, uncirculating. Purpose yearns after and secures artistic culture. It gathers, as by a strong suction, all things which it needs into itself. It often invests art with a moral and religious aspect . . .

Crabbe's artistic object is tolerably clear, and has been already indicated. His moral purpose is not quite so apparent. Is it to satirize, or is it to reform vice? Is it pity, or is it contempt, that actuates his song? What are his plans for elevating the lower classes in the scale of society? Has he any, or does he believe in the possibility of their permanent elevation? Such questions are more easily asked than answered. We must say that we have failed to find in him any one overmastering, and earnest object, subjugating everything to itself, and producing that unity in all his works which the trunk of a tree gives to its smallest, its remotest, to even its withered leaves. And yet, without apparent intention, Crabbe has done good moral service. He has shed much light upon the condition of the poor. He has spoken in the name and stead of the poor dumb mouths that could not tell their own sorrows or sufferings to the world. He has opened the 'mine,' which Ebenezer Elliott and others, going to work with a firmer and more resolute purpose, have dug to its depths.

2dly, His originality.—This has been questioned by some critics. He has been called a version, in coarser paper and print, of Goldsmith, Pope, and Cowper. His pathos comes from Goldsmith—his wit and satire from Pope—and his minute and literal description from Cowper. If this were true, it were as complimentary to him as his warmest admirer could wish. To combine the characteristic excellences of three true poets is no easy matter. But Crabbe has not combined them. His pathos wants altogether the naiveté of sentiment, and *curiosa felicitas* of expression which distinguish Goldsmith's *Deserted Village*. He has something of Pope's terseness, but little of his subtlety, finish, or brilliant malice. And the motion of Cowper's mind and style in description differs as much from Crabbe's as the playful leaps and gambols of a kitten from the measured, downright, and indomitable pace of a hound—the one is the easiest, the other the severest, of describers. Resemblances, indeed, of a minor kind are to be found; but, still, Crabbe is as distinct from Goldsmith, Cowper, and Pope, as Byron from Scott, Wordsworth, and Coleridge.

Originality consists of two kinds—one, the power of inventing new materials; and the other, of dealing with old materials in a new way. We do not decide whether the first of these implies an act of absolute creation; it implies all we can conceive in an act of creative power, from elements bearing to the result the relation which the Alphabet does to the *Iliad*—genius brings forth its bright progeny, and we feel it to be new. In this case, you can no more anticipate the effect from the elements than you can, from the knowledge of the letters, anticipate the words which are to be compounded out of them. In the other kind of originality, the materials bear a large proportion to the result—they form an appreciable quantity in our calculations of what it is to be. They are found for the poet, and all he has to do is, with skill and energy, to construct them. Take, for instance, Shakspeare's *Tempest*, and Coleridge's 'Anciente Marinere'—of what more creative act can we conceive than is exemplified in these? Of course, we have all had beforehand ideas similar to a storm, a desert island, a witch, a magician, a mariner, a hermit, a wedding-guest; but these are only the Alphabet to the spirits of Shakspeare and Coleridge.

. . . Take Creation as meaning, not so much Deity bringing something out of nothing, as *filling the void with his Spirit*, and genius will seem a lower form of the same power.

The other kind of originality is, we think, that of Crabbe. It is magic at second-hand. He takes, not makes, his materials. He finds a good foundation—wood and stone in plenty—and he begins laboriously, successfully, and after a plan of his own, to build. If in any of his works he approaches to the higher property, it is in 'Eustace Grey,' who moves here and there, on his wild wanderings, as if to the rubbing of Aladdin's lamp.

This prepares us for coming to the third question, what is Crabbe's relative position to his great contemporary poets? We are compelled to put him in the second class. He is not a philosophic poet, like Wordsworth. He is not, like Shelley, a Vates, moving upon the uncertain but perpetual and furious wind of his inspirations. He is not, like Byron, a demoniac exceeding fierce, and dwelling among the tombs. He is not, like Keats, a sweet and melancholy voice, a tune bodiless, bloodless— dying away upon the waste air, but for ever to be remembered as men remember a melody they have heard in youth. He is not, like Coleridge, all these almost by turns, and, besides, a Psalmist, singing at times strains so sublime and holy, that they might seem snatches of the song of Eden's cherubim, or caught in trance from the song of Moses and the Lamb. To this mystic brotherhood Crabbe must not be added. He ranks with a lower but still lofty band—with Scott, (as a poet) and Moore, and Hunt, and Campbell, and Rogers, and Bowles, and James Montgomery, and Southey; and surely they nor he need be ashamed of each other, as they shine in one soft and peaceful cluster.

We are often tempted to pity poor posterity on this score. How is it to manage with the immense number of excellent works which this age has bequeathed, and is bequeathing it? How is it to economize its time so as to read a tithe of them? And should it in mere self-defence proceed to decimate, with what principle shall the process be carried on, and who shall be appointed to preside over it? Critics of the twenty-second century, be merciful as well as just. Pity the *disjecta membra* of those we thought mighty poets. Respect and fulfil our prophecies of immortality. If ye must carp and cavil, do not, at least, in mercy, abridge. Spare us the prospect of this last insult, an abridged copy of the *Pleasures of Hope*,[1] or *Don Juan*, a *new* abridgement. If ye must operate in this way, be it on *Madoc Thehama*,[2] or the *Course of Time*.[3] Generously leave room for 'O'Connor's Child'[4] in the poet's corner of a journal, or for 'Eustace Grey' in the space of a crown piece. Surely, living in the Millenium, and resting under your vines and fig-trees, you will have more time to read than we, in this bustling age, who move, live, eat, drink, *sleep, and die*, at railway speed. If not, we fear the case of many of our poets is hopeless, and that others, besides Satan Montgomery[5] and the author of 'Silent Love,'[6] would be wise to enjoy their present laurels, for verily there are none else for them.

Seriously, we hope that much of Crabbe's writing will every year become less and less readable, and less and less easily understood; till, in the milder day, men shall have difficulty in believing that such physical, mental, and moral degradation, as he describes, ever existed in Britain; and till, in future Encyclopædias, his name be found recorded as a powerful but barbarous writer, writing in a barbarous age. . . .

[1] Thomas Campbell (1777–1844), *The Pleasures of Hope*, 1799.

[2] This appears to be a reference to Robert Southey who published *Madoc* in 1805 and *The Curse of Kehama* in 1810.

[3] Robert Pollok (1798–1827), *The Course of Time*, 1827.

[4] By Thomas Campbell.

[5] Robert Montgomery (1807–55), *Satan, a Poem*, 1830.

[6] By James Wilson.

66. Another American view

1850

Henry Giles (1809–82), a Scotsman of Unitarian persuasions who emigrated to America in 1840, published *Lectures and Essays*, Vol. I, Boston, 1850. The essay on Crabbe (pp. 45–92) is, in its own words, 'criticism which is not merely literary, but moral also' (p. 54). The extract below is from the middle section (pp. 62–72).

The poems of Crabbe may be classed under three distinct designations, as tragic, moral, and satirical; and, by the laws that respectively govern these, we must regulate our criticism and form our decision. If we regard Crabbe as a tragic writer, we must not complain that he is gloomy; if we take him as a moralist, we must not wonder at his severity; if we turn to him as a satirist, we must expect often to find him bitter or sarcastic.

Crabbe is a writer of harrowing, tragic power; his narratives are so vivid, as almost to be dramatic; you not only follow the incidents of a story, but you conceive the presence of an action. He lays bare the human heart, and shows the loves and hatreds, the vices and the virtues, that work within it, the agonies and fears that wreck and break it. He observes the passions in their modifications, he traces them in all their stages, he portrays them in all their consequences; the love that lingers guileless to the grave, or shivers the brain in madness; the revenge that never quits its deadly thought, until it is perfected in the horrid deed; the remorse that follows sin, that haunts the affrighted conscience through existence.

Never has didactic poet more effectively than Crabbe, exhibited his teachings in dramatic example. His characters are drawn with such fidelity, that you behold them with all their living peculiarities. In both the description of scenes and the portraiture of characters, we observe evidence of mournful thoughtfulness, of accurate inspection; of scrupulous reality, of careful coloring.

Fishermen and smugglers are frequently his personages, and with

these, and their fortunes, he constantly links descriptions of the ocean
which are fearful and sublime. With ruthless fidelity, he paints dreary
portions of the shore with most mournful accessories; the desert beach;
the chilly and the slimy strand; muscle-gatherers prowling through the
mud; smugglers preparing to brave the tempest and the deep; wreckers
watching for their prey. Taking a barren field adjacent to the sea, by a
few salient touches,—such as a ragged child torn by brambles, a group
of scattered hats, a company of gypsies, a straggling poacher, a gaudy
weed, a neglected garden,—he will make a picture of sadness, that shall
oppress you as a thing of sense.

His style corresponds to his thoughts; austere and simple, he entrusts
entirely to the naked force of meaning, and that meaning it is impossible
to mistake. The wickedness of sin, the wreck of passion, appear more
fearful when they are not so much described as displayed by this color-
less language, which, like the cloudless atmosphere, exhibits objects,
without exhibiting itself. Minuteness of touch is the characteristic which
critics commonly attribute to the moral pictures of Crabbe. Generally,
this may be correct, yet no writer can suggest more than Crabbe does,
at times, in few words, as where he describes the lady,

> wise, austere, and nice,
> Who showed her virtue, by her scorn of vice;
> [*The Parish Register*, III, 320–1]

Or, when he sets before us the pliant parson, who pleased his parishioners by never offending them; one of those good easy souls, who never
know the loss of appetite by the toils of thought; who bow and smile,
and always say 'yes;' whom an independent opinion would frighten, as
a ghost from the dead; and who would as soon mount a forlorn hope,
as venture on a sturdy contradiction.

> Fiddling and fishing were his arts; at times
> He altered sermons, and he aimed at rhymes.
> [*The Borough*, III, 102–3]

Crabbe's poetry is the tragedy of common life, and as tragedy we
must judge it. The tragic elements are in rude forms as well as ideal ones;
they are in humble conditions as well as in heroic situations. They belong to human nature in its essence, and the modes in which they show
themselves are but the accidents of art or circumstances. The tragic
genius naturally selects the sad and the terrible in our nature; most poets
have associated these elements with exalted condition or extraordinary

events. Crabbe has connected them with lowly individuals and un-romantic incidents. If we, therefore, call Crabbe gloomy, why should we not so designate every writer who is purely tragic? Does Crabbe, in his terrible scenes, intend to give a general picture of common life? No, assuredly. He no more intends this, than the writer of romantic tragedy intends to represent his impersonations as the veracity of history, or as the counterparts of elevated rank. Crabbe, most certainly would no more imply that Peter Grimes, a vulgar, but gloomy and atrocious man was common among fishermen, than Massinger would have it under-stood that Sir Giles Overreach was a frequent character among private gentlemen. Peter Grimes is in essence a tragic character, as well as Sir Giles Overreach. In what sense, then, is Crabbe a gloomy writer in which Massinger is not also? Is it that the personages of Crabbe are of low or every-day existence?

Whether these are proper subjects for tragic story is a question of criticism, that I cannot here discuss, and the discussion of it is not neces-sary to my subject. The *condition* of the characteristics does not in any way affect the spirit which they embody. Admitting much of nature in that sympathy with the sorrows of those raised above us, which we so strongly feel, I think there is also in it somewhat of prejudice. Feelings more genuine and more true, would teach us not to destroy the differ-ence but to lessen it. Some persons can feel for woe that weeps amidst gauze and gas light, and faints most gracefully in a spangled robe, while they will turn away in disgusted selfishness from vulgar want. Yet the record of such want, the knowledge that such want has being, ought more to touch our hearts than the genteelest agony that was ever printed upon vellum. Sensibility, which is moral rather than imagin-ative, which has its glow in the affections, rather than in the fancy, can approach rude suffering in its coarseness, and it can bear it in description.

Crabbe dispelled many illusions which the fiction and falsehood of our literature had maintained in reference to humble life. Nor was it unkindness to the poor, but rather benevolence, to dispel such decep-tions. The region of laborious life was, to poets and their patrons, an enchanted Eden; a fairy land, where some light from the golden age continued yet to linger; where passions were asleep, where tastes were simple, and where wants were few. The bards sang sweetly of poverty with blessed content; of innocence in rural vales, of shepherds that only dreamed of love, and hinds that whistled as they went for want of thought; of swains that tuned their oaten pipes, and maidens that listened in rapture to the sound; well pleased, the wealthy heard; sure never was lot so happy as the poor enjoyed; and while crime and misery were at their doors, they read only of contented Louisas and gentle Damons; then rushed to ball and banquet in the bliss of ignorance, and without one pang of charity.

Crabbe revealed other matters. He showed that sin and sorrow, guilt and passion, are doing their work at the base of society, as well as on its summit; he showed that the heart was much the same history in all conditions. This, so far, was novelty; and surely the novelty of truth is worth something, even when it is not so pleasant as we might desire; nor is that power manifested in vain, which shows us that the fearful strength of human nature which wrecks a throne, may spend as terrible a fury on a cottage hearth.

As a matter of taste, we may object to the social grade of Crabbe's personages: as matter of principle, I see not that we can. Neither can we object to him that he connects them with dark and destructive passions. The passions are essentially the same, whether in high life or low; and with those which are dark and destructive the tragic writer deals, whether he places the catastrophe in palace or in tent. The envy of Iago, the jealousy of Othello, the ambition of Macbeth, and the cruelty of Richard, are all the same envy, jealousy, ambition, and cruelty in so many peasants; and in peculiarity of circumstances they might be equally as tragic. Will it be said, that Crabbe deals with such passions exclusively? It is not so; passages of greater sweetness, passages more loving, gentle, tender, beautiful, than numbers to be found in Crabbe, poet has seldom written. Take, for instance, the story of Phœbe Dawson; the sketch of the young girl towards the close of *The Parish Register*, and her consumptive sailor lover; 'The Parting Hour,' and 'Farmer Ellis;' and if they have not moral truth and beauty, strong and devoted affections, I do not know what can be considered truth, beauty, or affection.

Crabbe is not ungentle, but he is sad. He has not the genial amplitude of Burns, and neither his constitution nor his circumstances tended to produce it. Burns with a rare affluence of soul, was trained among an intelligent, and, on the whole, independent population; with trials, to be sure, around them, that would often make them sad, but seldom the sordid wretchedness that could see no hope. Daily there was labor in the field, and sometimes there was sorrow on the hearth, but the cloud was not enduring; fun soon laughed at care again, and frolic danced as merrily as ever.

Crabbe in youth had but little pleasure; in London he was steeped in poverty to the very lips; in mature life his professional position, in neighbourhoods abounding with destitution, brought him continually into contact with the most forlorn ignorance, and the most hapless vice. He does not often rise to the raptures of enjoyment, but he has constantly gleams of the beautiful in human life; the fidelities of lowly attachment; the sensibilities and the grace, that nature gives to an unperverted woman; the glory that, in the hardest fortune, crowns the brave and honest man.

I would not say, however, that Crabbe never presents too gloomy an aspect of existence. His pictures of poverty, with its attendant evils, are often certainly too harsh; often as partial as they are discolored; pictures which evince a fearful power of causing pain, but which afford no moral compensation for the agony they excite. This remark applies very extensively to most of our poet's views of external nature. His eye is sicklied with hues of sorrow, and his ear is disordered with its sounds. The burden of lamentation intercepts from his hearing the music of paradise; the sun sets with glory in the heavens, but while he gazes, a mist of tears ascends from earth to dim it; the flower rejoices in the desert, but man is trodden in the crowd; the stream is clear in the solitude, but in habitable places it is the mirror of worn faces and blasted forms. Our poet wanders too much like a haunted man, meeting at too many turns a gaunt and remorseless spectre of crime and suffering. Intervals of release he has; intervals of many genial thoughts, when the sounds of the living world, if melancholy, are at least musical; when human goodness and human affections throw their beauty on his dream, and when the sympathies of love, undimmed by selfishness, come pictured from his fancy in pencillings of light.

As a moralist, Crabbe is most solemn and most impressive. The power of his description is equalled only by his truth of principle and his moveless integrity of purpose. Never has moralist exhibited more terribly than Crabbe the maledictions that fall upon the guilty. Never has moralist exhibited the awful law of right and wrong, in so many and impressive forms. Wherever he places sin, there is the reign of misery—in the rural cottage, in the city garret, on the midnight ocean, on the barren moor. Wherever he gives us the crime, he gives us the retributive calamity, that dogs it with certain step, and strikes when the clock of fate has tolled the hour of execution. He makes no compromise; he flatters no sin; he softens no sentence that it merits; he conceals no consequence of ruin that follows it; he confounds no distinctions of obligation; he sophisticates no principles of action; he loosens no bonds

393

of duty; he shakes no trust in virtue; he wrings our hearts, but he warns them; and while he moves us to sadness, he moves us to wisdom.

As a satirist, I do not remember much that I can commend in Crabbe. This aspect of his poetry is to me one of complete repulsion; one of harshness, that inflicts pain, and does not minister to correction. Crabbe wanted the gayety of heart, which enables the satirist to please as well as to chastise; he wanted that easy and sportive fancy, which adds grace even to censure; he wanted that exhilarating humor, which can prevent anger from deepening to malice or contempt, by a joyous and a humanizing laugh. Our author's son commends his satire; but satire does not, as I can perceive, suit either his temper or his subjects. His temper inclined him to the melancholy in our life and nature; his manner is therefore so uniformly serious, that satire, in its levity, would sound from him like laughter in a church. The gravity of satire is still more inconsistent with his subjects.

67. W. C. Roscoe on Crabbe's standing in mid-century

1859

Roscoe (1823–59) contributed to the *National Review*, edited by his brother-in-law, R. H. Hutton. This article appeared in January 1859 (No. xv, 1–32), reviewing the 1853 edition of *Life and Poems*.

The criticism of contemporary art cannot possibly be mature. No reader can avoid being influenced by the point of view from which he contemplates the subject of his observation. And as all art worthy of the name is, to some extent at least, permanent, it will always have a side addressed to ideas other than the prevailing ones of the time when it first appears; and where the poet is of a wider reaching imagination and insight than his critic, as every great poet almost always will be, this side will probably, for some time at least, be beyond the power of the latter to estimate, perhaps beyond his scope to perceive at all. Every new generation possesses new facilities for the estimation of a true poet. It can ascertain the judgment passed by those who have gone before; and it can bring its own new knowledge and the fresh conditions of its own position to test the permanent truthfulness, wisdom, and beauty of the poems delivered to the ears of generations gone by. The true Temple of Fame is long in building; every age reviews its proportions, adds a new stone, or tears down an unmerited decoration. Sometimes a hasty Tower of Babel soars into the skies in a brief ecstasy of popular applause, to be scattered for ever in scorn by the next comers; sometimes the moss gathers over a few well-laid stones, destined after long years to be reverentially cleared and made the foundation of a monument lasting as the heavens. The criticism of the literature of the day is, no doubt, the more immediate function of the Reviews of the day; but, even in the interests of such criticism, it is well to secure those elements of comparison which are to be obtained by the occasional discussion of the productions of other writers than those who now first appear upon the stage. We shall treat these latter more broadly and more justly if we preserve our familiarity with those who have preceded them; and, independently of this, it can never be without interest to record how a great poet appears to each new generation of readers.

It needs no apology, then, we conceive, to our readers, that we occupy our pages with some remarks on the poetry of Crabbe; which, however little it may coincide with the modern estimate of what is most delightful in the art of verse, can yet never fail to command respect and admiration. Nor shall we scruple to refresh their memories with a brief sketch of the life and personal habits of the author; not because we have any thing to offer on this subject derived from other than the existing resources of contemporary allusion and the excellent Memoir by his son, but because it is our object rather to examine the genius of the man than to attempt to measure out exact dues of praise or blame to his productions.

Both the biography and the works of Crabbe are less widely read than they deserve to be. The poet in his lifetime enjoyed a wide popularity, which narrowed somewhat suddenly after his decease. His writings, on their first appearance, had an extensive body of readers, and gained the suffrages of the best-qualified judges of his day. Burke first distinguished his rising genius. Fox and Johnson read him with pleasure, and condescended to correct him; for a condescension it was esteemed on both sides, though corrections made under the influence of an external authority of this kind rarely fail to operate as deteriorations. Canning and Dudley North were warm in their admiration; and Wilson and Jeffrey and Gifford agreed to applaud him. Sir Walter Scott, with his open-hearted enthusiasm, extolled him as a poet and welcomed him as a friend. Both *The Borough* and *The Village*, inferior as they are to the *Tales*, found readers throughout the breadth of the land; and Mr. Murray paid him £3,000 for the *Tales of the Hall* and the copyright of the poems already published. But though that work was too well received, the interest in Crabbe's poetry receded so rapidly that the bargain proved more liberal than prudent on the part of the publisher. Most poets experience an ebb of reputation after it has risen to its first height; and, indeed, their fame generally partakes of a periodical rise and fall, during which some are borne higher on every succeeding wave, and others gradually stranded.

It is low tide with Crabbe just at present: the times of late have not been favourable to the appreciation of writers of his school. He may be considered as the last great poet who made man and the lives of men the direct subject of his verse. Modern poetry has occupied itself not with men, but with the ideas, the passions, and the sentiments of men; not with their lives, and not with their characters, but with detached incidents of lives and special traits or sides of character. The concrete man and the actual life have been subordinated to, or displayed only to throw a more vivid light on, the elucidation of feelings and ideas; and often these have been simply the feelings and ideas of the poet himself. The colloquists of *The Excursion* are not very ingeniously contrived mouthpieces for the contemplative imagination and meditative genius of the author. Byron wrote to vent his own passions—his anger, his wit, his chagrin, his love of beauty; Burns is either lyrical or satirical; and Shelley, singing like his own sky-lark

> Till all the earth and air
> With his voice is loud,

soars like it too into a region of thin air, native to himself, but removed far away from the working-day aspects and actual arrangements of human affairs. Tennyson, with far more power than any of these of entering into other minds and sympathizing with varied feeling, is perhaps still less capable of dealing with complete character. He has painted not men, but present moods, and what may be called attitudes of mind, in men. In the softness of his outlines and the richness of his colouring he is most unlike the daguerreotypist; but he is like the manipulator in his main difference from a great painter. He gives a likeness from a fixed point of view; and, though a complete likeness, yet, one of only a single aspect of his subject: while a man like Rembrandt or Sir Joshua Reynolds, poring long upon a face, possesses the magic power of indicating something of the whole character in his one likeness of the countenance. Literary art for some years past, both in verse and prose fiction, has narrowed itself more and more exclusively to the exposition of the feelings and the description of nature. The thought itself which mingles in it is employed in reflecting on the influences of scenery and scrutinizing the working of the heart; and character has come to mean less what a man will think and do and appear under given circumstances than what he will feel. In such a school women are of course prominent, both as writers and subject-matter. The material is that with which they are specially qualified to deal both from knowledge and inclination, and of which they themselves furnish a complex, varied, and interesting part. Their conceptions, it is true, are often concrete and real; but they occupy themselves with but one-half of our nature, and always the same half. They are not alone, however; the closest observer and ablest reproducer of life and manners among modern writers[1] wades deeper every step in the same direction. He has long been at a dead-lock in *The Virginians*, and threatens to surrender himself entirely to describing sentiment and uttering caustic and humorous sayings about sentiment. The humour of Dickens has always lain in the caricature of special traits and the exaggeration of engaging excellences; and Bulwer, tired of his old ideals, solicits a female audience, and striking boldly into the current of the day, devotes himself to the domestic affections. Modern poets are not simply lyrical; they do not utter themselves directly. They are contemplative, but contemplate themselves; they frame outward delineations, but use them as machinery for displaying the results of introspection. *Aurora Leigh* is a vivisection on the bookseller's counter; Coventry Patmore, in a poem devoted to the deification of woman, tells us how he felt during his courtship; and, to descend lower, Alexander Smith and Gerald Massey, as they have the less command of external resources, are all the more assiduous in digging in their own natures.

[1] Thackeray.

It may be questioned, however, whether a reaction be not at hand. At any rate, we think the world of readers is ripe for it, if any writer shall be found powerful enough to raise the standard of revolt. War has shaken up the energies of the nation; and we should not be surprised if it and some other influences should be found potent to disperse the too exclusive devotion to the affections which has long distinguished English art.

Should our poetry turn to contemplate the more practical and every-day aspects of human life,—should it turn, we mean, from the passions and sentiments on which life revolves to the activities in which it is spent; should it take to scanning moralities rather than feelings, and doings rather than contemplations,—it is probable that Crabbe will gain some meed of real attention more valuable than the uninformed acquiescence in eulogy which is pretty universally conceded to him.

[There follows a section devoted to the *Life*.]

It is a common, almost a universal idea, that a love of beauty is essential to the character of a poet. Some have even gone so far as to make this passion the basis of their theories of his art. It is obvious that a classification thus grounded goes far to exclude some branches which universally accepted language has always comprehended within the name of poetry. It is difficult to see the beauty of satire and epigram; it is not very precise to ascribe that quality to wit or humour; yet no restrictions of the theorist can avail to put Butler, Dryden, and Pope out of the category of poets. Crabbe presents difficulties still greater to the prevalent ideas on this subject. His position is perhaps more anomalous than that of any other English poet; yet few, if any, will deny that he has an incontrovertible claim to the title. There is a sense in which he is the least poetical of poets; there is another in which he is one of the most so. He is the plainest of all poets,—deals the least in ornament. When he gives you a simile,—as he sometimes thinks it his duty to do,—he puts it in perspicuously, adds it ostentatiously, like a Quaker sticking a flower in his button-hole. To a great poet metaphor is a more refined language, through which alone he can express his deeper meanings and hint his more refined ones. But Crabbe has no profound ideas, and no subtle ones. The common language of common men is abundantly sufficient to express what he has to say; and it is rarely indeed that he travels beyond it. And yet he is a poet. He is a poet, moreover, without passion, and with only a steady tempered sympathy with the affections he displays and the characters he presents in his poems. He has none of that constructive genius which turns all the things it touches into harmonious wholes, and contrives to shed a grace of external form over the veriest trifles. He has no wit and no humour; and without all this he is a poet. He is the last man to make himself, and the display of his own character, life, or feelings, the source of interest to others. He gives no voice to our profounder thoughts; he neither interprets nature, nor reproduces her aspects of beauty with that richness of colouring which is the characteristic of modern poetry. He is much further from Tennyson, Wordsworth, Burns, Byron, and Keats, than any one of these poets is from another. In the plainness and common-placeness of his ideas and language, in his absence of passion and profound insight, in his total disregard of beauty, Crabbe was no poet. Some will say nothing remains to make him one. We say, on the contrary, that he had in a high degree the one essential quality which all poets must have in common; and that those things in which we have marked him as deficient, important and valuable as they are, are the accidents, not the essentials, of poetry. He had imagination. That man is a poet (though there may be no limit to his poverty and triteness) who takes up into the receptive imagination any matter whatever, and reproduces it in language under any of those rhythmical conditions which are accepted as forms of verse. There is no limit to this definition. A train of argument is not poetry; and if there be such a thing as a man arriving at logical conclusions in rhyme, he is not making poetry. But a man who gives a metrical form to a conceived train of thought (as Dryden in the *Religio Laici*) is writing poetry; and he who describes in the barest words the very commonest object he has once seen and formed a concrete idea of, is an artist and, if he uses verse, a poet; he is a poet, that is, by definition. To be a great poet, indeed to be a poet at all in the higher sense in which we usually employ the term, a man must have a creative imagination: he must be able to make some new thing out of those impressions which he has received,—to 'body forth the shapes of things unseen,' and by the fire of his genius to fuse and transmute into new forms the results of his experience, his insight, and his intuition.

It is imagination that constitutes the poet; and one half of imagination consists in the power to form vivid mental conceptions of the things which do exist; in the power of gathering in a harvest of one's own from the external world. It is the high, the almost unexampled degree in which Crabbe possesses this power which gives him his place

as a poet. He has little of the true creative power; he is only just removed from an actual transcriber; but he has a wealth of materials,
a treasury of exact conceptions of existing things, which goes far to
compensate a want of ingenuity in framing things new. We have
spoken of the receptive imagination, and this adjective indicates the
nature of the faculty in most minds; it is generally to a great extent
passive, and partakes of the nature of a mirror in which the images of
outer things are reflected. But in some men it is a more active and
aggressive power; and this was particularly the case with Crabbe. His
was a grasping tenacious imagination. Little Hartley Coleridge would
have called it a 'catch-me-fast' faculty. He was a man of keen observation, but also something farther; he did more than see things; he laid
fast hold of them, and held them up as it were to himself for contemplation; cast a vivid light on them; and when he gave them forth again,
he gave not the crude fact, but the impression he had taken of it. If he
did not transmute experience into poetry, he yet did something more
than simply translate it into verse.

He has not, indeed, that power which Giorgione among painters
possesses in so high a degree, of making the image of an outward thing
wear and express the mood of the artist's own mind; as where he
steeps in sadness, and almost in despair, the picture of a man playing,
and two women singing, seated on the grass. Such an artist is like one
who moulds gold, and stamps his own image on it; but Crabbe uses,
as it were, his own mind for the material, and stamps images of
the external world on it. Every work of art is part gathered from the
external world, part the artist's own. In the first case we have cited, the
artist shows himself in the superscription he leaves on his material; in
the latter, he shows himself in the sort of substance in which the work
is done. And this comparison of Crabbe's productions to a piece of
metal bearing a defined impress may serve to contrast him also with
another class of poetical minds. Some imaginations are like a sheet of
clear water, in whose bosom is reflected the landscape around it and
the sky above. As the water itself is part of the scene, so the man's
nature seems to mingle with and be part of all that he conceives; and
all things around him lean over him, and leave their shapes mirrored
within him with softened wavering outlines, like the trees and towers
in the lake, which partly seem watery images, and partly the water
seems an inverted picture of the land. If the nature be deep and pure,
and broad enough, such an imagination is great indeed; but if it be
easily ruffled, or clouded, or small, it reflects but evanescent patches

of truth and loveliness. Other minds,—and of such was Crabbe's,—have metal imaginations; the man himself takes hold of a thing as it were, and himself stamps it on the cold and hard but still receptive and tenacious material. The image remains, sharp, distinct, lasting; but rigid, colourless, and detached; and bearing with it in the very substance in which it is impressed an indisseverable and unmistakable evidence of the poet's own nature.

Crabbe has nothing of the fiery and alert imagination. He cannot 'turn and wind a fiery Pegasus;' but drives a steady unwinged horse at an even trot from period to period. His genius is no swift sparkling brook or broad shining river hastening through scenes of beauty to the sea; but is like the stream familiar to his childhood, rolling, placidly and somewhat heavily along between its banks, laden with the common things appertaining to common men—hoys and brigantines and trading sloops.

Yet a strong imagination he undoubtedly had; and, what seems singular in looking at his writings, a musing temperament and a retiring nature. In reading Crabbe, one would naturally draw the conclusion that he had studied men from very close acquaintance with individuals, and had consorted with them much and familiarly. It is clear, however, that this was by no means the case. It is clear that he was never much at home in the society of others,—even the poor of his own parish; that he loved best to be alone with his own pursuits. He observed men closely; but it was as an outside spectator. 'The author-rector,' says his son, 'is in all points the similitude of Mr. Crabbe himself, except in the subject of his lucubrations:'

Then came the *author-rector*: his delight . . .
[*The Parish Register*, III, 865–84]

When he was a boy, he did not mingle in the sports and occupations of those of his own age, but neglected school and playground alike for occupations and pleasures which indicate very clearly the peculiar character of his genius. He lived a life of the imagination as truly as any other young poet has done; but his was not an imagination which could feast on its own dreams or soar unaided in the skies. It renewed its vigour by the touch of earth; it required a constant contact with reality, and sought an ever-fresh excitement in the transactions of men and the changes of nature.

I sought the town, and to the ocean gave . . .
[*Tales of the Hall*, IV, 295–410]

In the shop of the craftsman, by the inn fireside, with the shepherds on the heath, even at the smugglers' hut between the rocks, the observant curious boy was to be found; and in lines more full of poetic feeling than are common in his writings, he describes his companionship with nature: though here too he does not leave without a witness, as in his reference to the salt *taste* of the spray, his fondness for the recording of minute observations:

> I loved to walk where none had walked before, . . .
> [*ibid.*, 447–85]

The fact is, the opportunities possessed by Crabbe for the study of life and character were, both from circumstance and temperament, much narrower than any one would conceive who judged from his writings. And thus he was in reality thrown more upon his imagination than we are apt to suppose. If he did not use it to create, he necessarily fell back upon it to piece out true conceptions from the hints which fell in his way. Like Professor Owen constructing a mastodon from a tooth, he employed himself in making out character from the casual traits which came under his notice. Invention in poetry is a cooler word of our forefathers for what we call creation; but, used in its etymological sense, it would serve well to describe Crabbe's mode of working. Observation was his ruling passion, and he carried into poetry exactly the same habits and indulged the same tastes as in natural history. In both alike he was intolerant of system and careless of inductions. The Vicar of the *Tales of the Hall*, contradictory as the descriptions may seem in some respects, is no less like him than the Author-Rector of *The Parish Register*:

> The Vicar's self, still further to describe, . . .
> [*ibid.*, VI, 40–81]

It is with the poor, and those who constitute the lower half of the middle class, that Crabbe chiefly deals. He says truly that these possess in their conditions of life more room for rigorous individual growth, and are less compressed by conventional habits into set shapes, than any others; but there was, if not a better, a more practical reason for his drawing from them. He had seen more of them, and therefore knew them better. With the exception of his brief stay in London and at Beaconsfield and Belvoir, he had, when he wrote, lived the life either of a country surgeon or a country clergyman, and had mingled little, if at all, in what the world calls society. Nor, if had done so, was his a mind or an imagination to take cognisance of the finer *nuances* in which differences of character there display themselves. He could scarcely have studied men through their manners. He required marked differences, though they might be minute, showing themselves in marked characteristics, though they might not be obvious to a less close observer. It may even be said further that he lacked the power to appreciate any very finished degree of culture or extended reach of intellect. He reverenced and admired Burke and Fox; but they made no deep and abiding impression on him. When Moore and Rogers, anxious to secure any recollections of Burke which could be gathered from contemporary sources, came to consult Crabbe as to the conversation of his great patron, he could tell them nothing. He absolutely seems never to have formed an idea of the sort of men they really were. But he could draw with an unerring pencil a Sir Denis Brand or an Isaac Ashford; he explored with wonderful accuracy the depths and shallows of minds, however singular, which were of a certain calibre only. His eyes were always directed on a level or downwards. Nothing escaped their keen and penetrating gaze but what was set too far above or beyond their scope. Within certain narrow limits of range he has displayed a greater faculty for marking and describing nice distinctions in human character than any poet since Shakespeare. But it is not to be supposed he resembles Shakespeare. On the contrary, he stands as far apart from him as it is possible to do; and this not only by the whole interval between richness and poverty of fancy, but by another characteristic, important indeed, but not very easy to describe. Shakespeare cannot touch a thread in the vast network of the universe, but the whole web seems to quiver under his hands and to vibrate in his imagination; some haunting image of the whole breaks through and shines in each particular fancy. What most distinguishes him from every other poet is his strange intimacy with all the various relations borne by the matter he is handling to all other things, and his power by some rapid side-glance of indicating these relations, however remote and subtle. It would need his own command of language to describe exactly what his power is. We must be content to feel it, and to say, that it is as if he never detached a portion of the whole world of things, to deal with it; but only occupied a part of it, leaving all its connecting links and clues of association unsevered and even undisturbed: as if he played each play of his on some plot of forest ground marked out only by the surrounding trees, between which, and through shrub and quivering foliage, we glance along the shifting and interminable vistas which penetrate the unbounded woodland.

Crabbe is the reverse of all this. His genius works in things limited and disconnected. He cuts you off a piece of human nature, and holds it in his hand for you to look at. He builds up separate little brick cottages of mortal characteristics, and is glad when he can get them to stand in a row; then he makes a book of them. But his are no sham structures, no lath and plaster; all his bricks are moulded of real human clay, his timbers are taken from the events of real life; he bodies forth nothing but the shapes of things as they are. He is the antipodes of Shakespeare, because he is the plainest, the most detached, the most matter-of-fact of poets; but he is the antipodes of Byron, because he is the most truthful and the most conscientious of poets. Byron's imagination was like some great bright reflector, of shining but uneven surface, in which are shaped brilliant but distorted images; Crabbe's was like a little square flat Dutch glass, which reflects a small area, but that exactly.

Closely connected with this side of his genius is another of the main characteristics of his poetry—the way in which all the more fine threads of intellectual effort and moral character in men are ignored—the manner in which every thing is stripped of the atmosphere which surrounds it and unites it to other things, and exhibited square and naked, without the softened outline and the grace which particular things derive from the fineness of the shades with which they pass into something else. He has no eye for the aerial softness and blended colouring of nature. He describes with a hard resolute pen, idealizing nothing; but, on the contrary, often omitting all that casts a veil over meanness and deformity. Yet it is a mistake to speak of Crabbe's pictures of life as gloomy; and Byron characterized him still less aptly when he styled him 'nature's sternest painter.' There is nothing stern either in his disposition or his writings. A quiet kindliness prevails in both; he makes full, one might almost sometimes say undue, allowance for the frailties of human nature. He is neither exacting in his demands nor severe in his reprehensions. It is the very want of a high ideal and of the softening and refining influence of a lofty imagination which give to his poetry that distinguishing character which is in reality neither gloom nor sternness, but rudeness, if it is to be characterized in one word. He had a mild disposition, but a certain harshness of mind. His pictures of nature are naked, and in the worse sense of nakedness. He had nothing of that eye by which the sculptor sees in the figure of man the suggestion of the Apollo Belvidere; he had not the power to pierce beyond the mixed deformities of human organization; he had not even a pleasure in studying its higher types. Had he been a sculptor, he would have modelled the ungainly ploughboy or the warped artisan, not the athlete or the hunter. The stamp of his birth and early education was effaced from his manners and his ordinary modes of thought, but was ineffaceably impressed in the deeper parts of his nature. There is a something in seaside-dwelling men, especially of towns and of our eastern coasts, as if the salt spray and heavy winds had helped to mould them; it is not so much native coarseness as a sort of weather-beaten cast. Such men are resolute, but stubborn; they are daring, with a sort of moody contempt of danger, which they neither love nor care to avoid; hard, self-dependent, intolerant of weakness,—men who are accustomed to contend with difficulties below themselves rather than to avail themselves of advantages to rise; they have a nature tenacious, claylike—like clay too in being at once common and valuable. Doubtless Crabbe was very different from such men; but, softened and refined as he was, something both of the rudeness and the strength of this salt Suffolk blood lay about the base of his character.

He handles life so as to take the bloom off it. His way of viewing things is one which recommends itself to many minds, and in some moods to us all. Sometimes we cannot take wings, and ascend to the higher truths of existence and the more essential and more refined aspects of things. We ask for the coarse substantial certainties of common experience,—for sense, not only common sense but vulgar sense; we acknowledge our appetites,—bread, beef, and beer seem valuable; we lay hold of tangible ponderable certainties; we look on the landscape with an eye to crops, the great sea as a place to fish in and wherein to float steamers, and 'the glorious sun himself' seems made to shine in at window. Such thoughts and feelings are good for us at times; these sort of things are the rude foundation-stones of our lives, let them rise to whatever lofty purposes and spring with whatever beauty of carved arch and aspiring pinnacle into the heavens. It is steadying and sobering to turn sometimes to them, though it would be debasing to live too much among them. And Crabbe, with all his excellencies, his genuine simplicity, his uncompromising moral tone, his kindliness, his manliness, cannot be said to be an elevating poet, or to exercise a refining influence. He paints correctly, but inadequately; as if one should copy the Venus de' Medici with exactness, but in sandstone. Hence that disenchanting air which hangs over his works. He rises above it sometimes; but it is the prevailing tone, and as such, has universally made itself felt. The swift aspirations, the winged hopes, the impassioned affections of men, the mystery of life, the problem of death,—you must not look to see these things touched upon; but instead of it an unshrinking hand laid on all that lies bare to our sight, and a calm unharassed contentment to abide in the common and obvious conditions of human life. In his preaching as in his verse he was fond of what was tangible, plain, and practical. He was a tolerant man; but the thing he had least tolerance for was enthusiasm, and the fervour of the Methodists and their sudden conversions were just the things to annoy him,—he wrote and preached against them with vehemence. On the other hand, he himself,—and it is significant of the state of the church in his day—, earned the appellation of a 'Gospel preacher,' implying that he was a little overstrained in his notions; and this because he had some conviction of the intrinsic importance of religion, and preached a doctrine of future rewards and punishments, instead of simply drawing attention to the worldly advantages which follow in the train of prudent and not overstrained virtue.

He was a man rather of affectionate nature than of deep feelings, and it is very rarely indeed that he ventures on the delineation of strong passion or uncontrolled emotion. He may describe the consequences of such things; but he nowhere, so far as we can remember, gives them a direct voice. 'Sir Eustace Grey,' indeed, contains a forcible picture of terrors; but it is an enumeration of past terrors, nor can we acquiesce in the place Gifford[1] assigns it. Like every thing of Crabbe's, it is too defined, too explicit and limited. But the essence of terror lies in dim imaginations, in appeals to an unascertained capacity of suffering, in the stirring of dread and uncomprehended possibilities of pain. When we can gaze on even the worst forms of anguish in the face, they lose much of their power of exciting terror. Sir Eustace catalogues the miseries of his madness and despair, and details the tortures inflicted on him by the fiends:

> Those fiends upon a shaking fen . . .
> ['Sir Eustace Grey', 268–91]

This is forcible and frightful; but it does not shake the spirit and make quail the heart, like some parts of De Quincy's description of the 'Mater Tenebrarum.' The only passion which Crabbe really moves deeply is the one to which he was himself most accessible, that of pity. A sort of quiet compassion is the mood in which he contemplates the

[1] See the *Quarterly Review* article, No. 27 above.

sorrows and troubles of mortality; and he excites the same feeling in his readers, not by any direct appeal, but by the tenor of his narrative and the contagious influence of his own temper. The description in 'Resentment'[1] of the abject wretchedness of the broken merchant contrasted with the unfeeling rigour of his prosperous wife, and especially those last lines in which the soft-hearted maid-servant has no eyes for the faults of her mistress in her remorse for the slowness of her own compassion, afford perhaps the best instance of his power in this direction.

It is curious that, with so sound a mind of his own, Crabbe loves to speak of and describe a disordered intellect; and it is a proof of his penetration, that he traces the disordering influence of sin on the mind, and is not content with telling us how it affects the feelings only. In this direction he shows more insight than in any other; and 'Edward Shore'[2] and 'Peter Grimes'[3] will always rank among his master-pieces. The former is a narrative the more striking perhaps from the unexaggerated diction in which it is clothed, and the homely simplicity of the reflections which accompany it. It shows how genius, grace, proud thoughts, and aspiring hopes to live true to a high ideal, may be no charm to secure their owner from the depths of human degradation, if they be but the furnishings of a self-centered heart and want the basis of pure principle to sustain them. It is useless to attempt to epitomize Crabbe's poems, and few can be ignorant of that remarkable history of genius and ambition traced through their alliance with unfenced passion and indulged pride to their setting in idiocy. It is in describing an unsettled brain that Crabbe most often rises above the level of his ordinary strain, not only in his matter but in his utterance:

> That gentle maid, whom once the youth had loved, . . .
> [*Tales*, XI, 446–67]

The story of 'The Parish Clerk,' long proud in his integrity, and boastful of his superiority to the weaknesses of those around him, betrayed into a system of pilfering the church offerings, and convicted at the altar before the whole congregation, is another instance of the same kind; and the description of the effect upon the man furnishes one of the finest examples of Crabbe's poetical capacity, and of the power of his unadorned but vigorous imagination:

> He lived in freedom, but he hourly saw . . .
> [*The Borough*, XIX, 262–300]

---

[1] *Tales*, XVII.   [2] *Tales*, XI.   [3] *The Borough*, XXII.

'Peter Grimes' portrays the influence of a savage sort of remorse on a coarse and brutal nature. It is powerful but rude drawing, and a far more vivid and terror-inspiring picture of raving alienation of intellect than that contained in 'Sir Eustace Grey.' The image of the depraved and sullen criminal floating in his boat along some solitary reach of the stagnant river, and gazing on the water until the shapes of those he has murdered rise to taunt him with his sin, is oppressive in its vividness and in the unsparing fidelity with which all the sad and foul aspects of the scene are catalogued, as if all the nature about him were in harmony with the callous heart of the sufferer.

Crabbe's writings cannot be said to be distinguished either by wit or humour. He sees the comic aspect of a matter sometimes, and reports it in a matter-of-fact deliberate way that has a pleasant air of quaintness, such as distinguishes 'The Frank Courtship;'[1] but there is nothing in his writings to laugh at. His bent is in another direction—to moralize; and it may be said that all of his poetry which does not consist in direct scrutiny of men themselves, is made up of observations on the moral phenomena resulting from their characters and actions. And here the same mind shows itself as elsewhere: you are not to expect what is subtle or profound, but what is sensible, keen, direct, and sagacious. Here, as elsewhere, he displays great acuteness, and little delicacy of perception. His remarks are all detached, and made without any view to general deductions. He collected the materials for his poetry in just the same way as he collected his facts in science; and both in poetry and science he showed himself absolutely destitute of the philosophic spirit. What he called botany, was gathering plants and knowing their names; entomology was collecting specimens of insects without even arranging them. He was satisfied with single links of knowledge, and never cared to discover how they made parts of a chain. He never reasons. He says many shrewd things, and some things, occasionally wise things, about human life, especially its moral conditions; but they are always things he has seen and noted, never conclusions he has deduced. Reading him is like going into a museum; you are introduced to a collection of human traits and experiences. He absolutely adds not so much to your knowledge of human nature as to your opportunities of studying it. He supplies you with new information; but, just as is the case in a museum, the pleasure and advantage are limited. Once become sufficiently familiar with Crabbe to know what he has written, and there is nothing more to be gained from him. It is all patent. A man may read

1 *Tales*, VI.

Lear ten, twenty, and a hundred times; and if his mind be awake, he will every time find something fresh, something he did not before know was there said, or implied, or hinted at. No man has a right to say he knows a single speech written by Shakespeare until he has learned it by heart, and thought on it night and morning. A man may read a page of Wordsworth, and think it commonplace; but, musing on it quietly and long, he will find a depth beneath its apparent platitude, and a harmony under its seeming ungainliness, which will find him food for his deepest meditations, and which daily converts sceptics of his genius into worshippers, the more inclined to blindness because they seem to work with the poet to their results. But Crabbe—you may read him twice; but you must be gifted with a short memory to enjoy him after this, except in some isolated passages which rise above his ordinary strain. 'The Convert' is a clear piece of drawing; but one does not recur to the moral again and again:

> Unhappy Dighton! had he found a friend . . .
> [*Tales*, XIX, 448–61]

We are afraid Mr. Crabbe preached like that. Irreproachable sermonizing, 'sound,' and so forth; but rather in what has irreverently been called the 'chopped-hay' school, and, at any rate, not good poetry. This sort of commonplace is, no doubt, interspersed with shrewd telling observations; still, they are of the kind which bear their full meaning on the surface. You are not drawn into deeper thought; but, on the other hand, as we have said, you often positively add to your knowledge about the habits of human beings. It is a sort of moral 'animated nature.' Thus:

> The boy indeed was at the grandam's side . . .
> [*Tales*, XXI, 91–105]

For details he had a sort of passion, and his interest in them was proportioned to their smallness. Of all observers he is the minutest. In the world of natural history, of whose study, in a certain way he was no mean proficient, he was always occupied in finding out and studying the small and insignificant tribes. Beauty invited him not the least. Among plants he studied grasses and lichens, or the least marked of the roadside flowers; not, apparently, interested in plants like the cryptogams or others which might be supposed to invite by the singularity of their modes of growth, but attracted absolutely by insignificance and vulgarity. He loved weeds for their own sake. In zoology he took to entomology, and hunted down small beetles and flies. In his writings the same spirit is observable. He found no subject too insignificant to be dwelt on, no trait too minute to be recorded. Hence a certain air of narrowness and pettiness distinguishes his writings. And he was moreover very insensible to the claims of proportion, and showed no skill in adjusting the detail of his treatment to the claims of the several parts of his stories. His son has some very just observations on this aspect of his mind:

In fact, [he says,] he neither loved order for its own sake, nor had any very high opinion of that passion in others; witness his words in the tale of Stephen Jones, the 'Learned Boy':

> The *love of order*—I the thing receive
> [*Tales*, XXI, 309–12, 319–27]

But he had a passion for science,—the science of the human mind, first; then, that of nature in general; and lastly, that of abstract quantities. [*Life*, chapter 7]

By 'science' as here used must be understood knowledge of facts; for Mr. Crabbe, as we have said, had not the least taste for the investigation of laws. In corroboration of his indifference to the charms of external nature, may be cited a saying of his own, that he loved better to walk in the streets and observe the faces of the passers-by than to gaze on the finest natural scene.

The style of Crabbe is no less characteristic than his matter. It is not, however, so purely his own; and though he makes it the faithful instrument of his purposes, it always bears the traces of the model on which it was formed. Horace Smith called him 'Pope in worsted stockings.' It would have been more to the purpose to say he was a new poet in Pope's stockings; for the likeness is in the superficies, and the contrast is in the substance. Crabbe formed himself on Pope's style, deliberately studied his mode of expression, and sought to catch his pointed way of putting things, in which, and not in the flow of his verse, lies the characteristic excellence of Pope's style. And Crabbe did attain this excellence to a certain extent. The points are much blunter, the polish is vastly inferior: but there is the same effort to afford a share of emphasis to every sentence, to give a sharp decisive accent of meaning to correspond with the marked accent of the verse; and a considerable degree of success attends the effort. It was an excellent school for Crabbe to be exercised in; his natural bent was to be dull, minute, and prolix. The study of Pope made him look out for rest at brief intervals, for contrast and relief. If we read some of his prefaces, we shall see what he might have been in verse had he not contended against his native propensities. He emancipated himself from being a proser. Poets, even good poets, have not always done this. Rogers is a refined proser; Wordsworth is a profound, a sagacious, a harmonious, and a most interminable proser. But, in substance, Crabbe differs widely from Pope. Pope is always employed in giving a specific shape to generalities; Crabbe is occupied with things as they are. Pope, except when personal, was always working out results and deductions, making up thoughts and giving them a taking form; Crabbe never wished to do more than describe graphically and agreeably (according to his notions of the agreeable in verse) what things he had seen and known. Pope's business, as he himself says, was to find rhymes for sense; Crabbe's was, to find rhymes for facts. Pope studied society, manners, and man; Crabbe studied social life, moral habits, and men. If he ever imitated Pope's matter, it was only in his very early poems; and even his style lost its influence over his later poems, and very much to their disadvantage. He is not a master of expression. His language is the very reverse of suggestive. It is so bald and dry, that the reader must furnish all accessories from his own imagination. He must give colour and shading to the thought, he must improve the hint, and clothe the naked idea. Crabbe writes like one who draws outlines with a hard pencil; and he who reads must employ a vivid fancy to fill them up. Moreover he has none of that power by which a great poet gathers up and compresses the details of his subject within the limits of the briefest general description. He is not a pregnant writer; what he has to say, he says *in extenso*; and though he is often curt, it is only as a way of filling up interstices and introducing or connecting pieces of prolix detail. Yet it is wonderful how much he contrives by this process to get into a small compass. This is particularly the case in his portrait-painting. He packs a complete and characteristic picture in very small space, and after a peculiar fashion. He does not, like Ben Jonson, and sometimes Dickens, take a distinguishing humour or trait, or a set of these, and call them a man: his people are real living people; mere sketches often, no doubt, but exact, defined, and likenesses. Though he may imitate Pope in his style, he has none of his epigrammatic way of pinning a character down by a single prominent trait; none of Wordsworth's habit of slowly winding it off as if it were a hank of cotton, and his poem a reel to wind it on. He sets to work in a way of his own, giving a brief, forcible, general description, and illustrating it by some dramatic speech or minor piece of description at full length. His pictures are like one of Grüner's plates

of a painted ceiling, the whole drawn in outline and a corner filled up
in colours. It is true, his early attempts savour more of direct and
elaborate description both of things and persons, and that, where the
subject suits him, he has few rivals in the skill with which he selects
distinguishing points, or the aptness with which he conveys their
effect through the medium of language. But when he is at his best, as
in the *Tales*, the dramatic element holds a considerable space in his
delineation of persons, and the peculiar style we have mentioned is seen
in its perfection; fading down in the *Tales of the Hall* into something
too much of prolixity and mere conversation in verse.

Our limits afford no space for a detailed survey of his various
writings. It was not until he discovered that his strength lay in the
minute illustration of human character that he really enrolled himself
among English poets. In his early poems, often even in *The Borough*, he
shows too clearly that he is hunting about for matter for his rhymes,
and making prize of every idea he can lay his hands on. As long as he is
occupied with general ideas and thoughts, Crabbe is insufferably
commonplace and dull. For one sound and novel aphorism, brightly
and aptly expressed,—the sort of thing with which Pope's pages teem,—
his imitator (for when thus employed Crabbe is a direct imitator of
Pope) gives us a hundred heavy disconnected sentences, which prance
awkwardly up and down the verse like a cart-horse cantering after a
thorough-bred. Thus, to quote the first specimen that offers:

> Law was design'd to keep a state in peace; . . .
> [*The Borough*, VI, 149–73]

The Library is pompous, pointless, and commonplace; and the only
thing that men have found worth remembrance in it is the description
of the binding of old folios. Once or twice only in the whole course of
it is to be found some stray couplet which points in the direction of the
author's real insight; such lines, for instance, as

> For transient vice bequeaths a lingering pain,
> Which transient virtue strives to heal in vain.
> [*The Library*, 345–6]

However unadorned in statement, such a dictum indicates much of
observation and something of wisdom in the writer.

The Newspaper is full of platitudes and pumped-up thought. It is a
satire unrecommended by the force and brilliancy which alone can
make satire endurable. The minor poems are simply unreadable. *The*

Library, indeed, was published under the auspices of Burke; but if upon this poem alone he had formed his estimate of the author's genius, one would have said either that he had a very low idea of the requisites of poetry, or an almost supernatural insight into the germs of future success which lay hidden in the poem in question. But it seems it was on some very different lines, in *The Village*, that Burke rested his high opinion of the powers of his young client. They are lines which amply justify the prophecy of success; and, indeed, *The Village* stands quite alone among Crabbe's earlier writings. In it he spoke straight from his own personal convictions, he described directly what he had seen and known. The complexion of it differs from that of his other poems. It alone of his writings may with some degree of justice be called stern and gloomy. The struggle and the painful experience through which he was himself passing coloured the medium through which he looked. His picture of the life and sufferings of the poor in this poem leaves an indelible impression on the mind of every reader. It is not only that it is uncompromising, that it tears off and scornfully casts aside the old stage-costume of Corydon and Phyllis; but that it keeps aloof from all the sources of comfort and consolation, the common assuagements which are not denied even to the lowest aspects of human life, and builds in its forcible lines so sad a picture of unrequited and incessant toil, deserted old age, and miserable death, as none can look at without a shudder. And when, in the second part, he turns professedly to contemplate the

> Gleams of transient mirth and hours of sweet repose,
> [II, 4]

the subject leads him instantly to the vices which form or accompany the amusements of the poor, and he immediately becomes absorbed in this, to him, more attractive subject. For force, aptness of language, fervour, and directness, the first part of *The Village* stands unapproached among Crabbe's early poems.

The Borough, with many parts and detached passages of first-class excellence, is a very unequal performance; and it is not until the first series of the *Tales* that Crabbe's genius displays itself in its full power, and maintains a sustained and unwavering flight. It is on *The Village*, on detached parts of *The Borough*, and on the *Tales* (the second series of which is less fresh, graphic, and pointed than the first), that the permanent reputation of Crabbe rests. The posthumous poems cannot be said to be destitute of his peculiar merits; but they must be confessed,

413

on the other hand, to be very unworthy of what had preceded them.

The common feature throughout all his works which gives this author his hold upon his readers is his singular insight into the minute working of character, his wondrous familiarity with so vast a number of various dispositions, and the unerring fidelity with which he traces their operations and discerns their attitudes under every sort of circumstance. It would be difficult in the whole range of literature to point to more than two or three who have rivalled him in this respect. Chaucer is one; and a curious and not uninteresting comparison might be instituted between the two, though the old poet far surpasses the modern one in love of beauty, liveliness of fancy, and breadth of genius. Crabbe knew where his own strength lay, and in some lines in *The Borough* has aptly described both the bent and the animus of his poetic powers:

For this the poet looks the world around, . . .
[XXIV, 426–43]

One great source of his strength is, that he dared to be true to himself, and to work with unhesitating confidence his own peculiar vein. This originality is not only great, but always genuine. A never-failing charm lies in the clear simplicity and truthfulness of nature which shines through all his writings. Nothing false or meretricious ever came from his pen; and if his works want order and beauty, neither they nor his life are destitute of the higher harmony which springs from a character naturally single and undeteriorated by false aims and broken purposes.

68. Fiction—in prose or verse?

1864

From the *Saturday Review*, 28 September 1864, pp. 394–6.

So long as poets only write occasional pieces, and come quickly to an end of what they have to say, it is very easy for them to manage with no other subject than their own feelings, sorrows, or fancies. But if they are to make a sustained effort, they must have a subject external to themselves, which they propose to treat in the manner that pleases them. Epic poets choose subjects great enough for epics, and idyllic poets choose such subjects as are suitable for idyls—that is, tales of human adventure or suffering where the interest is not quite up to the higher level of the epic. Of these subjects none are more natural to the modern mind than tales of contemporary life. The same feelings which prompt us to depict ourselves in prose fiction also lead us to describe in verse incidents chosen from that daily life in which we take so strong an interest. But it is obvious that these incidents of daily and hourly life may be treated in very different ways, according to the bias of the mind that treats them. The poet may stand in a hundred different relations to the characters whom he introduces into his tale. He may, for instance, make them and their story the vehicle for his own thoughts and feelings. They may come to be almost lost in their narrator, as, for example, the persons described in *The Excursion* are lost and swallowed up in Wordsworth. There is not much of incident in these stories of *The Excursion*, there is not much that can be called distinctively poetry in the treatment, but there is an unending flux of poetical philosophy, very lengthily, but sometimes powerfully, expressed. In *Enoch Arden*, Mr. Tennyson seldom wanders away from the tale he has to tell, but he always, or at any rate in the better passages, gives his tale a poetical form. He is the poet telling a tale, whereas Wordsworth is a poet seeking in the outlines of a tale the form or excuse for his philosophical

415

meditations. It is interesting to compare with both of them a writer of a wholly different turn—a poet who tells a tale as a tale and nothing more, who looks on it neither as the vehicle of philosophy nor of poetry, but who simply tries to produce fiction in metre. The merits of Crabbe are great when once we take him on the level where he himself was content to stand. He was not a philosopher, nor in any high sense a poet, but he could tell a tale, and he had a very just perception of the consequences which ought to follow on the attempt to tell a tale in verse. He knew when metre was a gain and when it was a loss to him. Perhaps, in mere power of conceiving character and arranging incidents, he was about equal to Miss Austen as a writer of fiction, and numerous points of resemblance between the two writers will present themselves to any one who will compare their respective works. In some respects, verse, as a vehicle for narration, rises above prose, and then Crabbe is superior to Miss Austen. In many and in more respects, prose is a better vehicle for the purposes of fictitious narrative than verse is, and in these respects Miss Austen rises above Crabbe. Verse is briefer, more taking, more incisive than prose. It drives little epigrammatic points more directly home. It arrests the attention to conversation and incidents by the artificial construction of metre; but, on the other hand, characters are less drawn out, mistakes, blunders, and oddities are less shaded off, the tone of everything is much further from the tone of real life. It is a greater effort to keep up with verse than with prose; it is harder to understand, and it makes us exert ourselves to fill up the blanks it leaves. Therefore, narrative in verse, as mere narrative, will never be so popular as narrative in prose, and Miss Austen has a hundred readers where Crabbe has one.

The *Tales of the Hall* were published when Crabbe was an elderly man, and were not only recognized at once as among the best and most characteristic of his productions, but as embodying in a moderate compass all his leading views of life and morals. They had been gradually worked out during many years, and were touched and retouched until they satisfied his judgment. They summed up to him and to his readers the fruits of his experience and of his feeling, and it is one of their great charms that they exhibit with so much fidelity and simplicity what their author had learnt to think of men and women in the sphere of English life with which he was acquainted. Crabbe's view of the world was not what would generally be called a poetical view. It seemed to him a place full of stupid mistakes, bungles, and errors. The men he paints are easily led away by temptation, the facile prey of deceit, full of meanness as well as of better things, silly in their religion as in their worldly conduct, and in every way a very unheroic set. His women are almost all weak, and almost all coquettes. That women say what they do not mean, and mean what they do not say, was the great truth which sixty years of observation of the female sex had taught him. No one, he thought, need expect to be happy in this world; for, if worse misfortunes do not overtake him, his own folly and the folly of his neighbours assure him a constant crop of troubles. There are some very bad women in the world, he lets us know, though he very seldom notices them; and a great many bad men, of whom village ruffians moved his deepest anger and pity, and village fanatics his deepest scorn. But the world, as a whole, is not so much bad as silly, and life is not so much terrible as trivial and disappointing. Still, the gloom is relieved by some bright spots. In the first place, there is family affection, and especially there is the unfailing kindness of those bound to each other by near ties of blood. As to husbands and wives, Crabbe's philosophy seems to have revealed to him that, in nine cases out of ten, they are fated to get tired of each other. That love, in the long run, discovers its own mistake, was almost an axiom with him; but he is never tired of painting the effusive affection of English sisters, or the reserved but trustworthy friendship of English brothers. Life, too, was to him full of quiet fun. He saw the oddities, the queerness, the little ludicrous follies and vanities of ordinary people, and he loved to laugh at them in a shrewd gentle way. There was a comedy of errors going on all around him; and although he deplored the errors, he enjoyed the comedy. Lastly, he had a profound belief in the healing and sustaining power of religion. He had very little theological depth, but he had an abiding conviction that people who tried to be good Christians were the only happy people, and that somehow their miseries and their sufferings were always made up to them. A man who views life in such a temper views it, on the whole, aright. Crabbe's notions are sound notions. There is much crime and misery, and much fun in the world; and religion, if it can but be got of the right sort, is a pearl of great price. No one can quarrel with such a view. It may not embrace all that is to be said of rural society in modern England, but, so far as it goes, it is unassailable.

At any rate, it is a view of life which eminently suits the teller of tales. Crabbe's philosophy gave a thread on which he could easily string together the incidents of a story. And he had also a keen sense of how a story ought to be told, when to be brief and when to be lengthy, how far to be comic and how far to be pathetic, how far description can really describe, and what expressions will best convey the character of the person to whom they are attributed. He very rarely fails in the management of his machinery, and in none of his stories is there any uncertainty as to the sort of persons of whom he is speaking. He generally sets himself to work out a lesson, and although he often chooses to work out lessons of a very humble kind, he succeeds in bringing home to us the lesson, such as it is. One of the best of the *Tales of the Hall* is called 'Delay has Dangers.'[1] The moral is, that weak young men, when they are engaged, had better marry quickly, or they will flirt with some one else until they lose their old love. This is not a very elevating subject for a poet to take, but it is a truth of daily life, and, having set himself to illustrate it, Crabbe enforces it with great point and vivacity. At the outset of the story he does indeed indulge himself with an excursus disproportionately long on the true meaning of a lady's 'No.' This is exactly one of the points on which he displays an almost comical earnestness. He is never more business-like and serious than when he unfolds his reasons for not believing too hastily what women say. . . .

> A downright *No*! would make a man despair, . . .
> [*Tales of the Hall*, XIII, 106–26, 245–60, 381–98]

We need not pursue the story, but these extracts show the power which Crabbe had of making verse serve his purpose. He does by means of it what he could not have done in prose. What he writes can scarcely be called poetry. Prose could produce exactly the same impression. Miss Austen, for example, could have sketched Cecilia, and Fanny, and Henry's feelings towards both, so that, as a description of character and feeling, there would have been no difference between her sketch and that of Crabbe. But verse, and his command of verse, enable Crabbe to draw the sketch in a much brighter and more effective way; and a command of verse, and an apprehension of the purposes it may serve, are part of the poet's art, if not a very high part. But it would be unfair to say that Crabbe was only in this sense a poet. He often gives vent to feelings that every one would call poetical. More especially the poetical sentiment was awakened in him by the contrast between man and nature—by the indifference with which nature regards the feelings of the heart, and by the changes which man sees in nature according to his own state. For example, the following lines, describing Henry's feelings as he looks on the scenes where at the beginning of his visit he

[1] XIII.

used to see Cecilia in everything, and where he now sees the record of his loss, are full of pathos and of a quaint poetical observation:—

> That evening all in fond discourse was spent, . . .
> [XIII, 698–724]

The notion of a lover finding things more dreary because it happened to be the time when the young birds had just been fledged, could only have occurred to a man as fond of watching rural sights and sounds as Crabbe was, but it also could only have occurred to a man who watched the common operations of nature with a sympathetic interest. In one of the earlier tales he describes his own early youth while pretending to describe the youth of one of the characters of his fiction, and the genuineness of his feeling and the nicety of his observation are attested by the confession of humiliation which he underwent under the unconcern of the wild birds around him:—

> I loved to walk where none had walked before
> About the rocks that ran along the shore;
> Or far beyond the sight of men to stray,
> And take my pleasure when I lost my way;
> For then 'twas mine to trace the hilly heath,
> And all the mossy moor that lies beneath;
> Here had I favourite stations, where I stood
> And heard the murmurs of the ocean-flood,
> With not a sound beside, except when flew
> Aloft the lapwing, or the gray curlew,
> Who with wild notes my fancied power defied,
> And mock'd the dreams of solitary pride.
> [*Tales of the Hall*, IV, 447–58]

The strength as well as the weakness of Crabbe are exhibited in these lines. Most of the lines are clear, simple, and vigorous, and the feeling described in them rises above his usual height. But the line,

> And take my pleasure when I lost my way,

is an instance of that almost childish love of little turns of language and plays upon words which was so happily ridiculed in *Rejected Addresses*. It was not much of an exaggeration when the sham Crabbe of the *Addresses* was made to say, of the lamps lit in the evening, that they

> Start into light, and make the lighter start.

Crabbe was seldom more successful than when describing the

characters he introduces to us. Ordinarily prose narration breaks down here, and the description of heroes and heroines, and even of comic characters, is proverbially tedious. But verse, with its superior liveliness and brevity, can succeed, although prose fails. There are many excellent sketches of character which Crabbe manages to give in a few lines, and he is especially successful where he is intentionally comic. A lover described in 'The Sisters' may serve as an example:—

'Thus thinking much, but hiding what he thought. . . .'
[*Tales of the Hall*, VIII, 206–23]

This is a picture of a young man which immediately commends itself to us as consistent and complete; and yet his inveterate snobbishness, and the different feelings he awakens in the tamer and the more romantic sister respectively, are touched off in a very short space. But perhaps the best sketch in the *Tales* is drawn from still humbler life, and it is hard to believe that any one except an incumbent of an agricultural parish could have painted the village swell so graphically as Crabbe paints his William Bailey:—

But, with our village hero to proceed— . . .
[*Tales of the Hall*, XIX, 127–48, 157–64]

This is amusing, and, indeed, Crabbe is hardly ever dull. He seldom interests us profoundly, but he tells tales in verse which are readable as tales, and very few writers of tales in verse have done this. He entertains, interests, and diverts us, and sometimes thrills us with a touch of unexpected power or poetry. But he is not widely read, and it is not likely that he ever will be. Fiction in verse, as fiction, is not equal to fiction in prose, and he is not great enough as a poet to make his tales read for their poetry. *The Excursion* is dreary and prolix, but it breathes the spirit of a great mind, and is full of flashes of high and unquestionable poetry. We cannot know what Wordsworth was unless we read and study it. But then it is worth while to go through much trouble and pain to understand Wordsworth, whereas reading or not reading Crabbe is only like reading or not reading an excellent but forgotten novel. It is pleasant and admirable if we take it up, but it remains almost an accident whether we take it up or not.

69. Fifty years after

1869

From *St. James's Magazine*, February 1869, n.s. ii, 677–88. On the fiftieth anniversary of the publication of *Tales of the Hall*. The passage quoted comes from pages 684–6.

To a place among the first class of English poets the writer of *The Borough* has no claim. It may even be doubted by some whether he has a right, in the second class, to a place beside the lighter, more graceful, and more elegant melodies of Campbell, Scott, and Moore, whose friendship he lived to enjoy. But though his verse may lack refinement and smoothness, though it fail in point of humour, and be deficient in stirring those deeper emotions and profounder mysteries of man's being, which Byron, Wordsworth, and Tennyson have plumbed to their inmost depths; yet, keenness and truth of observation, wondrous power of imagination, intense honesty of purpose, firm love of truth, hatred of all shams, and a power of reproducing the aspect of common things; the hard, exact features of the daily life which went on about him,—were his to a degree rarely excelled. These he put to the readiest and best use that he knew and understood, and on them must rest his claims as a poet. It may only be a picture of outer, common, life; but it is a true picture, and as such, is worthy of life, and *must* live. It may be painted only in the boldest, plainest, commonest words; but it is the work of a true artist, and has a clear right to a place in the gallery of genius.

A man must be judged not only by what he is *not*, but by what he is. Turner, with all his glowing poetry of earth, sea and sky, must hang beside the gloomy grandeur of G. Poussin; the gorgeous lights and shadows of Rembrandt, or the crude, startling, yet living abruptness of Van Eyck. Each speaks with the native power, passion, and skill that make up his own individual identity; all differently, yet all as true *artists* and *poets*;—the two terms being in their highest, truest, sense, synonymous.

Nine-tenths of the things and men described by Crabbe, we have all seen a thousand times. Yet he charms us by the freshness, brightness, and reality of his picture. It may be but a room in the village workhouse, a noisy, drunken brawl at a tavern; a dingy jail; a profligate tailor; a miserable poacher, without a particle of sentiment, or a spark of grace in him, to redeem the paltry corruption of the entire man. It may be at times disagreeable, annoying, or even repulsive, to have such pictures thrust upon one, still—whether disagreeable or not—they are eminently true. They are excellent of their kind; no matter what be their exact intrinsic excellence. Within the bounds we have assigned to the poet, they are perfect; in the very sense in which Aristotle outlines for us what he calls κλεπτὴν τέλειον *i.e. a perfect thief*; or Mr. Howship, on Indigestion, talks rapturously of a certain sore, as 'a beautiful ulcer.'

Jeffrey, the arch critic, who despised the poetry of Cockaigne, disliked the 'Lakers,' and had no great affection for what he calls 'the vulgar fine country of England,'—in general, pours out a string of regrets that Crabbe had never seen the lakes and woods of incomparable Caledonia, and found in them a nobler theme for his keen and imaginative muse. But, graphic and true to nature, as some of the landscapes of Crabbe are, his eye caught at, and his mind stored up with far greater readiness, the points of human living interest. He sketched the outside of the poor-house, but his full power flashes out only when he comes to deal with the degraded, miserable, hapless beings who lived and died by inches within its dreary walls. If Crabbe had visited Scotland, he would not have trod in the glowing footsteps of Walter Scott, or soared into living song concerning the

> Land of brown heath and shaggy wood,
> Land of the mountain and the flood.
> [Scott, *The Lay of the Last Minstrel*, VI, stanza 2]

We should have had minute, bold, racy, coarse pictures of Sandie 'fou at night,' and 'sair and sober at the morn;' glimpses of the Canongate, the snuffy, whiskey-drinking, ranting ruffians of the dens and closes of Edinburgh and Glasgow; the half-starved shepherd on the hills; the hungry exciseman; the hungrier Scotch attorney; the jail-birds, crimes, miseries, and hardships of northern life, far more than the romantic beauties of Loch Katrine, or the rocky glories of Arthur's seat.

'*Cuique suum;*' Crabbe was meant and made for what he did: to be the poet of the poorer, darker, rougher side of humanity, and not only to draw the picture, but to say all that he felt and could to soothe and to relieve the burden, to expose the folly, to lay bare the fraud; and he did it well. He accomplished his brave and true task as perfectly as our own immortal Tupper has in these later days of multitudinous thought accomplished *his*, of sending forth for the comfort of mankind that endless tide of Solomon and water—

> In which the feeblest, faintest, intellect
> Can bathe with joy.

The mystery is that for two such perfect men—the one the quintessence of keen original perception, and incomparable good sense, and the other, of redundant verbosity, and of watery bathos,—so widely different a destiny should be prepared. The age that tolerates Tupper, consents to forget Crabbe. After all, Nemesis is just. The latter will be read and enjoyed by thousands, when the former darling clings fondly to the interior of our portmanteaus in desperate tenacity for bare life.

70. Crabbe and the eighteenth century: an American estimate

1872

North American Review, July 1872, cxv, 48–65, by Frederick Sheldon.

Crabbe's first appearance before the public was in the iron age of letters, when a poor author thought himself comparatively lucky to be a 'bookseller's hack.' It was better to shiver in a garret in his 'tattered nightgown and the breeches of a heathen philosopher,' than to wait for hours in an antechamber with a dedication, on the chance that a noble Mecænas might bestow a gratuity, or, rather, an alms. The Muse found

Crabbe as she did Scroggen, 'stretched beneath a rug,' and watched him as he went shabby and hungry to the shops of booksellers, and to the doors of great people. He was at last fortunate enough to attract the notice of Edmund Burke, who persuaded him to take orders, and placed him in a comfortable nook in the Church.

> Give poets claret, they grow idle soon.
> [*The Newspaper*, 281]

So sang Crabbe, and so he did. He put aside authorship and disappeared in the obscurity of village life. After an eclipse of twenty-two years,—from 1785 to 1807, only remembered by one or two passages in the *Elegant Extracts*, a collection of English poetry which some of our older readers will recollect in every family who considered books a necessary part of furniture,—Crabbe reappeared in a world, separated from his former state of probation by the French Revolution and the victories of Napoleon. He brought his old poems with him, and others very like them,—a literary Rip Van Winkle,—but the new public did not think him old-fashioned, or his poems rusty. On the contrary, the young *Edinburgh* and *Quarterly* praised him, new editions were called for, and the comely old gentleman of sixty was received with open arms by the great writers of that remarkable period, and became a lion, invited to the breakfasts and dinners of the fashionable.

Forty years full of great events, and productive of many books, have passed since Crabbe died. He was not a man of genius, hardly a poet, in the strict sense of the word, yet among the mediocrists of England, as Pope calls them, no one, on the whole, shows more signs of vitality. He turned out no first-rate, thoroughly finished work, such as 'The Castle of Indolence,' or Shenstone's 'Schoolmistress,' or Campbell's 'Hohenlinden'; but his *Tales* will be looked over with interest, while 'The Seasons' and 'Gertrude of Wyoming' stand untouched upon the shelves.

The fashion in metrical composition which Pope carried to perfection had gradually deteriorated in the hands of weak imitators to Darwin's *Loves of the Plants*, and Hayley's *Triumphs of Temper*. The revival in literature is generally dated from Cowper's 'Task,' published in 1785. A clever lady critic has ascribed this reaction to the example set by Cowper, and, with the habit of exaggeration constitutional in the sex, has written, 'It is safe to say that, without Cowper, Wordsworth could scarcely have been.' It is much safer not to say so. Had there been no Cowper, things would have turned out very much as they have done. The *homme nécessaire* has less existence in literature than elsewhere. The reaction from the artificial school began before 'The Task.' Burns, for instance, was already known to his neighbours a year or two earlier as 'a writer of some good songs'; and in 1782, Crabbe, then a medical man like Goldsmith, but unlike that sunshiny musical Bohemian in everything but poverty and want of skill in his profession, published his *Village*, a protest against the sweetness of Auburn, and against those mere 'creatures of the author's pen,'

> Borrowed and again conveyed
> From book to book, the shadows of a shade.
> [*The Borough*, XIX, 19–20]

[There follows a sketch of Crabbe's life and works.]

He was a bard with but one string to his lyre; he sang the same tune throughout his long life. The *Tales of the Hall*, published in 1822,[1] and a volume of *Posthumous Tales*, present the same minute sketches of low character and the same peculiarities of style. The impression made upon his mind by the misery of his early surroundings was never effaced. It was not the imaginary and almost maudlin misery of Dickens when he spoke of his month or two in the blacking business, but an indelible scar left upon his brain by the suffering of his youth. Even in his London days, when smiles, flattery, and good dinners were offered him daily, those Aldborough scenes would revisit him in his dreams; 'asleep all was misery and degradation.' As his Muse was truly the daughter of Memory, when he describes a village, his mind always reverted to those two unpaved streets running between mean and scrambling houses, the homes of squalid, commonplace want. In his sketches of scenery he is never vivid, except when he paints the ocean and the open sandy commons, the sterile half-cultivated farms, and the dreary marshes of Aldborough. The half-savage men who spent their days in cheerless toil and their nights in drunkenness are always present in his pages. He found others more or less like them in his country parish, and opportunity as well as inclination led him to study their achromatic existence, made up of shop, table, and bed, with a dark background of almshouse and prison. It has been said of him that he handled human nature so as to take the bloom off; but it was rather that he selected for a subject human nature that had lost its bloom.

Crabbe had probably less imagination than any man who ever wrote verses after the age of twenty; he confessed with his usual honesty that

[1] 1819.

he had no taste for music, art, or architecture. His mind was like a camera, receiving every impression, and rendering it exactly. Those 'painted clouds that beautify our days' were seldom seen in his sky; the bright ideal side of human nature that redeems 'man's life from being cheap as beasts'' was beyond his ken. Like Lucian's Menippus, when Mercury points out to him in Hades, Leda, Helen of Troy, and other celebrated fair ones, he could see nothing but skulls and bones naked of flesh. Hence his pictures are photographs in their accuracy and in their want of color. His realism is complete and unmitigated, not like the spiritualized realism of the Pre-Raphaelite school. The 'Dead Stone-Breaker' is painted to the last button like Crabbe's pauper in the village workhouse; but the body of the stone-breaker is transfigured by 'a light that knows no waning.' We feel that the tears have been wiped away forever from the poor weary eyes. Crabbe's pauper lies upon the bier, a grim, ghastly, emaciated corpse.

This is his dreariest vein. In his more cheerful sketches he is frequently harsh and coarse. He has often been called the Hogarth of poetry, and indeed no better illustrator could be found for Crabbe than Hogarth. Bedlam, the Tavern, the Prison in the 'Rake's Progress,' Bridewell, the garret, and the gin-shop in 'Industry and Idleness,' might be bound up with his works. His tales often leave an after-taste of disgust in the mind like Hogarth's plates.

Crabbe was born a naturalist, with a strong bias for writing in verse. A keen botanist and entomologist, one might have expected from him a poem like *The Loves of the Plants*, chanting the emotions of the 'love-sick violet,' the 'virgin lily,' 'the jealous cowslip,' and 'the enamored woodbine'; but he liked to examine the motives of mankind even better than pistils and stamens. And as in science he devoted himself principally to common herbs and garden insects, so in character his speciality was peasants and village tradespeople,—

> Fixed like a plant on their peculiar spot,
> To draw nutrition, propagate, and rot.[1]

He picked up a Simon or a Phebe, put them under his microscope,— an almost perfect instrument,—classed them in genus *homo insipiens*, species *rusticus communis*; prepared them, and placed them in his collection. As you turn over his works you find a new specimen preserved on every page. He described their habitat and habits in a cool, scientific way. He had little more sympathy with them than with his beetles.

[1] Pope, *Essay on Man*, II, 64.

But he is always accurate and true. He never tries to make a beetle a butterfly. One may thank him for that.

In spite of his profession, the duties of which he fulfilled most conscientiously, Crabbe was a looker-on in the world rather than an actor. He was kind-hearted, charitable; in individual cases, no sympathy was like his; but he was with his flock, not of them. Their failings lay bare before him. He looked down upon the struggling creatures about him, each one wrapped in its own petty interests with a good-natured indulgence; much as a farmer looks upon the cattle and the corn he expects to harvest. They were his crop; as Heine says, 'his fool crop, all his own.' He never shows much feeling of any kind, except when he describes jacobinical radicals,

> Who call the wants of knaves the rights of man,
> [*The Parish Register*, I, 815–misquoted]

or noisy dissenters, like his 'serious toyman' who trod pretty often upon his clerical toes. He was not a satirist. A satirist has an object in his attack. Crabbe had none. He studied mankind; the particular specimen might be mean, ridiculous, wicked: it was indifferent to him.

There is little or no plot in Crabbe's stories, and a very moderate allowance of incident. Not a character ever stepped out of them into daily life, to become a household acquaintance. There is no grace of thought, no play of fancy. Even the few similes he used did not spring up spontaneously in his mind when heated by his subject. One can see the seams where he has patched them on. Jeffrey noticed this, and Crabbe admitted it in his simple, straightforward way. 'My usual method,' he said, 'has been to think of such illustrations and insert them after finishing a tale.' He told Mrs. Leadbeater that all his characters were drawn from life; 'there is not one of whom I had not in my mind the original.' 'Indeed I do not know that I could paint merely from my own fancy; and there is no cause why we should. Is there not diversity sufficient in society? And who can go even but a little into the assemblies of our fellow-wanderers from the way of perfect rectitude, and not find characters so varied and so pointed that he need not call upon his imagination?'[1]

Pope was his model in versification, but he never attained Pope's exquisite polish. In Crabbe one can always see the marks of the tools. James Smith, whose parody of Crabbe in the *Rejected Addresses* is one of the best ever written, called him, 'Pope in worsted stockings.' He has a

[1] *Life*, Ch. 9.

profusion of antithesis, and a tiresome fondness for alliteration and plays upon words, often mere puns. His metre is frequently rough and jolting, and his style a 'little word-bound,' as Addison expressed it. The verse does not flow smoothly, there is a perceptible effort; he evidently does not sing because he cannot help it.

In all his volumes, one can hardly find a hundred lines containing that subtle indefinable essence that constitutes poetry. On the other hand, very many are the merest prose run into the mould of Pope, simple to puerility, like these:—

> Grave Jonas Kindred, Sybil Kindred's sire,
> Was six feet high, and looked six inches higher.
> [*Tales*, VI, 1–2]

And these:—

> And I was asked and authorized to go
> To seek the firm of Clutterbuck & Co.
> [*Tales of the Hall*, VII, 472–3]

Others read like the rhymed rules for wise conduct of the Poor Richard school:—

> Who would by law regain his plundered store,
> Would pick up fallen mercury from the floor.
> [*Tales*, III, 113–14]

> We find too late, by stooping to deceit,
> It is ourselves, and not the world we cheat.
> [*Tales of the Hall*, XV, 451–2]

And occasionally he is guilty of a line that is not even verse, like this one:—

> I for your perfect acquiescence call.
> [*Ibid*, XX, 199]

The *naïveté* of his prefaces and notes, and his scruples lest by accident he should offend somebody or misrepresent something, are delightful. The

> Brick-floored parlor which the butcher lets,
> [*The Borough*, IX, 19]

'is so mentioned,' he tells the reader, 'because the lodger is vain.'

Crabbe exhibits the common people of England as they were, and describes their homes and habits, too often cheerless and wretched, as they had never been painted before. It was something quite original in the language. He first introduced into literature the real laboring man, ignorant, narrow-minded, overworked, rough in his manners, surly in his temper, dirty in his attire. He sketched from the life, and not from the conventional lay-figure. Before his time, peasants and paupers were introduced in fiction, like the chorus in an opera, dressed poorly but neatly, to echo with becoming humility the sentiments of the well-born and the rich. Crabbe showed the reading class (there was a property qualification in culture in those days) what George Stephenson, the engineer, announced more coarsely afterward, 'Strip us and we are all pretty much alike.' We must throw ourselves back some eighty or a hundred years in imagination to feel what revelation this must have been to ordinary minds. . . .

To novelty of subject Crabbe added freshness of treatment. His anatomy of character of the commonplace sort, the sort he studied, extends to the smallest moral fibre. He is the La Bruyère of the lower middle and lower classes. No detail of dress, decoration, or furniture in a cottage was lost upon him, and he noted with equal exactness the daily thoughts, habits, and feelings of the dwellers in the cottage. Nothing escaped him but the ethereal part. Crabbe's power of minute observation has never been surpassed; it was a kind of genius, it stood him instead of imagination. We get constant peeps behind the scenes of human nature, and often very pleasant ones. What an admirable catalogue of the symptoms of approaching age is this passage in the 'Old Bachelor,' one of the *Tales of the Hall*:—

> Six years had past, and forty ere the six . . .
> [X, 458–61, 466–79, 482–6]

Pope has a few lines on the same subject, which Lord Holland is said to have often quoted:—

> Years following years, steal something every day,
> At last they steal us from ourselves away.
> In one our follies, our amusements end;
> In one a mistress drops, in one a friend, etc.
> [*Imitations of Horace*, Bk II, Ep. II, 72–5]

Smooth, clever, but vague and ineffective compared with the vigorous minuteness of Crabbe.

Crabbe's sketches of women are numerous and always good. They range from the

> Tender, timid maid, who knows not how

> To pass a pig-sty or to face a cow;
> Smiling she comes with pretty talents graced,
> A fair complexion and a slender waist,
> [*Tales*, VII, 3-6]

to the stout-minded old spinster,—

> Who suffered no man her free soul to vex,
> Free from the weakness of her gentle sex.
> [*The Borough*, XVI, 210-11]

Crabbe loved the women, although he never could see them as angels. A clergyman and a family physician have unusual opportunities for studying the sex. He became more and more affectionate as he grew older. In 1819 his manner to the London ladies was so sweet, that Miss Spencer compared him to a frosted cake: 'The cake is very good but there is too much sugar to cut through in getting at it.' At the age of sixty-two he contemplated a second marriage. He was probably sorely beset. It would seem from this couplet that he had the usual experience of widowed clergymen:—

> O, 't is a precious thing, when wives are dead,
> To find such numbers who will serve instead.
> [*Tales*, XXI, 17-18]

As no man can write verses all his life without occasionally rising into poetry, Crabbe now and then accomplished it, especially in his descriptions of the sea, and in some tender little touches of human feeling that reach every heart. Age mellowed him: he was milder without growing weaker. Some of his best passages are in the *Posthumous Tales*. A sly humor and a shrewd way of saying things, good sense and sagacity that never fail him, make his stories pleasant reading to this day; and if he limped in numbers, and lacks grace, he has vigor, and could attain a power of epigrammatic expression not surpassed by Pope or by Dryden. Crabbe's quaint, homely style is utterly dissimilar from any other author. With all its awkwardness and mannerism, it has an agreeable flavor of the soil about it like *vin du pays*. He is as English as Chaucer; all his roots are in English ground: and if Cowper is to have a monument at Barkhampstead, there should be one erected to Crabbe at Aldborough.

We recommend Crabbe as an alternative to those who have read too much of the poetry of our day. His hard realism is a capital tonic for minds surfeited with the vaporing verse of the nineteenth century, curiously compounded as it is of mysticism and metaphysics, fault-finding and sensuality. It is refreshing to turn from the discordant obscurity of Browning, from Tennyson's feminine prettiness, from the chaotic licentiousness and affectations of Swinburne and Rossetti, and the neat, nicely combed and curled plaints of Matthew Arnold, to plain, robust, keen old Crabbe. He at least was equal to his times. The world, with its trials and its mysteries, was good enough for him. He 'saw it whole' and had a contented and healthy appreciation of it as it was; not a paradise, by any means, but he had never heard of 'world sorrow' or of 'longings,' nor did he think it a merit to 'sit apart' from his fellow-men, impatient and disgusted with them and with their doings. . . .

71. A third-rate poet

1873

Joseph Devey (c. 1843–97), *A Comparative Estimate of Modern English Poets*, 1873, pp. 368–75.

It is rarely, when clergymen venture into the regions of the Muses, that they cut a very conspicuous figure there. I only know of two, who, as poets, have left behind them a brilliant reputation, and their triumphs were achieved in defiance of the cloth which they wore. While Herrick and Churchill wrote their best pieces, they lived in direct hostility with their professional duties. It would seem that the daughters of memory cherish some secret antipathy to theological pursuits, or at least they have no feelings of sympathy with those who,

> To wander round the Muse's sacred hill,
> Let the salvation of mankind stand still.
> [Churchill, Dedication to the *Sermons*, 125–6]

We all know that Young did not get on very well with them, even when he moralized his song; and Bowles, in the list of those who have

acquired fame during the present century, is, perhaps, the least entitled
to it. Home, who was turned out of the Presbytery for writing dramas,
occupies a still lower position. Crabbe, though a poet of far more
respectable pretensions, still labours under the disadvantages of his profession. Had he or Young been trained divines, it is probable what little
poetical capacity either possessed would have been squeezed out of
them. But both entered the Church in mature age. They brought into
the ministry a full knowledge of the world, a practical acquaintance
with the miseries of life and vicissitudes of fortune. This experience was
the grand storehouse of Young's and Crabbe's muse. But they brought
to the manipulation of the raw material the contracted views of their
new profession. Human life was painted in all its shivering nakedness.
The world outside the Church was the vestibule of hell. The responsi-
bilities of the wealthy made life burdensome, the labours of the poor
made life miserable. That spirit of Greek joyousness which casts such
broad sunshine over Helicon, hardly illumines a single line they have
written. The sense of beauty suffers in them a complete eclipse. There
is no outlet from the calamities of existence except spare living, a grave
demeanour, reading one's Bible, and keeping a clear look-out against
the evils which are always impending over us. The world is a sort of
penitentiary, and they conduct us into its wards, with black staves, in
crape bands, with the starch solemnity of decorum, as if they were
ushering us into a house of mourning, and nature had no feeling but
sorrow.

But Crabbe, in addition to the gloom imparted by his professional
bias, allowed his early miseries to impart a peculiar hypochondriac tone
to his poetry. The feelings he excites are mentally depressing. He is a
mere anatomist of moral diseases. We go through his poems as we
would through a lazar-house or hospital. The characters are drawn to
the life. But each is the subject of a moral diagnosis. His early practice
as a village doctor would seem to have inured his mind to the Æsculapian
habit of probing moral diseases to their root. We admit the truth of the
picture, but feel that the poet has drawn his subjects from the darkest
side of human life. Crabbe has been called the Hogarth of poets. But
this is hardly correct, for he shuns licentious revels. He does not picture
vice in the acme of enjoyment, but in the agonies of its fall. He surrounds himself with nothing but miseries, and never seems so happy as
when he is recounting the griefs of his neighbours. The poet has no
philosophical opinions or æsthetic views of any kind. The area of his
mind might be covered by the village catechism. It is owing to this lack

of comprehensiveness, no less than to the sombre nature of his muse, that Crabbe has long since fallen from the high place he once held among his contemporaries.

It is, I suppose, in consequence of this contracted range of his thoughts, that Crabbe does not flourish in abstract themes, but only in painting objective individualities. When he generalizes, he becomes trite and heavy. But to his portraits he imparts the finished touches and the marvellous shades of Rembrandt. His *Library* and *Newspaper* are two of his most general, and two of his worst, poems. His *Parish Register* is the most individual, and therefore the best of his productions. He even seems incompetent to deal with specific facts, unless such as are actually floating before his eyes. For nearly all his pictures are the result of visual observation. Perhaps, there is no instance of any other poet, who has risen to greatness, with so contracted a sphere for his muse. Nearly all his poems are so many different photographs of the same subject. His *Parish Register* is only a prolongation of his *Village*. His *Borough* is a still further expansion of the same subject. They both consist of masterly analyses of character and delineations of social life, in its most prosaic and repulsive aspects. In the *Tales of the Hall*, Crabbe is much more discursive; but they are all only so many episodes of provincial life. And even here, his lymphatic constitution predominates. There is a sickly air of melancholy, and sombre tinge of cloistered morality over all his narratives. He seems, even upon amatory subjects, to have felt that his whole strength lay in subduing the soul by pity. The purifying tendencies of this feeling, so present to the Greek mind, doubtless led him to think that, in giving his poems this turn, he was employing the Muses as the moral regenerators of mankind.

In vivid sketches of individual suffering, drawn from the humbler ranks of life, and in exciting sympathy for such suffering among a class too brazened by affluence and custom to be impressed by the sight of it, Crabbe appears to have found his peculiar mission. Out of such materials he contrives to extract more genuine feeling than any other poet. Wordsworth, who closely followed him in this line, certainly did not improve upon his master. The descriptions of Crabbe are more terse, the portraits more life-like, his language more vigorous, his details more striking, and the thorn of sorrow rankles deeper in the heart, when barbed by a man who had himself experienced the miseries which he conveys. In the following description of the heroine of a milliner's shop, as in most of his other portraits, the poet seems not to have been drawing from his imagination so much as sketching from real life:—

433

And who that poor, consumptive, wither'd thing, . . .
[*The Borough*, XII, 123-44]

Here the poet produces his results by simply adhering to nature.
There is no exaggeration of any kind, no apparent struggle to produce
effect. The 'Story of Phoebe Dawson'[1] is still more effective than that
of the 'Musical Heroine,' and the description of the 'Miller's Daughter'[2]
is more vigorous than either. 'Ruth'[3] and 'Ellen Orford'[4] belong to the
same gallery of portraits; yet there is a particularity about them which
makes them as individual as the rest. The 'History of Thomas, the
Consumptive Sailor Boy,'[5] who comes back from Greenland to die in
the arms of Sally, is, as far as the materials of the tale go, trite enough.
But in the hands of Crabbe it is invested with more plaintive tenderness
than any other similar story in our language. Throughout all this class
of subjects, Crabbe shows himself an easy master of those graphic traits
and salient touches which make the individual character walk out, as it
were, from the framework of the narrative; and in using such materials
for evoking sympathy he rules supreme. But these qualities alone would
not place a man very high in the roll of British poets, and had it not
been for adventitious circumstances, this poet would never have occupied that position in the eyes of his competitors.

Crabbe was singularly fortunate during his life, in reuniting in his
favour the suffrages of the two dispensers of poetical reputation,—
Gifford and Jeffrey, who vied with each other in chanting his praises
and descanting on his merits. There has been no such union of rival
political factions, in setting a poet upon a pedestal, since the days of
Addison. Crabbe owed this success not less to the anti-democratic
tendencies of his muse than to the solid advantages which the patronage
of Burke conferred upon him. It certainly is another proof of the
prescient sagacity of Burke's penetrating mind, that when no editor
would receive Crabbe's wares when all the booksellers to a man repudi-
ated his pretensions, when every door was shut against him, Burke
recognized his merit, and received the poet into his family, until some
provision could enable him to woo the muses without experiencing the
fate of an Otway or a Savage. Such was the expansiveness of that great
man's heart, that to know Burke was to know the large circle of his
acquaintance. By him he was introduced to Johnson, and found himself
at the easel of Sir Joshua Reynolds. Thenceforth he shot up like a rocket
into the heaven of renown. Booksellers competed for the honour of

[1] *The Parish Register*, II.   [2] *Ibid.*, I.   [3] *Tales of the Hall*, V.
[4] *The Borough*, XX.   [5] *Ibid.*, II.

publishing what a few years before they had scornfully rejected. Fox soothed the hours of sickness by turning over the leaves of *The Parish Register*, where he read of miseries deeper than his own. Even the tough heart of Thurlow was taught, by the same work, to melt at the sight of others' woe. He gave the poet a benefice. Sir Walter Scott re-echoed the general acclamation. Even the youthful Byron caught the infection so deeply as to place him in the first rank of existing poets:

> This fact in Virtue's name let Crabbe attest;
> Though Nature's sternest painter, yet the best.
> [*English Bards and Scotch Reviewers*, 857–8]

But this general eulogy was too exalted to be sustained. In the next generation Crabbe rapidly declined in favour, and now he is as virtually laid on the shelf as Rogers or Southey himself. But a calm and dispassionate criticism will equally learn to reduce factitious renown to its true value, while it rescues the poet's memory from the injustice of neglect.

No poet in our literature carved out for himself a more special province than Crabbe, and adhered to it with more fidelity. This, perhaps, is one of the best proofs of his original genius. While adhering to the old poetical establishment with respect to his style, with respect to his matter, he resolved to follow nature, to discard the hackneyed poetical commonplaces,—to sing of nothing but the natural results of his own experience. Life must be painted as it actually is, and not as it is depicted by a too heated imagination. As his predecessors revelled with buskined nymphs and swains in Idæan valleys or in Olympian groves, he reproduced the outcasts of cellars, the inmates of almshouses, and the victims of depravity, wrestling with misery in the squalid haunts of impoverished towns. No subject was too low for his muse. Every rank and grade of life was ransacked to afford him instances of the miseries and the vices of the class from which he sprung. But these are treated in the elaborate style which the Queen Anne poets applied to a far different kind of subjects. Hence, he has been called Pope in worsted stockings. But this is hardly fair to either poet, for both have distinct peculiarities, which keep them as wide apart as any two poets in our literature. If Crabbe has none of the passion, or sublimity, or recondite thought, or ingenious fancy, he has few of the artificial airs of his master. He rarely substitutes words for thoughts. If his language is polished, it is always terse, manly, unostentatious,—always revealing the matter, never itself. He never attempts to hide prosaic conceptions behind brilliant antitheses. But we rarely get more than the simple picture of the object which Crabbe presents to us, or if the poet helps us to anything out of his own mind, it simply consists of wise saws of prudence, moral hints, and religious admonitions. In this respect he is the most objective poet in any literature.

I must, therefore, set down Crabbe as wanting in all the qualities of first-class poetry. Ideality, passion, constructiveness, invention upon any imposing scale, brilliant fancy,—he has none of these: hence, he rarely attempts any other form of verse except the simple idyll, or any other metre than the pentameter. In extracting pathos out of scenes mainly drawn from humble life, he is unrivaled. Here his strength lay. He is also hardly less successful in graphic delineation of the provincial life with which he was familiar. Crabbe from a boy was a keen observer of everything which passed under his notice. He has drawn his own portrait in this respect in the adventures of Richard,[1] the poor lad who daily brought to his widowed mother's home the results of his rambles through the neighbouring fishing village, and also contrived, from the quay and the street, from the mechanic's shop and the smuggler's cave, from the fisher's hut and the tavern fireside, from the screaming gulls and the clashing waves, to extract themes for his muse and principles for his guidance, in after life. In reproducing these varied experiences, and in surrounding them with details which imparted to them life and freshness, no poet could have been more successful than Crabbe; but here his triumph ends. In describing the lower phases of the actual, he distances all his competitors. But when he comes to warmth of colouring, to passionate imagination, to sublime philosophic invention; in fine, to any of those qualities which invest the actual with the ideal, here Crabbe touches ground. It is not that he fails in any of these great qualities, so much as he never attempts to exhibit them. Hence Crabbe's stories can never occupy the top rank of idyllic literature, nor entitle their author to more than a respectable place in the middle group of our third-class poets.

[1] *Tales of the Hall*, IV.

72. Leslie Stephen on Crabbe

1874

Stephen (1832–1904) wrote for the *Cornhill* from 1866, becoming its editor in 1871. This paper appeared in 1874, Vol. xxx, pp. 454–73. It was reprinted in *Hours in a Library*, 2nd series, 1876; new edition, 1892.

It is nearly a century since George Crabbe, then a young man of five-and-twenty, put three pounds in his pocket and started from his native town of Aldborough with a box of clothes and a case of surgical instruments to make his fortune in London. Few men have attempted that adventure with less promising prospects. Any sensible adviser would have told him to prefer starvation in his native village to starvation in the back lanes of London. . . .

The interstices of the box of clothing which went with him from Aldborough to London were doubtless crammed with much waste paper scribbled over with feeble echoes of Pope's Satires, and with appeals to nymphs, muses, and shepherds. Crabbe was one of those men who are born a generation after their natural epoch, and was as little accessible to the change of fashion in poetry as in costume. When, therefore, he finally resolved to hazard his own fate and Mira's upon the results of his London adventure, the literary goods at his disposal were already somewhat musty in character. The year 1780, in which he reached London, marks the very nadir of English poetry. From the days of Elizabeth to our own there has never been so absolutely barren a period. People had become fairly tired of the jingle of Pope's imitators, and the new era had not dawned. Goldsmith and Gray, both recently dead, serve to illustrate the condition in which the most exquisite polish and refinement of language has been developed until there is a danger of sterility. The *Elegy* and *The Deserted Village* are inimitable poems: but we feel that the intellectual fibre of the poets has become dangerously delicate. The critical faculty could not be stimulated further without destroying all spontaneous impulse. The reaction to a more

masculine and passionate school was imminent; and if the excellent
Crabbe could have put into his box a few of Burns's lyrics, or even a copy
of Cowper's 'Task,' one might have augured better for his prospects. But
what chance was there for a man who could still be contentedly
invoking the muse and stringing together mechanic echoes of Pope's
couplets? How could he expect to charm the jaded faculties of a
generation which was already beginning to heave and stir with a longing
for some fresh excitement?

[There follows some account of his experience in London and of his
courtship of 'Mira', his future wife, in her uncle Tovell's household,
where, Stephen suggests, Crabbe met some of the originals of his
characters. There is a reference to this passage in Woodberry's essay—
see p. 452 below.]

In his long portrait gallery there are plenty of virtuous people, and
some people intended to be refined; but features indicative of coarse
animal passions, brutality, selfishness, and sensuality are drawn to the
life, and the development of his stories is generally determined by some
of the baser elements of human nature. 'Jesse and Colin' are described
in one of the *Tales*[1]; but they are not the Jesse and Colin of Dresden
china. They are such rustics as ate fat bacon and drank 'heavy ale and
new;' not the imaginary personages who exchanged amatory civilities
in the old-fashioned pastorals ridiculed by Pope and Gay.

Crabbe's rough style is indicative of his general temper. It is in places
at least the most slovenly and slipshod that was ever adopted by any
true poet. The authors of the *Rejected Addresses* had simply to copy,
without attempting the impossible task of caricaturing. One of their
familiar couplets, for example, runs thus:—

> Emmanuel Jennings brought his youngest boy
> Up as a corn-cutter, a safe employ!

And here is the original Crabbe:—

> Swallow, a poor attorney, brought his boy
> Up at his desk, and gave him his employ.
> [*The Borough*, VI, 200–1]

When boy cannot be made to rhyme with employ, Crabbe is very fond
of dragging in a hoy. In *The Parish Register* he introduces a narrative
about a village grocer and his friend in these lines:—

[1]XIII.

> Aged were both, that Dawkins, Ditchem this,
> Who much of marriage thought and much amiss.
>
> [I, 514–15]

Or to quote one more opening of a story:—

> Counter and Clubb were men in trade, whose pains,
> Credit, and prudence, brought them constant gains;
> Partners and punctual, every friend agreed
> Counter and Clubb were men who must succeed.
>
> [*Tales*, XVIII, 1–4]

But of such gems anyone may gather as many as he pleases by simply turning over Crabbe's pages. In one sense, they are rather pleasant than otherwise. They are so characteristic and put forward with such absolute simplicity that they have the same effect as a good old provincialism in the mouth of a genuine countryman. It must, however, be admitted that Crabbe's careful study of Pope had not initiated him in some of his master's secrets. The worsted stockings were uncommonly thick. If Pope's brilliance of style savours too much of affectation, Crabbe never manages to hit off an epigram in the whole of his poetry. The language seldom soars above the style which would be intelligible to the merest clodhopper; and we can understand how, when in his later years Crabbe was introduced to wits and men of the world, he generally held his peace, or, at most, let fall some bit of dry quiet humour. At rare intervals he remembers that a poet ought to indulge in a figure of speech, and laboriously compounds a simile which appears in his poetry like a bit of gold lace on a farmer's homespun coat. He confessed as much in answer to a shrewd criticism of Jeffrey's, saying that he generally thought of such illustrations and inserted them after he had finished his tale. There is one of these deliberately concocted ornaments, intended to explain the remark that the difference between the character of two brothers came out when they were living together quietly:—

> As various colours in a painted ball,
> While it has rest are seen distinctly all;
> Till, whirl'd around by some exterior force,
> They all are blended in the rapid course;
> So in repose and not by passion swayed
> We saw the difference by their habits made;
> But, tried by strong emotions, they became
> Filled with one love, and were in heart the same.
>
> [*Tales of the Hall*, II, 25–32]

The conceit is ingenious enough in one sense, but painfully ingenious. It requires some thought to catch the likeness suggested, and then it turns out to be purely superficial. The resemblance of such a writer to Pope obviously does not go deep. Crabbe imitates Pope because everybody imitated him at that day. He adopted Pope's metre because it had come to be almost the only recognized means of poetical expression. He stuck to it after his contemporaries had introduced new versification, partly because he was old-fashioned to the backbone and partly because he had none of those lofty inspirations which naturally generate new forms of melody. He seldom trusts himself to be lyrical, and when he does his versification is nearly as monotonous as in his narrative poetry. We must not expect to soar with Crabbe into any of the loftier regions; to see the world 'apparelled in celestial light,' or to descry

> Such forms as glitter in the muses' ray,
> With orient hues, unborrowed of the sun.
> [Gray, 'The Progress of Poesy', 119–20]

We shall find no vehement outbursts of passion, breaking loose from the fetters of sacred convention. Crabbe is perfectly content with the British Constitution, with the Thirty-nine Articles, and all respectabilities in Church and State, and therefore he is quite content also with the good old jogtrot of the recognized metres; his language, halting unusually, and for the most part clumsy enough, is sufficiently differentiated from prose by the mould into which it is run, and he never wants to kick over the traces with his more excitable contemporaries.

> The good old rule
> Sufficeth him, the simple plan
> [Wordsworth, 'Rob Roy's Grave', 37–8]

that each verse should consist of ten syllables, with an occasional Alexandrine to accommodate a refractory epithet, and should rhyme peaceably with its neighbour.

From all which it may be too harshly inferred that Crabbe is merely a writer in rhyming prose, and deserving of no attention from the more enlightened adherents of a later school. The inference, I say, would be hasty, for it is impossible to read Crabbe patiently without receiving a very distinct and original impression. If some pedants of æsthetic philosophy should declare that we ought not to be impressed because Crabbe breaks all their rules, we can only reply that they are mistaking their trade. The true business of the critic is to discover from observation what are the conditions under which art appeals to our sympathies, and, if he finds an apparent exception to his rules, to admit that he has made an oversight, and not to condemn the facts which persist in contradicting his theories. It may, indeed, be freely granted that Crabbe has suffered seriously by his slovenly methods and his insensibility to the more exquisite and ethereal forms of poetical excellence. But however he may be classified, he possesses the essential mark of genius, namely, that his pictures, however coarse the workmanship, stamp themselves on our minds indelibly and instantaneously. His pathos is here and there clumsy, but it goes straight to the mark. His characteristic qualities were first distinctly shown in *The Village*, which was partly composed under Burke's eye, and was more or less touched by Johnson. It was, indeed, a work after Johnson's own heart, intended to be a pendant, or perhaps a corrective, to Goldsmith's *Deserted Village*. It is meant to give the bare blank facts of rural life, stripped of all sentimental gloss. To read the two is something like hearing a speech from an optimist landlord and then listening to the comments of Mr. Arch.[1] Goldsmith, indeed, was far too exquisite an artist to indulge in mere conventionalities about agricultural bliss. If his 'Auburn' is rather idealized, the most prosaic of critics cannot object to the glow thrown by the memory of the poet over the scene of now ruined happiness, and, moreover, Goldsmith's delicate humour guards him instinctively from laying on his rose-colour too thickly. Crabbe, however, will have nothing to do with rose-colour, thick or thin. There is one explicit reference in the poem to his predecessor's work, and it is significant. Everybody remembers, or ought to remember, Goldsmith's charming pastor, to whom it can only be objected that he has not the fear of political economists before his eyes. This is Crabbe's retort, after describing a dying pauper in need of spiritual consolation:—

> And doth not he, the pious man, appear . . .
> [*The Village*, I, 302–13]

The ultimate fate of the worn-out labourer is the poorhouse, described in lines, of which it is enough to say that Scott and Wordsworth learnt them by heart, and the melancholy death-bed already noticed. Are we reading a poem or a Blue Book done into rhyme? may possibly be the question of some readers. The answer should perhaps be that a good many Blue Books contain an essence which only requires to be properly extracted and refined to become genuine poetry. If Crabbe's verses

---

[1] Leader of the Agricultural Workers' Union.

retain rather too much of the earthly elements, he is capable of transmuting his minerals into genuine gold, as well as of simply collecting them. Nothing, for example, is more characteristic than the mode in which the occasional descriptions of nature are harmoniously blended with the human life in his poetry. Crabbe is an ardent lover of a certain type of scenery, to which justice has not often been done. We are told how, after a long absence from Suffolk, he rode sixty miles from his house to have a dip in the sea. Some of his poems appear to be positively impregnated with a briny, or rather perhaps a tarry odour. The sea which he loved was by no means a Byronic sea. It has no grandeur of storm, and still less has it the Mediterranean blue. It is the sluggish muddy element which washes the flat shores of his beloved Suffolk. He likes even the shelving beach, with fishermen's boats and decaying nets and remnants of stale fish. He loves the dreary estuary, where the slow tide sways backwards and forwards, and whence

> High o'er the restless deep, above the reach
> Of gunner's hope, vast flocks of wildfowl stretch.
> [*The Borough*, I, 218-19]

The coming generation of poets took to the mountains; but Crabbe remained faithful to the dismal and yet, in his hands, the impressive scenery of his native salt-marshes. His method of description suits the country. His verses never become melodramatic, nor does he ever seem to invest nature with the mystic life of Wordsworth's poetry. He gives the plain prosaic facts which impress us because they are in such perfect harmony with the sentiment. Here, for example, is a fragment from *The Village*, which is simply a description of the neighbourhood of Aldborough:—

> Lo! where the heath, with withering brake grown o'er . . .
> [*The Village*, I, 63-76]

The writer is too obviously a botanist; but the picture always remains with us as the only conceivable background for the poverty-stricken population whom he is about to describe. The actors in *The Borough* are presented to us in a similar setting; and it may be well to put a sea-piece beside this bit of barren common. Crabbe's range of descriptive power is pretty well confined within the limits so defined. He is scarcely at home beyond the tide-marks:—

> Be it the summer noon: a sandy space . . .
> [*The Borough*, I, 173-89, omitting 177-8]

I have omitted a couplet which verges on the scientific; for Crabbe is unpleasantly anxious to leave nothing unexplained. The effect is, in its way, perfect. Any one who pleases may compare it with Wordsworth's calm in the verses upon Peele Castle, where the sentiment is given without the minute statement of facts, and where, too, we have the inevitable quotation about the 'light that never was on sea or land,' and is pretty nearly as rare in Crabbe's poetry. What he sees, we can all see, though not so intensely; and his art consists in selecting the precise elements that tell most forcibly towards bringing us into the required frame of mind. To enjoy Crabbe fully, we ought perhaps to be acclimatized on the coast of the Eastern counties; we should become sensitive to the plaintive music of the scenery, which is now generally drowned by the discordant sounds of modern watering-places, and would seem insipid to a generation which values excitement in scenery as in fiction. Readers, who measure the beauty of a district by its average height above the sea-level, and who cannot appreciate the charm of a 'waste enormous marsh,' may find Crabbe uncongenial.

The human character is determined, as Mr. Buckle and other philosophers have assured us, by the climate and the soil. A little ingenuity, such as those philosophers display in accommodating facts to theory, might discover a parallel between the type of Crabbe's personages and the fauna and flora of his native district. Declining a task which might lead to fanciful conclusions, I may assume that the East Anglian character is sufficiently familiar, whatever the causes by which it has been determined. To define Crabbe's poetry we have simply to imagine ourselves listening to the stories of his parishioners, told by a clergyman brought up amongst the lower rank of the middle classes, scarcely elevated above their prejudices, and not willingly leaving their circle of ideas. We must endow him with that simplicity of character which gives us frequent cause to smile at its proprietor, but which does not disqualify him from seeing a great deal further into his neighbours than they are apt to give him credit for doing. Such insight, in fact, is due not to any great subtlety of intellect, but to the possession of deep feeling and sympathy. Crabbe saw little more of Burke than would have been visible to an ordinary Suffolk farmer. When transplanted to a ducal mansion, he only drew the pretty obvious inference, inferred in a vigorous poem, that a patron is a very disagreeable and at times a very mischievous personage. The joys and griefs which really interest him are of the very tangible and solid kind which affect men and women to whom the struggle for existence is a stern reality. Here and there his good-humoured but rather clumsy ridicule may strike some lady to whom some demon has whispered 'have a taste;' and who turns up her nose at the fat bacon on Mr. Tovell's table. He pities her squeamishness, but thinks it rather unreasonable. He satirizes too the heads of the rustic aristocracy; the brutal squire who bullies his nephew, the clergyman, for preaching against his vices, and corrupts the whole neighbourhood; or the speculative banker who cheats old maids under pretence of looking after their investments. If the squire does not generally appear in Crabbe in the familiar dramatic character of a rural Lovelace, it is chiefly because Crabbe has no great belief in the general purity of the inferior ranks of rural life. But his most powerful stories deal with the tragedies—only too lifelike—of the shop and the farm. He describes the temptations which lead the small tradesman to adulterate his goods, or the parish clerk to embezzle the money subscribed in the village church, and the evil effects of dissenting families who foster a spiritual pride which leads to more unctuous hypocrisy; for though he says of the wicked squire, that

> His worship ever was a churchman true,
> And held in scorn the methodistic crew,
> [*The Borough*, XVI, 96–7]

the scorn is only objectionable to him in so far as it is a cynical cloak for scorn of good morals. He tells how boys run away to sea, or join strolling players, and have in consequence to beg their bread at the end of their days. The almshouse or the county gaol is the natural end of his villains, and he paints to the life the evil courses which generally lead to such a climax. Nobody describes better the process of going to the dogs. And most of all, he sympathizes with the village maiden who has listened too easily to the voice of the charmer in the shape of a gay sailor or a smart London footman, and has to reap the bitter consequences of her too easy faith. Most of his stories might be paralleled by the experience of any country clergyman who has entered into the life of his parishioners. They are as commonplace and as pathetic as the things which are happening round us every day, and which fill a neglected paragraph in a country newspaper. The treatment varies from the purely humorous to the most deep and genuine pathos; though it seldom takes us into the regions of the loftier imagination.

The more humorous of these performances may be briefly dismissed. Crabbe possessed the faculty, but not in any eminent degree; his hand is a little heavy, and one must remember that Mr. Tovell and his like were of the race who require to have a joke driven into their heads with a sledge hammer. Once or twice we come upon a sketch which may help to explain Miss Austen's admiration. There is an old maid devoted to Mira, and rejoicing in stuffed puppies and parrots, who might have been another Emma Woodhouse, and a parson who would have suited the Eltons admirably:

> Fiddling and fishing were his arts; at times
> He altered sermons and he aimed at rhymes;
> And his fair friends, not yet intent on cards,
> Oft he amused with riddles and charades.
> [*The Borough*, III, 102-5]

Such sketches are a pleasant relief to his more sombre portraiture; but it is in the tragic elements that his true power comes out. The motives of his stories may be trivial, but never the sentiment. The deep manly emotion makes us forget not only the frequent clumsiness of his style but the pettiness of the incident, and, what is more difficult, the rather bread-and-butter tone of morality. If he is a little too fond of bringing his villains to the gallows, he is preoccupied less by the external consequences than by the natural working of evil passions. With him sin is not punished by being found out, but by disintegrating the character and blunting the higher sensibilities. He shows—and the moral, if not new, is that which possesses the really intellectual interest— how evil-doers are tortured by the cravings of desires that cannot be satisfied, and the lacerations inflicted by ruined self-respect. And there-fore there is a truth in Crabbe's delineations which is quite independent of his more or less rigid administration of poetical justice. His critics used to accuse him of having a low opinion of human nature. It is quite true that he assigns to selfishness and brutal passion a very large part in carrying on the machinery of the world. Some readers may infer that he was unlucky in his experience and others that he loved facts too unflinchingly. His stories sometimes remind one of Balzac's in the descriptions of selfishness triumphant over virtue. One, for example, of his deeply pathetic poems is called 'The Brothers;'[1] and repeats the old contrast given in Fielding's Tom Jones and Blifil. The shrewd sly hypocrite has received all manner of kindnesses from the generous and simple sailor, and when, at last, the poor sailor is ruined in health and fortune, he comes home expecting to be supported by the gratitude of the brother, who has by this time made money and is living at his ease.

[1] *Tales*, XX.

Nothing can be more pathetic or more in the spirit of some of Balzac's stories than the way in which the rich man receives his former bene- factor; his faint recognition of fraternal feelings gradually cools down under the influence of a selfish wife; till at last the poor old sailor is driven from the parlour to the kitchen, and from the kitchen to the loft, and finally deprived of his only comfort, his intercourse with a young nephew not yet broken into hardness of heart. The lad is not to be cor- rupted by the coarse language of his poor old uncle. The rich brother suspects that the sailor has broken this rule, and is reviling him for his ingratitude, when suddenly he discovers that he is abusing a corpse. The old sailor's heart is broken at last; and his brother repents too late. He tries to comfort his remorse by cross-examining the boy, who was the cause of the last quarrel:—

'Did he not curse me, child?' 'He never cursed,
But could not breathe, and said his heart would burst.'
'And so will mine——' 'But, father, you must pray;
My uncle said it took his pains away.'
[*Tales*, XX, 391–4]

Praying, however, cannot bring back the dead; and the fratricide, for such he feels himself to be, is a melancholy man to the end of his days. In Balzac's hands repentance would have had no place, and selfishness been finally triumphant and unabashed. We need not ask which would be the most effective or the truest treatment; though I must put in a word for the superior healthiness of Crabbe's mind. There is nothing morbid about him. Still it would be absurd to push such a comparison far. Crabbe's portraits are only spirited vignettes compared with the elaborate full-lengths drawn by the intense imagination of the French novelist; and Crabbe's whole range of thought is narrower. The two writers have a real resemblance only in so far as in each case a powerful accumulation of life-like details enables them to produce a pathos, powerful by its vivid reality.

The singular power of Crabbe is in some sense more conspicuous in the stories where the incidents are almost audaciously trifling. One of them begins with this not very impressive and very ungrammatical couplet:—

With our late Vicar, and his age the same,
His clerk, hight Jachin, to his office came.
[*The Borough*, XIX, 1–2]

Jachin is a man of oppressive respectability; so oppressive, indeed, that some of the scamps of the borough try to get him into scrapes by temptations of a very inartificial kind, which he is strong enough to resist. At last, however, it occurs to Jachin that he can easily embezzle part of the usual monthly offerings while saving his character in his own eyes by some obvious sophistry. He is detected and dismissed, and dies after coming upon the parish. These materials for a tragic poem are not very promising; and I do not mean to say that the sorrows of poor Jachin effect [sic] us as deeply as those of Gretchen in *Faust*. The parish clerk is perhaps a fit type of all that was least poetical in the old social order of the country, and virtue which succumbs to the temptation of taking two shillings out of a plate scarcely wants a Mephistophiles to overcome it. We may perhaps think that the apologetic note which the excellent Crabbe inserts at the end of his poem, to the effect that he did not mean by it to represent mankind as 'puppets of an overpowering destiny,' or 'to deny the doctrine of seducing spirits,' is a little superfluous. The fact that a parish-clerk has taken to petty pilfering can scarcely justify those heterodox conclusions. But when we have smiled at Crabbe's philosophy, we begin to wonder at the force of his sentiment. A blighted human soul is a pathetic object, however paltry the temptation to which it has succumbed. Jachin has the dignity of despair, though he is not quite a fallen archangel; and Crabbe's favourite scenery harmonizes with his agony.

> In each lone place dejected and dismay'd, . . .
> [*The Borough*, XIX, 270–8]

Nor would he have been a more pitiable object if he had betrayed a nation or sold his soul for a garter instead of the pillage of a subscription plate. Poor old Jachin's story may seem to be borrowed from a commonplace tract; but the detected pilferer, though he has only lost the respect of the parson, the overseer, and the beadle, touches us deeply as the Byronic hero who has fallen out with the whole system of the world.

If we refuse to sympathize with the pang due to so petty a catastrophe —though our sympathy should surely be proportioned to the keenness of the suffering rather than the absolute height of the fall—we may turn to tragedy of a deeper dye.—Peter Grimes [which is then summarized].

Of all haunted men in fiction, it is not easy to think of a case where the horror is more terribly realized. The blood-boulter'd Banquo tortured a noble victim, but scarcely tortured him more effectually. Peter Grimes was doubtless a close relation of Peter Bell. Bell having the advantage of Wordsworth's interpretation, leads us to many thoughts which lie altogether beyond Crabbe's reach; but, looking simply at the sheer tragic force of the two characters, Grimes is to Bell what brandy is to small beer. He would never have shown the white feather like his successor, who,

> after ten months' melancholy,
> Became a good and honest man.
> [*Peter Bell*, 1134–5]

If, in some sense, Peter Grimes is the most effective of Crabbe's heroes, he would, if taken alone, give a very distorted impression of the general spirit of the poetry. It is only at intervals that he introduces us to downright criminals. There is, indeed, a description of a convicted felon, which, according to Macaulay, has made 'many a rough and cynical reader cry like a child,' and which, if space were unlimited, would make a striking pendant to the agony of the burdened Grimes. But, as a rule, Crabbe can find motives enough for tenderness in sufferings which have nothing to do with the criminal law, and of which the mere framework of the story is often interesting enough. His peculiar power is best displayed in so presenting to us the sorrows of commonplace characters as to make us feel that a shabby coat and a narrow education, and the most unromantic causes, need not cut off our sympathies with a fellow-creature; and that the dullest tradesman who treads on our toes in an omnibus may want only a power of articulate expression to bring before us some of the deepest of all problems. The parish clerk and the grocer—or whatever may be the proverbial epitome of human dullness—may swell the chorus of lamentation over the barrenness and the hardships and the wasted energies and the harsh discords of life which is always 'steaming up' from the world, and to which it is one, though perhaps not the highest, of the poet's functions to make us duly sensible. Crabbe, like all realistic writers, must be studied at full length, and therefore quotations are necessarily unjust. It will be sufficient if I refer—pretty much at random—to the short stories of 'Phœbe Dawson' in *The Parish Register*, to the more elaborate stories of 'Edward Shore' and 'The Parting Hour' in the *Tales*, or to the story of 'Ruth' in the *Tales of the Hall*, where again the dreary pathos is strangely heightened by Crabbe's favourite seaport scenery, to prove that he might be called as truly as Goldsmith *affectuum potens*, though scarcely *lenis, dominator*.

It is time, however, to conclude by a word or two as to Crabbe's peculiar place in the history of English literature. I said that, unlike his contemporaries, Cowper and Burns, he adhered rigidly to the form of the earlier eighteenth century school, and partly for this reason excited the wayward admiration of Byron, who always chose to abuse the bridge which carried him to fame. But Crabbe's clumsiness of expression makes him a very inadequate successor of Pope or of Goldsmith, and his claims are really founded on the qualities which led Byron to call him 'nature's sternest painter, yet her best.' On this side he is connected with some tendencies of the school which supplanted his early models. So far as Wordsworth and his followers represented the reaction from an artificial to a love of unsophisticated nature, Crabbe is entirely at one with them. He did not share that unlucky taste for the namby-pamby by which Wordsworth annoyed his contemporaries, and spoilt some of his earlier poems. Its place was filled in Crabbe's mind by an even more unfortunate disposition for the simply humdrum and commonplace, which, it must be confessed, makes it almost as hard to read a good deal of his verses as to consume large quantities of suet pudding, and has probably destroyed his popularity with the present generation. Still Crabbe's influence was powerful as against the old conventionality. He did not, like his predecessors, write upon the topics which interested 'persons of quality,' and never gives us the impression of having composed his rhymes in a full-bottomed wig or even in a Grub Street garret. He has gone out into country fields and village lanes, and paints directly from man and nature, with almost a cynical disregard of the accepted code of propriety. But the points on which he parts company with his more distinguished predecessors is equally obvious. Mr. Stopford Brooke has lately been telling us with great eloquence what is the theology which underlies the poetical tendencies of the last generation of poets.[1] Of that creed, a sufficiently vague one, it must be admitted, Crabbe was by no means an apostle. Rather one would say he was as indifferent as a good old-fashioned clergyman could very well be to the existence of any new order of ideas in the world. The infidels, whom he sometimes attacks, read Bolingbroke, and Chubb, and Mandeville, and have only heard by report even of the existence of Voltaire. The Dissenters, whom he so heartily detests, have listened to Whitefield and Wesley, or perhaps to Huntington, S.S.— that is, as it may now be necessary to explain, Sinner Saved. Every newer development of thought was still far away from the quiet pews of Aldborough, and the only form of Church restoration of which he

[1] *Theology in the English Poets*, 1874.

has heard is the objectionable practice of painting a new wall to represent a growth of lichens.[1] Crabbe appreciates the charm of the picturesque, but has never yet heard of our elaborate methods of creating modern antiques. Lapped in such ignorance, and with a mind little given to speculation, it is only in character that Crabbe should be totally insensible to the various moods of thought represented by Wordsworth's pantheistic conceptions of nature, or by Shelley's dreamy idealism, or Byron's fierce revolutionary impulses. Still less, if possible, could he sympathize with that love of beauty, pure and simple, of which Keats was the first prophet. He might, indeed, be briefly described by saying that he is at the very opposite pole from Keats. The more bigoted admirers of Keats—for there are bigots in all matters of taste or poetry as well as in science or theology or politics—would refuse the title of poet to Crabbe, altogether on the strength of the absence of this element from his verse. Like his most obvious parallels in painting, he is too fond of boors and pothouses to be allowed the quality of artistic perception. I will not argue the point, which is, perhaps, rather a question of classification than of intrinsic merit; but I will venture to suggest a test which will, I think, give Crabbe a very firm, though, it may be, not a very lofty place. I should be unwilling to be reckoned as one of Macaulay's 'rough and cynical readers.' I admit that I can read the story of the convicted felon, or of Peter Grimes without indulging in downright blubbering. Most readers, I fear, can in these days get through pathetic poems and novels without absolutely using their pocket-handkerchiefs. But though Crabbe may not prompt such outward and visible signs of emotion, I think that he produces a more distinct titillation of the lachrymatory glands than almost any poet of his time. True, he does not appeal to emotions, accessible only through the finer intellectual perceptions, or to the thoughts which 'lie too deep for tears.' That prerogative belongs to men of more intense character, greater philosophical power, and more delicate instincts. But the power of touching readers by downright pictures of homespun griefs and sufferings is one which, to my mind, implies some poetical capacity, and which clearly belongs to Crabbe.

[1] *The Borough*, II.

73. A last American judgment

1880

George E. Woodberry was Professor of English at Nebraska University between 1877 and 1882 and at Columbia from 1891 to 1904. He contributed to the *Atlantic Monthly* from 1876 to 1891, this article appearing in Vol. xlv (May 1880), pp. 624–9. It was later collected in *Studies in Letters and Life*, 1890.

We have done with Crabbe. His tales have failed to interest us. Burke and his friends, as we all know, held a different opinion from ours; and their praise is not likely to have been ill founded. The cultivated taste of Holland House, thirty years later, is also against our decision. Through two generations of markedly different literary temper Crabbe pleased the men best worth pleasing. . . .

Without reckoning the approval of others, what was the strong attraction in Crabbe's work for Scott and Fox? Their judgment was not so worthless that it can be disregarded with the complacent assurance with which the decisions of Gifford and Jeffrey are set aside; on the contrary, Scott had such health and Fox such refinement that their judgment ought to raise a doubt whether our generation is not making a mistake and missing pleasure through its neglect of Crabbe.

Crabbe is a story-teller. He describes the life he saw,—common, homely life, sometimes wretched, not infrequently criminal; the life of the country poor, with occasional light and shadow from the life of the gentlefolk above them. He had been born into it, in a village on the Suffolk coast, amid stern and cheerless natural scenes: landward, the bramble-overgrown heath encompassing crowded and mean houses; eastward,—

> Stakes and sea-weed withering on the mud.
>
> [*The Borough*, I, 42]

Here he had passed his boyhood, in the midst of human life equally barren and stricken with the ugliness of poverty, among surly and sordid fishers given to hard labor and rough brawl,—

A joyless, wild, amphibious race,
With sullen woe displayed in every face,—
[*The Village*, I, 85–6]

and the sight had been a burden to him. . . .

In his later tales he dealt less in unrelieved gloom and bitter misery, and at times made a trial at humor. There are glimpses of pleasant English life and character, but these are only glimpses; the ground of his painting is shadow,—the shadow that rested on the life of the English poor in his generation.

Where else would one turn for an adequate description of that life, or gain so direct an insight into the social sources and conditions of the Methodist revival, or into the motives and convictions of reformers like Mary Wollstonecraft? Where would one obtain so keen a sense of the vast change which has taken place in the conditions of humble human life within this century? Mr. Leslie Stephen, in that essay which is so good-humoured but so unsuccessful an attempt to appreciate Crabbe, mentions the few illustrations in modern literature of the life Crabbe described; it is seen in Charlotte Brontë's Yorkshiremen, and George Eliot's millers, and in a few other characters, 'but,' he says, 'to get a realistic picture of country life as Crabbe saw it, we must go back to Squire Western, or to some of the roughly-hewn masses of flesh who sat to Hogarth.' The setting of Crabbe's tales has this special historic interest. This historic value of the tales, however, great as it is to the student of manners, is secondary to their poetic value, which lies in the sentiment, feeling, and pathos with which the experience of life embodied in them, the workings of simple human nature, in however debased surroundings, is set forth. It is an experience which results usually from the interplay of low and selfish motives, and of ignoble or weak passions; it is, too often, the course of brutal appetite, thoughtless or heartless folly, avarice, sensuality, and vice, relieved too seldom by amiable character, sympathy, charity, self-sacrifice, or even by the charm of natural beauty. Yet if all the seventy tales be taken into account, they contain nearly all varieties of character and circumstance among the country poor; and, though the darker side may seem to be more frequently insisted upon, it is because the nature of his subject made it necessary, because he let his light, as Moore said,—

Through life's low, dark interior fall,
Opening the whole, severely bright,
['Verses to the Poet Crabbe's Inkstand', 23–4]

rather than because he had any lack of cheerfulness of temper.

Crabbe does not, in a true sense, give expression to the life of the poor; he merely narrates it. Here and there, throughout the poems, are episodes written out of his own life; but usually he is concerned with the experience of other men, which he had observed, rather than with what his own heart had felt. A description of life is of course far inferior to an utterance of it, such as was given to us by Burns, who dealt with the life of the poor so much more powerfully than Crabbe; and a realistic description has less poetic value than an imaginative one, such as was given to us by Wordsworth at his best. Crabbe's description is perhaps the most nakedly realistic of any in English poetry; but it is an uncommonly good one. Realism has a narrow compass, and Crabbe's powers were confined strictly within it; but he had the best virtues of a realist. His physical vision—his sight of what presents itself to the eye—was almost perfect; he saw every object, and saw it as it was. Perhaps the minuteness with which he saw was not altogether an advantage, for he does not seem to have taken in the landscape as a whole, but only as a mosaic of separate objects. He never gives general effects of beauty or grandeur; indeed, he seldom saw the beauty of a single object; he did little more than catalogue the things before him, and employ in writing poetry the same faculty in the same way as in pursuing his favorite studies of botany and entomology. Yet, with these limitations, what realist in painting could exceed in truthfulness and carefulness of detail this picture of a fall morning?—

> It was a fair and mild autumnal sky . . .
> [*Tales of the Hall*, IV, 46–7, 50–3, 59–60]

and

> That window view!—oil'd paper and old glass . . .
> [*The Borough*, XVIII, 354–61]

Nor is this carefulness of detail a trick, such as is sometimes employed, to give the appearance of reality to unreal human life. Crabbe's mental vision, his sight into the workings of the passions and the feelings, although not so perfect as his physical vision, was yet at its best very keen and clear; the sentiments, moods, reflections, and actions of his characters are seldom contrary to nature. It would be difficult to show a finer delineation of its kind than his description of the meeting of two long-parted brothers.

> How shall I now my unknown way explore, . . .
> [*Tales of the Hall*, I, 295–8, 302–17, 320–3, 328–33, 338–9, 342–4]

These qualities of fine, true physical and mental vision are the essential qualities for valuable realistic work; if there be room for regret in Crabbe's share of them, it is because their range is contracted. The limitations of his physical vision have been mentioned; in respect to his mental vision Crabbe saw only a few and comparatively simple operations of human nature,—the workings of country-bred minds, not finely or complexly organized, but slow-motioned, and perplexed, if if perplexed at all, not from the difficulty of the problem, but from their own dullness. Yet within these limits his characters are often pathetic, sometimes tragic, or even terrible, in their energy of evil passion or remorse.

One other quality, without which clear mental and physical vision would be ineffective, is essential to realism like Crabbe's,—transparency, the quality by virtue of which life is seen through the text plainly and without distortion; and this is the quality which Crabbe possessed in most perfection. He not only saw the object as it was; he presented it as it was. He neither added nor took away; he did not unconsciously darken or heighten colour, soften or harden line. Whatever was before his mind—the conversation of a gossip, the brutality of a ruffian, the cant of a convert—he reproduced truthfully; whatever was the character of his story, mean or tragic, trivial or pathetic, he did not modify it. There was no veil of fancy, no glamour of amiable deception or dimness of charitable tears, to obscure his view: if he found nudity and dirt, they reappeared in his work nudity and dirt still; if he found courage and patience, he dealt the same even-handed justice. His distinction is that he told a true story.

It was, perhaps, because he was thus able to present accurately and faithfully the human life which he saw so clearly that he won such admiration from Scott; for Scott had the welcome of genius for any new glimpse of humanity, and he knew how rare, and consequently how valuable, is the gift of simple and direct narration of what one sees. Fox had great sensibility and tenderness of heart; and Crabbe presented the lot of the poor so vividly, so lucidly, so immediately, that he stirred in Fox the same feelings with which a better poet would have so charged his verses that natures not so finely endowed as Fox would have been compelled to feel them too. Scott and Fox knew what a valuable acquisition this realistic sketch of humble life in their generation was, so faithful, minute, and trustworthy; they felt that their experience was enlarged, that real humanity had been brought home to them, and in the sway of those emotions, which Crabbe did not infuse into his work, but which his work quickens in sympathetic hearts, they could forgive him his tediousness, his frequent commonplace, his not unusual absurdity of phrase, his low level of flight with its occasional feebleness of wing.

In their minds, too, his style must have had more influence than we are apt to think,—the style of the great school which died with him, the form and versification which they had been taught to believe almost essential to the best poetry, and from a traditional respect for which they could hardly free their minds as easily as ourselves. Crabbe used the old heroic rhymed couplet, that simplest form of English verse music, which could rise, nevertheless, to the almost lyric loftiness of the last lines of *The Dunciad*; so supple and flexible; made for easy simile and compact metaphor; lending itself so perfectly to the sudden flash of wit or turn of humor; the natural shell of an epigram; compelling the poet to practice all the virtues of brevity; checking the wandering fancy, and repressing the secondary thought; requiring in a masterly use of it the employment of more mental powers than any other metrical form; despised and neglected now because the literature which is embodied in it is despised and neglected, yet the best metrical form which intelligence, as distinct from poetical feeling, can employ. Crabbe did not handle it in any masterful way; he was careless, and sometimes slip-shod; but when he chose he could employ it well, and should have credit for it. To take one more example from his poems, how excellently he uses it in this passage!—

> Where is that virtue that the generous boy . . .
> [*Tales of the Hall*, III, 336–45, 348–9, 352–9]

Scott felt an attraction in such poetic form which we have perhaps ceased to feel; and Fox, had he lived to read it, would equally have acknowledged its power.

But Wordsworth said Crabbe was unpoetical; he condemned him for 'his unpoetical mode of considering human nature and society;' and, after all, the world has agreed with Wordsworth, and disagreed with Scott and Fox. Wordsworth told Scott an anecdote in illustration of his meaning.[1] Sir George Beaumont, sitting with himself and Crabbe one day, blew out the candle which he had used in sealing a letter. Sir George and Wordsworth, with proper taste, sat watching the smoke rise from the wick in beautiful curves; but Crabbe seeing—or rather smelling—the object, and not seeing the beauty of it, put on the extinguisher. Therefore, said Wordsworth, Crabbe is unpoetical,—as

---

[1] See above, pp. 290 and 291.

fine a bit of æsthetic priggishness as is often met with. Scott's opinion was not much affected by the anecdote, and Wordsworth was on the wrong track. It is true, however, that Crabbe was unpoetical in Wordsworth's sense. Crabbe had no imaginative vision,—no such vision as is shown in that stormy landscape of Shelley's, in the opening of *The Revolt of Islam*, which lacks the truth of actuality, but possesses the higher imaginative truth, like Turner's painting, or as is shown in that other storm in 'Pippa Passes.' Crabbe saw sword-grass and saltwort and fen, but he had no secret of the imagination by which he could mingle them into harmonious beauty; there is loveliness in a salt marsh, but Crabbe could not present it, nor even see it for himself. As in landscape so in life. Goldsmith was untrue to the actual Auburn, but he was faithful to a far more precious truth, the truth of remembered childhood, and he revealed with the utmost beauty the effect of the subtlest working of the spirit of man on practical fact; it is his fidelity to this psychological and spiritual truth which makes Auburn the 'loveliest village of the plain.' Crabbe exhibited nothing of this imaginative transformation of the familiar and the commonplace, perhaps saw nothing of it; he described the fishing village of Aldborough as any one with good powers of perception, who took the trouble, might see it. Through these defects of his powers he loses in poetic value; his poetry is, as he called it, poetry without an atmosphere; it is a reflection, almost mirror-like, of plain fact.

Men go to poetry too often with a preconceived notion of what the poet ought to give, instead of with open minds for whatever he has to give. Too much is not to be expected from Crabbe. He was only a simple country clergyman, half educated, with no burning ideals, no reveries, no passionate dreams; his mind did not rise out of the capabilities and virtues of respectability. His life was as little poetical, in Wordsworth's sense, as his poetry. Yet his gift was not an empty one. Moore, Scott, and Byron were story-tellers who were poetical, in Wordsworth's sense; but is Crabbe's true description of humble life less valuable than Scott's romantic tradition, or Moore's melting, sensuous Oriental dream, or Byron's sentimental, falsely-heroic adventure? It is far more valuable, because there is more of the human heart in it; because it contains actual suffering and joy of fellow-men; because it is humanity, and calls for hospitality in our sympathies and charities. Unpoetical? Yes; but it is something to have real life brought home to our tears and laughter, although it be presented barely, and the poet has trusted to the rightness and tenderness of our hearts for those feelings the absence of which in his verse led Wordsworth to call these tales unpoetical. But it is only when Crabbe is at his best that his verse has this extraordinary power.

74. FitzGerald as Crabbe's Champion

1882

Edward FitzGerald (1809–83), translator of *Omar Khayyam*, knew Crabbe's son (the biographer) and grandson and did much in later years (see above, No. 63(g)) to revive interest in the poet. The following passage comes from his introduction to *Readings in Crabbe* (*Tales of the Hall*), privately printed, 1879. It was reprinted in *Letters and Literary Remains*, ed. W. Aldis Wright, 1889 under the date 1883, and it is from this work (Vol. III, 480–9) that the text below is taken.

[Begins with quotation of Crabbe's letter to Mary Leadbeater, 30 October 1817, followed by an extract from Jeffrey's *Edinburgh Review* article on *Tales of the Hall* in 1819.]

When he wrote the letter above quoted (two years before the publication of his book) he knew not whether his tragic exceeded the lighter stories in quantity, though he supposed they would leave the deeper impression on the reader. In the completed work I find the tragic stories fewer in number, and, to my thinking, assuredly not more impressive than such as are composed of that mingled yarn of grave and gay of which the kind of life he treats of is, I suppose, generally made up. 'Nature's sternest Painter' may have mellowed with a prosperous old age, and from a comfortable grand-climacteric, liked to contemplate and represent a brighter aspect of humanity than his earlier life afforded him. Anyhow, he has here selected a subject whose character and circumstance require a lighter touch and shadow less dark than such as he formerly delineated.

Those who now tell their own as well as their neighbours' stories are much of the Poet's own age as well as condition of life, and look back (as he may have looked) with what Sir Walter Scott calls a kind of humorous retrospect over their own lives, cheerfully extending to others the same kindly indulgence which they solicit for themselves. The book, if I mistake not, deals rather with the follies than with the vices of men, with the comedy rather than the tragedy of life. Assuredly there is scarce anything of that brutal or sordid villainy, of which one has more than enough in the Poet's earlier work. And even the more sombre subjects of the book are relieved by the colloquial intercourse of the narrators, which twines about every story, and, letting in occasional glimpses of the country round, encircles them all with something of dramatic unity and interest, insomuch that of all the Poet's works this one alone does not leave a more or less melancholy impression upon me; and, as I am myself more than old enough to love the sunny side of the wall, is on that account, I do not say the best, but certainly that which best I like, of all his numerous offspring.

Such, however, is not the case, I think, with Crabbe's few readers, who, like Lord Byron, chiefly remember him by the sterner realities of his earlier work. Nay, quite recently Mr. Leslie Stephen in that one of his admirable essays which analyses the Poet's peculiar genius says:

The more humorous of these performances may be briefly dismissed. Crabbe possesses the faculty, but not in any eminent degree; his hand is a little heavy, and one must remember that Mr. Tovell and his like were of the race who require to have a joke driven into their heads with a sledge-hammer. Once or twice we come upon a sketch which may help to explain Miss Austen's admiration. There is an old maid[1] devoted to china, and rejoicing in stuffed parrots and puppies, who might have been ridiculed by Emma Woodhouse; and a Parson who would have suited the Eltons admirably.[2]

The spinster of the stuffed parrot indicates, I suppose, the heroine of 'Procrastination' in another series of tales.[3] But Miss Austen, I think, might also have admired another, although more sensible, spinster in these, who tells of her girlish and only love while living with the grandmother who maintained her gentility in the little town she lived in at the cost of such little economies as 'would scarce a parrot keep;'[4]

[1] Catherine Lloyd, *The Parish Register*, III, 312–412.   [2] *The Borough*, III.
[3] No. See my identification under note 1.   [4] *Tales of the Hall*, XI.

and the story of the romantic friend who, having proved the vanity of human bliss by the supposed death of a young lover, has devoted herself to his memory, insomuch that as she is one fine autumnal day protesting in her garden that, were he to be restored to her in all his youthful beauty, she would renounce the real rather than surrender the ideal Hero awaiting her elsewhere—behold him advancing toward her in the person of a prosperous, portly merchant, who reclaims, and, after some little hesitation on her part, retains her hand.

There is also an old Bachelor[1] whom Miss Austen might have liked to hear recounting the matrimonial attempts which have resulted in the full enjoyment of single blessedness; his father's sarcastic indifference to the first, and the haughty defiance of the mother of the girl he first loved. And when the young lady's untimely death has settled that question, his own indifference to the bride his own mother has provided for him And when that scheme has failed, and yet another after that, and the Bachelor feels himself secure in the consciousness of more than middle life having come upon him, his being captivated—and jilted— by a country Miss, toward whom he is so imperceptibly drawn at her father's house that

> Time after time the maid went out and in,
> Ere love was yet beginning to begin;
> The first awakening proof, the early doubt,
> Rose from observing she went in and out.
> [*Tales of the Hall*, X, 651–4]

Then there is a fair Widow, who, after wearing out one husband with her ruinous tantrums, finds herself all the happier for being denied them by a second. And when he too is dead, and the probationary year of mourning scarce expired, her scarce ambiguous refusal (followed by acceptance) of a third suitor, for whom she is now so gracefully wearing her weeds as to invite a fourth.[2]

If 'Love's Delay'[3] be of a graver complexion, is there not some even graceful comedy in 'Love's Natural Death';[4] some broad comedy—too true to be farce—in 'William Bailey's' old housekeeper;[5] and up and down the book surely many passages of gayer or graver humour; such as the Squire's satire on his own house and farm;[6] his brother's account of the Vicar, whose daughter he married;[7] the gallery of portraits in

---

[1] *Ibid.*, X.   [2] *Ibid.*, XVII.   [3] *Ibid.*, XIII.   [4] *Ibid.*, XIV.
[5] *Ibid.* XIX.   [6] *Ibid.*, IV, 78 ff.   [7] *Ibid.*, VI, 41–83.

the 'Cathedral Walk,'[1] besides many a shrewd remark so tersely put that I should call them epigram did not Mr. Stephen think the Poet incapable of such; others so covertly implied as to remind one of old John Murray's remark on Mr. Crabbe's conversation—that he said uncommon things in so common a way as to escape notice, though assuredly not the notice of so shrewd an observer as Mr. Stephen if he cared to listen, or to read?

Nevertheless, with all my own partiality for this book, I must acknowledge that, while it shares with the Poet's other works in his characteristic disregard of form and diction—of all indeed that is now called 'Art'—it is yet more chargeable with diffuseness, and even with some inconsistency of character and circumstance, for which the large canvas he had taken to work on, and perhaps some weariness in filling it up, may be in some measure accountable. So that, for one reason or another, but very few of Crabbe's few readers care to encounter the book. And hence this attempt of mine to entice them to it by an abstract, omitting some of the stories, retrenching others, either by excision of some parts, or the reduction of others into as concise prose as would comprehend the substance of much prosaic verse.

Not a very satisfactory sort of medley in any such case; I know not if more or less so where verse and prose are often so near akin. I see, too, that in some cases they are too patchily intermingled. But I have tried, though not always successfully, to keep them distinct, and to let the Poet run on by himself whenever in his better vein; in two cases—that of the 'Widow' and 'Love's Natural Death'[2]—without any interruption of my own, though not without large deductions from the author in the former story.

On the other hand, more than as many other stories have shrunk under my hands into seeming disproportion with the Prologue by which the Poet introduces them, insomuch as they might almost as well have been cancelled were it not for carrying their introduction away with them.*

And such alterations have occasionally necessitated a change in some initial article or particle connecting two originally separated paragraphs; of which I subjoin a list, as also of a few that have inadvertently crept

---

* As 'Richard's Jealousy,' 'Sir Owen Dale's Revenge,' the 'Cathedral Walk,' in which the Poet's diffuse treatment seemed to me scarcely compensated by the interest of the story. [*Tales of the Hall*, VI, XII, XX].

---

[1] *Tales of the Hall*, XX.   [2] *Ibid.*, XVII, XIV.

into the text from the margin of my copy; all, I thought, crossed out before going to press. For any poetaster can amend many a careless expression which blemishes a passage that none but a poet could indite.

I have occasionally transposed the original text, especially when I thought to make the narrative run clearer by so doing. For in that respect, whether from lack or laxity of constructive skill, Crabbe is apt to wander and lose himself and his reader. This was shown especially in some prose novels, which at one time he tried his hand on, and (his son tells us), under good advice, committed to the fire.

I have replaced in the text some readings from the Poet's original MS. quoted in his son's standard edition, several of which appeared to me fresher, terser, and (as so often the case) more apt than the second thought afterward adopted.*

Mr. Stephen has said—and surely said well—that, with all its short and long-comings, Crabbe's better work leaves its mark on the reader's mind and memory as only the work of genius can, while so many a more splendid vision of the fancy slips away, leaving scarce a wrack behind. If this abiding impression result (as perhaps in the case of Richardson or Wordsworth) from being, as it were, soaked in through the longer process by which the man's peculiar genius works, any abridgement, whether of omission or epitome, will diminish from the effect of the whole. But, on the other hand, it may serve, as I have said, to attract a reader to an original, which, as appears in this case, scarce anybody now cares to venture upon in its integrity.

I feel bound to make all apology for thus dealing with a Poet whose works are ignored, even if his name be known, by the readers and writers of the present generation. 'Pope in worsted stockings,' he has been called. But, in truth, the comparison, such as it is, scarcely reaches beyond Crabbe's earliest essays. For in *The Village*, which first made him popular, he set out with Goldsmith rather than with Pope, though toward a very different object than 'Sweet Auburn.' And then, after nearly twenty years' silence (a rare interval for a successful author),

---

* A curious instance occurs in that fair Widow's story, when the original

'Would you believe it, Richard, that fair she
Has had three husbands? I repeat it, three!'

is supplanted by the very enigmatical couplet:

'No need of pity, when the gentle dame
Has thrice resign'd and re-assumed her name.'

[*Tales of the Hall*, XVII, 40–1.]

appeared a volume of *Tales*;[1] and after them *The Parish Register*, accompanied with 'Sir Eustace Grey', and by-and-by followed by *The Borough*: in all of which the style differed as much from that of Pope as the character and scene they treated of from the Wits and Courtiers of Twickenham and Hampton Court. But all so sharply delineated as to make Lord Byron, according to the comprehensive and comfortable form of decision that is never out of date, pronounce him to be Nature's best, if sternest, painter.

In the present *Tales of the Hall*, the poet, as I have said, has in some measure shifted his ground, and Comedy, whose shrewder—not to say more sardonic—element ran through his earlier work, here discovers something of her lighter humour. Not that the Poet's old Tragic power, whether of Terror or Pity, is either absent or abated; as witness the story of 'Ruth';[2] and that of 'The Sisters,'[3] of whom one, with the simple piety that has held her up against the storm which has overtaken them both, devotes herself to the care of her whom it has bewildered, as she wanders alone in the deepening gloom of evening,

> Or cries at mid-day, 'Then Good-night to all!'
> [VIII, 798]

And to prove how the Poet's landscape hand has not slackened in its cunning, we may accompany the Brothers in their morning ramble to the farm;[4] or Richard on his horse to the neighbouring town;[5] or at a respectful distance observe those two spinsters conversing in their garden on that so still autumnal day,

> When the wing'd insect settled in our sight,
> And waited wind to recommence her flight,
> [XI, 794-5]

till interrupted by the very substantial apparition of him who ought long ago to have been a Spirit in heaven.

But 'Tragedy, Comedy, Pastoral,' all that, applauded as it was by contemporary critics and representatives of literature, contributed to make this writer generally read in the first quarter of this century, has left of him to the present generation but the empty echo of a name, unless such as may recall the

John Richard William Alexander Dwyer

---

[1] FitzGerald has mistaken the order of publication here. *Tales* did not appear until 1812, after all those he mentions later.

[2] V.   [3] VIII.   [4] IV.   [5] XIII.

of the *Rejected Addresses*. Miss Austen, indeed, who is still so much renowned for her representation of genteel humanity, was so unaccount-
ably smitten with Crabbe in his worsted hose, that she playfully
declared she would not refuse him for her husband. That Sir Walter
Scott, with his wider experience of mankind, could listen to the reading
of him when no longer able to hold the book for himself, may pass for
little in these days when the Lammermoors and Midlothians are almost
as much eclipsed by modern fiction as *The Lady of the Lake* and *Marmion*
by the poetic revelations which have extinguished Crabbe. Nevertheless, among the many obsolete authorities of yesterday, there is yet
one—William Wordsworth—who now rules, where once he was least,
among the sacred Brotherhood to which he was exclusive enough in
admitting others, and far too honest to make any exception out of
compliment to anyone on any occasion; he did, nevertheless, thus write
to the Poet's son and biographer in 1834: 'Any testimony from me to
the merit of your revered father's works would, I feel, be superfluous,
if not impertinent. They will last, from their combined merits as poetry
and truth, full as long as anything that has been expressed in verse since
they first made their appearance'[1]—a period which, be it noted, includes
all Wordsworth's own volumes except 'Yarrow Revisited,' *The Prelude*,
and *The Borderers*. And Wordsworth's living successor to the laurel no
less participates with him in his appreciation of their forgotten brother.
Almost the last time I met him he was quoting from memory that fine
passage in 'Delay has Danger,' where the late autumn landscape seems
to borrow from the conscience-stricken lover who gazes on it the
gloom which it reflects upon him;[2] and in the course of further conversation on the subject, Mr. Tennyson added, 'Crabbe has a world of
of his own;'[3] by virtue of that original genius, I suppose, which is said
to entitle, and carry, the possessor to what we call Immortality.

Mr. Mozley, in his *Recollections of Oriel College*, has told us that
Cardinal Newman was a great reader of Crabbe in those earlier days;
and the Cardinal himself, in one of his 'Addresses to the Catholics of
Dublin,' published in 1873, tells us that so he continued to be, and, for
one reason, *why*. For in treating of what may be called his Ideal of a
University, he speaks of the insufficiency of mere Book-learning toward
the making of a Man, as compared with that which the Richard of these
Tales unconsciously gathered in the sea-faring village where his boyhood

---

1 But see also above p. 455 and references under note 1 on that page.
2 *Tales of the Hall*, XIII, 701 ff.
3 See above p. 368.

passed; and where—not from books (of which he had scarce more than a fisherman's cottage supplied), but from the seamen on the shore, and the solitary shepherd on the heath, and a pious mother at home— 'he contrived to fashion a philosophy and poetry of his own;' which, followed as it was by an active life on land and sea, made of him the man whom his more educated and prosperous brother contemplated with mingled self-regret and pride. And the poem in which this is told is considered by Cardinal Newman as, 'whether for conception or execution, one of the most touching in our language,' which having read 'on its first publication with extreme delight,' and again, thirty years after, with even more emotion, and yet again, twenty years after *that*, with undiminished interest: he concludes by saying that 'a work which can please in youth and age seems to fulfil (in logical language) the *accidental* definition of a classic.'[1]

For a notice of this passage (which may be read at large in Cardinal Newman's sixth Discourse delivered to the Catholics of Dublin, p. 150, Edit. 1873) I am indebted to Mr. Leslie Stephen, against whom I ventured to break a lance, and who has thus supplied me with one that recoils upon myself for having mutilated a poem which so great an authority looks on as so perfect.

[1] See above, p. 361.

75. Patmore contrasts Crabbe and Shelley

1887

This article by Coventry Patmore (1823–96) appeared in *St. James's Gazette*, 16 February 1887 and was later reprinted in *Principle in Art*, 1889.

Things, it is said, are best known by comparison with their opposites; and, if so, surely Crabbe must be the best illustrated by Shelley and Shelley by Crabbe. Shelley was an atheist and profoundly immoral; but his irreligion was radiant with pious imagination, and his immorality delicately and strictly conscientious. Crabbe was a most sincere Christian in faith and life; but his religion and morality were intolerant, narrow, and scrupulous, and sadly wanting in all the modern graces. Shelley had no natural feeling or affection and the greatest sensitiveness; Crabbe had the tenderest and strongest affections, but his nerves and æsthetic constitution were of the coarsest. Shelley's taste often stood him in the stead of morality. He would have starved rather than write begging letters to Thurlow, Burke, and other magnates, as Crabbe did when he wanted to better his condition as an apothecary's apprentice. Crabbe's integrity produced some of the best effects of taste, and made him at once an equal in manners with the dukes and statesmen with whom he associated as soon as he had been taken from his beggary by Burke. Through years and years of poverty and almost hopeless trial Crabbe was a devoted and faithful lover, and afterwards as devoted and faithful a husband to his 'Myra,' whom he adored in verses that justified some one's description of his style as 'Pope in worsted stockings.' Shelley breathes eternal vows in music of the spheres, to woman after woman, whom he will abandon and speak or write of with hatred and contempt as soon as their persons have ceased to please him. Crabbe knew nothing of the 'ideal,' but loved all actualities, especially unpleasant ones, upon which he would turn the electric light of his peculiar powers of perception till the sludge and dead dogs of a tidal river shone. Jeffrey described the true position of Crabbe among poets better than any one else has done when he wrote, 'He has represented his villagers and humble burghers as altogether as dissipated and more dishonest and discontented than the profligates of higher life. . . . He may be considered as the satirist of low life—an occupation sufficiently arduous, and in a great degree new and original in our language.' In this his proper vocation Crabbe is so far from being a 'Pope in worsted stockings,' that his lines often resemble the strokes of Dryden's sledge-hammer rather than the stings of his successor's cane. But, when uninspired by the intensely disagreeable or vicious, Crabbe's 'diction' is to modern ears, for the most part, intolerable. In his cooler moments he poured forth thousands of such couplets as

> It seems to us that our Reformers knew
> Th' important work they undertook to do.
> [*The Borough*, IV, 84–5]

And to such vile newspaper prose he not only added the ghastly adornment of verse, but also frequently enlivened it with the 'poetic licences' and Parnassian 'lingo' of the Pope period. What a contrast with Shelley! He erred quite as much as Crabbe did from the imaginative reality which is the true ideal; but it was all in the opposite way. If Crabbe's eye, in its love for the actual and concrete, dwelt too habitually upon the hardness and ugliness of the earth on which he trod, Shelley's thoughts and perceptions were for the most part

> Pinnacled dim in the intense inane
> [*Prometheus Unbound*, III, iii, 204]

of a fancy which had no foundation in earth or heaven. His poetry has, however, the immortal reality of music; and his songs *are* songs, though they may be often called 'songs without words,' the words meaning so little though they sound so sweet.

This 'parallel'—as lines starting and continued in opposite directions have got to be called—might be carried much further with advantage to the student of poetry; and the comparison might be still more profitable if the best poems of Coleridge were examined as illustrations of the true poetic reality from which Crabbe and Shelley diverge equally, but in contrary ways. Crabbe mistakes actuality for reality; Shelley's imagination is unreal. Coleridge, when he is himself, whether he is in the region of actuality, as in 'Genevieve,' or in that of imagination, as in 'Christabel,' is always both real and ideal in the only true poetic sense, in which reality and ideality are truly one. In each of these poems, as in every work of true art, there is a living idea which expresses itself in

every part, while the complete work remains its briefest possible expression, so that it is as absurd to ask What is its idea? as it would be to
ask what is the idea of a man or of an oak. This idea cannot be a simple
negation; and simple evil—which is so often Crabbe's theme—*is* simple
negation. On the other hand, good, in order to be the ground of the
ideal in art, must be intelligible—that is to say, imaginatively credible,
though it may want the conditions of present actuality. But is there any
such ideal as this in Shelley?

76. Final verdicts (I): Crabbe as a 'Great Writer'

1888

From Thomas E. Kebbel (1827 ?), *George Crabbe*, 1888, in the
Great Writers series, pp. 108–11, 140–51.

The truth is, that Cowper did not occupy at all the same position as
Crabbe. Not only did he move in a more contracted sphere, but he did
not present himself to the world as a disciple of the Augustan school. In
enumerating the poets who had handed down the torch to the beginning of the present century, Byron does not include Cowper. Cowper
wrote admirably in rhyme, though his best-known works are in blank
verse. But it is not the rhyme of Pope or Campbell. It is as different
from these as the hexameters of Catullus are from the hexameters of
Virgil. Cowper, in fact, claimed rather to be the founder of a new
school; whereas it was Crabbe's glory *stare super vias antiquas*. Cowper
had much of the simplicity and reality which the Lake school required,
as well as Crabbe; but then in Cowper it was purchased by the sacrifice
of the old style. In Crabbe, it was not. He combined rare fidelity to
nature with a highly artificial mode of expression.

Further than that, while Cowper surpassed Crabbe in refinement,
gentleness, and spiritual fervour, he was infinitely inferior to Crabbe in

his knowledge of human nature, and power of delineating individuals. He never attempted tales, and I cannot think any of his characters in 'The Progress of Error,' 'Truth,' 'Hope,' and 'Conversation,' equal to those in *The Borough* and *Tales of the Hall*. Moreover, he did not look round him with the observant glance of Crabbe, who, as Lockhart says, never opened his eyes in vain. Like many other invalids, or hypochon-driacs, surrounded with comforts themselves, he had little deep sympathy with physical suffering and hardship. He too, like Crabbe, understood the falsity of those conventional pictures of rural felicity to which the world had so long been accustomed. And there are lines in the 'Winter Evening' following out much the same train of thought as we find in the opening of *The Village*. Sometimes, indeed, the resemblance is so close as to suggest something more than a merely accidental coin-cidence. *The Village* was published in May 1783, and 'The Task' in June 1785, and the reference to the golden age of Maro, which occurs in both, might warrant the conjecture that the author of the later poem was no stranger to the earlier. So too Cowper's lines—

> The frugal housewife trembles when she lights
> Her scanty stock of brushwood,
> > ['The Task', IV, 380–1]

are very near to Crabbe's—

> Or her[s], that matron pale, whose trembling hand
> Throws on the wretched hearth the expiring brand.
> > [*The Village*, I, 179–80]

But be that as it may, Cowper's grasp of the subject is very different from Crabbe's. He too describes the interior of a labourer's cottage, 'and the misery of a stinted meal.' But in what a different tone! In Cowper we see only the gentle compassion of a kind-hearted gentleman for trials which he regarded as inevitable. In Crabbe we see the *sæva indignatio* of the satirist, angry with a world and a society in which such things could be, and with the lying poets who had so long disguised the truth. More-over, Cowper's picture of the agricultural labourer is, on the whole, a cheerful one. The waggoner and his horses, the woodman and his dog, the wife and her poultry, are all described in tones which rather favour than condemn those views of rural life which Crabbe had set himself to expose. Had Crabbe described the waggoner or the woodman, we should have heard something about ague, rheumatism, and fever. . . .

It has been necessary to say these few words on the position of Cowper, because, at first sight, it might appear that he and Crabbe travelled along the same road, and represented the same class of ideas. Nothing can be more untrue. They touch each other at certain points. But they neither start from the same source, nor make for the same port, nor, as I have already said, belong to the same school. My own opinion is that the English writer with whom Crabbe has most in common is George Eliot. The story of Hetty Sorel he would have told to perfection. Mr. Dempster, Squire Cass, Mr. Tulliver, are all characters after Crabbe's own heart; and the mingled village tragedy and comedy, with the vices, virtues, and humours of the middle class, which George Eliot understood so well, were equally familiar to the author of *The Parish Register* and the *Tales in Verse*. . . .

They both drew from the same source, and both depend on the deeper springs of human action for awakening our interest in their characters. But as regards external'conditions, there is one point on which they differ, with which I have frequently been struck. In all George Eliot's tales of rural life no suggestion escapes her of that extreme depression among the agricultural poor, on which Crabbe is so eloquent. She had lived among them in her youth, and knew all their traditions, prejudices, and grievances. It is curious that she drops no hint of any misery or discontentment prevailing among them—says nothing of their hardships or their penury, their stinted meals and fireless grates— of the aches and pains which await them in their old age, and the work-house which receives them in the end. I have often remarked on the absence of any such topics in George Eliot's writings, and a reperusal of Crabbe has made it seem more singular than ever.

Of the construction and incidents of Crabbe's Tales there is little to say. They usually narrate the fortunes or adventures of not more than two or three persons in a simple and direct manner, independently of mystery or catastrophe. The principal exception to this rule is in the 'Tale of Smugglers and Poachers,' in *Tales of the Hall*, and perhaps the scheme of the two brothers, on which the whole series rests, may be thought another. Yet Crabbe is essentially a story-teller. Pope's characters are either portraits—rarely drawn, no doubt—or else pegs on which to hang certain illustrations of human nature, exquisitely painted, but not representing living, breathing human beings. Nobody, for instance, can be interested in Sir Balaam as an individual, however we admire him as a type. But Crabbe *interests* us in his characters. We follow their footsteps with curiosity, and make their troubles and successes our own.

Crabbe was possessed, in no common degree, of that peculiar power by which compassion, horror, scorn, despair, and indignation are excited. Wordsworth says that these feelings are less easily aroused in us by verse than by prose; and he compares the most tragic scenes in Shakespeare with the sorrows of Richardson's *Clarissa*, and says that while we can read the former without any painful emotion, we shrink from returning to the latter a second time, in dread of its agitating effect. The remark is true; and the reason given for it, namely, that the pleasure which we derive from verse composition distracts our attention from the painful nature of the subject, is on the whole just. Yet Crabbe has levelled even these distinctions. For not all the beauty of the verse can enable us to read the workhouse scene in *The Village*, the mother's death in *The Parish Register*, the wreck in 'The Boat Race,' or the gipsy woman's story in 'The Hall of Justice,' without sensations being raised in us which we do not care to experience too often.

The moral inculcated by Crabbe is simple. He shows, as Mary Leadbeater has observed, the real consequences of vice—here again resembling George Eliot—and rebuking the insidious voice, which whispers to every man and woman on the verge of doing wrong, 'Thou shalt not surely die.' Thackeray laughs at this simple morality, as he calls it. Jack was a good boy and had plum-cake: Harry was a bad boy, and was eaten by wild beasts. But I don't know what can be substituted for it. Virtue, it is true, is not always rewarded, nor vice punished, in this world. Neither do industry and frugality invariably make a man rich, nor idleness and self-indulgence poor. But all we can do is to show that virtue, industry, and frugality are the best policy on the whole. Probability, the guide of life, as Butler says, is in their favour. And in matters of action, the balance of probability, though it weigh down the scale only by the weight of a feather, is enough to determine us. Crabbe shows that impatience, imprudence, vanity, passion, and a selfish disregard of others, no less than down-right violence and crime, often land us in very pitiable predicaments.

Crabbe was ridiculed in *Rejected Addresses*, where he is called Pope in worsted stockings. The satire is misdirected, though the parody, as Crabbe himself allowed, is excellent. To my mind Crabbe, though the last of Pope's school, and specially interesting on that account, is very unlike Pope. His turn of thought is not the same. He looks out upon the world with different eyes, and, what is more, he is guilty of faults of style, and breaches of good taste, at which Pope would have shuddered. The great fault of his versification is a too frequent straining after antithesis, when the sense is not improved by it, and the effect is purely verbal. Examples of what I mean are the following:—

> Here are no wheels for either wool or flax,
> But packs of cards, made up of various packs.
> [*The Parish Register*, I, 230–1]

A lady's brother interferes to prevent a gentleman from trifling with his sister's affections—

> Yet others tell the captain fixed they doubt,
> He'd call thee brother, or he'd call thee out.
> [*ibid.*, II, 272–3]

Of Lucy Collins, captivated by footman Daniel in his smart livery, we are told—

> But from that day, the fatal day, she spied
> The pride of Daniel, Daniel was her pride.
> [*ibid.*, II, 319–20]

Of Abel Keene—

> A quiet, simple man was Abel Keene,
> He meant no harm, nor did he often mean.
> [*The Borough*, XXI, 1–2]

But a still greater drawback to the enjoyment of Crabbe's poetry is the fault to which we have already referred—the bad taste which mars some of his finest passages. One can never be sure of him. As we move slowly through some beautiful description, or some melancholy tragedy, enchanted by the sweetness and fidelity of the one, or the pathos and passion of the other, we are always apt to be tripped up by some literary *gaucherie* which interrupts the illusion, and brings us down again to the common day. In the description of the ruined monastery, amid a crowd of beautiful images and romantic associations which the poet brings together in this passage, we read—

> That oxen low, where monks retired to eat.
> [*ibid.*, IV, 150]

This is shocking. What follows is, if possible, even worse. [In] 'The Felon's Dream,' a passage dark with all the horrors of death and hell, and looking all the more dreadful for the flash of dream-light thrown across them, . . . the poet must needs tell us that when the sleeping criminal saw his native village, he saw too

The house, the chamber, where he once arrayed
His youthful person.

[*ibid.*, XXIII, 277–8]

Again, in the description of the girl taking leave of her lover who is going to sea, and returns only to die in her arms, the care which she bestowed upon his wardrobe is one of the principal particulars—

White was his better linen, and his check
Was made more trim than any on the deck.

[*ibid.*, II, 192–3]

It is no pleasure to multiply examples of this unlucky deficiency, or many might be given, some far more ludicrous than the above. It is more interesting to speculate on the source of this singular anomaly. Crabbe, it is said, was to the last, inaccessible to the charms of order, congruity, and regularity. He has satirized the love of order in 'The Learned Boy.'[1] He had no ear for music, and no eye for proportion or perspective. He did not understand architecture, and, except for the general effect, would have seen little difference between Westminster Abbey and Buckingham Palace. He liked to accumulate specimens of insects, grasses, and fossils; but he derived no pleasure from classifying them according to their species. Weeds and flowers of the most diverse characters all grew together in his garden in wild confusion. It was enough that they were there. To arrange them according to their kinds, or to mingle their various hues so as to produce the best effect, was what never occurred to him for a moment. We see the same tendency at work in his poetry. His descriptions are often overcharged from the desire to omit nothing, and remind us of the shepherd who thought that a landscape painting ought to be as complete as an ordnance map. Thus we can understand that he might have been comparatively indifferent to the frequency with which incongruous ideas and conflicting moods refuse to blend together in his poetry, and quite unconscious of the shock which the intrusion of commonplace or vulgar thoughts into passages of highly-wrought sentiment is calculated to inflict on palates of greater literary nicety.

His son and biographer laments his father's want of taste, and tells us even that he had little appreciation of 'what the painter's eye considers as the beauties of landscape.' This is very singular, when we consider his power of describing natural beauty. He was certainly one of the closest observers of nature, and especially of the sea in all its moods, which our

[1] *Tales*, XXI.

literature can show. Some of his little sea pieces are decidedly picturesque, and this effect could hardly be produced by one who had no eye
for colour, for light, shade, or movement. The truth is, that the quality
in which Crabbe's poetry is deficient is elegance, admirably described
by Johnson as the beauty of propriety. The picturesque may be produced by a single happy touch, as in the lines descriptive of the waves
in a calm:—

> That tap the tarry boat with gentle blow,
> And back return in silence smooth and slow.
> [*ibid.*, I, 183–4]

But elegance is the result of selection, combination, and arrangement;
all, in fact, that in a painting is called composition—the beauty of order,
the beauty of harmony. To accuse Crabbe in general terms, therefore,
of a want of taste, is to bring too sweeping a charge against him. His
taste was imperfect, but it was rather in the discriminative than the
appreciative faculty of taste that the defect lay. Hence the uncertainty
of which I have already spoken—the constant doubt in reading his
finest passages, whether we may not suddenly stumble over some
utterly inappropriate image, or some wretched triviality, which destroys half the effect of it. It is not purple patches that offend the reader
in Crabbe, but the beads of clay strung at intervals upon the chain of
pearls.

It is remarkable that Crabbe's versification grew worse as he grew
older. In his three earliest poems there are passages which have really
some pretensions to elegance, the result, I suppose, of assiduous labour
when he was just fresh from the study of Pope. In his later works such
passages grow less and less frequent, though still occasionally to be met
with. When asked by Rogers what was the reason for this difference,
Crabbe very candidly replied that in his youthful compositions he was
on his promotion, but that when his popularity was assured, he no
longer felt it necessary to take so much trouble. No real lover of style
as such would ever have given this reply.

With Crabbe, as I have said, the old dynasty of poets, who ruled
English literature for a hundred years, came to an end, amid the mur-
mured regrets of many who, for a long time, refused allegiance to its
successors. That controversy is over now; and the heroic school of
poetry is as dead as the house of Stuart. But a peculiar, and even a
romantic, interest attaches to its last representative, who connects the age
of Johnson with the age of Tennyson, and prolonged nearly to the

reign of Victoria the literary form and method which ripened in the reign of Anne. Crabbe, however, could not seclude himself from the operation of the new forces at work within his own era; and the distinctive mark of his poetry is the attempt to marry the new ideas of a revolutionary epoch, which was just beginning, to the old style of a strictly conservative period, which was just ending. He, in fact, accomplished the great feat of pouring new wine into old bottles, if not without occasional breakage, yet, on the whole, with eminent success; and those who can admire his poetry for nothing else may at least admire it as a wonderful *tour de force*. But Crabbe has far other claims upon us than those of a dexterous versifier, subduing to the heroic metre thoughts, scenes, and actions which had hitherto rejected it. He is a great moral writer, and one of the greatest English satirists. He was almost the first to paint in colours that will last the tragedy of humble life; and though inferior both in humour and psychological insight to George Eliot, he has anticipated her in drawing from the short and simple annals of the poor the materials of domestic dramas almost as touching as her own. In his knowledge of human nature, in the ordinary sense of the term, he was quite her equal, and I think Pope's superior; while it must also be remembered that he too anticipated George Eliot in discerning the rich harvest of literary wealth to be gathered from the middle-classes, or those which, a hundred years ago, lay between the gentry and the tradespeople, and supplied the authoress of *Adam Bede* with her Tulliver and Pullets, which will live for ever with Jane Austen's Norrises and Eltons, taken from the class just above them.

Crabbe came upon the stage at a lucky moment for his own immediate popularity; but I am not so sure that it was a lucky one for his popularity with posterity. The combination of qualities which made his poetry so attractive to men like Jeffrey and Byron owed its charm to the fact that it represented a transition period, when the old and new styles were just melting into each other. But the general public, I think, has, upon the whole, preferred to take them separately, thinking Pope very good, and Wordsworth very good, but not caring much about the mixture. What helped Crabbe so much with the critics of his own time has rather been against him in ours, and has interfered with the due appreciation of his real greatness, which is quite independent of rhymes and metres. We have only to read 'The Hall of Justice' to see how near he was to what is called the modern spirit. Change the metre, and we can imagine its occurring in the latest volume of Lord Tennyson. It is curious, too, that when Crabbe uses any lyric metre, he is totally free from all those puerile conceits which disfigure his heroics. Nobody would ever dare to parody Crabbe's lyrics; and it may be a question after all whether he was not doing some violence to the natural bent of his genius in resolving to be a disciple of Pope.

However this may be, he has left behind him a body of poetry, which, whether we regard the delineation of manners, the knowledge of character, the strength of passion, or the beauty of description combined in it, need not shrink from comparison with works of which the fame is much more widely extended. Dryden, Pope, Goldsmith, Johnson, to say nothing of the later poets, each, no doubt, excelled Crabbe in some of these particulars; but they are not united to the same extent in any one of them. This distinction does not necessarily make him either so delightful a companion, or so great a poet, as those that I have named. But it qualifies him to take rank with the best of them as a Great Writer.

77. Final verdicts (II): Saintsbury not so enthusiastic

1890

From George Saintsbury (1845–1933), *Essays in English Literature, 1780–1860*, 1890, pp. 1–32. This was one of Saintsbury's best works, but he is not very sympathetic towards Crabbe.

There is a certain small class of persons in the history of literature the members of which possess, at least for literary students, an interest peculiar to themselves. They are the writers who having attained, not merely popular vogue, but fame as solid as fame can ever be, in their own day, having been praised by the praised, and having as far as can be seen owed this praise to none of the merely external and irrelevant causes—politics, religion, fashion or what not—from which it sometimes arises, experience in a more or less short time after their death the fate of being, not exactly cast down from their high place, but left respectfully alone in it, unvisited, unincensed, unread. Among these writers, over the gate of whose division of the literary Elysium the famous, 'Who now reads Bolingbroke?' might serve as motto, the author of *The Village* and *Tales of the Hall* is one of the most remarkable. As for Crabbe's popularity in his own day there is no mistake about that. It was extra-ordinarily long, it was extremely wide, it included the select few as well as the vulgar, it was felt and more or less fully acquiesced in by persons of the most diverse taste, habits, and literary standards. His was not the case, which occurs now and then, of a man who makes a great reputation in early life and long afterwards preserves it because, either by accident or prudence, he does not enter the lists with his younger rivals, and therefore these rivals can afford to show him a reverence which is at once graceful and cheap. Crabbe won his spurs in full eighteenth century, and might have boasted, altering Landor's words, that he had dined early and in the best of company, or have parodied Goldsmith, and said, 'I have Johnson and Burke: all the wits have been here.' But when his studious though barren manhood was passed, and he again began, as almost an old man, to write poetry, he entered into full competition with the giants of the new school, whose ideals and whose education were utterly different from his. While *The Library* and *The Village* came to a public which still had Johnson, which had but just lost Goldsmith, and which had no other poetical novelty before it than Cowper, *The Borough* and later *Tales* entered the lists with *Marmion* and *Childe Harold*, with 'Christabel' and *The Excursion*, even with *Endymion* and *The Revolt of Islam*. Yet these later works of Crabbe met with the fullest recognition both from readers and from critics of the most opposite tendencies. Scott, the most generous, and Wordsworth, the most grudging, of all the poets of the day towards their fellows, united in praising Crabbe; and unromantic as the poet of *The Village* seems to us he was perhaps Sir Walter's favourite English bard. Scott read him constantly, he quotes him incessantly; and no one who has read it can ever forget how Crabbe figures in the most pathetic biographical pages ever written—Lockhart's account of the death at Abbotsford. Byron's criticism was as weak as his verse was powerful, but still Byron had no doubt about Crabbe. The utmost flight of memory or even of imagination can hardly get together three contemporary critics whose standards, tempers, and verdicts, were more different that those of Gifford, Jeffrey, and Wilson. Yet it is scarcely too much to say that they are all in a tale about Crabbe. In this unexampled chorus of eulogy there rose (for some others who can hardly have admired him much were simply silent) one single note, so far as I know, or rather one single rattling peal of thunder on the other side. It is true that this was significant enough, for it came from William Hazlitt.

Yet against this chorus, which was not, as has sometimes happened, the mere utterance of a loud-voiced few, but was echoed by a great multitude who eagerly bought and read Crabbe, must be set the almost total forgetfulness of his work which has followed. . . .

[There follows a long section on Crabbe's life.]

Crabbe, though by no means always at his best, is one of the most curiously equal of verse-writers. *Inebriety* and such other very youthful things are not to be counted; but between *The Village* of 1783 and the *Posthumous Tales* of more than fifty years later, the difference is surprisingly small. Such as it is, it rather reverses ordinary experience, for the later poems exhibit the greater play of fancy, the earlier the exacter graces of form and expression. Yet there is nothing really wonderful in this, for Crabbe's earliest poems were published under severe surveillance of himself and others, and at a time which still thought nothing of such value in literature as correctness, while his later were written under no particular censorship, and when the Romantic revival had already, for better or worse, emancipated the world. The change was in Crabbe's case not wholly for the better. He does not in his later verse become more prosaic, but he becomes considerably less intelligible. There is a passage in 'The Old Bachelor,'[1] too long to quote but worth referring to, which, though it may be easy enough to understand it with a little goodwill, I defy anybody to understand in its literal and grammatical meaning. Such welters of words are very common in Crabbe, and Johnson saved him from one of them in the very first lines of *The Village*. Yet Johnson could never have written the passages which earned Crabbe his fame. The great lexicographer knew man in general much better than Crabbe did; but he nowhere shows anything like Crabbe's power of seizing and reproducing man in particular. Crabbe is one of the first and certainly one of the greatest of the 'realists' who, exactly reversing the old philosophical signification of the word, devote themselves to the particular only. Yet of the three small volumes by which he, after his introduction to Burke, made his reputation, and on which he lived for a quarter of a century, the first and the last display comparatively little of this peculiar quality. *The Library* and *The Newspaper* are characteristic

[1] *Tales of the Hall*, X.

pieces of the school of Pope, but not characteristic of their author. . . .
In *The Village*, on the other hand, contemporaries and successors alike
have agreed to recognize Crabbe in his true vein. The two famous passages which attracted the suffrages of judges so different as Scott and
Wordsworth, are still, after more than a hundred years, fresh, distinct,
and striking. Here they are once more:—

[*The Village*, I, 228–39, 276–95.]

The poet executed endless variations on this class of theme, but he
never quite succeeded in discovering a new one, though in process of
time he brought his narrow study of the Aldborough fishermen and
townsfolk down still more narrowly to individuals. His landscape is
always marvellously exact, the strokes selected with extraordinary skill
ad hoc so as to show autumn rather than spring, failure rather than hope,
the riddle of the painful earth rather than any joy of living. Attempts
have been made to vindicate Crabbe from the charge of being a gloomy
poet, but I cannot think them successful; I can hardly think that they
have been quite serious. Crabbe, our chief realist poet, has an altogether
astonishing likeness to the chief prose realist of France, Gustave Flaubert,
so far as his manner of view goes, for in point of style the two have
small resemblance. One of the most striking things in Crabbe's biography is his remembrance of the gradual disillusion of a day of pleasure
which, as a child, he enjoyed in a new boat of his father's. We all of us,
except those who are gifted or cursed with the proverbial duck's back,
have these experiences and these remembrances of them. But most men
either simply grin and bear it, or carrying the grin a little farther, console themselves by regarding their own disappointments from the ironic
and humorous point of view. Crabbe, though not destitute of humour,
does not seem to have been able or disposed to employ it in this way.
Perhaps he never quite got over the terrible and, for the most part unrecorded, year in London: perhaps the difference between the Mira of
promise and the Mira of possession—the 'happiness denied'—had something to do with it: perhaps it was a question of natural disposition with
him. But when, years afterwards, as a prosperous middle-aged man, he
began his series of published poems once more with *The Parish Register*,
the same manner of seeing is evident, though the minute elaboration of
the views themselves is almost infinitely greater. Nor did he ever succeed in altering this manner, if he ever tried to do so.

With the exception of his few Lyrics, the most important of which,
'Sir Eustace Grey' (one of his very best things), is itself a tale in different

metre, and a few other occasional pieces of little importance, the entire work of Crabbe, voluminous as it is, is framed upon a single pattern, the vignettes of *The Village* being merely enlarged in size and altered in frame in the later books. The three parts of *The Parish Register*, the twenty-four Letters of *The Borough*, some of which have single and others grouped subjects, and the sixty or seventy pieces which make up the three divisions of *Tales*, consist almost exclusively of heroic couplets, shorter measures very rarely intervening. They are also almost wholly devoted to narratives, partly satirical, partly pathetic, of the lives of individuals of the lower and middle class chiefly. Jeffrey, who was a great champion of Crabbe and allotted several essays to him, takes delight in analysing the plots or stories of these tales; but it is a little amusing to notice that he does it for the most part exactly as if he were criticizing a novelist or a dramatist. 'The object,' says he, in one place, 'is to show that a man's fluency of speech depends very much upon his confidence in the approbation of his auditors': 'In Squire Thomas we have the history of a mean domineering spirit,' and so forth. Gifford in one place actually discusses Crabbe as a novelist. I shall make some further reference to this curious attitude of Crabbe's admiring critics. For the moment I shall only remark that the singularly mean character of so much of Crabbe's style, the 'style of drab stucco,' as it has been unkindly called, which is familiar from the wicked wit that told how the youth at the theatre

> Regained the felt and felt what he regained,
> [*Rejected Addresses*]

is by no means universal. The most powerful of all his pieces, the history of Peter Grimes, the tyrant of apprentices, is almost entirely free from it, and so are a few others. But it is common enough to be a very serious stumbling-block. In nine tales out of ten this is the staple:—

> Of a fair town where Dr. Rack was guide,
> His only daughter was the boast and pride.
> [*Tales*, IX, 1–2]

Now that is unexceptional verse enough, but what is the good of putting it in verse at all? Here again:—

> For he who makes me thus on business wait,
> Is not for business in a proper state.
> [*Tales of the Hall*, VII, 515–16]

It is obvious that you cannot trust a man who, unless he is intending a burlesque, can bring himself to write like that. Crabbe not only brings himself to it, but rejoices and luxuriates in the style. The tale from which that last luckless distich is taken, 'The Elder Brother,' is full of pathos and about equally full of false notes. If we turn to a far different subject, the very vigorously conceived 'Natural Death of Love,' we find a piece of strong and true satire, the best thing of its kind in the author, which is kept up throughout. Although, like all satire, it belongs at best but to the outer courts of poetry, it is so good that none can complain. Then the page is turned and one reads:—

> 'I met', said Richard, when returned to dine,
> 'In my excursion with a friend of mine.'
> [*ibid.*, XV, 1–2]

It may be childish, it may be uncritical, but I own that such verse as that excites in me an irritation which destroys all power of enjoyment, except the enjoyment of ridicule. Nor let any one say that pedestrian passages of the kind are inseparable from ordinary narrative in verse and from the adaptation of verse to miscellaneous themes. If it were so the argument would be fatal to such adaptation, but it is not. Pope seldom indulges in such passages, though he does sometimes: Dryden never does. He can praise, abuse, argue, tell stories, make questionable jests, do anything in verse that is still poetry, that has a throb and a quiver and a swell in it, and is not merely limp, rhythmed prose. In Crabbe, save in a few passages of feeling and a great many of mere description—the last an excellent setting for poetry but not necessarily poetical—this rhythmed prose is everywhere. The matter which it serves to convey is, with the limitations above given, varied, and it is excellent. No one except the greatest prose novelist has such a gallery of distinct, sharply etched characters, such another gallery of equally distinct scenes and manner-pieces, to set before the reader. Exasperating as Crabbe's style sometimes is, he seldom bores—never indeed except in his rare passages of digressive reflection. It has, I think, been observed, and if not the observation is obvious, that he has done with the pen for the neighbourhood of Aldborough and Glemham what Crome and Cotman have done for the neighbourhood of Norwich with the pencil. His observation of human nature, so far as it goes, is not less careful, true, and vivid. His pictures of manners, to those who read them at all, are perfectly fresh, and in no respect grotesque or faded, dead as the manners themselves are. His pictures of motives and of facts, of vice and virtue, never can fade, because the subjects are perennial and are truly caught. Even his plays on words, which horrified Jeffrey—

> Alas! your reverence, wanton thoughts I grant
> Were once my motive, now the thoughts of want,
> [*The Parish Register*, I, 453–4]

and the like—are not worse than Milton's jokes on the guns. He has immense talent, and he has the originality which sets talent to work in a way not tried by others, and may thus be very fairly said to turn it into genius. He is all this and more. But despite the warnings of a certain precedent I cannot help stating the case which we have discussed in the old form, and asking, was Crabbe a poet?

And thus putting the question, we may try to sum up. It is the gracious habit of a summing-up to introduce, if possible, a dictum of the famous men our fathers that were before us. I have already referred to Hazlitt's criticism on Crabbe in *The Spirit of the Age*, and I need not here urge at very great length the cautions which are always necessary in considering any judgment of Hazlitt's. Much that he says even in the brief space of six or eight pages which he allots to Crabbe is unjust; much is explicably, and not too creditably, unjust. Crabbe was a successful man, and Hazlitt did not like successful men: he was a clergyman of the Church of England, and Hazlitt did not love clergymen of the Church of England: he had been a duke's chaplain, and Hazlitt loathed dukes: he had been a Radical, and was still (though Hazlitt does not seem to have thought him so) a Liberal, but his Liberalism had been Torified into a tame variety. Again, Crabbe, though by no means squeamish, is the most unvoluptuous and dispassionate of all describers of inconvenient things; and Hazlitt was the author of *Liber Amoris*. Accordingly there is much that is untrue in the tissue of denunciation which the critic devotes to the poet. But there are two passages in this tirade which alone might show how great a critic Hazlitt himself was. Here in a couple of lines ('they turn, one and all, on the same sort of teasing, helpless, unimaginative distress') is the germ of one of the most famous and certainly of the best passages of the late Mr. Arnold; and here again is one of those critical taps of the finger which shivers by a touch of the weakest part a whole Rupert's drop of misapprehension. Crabbe justified himself by Pope's example. 'Nothing,' says Hazlitt, 'can be more dissimilar. Pope describes what is striking: Crabbe would have described merely what was there. . . . In Pope there was an appeal to the imagination, you see what was passing *in a poetical point of view*.'

Even here (and I have not been able to quote the whole passage) there is one of the flaws, which Hazlitt rarely avoided, in the use of the word 'striking'; for, Heaven knows, Crabbe is often striking enough. But the description of Pope as showing things 'in a poetical point of view' hits the white at once, wounds Crabbe mortally, and demolishes realism, as we have been pleased to understand it for the last generation or two. Hazlitt, it is true, has not followed up the attack, as I shall hope to show in an instant; but he has indicated the right line of it. As far as mere treatment goes, the fault of Crabbe is that he is pictorial rather than poetic, and photographic rather than pictorial. He sees his subject steadily, and even in a way he sees it whole; but he does not see it in the poetical way. You are bound in the shallows and the miseries of the individual; never do you reach the large freedom of the poet who looks at the universal. The absence of selection, of the discarding of details that are not wanted, has no doubt a great deal to do with this—Hazlitt seems to have thought that it had everything to do. I do not quite agree with him there. Dante, I think, was sometimes quite as minute as Crabbe; and I do not know that any one less hardy than Hazlitt himself would single out, as Hazlitt expressly does, the death-bed scene of Buckingham as a conquering instance in Pope to compare with Crabbe.[1] We know that the bard of Twickenham grossly exaggerated this. But suppose he had not? Would it have been worse verse? I think not. Although the faculty of selecting instead of giving all, as Hazlitt himself justly contends, is one of the things which make *poesis non ut pictura*, it is not all, and I think myself that a poet, if he is a poet, could be almost absolutely literal. Shakespeare is so in the picture of Gloucester's corpse. Is that not poetry?

The defect of Crabbe, as it seems to me, is best indicated by reference to one of the truest of all dicta on poetry, the famous maxim of Joubert —that the lyre is a winged instrument and must transport. There is no wing in Crabbe, there is no transport, because as I hold (and this is where I go beyond Hazlitt), there is no music. In all poetry, the very highest as well as the very lowest that is still poetry, there is something which transports, and that something in my view is always the music of the verse, of the words, of the cadence, of the rhythm, of the sounds superadded to the meaning. When you get the best music married to the best meaning, then you get, say, Shakespeare: when you get some music married to even moderate meaning, you get, say, Moore. Wordsworth can, as everybody but Wordsworthians holds, and as some even

[1] Crabbe himself referred to these lines in the Preface to the *Tales* (1812).

of Wordsworthians admit, write the most detestable doggerel and platitude. But when any one who knows what poetry is reads—

> Our noisy years seem moments in the being
> Of the eternal silence,
> ['Ode: Intimations of Immortality', 155–6]

he sees that, quite independently of the meaning, which disturbs the soul of no less a person than Mr. John Morley, there is one note added to the articulate music of the world—a note that never will leave off resounding till the eternal silence itself gulfs it. He leaves Wordsworth, he goes straight into the middle of the eighteenth century, and he sees Thomson with his hands in his dressing-gown pockets biting at the peaches, and hears him between the mouthfuls murmuring—

> So when the shepherd of the Hebrid Isles,
> Placed far amid the melancholy main,
> [Thomson, *The Castle of Indolence*, I, st. 30]

and there is another note, as different as possible in kind yet still alike, struck for ever. Yet again, to take example still from the less romantic poets, and in this case from a poet, whom Mr. Kebbel[1] specially and disadvantageously contrasts with Crabbe, when we read the old schoolboy's favourite—

> When the British warrior queen,
> Bleeding from the Roman rods,
> [Cowper, 'Boadicea']

we hear the same quality of music informing words, though again in a kind somewhat lower, commoner, and less. In this matter, as in all matters that are worth handling at all, we come of course *ad mysterium*. Why certain combinations of letters, sounds, cadences, should almost without the aid of meaning, though no doubt immensely assisted by meaning, produce this effect of poetry on men no man can say. But they do; and the chief merit of criticism is that it enables us by much study of different times and different languages to recognize some part of the laws, though not the ultimate and complete causes, of the production.

Now I can only say that Crabbe does not produce, or only in the rarest instances produces, this effect on me, and what is more, that on ceasing to be a patient in search of poetical stimulant and becoming merely a gelid critic, I do not discover even in Crabbe's warmest

---

[1] See No. 76 above.

admirers any evidence that he produced this effect on them. . . . I observe that the eulogists either discreetly avoid saying what they mean by poetry, or specify for praise something in Crabbe that is not distinctly poetical. Cardinal Newman said that Crabbe 'pleased and touched him at thirty years' interval,' and pleaded that this answers to the 'accidental definition of a classic.' Most certainly; but not necessarily to that of a poetical classic. Jeffrey thought him 'original and powerful.' Granted; but there are plenty of original and powerful writers who are not poets. Wilson gave him the superlative for 'original and vivid painting.' Perhaps; but is Hogarth a poet? Jane Austen 'thought she could have married him.' She had not read his biography; but even if she had would that prove him to be a poet? Lord Tennyson is said to single out the following passage, which is certainly one of Crabbe's best, if not his very best:—

> Early he rose, and look'd with many a sigh . . .
> [*Tales of the Hall*, XIII, 701–24]

It is good: it is extraordinarily good: it could not be better of its kind. It is as nearly poetry as anything that Crabbe ever did—but is it quite? If it is (and I am not careful to deny it) the reason, as it seems to me, is that the verbal and rhythmical music here, with its special effect of 'transporting', of 'making the common as if it were uncommon,' is infinitely better than is usual with Crabbe, that in fact there is music as well as meaning. Hardly anywhere else, not even in the best passages of the story of Peter Grimes, shall we find such music; and in its absence it may be said of Crabbe much more truly than of Dryden (who carries the true if not the finest poetical undertone with him even into the rant of Almanzor and Maximin, into the interminable arguments of *Religio Laici* and *The Hind and the Panther*) that he is a classic of our prose.

Yet the qualities which are so noteworthy in him are all qualities which are valuable to the poet, and which for the most part are present in good poets. And I cannot help thinking that this was what actually deceived some of his contemporaries and made others content for the most part to acquiesce in an exaggerated estimate of his poetical merits. It must be remembered that even the latest generation which, as a whole and unhesitatingly, admired Crabbe, had been brought up on the poets of the eighteenth century, in the very best of whom the qualities which Crabbe lacks had been but sparingly and not eminently present. It must be remembered too, that from the great vice of the poetry of the eighteenth century, its artificiality and convention, Crabbe is conspicuously free. The return to nature was not the only secret of the return to poetry; but it was part of it, and that Crabbe returned to nature no one could doubt. Moreover he came just between the school of prose fiction which practically ended with *Evelina* and the school of prose fiction which opened its different branches with *Waverley* and *Sense and Sensibility*. His contemporaries found nowhere else the narrative power, the faculty of character-drawing, the genius for description of places and manners, which they found in Crabbe; and they knew that in almost all, if not in all the great poets there is narrative power, faculty of character-drawing, genius for description. Yet again, Crabbe put these gifts into verse which at its best was excellent in its own way, and at its worst was a blessed contrast to Darwin or to Hayley. Some readers may have had an uncomfortable though only half-conscious feeling that if they had not a poet in Crabbe they had not a poet at all. At all events they made up their minds that they had a poet in him.

But are we bound to follow their example? I think not. You could play on Crabbe that odd trick which used, it is said, to be actually played on some mediæval verse chroniclers and unrhyme him—that is to say, put him into prose with the least possible changes—and his merits would, save in rare instances, remain very much as they are now. You could put other words in the place of his words, keeping the verse, and it would not as a rule be much the worse. You cannot do either of these things with poets who are poets. Therefore I shall conclude that save at the rarest moments, moments of some sudden gust of emotion, some happy accident, some special grace of the Muses to reward long and blameless toil in their service, Crabbe was not a poet. But I have not the least intention of denying that he was great, and all but of the greatest among English writers.

Select Bibliography

BROMAN, W. E., 'Factors in Crabbe's eminence in the early nineteenth century', *Modern Philology*, li, August 1953, 42–9: summarizes contemporary criticism, but with purpose of identifying Romantic strains in his work.

HAYDON, J. O., *The Romantic Reviewers, 1802–24*, 1969: Part I surveys the reviews of the period; Part II has a section on the treatment of Crabbe.

HODGART, P. and REDPATH, T., *Romantic perspectives: the work of Crabbe, Blake, Wordsworth and Coleridge as seen by their contemporaries and by themselves*, 1964.

HUCHON, R., *George Crabbe and His Times 1754–1832*, 1907: standard biography in substantial detail. Better on information than interpretation. Contains sections dealing with the contemporary reception of Crabbe's poetry.

Index

(Bold type indicates comment by the person mentioned.)

Abel, Carl, 24
Addison, Joseph, 434
Ainger, Alfred, 25
Allan, David, 317, 352
Arch, Joseph, 441
Ariosto, 153, 317
Arnold, Matthew, 366, 431, 481
Austen, Jane, **295**, 347, 364, 416, 418, 445, 458, 463, 474, 484–5

Balzac, Honoré de, 445
Baring, Maurice, 24
Baudry, 23–4
Beaumont, Sir George, 291, 455
Birrell, Augustine, 16
Blair, Robert, 69, 72–3
Bloomfield, Robert, 217
Blunden, Edmund, 26
Boccaccio, 149–50, 156, 259
Boileau, Nicolas, 25
Bowles, W. L., 387, 431
Brettell, John, 4
Broman, W. E., 486
Brontë, Charlotte, 452
Brooke, Stopford, 449
Brougham, Henry, Lord, 54
Browning, Elizabeth B., 397
Browning, Robert, 3, 431, 456
Brownrigg, Elizabeth, 110 & n, 114
Bryant, W. C., 369
Brydges, Sir Egerton, 335n
Bulwer, Lytton, 397
Bunyan, John, 215
Burke, Edmund, 63, 273, 321, 335, 350, 395, 403, 424, 434, 443, 451, 465, 476
Burn, Richard, 214

Burney, Charles, **46 ff**
Burney, Fanny, 485
Burns, Robert, 16, 20, 25, 166, 218–21, 298, 308, 311–12, 377, 392, 396, 399, 425, 438, 449, 453
Butler, Joseph, 470
Butler, Samuel, 256, 278, 398
Byron, Lord, 16, 20, 24, 216, 248–9, 270–1, **294–5**, 315, 317–19, 322, 335, 348, 371–2, 377, 383, 386–7, 396, 399, 404, 421, 435, 449–50, 456, 458, 462, 467, 474, 476

Campbell, Thomas, 20, 25, 97, 144, 197–8, 294, 387–8, 421, 424, 467
Canning, George, 315, 396
Carlyle, Thomas, 20, **296**, 371
Cartwright, Edmund, 5, **33, 39, 42**
Cervantes, M. de, 156, 317, 364
Chamberlain, R. L., 27
Chasles, Philarète, 25
Chatterton, Thomas, 195
Chaucer, Geoffrey, 13, 112, 149–50, 152, 156–9, 297, 430
Child, F. J., 361
Churchill, Charles, 54, 256, 296, 431
Cicero, 192
Clare, John, **297–8**
Claude Lorrain, 240
Clough, A. H., 21, **361**
Coleridge, Hartley, 22, 400
Coleridge, S. T., 20, 22, 56, **298**, 352, 377, 386–7, 466, 476
Cotman, J. S., 480
Cowley, Abraham, 126
Cowper, William, 2, 25, 55, 67, 88, 155, 178, 210, 248–9, 296–7, 302,

II. CRABBE: WORKS

(Bold type indicates a review of the poem concerned.)

III. CRABBE: CHARACTERISTICS

IV. PERIODICALS

(Bold type indicates first page of extracts from the periodical.)

DATE DUE

UPI			Printed in USA

THE CRITICAL HERITAGE SERIE

GENERAL EDITOR: B. C. SOUTHAM

Volumes published and forthcoming

Continued